# Triumph Daytona, Speed Triple, Sprint & Tiger
## Service and Repair Manual

# by Matthew Coombs and Phil Mather

*(3755-368-11AE1)*

### Models covered
T595/955i Daytona. 955cc. 1997 to 2005
T509 Speed Triple. 885cc. 1997 to 1998
955i Speed Triple. 955cc. 1999 to 2004
Sprint ST. 955cc. 1999 to 2004
Sprint RS. 955cc. 2000 to 2003
Tiger. 885cc. 1999 to 2000
Tiger. 955cc. 2001 to 2005

**Note:** *The 1050cc Speed Triple and Sprint are not covered by this manual.*

© Haynes Publishing 2006

A book in the **Haynes Service and Repair Manual Series**

ABCDE

ISBN **978 0 85733 939 3**

**British Library Cataloguing in Publication Data**
A catalogue record for this book is available from the British Library

**Library of Congress Control Number – 2005934811**

Printed in the USA

**Haynes Publishing**
Sparkford, Yeovil, Somerset BA22 7JJ, England

**Haynes North America, Inc**
861 Lawrence Drive, Newbury Park, California 91320, USA

*Printed using 33-lb Resolute Book 65 4.0 from Resolute Forest Products Calhoun, TN mill. Resolute is a member of World Wildlife Fund's
Climate Savers programme committed to significantly reducing GHG emissions. This paper uses 50% less wood fibre than traditional offset. The
Calhoun Mill is certified to the following sustainable forest management and chain of custody standards: SFI, PEFC and FSC Controlled Wood.*

# Contents

## LIVING WITH YOUR TRIUMPH

### Introduction

### Daily (pre-ride) checks

## MAINTENANCE

### Routine maintenance and servicing

# Contents

## REPAIRS AND OVERHAUL

### Engine, transmission and associated systems

### Chassis and bodywork components

### Electrical system

### Wiring diagrams

## REFERENCE

### Index

# A Phoenix from the ashes

by Julian Ryder

Where is the most modern motorcycle factory in the World? Tokyo? Berlin? Turin, maybe? No, it's in Hinckley, Leicestershire. Improbable as it may seem, the Triumph factory in the Midlands of England is a more advanced production facility than anything the mighty Japanese industry, German efficiency or Italian flair can boast. Still more amazingly, the first motorcycle rolled off the brand new production line in July 1991, nine years after the last of the old Triumphs had trickled out of the old Meriden factory.

It's important to realise that the new Triumph company has very little to do with the company that was a giant on the world stage in the post-war years when British motorcycle makers dominated the global markets. It is true that new owner John Bloor bought the patents, manufacturing rights and, most importantly, trademarks when the old factory's assets were sold in 1983, but the products of the old and new companies bear no relation at all to one another. Apart, of course, from the name on the tanks. Bloor's research-and-development team started work in Collier Street, Coventry and in 1985 work started on the ten-acre green-field factory site

which was occupied for the first time the following year.

The R & D team soon dispensed with the old Meriden factory's project for a modern DOHC, eight-valve twin known within the factory as the Diana project (after Princess Di) but shown at the NEC International Bike Show in 1982 as the Phoenix. The world got to see the new Triumphs for the first time at the Cologne Show in late 1990. The company was obviously anxious to distance itself from the old, leaky, unreliable image of the traditional British motorcycle, but it was equally anxious not to engage in a head-on technology war with the big four Japanese factories. The new motto was 'proven technology', the new engines were in-line threes and fours with double overhead camshafts and four valves per cylinder. They were all housed in a universal steel chassis with a large-diameter tubular backbone, and interestingly the new bikes would all carry famous model names from Triumph's past.

If you were looking to compare the technology level with an established machine, you'd have to point to the Kawasaki GPZ900R launched back in '84. Do not take this as a suggestion, current in '91, that the new

Triumphs were in some way Kawasakis in disguise because the cam chain was sited on the right-hand side of the motor rather than between the middle cylinders. Yes, of course Triumph had looked at the technology and manufacturing of the Japanese companies and naturally found that an in-line multi-cylinder motor was the most economical way to go. It's just the same in the car world, the straight four is cheaper than the V6 because it uses fewer, simpler parts. In fact the layout of the new motor would seem to indicate that designers from the car world had been brought in by John Bloor. If anyone still harbours the belief that Triumph copied or co-operated with Kawasaki, try and find a contemporary Kawasaki that used wet liners (cylinder liners in direct contact with coolant as opposed to sleeves fitted into the barrels).

But if Triumph's technology wasn't exactly path-breaking it was certainly very clever. The key concept was the modular design of the motor based around long and short-throw crankshafts in three and four-cylinder configurations. Every engine used the common 76 mm bore with either 55 or 65 mm throw cranks so that the short-stroke engine would be 750 cc in

**1999 955i Daytona**

**2002 955i Daytona**

three-cylinder form and 1000 cc as a four. Put the long-stroke crank in and you get a 900 cc triple and a 1200 cc four. The first bike to hit the shops was the 1200 Trophy, a four-cylinder sports tourer which was immediately competitive in a very strong class. There was also a 900 cc, three-cylinder Trophy. The 750 and 1000 Daytonas used the short-stroke motor in three and four-cylinder forms in what were intended to be the sportsters of the range. The other two models, 750 and 900 cc three-cylinder Tridents, cashed in on the early-'90s fad for naked retro bikes that followed the world-wide success of the Kawasaki Zephyr.

The reborn Triumphs were received with acclaim from the motorcycle press – tinged with not a little surprise. They really were very good motorcycles, the big Trophy was a match for the Japanese opposition in a class full of very accomplished machinery. The fact it could live with a modern day classic like the Yamaha FJ1200 straight off the drawing board was a tribute to John Bloor's designers and production engineers. The bike was big, fast, heavy and quite high, but it worked and worked well. And it didn't leak oil or break down, it was obvious that whatever else people were going to say about Triumphs they weren't going to able to resurrect the old jokes about British bangers leaving puddles of lubricant under them. As the rest of the range arrived and tests of them got into print, the star of the show emerged; it was the long-stroke, three-cylinder, 900 cc motor. It didn't matter how it was dressed up, the big triple had that indefinable quality – character. It was the motor the Japanese would never have made, very torquey but with a hint of vibration that endears rather than annoys. Somewhere among the modern, water-cooled, multi-valve technology, the 900-triple had the genes of the old

air-cooled OHV Triumph Tridents that appeared in 1969 and stayed in production until '75.

The range stayed basically unchanged for two years, until the Cologne Show of '92. Looking back at the first range it is now easy to see – hindsight again – that the identity of all the models was far too close. The sports tourer Trophy models were reckoned to be a little too sporting, the basic Tridents still had the handlebar and footrest positions of faired bikes. Triumph management later agreed that the first range evinced a certain lack of confidence, that was certainly not the case with the revamped 1993 range.

Visitors to the Cologne Show in September '92 agreed that the Triumphs were the stars, any lack of confidence there may have been two years earlier was completely gone. Any shyness the management may have felt about the Triumph name's past was shaken off as the new Tridents went retro style. Overall, the identities of the original bikes became more individual and more obviously separated; the Trophy models became more touring oriented, the Daytona more sporty looking and the Trident models more traditional. The factory even had the confidence to put small Union Flag emblems on the side panels of

**2002 955i Daytona Centennial**

each model, no more apologising for the imagined shortcomings of British engineering. Despite this spreading of the range's appeal, all these bikes were still built on the original modular concept.

There was, however, an exception to this rule of uniformity in the shape of a brand new bike, the Tiger 900. This model was in the enduro/desert-racer style much favoured on Continental Europe but not at all popular at home in the UK. Here was a Triumph with a 19-inch front tyre, wire wheels and a lower power output than the other 900s. Both the chassis and engine parts were slightly different from the rest of the range. Judging their market

**1999 955i Speed Triple**

**2003 955i Speed Triple**

**2004 Sprint ST**

**2000 Sprint RS**

as cleverly as ever, the factory held back another new model for the International Bike Show at the Birmingham NEC. This was the Daytona 1200, an out and out speed machine with a hidden political agenda. Its high-compression, 147 PS engine gave it brutal straight-line performance in much the same way as the big Kawasakis of the mid-'80s, and like them it wasn't too clever in the corners because of its weight and length. The bike was built as much to show that Triumph could do it as to sell in big numbers, it also had the secondary function of thumbing the corporate nose at the UK importers' gentlemen's agreement not to bring in bikes of over 125 PS.

Next year's NEC show saw two more new Triumphs, both reworkings of what was now regarded as a modern classic, the 900 triple. The Speed Triple was a clever reincarnation of the British cafe racer style, complete with clip-on handlebars and rear-set footrests. The big three-cylinder engine in standard tune got an all-black finish with black chrome pipes and silencers for the appropriately mean look. Black wheel rims and new bodywork completed a superbly styled bike available with black or yellow bodywork, the Speed Triple was the star of the show, a bike with an attitude.

The other newcomer was a more radical project, the Daytona Super III. Externally the motor looked like the usual 900 three, but a lot of work by Cosworth Engineering was hidden under the cases. The result was 115 PS as opposed to the standard 900 Daytona's 98 PS.

Triumph's next big step was into the US market, where the old company was so strong in the post-war years when the only competition was Harley-Davidson and where there is considerable affection for the marque. The name Triumph chose to spearhead this new challenge was Thunderbird, a trademark sourced in Native American mythology. This

time the famous name adorned yet another version of the 900 triple but this time heavily restyled and in a retro package. Dummy cooling fins give it the look of an air-cooled motor, the logo was cast into the clutch cover, and there were soft edges and large expanses of polished alloy. Inside those restyled cases, the motor was retuned even more than the Tiger's for a very user-friendly dose of low-down punch and mid-range power. The cycle parts were given an equally radical redesign, although the retro style stopped short of giving the Thunderbird twin rear shock absorbers. But everything else, the shape of the tank, the chrome headlight and countless other details, harks back to the original Thunderbird and nothing does so as shamelessly as the 'mouth-organ' tank badge, a classic icon if ever there was one.

The first Thunderbird derivative, the Adventurer, appeared for 1996 with a different rear subframe and rear-end styling including a sissy bar and single seat. That same year, the short-stroke 750 cc motor bowed out of the range, but it went with a bang not a whimper not in a final batch of Tridents but in a limited-edition run of 750 Speed Triples. The bigger Speed Triple's motor was inserted in the Sprint and the result called the Sprint Sport. The reason for using up all those motors was the advent of the new range of fuel-injected and heavily revised three-cylinder engines that first powered the T509 Speed Triple and T595 Daytona of 1997.

The first fuel-injected Triumph, the Daytona T595, was a major milestone for the Factory. It represented a change of policy, the first time Triumph would venture to confront their opposition on the cutting edge of technology. In early 1997, the Honda FireBlade and Ducati 916 ruled. The T595 was able to play in the same ball park. Only on a race track could the Japanese and Italian machines be shown to be

better. In the real world the T595 was at least as good a bike. The old long stroke of 65 mm was retained but everything else was new, it was a radical departure from the modular concept that had dominated production until now. You could see how the new motor was a lightened version of the old triple, but fuel injection was new and the frame was a radical departure from previous practice. Serpentine tubing ran from steering head to swingarm pivot and it was aluminium. Bodywork looked tasty too. Despite what Triumph had said about not taking on the Japanese back in 1991, the T595 came out of comparative tests with the 'Blade and 916 on equal terms. The new bike was also given the Speed Triple treatment and adorned with bug-eyed twin headlights in the fashionable 'streetfighter' style. You liked it or loathed it, but you couldn't ignore it.

The trouble with the Supersports end of the market is that the goal posts keep moving, so Triumph hedged their bets by softening the 955i's nominal 128 PS to 108, housing it in a simpler twin-beam frame and calling the result the Sprint ST. This continuation of the original Sprint concept was one of the hits of 1999. As a sports tourer, the fuel-injected Sprint ST was right up there with Honda's classic class leader, the VFR. Some magazines even preferred the British bike – high praise indeed. The Tiger got the fuel-injected 855 cc motor in '99. The result was a much more svelte machine than the original carburetted model, but Britain still refused to fall in love with the concept. Not that development of the carburetted bikes was neglected. Triumph got a Thunderbird derivative right in 1998 with the Thunderbird Sport. The Legend TT is the same bike with a different exhaust system and graphics.

Up to 1999 Triumph concentrated on big bikes but then they took another giant step towards the big time by taking on the Japanese in the most competitive market sector of them all, Supersports 600, with the TT600. For 2001 the most famous name of all was bought out of retirement: Bonneville. And it was an air-cooled twin! From a standing start in 1991, the Hinckley factory was competing in all the major motorcycle market sectors. Much bigger production volumes meant the original modular concept was no longer a necessity. By the dawn of the 21$^{st}$ Century Triumph had sold over 100,000 motorcycles.

Then the factory was struck by one of the biggest fires ever at a British industrial site. In March 2002 the production line, moulding shop and stores were destroyed and many other parts of the plant severely damaged. Just six months later the rebuilt factory was running at full capacity. The first new product out of the doors was the Daytona 600, a replacement for the TT600. Where the first Supersports 600 Triumph had failed to compete with the Japanese this one was good enough to win a TT in the hands of Kiwi Isle of Man hero Bruce Anstey.

By this time the now nicely differentiated range was well established: Triumph call the Daytonas, Sprints and Tiger 'Urban Sports' while the Bonneville and its derivatives, including the lively café racer styled 900 cc Thruxton, are billed as 'Modern Classics'. With an eye on America Triumph Triumph then unleashed their most audacious bike yet: the Rocket III. (Whisper it, but Rocket III was actually a BSA model name back in the 1970s.) They call it a cruiser but behemoth would be a better description, it's the first production bike to boast a capacity of over two litres and the bike that can make a Harley V-Rod look shy and retiring.

In less than 15 years Triumph has gone from hesitant newcomer (or it could be said, returnee) to a significant player on the world motorcycling stage. To anyone who remembers the state of the British industry when the original Triumph factory closed its doors, that is nothing short of a miracle.

# Acknowledgements

Our thanks are due to Bridge Motorcycles of Exeter and Fowlers Motorcycles of Bristol who supplied the machines featured in the illustrations throughout this manual. We would also like to thank NGK Spark Plugs (UK) Ltd for supplying the colour spark plug condition photographs, the Avon Rubber Company for supplying information on tyre fitting, and Draper Tools for supplying many of the tools shown in the photographs.

Thanks are also due to Julian Ryder for providing the introductory copy – A Phoenix from the ashes. We would also like to extend thanks to Triumph Motorcycles, Hinckley, for permission to use pictures of the Triumph models. Triumph Motorcycles Limited bears no responsibility for the content of this book, having had no part in its origination or preparation.

# About this manual

The aim of this manual is to help you get the best value from your motorcycle. It can do so in several ways. It can help you decide what work must be done, even if you choose to have it done by a dealer; it provides information and procedures for routine maintenance and servicing; and it offers diagnostic and repair procedures to follow when trouble occurs.

We hope you use the manual to tackle the work yourself. For many simpler jobs, doing it yourself may be quicker than arranging an appointment to get the motorcycle into a dealer and making the trips to leave it and pick it up. More importantly, a lot of money can be saved by avoiding the expense the shop must pass on to you to cover its labour and overhead costs. An added benefit is the sense of satisfaction and accomplishment that you feel after doing the job yourself.

References to the left or right side of the motorcycle assume you are sitting on the seat, facing forward.

**We take great pride in the accuracy of information given in this manual, but motorcycle manufacturers make alterations and design changes during the production run of a particular motorcycle of which they do not inform us. No liability can be accepted by the authors or publishers for loss, damage or injury caused by any errors in, or omissions from, the information given.**

## Illegal Copying

It is the policy of Haynes Publishing to actively protect its Copyrights and Trade Marks. Legal action will be taken against anyone who unlawfully copies the cover or contents of this Manual. This includes all forms of unauthorised copying including digital, mechanical, and electronic in any form. Authorisation from Haynes Publishing will only be provided expressly and in writing. Illegal copying will also be reported to the appropriate statutory authorities.

**1999 885i Tiger**

**2005 955i Tiger**

## Weights and dimensions

| | Daytona | Speed Triple |
|---|---|---|
| Overall length | | |
| 1997 to 2001 models | 2115 mm (83.2 in) | 2115 mm (83.2 in) |
| 2002-on models | 2072 mm (81.6 in) | 2115 mm (83.2 in) |
| Overall width | | |
| 1997 to 2000 models | 800 mm (31.4 in) | 860 mm (33.9 in) |
| 2001 models | 720 mm (28.3 in) | 790 mm (31.1 in) |
| 2002-on models | 725 mm (28.5 in) | 780 mm (30.7 in) |
| Overall height | | |
| 1997 to 2001 models | 1170 mm (46.1 in) | 1230 mm (48.4 in) |
| 2002-on models | 1165 mm (45.8 in) | 1250 mm (49.2 in) |
| Wheelbase | | |
| 1997 to 2000 models | 1440 mm* (56.7 in) | 1440 mm (56.7 in) |
| 2001 models | 1431 mm (56.3 in) | 1440 mm (56.7 in) |
| 2002 models | 1417 mm (55.8 in) | 1429 mm (56.2 in) |
| 2002 Centennial Edition models | 1426 mm (56.1 in) | |
| 2003-on models | 1426 mm (56.1 in) | 1429 mm (56.2 in) |
| Seat height | | |
| 1997 to 2001 models | 800 mm (31.4 in) | 800 mm (31.4 in) |
| 2002-on models | 815 mm (32.0 in) | 815 mm (32.0 in) |
| Dry weight (no fuel and oil) | | |
| 1997 to 2001 models | 198 kg (437 lb) | 196 kg (432 lb) |
| 2002 | 188 kg (414 lb) | 189 kg (416 lb) |
| 2002 Centennial Edition models | 191 kg (420 lb) | |
| 2003-on models | 191 kg (420 lb) | 189 kg (416 lb) |
| Max. payload (rider, passenger, luggage, accessories) | 185 kg (408 lb) | 185 kg (408 lb) |

*Wheelbase of 1431 mm (56.3 in) from VIN 89737

## Weights and dimensions

| | Sprint ST |
|---|---|
| Overall length | 2160 mm (85.0 in) |
| Overall width | |
| 1999 to 2000 models | 750 mm (29.5 in) |
| 2001 to 2004 models | 735 mm (28.9 in) |
| Overall height | 1220 mm (48.0 in) |
| Wheelbase | |
| 1999 to 2002 | 1470 mm (57.9 in) |
| 2003 to 2004 | 1475 mm (58.1 in) |
| Seat height | |
| 1999 to 2002 models | 800 mm (31.4 in) |
| 2003 to 2004 models | 805 mm (31.7 in) |
| Dry weight (no fuel and oil) | 207 kg (456 lb) |
| Max. payload (rider, passenger, luggage, accessories) | 217 kg (478 lb) |

## Weights and dimensions

| | Sprint RS |
|---|---|
| Overall length | |
| 2000 | 2160 mm (85.0 in) |
| 2001 to 2003 | 2120 mm (83.5 in) |
| Overall width | |
| 2000 | 750 mm (29.5 in) |
| 2001 to 2003 | 735 mm (28.9 in) |
| Overall height | |
| 2000 | 1250 mm (49.2 in) |
| 2001 to 2003 | 1170 mm (46.1 in) |
| Wheelbase | 1470 mm (57.9 in) |
| Seat height | 805 mm (31.7 in) |
| Dry weight (no fuel and oil) | 199 kg (439 lb) |
| Max. payload (rider, passenger, luggage, accessories) | 217 kg (478 lb) |

## Weights and dimensions

| | Tiger |
|---|---|
| Overall length | |
| 1999 to 2002 | 2175 mm (85.6 in) |
| 2003 to 2005 | 2250 mm (88.6 in) |
| Overall width | 860 mm (33.9 in) |
| Overall height | |
| 1999 to 2002 | 1345 mm (53.0 in) |
| 2003 to 2004 | 1370 mm (53.9 in) |
| 2005 | 1390 mm (54.7 in) |
| Wheelbase | |
| 1999 to 2001 | 1550 mm (61.0 in) |
| 2002 to 2005 | 1515 mm (59.6 in) |
| Seat height | 840 to 860 mm (33.1 to 33.9 in) |
| Dry weight (no fuel and oil) | 215 kg (474 lb) |
| Max. payload (rider, passenger, luggage, accessories) | 207 kg (456 lb) |

## Engine

| | |
|---|---|
| Type | Liquid-cooled, 12 valve in-line three cylinder |

Capacity (bore x stroke)

| | |
|---|---|
| T509 Speed Triple and 1999 to 2000 Tiger | 885 cc (76 x 65 mm) |
| Daytona, 955i Speed Triple, Sprint ST/RS and 2001-on Tiger | 955 cc (79 x 65 mm) |

Compression ratio

| | |
|---|---|
| 1997 to 2001 Daytona | 11.2 to 1 |
| 2002 to 2005 Daytona | 12.0 to 1 |
| T509 Speed Triple | 11.0 to 1 |
| 1999 to 2001 955i Speed Triple | 11.2 to 1 |
| 2002 to 2004 955i Speed Triple | 12.0 to 1 |
| 1999 to 2001 Sprint ST | 11.2 to 1 |
| 2002 to 2004 Sprint ST | 12.0 to 1 |
| 2000 to 2001 Sprint RS | 11.2 to 1 |
| 2002 to 2003 Sprint RS | 12.0 to 1 |
| 1999 to 2000 Tiger | 11.3 to 1 |
| 2001 Tiger | 11.2 to 1 |
| 2002 to 2005 Tiger | 11.65 to 1 |
| Camshafts | DOHC, chain-driven from the right-hand end of the crankshaft |
| Engine management system | Multipoint sequential fuel injection, digital inductive ignition |
| Clutch | Wet multi-plate, cable-operated |
| Gearbox | 6-speed constant mesh |
| Final drive chain size | 530 |

## Chassis

Frame type

| | |
|---|---|
| Daytona and Speed Triple | Twin spar oval-section aluminium tube frame |
| Sprint ST/RS | Twin spar box-section aluminium frame |
| Tiger | Steel tube perimeter frame |

Rake and trail

| | |
|---|---|
| 1997 to 2001 Daytona | 24.0°, 86.0 mm |
| 2002 Daytona | 22.8°, 81.0 mm |
| 2002 Daytona Centennial Edition | 22.5°, 78.7 mm |
| 2003 to 2005 Daytona | 22.5°, 78.7 mm |
| 1997 to 2001 Speed Triple | 24.0°, 86.0 mm |
| 2002 to 2004 Speed Triple | 23.5°, 84.0 mm |
| Sprint ST | 25.0°, 92.0 mm |
| 2000 Sprint RS | 25.0°, 92.0 mm |
| 2001 to 2003 Sprint RS | 24.5°, 89.0 mm |
| 1999 to 2000 Tiger | 28.0°, 95.0 mm |
| 2001 to 2004 Tiger | 28.0°, 92.0 mm |
| 2005 Tiger | 25.8°, 87.9 mm |

Front suspension

| | |
|---|---|
| Daytona and Speed Triple | 45 mm cartridge forks with preload, rebound and compression damping adjustment |
| Sprint ST/RS and Tiger | 43 mm conventional forks, preload adjustment on Sprint |

Rear suspension

| | |
|---|---|
| 1997 to 2001 Daytona | Single-sided swingarm, single shock with rising-rate linkage |
| 2002 Daytona | Twin-sided swingarm, single shock, rising-rate linkage |
| 2002 Daytona Centennial Edition | Single-sided swingarm, single shock with rising-rate linkage |
| 2003 to 2005 Daytona | Single-sided swingarm, single shock with rising-rate linkage |
| Speed Triple | Single-sided swingarm, single shock with rising-rate linkage |
| Sprint ST | Single-sided swingarm, single shock with rising-rate linkage |
| Sprint RS and Tiger | Twin-sided swingarm, single shock, rising-rate linkage on Sprint RS |

Wheels

| | |
|---|---|
| 1999 to 2004 Tiger | Front – 36-spoke alloy rim 19 x 2.5", Rear – 40-spoke alloy rim 17 x 4.25" |
| 2005 Tiger | 14-spoke cast alloy – Front 19 x 2.5", Rear 17 x 4.25" |
| 2002 Daytona (except Centennial Edition), 2001 to 2003 Sprint RS | 3-spoke cast alloy – Front 17 x 3.5", Rear 17 x 5.5" |
| All other models | 3-spoke cast alloy – Front 17 x 3.5", Rear 17 x 6.0" |

Tyres*

| | |
|---|---|
| Speed Triple models | Front – 120/70-17, Rear – 190/50-17 |

Daytona models

| | |
|---|---|
| 2002 model with twin-sided swingarm | Front – 120/70-17, Rear – 180/55-17 |
| All other models | Front – 120/70-17, Rear – 190/50-17 |
| Sprint models | Front – 120/70-17, Rear – 180/55-17 |
| Tiger models | Front – 110/80-19, Rear – 150/70-17 |

*Refer to the owners handbook, the tyre information label on the swingarm, or your Triumph dealer or a tyre specialist for approved tyre brands and ratings.

Front brakes

| | |
|---|---|
| Daytona, Speed Triple and Sprint ST/RS | 2 x 320 mm discs with 4-piston calipers |
| Tiger | 2 x 310 mm discs with 2-piston calipers |

Rear brake

| | |
|---|---|
| 2002 Daytona (except Centennial Edition) | 1 x 220 mm disc with 1-piston caliper |
| Speed Triple and all other Daytona models | 1 x 220 mm disc with 2-piston caliper |
| Sprint ST/RS | 1 x 255 mm disc with 2-piston caliper |
| Tiger | 1 x 285 mm disc with 2-piston caliper |

## Daytona

The T595 was Triumph's first fuel-injected motorcycle and represented a clear departure from the modular design concept on which the previous Daytona model and all other carburettor-engined models were based.

Fuelling and ignition were controlled by a Sagem electronic engine management system and the ignition coils were integral with the spark plug caps. The engine was a stressed member in the wrap-around style, twin spar aluminium tube frame, constructed of oval section tubing. Suspension was of Showa manufacture, with cartridge type forks at the front and a single shock at the rear connected via a linkage to a single-sided swingarm. The front forks were adjustable for spring preload, rebound and compression damping, and the rear shock for rebound and compression damping. Brakes were of Nissin manufacture, with four-piston calipers at the front and a two-piston opposed caliper at the rear.

The T595 was renamed 955i for the 1999 model year and improvements were made to the engine, airbox, exhaust system and rear shock.

The engine and transmission, fuel injection and electrical systems were redesigned for the 2002 model year, resulting in a lower overall weight and increased power output. Valve sizes and valve angles were modified and the intake and exhaust ports were redesigned for better gas flow. New cast pistons fitted in steel cylinder liners increased the compression ratio, the alternator was located on the left-hand end of the crankshaft and the crankcases were high-pressure die-cast for strength and lightness. A larger, re-shaped air filter housing was part of the new closed-loop fuel injection system which featured smaller, lighter injectors.

The instrumentation, headlight, bodywork, exhaust system and radiator were also re-worked in 2002. A twin-sided aluminium swingarm and single piston rear brake caliper were fitted to the standard Daytona model for that year only. To celebrate 100 years of Triumph motorcycles, a Centennial Edition Daytona finished in Aston Green paintwork was produced with slightly differing specifications which were adopted by the standard models in the following year.

The 2003 model reverted to the single-sided swingarm and two-piston opposed brake caliper at the rear.

The 2004 model received minor cosmetic alterations, most noticeably to the headlight and fairing, mirrors and rider's footrests. An all-black special edition Daytona was available.

## Speed Triple

Introduced first as the T509 in 1997, the Speed Triple represented Triumph's attempt at creating a machine in the Streetfighter image.

Although essentially a Daytona T595 without the fairing, the most significant difference between the two models was the Speed Triple's smaller 885 cc engine, de-tuned for more mid-range power. Apart from having a different oil cooler and the option of either one-piece handlebars or clip-ons, in all other respects the Speed Triple used the same components as the Daytona.

The T509's engine was uprated to 955 cc for the 1999 model year and the model was renamed 955i Speed Triple.

The redesigned 955 cc engine was fitted in 2002, together with all the other uprated ancillary components. An all-black special edition Speed Triple was available in 2004, the final year for the 955-engined Speed Triple.

## Sprint ST

The Sprint ST was introduced in 1999 as an all-round sports tourer and immediately superseded the previous carburettor-engined Sprint model.

The ST used the 955i engine from the Daytona and Speed Triple, de-tuned by Triumph's engineers to ensure better mid-range performance with the loss of a little top-end power. This was achieved by changes to cam lift, valve timing, fuel injection mapping and exhaust design. Also cast pistons and steel liners replaced the forged pistons and coated aluminium liners used on the higher performance models.

The all-new aluminium twin-spar frame had a longer wheelbase than the wrap-around frame of the Daytona and provided better straight-line stability. Suspension was of Showa manufacture with conventional telescopic forks (adjustable for pre-load) at the front and a single shock and linkage at the rear. It shared the single-sided swingarm and brake components used on the Daytona and Speed Triple.

The redesigned 955 cc engine was fitted in 2002, together with all the other uprated ancillary components.

## Sprint RS

The Sprint RS was introduced for the 2000 model year and aimed at riders who wanted a more sporty version of the Sprint ST.

Based heavily on the ST, the changes were most evident in the bodywork and chassis. Most noticeable were the half-fairing and con-ventional twin-sided swingarm which resulted in a weight saving of 8 kg. The frame was unchanged, but the more sporty riding position was achieved by fitting lower handlebars, different suspension springing and damping characteristics. Ground clearance was increased by redesigning the exhaust system, and the centrestand of the ST model was omitted. The RS featured a modified instrument panel, with digital displays for the speedometer and coolant temperature; the fuel gauge of the ST model was replaced by a fuel level warning light.

The redesigned 955 cc engine was fitted in 2002, together with all the other uprated ancillary components. The single-sided swingarm was fitted to later RS models.

## Tiger

The fuel-injected Tiger introduced for the 1999 model year bears little resemblance to its carburettor-engine predecessor – it was a completely new model which used a re-tuned version of the 885 cc engine from the T509 Speed Triple. The engine was housed in a steel tube perimeter frame.

Suspension was taken care of by non-adjustable, 43 mm conventional front forks, and a single rear shock which had a remote preload adjuster and rebound damping adjuster. There was no suspension linkage as on the other models, the rear shock connecting directly to the frame and conventional twin-sided swingarm with integral eccentric drive chain adjusters. Brakes were of Nissin manufacture, although two-piston sliding calipers were used at the front rather than the four-piston type fitted to all other models.

The 24 litre fuel tank ensured a good touring range. Rider comfort and protection from the elements was provided by a handlebar fairing with small fly screen, hand guards over the levers, three-position adjustable seat height and a small luggage rack. Instrumentation was from the Sprint ST.

In 2001, an early variant of the redesigned 955 cc engine was fitted on the Tiger models. This combined the existing design of cylinder head, fuel and exhaust systems, used with the revised crankcases, alternator and starter motor set-up that were to be introduced on the Daytona, Speed Triple and Sprint models the following year.

In 2005 the Tiger's wire-spoked wheels were replaced by 14-spoke cast aluminium wheels designed to take tubeless tyres and the frame dimensions and suspension set-up were altered to enhance the bike's off-road performance. A new design of swingarm was fitted with conventional chain adjusters.

Professional mechanics are trained in safe working procedures. However enthusiastic you may be about getting on with the job at hand, take the time to ensure that your safety is not put at risk. A moment's lack of attention can result in an accident, as can failure to observe simple precautions.

There will always be new ways of having accidents, and the following is not a comprehensive list of all dangers; it is intended rather to make you aware of the risks and to encourage a safe approach to all work you carry out on your bike.

## Asbestos

● Certain friction, insulating, sealing and other products - such as brake pads, clutch linings, gaskets, etc. - contain asbestos. Extreme care must be taken to avoid inhalation of dust from such products since it is hazardous to health. If in doubt, assume that they do contain asbestos.

## Fire

● Remember at all times that petrol is highly flammable. Never smoke or have any kind of naked flame around, when working on the vehicle. But the risk does not end there - a spark caused by an electrical short-circuit, by two metal surfaces contacting each other, by careless use of tools, or even by static electricity built up in your body under certain conditions, can ignite petrol vapour, which in a confined space is highly explosive. Never use petrol as a cleaning solvent. Use an approved safety solvent.

● Always disconnect the battery earth terminal before working on any part of the fuel or electrical system, and never risk spilling fuel on to a hot engine or exhaust.

● It is recommended that a fire extinguisher of a type suitable for fuel and electrical fires is kept handy in the garage or workplace at all times. Never try to extinguish a fuel or electrical fire with water.

## Fumes

● Certain fumes are highly toxic and can quickly cause unconsciousness and even death if inhaled to any extent. Petrol vapour comes into this category, as do the vapours from certain solvents such as trichloro-ethylene. Any draining or pouring of such volatile fluids should be done in a well ventilated area.

● When using cleaning fluids and solvents, read the instructions carefully. Never use materials from unmarked containers - they may give off poisonous vapours.

● Never run the engine of a motor vehicle in an enclosed space such as a garage. Exhaust fumes contain carbon monoxide which is extremely poisonous; if you need to run the engine, always do so in the open air or at least have the rear of the vehicle outside the workplace.

## The battery

● Never cause a spark, or allow a naked light near the vehicle's battery. It will normally be giving off a certain amount of hydrogen gas, which is highly explosive.

● Always disconnect the battery ground (earth) terminal before working on the fuel or electrical systems (except where noted).

● If possible, loosen the filler plugs or cover when charging the battery from an external source. Do not charge at an excessive rate or the battery may burst.

● Take care when topping up, cleaning or carrying the battery. The acid electrolyte, evenwhen diluted, is very corrosive and should not be allowed to contact the eyes or skin. Always wear rubber gloves and goggles or a face shield. If you ever need to prepare electrolyte yourself, always add the acid slowly to the water; never add the water to the acid.

## Electricity

● When using an electric power tool, inspection light etc., always ensure that the appliance is correctly connected to its plug and that, where necessary, it is properly grounded (earthed). Do not use such appliances in damp conditions and, again, beware of creating a spark or applying excessive heat in the vicinity of fuel or fuel vapour. Also ensure that the appliances meet national safety standards.

● A severe electric shock can result from touching certain parts of the electrical system, such as the spark plug wires (HT leads), when the engine is running or being cranked, particularly if components are damp or the insulation is defective. Where an electronic ignition system is used, the secondary (HT) voltage is much higher and could prove fatal.

## Remember...

✗ **Don't** start the engine without first ascertaining that the transmission is in neutral.

✗ **Don't** suddenly remove the pressure cap from a hot cooling system - cover it with a cloth and release the pressure gradually first, or you may get scalded by escaping coolant.

✗ **Don't** attempt to drain oil until you are sure it has cooled sufficiently to avoid scalding you.

✗ **Don't** grasp any part of the engine or exhaust system without first ascertaining that it is cool enough not to burn you.

✗ **Don't** allow brake fluid or antifreeze to contact the machine's paintwork or plastic components.

✗ **Don't** siphon toxic liquids such as fuel, hydraulic fluid or antifreeze by mouth, or allow them to remain on your skin.

✗ **Don't** inhale dust - it may be injurious to health (see Asbestos heading).

✗ **Don't** allow any spilled oil or grease to remain on the floor - wipe it up right away, before someone slips on it.

✗ **Don't** use ill-fitting spanners or other tools which may slip and cause injury.

✗ **Don't** lift a heavy component which may be beyond your capability - get assistance.

✗ **Don't** rush to finish a job or take unverified short cuts.

✗ **Don't** allow children or animals in or around an unattended vehicle.

✗ **Don't** inflate a tyre above the recommended pressure. Apart from over-stressing the carcass, in extreme cases the tyre may blow off forcibly.

✔ **Do** ensure that the machine is supported securely at all times. This is especially important when the machine is blocked up to aid wheel or fork removal.

✔ **Do** take care when attempting to loosen a stubborn nut or bolt. It is generally better to pull on a spanner, rather than push, so that if you slip, you fall away from the machine rather than onto it.

✔ **Do** wear eye protection when using power tools such as drill, sander, bench grinder etc.

✔ **Do** use a barrier cream on your hands prior to undertaking dirty jobs - it will protect your skin from infection as well as making the dirt easier to remove afterwards; but make sure your hands aren't left slippery. Note that long-term contact with used engine oil can be a health hazard.

✔ **Do** keep loose clothing (cuffs, ties etc. and long hair) well out of the way of moving mechanical parts.

✔ **Do** remove rings, wristwatch etc., before working on the vehicle - especially the electrical system.

✔ **Do** keep your work area tidy - it is only too easy to fall over articles left lying around.

✔ **Do** exercise caution when compressing springs for removal or installation. Ensure that the tension is applied and released in a controlled manner, using suitable tools which preclude the possibility of the spring escaping violently.

✔ **Do** ensure that any lifting tackle used has a safe working load rating adequate for the job.

✔ **Do** get someone to check periodically that all is well, when working alone on the vehicle.

✔ **Do** carry out work in a logical sequence and check that everything is correctly assembled and tightened afterwards.

✔ **Do** remember that your vehicle's safety affects that of yourself and others. If in doubt on any point, get professional advice.

● If in spite of following these precautions, you are unfortunate enough to injure yourself, seek medical attention as soon as possible.

## Frame and engine numbers

The engine number is stamped into the top of the crankcase on the right-hand side of the engine. The VIN (vehicle identification number) is stamped into the right-hand side of the steering head and is duplicated on a plate riveted to the right-hand side of the frame behind the steering head on Daytona, Speed Triple and Sprint models, and to the frame cross-member under the rider's seat on Tiger models. These numbers should be recorded and kept in a safe place so they can be furnished to law enforcement officials in the event of a theft.

The VIN, engine number, and model code should be recorded and kept in a handy place (such as with your driver's licence) so that they are always available when purchasing or ordering parts for your machine.

The procedures in this manual identify the bikes by model (e.g. 955i Daytona). If a model has been modified during its production life, then the VIN is used to differentiate between the versions.

## Buying spare parts

Once you have found the identification numbers, record them for reference when buying parts. Since the manufacturers change specifications, parts and vendors (companies that manufacture various components on the machine), providing the ID numbers is the only way to be reasonably sure that you are buying the correct parts.

Whenever possible, take the worn part to the dealer so direct comparison with the new component can be made. Along the trail from the manufacturer to the parts shelf, there are numerous places that the part can end up with the wrong number or be listed incorrectly.

The two places to purchase new parts for your motorcycle – the accessory store and the franchised dealer – differ in the type of parts they carry. While dealers can obtain virtually every part for your motorcycle, the accessory dealer is usually limited to normal high wear items such as shock absorbers, tune-up parts, various engine gaskets, cables, chains, brake parts, etc. Rarely will an accessory outlet have major suspension components, cylinders, transmission gears, or cases.

Used parts can be obtained for roughly half the price of new ones, but you can't always be sure of what you're getting. Once again, take your worn part to the breaker's yard for direct comparison.

Whether buying new, used or rebuilt parts, the best course is to deal directly with someone who specialises in parts for your particular make.

The engine number is stamped into the crankcase on the right-hand side of the engine

The VIN is stamped into the right-hand side of the steering head

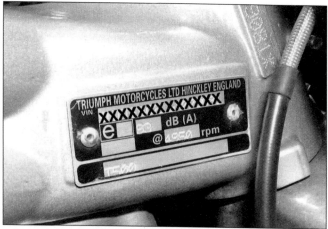

The VIN is duplicated on an information plate behind the steering head (Daytona, Speed Triple and Sprint models) . . .

. . . or on the frame cross-member under the rider's seat (Tiger model)

**Note:** *The daily (pre-ride) checks outlined in the owners handbook cover those items which should be inspected on a daily basis and at the same time as all routine maintenance intervals.*

# Engine oil level

## The correct oil
● Modern, high-revving engines place great demands on their oil. It is very important that the correct oil for your bike is used.
● Always top up with a good quality oil of the specified type and viscosity and do not overfill the engine. Triumph recommend using Mobil 1 Racing 4T oil.
*Caution: Do not mix any chemical additives with the oil, however good they may sound, as they could cause clutch slip. Never use mineral, vegetable, non-detergent or castor based oils.*

| Oil type | Semi or fully synthetic motorcycle engine oil, API grade SH or higher |
| --- | --- |
| Oil viscosity | SAE 10W/40 or 15W/50 |

## Before you start:
✔ Support the motorcycle in an upright position – don't check the oil level with the bike on its sidestand. Make sure it is on level ground.
✔ Start the engine and let it idle for several minutes to allow it to reach normal operating temperature.
*Caution: Do not run the engine in an enclosed space such as a garage or workshop.*
✔ Stop the engine and leave the motorcycle undisturbed for a few minutes to allow the oil level to stabilise.

## Bike care:
● If you have to add oil frequently, you should check whether you have any oil leaks. If there is no sign of oil leakage from the joints and gaskets the engine could be burning oil (see Fault Finding).

**1** On early engines, wipe the oil level inspection window, located in the bottom of the clutch cover on the right-hand side of the engine . . .

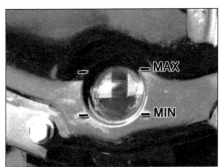

**2** . . . then check that the oil level is between the MAX and MIN level lines on the window . . .

**3** . . . and if the level is low remove the filler cap from the top of the clutch cover to top up.

**4** On later engines, unscrew the oil filler dipstick on the rear of the clutch cover on the right-hand side of the engine. Wipe off the oil, screw the cap fully home, then unscrew it again . . .

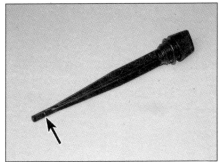

**5** . . . and check that the oil is visible up to the top of the hatched area at the bottom of the dipstick (arrowed).

**6** If required, top up the engine oil to the correct level with the recommended grade and type of oil.

# Coolant level

## Before you start:

✔ Make sure you have a supply of coolant available – a mixture of 50% distilled water and 50% corrosion inhibited ethylene glycol anti-freeze is needed.
✔ Always check the coolant level when the engine is cold.
✔ Support the motorcycle in an upright position, using an auxiliary stand if required. Make sure it is on level ground.

## Bike care:

● Use only the specified coolant mixture. It is important that anti-freeze is used in the system all year round, and not just in the winter. Do not top the system up using only water, as the system will become too diluted.
● Do not overfill the reservoir. If the coolant is significantly above the FULL level line at any time, the surplus should be siphoned or drained off to prevent the possibility of it being expelled out of the overflow hose.
● If the coolant level falls steadily, check the system for leaks (see Chapter 1). If no leaks are found and the level continues to fall, it is recommended that the machine be taken to a Triumph dealer for a pressure test.

## Tiger models

**1** The reservoir is mounted in the fairing on the right-hand side, and is visible by turning the steering to full right lock.

**2** The coolant level can also be viewed through the cutout in the fairing turn signal panel.

**3** If the coolant level does not lie between the MAX and MIN level lines, remove the reservoir filler cap from the panel.

**4** Top the coolant level up with the recommended coolant mixture. Fit the cap securely.

## Daytona and Speed Triple models

**1** Remove the seat (see Chapter 7). The coolant MAX and MIN level lines are marked on the reservoir.

**2** If the coolant level does not lie between the MAX and MIN level lines, remove the reservoir filler cap.

**3** Top the coolant level up with the recommended coolant mixture. Fit the cap securely, then install the seat (see Chapter 7).

## Sprint models

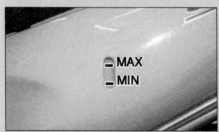

**1** The reservoir is mounted behind the seat cowling on the left-hand side, and is visible via the aperture in the cowling.

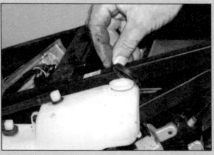

**2** If the coolant level does not lie between the MAX and MIN level lines, remove the seat cowling and filler cap.

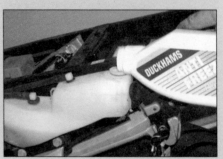

**3** Top the coolant level up with the recommended coolant mixture. Fit the cap securely, then install the seat cowling.

# Brake fluid level

> ⚠️ **Warning: Brake hydraulic fluid can harm your eyes and damage painted surfaces, so use extreme caution when handling and pouring it and cover surrounding surfaces with rag. Do not use fluid that has been standing open for some time, as it absorbs moisture from the air which can cause a dangerous loss of braking effectiveness.**

## Before you start:

✔ Make sure you have the correct hydraulic fluid. DOT 4 is recommended.

✔ Support the motorcycle in an upright position, using an auxiliary stand if required. Turn the handlebars until the top of the front master cylinder is as level as possible.

✔ The rear master cylinder reservoir is located behind the seat cowling or side panel on the right-hand side. On Daytona, Speed Triple and Sprint models remove the seat cowling, and on Tiger models remove the right-hand side panel (see Chapter 7).

## Bike care:

● The fluid in the reservoirs will drop slightly as the brake pads wear down. If any fluid reservoir requires repeated topping-up this is an indication of an hydraulic leak somewhere in the system.

● Check for signs of fluid leakage from the hydraulic hoses and brake system components – if found, rectify immediately (see Chapter 6).

● Check brake operation; if there is evidence of air in the system (spongy feel to lever or pedal), it must be bled as described in Chapter 6.

---

### FRONT BRAKE FLUID LEVEL – DAYTONA, SPEED TRIPLE AND SPRINT MODELS

**1** The front brake fluid level must be between the level lines. To top up, remove the clamp screw (A) and cap (B), then remove the plate and diaphragm.

**2** Top up with new DOT 4 hydraulic fluid, until the level is between the LOWER and UPPER level lines – do not overfill.

**3** Ensure that the diaphragm is correctly seated before installing the plate and cap. Secure the cap with its clamp.

---

### FRONT BRAKE FLUID LEVEL – TIGER MODELS

**1** The front brake fluid level is visible through the window in the reservoir body – it must be above the LOWER level line.

**2** If the level is low, undo the reservoir cover screws and remove the cover and the diaphragm.

**3** Top up with new DOT 4 hydraulic fluid, until the level is up to the UPPER level line (arrowed) inside the reservoir.

**4** Ensure that the diaphragm is correctly seated before installing the cover. Secure the cover with its screws.

---

### REAR BRAKE FLUID LEVEL – ALL MODELS

**1** The rear brake fluid level is visible through the reservoir body – it must be between the UPPER and LOWER level lines.

**2** If the level is low, remove the reservoir cap, plate and diaphragm, then top up with new DOT 4 hydraulic fluid – do not overfill.

**3** Ensure that the diaphragm is correctly seated before installing the plate and cap. Tighten the cap securely.

# Tyre checks

### The correct pressures

● The tyres must be checked when cold, not immediately after riding. Note that low tyre pressures may cause the tyre to slip on the rim or come off. High tyre pressures will cause abnormal tread wear and unsafe handling.
● Use an accurate pressure gauge. Many garage forecourt gauges are wildly inaccurate. If you buy your own, spend as much as you can justify on a quality gauge.
● Correct air pressure will increase tyre life and provide maximum stability, handling capability and ride comfort.

### Tyre care

● Check the tyres carefully for cuts, tears, embedded nails or other sharp objects and excessive wear. Operation of the motorcycle with excessively worn tyres is extremely hazardous, as traction and handling are directly affected. Also check the wheels for signs of damage and distortion.

● Check the condition of the tyre valve and ensure the dust cap is in place.
● Pick out any stones or nails which may have become embedded in the tyre tread. If left, they will eventually penetrate through the casing and cause a puncture.
● If tyre damage is apparent, or unexplained loss of pressure is experienced, seek the advice of a tyre fitting specialist without delay.

| Front | Rear |
|-------|------|
| 36 psi (2.50 Bar) | 42 psi (2.90 Bar) |

1 Check the tyre pressures when the tyres are cold and keep them properly inflated.

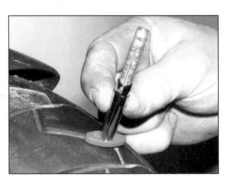

2 Measure tread depth at the centre of the tyre using a tread depth gauge.

3 Tyre tread wear indicator bar and its location marking (usually either an arrow, a triangle or the letters TWI) on the sidewall.

### Tyre tread depth

● At the time of writing UK law requires that tread depth must be at least 1 mm over 3/4 of the tread breadth all the way around the tyre, with no bald patches. Many riders, however, consider 2 mm tread depth minimum to be a safer limit. Triumph recommend a minimum of 2 mm for normal riding, or 3 mm on the rear tyre for speeds over 80 mph (130 km/h).
● Many tyres now incorporate wear indicators in the tread. Identify the triangular pointer or TWI mark on the tyre sidewall to locate the indicator bar and renew the tyre if the tread has worn down to the bar.

# Suspension, steering and final drive checks

### Final drive

● Check that the chain slack isn't excessive, and adjust it if necessary (see Chapter 1).
● If the chain looks dry, lubricate it (see Chapter 1).

### Suspension and Steering

● Check that the front and rear suspension operates smoothly without binding. Check that there are no fluid leaks from the front fork seals or rear shock seals.

● Check that the suspension is adjusted as required.
● Check that the steering moves smoothly from lock-to-lock.

# Legal and safety checks

### Lighting and signalling

● Take a minute to check that the headlight, tail light, brake light, instrument lights and turn signals all work correctly.
● Check that the horn sounds when the switch is operated.
● A working speedometer graduated in mph is a statutory requirement in the UK.

### Safety

● Check that the throttle grip rotates smoothly and snaps shut when released, in all steering positions. Also check for the correct amount of freeplay (see Chapter 1).
● Check that the engine shuts off when the kill switch is operated.
● Check that sidestand return spring holds the stand securely up when retracted.
● Check that the clutch cable is working smoothly and with the correct freeplay (see Chapter 1).
● Check for any nuts and bolts that may have worked loose.

### Fuel

● This may seem obvious, but check that you have enough fuel to complete your journey. Check for signs of fuel leakage – if any are found, rectify the cause immediately.
● Ensure you use the correct grade fuel – see Chapter 4 Specifications.

# Chapter 1
# Routine maintenance and servicing

## Contents

## Degrees of difficulty

| | | | | |
|---|---|---|---|---|
| **Easy,** suitable for novice with little experience  | **Fairly easy,** suitable for beginner with some experience  | **Fairly difficult,** suitable for competent DIY mechanic | **Difficult,** suitable for experienced DIY mechanic | **Very difficult,** suitable for expert DIY or professional  |

## Engine

Spark plugs
   1997 to 2001 Daytona, Speed Triple and Sprint, and all Tiger models
      Type ......................................................... NGK DPR8EA-9
      Electrode gap ............................................. 0.8 to 0.9 mm
   2002-on Daytona, Speed Triple and Sprint models
      Type ......................................................... NGK CR9EK
      Electrode gap ............................................. 0.7 mm
Engine idle speed
   T595 Daytona, T509 Speed Triple, 1999 to 2001 Sprint and Tiger .. 1150 to 1250 rpm
   1999 to 2001 955i Daytona and 955i Speed Triple .............. 1050 to 1150 rpm
   2002-on Daytona, Speed Triple, Sprint and Tiger .............. 1200 rpm
Cylinder identification .......................................... numbered 1 to 3 from left to right
Valve clearances (COLD engine)
   1997 to 2001 Daytona, Speed Triple and Sprint, and all Tiger models
      Intake valves ............................................. 0.10 to 0.15 mm
      Exhaust valves ........................................... 0.15 to 0.20 mm
   2002-on Daytona, Speed Triple and Sprint models
      Intake valves ............................................. 0.10 to 0.20 mm
      Exhaust valves ........................................... 0.20 to 0.30 mm
Cam chain stretch limit – 2002-on Daytona, Speed Triple and Sprint .. 147.63 mm
Engine oil pressure ............................................. 40 psi (2.8 Bar) @ 5000 rpm, oil @ 80°C

## Cycle parts

Brake pad minimum thickness .................................. 1.5 mm
Drive chain slack – Daytona, Speed Triple and Sprint models
   1997 to 2001 models ........................................ 35 to 40 mm
   2002 to 2005 models with single-sided swingarm .............. 35 to 40 mm
   2002 Daytona with twin-sided swingarm ...................... 30 to 35 mm
   2002-03 Sprint RS with twin-sided swingarm ................. 25 to 35 mm
Drive chain slack – all Tiger models ............................ 35 to 40 mm
Chain stretch limit ............................................. 321 mm
Throttle cable freeplay ......................................... 2 to 3 mm
Clutch cable freeplay .......................................... 0.4 to 0.8 mm
Tyre pressures (cold) .......................................... see *Daily (pre-ride) checks*

## Recommended lubricants and fluids

Engine oil type ................................................ Semi or fully synthetic motorcycle engine oil, SAE 10W/40 or 15W/50, API grade SH or higher – Triumph recommend Mobil 1 racing 4T

Engine oil capacity – dry engine, new filter
   1997 to 2001 Daytona, Speed Triple and Sprint, and all Tiger models .. 4.0 litres
   2002-on Daytona, Speed Triple and Sprint models ............. 3.5 litres
Coolant type .................................................. 50% distilled water, 50% corrosion inhibited ethylene glycol anti-freeze
Coolant capacity .............................................. 2.8 litres
Brake fluid ................................................... DOT 4
Drive chain ................................................... Chain lubricant suitable for O-ring chains – Triumph recommend Mobil Chain Spray or Mobilube HD 80
Steering head bearings ........................................ Mobil Grease HP 222 or Lithium-based multi-purpose grease
Swingarm pivot and bearings, suspension linkage bearings ......... Mobil Grease HP 222 or Lithium-based multi-purpose grease
Wheel bearings and seal lips .................................. Mobil Grease HP 222 or Lithium-based multi-purpose grease
Gearchange lever/clutch lever/front brake lever/
   rear brake pedal/sidestand pivots ........................... Mobil Grease HP 222 or Lithium-based multi-purpose grease
Cables ....................................................... Aersol cable lubricant
Throttle grip ................................................. Multi-purpose grease or dry film lubricant

## Torque wrench settings

| | |
|---|---|
| Drive chain adjuster clamp bolt – all models with single-sided swingarm | 55 Nm |
| Drive chain adjuster clamp bolts – 1999 to 2004 Tiger models | 35 Nm |
| Rear axle nut – Sprint RS and Daytona models with double-sided swingarm and 2005 Tiger models | 110 Nm |
| Oil drain plug | 25 Nm |
| Oil filter | |
|    1997 to 2001 Daytona, Speed Triple and Sprint, all Tiger models | 12 Nm |
|    2002-on Daytona, Speed Triple and Sprint models | 10 Nm |
| Fuel pump mounting plate bolts | 5 Nm |
| Ignition coil/spark plug cap screws | 10 Nm |
| Spark plugs | 20 Nm |
| Secondary air injection valve cover bolts | 9 Nm |
| Valve shim replacement tool mounting bolts and leg bolts – early engines | 7 Nm |
| Centre stand pivots – Sprint ST models | 36 Nm |
| Steering stem nut | |
|    1997 to 2001 Daytona models | 40 Nm |
|    2002 to early 2004 Daytona models | 65 Nm |
|    2004-on Daytona and Speed Triple models | 90 Nm |
|    Speed Triple models up to VIN 172426 and VIN 173398 to 173815 | 40 Nm |
|    Speed Triple models VIN 172427 to 2003 (except 173398 to 173815) | 65 Nm |
|    Sprint and Tiger models | 65 Nm |
| Fork clamp bolts (top yoke) | 20 Nm |
| Handlebar clamp bolts | |
|    Daytona and Speed Triple models with separate handlebars | |
|       6 mm bolts (up to VIN 47600 and from VIN 49061 to 49165) | 20 Nm |
|       8 mm bolts (from VIN 47601 to 63315 except VIN 49061 to 49165) | 25 Nm |
|       8 mm bolts (from VIN 63316) | 35 Nm |
| Handlebar retaining bolts – Daytona and Speed Triple models with separate handlebars (from VIN 105633) | 11 Nm |
| Handlebar positioning bolts – Sprint models | |
|    1999 to 2001 models | 22 Nm |
|    2002-on models | 26 Nm |
| Handlebar clamp bolts – Sprint models | |
|    1999 to 2001 models | 22 Nm |
|    2002-on models | 26 Nm |
| Cooling system drain plug | 13 Nm |
| Cooling system bleed-hole bolt – 1997 to 2001 Daytona, Speed Triple and Sprint, and all Tiger models | 7 Nm |
| Cooling system bleed-hole screw | |
|    2002-on Daytona and Speed Triple models | 12 Nm |
|    2002-on Sprint models | 9 Nm |
| Fuel hose banjo bolts (Daytona to VIN 71698 and 885cc Speed Triple models) | 20 Nm |
| Fuel delivery hose union bolts (all other models) | 5 Nm |
| Fuel hose sockets in pump mounting plate | 5 Nm |

# Maintenance schedule – 1997 to 2001 Daytona, Speed Triple and Sprint models, all Tiger models

**Note:** *The daily (pre-ride) checks outlined in the owner's manual covers those items which should be inspected on a daily basis. Always perform the pre-ride inspection at every maintenance interval (in addition to the procedures listed). The intervals listed below are the intervals recommended by the manufacturer for each particular operation during the model years covered in this manual. Your owner's manual may have different intervals for your model.*

## Daily (pre-ride)
☐ See Daily (pre-ride) checks at the beginning of this manual.

## After the initial 500 miles (800 km)
**Note:** *This check is usually performed by a Triumph dealer after the first 500 miles (800 km) from new. Thereafter, maintenance is carried out according to the following intervals of the schedule.*

## Every 200 miles (300 km)
☐ Check, adjust and lubricate the drive chain (Section 1)

## Every 500 miles (800 km)
☐ Check the drive chain for wear and stretch and the sprockets for wear (Section 2)

## Every 6000 miles (10,000 km) or 12 months (whichever comes sooner)
☐ Change the engine oil and filter and check the oil cooler (Section 3)
☐ Check the engine management system (Section 4)
☐ Check and adjust the throttle cable (Section 5)
☐ Check the cooling system (Section 6)
☐ Check the fuel system (Section 7)
☐ Check the suspension (Section 8)
☐ Check the brake pads (Section 9)
☐ Check the brake system and brake light switch operation (Section 10)
☐ Check the tightness of all nuts, bolts and fasteners (Section 11)
☐ Check the condition of the wheels and tyres (Section 12)
☐ Check the clutch (Section 13)
☐ Check the battery (Section 14)
☐ Check the drive chain slider (Section 15)

## Every 12,000 miles (20,000 km) or two years (whichever comes sooner)
*Carry out all the items under the 6000 mile (10,000 km) check, plus the following*
☐ Check the spark plugs (Section 16)
☐ Check/adjust the throttle body synchronisation (Section 17)
☐ Renew the air filter element (Section 18)
☐ Check the secondary air injection system (Section 19)
☐ Check and adjust the valve clearances (Section 20)
☐ Renew the fuel filter (Section 21)
☐ Check and adjust the steering head bearings (Section 22)
☐ Change the front fork oil (Section 23)
☐ Check the wheel bearings (Section 24)
☐ Lubricate the clutch and brake levers, gearchange lever linkage, brake pedal pivot and sidestand pivots and the throttle and clutch cables (Section 26)

## Every two years
☐ Change the coolant (Section 27)
☐ Change the brake fluid (Section 28)
☐ Renew the brake master cylinder and caliper seals (Section 29)

## Every 24,000 miles (40,000 km) or three years (whichever comes sooner)
*Carry out all the items under the 12,000 mile (20,000 km) check, plus the following*
☐ Lubricate the swingarm and suspension linkage bearings (see Section 30)

## Every 24,000 miles (40,000 km) or four years (whichever comes sooner)
*Carry out all the items under the 12,000 mile (20,000 km) check, plus the following*
☐ Renew the spark plugs (see Section 31)

## Every four years
☐ Renew the brake hoses (Section 33)
☐ Renew the fuel system hoses (Section 34)

## Non-scheduled maintenance
☐ Check the stand (Section 35)
☐ Check and adjust the headlight aim (Section 36)
☐ Check the cylinder compression (Section 37)

# Maintenance schedule – 2002-on Daytona, Speed Triple and Sprint models

**Note:** *The daily (pre-ride) checks outlined in the owner's manual covers those items which should be inspected on a daily basis. Always perform the pre-ride inspection at every maintenance interval (in addition to the procedures listed). The intervals listed below are the intervals recommended by the manufacturer for each particular operation during the model years covered in this manual. Your owner's manual may have different intervals for your model.*

## Daily (pre-ride)
- [ ] See *Daily (pre-ride) checks* at the beginning of this manual.

## After the initial 500 miles (800 km)
**Note:** *This check is usually performed by a Triumph dealer after the first 500 miles (800 km) from new. Thereafter, maintenance is carried out according to the following intervals of the schedule.*

## Every 200 miles (300 km)
- [ ] Check, adjust and lubricate the drive chain (Section 1)

## Every 500 miles (800 km)
- [ ] Check the drive chain for wear and stretch and the sprockets for wear (Section 2)

## Every 6000 miles (10,000 km) or 12 months (whichever comes sooner)
- [ ] Change the engine oil and filter and check the oil cooler (Section 3)
- [ ] Check the engine management system (Section 4)
- [ ] Check and adjust the throttle cable (Section 5)
- [ ] Check the cooling system (Section 6)
- [ ] Check the fuel system (Section 7)
- [ ] Check the suspension (Section 8)
- [ ] Check the brake pads (Section 9)
- [ ] Check the brake system and brake light switch operation (Section 10)
- [ ] Check the tightness of all nuts, bolts and fasteners (Section 11)
- [ ] Check the condition of the wheels and tyres (Section 12)
- [ ] Check the clutch (Section 13)
- [ ] Check the drive chain slider (Section 15)
- [ ] Check the spark plugs (Section 16)

## Every 12,000 miles (20,000 km) or two years (whichever comes sooner)
*Carry out all the items under the 6000 mile (10,000 km) check, plus the following*
- [ ] Check/adjust the throttle body synchronisation (Section 17)
- [ ] Renew the air filter element (Section 18)
- [ ] Check the secondary air injection system (Section 19)
- [ ] Check and adjust the valve clearances (Section 20)
- [ ] Renew the fuel filter (Section 21)
- [ ] Check and adjust the steering head bearings (Section 22)
- [ ] Change the front fork oil (Section 23)
- [ ] Check the wheel bearings (Section 24)
- [ ] Lubricate the rear wheel bearing – models with single-sided swingarm (Section 25)
- [ ] Lubricate the clutch and brake levers, gearchange lever linkage, brake pedal pivot and sidestand pivots and the throttle and clutch cables (Section 26)

## Every two years
- [ ] Change the coolant (Section 27)
- [ ] Change the brake fluid (Section 28)

## Every 18,000 miles (30,000 km) or three years (whichever comes sooner)
*Carry out all the items under the 6000 mile (10,000 km) check, plus the following*
- [ ] Lubricate the swingarm and suspension linkage bearings (Section 30)
- [ ] Renew the spark plugs (Section 31)

## Every 24,000 miles (40,000 km) or four years (whichever comes sooner)
*Carry out all the items under the 12,000 mile (20,000 km) check, plus the following*
- [ ] Check the cam chain (Section 32)

## Every four years
- [ ] Renew the brake hoses (Section 33)
- [ ] Renew the brake master cylinder and caliper seals (see Section 29)
- [ ] Renew the fuel system hoses (Section 34)

## Non-scheduled maintenance
- [ ] Check the stand (Section 35)
- [ ] Check and adjust the headlight aim (Section 36)
- [ ] Check the cylinder compression (Section 37)

## Component locations – Daytona and Speed Triple models

| | | | |
|---|---|---|---|
| 1 Clutch cable upper adjuster | 4 Air filter | 9 Coolant reservoir | 13 Oil filter |
| 2 Steering head bearing adjuster | 5 Battery | 10 Rear brake fluid reservoir | 14 Oil level window (early engine) |
| 3 Cooling system pressure cap | 6 Drive chain adjuster | 11 Clutch cable lower adjuster | 15 Oil filler cap (dipstick on later engine) |
| | 7 Oil drain plug | 12 Front brake fluid reservoir | |
| | 8 Coolant drain plug | | |

## Component locations – Sprint models

1 Clutch cable upper adjuster
2 Steering head bearing
   adjuster
3 Air filter
4 Battery

5 Coolant reservoir
6 Drive chain adjuster – RS type
   shown
7 Oil drain plug
8 Coolant drain plug

9 Cooling system pressure cap
10 Rear brake fluid reservoir
11 Clutch cable lower adjuster
12 Front brake fluid reservoir
13 Oil filter

14 Oil level window (early engine)
15 Oil filler cap (dipstick on later
   engine)
16 Drive chain adjuster –
   RS type shown

## Component locations – Tiger model

1 Clutch cable upper adjuster
2 Air filter
3 Drive chain adjuster
4 Oil drain plug
5 Coolant drain plug

6 Cooling system pressure cap
7 Rear brake fluid reservoir
8 Battery
9 Clutch cable lower adjuster

10 Front brake fluid reservoir
11 Coolant reservoir
12 Steering head bearing adjuster
13 Oil filter

14 Oil level window (early engine)
15 Oil filler cap (dipstick on later engine)
16 Drive chain adjuster – 1999 to 2004 type shown

1 This Chapter is designed to help the home mechanic maintain his/her motorcycle for safety, economy, long life and peak performance.

2 Deciding where to start or plug into the routine maintenance schedule depends on several factors. If the warranty period on your motorcycle has just expired, and if it has been maintained according to the warranty standards, you may want to pick up routine maintenance as it coincides with the next mileage or calendar interval. If you have owned the machine for some time but have never performed any maintenance on it, then you may want to start at the beginning and include all frequent procedures to ensure that nothing important is overlooked. If you have just had a major engine overhaul, then you should start the engine maintenance routines from the beginning. If you have a used machine and have no knowledge of its history or maintenance record, you should combine all the checks into one large initial service and then settle into the maintenance schedule prescribed.

3 Before beginning any maintenance or repair, the machine should be cleaned thoroughly, especially around the oil filter, spark plugs, valve cover, side panels, etc. Cleaning will help ensure that dirt does not contaminate the engine and will allow you to detect wear and damage that could otherwise easily go unnoticed.

4 Many of the bolts used in the building of the engine are of the Torx type. Unless you are already equipped with a good range of Torx bits, you are advised to obtain a set. Make sure you get bits that can be used in conjunction with a socket set so that a torque wrench can be applied – a Torx key set will not be adequate on its own, though will be useful in addition to the bits.

5 Certain maintenance information is sometimes printed on decals attached to the motorcycle. If any information on the decals differs from that included here, use the information on the decal.

6 Note that in many cases, Triumph use the machine's VIN number as a means of identification rather than the year of manufacture. Always check the VIN number against the details given in this manual to ensure you follow the correct procedure.

# Maintenance procedures

## 1 Drive chain check, adjustment and lubrication

### Check

1 As the chain stretches with wear, adjustment will periodically be necessary. A neglected drive chain won't last long and can quickly damage the sprockets. Routine chain adjustment and lubrication isn't difficult and will ensure maximum chain and sprocket life.

2 To check the chain, support the bike upright using an auxiliary stand or the centrestand (Sprint ST only), so that the rear wheel is off the ground. Make sure the transmission is in neutral.

3 Push up on the bottom run of the chain and measure the slack midway between the two sprockets (see illustration), then compare your measurement to that listed in this Chapter's Specifications. Since the chain will rarely wear evenly, resulting in a tight spot, rotate the rear wheel so that another section of chain can be checked; do this several times to check the entire length of chain. Any adjustment should be based upon the measurement taken at the tightest point.

4 In some cases where lubrication has been neglected, corrosion and galling may cause the links to bind and kink, which effectively shortens the chain's length. Any such links should be thoroughly cleaned and worked free. If the chain is tight between the sprockets, rusty or kinked, it's time to renew it. If you find a tight area, mark it with felt pen or paint, and repeat the measurement after the bike has been ridden. If the chain's still tight in the same area, it may be damaged or worn. Because a tight or kinked chain can damage the transmission output shaft bearing, it's a good idea to renew it (see Chapter 5).

### Adjustment

5 Support the bike upright using an auxiliary stand or the centrestand (Sprint ST only), so that the rear wheel is off the ground. Make sure the transmission is in neutral. Rotate the rear wheel until the chain is positioned with the tightest point at the centre of its bottom run.

### Daytona, Speed Triple, Sprint ST and RS models – single-sided swingarm

6 Slacken the adjuster clamp bolt (see illustration).

7 Locate the C-spanner supplied in the bike's toolkit, or a suitable alternative, into the notches in the eccentric adjuster in the hub and turn it until the amount of freeplay specified at the beginning of the Chapter is obtained at the centre of the bottom run of the chain (see illustration). If you are tightening the chain, locate the tool on the underside of the adjuster and turn it anti-clockwise (see illustration). If you are slackening the chain, locate the tool on the top of the adjuster and turn it clockwise.

1.3 Push up on the chain and measure the slack

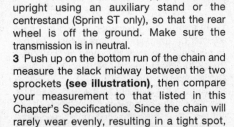

1.6 Chain adjuster clamp bolt (arrowed)

1.7a This adjustment tool is supplied in the bike's toolkit, and locates into the notches in the adjuster

1.7b Turn the adjuster anti-clockwise to tighten the chain

1.8 Tighten the clamp bolt to the specified torque

1.9 Slacken the rear axle nut (arrowed)

1.10a Slacken the locknut (A) and turn the adjuster (B) as required

8 When the correct amount of freeplay is obtained, tighten the adjuster clamp bolt to the torque setting specified at the beginning of the Chapter (see illustration). Rotate the rear wheel and recheck the adjustment.

### Daytona, Sprint RS and 2005 Tiger models – double-sided swingarm

9 Slacken the axle nut (see illustration).
10 Slacken the adjuster locknut on each side of the swingarm, then turn the adjusters evenly until the amount of freeplay specified at the beginning of the Chapter is obtained at the centre of the bottom run of the chain (see illustration). Following chain adjustment, check that the back edge of each chain adjustment marker is in the same position in relation to the marks on the swingarm (see illustration). It is important each adjuster aligns with the same mark; if not, the rear

wheel will be out of alignment with the front. Also check that there is no clearance between the adjuster and the front of the adjustment marker – push or kick the wheel forwards to eliminate any freeplay.

> **HAYNES HiNT** Refer to Chapter 6 for information on checking wheel alignment.

11 If there is a discrepancy in the chain adjuster positions, adjust one of them so that its position is exactly the same as the other. Check the chain freeplay as described above and readjust if necessary.
12 Tighten the axle nut to the torque setting specified at the beginning of the Chapter, then tighten the adjuster locknuts securely. Recheck the adjustment.

### 1999 to 2004 Tiger models

13 Slacken the adjuster clamp bolt on each end of the swingarm (see illustration).
14 Using two Allen keys, turn each eccentric adjuster simultaneously until the amount of freeplay specified at the beginning of the Chapter is obtained at the centre of the bottom run of the chain (see illustration). Following adjustment, check that each adjuster is in the same position in relation to the swingarm, otherwise the wheels could be out of alignment – the adjusters should naturally turn equally and simultaneously, but it is worth double-checking in case one has become tight due to corrosion.
15 If there is a discrepancy in the chain adjuster positions, adjust one of them so that its position is exactly the same as the other. Check the chain freeplay as described above and readjust if necessary.
16 Tighten the adjuster clamp bolts to the torque setting specified at the beginning of the Chapter (see illustration 1.13). Rotate the rear wheel and recheck the adjustment.

### Lubrication

17 If required, wash the chain in paraffin (kerosene), then wipe it off and allow it to dry, using compressed air if available. If the chain is excessively dirty it should be removed from the machine and allowed to soak in the paraffin (see Chapter 5).
*Caution: Don't use petrol (gasoline), solvent or other cleaning fluids which might damage the internal sealing properties of the chain. Don't use high-pressure water. The entire process shouldn't take longer than ten minutes – if it does, the O-rings in the chain rollers could be damaged.*
18 For routine lubrication, the best time to lubricate the chain is after the motorcycle has been ridden. When the chain is warm, the lubricant will penetrate the joints between the side plates better than when cold. **Note:** *Use chain lube which is marked as being suitable for O-ring chains; other types may contain solvents that could damage the O-rings.* Apply the lubricant to the area where the side plates overlap – not the middle of the rollers (see illustration). **Note:** *Triumph recommend that the bike should not be ridden for 8 hours after*

1.10b Check the relative position of the back edge of the adjustment marker (arrowed) with the marks on the swingarm

1.13 Slacken the clamp bolt (arrowed) on each end of the swingarm

1.14 Turn each eccentric adjuster equally using a pair of Allen keys, one in each side

1.18 Apply the lubricant to the overlap between the sideplates

*applying lubricant to allow it to penetrate between the chain components.*

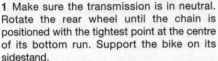

**HAYNES HiNT** *Apply the lubricant to the top of the lower chain run, so centrifugal force will work it into the chain when the bike is moving. After applying the lubricant, let it soak in for a few minutes, then wipe off any excess.*

## 2 Drive chain and sprockets wear and stretch check

**1** Make sure the transmission is in neutral. Rotate the rear wheel until the chain is positioned with the tightest point at the centre of its bottom run. Support the bike on its sidestand.

**2** Check the entire length of the chain for damaged rollers, loose links and pins, and missing O-rings. Fit a new chain if damage is found (see Chapter 5). **Note:** *Never install a new chain on old sprockets, and never use the old chain if you install new sprockets – replace the chain and sprockets as a set.*

**3** To check the amount of chain wear (stretch), obtain a 10 to 20 kg (20 to 40 lb) weight and hang it from the middle of the bottom run of the chain **(see illustration)**. Remove the chainguard. Measure along the top run the length of 21 pins (from the centre of the 1st pin to the centre of the 21st pin) and compare the result with the service limit specified at the beginning of the Chapter. Rotate the wheel so that several sections of the chain are measured, then calculate the average. If the chain exceeds the service limit it must be replaced with a new one (see Chapter 5).

**4** Remove the front sprocket cover (see Chapter 5). Check the teeth on the front and rear sprockets for wear **(see illustration)**.

**5** Inspect the drive chain slider on the swingarm for excessive wear and renew it if worn (see Chapter 5).

## 3 Engine oil and filter change

⚠️ **Warning:** *Be careful when draining the oil, as the exhaust pipes, the engine, and the oil itself can cause severe burns.*

**1** Consistent routine oil and filter changes are the single most important maintenance procedure you can perform on a motorcycle. The oil not only lubricates the internal parts of the engine, transmission and clutch, but it also acts as a coolant, a cleaner, a sealant, and a protector. Because of these demands, the oil takes a terrific amount of abuse and

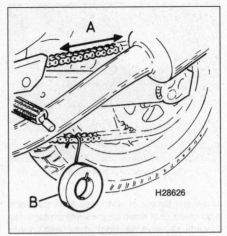

**2.3 Check the amount of stretch using a weight and by measuring as shown**
*A  21 pin length      B  Weight*

should be changed often with new oil of the recommended grade and type. Saving a little money on the difference in cost between a good oil and a cheap oil won't pay off if the engine is damaged. The oil filter should be changed with every oil change.

**2** Before changing the oil, warm up the engine so the oil will drain easily. Support the motorcycle upright on level ground using an auxiliary stand or the centrestand (Sprint ST only), making sure it is secure.

**3** Position a clean drain tray below the engine. Unscrew the oil filler cap from the

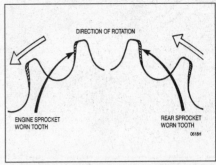

**2.4 Check the sprockets in the areas indicated to see if they are worn excessively**

clutch cover to vent it and to act as a reminder that there is no oil in the engine **(see illustration)**.

**4** Unscrew the oil drain plug from the underside of the engine and allow the oil to flow into the drain tray **(see illustrations)**. Discard the sealing washer on the drain plug as a new one must be fitted.

**5** When the oil has completely drained, fit the plug into the crankcase, using a new sealing washer, and tighten it to the torque setting specified at the beginning of the Chapter **(see illustration)**. Avoid overtightening, as you will damage the sump.

**6** Now place the drain tray below the oil filter, which is also under the engine. Unscrew the filter using a filter removal tool or a strap wrench and tip any residual oil into the drain

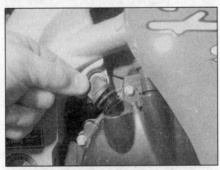

**3.3 Remove the oil filler cap from the clutch cover**

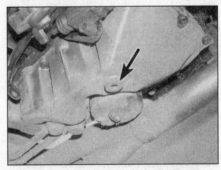

**3.4a Unscrew the oil drain plug (arrowed) . . .**

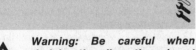

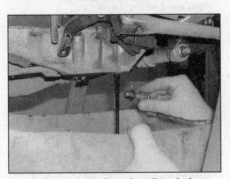

**3.4b . . . and allow the oil to drain**

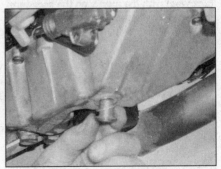

**3.5 Install the drain plug, using a new sealing washer if necessary, and tighten it to the specified torque**

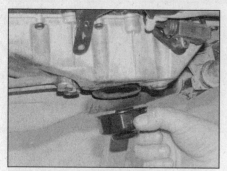

**3.6a A filter adaptor is the best tool for unscrewing the oil filter**

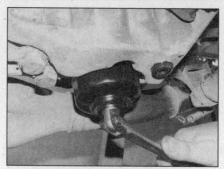

**3.6b Unscrew the filter . . .**

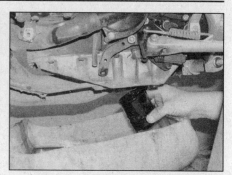

**3.6c . . . and drain it into the tray**

tray **(see illustrations)**. Triumph provides a suitable oil filter tool (Part No. T3880311).

7 Smear clean engine oil onto the rubber seal on the new filter, then manoeuvre it into position and screw it onto the engine until the seal just seats **(see illustrations)**. If a filter tool is available, tighten the filter to the torque setting specified at the beginning of the Chapter. Otherwise, tighten the filter as tight as possible by hand, or by the number of turns specified on the filter or its packaging. **Note:** *Do not use a strap or chain type removing tool to tighten the filter as you will damage the filter body.*

8 Refill the engine to the proper level, either on the inspection window or the dipstick as appropriate, using the recommended type and amount of oil (see *Daily (pre-ride) checks*). Install the filler cap, using a new O-ring if the old one is damaged, deformed or deteriorated **(see illustration 3.3)**. Start the engine and let it run for two or three minutes. Stop the engine, wait a few minutes, then check the oil level. If necessary, add more oil to bring the level up to the maximum level line. Check that there are no leaks around the drain plug. Similarly check the filter and tighten it some more if there are leaks.

9 Follow the procedure in Chapter 2A, Section 20, or Chapter 2B, Section 21, and check the oil cooler and oil hoses for damage and leaks. Renew any components as necessary – if removed, always use new sealing washers on each side of the banjo unions.

10 The old oil drained from the engine cannot be re-used and should be disposed of properly. Check with your local refuse disposal company, disposal facility or environmental agency to see whether they will accept the used oil for recycling. Don't pour used oil into drains or onto the ground. Remember to drain all the old oil from the filter (you can punch a hole in the filter to ensure it drains fully) into the drain pan. Note that the old filter should be taken to the oil disposal facility rather than disposed of with the household rubbish.

> **HAYNES HINT**
> *Check the old oil carefully – if it is very metallic coloured, then the engine is experiencing wear from break-in (new engine) or from insufficient lubrication. If there are flakes or chips of metal in the oil, then something is drastically wrong internally and the engine will have to be disassembled for inspection and repair. If there are pieces of fibre-like material in the oil, the clutch is experiencing excessive wear and should be checked.*

**OIL CARE** FOLLOW THE CODE

OIL BANK LINE
**0800 66 33 66**
www.oilbankline.org.uk

*In the USA, note that any oil supplier must accept used oil for recycling*

**Note:** *It is antisocial and illegal to dump oil down the drain. To find the location of your local oil recycling bank, call this number free.*

## 4 Engine management system check

**Note:** *The idle speed is controlled by the idle air control valve, which in turn is controlled by the electronic control module (ECM). Idle speed cannot be manually adjusted – it can only be done using the diagnostic tool.*

1 The engine management system should be checked for any stored diagnostic fault codes. To do this, the Triumph diagnostic tool is essential. Take your machine to a dealer and have them check the system – it should not take them long. Note that this task is impracticable for the DIY mechanic, not only because the diagnostic tool would be prohibitively expensive, but because an authorisation code is required to operate it and the codes are only available to Triumph dealers.

2 If any problems with the system occur during use, the malfunction indicator light (MIL) in the instrument cluster will illuminate. If this happens, the management system switches itself into 'limp home' mode, so that in theory you should not be left stranded. Depending on the problem, it is possible that you will notice no difference in the running of the motorcycle. In order to diagnose the fault and to turn the MIL off, the diagnostic tool is essential, so the machine must be taken to a Triumph dealer.

3 Further information on the system, including all tests and checks that can be performed without the Triumph diagnostic tool, is contained in Chapter 4.

## 5 Throttle cable check

**Note:** *1997 to 2001 Daytona, Speed Triple and Sprint models and all Tiger models are fitted with one throttle cable; 2002-on Daytona, Speed Triple and Sprint models are fitted with two (opening and closing) cables.*

1 Make sure the throttle twistgrip rotates easily from fully closed to fully open with the front wheel turned at various angles. The

**3.7a Smear some clean oil onto the seal . . .**

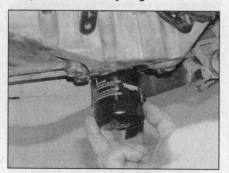

**3.7b . . . then thread the filter into the engine and tighten it as described**

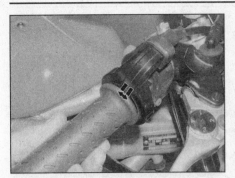

**5.3 Measure the amount of freeplay in the throttle twistgrip as shown**

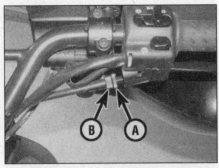

**5.4a Throttle cable adjuster locknut (A) and adjuster (B) – Tiger models**

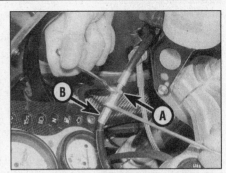

**5.4b Throttle cable adjuster locknut (A) and adjuster (B) – all other models**

twistgrip should return automatically from fully open to fully closed when released.

**2** If the throttle sticks, this is probably due to a cable fault. Remove the cable (see Chapter 4) and lubricate it (see Section 26). If the inner cable still does not run smoothly in the outer cable, renew it. With the cable removed, check that the twistgrip runs smoothly and freely around the handlebar – dirt and debris combined with a lack of lubrication can cause the action to be stiff. Install the lubricated or new cable, making sure it is correctly routed (see Chapter 4). If this falls to improve the operation of the throttle, the fault could lie in the throttle bodies. Remove the airbox and check the action of the throttle linkage and butterflies (see Chapter 4).

**3** With the throttle operating smoothly, check for a small amount of freeplay in the cable(s), measured in terms of the amount of twistgrip rotation before the throttle opens, and compare the amount to that listed in this Chapter's Specifications **(see illustration)**. If it's incorrect, adjust the cable(s) as follows.

### Single throttle cable

**4** An adjuster is incorporated at the twistgrip end of the cable, either as it leaves the twistgrip housing (Tiger models), or part-way along the cable (all other models). Slacken the locknut, then turn the adjuster until the specified amount of freeplay is obtained (see this Chapter's Specifications), then retighten the locknut **(see illustrations)**. Turn the adjuster in to increase freeplay and out to reduce it.

**5** If the adjuster has reached its limit of adjustment, reset it so that it is half way along its adjustment limit, then adjust the cable at the throttle body end as follows. Remove the fuel tank and the airbox (see Chapter 4).

**6** Slacken the locknuts holding the cable in the bracket, then turn the adjuster while holding the locknuts until the specified amount of freeplay is obtained **(see illustration)**. Turn the adjuster in to increase freeplay, and out to decrease it. Tighten the locknuts onto the bracket on completion. Further adjustments can now be made at the twistgrip end. If the cable cannot be adjusted as specified, renew the cable (see Chapter 4).

**7** Check that the throttle twistgrip operates smoothly and snaps shut quickly when released. Install the airbox and fuel tank (see Chapter 4).

### Opening and closing throttle cables

**8** An adjuster is incorporated at the twistgrip end of the opening cable. Slacken the locknut on the opening cable adjuster, then turn the adjuster until the specified amount of freeplay is obtained (see this Chapter's Specifications), then retighten the locknut **(see illustration)**. Turn the adjuster in to increase freeplay and out to reduce it.

**9** If the opening cable adjuster has reached its limit of adjustment, reset it so that it is half way along its adjustment limit, then adjust both cables at the throttle body end as follows. Remove the fuel tank and the airbox (see Chapter 4).

**10** Slacken the locknut holding the opening

(rear) cable in the bracket, then turn the adjuster on the opening cable until the specified amount of freeplay is obtained **(see illustration 5.6)**. Turn the adjuster in to increase freeplay, and out to decrease it. Tighten the locknut onto the bracket on completion. With the throttle fully closed, ensure that there is the specified amount of freeplay in the closing (front) cable and adjust it at the bracket as necessary.

**11** Further adjustments can now be made at the twistgrip end. If the cables cannot be adjusted as specified, renew them (see Chapter 4).

**12** Check that the throttle twistgrip operates smoothly and snaps shut quickly when released. Install the airbox and fuel tank (see Chapter 4).

> ⚠ **Warning: Turn the handlebars all the way through their travel with the engine idling. Idle speed should not change. If it does, the cable may be routed incorrectly. Correct this condition before riding the bike.**

## 6  Cooling system checks

> ⚠ **Warning: The engine must be cool before beginning this procedure.**

**1** Check the coolant level (see *Daily (pre-ride) checks*).

**2** The entire cooling system should be checked for evidence of leaks. On 1997 to 2001 Daytona and Speed Triple models remove the fuel tank cover (see Chapter 4) and on Daytona models also remove the left-hand fairing side panel (see Chapter 7). On 2002-on Daytona and Sprint models remove both fairing side panels (see Chapter 7). On all Tiger models remove the fuel tank (see Chapter 4).

**3** Examine each rubber coolant hose along its entire length. Look for cracks, abrasions and other damage. Squeeze each hose at various points. They should feel firm, yet pliable, and return to their original shape when released. If they are dried out or hard, replace them with new ones.

**4** Check for evidence of leaks at each cooling

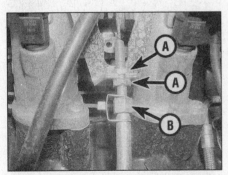

**5.6 Slacken the locknuts (A), then hold them and turn the adjuster (B) as required**

**5.8 Opening throttle cable adjuster**

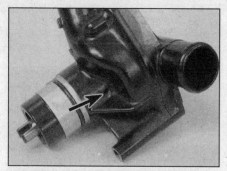

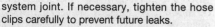

6.5 Check the drainage hole (arrowed) on the underside of the pump for signs of leakage

6.8a  Remove the pressure cap from the thermostat housing . . .

6.8b  . . . or the radiator filler neck as described

system joint. If necessary, tighten the hose clips carefully to prevent future leaks.

5 To prevent leakage of water from the cooling system to the lubrication system and vice versa, two seals are fitted on the pump shaft. On the bottom of the pump there is a drain hole **(see illustration)**. If either seal fails, the drain allows the coolant or oil to escape and prevents them mixing. The seal on the water pump side is of the mechanical type which bears on the rear face of the impeller. The second seal, which is mounted behind the mechanical seal is of the normal feathered lip type. If on inspection the drain hole shows signs of coolant leakage, remove the pump and replace it with a new one – the seals are not available individually. Refer to Chapter 3 for pump renewal.

6 Check the radiator for leaks and other damage. Leaks in the radiator leave tell-tale scale deposits or coolant stains on the outside of the core below the leak. If leaks are noted, remove the radiator (see Chapter 3) and either have it repaired by a professional or replace it with a new one.

*Caution: Do not use a liquid leak stopping compound to try to repair leaks.*

7 Check the radiator fins for mud, dirt and insects, which may impede the flow of air through the radiator. If the fins are dirty, remove the radiator (see Chapter 3) and clean it using water or low pressure compressed air directed through the fins from the rear face of the radiator. If the fins are bent or distorted, straighten them carefully with a screwdriver. If the air flow is restricted by bent or damaged fins over more than 30% of the radiator's surface area, install a new radiator.

8 Remove the pressure cap from the filler neck in the thermostat housing or the radiator as applicable **(see illustrations)**. Turn the cap anti-clockwise until it reaches a stop – if you hear a hissing sound (indicating there is still pressure in the system), wait until it stops. Now press down on the cap and continue turning it until it can be removed. Check the condition of the coolant in the system. If it is rust-coloured or if accumulations of scale are visible, drain, flush and refill the system with new coolant (See Section 27). Check the cap seal for cracks and other damage. If in doubt

about the pressure cap's condition, have it tested by a Triumph dealer or replace it with a new one. Install the cap by turning it clockwise until it reaches the first stop then push down on the cap and continue turning until it can turn further.

9 Check the antifreeze content of the coolant with an antifreeze hydrometer. Sometimes coolant looks like it's in good condition, but might be too weak to offer adequate protection. If the hydrometer indicates a weak mixture, drain, flush and refill the system (see Section 27).

10 Start the engine and let it reach normal operating temperature, then check for leaks again. As the coolant temperature increases beyond normal, the fan should come on automatically and the temperature should begin to drop. If it doesn't, refer to Chapter 3 and check the fan motor and fan circuit carefully, then if the fan still does not work, refer to Chapter 4 and check the engine coolant temperature sensor and the engine management system, which control the fan. Note that if the engine is switched off while the fan is running, the fan should continue to run until the coolant temperature has dropped to a normal level.

11 If the coolant level is consistently low, and no evidence of leaks can be found, have the entire system pressure checked by a Triumph dealer.

## 7  Fuel system checks

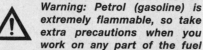

⚠ *Warning: Petrol (gasoline) is extremely flammable, so take extra precautions when you work on any part of the fuel system. Don't smoke or allow open flames or bare light bulbs near the work area, and don't work in a garage where a natural gas-type appliance is present. If you spill any fuel on your skin, rinse it off immediately with soap and water. When you perform any kind of work on the fuel system, wear safety glasses and have a fire extinguisher suitable for a Class B type fire (flammable liquids) on hand.*

### Fuel system

1 Remove the fuel tank (see Chapter 4). Check the entire system for signs of leaks, deterioration or damage; in particular check that there are no leaks from the fuel feed and return hoses and their sockets, fuel rail and connectors, and from the fuel pump assembly gasket on the fuel tank. Renew any hoses which are cracked or have deteriorated (see Section 34). **Note:** *On Daytona, Speed Triple and Sprint models from VIN 207555-on, and Tiger models from VIN 207447-on, only a fuel feed hose is fitted.*

2 The fuel hoses and their sockets incorporate a self-sealing valve that prevents residual fuel leaking when the tank is removed. Check that there are no leaks from the hose end. If there are, the valve has failed and the hose must be renewed. Check the condition of the O-ring on each fuel hose connector. If there are any signs of fuel leakage when the tank is installed, replace the O-rings with new ones – they should really be renewed every time the tank is removed.

3 Refer to Chapter 4 for removal of the fuel rail.

4 On all models fitted with a fuel feed and return hose, if the fuel hose sockets in the pump mounting plate are leaking, remove the tank and drain it (see Chapter 4), then unscrew the sockets and replace them with new ones, tightening them to the specified torque setting. Do not overtighten them as the threads will be damaged and further leakage will occur.

5 If the tank has been leaking from the fuel pump gasket, tightening the mounting plate bolts may help. To ensure the plate is evenly seated, slacken the bolts a little first, then tighten them evenly and a little at a time to the torque setting specified at the beginning of the Chapter. If leaks persists, remove the pump assembly and replace the seal with a new one (see Chapter 4).

6 Check the Idle Air Control circuit hoses running between the throttle bodies and the valve for loose connections, cracks and deterioration, and replace them with new ones if necessary.

7 On California models, check the EVAP system hoses for loose connections, cracks

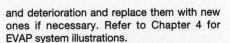

**8.8a Checking for play in the swingarm bearings**

**8.8b Checking for play in the suspension linkage bearings**

and deterioration and replace them with new ones if necessary. Refer to Chapter 4 for EVAP system illustrations.

8 If fitted, check the secondary air injection system hoses (see Section 19).

## Fuel strainer and filter

9 A fuel strainer and in-line fuel filter are mounted in the tank (see illustration 21.2). Cleaning of the strainer is advised after a high mileage has been covered. It is also necessary if fuel starvation is suspected. Remove the fuel pump assembly (see Chapter 4). Clean the gauze strainer to remove all traces of dirt and fuel sediment. If the strainer is dirty, check the condition of the inside of the tank – if there is evidence of rust, drain and clean the tank (see Chapter 4).

10 The in-line filter must be replaced with a new one at the specified service interval (see Section 21).

## 8 Suspension checks

1 The suspension components must be maintained in top operating condition to ensure rider safety. Loose, worn or damaged suspension parts decrease the motorcycle's stability and control.

## Front suspension

2 While standing alongside the motorcycle,

apply the front brake and push on the handlebars to compress the forks several times. See if they move up-and-down smoothly without binding. If binding is felt, the forks should be disassembled and inspected (see Chapter 5).

3 Where fitted, slacken the fork protector clamp bolt and slide the protector up the fork. On Tiger models, slacken the lower gaiter clamp and slide the gaiter up the fork. Check the gaiter for cracks, splits and general deterioration.

4 Inspect the bottom of the inner tube for signs of scratches, corrosion and pitting, and oil leakage, then carefully lever off the dust seal using a flat-bladed screwdriver and inspect the area around the fork oil seal. Any scratches, corrosion and pitting will cause premature seal failure. If the damage is excessive new tubes should be installed (see Chapter 5). If oil leaks are evident, new oil seals must be fitted (see Chapter 5).

5 Check the tightness of all suspension nuts and bolts to be sure none have worked loose, referring to the torque settings specified at the beginning of Chapter 5.

## Rear suspension

6 Inspect the rear shock for fluid leaks at the top of the damper rod. If leaks are found, a new shock should be installed (see Chapter 5).

7 With the aid of an assistant to support the bike, compress the rear suspension several times. It should move up and down freely

without binding. If any binding is felt, the worn or faulty component must be identified and renewed. The problem could be due to the shock absorber, the suspension linkage components or the swingarm.

8 Support the motorcycle using an auxiliary stand so that the rear wheel is off the ground. Grab the swingarm and rock it from side to side – there should be no discernible movement at the rear (see illustration). If there's a little movement or a slight clicking can be heard, inspect the tightness of all the rear suspension mounting bolts and nuts, referring to the torque settings specified at the beginning of Chapter 5, and re-check for movement. Next, grasp the top of the rear wheel and pull it upwards – there should be no discernible freeplay before the shock absorber begins to compress (see illustration). Any freeplay felt in either check indicates worn bearings in the suspension linkage or swingarm, or worn shock absorber mountings. The worn components must be renewed (see Chapter 5).

9 To make an accurate assessment of the swingarm bearings, remove the rear wheel (see Chapter 6) and the bolt securing the suspension linkage to the swingarm (see Chapter 5). Grasp the rear of the swingarm with one hand and place your other hand at the junction of the swingarm and the frame. Try to move the rear of the swingarm from side-to-side. Any wear (play) in the bearings should be felt as movement between the swingarm and the frame at the front. If there is any play the swingarm will be felt to move forward and backward at the front (not from side-to-side). Next, move the swingarm up and down through its full travel. It should move freely, without any binding or rough spots. If any play in the swingarm is noted or if the swingarm does not move freely, remove the swingarm and inspect the bearings (see Chapter 5).

10 Check the tightness of all suspension nuts and bolts to be sure none have worked loose, referring to the torque settings specified at the beginning of Chapter 5.

## 9 Brake pad check

1 Each brake pad has wear indicators that can be viewed without removing the pads from the caliper (see illustrations). Note that on some models it may be necessary to displace the caliper to check pad wear (see Chapter 6). If the pads are dirty, or you are in doubt as to the amount of friction material remaining, remove them for inspection (see Chapter 6).

2 The grooves in the brake pad friction material form the wear indicators – when the friction material has worn to the bottom of the grooves, the pads must be renewed (see

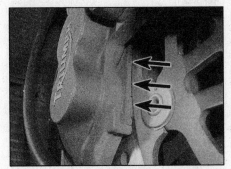

**9.1a Front brake pad wear indicator grooves (arrowed) – Daytona, Speed Triple and Sprint type shown**

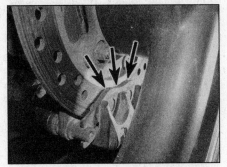
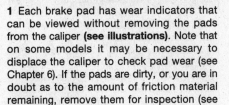

**9.1b Rear brake pad wear indicator grooves (arrowed) – Daytona, Speed Triple and Sprint type shown**

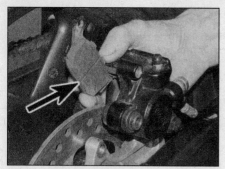

**9.2 Renew the pads when they are worn to the bottom of the wear indicator groove (arrowed)**

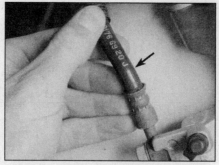

**10.3 Flex the brake hose (arrowed) and check for cracks, bulges and leaking fluid**

**10.5 Hold the brake light switch (A) and turn the adjuster nut (B)**

**illustration)**. If required, measure the amount of friction material remaining – the minimum is 1.5 mm. **Note:** *Some after-market pads may use different indicators (such as a groove cut into the top edge of the friction material); the pad is worn when the groove is no longer visible.*
**Caution: Do not allow the pads to wear beyond the groove.**
**3** Always renew brake pads in sets and renew the pads in both front brake calipers at the same time. If the pads appear to be wearing unevenly, remove the caliper and check the operation of the pistons (see Chapter 6).

## 10 Brake system checks

**1** A routine general check of the brake system will ensure that any problems are discovered and remedied before the rider's safety is jeopardised.
**2** Check the brake lever and pedal for looseness, improper or rough action, excessive play, bends, and other damage. Replace any damaged parts with new ones (see Chapter 5). Clean and lubricate the lever and pedal pivots if their action is stiff or rough (see Section 26).
**3** Make sure all brake fasteners are tight. Check the brake pads for wear (see Section 9) and make sure the fluid level in the reservoirs is correct (see *Daily (pre-ride) checks*). Check that there is no sign of fluid leakage at the

hose connections and that the hoses are not cracked or damaged **(see illustration)**. If the lever or pedal is spongy bleed the brakes (see Chapter 6). The brake fluid should be changed every two years (see Section 28) and the hoses renewed if they deteriorate, or every four years irrespective of their condition (see Section 33). The master cylinder and caliper seals should be renewed every two or four years (according to model) or if leakage from them is evident (see Section 29).
**4** Make sure the brake light operates when the front brake lever is pulled in. The front brake light switch, mounted in the lever bracket, is not adjustable. If it fails to operate properly, check it (see Chapter 8).
**5** Make sure the brake light is activated just before the rear brake takes effect. On Sprint and Tiger models, the switch is operated hydraulically and is not adjustable. If it fails to operate properly, check it (see Chapter 8). On Daytona and Speed Triple models, the switch is operated mechanically by a spring connected to the brake pedal. If it fails to operate properly, first check that the spring is still attached to both the pedal and the switch pullrod. If adjustment is necessary, hold the switch and turn the adjuster nut on the switch body until the brake light is activated when required **(see illustration)**. If the brake light comes on too late, turn the nut clockwise. If the brake light comes on too soon or is permanently on, turn the nut anti-clockwise. If the switch doesn't operate the brake light, check it (see Chapter 8).
**6** On Daytona, Speed Triple and Sprint

models, the front brake lever has a span adjuster which alters the distance of the lever from the handlebar to suit different hand sizes. Each setting is identified by a number on the adjuster which aligns with the arrow on the lever bracket. Pull the lever away from the handlebar and turn the adjuster ring until the setting which best suits the rider is obtained **(see illustration)**. There are four settings – setting 1 gives the largest span, and setting 4 the smallest. When making adjustment ensure that the pin set in the lever bracket is engaged in its detent in the adjuster.
**7** Check that the position of the brake pedal is correctly set for you **(see illustration)**. If you want to adjust the pedal height, slacken the clevis locknut on the master cylinder pushrod, then turn the pushrod using a spanner on the hex at the top of the rod until the pedal is at the correct or desired height **(see illustration)**. After adjustment check that the pushrod end is still visible in the hole in the clevis. On completion tighten the locknut securely. Adjust the rear brake light switch (Daytona and Speed Triple only) after adjusting the pedal height (see Step 5).

## 11 Nuts and bolts tightness check

**1** Since vibration of the machine tends to loosen fasteners, all nuts, bolts, screws, etc. should be periodically checked for proper tightness. If you feel the engine vibrating more

**10.6 Adjusting the front brake lever span**

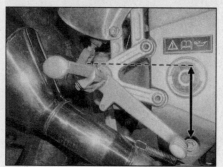

**10.7a If you want to adjust the height of the brake pedal relative to the footrest . . .**

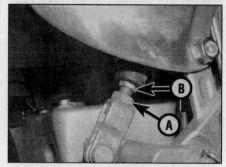

**10.7b . . . slacken the locknut (A) and turn the pushrod using the hex (B) as required**

than usual, check all the mountings before assuming there are extensive internal problems.

**2** Pay particular attention to the following:

*Spark plugs*

*Engine oil drain plug*

*Gearchange lever, brake and clutch lever, and brake pedal bolts*

*Footrest and stand bolts*

*Engine mounting bolts*

*Shock absorber and suspension linkage bolts and swingarm pivot bolts*

*Handlebar clamp bolts*

*Front axle bolt and axle clamp bolts*

*Front fork clamp bolts (top and bottom yoke)*

*Rear axle nut*

*Brake caliper mounting bolts*

*Brake hose banjo bolts and caliper bleed valves*

*Brake disc bolts*

*Exhaust system bolts/nuts*

**3** If a torque wrench is available, use it along with the torque specifications at the beginning of this and other Chapters.

## 12 Wheels and tyres check

### Tyres

**1** Check the tyre condition and tread depth thoroughly – see *Daily (pre-ride) checks.*

### Wheels

**2** Cast wheels as fitted to all Daytona, Speed Triple and Sprint models, and Tiger models from VIN 198875-on, are virtually maintenance free, but they should be kept clean and checked periodically for cracks and other damage. Also check the wheel runout and alignment (see Chapter 6). Never attempt to repair damaged cast wheels; they must be replaced with new ones. Check the valve rubber for signs of damage or deterioration and have it renewed by a motorcycle tyre fitting specialist if necessary. Also, make sure the valve stem cap is in place and tight.

**3** On Tiger models with wire-spoked wheels,

visually check the spokes for damage, breakage or corrosion. A broken or bent spoke must be renewed immediately because the load taken by it will be transferred to adjacent spokes, which may in turn fail.

**4** If you suspect that any of the spokes are incorrectly tensioned, tap each one lightly with a screwdriver and note the sound produced. Properly tensioned spokes will make a sharp pinging sound, loose ones will produce a lower pitch, and overtightened ones will be higher pitched. A spoke wrench will be needed if any of the spokes require adjustment. Unevenly tensioned spokes will promote rim misalignment – check the wheel runout and alignment (see Chapter 6) and seek the help of a wheel building expert if this is suspected.

## 13 Clutch check

**1** Check that the clutch lever operates smoothly and easily.

**2** If the lever action is heavy or stiff, remove the cable (see Chapter 2) and lubricate it (see Section 26). If the inner cable still does not run smoothly in the outer cable, replace it with a new one. Install the lubricated or new cable (see Chapter 2). If the action is still stiff, remove the lever and check for damage or distortion, or any other cause, and remedy as necessary. Clean and lubricate the pivot and contact areas (see Section 26). If the lever is good, refer to Chapter 2 and check the release mechanism in the cover and the clutch itself.

**3** With the cable operating smoothly, check that it is correctly adjusted. Periodic adjustment is necessary to compensate for wear in the clutch plates and stretch of the cable. Check that the amount of freeplay in the cable is within the specifications listed at the beginning of the Chapter – freeplay is measured in terms of the clearance between the lever and its bracket before the clutch is actuated **(see illustration)**.

**4** If adjustment is required, slacken the

adjuster lockring, then turn the adjuster in or out until the required amount of freeplay is obtained **(see illustration)**. To increase freeplay, turn the adjuster clockwise (into the lever bracket). To reduce freeplay, turn the adjuster anti-clockwise (out of the lever bracket). Tighten the lockring securely.

**5** If all the adjustment has been taken up at the lever, reset the adjuster to give the maximum amount of freeplay by screwing it into the bracket, then set freeplay to between 2 to 3 mm using the adjuster nuts on each end of the threaded section in the cable bracket on the right-hand side of the engine. On Daytona and Sprint ST models, remove the right-hand fairing side panel to access it (see Chapter 7). To increase freeplay, slacken the front nut, then thread the rear nut up the cable until the freeplay is correct **(see illustration)**. To decrease freeplay, slacken the rear nut, then thread the front nut down the cable towards the bracket until the freeplay is correct. Now use the adjuster at the clutch lever bracket to set the specified clearance of 0.4 to 0.8 mm between the clutch lever and its bracket.

*Caution: The specified clearance is very small and care must be taken to ensure that there is actually some freeplay in the cable, albeit a small amount, otherwise the clutch may slip.*

## 14 Battery checks

**1** T595 Daytona and T509 Speed Triple models are fitted with a standard battery which requires regular checks of the electrolyte level. Remove the battery (see Chapter 8). The electrolyte level is visible through the translucent battery case – it should be between the UPPER and LOWER level marks. If the electrolyte is low, remove the cell caps and fill each cell to the upper level mark with distilled water. Do not use tap water (except in an emergency), and do not overfill. The cell holes are quite small, so it may help to use a clean plastic squeeze bottle with a small spout to add the water. Install the

**13.3 Check the amount of freeplay in the cable as shown**

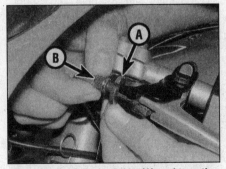

**13.4 Slacken the lockring (A) and turn the adjuster (B) as described to set the correct freeplay**

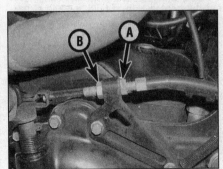

**13.5 Front nut (A), rear nut (B)**

**15.2 Clean the chain slider (arrowed) and check for wear**

**15.5 Removing the drive chain slider**

battery cell caps, tightening them securely, then install the battery. Note that Triumph supply a conversion kit for these models to enable them to use the maintenance-free battery used on later models.

**2** All other models are fitted with a maintenance-free (sealed) battery which requires no maintenance. **Note:** *Do not attempt to remove the battery caps to check the electrolyte level or battery specific gravity. Removal will damage the caps, resulting in electrolyte leakage and battery damage.* All that should be done is to check that the terminals are clean and tight and that the casing is not damaged or leaking. See Chapter 8 for further details

*Caution: Be extremely careful when handling or working around the battery. The electrolyte is very caustic and an explosive gas (hydrogen) is given off when the battery is charging.*

**3** If the machine is not in regular use, disconnect the battery and give it a refresher charge every month to six weeks (see Chapter 8).

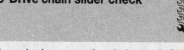

## 15 Drive chain slider check

**1** If required, remove the chainguard. Clean the chain slider with a suitable solvent to remove all traces of grease and road dirt.
**2** Inspect the surface of the slider – if it is deeply grooved or damaged it must be renewed **(see illustration)**.
**3** Remove the front sprocket cover (see Chapter 5, Section 16). On models fitted with a double-sided swingarm, remove the rear wheel (see Chapter 6).
**4** Undo the bolts securing the slider to the

swingarm – note that on single-sided swingarm models the slider is retained by one bolt on the top edge and one bolt on the underside of the arm, on other models the slider is retained by the chainguard fixings.
**5** Unclip the slider from the swingarm and draw it off **(see illustration)**.
**6** Installation is the reverse of removal.

## 16 Spark plug gap check

**1** Make sure your spark plug socket is the correct size before attempting to remove the plugs – a suitable one is supplied in the motorcycle's toolkit which is stored under the seat; an 18 mm hex size is required for 1997 to 2001 Daytona, Speed Triple and Sprint, and all Tiger models, and a 16 mm hex size is required for 2002-on Daytona, Speed Triple and Sprint models. The socket fits onto the end of a large hex key, which is used to turn the socket – a similar but smaller socket can be fitted onto the short end of the hex key as a handle for extra leverage. Make sure the ignition is switched OFF. Remove the fuel tank and airbox (see Chapter 4). On all models, the ignition coil is integral with the spark plug cap.
**2** Clean the area around the coils/caps to prevent any dirt falling into the spark plug channels. Check that the cylinder location is marked on each ignition coil/spark plug cap wiring connector and mark them accordingly if not.
**3** Disconnect the ignition coil/cap wiring connectors **(see illustration)**. Where fitted, undo the Torx screws securing the coils/caps to the valve cover **(see illustration)**. Pull the coils/caps off the spark plugs **(see illustration)**.
**4** Using compressed air if available, clean the area around the base of the spark plugs to prevent any dirt falling into the engine when they are removed.
**5** Using either the plug removing tool supplied in the bike's toolkit or a deep socket type wrench, unscrew the plugs from the cylinder head and remove them **(see illustrations)**. Lay each plug out in relation to its cylinder – if any plug shows up a problem it will then be easy to identify the troublesome cylinder.

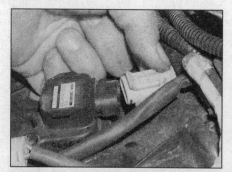

**16.3a Disconnect the wiring connector**

**16.3b Where fitted, undo the screws securing the coil/cap to the valve cover**

**16.3c Pull the coil/cap off the spark plug**

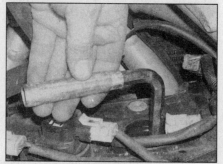

**16.5a Unscrew the plug . . .**

**16.5b . . . and remove it from the head**

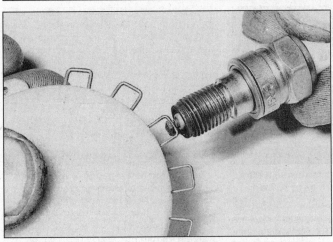

16.9a Using a wire type gauge to measure the spark plug electrode gap

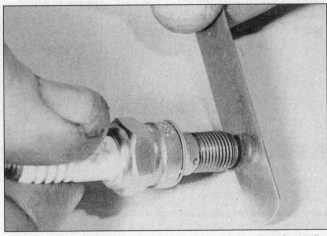

16.9b Using a feeler gauge to measure the spark plug electrode gap

**6** Inspect the electrodes for wear. Both the centre and side electrodes should have square edges and the side electrode should be of uniform thickness. Look for excessive deposits and evidence of a cracked or chipped insulator around the centre electrode. Compare your spark plugs to the colour spark plug reading chart at the end of this manual. Check the threads, the washer and the ceramic insulator body for cracks and other damage. Note that the NGK CR9EK plugs fitted to 2002-on Daytona, Speed Triple and Sprint models have two side electrodes.

**7** If the electrodes are not excessively worn, and if the deposits can be easily removed with a wire brush, and there are no cracks or chips visible in the insulator, the plugs can be re-gapped and re-used. If in doubt concerning the condition of the plugs, replace them with new ones, as the expense is minimal.

**8** Cleaning spark plugs by sandblasting is permitted, provided you clean the plugs with a high flash-point solvent afterwards.

**9** Before installing the plugs, make sure they are the correct type and heat range and check the gap between the electrodes **(see illustrations)**. Compare the gap to that specified and adjust as necessary. If the gap must be adjusted, bend the side electrodes only and be very careful not to chip or crack the insulator nose **(see illustration)**. Make

sure the sealing washer is in place on the plug before installing it.

**10** Since the cylinder head is made of aluminium, which is soft and easily damaged, thread the plugs into the heads turning the tool by hand **(see illustration 16.5b)**. Once the plugs have seated and are finger-tight, tighten them by 1/4 to 1/2 turn more, using the tool supplied or a socket drive **(see illustration 16.5a)**. Do not over-tighten them.

**HAYNES HiNT** *As the plugs are quite deeply recessed, you can slip a short length of hose over the end of the plug to use as a tool to thread it into place. The hose will grip the plug well enough to turn it, but will start to slip if the plug begins to cross-thread in the hole – this will prevent damaged threads.*

**11** Fit the coils/caps onto the spark plugs; where fitted, tighten their screws to the torque setting specified at the beginning of the Chapter **(see illustration 16.3c and b)**. Connect the coil/cap wiring connectors, making sure each goes to its correct cylinder **(see illustration 16.3a)**.

**12** Install the airbox and fuel tank (see Chapter 4).

**HAYNES HiNT** *Stripped plug threads in the cylinder head can be repaired with a Heli-Coil thread insert – see 'Tools and Workshop Tips' in the Reference section.*

## 17 Throttle body synchronisation

**Warning: Petrol (gasoline) is extremely flammable, so take extra precautions when you**

*work on any part of the fuel system. Don't smoke or allow open flames or bare light bulbs near the work area, and don't work in a garage where a natural gas-type appliance is present. If you spill any fuel on your skin, rinse it off immediately with soap and water. When you perform any kind of work on the fuel system, wear safety glasses and have a fire extinguisher suitable for a Class B type fire (flammable liquids) on hand.*

**Warning: Take great care not to burn your hand on the hot engine unit when accessing the gauge take-off points on the intake manifolds. Do not allow exhaust gases to build up in the work area; either perform the check outside or use an exhaust gas extraction system.**

**1** Throttle body synchronisation is simply the process of adjusting the throttle bodies so they pass the same amount of fuel/air mixture to each cylinder. This is done by measuring the vacuum produced in each cylinder. Throttle bodies that are out of synchronisation will result in decreased fuel mileage, increased engine temperature, less than ideal throttle response and higher vibration levels. Before synchronising the throttle bodies, make sure the valve clearances are properly set.

**2** To properly synchronise the throttle bodies you will need a set of vacuum gauges or a manometer. These instruments measure engine vacuum, and can be obtained from motorcycle dealers or mail order parts suppliers. The equipment used should be suitable for a three cylinder engine and come complete with the necessary adapters and hoses to fit the unions.

**Note 1:** *Because of the nature of the synchronisation procedure and the need for special instruments, most owners leave the task to a Triumph dealer. Triumph recommend using the Souriau Indiana digital inlet vacuum analyser, or a similar digital device, as they are more accurate than analogue gauges and*

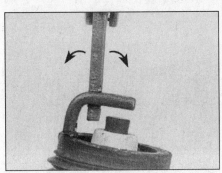

16.9c Adjust the electrode gap by bending the side electrode only

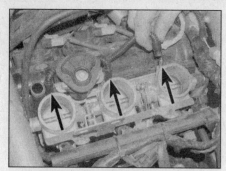

17.4a Detach the idle air control hoses from their unions (arrowed) on the throttle bodies . . .

17.4b . . . or the unions (arrowed) on the back of the cylinder head as described . . .

17.5 . . . and fit the gauge or manometer hoses in their place

manometers. *They are also far more expensive!*

**Note 2:** *Although it is possible to check and synchronise the throttle bodies on Daytona, Speed Triple and Sprint 2002-on year models, the idle air control valve and idle setting can only be checked and adjusted by a Triumph dealer equipped with the Triumph engine management system diagnostic tool.*

3 Remove the fuel tank and the airbox (see Chapter 4).

4 Disconnect the idle air control valve hoses from their unions on the throttle bodies (1997 to 2001 Daytona, Speed Triple and Sprint models and all Tiger models) or the back of the cylinder head (2002-on Daytona, Speed Triple and Sprint models) – mark each hose according to the throttle body it is attached to so that it can be correctly installed later **(see illustrations)**.

5 Attach the gauge or manometer hoses to the unions **(see illustration)**. Make sure the No. 1 gauge is attached to the hose from the No. 1 (left-hand) throttle body, and so on.

6 Temporarily install the fuel tank (see Chapter 4), but note that a kit which allows the tank to be used remotely during this procedure is available from Triumph dealers, and will make the synchronisation process much easier. Alternatively, place a secure support, such as a table, alongside the bike and position the tank on it, with the fuel hose and pump connectors positioned close to the hoses and leads. It is best to keep the tank off the bike as it will hinder access to the throttle bodies.

7 Start the engine, noting that as the idle air

control hoses have been disconnected, it will be necessary to hold the throttle open slightly in order to achieve the required idle speed of around 1200 rpm. If the gauges are fitted with damping adjustment, set this so that the needle flutter is just eliminated but so that they can still respond to small changes in pressure.

8 The vacuum readings for all cylinders should be the same **(see illustration)**. If the vacuum readings differ, proceed as follows.

### 1997 to 2001 Daytona, Speed Triple and Sprint models and all Tiger models

9 The throttle bodies are synchronised by turning the synchronising screws situated in-between each throttle body pair in the throttle linkage **(see illustration)**. On some models the idle air control valve may obstruct access to one of the synchronising screws. If this is the case, remove the screws securing the valve and displace it **(see illustration)**. If there is any sealant around the screws, remove it (Triumph specify to remove the old sealant before synchronisation, and to apply new afterwards. However on the models we examined, there was no evidence of any sealant).

10 The left-hand (No. 1) throttle body is non-adjustable, so the other two must be synchronised to read the same as it. **Note:** *Do not press on the screws whilst adjusting them, otherwise a false reading will be obtained.* First synchronise No. 2 throttle body to No. 1 using the left-hand synchronising screw until

the readings are the same. Then synchronise No. 3 throttle body to No. 1 using the right-hand screw. As the adjustment made to one cylinder can affect the running of another, it may now be necessary to repeat the adjustments, and to do so until all bodies read the same. When all the bodies are synchronised, open and close the throttle quickly to settle the linkage, and recheck the gauge readings, readjusting if necessary.

11 When the adjustment is complete, remove the gauges. Where removed, re-apply some sealant to the synchronising screws. If displaced, install the idle air control valve and secure it with its screws **(see illustration 17.9b)**. Refit the idle air control hoses, making sure they are connected to their original cylinders and are correctly routed **(see illustration 17.4a)**. Install the airbox and fuel tank (see Chapter 4).

12 Start the engine and check that the idle speed is as specified at the beginning of the Chapter. If it is outside the specified range, take the motorcycle to a Triumph dealer equipped with the diagnostic tool, as the idle speed can only be adjusted using it – there is no mechanical adjuster.

### 2002-on Daytona, Speed Triple and Sprint models

13 The throttle bodies are synchronised by turning the synchronising screws that are situated along the rear edge of the throttle body assembly **(see illustration)**. If there is any sealant around the screws, remove it (Triumph

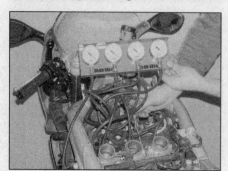

17.8 Checking and adjusting throttle body synchronisation

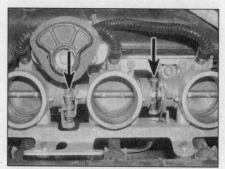

17.9a Throttle body synchronisation screws (arrowed)

17.9b Undo the screws (arrowed) and displace the idle air control valve if necessary

**17.13 Throttle body synchronisation screws (arrowed)**

specify to remove the old sealant before synchronisation, and to apply new afterwards. However on the models we examined, there was no evidence of any sealant).

**14** Use the vacuum analyser or gauge display to assess which cylinder(s) need adjusting and turn the screws only a small amount at a time until all bodies read the same.

**18.2a Undo the screws (arrowed) . . .**

**18.2b . . . and withdraw the filter housing from the airbox**

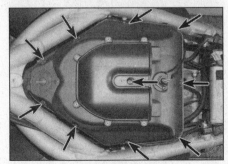

**18.11a Undo the screws . . .**

**15** The idle air control valve stepper position should now be checked using the Triumph diagnostic tool – if the read-out is outside the specified range, correct it by turning the synchronising screws.

**16** When the adjustment is complete, remove the gauges. Where removed, re-apply some sealant to the synchronising screws. Refit the idle air control hoses, making sure they are connected to their original cylinders and are correctly routed. Install the airbox and fuel tank (see Chapter 4).

**17** Start the engine and check that the idle speed is as specified at the beginning of the Chapter. If it is outside the specified range, use the Triumph diagnostic tool to adjust it.

**18 Air filter**

*Note: If the machine is continually ridden in dusty conditions, the filter should be cleaned in between renewal intervals (see Step 7).*

### 1997 to 2001 Daytona, Speed Triple and Sprint, and all Tiger models

**1** Remove the fuel tank (see Chapter 4).

**2** Remove the screws securing the air filter housing and withdraw it from the airbox, noting the sealing ring **(see illustrations)**. Separate the filter element from the housing, noting which way round it fits **(see illustration)**.

**3** Clean the housing and check it for signs of damage. Check the condition of the sealing ring and replace it with a new one if it is damaged, deformed or deteriorated.

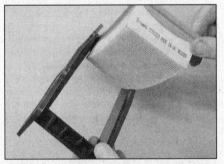

**18.2c Separate the filter from the housing**

**18.11b . . . and remove the airbox top . . .**

**4** Fit the new filter element into the housing, making sure it is the correct way round and seats properly **(see illustration 18.2c)**.

**5** Install the housing, making sure the rubber seal is in place, and secure it with the screws **(see illustration 18.2b and a)**.

**6** Check the crankcase breather hose between the engine and the airbox for loose connections, cracks and deterioration, and replace it with a new one if necessary.

**7** Install the fuel tank (see Chapter 4).

 **HAYNES HINT** *If the motorcycle is constantly used in dirty or dusty conditions, it is worth cleaning the element between renewal intervals. Remove it as described above, and tap it on a hard surface to dislodge any large particles of dirt. If compressed air is available, use it to clean the element, directing the air in the opposite direction of normal flow. If the element is torn or cannot be cleaned, or is obviously beyond further use, replace it with a new one.*

### 2002-on Daytona, Speed Triple and Sprint models

**8** Remove the fuel tank (see Chapter 4).

**9** Disconnect the intake air temperature wiring connector **(see illustration)**.

**10** Where fitted, disconnect the secondary air injection control valve hoses and the valve wiring connector.

**11** Remove the screws securing the top of the airbox and lift it off – don't forget to remove the central screw – then lift out the filter element **(see illustrations)**.

**12** Clean the inside of the airbox and check it

**18.9 Disconnect the intake air temperature wiring connector**

**18.11c . . . then lift out the filter element**

for signs of damage. Check the condition of the top sealing ring and replace it with a new one if it is damaged, deformed or deteriorated. Check that the airbox is correctly seated over the throttle body intakes – the airbox is secured over the intakes by spring clips which can become dislodged. If necessary, refer to the procedure in Chapter 4 and remove the airbox and install it correctly.

**13** Fit the new filter element into the airbox, then install the top, making sure the rubber seal is in place, and secure it with the screws **(see illustrations 18.11b and a).**

**14** Install the remaining components in the reverse order of removal.

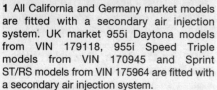

## 19 Secondary air injection system check

**1** All California and Germany market models are fitted with a secondary air injection system. UK market 955i Daytona models from VIN 179118, 955i Speed Triple models from VIN 170945 and Sprint ST/RS models from VIN 175964 are fitted with a secondary air injection system.

**2** The system consists of an electrically actuated solenoid valve located on the top of the airbox connected via hoses to reed valves on the top of the valve cover. At certain engine speeds, the electronic control module (ECM) opens the solenoid valve and feeds air into the exhaust ports via the reed valves. The introduced air promotes further combustion of the exhaust gases, reducing the level of pollutants.

### Solenoid valve and hoses

**3** Disconnect the battery negative (-ve) lead (see Chapter 8). Remove the fuel tank (see Chapter 4).

**4** Check the system hoses for loose connections, cracks and deterioration, and replace them with new ones if necessary.

**5** A faulty solenoid valve should be indicated by the malfunction indicator lamp in the instrument cluster, although it is impossible to access fault codes without the use of the Triumph engine management system diagnostic tool (see Chapter 4). Triumph provide no test procedure for the valve, however its function can be checked as follows.

**6** Trace the wiring from the valve and disconnect it at the connector. Release the clips and disconnect the three air outlet hoses, then remove the screw securing the valve to the airbox. Draw the valve out carefully, noting how it locates. Note the O-ring and discard it if it is damaged or deteriorated as a new one must be fitted.

**7** First blow into the valve inlet union and ensure no air comes out the outlet unions – the valve is closed. Now, using a fully charged 12 volt battery and two insulated jumper wires, connect the positive (+ve) battery terminal to the yellow/orange wire terminal in the valve wiring connector and the negative (-ve) battery terminal to the brown/pink wire terminal and check that the valve has opened. If the valve does not function as described, replace it with a new one.

**8** Installation is the reverse of removal. Ensure that the wiring connector terminals are clean and that the connector is firm.

### Reed valves

**9** Disconnect the battery negative (-ve) lead (see Chapter 8). Remove the airbox (see Chapter 4).

**10** Remove the fairing side panels (see Chapter 7).

**11** Remove the spark plug coils/caps (see Section 16).

**12** Mark the air hoses to aid installation, then release the clips and pull the hoses off the unions on the reed valve covers, noting how they fit.

**13** Undo the screws securing the airbox front bracket and remove the bracket.

**14** Release the trim clips securing the air deflector. Detach the clutch cable from the release lever on the clutch cover (see Chapter 2, Section 17). Pass the cable through the air deflector and lift off the deflector.

**15** Undo the bolts securing the reed valve covers and lift off the covers. The reed valves may come off with the covers or they may remain in the valve cover; lift them out carefully, noting which way round they fit.

**16** If required, clean any gum off the reeds and stopper plates with a suitable solvent, taking care not to distort the reeds. Inspect the seats – if they are damaged or deteriorated, renew the reed assemblies. Hold each reed up to the light and check that there is no gap between the reed and the seat.

**17** Installation is the reverse of removal. Ensure the reeds are fitted the correct way round and tighten the cover bolts to the specified torque setting. Don't forget to pass the clutch cable through the air deflector before installing the deflector. Ensure the air hoses are clipped securely to the cover unions and correctly positioned before the airbox is installed.

## 20 Valve clearance check

### Check

**1** The engine must be completely cool for this maintenance procedure, so let the machine sit overnight before beginning.

**2** Remove the spark plugs (see Section 16).

**3** Remove the valve cover (see Chapter 2A or 2B as applicable). Each cylinder is referred to by a number. They are numbered 1 to 3 from left to right. Make a chart or sketch of all valve positions so that a note of each clearance can be made against the relevant valve.

**4** The valve clearance can be measured when the cam lobe for that valve is pointing away from it. To turn the camshafts, place the motorcycle on an auxiliary stand, or its centrestand on Sprint ST models, so that the rear wheel is off the ground, select a high gear, and rotate the rear wheel by hand in its normal direction of rotation. Turn the wheel until the lobes above the valves being checked are pointing up. There is one point during the engine cycle where the lobes for all the valves for that cylinder will be pointing up – this is when the piston in that cylinder is at top dead centre (TDC) on the compression stroke, and all its valves are closed.

**5** Turn the engine until all the camshaft lobes above the No.1 cylinder are pointing away from the valves. The No. 1 cylinder is now at TDC on the compression stroke. Insert a feeler gauge of the same thickness as the correct valve clearance (see Specifications at the beginning of the Chapter) between the base of the camshaft lobe and the shim or cam follower of each valve in turn and check that it is a firm sliding fit – you should feel a slight drag when the you pull the gauge out **(see illustration).** If not, use the feeler gauges to obtain the exact clearance. **Note:** *On 1997 to 2001 Daytona, Speed Triple and Sprint models and all Tiger models, the valve shim is located in the top of the cam follower immediately below the cam lobe; on 2002-on Daytona, Speed Triple and Sprint models, the valve shim is located underneath the cam follower.* Record the measured clearance on the chart. Note that there is a difference in the clearance between the intake valves and the exhaust valves.

**6** Now turn the rear wheel until the camshaft lobes for the No. 2 cylinder are facing away from the valves. The No. 2 cylinder is now at TDC on the compression stroke. Measure the clearances of the valves using the method described in Step 5.

**7** Now turn the rear wheel until the camshaft lobes for the No. 3 cylinder are facing away from the valves. The No. 3 cylinder is now at TDC on the compression stroke. Measure the clearances of the valves using the method described in Step 5.

**8** When all clearances have been measured and charted, identify whether the clearance

**20.5 Make sure the cam lobes are facing up, then measure the clearance with the feeler gauge**

on any valve falls outside that specified. If it does, the valve shim on that particular valve must be replaced with one of a thickness which will restore the correct clearance.

## Adjustment – 1997 to 2001 Daytona, Speed Triple and Sprint, and all Tiger models

**9** Changing the shims requires the use of a special Triumph tool (Part No. T3880012) which when fitted holds a pair of valves open, creating clearance between the camshaft and shim so the shim can be removed. Note that if the tool is not available the camshafts must be removed to access the shims as described in Chapter 2. Place rags over the spark plug holes and the cam chain tunnel to prevent a shim from dropping into the engine on removal. Rotate the cam follower of the valve in question so that its shim removing slot faces backwards (exhaust valve) or forwards (inlet valve) **(see illustrations)**.

**10** To install the tool, first turn the engine using the rear wheel so that the lobes above the valve being worked on are depressing the valve so that it is fully open. The tool mounting plate bolts into two of the camshaft caps **(see illustration)**. If an intake valve is being worked on, the IN mark on the tool must face forwards. If an exhaust valve is being worked on, the EX mark on the tool must face backwards. Locate the tool so that one end is above the valve being worked on and bolt it onto the camshaft caps. Tighten the bolts to the torque setting specified at the beginning of the Chapter. Now fit the legs onto the tool, locating their lower ends against the rims of the followers, and making sure they are fitted to the side marked IN if working on an intake valve, and the side marked EX if working on an exhaust valve. Tighten the leg bolts to the specified torque, making sure they remain correctly located against the rim of the follower. **Note:** *The tool is designed so that the same valves (i.e. intake OR exhaust) on two adjacent cylinders can be adjusted without removing the tool mounting plate – simply unbolt the legs and move them to the other end of the plate, then bolt them into place.*

**11** With the tool installed, turn the engine using the rear wheel so that the lobes on the

**20.9a Turn each follower using a screwdriver . . . .**

**20.9b . . . until the shim removal notch (arrowed) faces towards the middle of the engine**

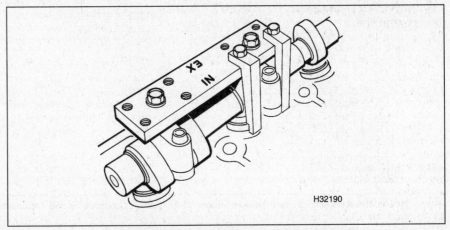

**20.10 Triumph tool installed on the intake camshaft**

camshaft move away from the legs and off the shims, until they point directly away from them, leaving the valve depressed and held open by the tool **(see illustration)**.

*Caution: Be sure to turn the rear wheel so that when the engine turns the lobes move away from the tool legs and not into them – if the lobes are forced against the legs, the camshafts, caps and tool could be damaged.*

**12** Pick the shim out of the top of the follower using either a magnet, a screwdriver with a dab of grease on it (the shim will stick to the grease), or, if the shim is tight, a small screwdriver to lever it out and a magnet or pair of pliers to grasp it **(see illustration)**. Do not allow the shim to fall into the engine.

**13** Measure the thickness of the shim using a micrometer and record it next to the clearance recorded earlier **(see illustration)**. A size mark should be stamped on the bottom face of the shim, however it is best to measure the shim in case it has worn. A shim marked 200 should be 2.00 mm thick.

**14** Using the appropriate shim selection

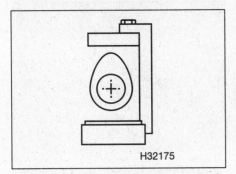

**20.11 Rotate the camshaft as described leaving the valve held open by the tool**

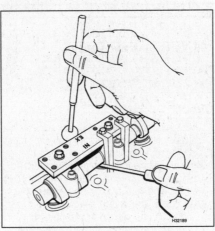

**20.12 Removing the shim from the follower**

**20.13 Measure the shim using a micrometer to confirm its size**

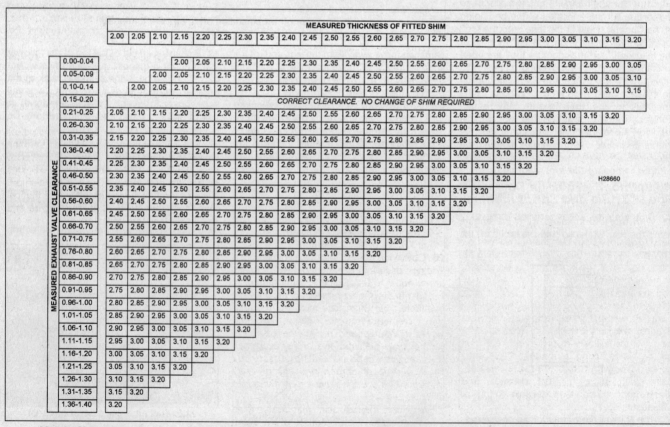

**Intake valves table**

| MEASURED INTAKE VALVE CLEARANCE | \ MEASURED THICKNESS OF FITTED SHIM → 2.00 | 2.05 | 2.10 | 2.15 | 2.20 | 2.25 | 2.30 | 2.35 | 2.40 | 2.45 | 2.50 | 2.55 | 2.60 | 2.65 | 2.70 | 2.75 | 2.80 | 2.85 | 2.90 | 2.95 | 3.00 | 3.05 | 3.10 | 3.15 | 3.20 |
|---|---|---|---|---|---|---|---|---|---|---|---|---|---|---|---|---|---|---|---|---|---|---|---|---|---|
| 0.00-0.04 | | | 2.00 | 2.05 | 2.10 | 2.15 | 2.20 | 2.25 | 2.30 | 2.35 | 2.40 | 2.45 | 2.50 | 2.55 | 2.60 | 2.65 | 2.70 | 2.75 | 2.80 | 2.85 | 2.90 | 2.95 | 3.00 | 3.05 | 3.10 |
| 0.05-0.09 | | 2.00 | 2.05 | 2.10 | 2.15 | 2.20 | 2.25 | 2.30 | 2.35 | 2.40 | 2.45 | 2.50 | 2.55 | 2.60 | 2.65 | 2.70 | 2.75 | 2.80 | 2.85 | 2.90 | 2.95 | 3.00 | 3.05 | 3.10 | 3.15 |
| 0.10-0.15 | *CORRECT CLEARANCE. NO CHANGE OF SHIM REQUIRED* | | | | | | | | | | | | | | | | | | | | | | | | |
| 0.16-0.20 | 2.05 | 2.10 | 2.15 | 2.20 | 2.25 | 2.30 | 2.35 | 2.40 | 2.45 | 2.50 | 2.55 | 2.60 | 2.65 | 2.70 | 2.75 | 2.80 | 2.85 | 2.90 | 2.95 | 3.00 | 3.05 | 3.10 | 3.15 | 3.20 | |
| 0.21-0.25 | 2.10 | 2.15 | 2.20 | 2.25 | 2.30 | 2.35 | 2.40 | 2.45 | 2.50 | 2.55 | 2.60 | 2.65 | 2.70 | 2.75 | 2.80 | 2.85 | 2.90 | 2.95 | 3.00 | 3.05 | 3.10 | 3.15 | 3.20 | | |
| 0.26-0.30 | 2.15 | 2.20 | 2.25 | 2.30 | 2.35 | 2.40 | 2.45 | 2.50 | 2.55 | 2.60 | 2.65 | 2.70 | 2.75 | 2.80 | 2.85 | 2.90 | 2.95 | 3.00 | 3.05 | 3.10 | 3.15 | 3.20 | | | |
| 0.31-0.35 | 2.20 | 2.25 | 2.30 | 2.35 | 2.40 | 2.45 | 2.50 | 2.55 | 2.60 | 2.65 | 2.70 | 2.75 | 2.80 | 2.85 | 2.90 | 2.95 | 3.00 | 3.05 | 3.10 | 3.15 | 3.20 | | | | |
| 0.36-0.40 | 2.25 | 2.30 | 2.35 | 2.40 | 2.45 | 2.50 | 2.55 | 2.60 | 2.65 | 2.70 | 2.75 | 2.80 | 2.85 | 2.90 | 2.95 | 3.00 | 3.05 | 3.10 | 3.15 | 3.20 | | | | | |
| 0.41-0.45 | 2.30 | 2.35 | 2.40 | 2.45 | 2.50 | 2.55 | 2.60 | 2.65 | 2.70 | 2.75 | 2.80 | 2.85 | 2.90 | 2.95 | 3.00 | 3.05 | 3.10 | 3.15 | 3.20 | | | | | | |
| 0.46-0.50 | 2.35 | 2.40 | 2.45 | 2.50 | 2.55 | 2.60 | 2.65 | 2.70 | 2.75 | 2.80 | 2.85 | 2.90 | 2.95 | 3.00 | 3.05 | 3.10 | 3.15 | 3.20 | | | | | | | |
| 0.51-0.55 | 2.40 | 2.45 | 2.50 | 2.55 | 2.60 | 2.65 | 2.70 | 2.75 | 2.80 | 2.85 | 2.90 | 2.95 | 3.00 | 3.05 | 3.10 | 3.15 | 3.20 | | | | | | | | |
| 0.56-0.60 | 2.45 | 2.50 | 2.55 | 2.60 | 2.65 | 2.70 | 2.75 | 2.80 | 2.85 | 2.90 | 2.95 | 3.00 | 3.05 | 3.10 | 3.15 | 3.20 | | | | | | | | | |
| 0.61-0.65 | 2.50 | 2.55 | 2.60 | 2.65 | 2.70 | 2.75 | 2.80 | 2.85 | 2.90 | 2.95 | 3.00 | 3.05 | 3.10 | 3.15 | 3.20 | | | | | | | | | | |
| 0.66-0.70 | 2.55 | 2.60 | 2.65 | 2.70 | 2.75 | 2.80 | 2.85 | 2.90 | 2.95 | 3.00 | 3.05 | 3.10 | 3.15 | 3.20 | | | | | | | | | | | |
| 0.71-0.75 | 2.60 | 2.65 | 2.70 | 2.75 | 2.80 | 2.85 | 2.90 | 2.95 | 3.00 | 3.05 | 3.10 | 3.15 | 3.20 | | | | | | | | | | | | |
| 0.76-0.80 | 2.65 | 2.70 | 2.75 | 2.80 | 2.85 | 2.90 | 2.95 | 3.00 | 3.05 | 3.10 | 3.15 | 3.20 | | | | | | | | | | | | | |
| 0.81-0.85 | 2.70 | 2.75 | 2.80 | 2.85 | 2.90 | 2.95 | 3.00 | 3.05 | 3.10 | 3.15 | 3.20 | | | | | | | | | | | | | | |
| 0.86-0.90 | 2.75 | 2.80 | 2.85 | 2.90 | 2.95 | 3.00 | 3.05 | 3.10 | 3.15 | 3.20 | | | | | | | | | | | | | | | |
| 0.91-0.95 | 2.80 | 2.85 | 2.90 | 2.95 | 3.00 | 3.05 | 3.10 | 3.15 | 3.20 | | | | | | | | | | | | | | | | |
| 0.96-1.00 | 2.85 | 2.90 | 2.95 | 3.00 | 3.05 | 3.10 | 3.15 | 3.20 | | | | | | | | | | | | | | | | | |
| 1.01-1.05 | 2.90 | 2.95 | 3.00 | 3.05 | 3.10 | 3.15 | 3.20 | | | | | | | | | | | | | | | | | | |
| 1.06-1.10 | 2.95 | 3.00 | 3.05 | 3.10 | 3.15 | 3.20 | | | | | | | | | | | | | | | | | | | |
| 1.11-1.15 | 3.00 | 3.05 | 3.10 | 3.15 | 3.20 | | | | | | | | | | | | | | | | | | | | |
| 1.16-1.20 | 3.05 | 3.10 | 3.15 | 3.20 | | | | | | | | | | | | | | | | | | | | | |
| 1.21-1.25 | 3.10 | 3.15 | 3.20 | | | | | | | | | | | | | | | | | | | | | | |
| 1.26-1.30 | 3.15 | 3.20 | | | | | | | | | | | | | | | | | | | | | | | |
| 1.31-1.35 | 3.20 | | | | | | | | | | | | | | | | | | | | | | | | |

H28659

**20.14a  Shim selection chart – intake valves (1997 to 2001 Daytona, Speed Triple and Sprint models and all Tiger models)**

**Exhaust valves table**

| MEASURED EXHAUST VALVE CLEARANCE | \ MEASURED THICKNESS OF FITTED SHIM → 2.00 | 2.05 | 2.10 | 2.15 | 2.20 | 2.25 | 2.30 | 2.35 | 2.40 | 2.45 | 2.50 | 2.55 | 2.60 | 2.65 | 2.70 | 2.75 | 2.80 | 2.85 | 2.90 | 2.95 | 3.00 | 3.05 | 3.10 | 3.15 | 3.20 |
|---|---|---|---|---|---|---|---|---|---|---|---|---|---|---|---|---|---|---|---|---|---|---|---|---|---|
| 0.00-0.04 | | | | 2.00 | 2.05 | 2.10 | 2.15 | 2.20 | 2.25 | 2.30 | 2.35 | 2.40 | 2.45 | 2.50 | 2.55 | 2.60 | 2.65 | 2.70 | 2.75 | 2.80 | 2.85 | 2.90 | 2.95 | 3.00 | 3.05 |
| 0.05-0.09 | | | 2.00 | 2.05 | 2.10 | 2.15 | 2.20 | 2.25 | 2.30 | 2.35 | 2.40 | 2.45 | 2.50 | 2.55 | 2.60 | 2.65 | 2.70 | 2.75 | 2.80 | 2.85 | 2.90 | 2.95 | 3.00 | 3.05 | 3.10 |
| 0.10-0.14 | | 2.00 | 2.05 | 2.10 | 2.15 | 2.20 | 2.25 | 2.30 | 2.35 | 2.40 | 2.45 | 2.50 | 2.55 | 2.60 | 2.65 | 2.70 | 2.75 | 2.80 | 2.85 | 2.90 | 2.95 | 3.00 | 3.05 | 3.10 | 3.15 |
| 0.15-0.20 | *CORRECT CLEARANCE. NO CHANGE OF SHIM REQUIRED* | | | | | | | | | | | | | | | | | | | | | | | | |
| 0.21-0.25 | 2.05 | 2.10 | 2.15 | 2.20 | 2.25 | 2.30 | 2.35 | 2.40 | 2.45 | 2.50 | 2.55 | 2.60 | 2.65 | 2.70 | 2.75 | 2.80 | 2.85 | 2.90 | 2.95 | 3.00 | 3.05 | 3.10 | 3.15 | 3.20 | |
| 0.26-0.30 | 2.10 | 2.15 | 2.20 | 2.25 | 2.30 | 2.35 | 2.40 | 2.45 | 2.50 | 2.55 | 2.60 | 2.65 | 2.70 | 2.75 | 2.80 | 2.85 | 2.90 | 2.95 | 3.00 | 3.05 | 3.10 | 3.15 | 3.20 | | |
| 0.31-0.35 | 2.15 | 2.20 | 2.25 | 2.30 | 2.35 | 2.40 | 2.45 | 2.50 | 2.55 | 2.60 | 2.65 | 2.70 | 2.75 | 2.80 | 2.85 | 2.90 | 2.95 | 3.00 | 3.05 | 3.10 | 3.15 | 3.20 | | | |
| 0.36-0.40 | 2.20 | 2.25 | 2.30 | 2.35 | 2.40 | 2.45 | 2.50 | 2.55 | 2.60 | 2.65 | 2.70 | 2.75 | 2.80 | 2.85 | 2.90 | 2.95 | 3.00 | 3.05 | 3.10 | 3.15 | 3.20 | | | | |
| 0.41-0.45 | 2.25 | 2.30 | 2.35 | 2.40 | 2.45 | 2.50 | 2.55 | 2.60 | 2.65 | 2.70 | 2.75 | 2.80 | 2.85 | 2.90 | 2.95 | 3.00 | 3.05 | 3.10 | 3.15 | 3.20 | | | | | |
| 0.46-0.50 | 2.30 | 2.35 | 2.40 | 2.45 | 2.50 | 2.55 | 2.60 | 2.65 | 2.70 | 2.75 | 2.80 | 2.85 | 2.90 | 2.95 | 3.00 | 3.05 | 3.10 | 3.15 | 3.20 | | | | | | |
| 0.51-0.55 | 2.35 | 2.40 | 2.45 | 2.50 | 2.55 | 2.60 | 2.65 | 2.70 | 2.75 | 2.80 | 2.85 | 2.90 | 2.95 | 3.00 | 3.05 | 3.10 | 3.15 | 3.20 | | | | | | | |
| 0.56-0.60 | 2.40 | 2.45 | 2.50 | 2.55 | 2.60 | 2.65 | 2.70 | 2.75 | 2.80 | 2.85 | 2.90 | 2.95 | 3.00 | 3.05 | 3.10 | 3.15 | 3.20 | | | | | | | | |
| 0.61-0.65 | 2.45 | 2.50 | 2.55 | 2.60 | 2.65 | 2.70 | 2.75 | 2.80 | 2.85 | 2.90 | 2.95 | 3.00 | 3.05 | 3.10 | 3.15 | 3.20 | | | | | | | | | |
| 0.66-0.70 | 2.50 | 2.55 | 2.60 | 2.65 | 2.70 | 2.75 | 2.80 | 2.85 | 2.90 | 2.95 | 3.00 | 3.05 | 3.10 | 3.15 | 3.20 | | | | | | | | | | |
| 0.71-0.75 | 2.55 | 2.60 | 2.65 | 2.70 | 2.75 | 2.80 | 2.85 | 2.90 | 2.95 | 3.00 | 3.05 | 3.10 | 3.15 | 3.20 | | | | | | | | | | | |
| 0.76-0.80 | 2.60 | 2.65 | 2.70 | 2.75 | 2.80 | 2.85 | 2.90 | 2.95 | 3.00 | 3.05 | 3.10 | 3.15 | 3.20 | | | | | | | | | | | | |
| 0.81-0.85 | 2.65 | 2.70 | 2.75 | 2.80 | 2.85 | 2.90 | 2.95 | 3.00 | 3.05 | 3.10 | 3.15 | 3.20 | | | | | | | | | | | | | |
| 0.86-0.90 | 2.70 | 2.75 | 2.80 | 2.85 | 2.90 | 2.95 | 3.00 | 3.05 | 3.10 | 3.15 | 3.20 | | | | | | | | | | | | | | |
| 0.91-0.95 | 2.75 | 2.80 | 2.85 | 2.90 | 2.95 | 3.00 | 3.05 | 3.10 | 3.15 | 3.20 | | | | | | | | | | | | | | | |
| 0.96-1.00 | 2.80 | 2.85 | 2.90 | 2.95 | 3.00 | 3.05 | 3.10 | 3.15 | 3.20 | | | | | | | | | | | | | | | | |
| 1.01-1.05 | 2.85 | 2.90 | 2.95 | 3.00 | 3.05 | 3.10 | 3.15 | 3.20 | | | | | | | | | | | | | | | | | |
| 1.06-1.10 | 2.90 | 2.95 | 3.00 | 3.05 | 3.10 | 3.15 | 3.20 | | | | | | | | | | | | | | | | | | |
| 1.11-1.15 | 2.95 | 3.00 | 3.05 | 3.10 | 3.15 | 3.20 | | | | | | | | | | | | | | | | | | | |
| 1.16-1.20 | 3.00 | 3.05 | 3.10 | 3.15 | 3.20 | | | | | | | | | | | | | | | | | | | | |
| 1.21-1.25 | 3.05 | 3.10 | 3.15 | 3.20 | | | | | | | | | | | | | | | | | | | | | |
| 1.26-1.30 | 3.10 | 3.15 | 3.20 | | | | | | | | | | | | | | | | | | | | | | |
| 1.31-1.35 | 3.15 | 3.20 | | | | | | | | | | | | | | | | | | | | | | | |
| 1.36-1.40 | 3.20 | | | | | | | | | | | | | | | | | | | | | | | | |

H28660

**20.14b  Shim selection chart – exhaust valves (1997 to 2001 Daytona, Speed Triple and Sprint models and all Tiger models)**

**20.21a Lift out the cam follower . . .**

**20.21b . . . and retrieve the shim (arrowed)**

chart, find where the measured valve clearance and existing shim thickness values intersect and read off the shim size required **(see illustrations)**. Shims are available in 0.05 mm increments from 2.00 mm to 3.20 mm and can be obtained from a Triumph dealer. **Note:** *If the required replacement shim is greater than 3.2 mm (the largest available), the valve is probably not seating correctly due to a build-up of carbon deposits and should be checked and cleaned or resurfaced as required (see Chapter 2).*

**15** Obtain the replacement shim, then lubricate it with clean engine oil and fit it into its recess in the top of the follower, with the size marking facing down **(see illustration 20.12)**. Check that the shim is correctly seated.

**16** Turn the engine using the rear wheel so that the lobes on the camshaft move down onto the shims and hold the valves open. Make sure the rear wheel is turned so the lobes do not contact the tool legs – see *Caution* above **(see illustration 20.11)**. Unbolt the tool from the camshaft caps and remove it.

**17** Repeat the procedure for any other valves until all the clearances are correct.

**18** Rotate the engine several turns to seat the new shim(s), then check the clearances again.

**19** Install the valve cover (see Chapter 2) and the spark plugs (see Section 16).

## Adjustment – 2002-on Daytona, Speed Triple and Sprint models

**20** Changing the shims requires removal of the camshafts (see Chapter 2B). There is no need to remove both camshafts if shims from only one side of the engine need changing. Place rags over the spark plug holes and the cam chain tunnel to prevent a shim dropping into the engine on removal.

**21** With the camshaft removed, remove the cam follower of the valve in question **(see illustration)**. Retrieve the shim from either the inside of the follower or pick it out of the top of the valve using a magnet or a small screwdriver with a dab of grease on it (the shim will stick to the grease) **(see illustration)**. Do not allow the shim to fall into the engine.

**22** The shim size may be marked on its upper

face but the shim should be measured with a micrometer to check that it has not worn **(see illustration 20.13)**. If the shim has worn undersize, this must be taken into account when calculating the valve clearance.

**23** The new shim thickness required can be calculated as follows – always aim to get the clearance at the mid-point of the specified range.

**24** If the valve clearance is less than specified, subtract the measured clearance from the specified clearance then deduct the result from the original shim thickness. For example:

### Sample calculation – intake valve clearance too small

Specified clearance:
  0.15 mm (0.10 to 0.20 mm)
Measured clearance: 0.08 mm
Difference: 0.07 mm
Shim thickness fitted: 2.575 mm
Correct shim thickness required
  is 2.575 – 0.07 = 2.505 mm

**25** If the valve clearance is greater than specified, subtract the specified clearance from the measured clearance, and add the result to the thickness of the original shim. For example:

### Sample calculation – exhaust valve clearance too large

Specified clearance:
  0.25 mm (0.20 to 0.30 mm)
Measured clearance: 0.37 mm
Difference: 0.12 mm
Shim thickness fitted: 1.975 mm
Correct shim thickness required
  is 1.975 + 0.12 = 2.095 mm

**26** Obtain the correct thickness shims from a Triumph dealer. Where the required thickness is not equal to the available shim thickness, round off the measurement to the nearest available size. Shims are available in 0.025 mm increments from 1.70 mm to 3.00 mm. **Note:** *If the required replacement shim is greater than 3.00 mm (the largest available), the valve is probably not seating correctly due to a build-up of carbon deposits or valve damage. Remove the valve for checking (see Chapter 2).*

**27** Lubricate the new shim with clean engine oil or molybdenum disulphide oil (a 50/50

mixture of molybdenum disulphide grease and engine oil) and fit it into its recess in the top of the valve with the size marking facing up. Check that the shim is correctly seated, then lubricate the follower with engine oil or molybdenum disulphide oil and install it onto the valve. Repeat the procedure for any other valves as required, then install the camshafts (see Chapter 2B).

**28** Rotate the engine several turns to seat the new shim(s), then check the clearances again.

**29** Install the remaining components in the reverse order of removal.

## 21 Fuel filter

> **Warning: Petrol (gasoline) is extremely flammable, so take extra precautions when you work on any part of the fuel system. Don't smoke or allow open flames or bare light bulbs near the work area, and don't work in a garage where a natural gas-type appliance is present. If you spill any fuel on your skin, rinse it off immediately with soap and water. When you perform any kind of work on the fuel system, wear safety glasses and have a fire extinguisher suitable for a Class B type fire (flammable liquids) on hand.**

**1** An in-line fuel filter is fitted to the pump assembly, which is housed inside the fuel tank. Remove the fuel tank, then remove the fuel pump assembly from it (see Chapter 4).

**2** Have a rag handy to soak up any residual fuel, then release the hose clamps and detach the hoses from the filter, noting which fits where **(see illustration)**. Remove the filter, noting which way round it fits, and discard it.

**3** Install the new filter so that its arrow points in the direction of fuel flow (i.e. away from the pump and towards the union on the pump assembly base). Fit the hoses onto the unions on the filter and secure them with the clamps.

**4** Install the fuel pump assembly and the fuel tank (see Chapter 4). Start the engine and check that there are no leaks.

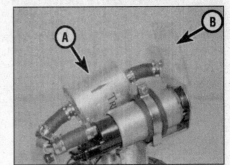

**21.2 Fuel filter (A), fuel strainer (B)**

**22.5 Checking for play in the steering head bearings**

**22.7a Location of the handlebar bracket retaining bolts (arrowed)**

**22.7b Handlebar clamp bolt (arrowed) – Daytona and some Speed Triple models**

## 22 Steering head bearing check, lubrication and adjustment

**1** Triumph specify that the steering head bearings must be re-greased at the same service interval as making checks and adjustments for freeplay. As re-greasing involves removing the steering stem, follow the procedure in Chapter 5 to remove and install the stem and adjust the bearings on reassembly.
**2** Note that steering head bearings can become dented, rough or loose during normal use of the machine – wear or damage will be noticeable in the way the bike handles. In extreme cases, worn or loose steering head bearings can cause steering wobble – a condition that is potentially dangerous. It is good practice to check the bearings on a regular basis and adjust them if necessary as described below.

### Check

**3** Using an auxiliary stand, support the motorcycle in an upright position so that the front wheel is off the ground.
**4** Point the front wheel straight-ahead and slowly move the handlebars from side-to-side. Any dents or roughness in the bearing races will be felt and the bars will not move smoothly and freely.
**5** Next, grasp the fork sliders and try to pull and push them forward and backward **(see**

illustration). Any looseness in the steering head bearings will be felt as front-to-rear movement of the forks. If play is felt in the bearings, adjust the steering head as follows.

> **HAYNES HiNT** *Freeplay in the fork due to worn fork bushes can be misinterpreted as steering head bearing play – do not confuse the two.*

### Adjustment

*Caution: Take great care not to apply excessive pressure when adjusting the bearings because this will cause premature bearing failure.*
**Note:** *Some models have a bearing adjuster nut and locknut fitted under the top yoke, others have an adjuster nut only, and from early 2004, Daytona and Speed Triple models had a tabbed washer and locknut fitted to the bearing adjuster nut – check which arrangement is fitted to your machine and follow the appropriate procedure below.*
**6** Remove the fuel tank (see Chapter 4) and, where fitted, the fairing (see Chapter 7). **Note:** *Although it is not strictly necessary to remove the fuel tank and fairing, doing so will prevent the possibility of damage should a tool slip.*

### Daytona and Speed Triple models

**7** On models with separate handlebars, check on the underside of the handlebar brackets for the location of a retaining bolt **(see illustration)**. Retaining bolts are fitted

from VIN 105633. If fitted, remove the retaining bolts. On all models, slacken the handlebar clamp bolts **(see illustration)**. On models up to VIN 105632, a pin in the handlebar bracket locates in a hole in the underside of the top yoke – slide the handlebars down the forks until the pins are clear of the holes. On all models, twist the bars round until the fork clamp bolts in the top yoke are accessible **(see illustration)**.
**8** On Speed Triple models with one-piece handlebars, displace the handlebars from the top yoke (see Chapter 5).
**9** Slacken the fork clamp bolts in the top yoke **(see illustration 22.7c)**.
**10** Slacken the steering stem nut – this requires the use of a special Triumph tool (Part No. T3880300), or a suitable equivalent to engage the drillings in the nut **(see illustration)**.
**11** Check to see if there is a bearing adjuster nut, adjuster nut and locknut, or adjuster nut, tabbed washer and locknut (2004-on models), under the top yoke. If there is only an adjuster nut, slacken the adjuster nut slightly until pressure is just released, then tighten it until all freeplay is removed, then tighten it a little more **(see illustration)**. This pre-loads the bearings. Now slacken the nut, then tighten it again, setting it so that all freeplay is just removed yet the steering is able to move freely from side to side. To do this tighten the nut only a little at a time, and after each tightening repeat the checks outlined above (see Steps 4 and 5) until the bearings are

**22.7c Fork clamp bolt (arrowed) – Daytona and some Speed Triple models**

**22.10 This special tool, or a home-made equivalent, must be used on Daytona and Speed Triple models**

**22.11 Adjusting the steering head bearings**

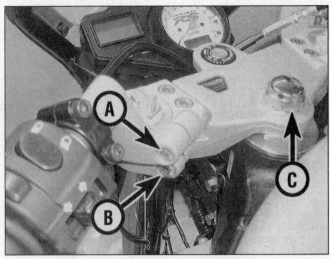

22.14a  Handlebar clamp bolt (A), fork clamp bolt (B), steering stem nut (C) – Sprint ST models

22.14b  Handlebar clamp bolt (A), fork clamp bolt (B), steering stem nut (C) – Sprint RS models

correctly set. The object is to set the adjuster nut so that the bearings are under a very light loading, just enough to remove any freeplay. Tighten the steering stem nut to the torque setting specified at the beginning of the Chapter, counter-holding the adjuster nut to prevent it turning as you do so. Now tighten the fork clamp bolts in the top yoke to the specified torque setting.

12  If there is an adjuster nut and locknut, follow the procedure in Steps 19 to 21. If there is an adjuster nut, tabbed washer and locknut (2004-on models), remove the steering stem nut and displace the top yoke. Remove the locknut, then lift off the tabbed washer. Triumph specify a torque setting for the adjuster nut, which can only be applied using their service tool (Part No. T3880024); with the torque wrench connected to the tool, apply a torque of 40 Nm to the adjuster nut – this will preload the bearings. Now slacken the nut and tighten it to the final torque setting of 15 Nm. If the service tool isn't available pre-load, then reset the adjuster nut as described in Step 11. Whichever method is used, once the setting is correct fit the tabbed washer and

the locknut and tighten the locknut to the torque setting specified at the beginning of the Chapter. Check the bearing adjustment (see Steps 4 and 5) and if they are correctly set install the top yoke and steering stem nut.

13  Tighten the steering stem nut, then tighten the fork clamp bolts, to the specified torque settings. Install the remaining components in the reverse order of removal.

### Sprint models

14  Slacken the handlebar clamp bolts, then slacken the fork clamp bolts in the top yoke and slacken the steering stem nut **(see illustrations)**.

15  Check to see if there is a bearing adjuster nut, or adjuster nut and locknut under the top yoke. If there is an adjuster nut and locknut, follow the procedure in Steps 19 to 21. If there is only an adjuster nut, slacken the adjuster nut slightly until pressure is just released, then tighten it until all freeplay is removed, then tighten it a little more **(see illustration 22.11)**. This pre-loads the bearings. Now slacken the nut, then tighten it again, setting it so that all freeplay is just removed yet the steering is able to move freely from side to side. To do

this tighten the nut only a little at a time, and after each tightening repeat the checks outlined above (see Steps 4 and 5) until the bearings are correctly set. The object is to set the adjuster nut so that the bearings are under a very light loading, just enough to remove any freeplay.

16  Tighten the steering stem nut to the torque setting specified at the beginning of the Chapter, counter-holding the adjuster nut to prevent it turning as you do so. Now tighten the fork clamp bolts in the top yoke to the specified torque setting and tighten the handlebar clamp bolts to the specified torque.

### Tiger models

17  Displace the handlebars from the top yoke (see Chapter 5).

18  Slacken the fork clamp bolts in the top yoke and slacken the steering stem nut **(see illustrations)**.

19  Use two suitable open-ended spanners to slacken the adjuster locknut under the top yoke while counter-holding the adjuster nut **(see illustration)**. Triumph service tools (thin spanners) can be obtained for this purpose (Part No. 3880140-T0301).

22.18a  Fork clamp bolts (arrowed) – Tiger models

22.18b  Steering stem nut (arrowed) – Tiger models

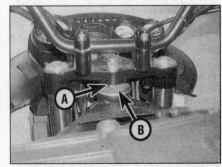

22.19  On Tiger models, slacken the locknut (A) while counter-holding the adjuster nut (B)

24.2 Checking for play in the wheel bearings

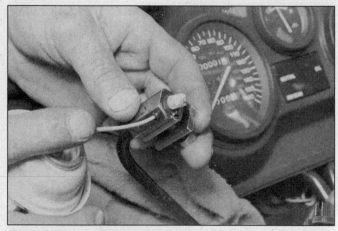

26.3 Lubricating a cable with a pressure lubricator. Make sure the tool seals around the inner cable

**20** Slacken the adjuster nut slightly until pressure is just released, then tighten it until all freeplay is removed, then tighten it a little more. This pre-loads the bearings. Now slacken the nut, then tighten it again, setting it so that all freeplay is just removed yet the steering is able to move freely from side to side. To do this tighten the nut only a little at a time, and after each tightening repeat the checks outlined above (see Steps 4 and 5) until the bearings are correctly set. The object is to set the adjuster nut so that the bearings are under a very light loading, just enough to remove any freeplay.
**21** Tighten the adjuster locknut against the adjuster nut while counter-holding the adjuster nut – it is important the adjuster nut does not turn with the locknut. If the service tools referred to in Step 19 are being used, a torque setting of 40 Nm can be applied to the locknut – the spanner has provision for attaching the torque wrench.
**22** Tighten the steering stem nut to the torque setting specified at the beginning of the Chapter. Now tighten the fork clamp bolts in the top yoke to the specified torque setting.
**23** Install the handlebars (see Chapter 5).

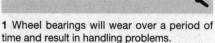

### 23 Front fork oil change

**1** Fork oil degrades over a period of time and loses its damping qualities.
**2** Remove the front forks from the yokes as described in Chapter 5, Section 6.
**3** On Sprint and Tiger models, follow steps 3 to 6 of Chapter 5, Section 7, to drain the oil, then steps 25 to 27 to refill with oil.
**4** On Daytona and Speed Triple models, follow steps 32 to 36 of Chapter 5, Section 7, to drain the oil, then steps 55 to 59 to refill with oil.
**5** Fork oil quantity, level and oil type are given in the Specifications at the beginning of Chapter 5.

### 24 Wheel bearing check

**1** Wheel bearings will wear over a period of time and result in handling problems.
**2** Support the motorcycle upright using an auxiliary stand. Check for any play in the bearings by pushing and pulling the wheel against the hub **(see illustration)**. Also spin the wheel and check that it rotates smoothly.
**3** If any play is detected in the wheel hub, or if the wheel does not rotate smoothly (and this is not due to brake or transmission drag), the wheel must be removed and the bearings inspected for wear or damage (see Chapter 6). Note that on Daytona, Speed Triple and Sprint ST models fitted with a single-sided swingarm, the rear wheel bearings are housing in the hub rather than the wheel itself (see Section 25). Do not remove the needle roller bearing on these models unless it is going to be replaced with a new one.

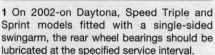

### 25 Rear wheel bearing lubrication

**1** On 2002-on Daytona, Speed Triple and Sprint models fitted with a single-sided swingarm, the rear wheel bearings should be lubricated at the specified service interval.
**2** Follow the procedure in Chapter 6 to remove the hub assembly. If required, remove the grease seal from the right-hand side of the hub and discard it if it is damaged or deteriorated.
**3** Clean off the old grease and inspect the condition of the bearings as described in Chapter 6 – note that if the left-hand bearing is sealed on both sides it cannot be cleaned or re-greased.
**4** Lubricate the bearings with the grease specified at the beginning of this Chapter. If

required, fit a new seal to the right-hand side of the hub, then follow the procedure in Chapter 6 and install the hub assembly.

### 26 Stand, lever pivots and cable lubrication

**1** Since the controls, cables and various other components of a motorcycle are exposed to the elements, they should be lubricated periodically to ensure safe and trouble-free operation.
**2** The footrests, clutch and brake levers, brake pedal, gearchange lever linkage and stand pivots should be lubricated frequently. In order for the lubricant to be applied where it will do the most good, the component should be disassembled and the recommended lubricant applied (see Specifications). However, if an aerosol spray lubricant is used, it can be applied to the pivot joint gaps and will usually work its way into the areas where friction occurs.
**3** To lubricate the throttle and clutch cables, disconnect the relevant cable at its upper end, then lubricate the cable with a pressure adapter **(see illustration)**. See Chapter 4 for the throttle cable removal procedures, and Chapter 2 for the clutch cable.

### 27 Coolant change

*Warning: Allow the engine to cool completely before performing this maintenance operation. Also, don't allow antifreeze to come into contact with your skin or the painted surfaces of the motorcycle. Rinse off spills immediately with plenty of water. Antifreeze is highly toxic if ingested. Never leave antifreeze lying around in an open container or in*

27.2a Remove the bleed bolt (arrowed) from the thermostat housing . . .

27.2b . . . or from the top of the radiator

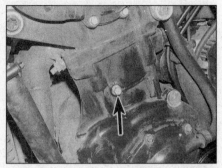

27.3a Unscrew the drain plug (arrowed) . .

*puddles on the floor; children and pets are attracted by its sweet smell and may drink it. Check with local authorities (councils) about disposing of antifreeze. Many communities have collection centres which will see that antifreeze is disposed of safely. Antifreeze is also combustible, so don't store it near open flames.*

## Draining

**1** On 1997 to 2001 Daytona and Speed Triple models, remove the fuel tank cover (see Chapter 7). On 1997 to 2001 Daytona and Sprint ST models, remove the lower fairing and the left-hand fairing side panel (see Chapter 7). On 2002-on Daytona and Sprint ST models, remove the left and right-hand fairing side panels (see Chapter 7). On Sprint RS models, remove the left-hand fairing side panel (see Chapter 7). On Tiger models, remove the fuel tank (see Chapter 4).

**2** Remove the pressure cap from the filler neck in the thermostat housing or the radiator as applicable by turning it anti-clockwise until it reaches a stop **(see illustration 6.8a or 8b)**. If you hear a hissing sound (indicating there is still pressure in the system), wait until it stops. Now press down on the cap and continue turning it until it can be removed. Also remove the filler cap from the coolant reservoir. Unscrew the bleed-hole bolt **(see illustrations)**.

**3** Position a suitable container beneath the drain plug on the left-hand side of the engine. Unscrew the drain plug and allow the coolant to completely drain from the system **(see illustrations)**. Retain the old sealing washer for use during flushing.

**4** On 1997 to 2001 Daytona, Speed Triple and Sprint models, and all Tiger models, position the container beneath the left-hand end of the radiator. Slacken the clamp securing the bottom coolant hose to the radiator and detach it, then point it down into the container and allow the coolant to drain **(see illustrations)**.

**5** On 2002-on Daytona, Speed Triple and Sprint models, slacken the clamp securing the bottom coolant hose to the water pump and detach it, then point it down into the container

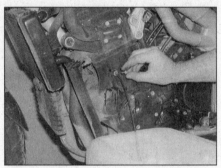

27.3b . . . and allow the coolant to drain

and allow the coolant to drain **(see illustration)**.

## Flushing

**6** Flush the system with clean tap water by inserting a garden hose in the filler neck. Allow the water to run through the system until it is clear and flows cleanly out. If the radiator is extremely corroded, remove it (see Chapter 3) and have it cleaned professionally.

**7** Clean the drain hole then install the drain plug using the old sealing washer. Attach the coolant hose to the radiator or water pump as applicable and tighten the clamp.

**8** Fill the cooling system with clean water mixed with a flushing compound. Make sure the flushing compound is compatible with aluminium components, and follow the manufacturer's instructions carefully. Install the pressure cap and the bleed-hole bolt. On

27.4a Slacken the hose clamp (arrowed) and detach the hose . . .

Tiger models, temporarily install the fuel tank (see Chapter 4).

**9** Start the engine and allow it to reach normal operating temperature. Let it run for about ten minutes.

**10** Stop the engine and let it cool for a while. On Tiger models, remove the tank again. Cover the pressure cap with a heavy rag and turn it anti-clockwise to the first stop, releasing any pressure that may be present in the system. Once the hissing stops, push down on the cap and remove it completely.

**11** Drain the system.

**12** Fill the system with clean water and repeat the procedure in Steps 9 to 11.

## Refilling

**13** Fit a new sealing washer onto the drain plug and tighten it to the torque setting specified at the beginning of the Chapter **(see**

27.4b . . . . and allow the coolant to drain

27.5 Detach the bottom coolant hose (arrowed) from the water pump

**27.13 Install the drain plug using a new sealing washer**

**27.14 Fill the system using the correct mixture as described**

**32.5 Inspect the cam chain plates where they pass over the sprockets (arrowed)**

**illustration)**. Attach the coolant hose to the radiator or water pump as applicable and tighten the clamp.

14 Fill the system via the filler neck with the proper coolant mixture (see this Chapter's Specifications) **(see illustration)**. **Note:** *Pour the coolant in slowly to minimise the amount of air entering the system.* When the system appears full, take the bike off its stand and shake it slightly to dissipate the coolant, then place the bike back on the stand and top the system up. Check that there is coolant visible in the bleed-hole. If there isn't, there could be an air-lock somewhere. Try shaking the bike again to disperse it.

15 Install the bleed-hole bolt, using a new sealing washer if the old one is damaged, deformed or deteriorated, and tighten it to the specified torque setting **(see illustration 27.2a or b)**. Install the pressure cap. Now fill the coolant reservoir to the MAX level line (see *Daily (pre-ride) checks*).

16 Start the engine and allow it to idle for 2 to 3 minutes. Flick the throttle twistgrip part open 3 or 4 times, so that the engine speed rises to approximately 4000 – 5000 rpm, then stop the engine. On 1997 to 2001 Daytona and Speed Triple models, it is worth squeezing and moving around the coolant hose that comes out of the top left-hand side of the radiator as there is a potential air-lock at the highest point of the hose. Any air trapped in the system should have bled back to the filler neck.

17 Let the engine cool then remove the pressure cap as described in Step 2. Check that the coolant level is still up to the top of the filler neck. If it's low, add the specified mixture until it reaches the top. Refit the pressure cap.

18 Check the coolant level in the reservoir and top up if necessary (see *Daily (pre-ride) checks*).

19 Check the system for leaks.

20 Do not dispose of the old coolant by pouring it down the drain. Instead pour it into a heavy plastic container, cap it tightly and take it into an authorised disposal site or service station – see **Warning** at the beginning of this Section.

21 Install the fuel tank/fuel tank cover/fairing panels as required according to your model (see Step 1).

## 28 Brake fluid change

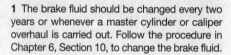

1 The brake fluid should be changed every two years or whenever a master cylinder or caliper overhaul is carried out. Follow the procedure in Chapter 6, Section 10, to change the brake fluid.

## 29 Brake master cylinder and caliper seal renewal

1 The seals will deteriorate over a period of time and lose their effectiveness, leading to sticky operation or fluid loss, or allowing the ingress of air and dirt. Refer to the appropriate Sections in Chapter 6 and dismantle the components for seal renewal every two years.

## 30 Swingarm and suspension linkage bearing lubrication

1 Over a period of time the grease will harden and dirt will penetrate the bearings.

2 The rear suspension components are not equipped with grease nipples. Remove the swingarm and the suspension linkage as described in Chapter 5 for re-greasing of the bearings.

## 31 Spark plug renewal

1 Remove the old spark plugs as described in Section 16 and install new ones.

## 32 Cam chain check

1 On 2002-on Daytona, Speed Triple and Sprint models, the cam chain should be inspected at the specified service interval.

2 Remove the spark plugs (see Section 15).

3 Follow the procedure in Chapter 2B to remove the valve cover.

4 To check the chain visually, place the motorcycle on an auxiliary stand, or its centrestand on Sprint ST models, so that the rear wheel is off the ground, select a high gear, and rotate the rear wheel by hand in its normal direction of rotation. Inspect the chain as it passes over the camshaft sprockets.

5 Inspect the chain plates for cracking and abrasion and inspect the inner plates for wear where they pass over the camshaft and crankshaft sprockets **(see illustration)**. Check for blue discolouration of the chain indicating excessive heat build-up. Examine the chain pins and ensure none are loose.

6 If there is any doubt about the condition of the chain, follow the procedure in Chapter 2B and remove it for further inspection (also check the cam chain tensioner and tensioner blade).

7 To measure chain stretch, hang the chain from a hook and attach a 13 kg (28 lb) weight to its lower end. Measure the length of 24 pins (from the centre of the 1st pin to the centre of the 24th pin) and compare the result to the service limit specified at the beginning of the Chapter. Reposition the chain so that another section can be measured. If the chain exceeds the service limit it must be replaced with a new one.

## 33 Brake hose renewal

1 The hoses will deteriorate with age and should be replaced with new ones every four years regardless of their apparent condition.

2 Refer to Chapter 6 and disconnect the hoses from the master cylinders and calipers. Always renew the banjo union sealing washers.

## 34 Fuel hose renewal

**⚠** *Warning: Petrol (gasoline) is extremely flammable, so take extra precautions when you work on any part of the fuel system. Don't smoke or allow open flames or bare light bulbs near the work area, and don't work in*

a garage where a natural gas-type appliance is present. If you spill any fuel on your skin, rinse it off immediately with soap and water. When you perform any kind of work on the fuel system, wear safety glasses and have a fire extinguisher suitable for a Class B type fire (flammable liquids) on hand.

1 Before commencing work, disconnect the fuel pump wiring connector (see Section 7), then turn the engine over on the starter for a few seconds – this reduces the pressure in the fuel rail and so prevents the fuel from being sprayed everywhere when the rail is removed or the hoses are detached.

2 Remove the fuel tank and airbox (see Chapter 4). Disconnect the fuel hoses from the fuel rail, noting which hose fits where (see Chapter 4 if required). **Note:** On Daytona, Speed Triple and Sprint models from VIN 207555-on, and Tiger models from VIN 207447-on, only a fuel feed hose is fitted.

3 On Daytona models to VIN 71698 and 885cc Speed Triple models, the hoses are secured by banjo fittings which use a sealing washer on each side of the union. All other models have the feed hose secured by two bolts and sealed by an O-ring, while the return hose slips over a union and is held by a clamp **(see illustration)**. When installing the new hoses, always use new sealing washers and/or O-rings according to model, and tighten the banjo bolts or union bolts to the torque setting specified at the beginning of the Chapter **(see illustration)**. Use a new clamp on the return hose on later models.

4 Run the engine and check that there are no leaks before taking the machine out on the road.

## 35 Stand checks

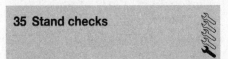

1 The sidestand return spring (and centrestand return spring on Sprint ST models) must be capable of retracting the stand fully and holding the stand retracted when the motorcycle is in use. If a spring is sagged or broken it must be replaced with a new one.

2 Lubricate the stand pivot regularly (see Section 26).

3 The sidestand switch prevents the

36.3a Horizontal adjuster (arrowed) – Daytona

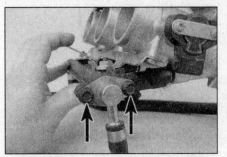

34.3a The supply hose to the fuel rail is secured by two bolts (arrowed) on later models

motorcycle being started if it is in gear and the stand is down, and cuts the engine if the stand is put down while it is running and in gear. Check its operation by shifting the transmission into neutral, retracting the stand and starting the engine. Pull in the clutch lever and select a gear. Extend the sidestand. The engine should stop as the sidestand is extended. If the sidestand switch does not operate as described, check its circuit (see Chapter 8). The clutch switch is also part of the same circuit – to check it, retract the sidestand, then select a gear. With the clutch lever pulled in, start the engine – if the engine starts, the switch is good. Otherwise, check the circuit (see Chapter 8).

## 36 Headlight aim

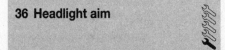

**Note:** An improperly adjusted headlight may cause problems for oncoming traffic or provide poor, unsafe illumination of the road ahead. Before adjusting the headlight aim, be sure to consult with local traffic laws and regulations – for UK models refer to MOT Test Checks in the Reference section.

1 The headlight beam can be adjusted both horizontally and vertically. Before making any adjustment, check that the tyre pressures are correct and the suspension is adjusted as required. Make any adjustments to the headlight aim with the machine on level ground, with the fuel tank half full and with an assistant sitting on the seat. If the bike is usually ridden with a passenger on the back, have a second assistant to do this.

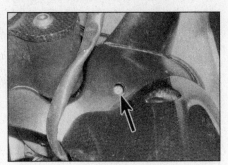

36.3b Access is through the hole in the fairing

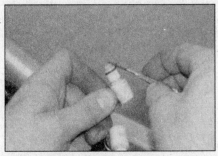

34.3b Use new O-rings on all connections which have them

### Daytona models

2 Vertical adjustment is made by turning the adjuster screw on the bottom inner corner of each headlight unit **(see illustration)**. Turn it anti-clockwise to raise the beam, and clockwise to lower it.

3 Horizontal adjustment is made by turning the adjuster screw on the top outer corner of each headlight unit **(see illustration)**; on 1997 to 2001 models, the adjuster is accessed via the aperture in the fairing **(see illustration)**. For the right-hand beam, turn it clockwise to move the beam to the right, and anti-clockwise to move it to the left. For the left-hand beam, turn it anti-clockwise to move the beam to the right, and clockwise to move it to the left.

### Speed Triple models

4 Vertical adjustment is made by slackening the clamp bolt on the headlight mounting and by pivoting the lights up or down as required – the beams can only be moved as a pair and are not individually adjustable **(see illustration)**. Tighten the bolt securely on completion.

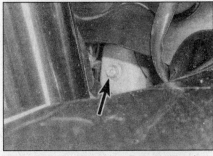

36.2 Vertical adjuster (arrowed) – Daytona

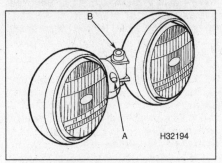

36.4 Vertical adjuster (A), horizontal adjuster (B) – Speed Triple

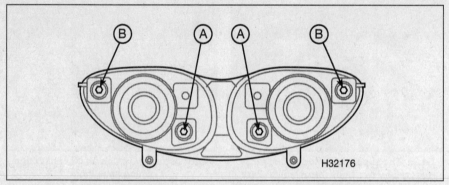

**36.7 Vertical adjusters (A), horizontal adjusters (B) – Sprint**

**5** Horizontal adjustment is made by slackening the pivot bolt on the headlight mounting and by pivoting the lights in or out as required – each beam can be adjusted independently of the other **(see illustration 36.4)**. Tighten the bolt securely on completion.

### Sprint models

**6** Remove the fairing (see Chapter 7).
**7** Vertical adjustment is made by turning the adjuster screw on the bottom inner corner of each headlight unit **(see illustration)**. Turn it anti-clockwise to raise the beam, and clockwise to lower it.
**8** Horizontal adjustment is made by turning the adjuster screw on the top outer corner of each headlight unit **(see illustration 36.7)**. For the right-hand beam, turn it clockwise to move the beam to the right, and anti-clockwise to move it to the left. For the left-hand beam, turn it anti-clockwise to move the beam to the right, and clockwise to move it to the left.

### Tiger models

**9** Remove the fairing (see Chapter 7).
**10** Vertical adjustment is made by turning the adjuster screw on the top inner corner of each headlight unit **(see illustration)**. Turn it clockwise to raise the beam, and anti-clockwise to lower it.

**11** Horizontal adjustment is made by turning the adjuster knob on the bottom outer corner of each headlight unit **(see illustration)**. For the right-hand beam, turn it clockwise to move the beam to the left, and anti-clockwise to move it to the right. For the left-hand beam, turn it anti-clockwise to move the beam to the left, and clockwise to move it to the right.

### 37 Cylinder compression check

**1** Among other things, poor engine performance may be caused by leaking valves, incorrect valve clearances, a leaking head gasket, or worn pistons, rings and/or cylinder liners. A cylinder compression check will help pinpoint these conditions and can also indicate the presence of excessive carbon deposits in the cylinder heads.
**2** The only tools required are a compression gauge and a spark plug wrench. A compression gauge with a threaded end for the spark plug hole is essential; a 12 mm thread size is required for 1997 to 2001 Daytona, Speed Triple and Sprint, and all Tiger models, and a 10 mm thread size for 2002-on Daytona, Speed Triple and Sprint models. Depending on the outcome of the initial test, a squirt-type oil can may also be needed.
**3** Make sure the valve clearances are correctly set (see Section 20) and that the cylinder head bolts are tightened to the correct torque setting (see Chapter 2A or 2B).
**4** Refer to *Fault Finding Equipment* in the Reference section for details of the compression test. Triumph do not provide any specific compression figures, but generally a range of 140 to 200 psi (10 to 14 Bar) is normal, while much above or below this can be considered high or low and should be investigated. Also, there should be no more than about 25 psi (1.7 Bar) difference between any of the cylinders, even if the figures for all cylinders are within the general limits.

**36.10 Vertical adjuster (arrowed) – Tiger**

**36.11 Horizontal adjuster (arrowed) – Tiger**

# Chapter 2A
## Engine, clutch and transmission – 1997 to 2001 models

*This chapter covers Daytona models up to VIN 132512, Speed Triple models up to VIN 141871, Sprint ST and RS models up to VIN 139276 and 885cc Tiger models*

## Contents

## Degrees of difficulty

| | | | | |
|---|---|---|---|---|
| **Easy,** suitable for novice with little experience  | **Fairly easy,** suitable for beginner with some experience  | **Fairly difficult,** suitable for competent DIY mechanic  | **Difficult,** suitable for experienced DIY mechanic | **Very difficult,** suitable for expert DIY or professional |

## Specifications

### General

Capacity
| | |
|---|---|
| T595 and 955i Daytona models | 955 cc |
| T509 Speed Triple models | 885 cc |
| 955i Speed Triple models | 955 cc |
| Sprint models | 955 cc |
| Tiger models | 885 cc |

Bore
| | |
|---|---|
| 885 cc engines | 76.0 mm |
| 955 cc engines | 79.0 mm |
| Stroke – all models | 65.0 mm |

Compression ratio
| | |
|---|---|
| T595 and 955i Daytona models | 11.2 to 1 |
| T509 Speed Triple models | 11.0 to 1 |
| 955i Speed Triple models | 11.2 to 1 |
| Sprint models | 11.2 to 1 |
| Tiger models | 11.3 to 1 |
| Cylinder numbering (from left side to right side of the bike) | 1-2-3 |
| Firing order | 1-2-3 |

## Camshafts, followers and cam chain

| | |
|---|---|
| Camshaft runout | 0.05 mm max. |
| Camshaft end-float | |
|   Standard | 0.03 to 0.13 mm |
|   Maximum | 0.2 mm |
| Camshaft bearing oil clearance | 0.12 mm max. |
| Camshaft journal diameter – all journals except outrigger | 22.90 to 22.93 mm |
| Camshaft journal diameter – outrigger journals (cam chain end) | 22.923 to 22.936 mm |
| Camshaft bearing bore diameter | 23.000 to 23.021 mm |
| Follower outside diameter | 27.987 to 27.993 mm |
| Follower bore diameter | 28.000 to 28.021 mm |
| Cam chain tensioner spring free length | 73.7 mm |
| Cam chain stretch limit | 442.9 mm |

## Valves, guides and springs

| | |
|---|---|
| Intake valve stem diameter | |
|   Standard | 5.475 to 5.490 mm |
|   Service limit | 5.47 mm |
| Exhaust valve stem diameter | |
|   Standard | 5.455 to 5.470 mm |
|   Service limit | 5.45 mm |
| Valve guide bore diameter – intake and exhaust | 5.500 to 5.515 mm |
| Valve stem-to-guide clearance – intake | |
|   Standard | 0.01 to 0.04 mm |
|   Service limit | 0.07 mm |
| Valve stem-to-guide clearance – exhaust | |
|   Standard | 0.03 to 0.06 mm |
|   Service limit | 0.09 mm |
| Valve face width | 1.8 to 2.5 mm |
| Valve seat width | |
|   Standard | 0.9 to 1.1 mm |
|   Service limit | 1.5 mm |
| Valve spring length | |
|   Inner spring | not less than 24.0 mm with 15 kg load |
|   Outer spring | not less than 26.5 mm with 41 kg load |

## Cylinder liners

| | |
|---|---|
| Cylinder liner ID | |
|   T509 Speed Triple to VIN 53779 (aluminium liners) | |
|     Standard | 75.985 to 76.003 mm |
|     Service limit | 76.053 mm |
|   T509 Speed Triple VIN 53780-on (cast iron liners) | |
|     Standard | 76.030 to 76.050 mm |
|     Service limit | 76.100 mm |
|   955i Daytona and Speed Triple, Sprint models | |
|     Standard | 79.030 to 79.050 mm |
|     Service limit | 79.10 mm |
|   Tiger models | |
|     Standard | 75.985 to 76.030 mm |
|     Service limit | 76.050 mm |

## Pistons

| | |
|---|---|
| Piston OD (measured 5 mm up from skirt, at 90° to piston pin axis) | |
|   885 cc engines | |
|     Cylinders 1 and 3 | |
|       Standard | 75.960 to 75.980 mm |
|       Service limit | 75.920 mm |
|     Cylinder 2 | |
|       Standard | 75.96 to 75.97 mm |
|       Service limit | 75.900 mm |
|   955 cc engines | |
|     Cylinders 1 and 3 | |
|       Standard | 78.960 to 78.980 mm |
|       Service limit | 78.920 mm |
|     Cylinder 2 | |
|       Standard | 78.96 to 78.97 mm |
|       Service limit | 78.900 mm |
| Piston pin bore diameter in piston | 19.002 to 19.008 mm |
| Piston pin diameter | 18.995 to 19.000 mm |
| Connecting rod small-end diameter | 19.016 to 19.034 mm |

## Piston rings

| | |
|---|---|
| Ring-to-groove clearance (top and second rings) . . . . . . . . . . . . . . . . . | 0.02 to 0.06 mm |
| End gap (installed) | |
|   885 cc engines | |
|     T509 Speed Triple | |
|       Top ring . . . . . . . . . . . . . . . . . . . . . . . . | 0.15 to 0.30 mm |
|       Second ring . . . . . . . . . . . . . . . . . . . . . | 0.26 to 0.41 mm |
|       Oil control ring side rails . . . . . . . . . . . . . . . . . | 0.20 to 0.70 mm |
|     Tiger | |
|       Top ring . . . . . . . . . . . . . . . . . . . . . . . . | 0.11 to 0.26 mm |
|       Second ring . . . . . . . . . . . . . . . . . . . . . | 0.26 to 0.41 mm |
|       Oil control ring side rails . . . . . . . . . . . . . . . . . | 0.20 to 0.70 mm |
|   955 cc engines | |
|     Top ring . . . . . . . . . . . . . . . . . . . . . . . . . . . | 0.15 to 0.30 mm |
|     Second ring . . . . . . . . . . . . . . . . . . . . . . . . . . . | 0.30 to 0.45 mm |
|     Oil control ring side rails . . . . . . . . . . . . . . . . . | 0.20 to 0.70 mm |

## Clutch

| | |
|---|---|
| Friction plates | |
|   Quantity . . . . . . . . . . . . . . . . . . . . . . . . . . . | 9 |
|   Thickness | |
|     Standard . . . . . . . . . . . . . . . . . . . . . . . . | 3.80 to 3.88 mm |
|     Service limit . . . . . . . . . . . . . . . . . . . . . . . . | 3.60 mm |
| Plain plates | |
|   Quantity . . . . . . . . . . . . . . . . . . . . . . . . . . . | 8 |
|   Warpage | |
|     Standard . . . . . . . . . . . . . . . . . . . . . . . . | 0.15 mm |
|     Service limit . . . . . . . . . . . . . . . . . . . . . . . . | 0.20 mm |
| Clutch shim clearance . . . . . . . . . . . . . . . . . . . . . . . . | 0.075 to 0.125 mm |
| Clutch cable freeplay . . . . . . . . . . . . . . . . . . . . . . . . | see Chapter 1 |

## Lubrication system

| | |
|---|---|
| Oil pressure @ 5000 rpm . . . . . . . . . . . . . . . . . . . . . . . . | 40 psi (2.76 Bars) at 80°C oil temp. |
| Oil pump rotor tip-to-outer rotor clearance | |
|   Standard . . . . . . . . . . . . . . . . . . . . . . . . . . . | 0.15 mm |
|   Service limit . . . . . . . . . . . . . . . . . . . . . . . . | 0.20 mm |
| Oil pump outer rotor-to-body clearance | |
|   Standard . . . . . . . . . . . . . . . . . . . . . . . . . . . | 0.15 to 0.22 mm |
|   Service limit . . . . . . . . . . . . . . . . . . . . . . . . | 0.35 mm |
| Oil pump rotor end-float | |
|   Standard . . . . . . . . . . . . . . . . . . . . . . . . . . . | 0.007 to 0.02 mm |
|   Service limit . . . . . . . . . . . . . . . . . . . . . . . . | 0.10 mm |

## Connecting rods and bearings

| | |
|---|---|
| Connecting rod side clearance | |
|   Standard . . . . . . . . . . . . . . . . . . . . . . . . . . . | 0.15 to 0.30 mm |
|   Service limit . . . . . . . . . . . . . . . . . . . . . . . . | 0.5 mm |
| Connecting rod big-end bearing oil clearance | |
|   Standard . . . . . . . . . . . . . . . . . . . . . . . . . . . | 0.036 to 0.066 mm |
|   Service limit . . . . . . . . . . . . . . . . . . . . . . . . | 0.1 mm |
| Connecting rod big-end journal diameter | |
|   Standard . . . . . . . . . . . . . . . . . . . . . . . . . . . | 40.946 to 40.960 mm |
|   Service limit . . . . . . . . . . . . . . . . . . . . . . . . | 40.932 mm |

## Crankshaft and main bearings

| | |
|---|---|
| Main bearing oil clearance | |
|   Standard . . . . . . . . . . . . . . . . . . . . . . . . . . . | 0.020 to 0.044 mm |
|   Service limit . . . . . . . . . . . . . . . . . . . . . . . . | 0.1 mm |
| Main bearing journal diameter | |
|   Standard . . . . . . . . . . . . . . . . . . . . . . . . . . . | 37.960 to 37.976 mm |
|   Service limit . . . . . . . . . . . . . . . . . . . . . . . . | 37.936 mm |
| Crankshaft end-float | |
|   Standard . . . . . . . . . . . . . . . . . . . . . . . . . . . | 0.05 to 0.20 mm |
|   Service limit . . . . . . . . . . . . . . . . . . . . . . . . | 0.40 mm |

## Transmission

Primary reduction ratio ........................................ 1.75 to 1 (105/60T)
Gear ratios (No. of teeth)
   First gear ................................................ 2.733 to 1 (41/15T)
   Second gear ............................................ 1.947 to 1 (37/19T)
   Third gear .............................................. 1.545 to 1 (34/22T)
   Fourth gear ............................................. 1.291 to 1 (31/24T)
   Fifth gear ............................................... 1.154 to 1 (30/26T)
   Sixth gear .............................................. 1.074 to 1 (29/27T)
Final reduction ratio
   T595 Daytona and 955i Daytona to VIN 89736 .......... 2.388 to 1 (43/18T)
   955i Daytona VIN 89737-on (except Germany) ............ 2.333 to 1 (42/18T)
   955i Daytona VIN 89737-on (Germany) ................... 2.263 to 1 (43/19T)
   T509 and 955i Speed Triple ............................ 2.388 to 1 (43/18T)
   Sprint ST (1999 models) ............................... 2.388 to 1 (43/18T)
   Sprint RS and ST (2000-on models) ..................... 2.263 to 1 (43/19T)
   Tiger ................................................... 2.666 to 1 (48/18T)
Selector fork end width
   Standard ............................................... 5.8 to 5.9 mm
   Service limit ........................................... 5.7 mm
Selector fork groove width in gears
   Standard ............................................... 6.0 to 6.1 mm
   Service limit ........................................... 6.25 mm
Selector fork-to-groove clearance ........................... 0.55 mm maximum

## Torque settings

Engine mounting bolts
   Daytona and Speed Triple models
      Engine mounting bracket-to-cylinder head bolts ............. 30 Nm
      All other mounting bolts
         Initial setting ...................................... 80 Nm
         Final setting ....................................... 95 Nm
      Suspension linkage-to-frame bolt ....................... 95 Nm
   Sprint models
      Mounting bolts ...................................... 95 Nm
      Adjuster bolts ....................................... 3 Nm
      Adjuster bolt locknuts ................................ 55 Nm
      Suspension linkage-to-frame bolt ....................... 48 Nm
   Tiger models
      Engine mounting bracket-to-cylinder head bolts ............. 30 Nm
      All other mounting bolts ............................... 95 Nm
      Swingarm pivot bolt .................................. 85 Nm
Ignition coil/spark plug cap screws ......................... 10 Nm
Valve cover bolts ......................................... 10 Nm
Cam chain tensioner mounting bolts ........................ 9 Nm
Cam chain tensioner end bolt .............................. 23 Nm
Camshaft sprocket bolts ................................... 15 Nm
Camshaft cap bolts ....................................... 10 Nm
Cam chain upper guide screws ............................. 10 Nm
Cam chain tensioner blade pivot bolt ...................... 18 Nm
Cam chain support bolt ................................... 10 Nm
Ignition timing rotor Allen bolt ............................ 27 Nm
Cylinder head bolts
   Stage 1 ................................................ 20 Nm
   Stage 2 ................................................ 27 Nm
   Stage 3 ................................................ Angle-tighten 90°
Cylinder head-to-cylinder block screws ..................... 12 Nm
External oil hose banjo bolts ............................... 25 Nm
Clutch centre nut ......................................... 105 Nm
Clutch pressure plate bolts ................................ 10 Nm
Clutch cover bolts ........................................ 9 Nm
Internal oil pipe banjo bolts ............................... 8 Nm
Sump bolts .............................................. 12 Nm
Oil cooler hose banjo bolts ................................ 25 Nm
Oil pressure relief valve ................................... 15 Nm
Crankcase 6 mm bolts (see text) .......................... 12 Nm
Crankcase 8 mm bolts (see text) .......................... 28 Nm
Crankcase breather disc screws ........................... 12 Nm

## Torque settings (continued)

| | |
|---|---|
| Connecting rod cap nuts | 14 Nm + 120° (see text) |
| Balancer shaft end cap(s) | 40 Nm |
| Oil pump driven gear screw | 9 Nm |
| Oil pump middle gear screw | 9 Nm |
| Oil pump mounting screws | 12 Nm |
| Gearchange mechanism centralising spring locating pin | 23 Nm |
| Selector drum bearing retainer bolt | 12 Nm |
| Selector drum detent cam screw | 12 Nm |
| Pawl retainer plate screws | 9 Nm |
| Neutral and gear stopper arm nuts | 9 Nm |
| Selector fork shaft retainer plate screw | 6 Nm |
| Starter clutch body bolts | 12 Nm |
| Idle/reduction gear shaft retainer bolt | 12 Nm |
| Alternator driveshaft needle bearing retainer screw | 10 Nm |
| Alternator driveshaft ball bearing retainer bolts | 12 Nm |
| Alternator driveshaft long bolt nut | 40 Nm |

## 1 General information

The engine/transmission is a water-cooled in-line three-cylinder design, fitted across the frame. The twelve valves are operated by double overhead camshafts, chain driven off the right-hand end of the crankshaft. The pistons run in removable liners, surrounded by a water jacket.

The engine/transmission is constructed in aluminium alloy with the crankcase divided horizontally. The crankcase incorporates a wet sump, pressure fed lubrication system, and houses a gear driven oil pump. An external oil feed pipe supplies oil to the cylinder head and cam components. A single balancer shaft is driven directly off a gear on the right-hand end of the crankshaft.

The clutch is of the wet multi-plate type and is gear driven off the crankshaft. An auxiliary gear on the back of the clutch drives the oil pump (and thence the water pump) and the alternator driveshaft.

The transmission is of the six-speed constant mesh type. Final drive to the rear wheel is by chain and sprockets.

Many of the bolts used on Triumph motorcycles are of the Torx type. Unless you are already equipped with a good range of Torx bits, you are advised to purchase a set before attempting work on the engine. Make sure you get bits that can be used in conjunction with a socket set so that a torque wrench can be applied – a Torx key set will not be adequate on its own, though will be a useful addition to the bits.

## 2 Operations possible with the engine in the frame

The components and assemblies listed below can be removed without having to remove the engine/transmission assembly from the frame. If however, a number of areas require attention at the same time, removal of the engine is recommended.

*Valve cover*
*Cam chain tensioner*
*Camshafts and followers*
*Cam chain and tensioner/guide blades*
*Cylinder head*
*Cylinder liners and pistons*
*Starter motor*
*Alternator*
*Water pump*
*Clutch*
*Oil cooler (where fitted)*
*Sump*
*Alternator*
*Alternator/starter clutch driveshaft (see Section 31)*

## 3 Operations requiring engine removal

It is necessary to remove the engine/transmission assembly from the frame and separate the crankcase halves to gain access to the following components.

*Starter clutch*
*Gearchange mechanism*
*Selector drum and forks*
*Transmission shafts*
*Crankshaft and bearings*
*Connecting rod assemblies and bearings*
*Oil pump and pressure relief valve*
*Balancer shaft*

## 4 Major engine repair – general note

**1** It is not always easy to determine when or if an engine should be completely overhauled, as a number of factors must be considered.
**2** High mileage is not necessarily an indication that an overhaul is needed, while low mileage, on the other hand, does not preclude the need for an overhaul. Frequency of servicing is probably the single most important consideration. An engine that has regular and frequent oil and filter changes, as well as other required maintenance, will most likely give many miles of reliable service. Conversely, a neglected engine, or one which has not been run in properly, may require an overhaul very early in its life.
**3** Exhaust smoke and excessive oil consumption are both indications that piston rings and/or valve guides are in need of attention, although make sure that the fault is not due to oil leakage.
**4** If the engine is making obvious knocking or rumbling noises, the connecting rod and/or main bearings are probably at fault.
**5** Loss of power, rough running, excessive valve train noise and high fuel consumption rates may also point to the need for an overhaul, especially if they are all present at the same time. If a complete tune-up does not remedy the situation, major mechanical work is the only solution.
**6** An engine overhaul generally involves restoring the internal parts to the specifications of a new engine. The piston rings and main and connecting rod bearings are usually renewed during a major overhaul. Generally the valve seats are reground, since they are usually in less than perfect condition at this point. The end result should be a like new engine that will give as many trouble-free miles as the original.
**7** Before beginning the engine overhaul, read through the related procedures to familiarise yourself with the scope and requirements of the job. Overhauling an engine is not all that difficult, but it is time consuming. Plan on the motorcycle being tied up for a minimum of two weeks. Check on the availability of parts and make sure that any necessary special tools, equipment and supplies are obtained in advance.
**8** Most work can be done with typical workshop hand tools, although a number of precision measuring tools are required for inspecting parts to determine if they must be

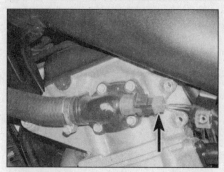

**5.6  Coolant temperature sensor wiring connector (arrowed) – Sprint models**

**5.8  Make an alignment mark with the slit in the clamp, then unscrew the bolt (arrowed) and slide the arm (or lever) off the shaft**

**5.11a  Unscrew the rear mounting bolt and detach the lead(s)**

renewed. Often a dealer will handle the inspection of parts and offer advice concerning reconditioning and renewal. As a general rule, time is the primary cost of an overhaul so it does not pay to install worn or substandard parts.

**9** As a final note, to ensure maximum life and minimum trouble from a rebuilt engine, everything must be assembled with care in a spotlessly clean environment.

## 5  Engine removal and installation

*Caution: The engine is very heavy. Engine removal and installation should be carried out with the aid of at least one assistant. Personal injury or damage could occur if the engine falls or is dropped. An hydraulic or mechanical floor jack should be used to support and lower or raise the engine if possible.*

### Removal

**1** Position the bike on its centrestand (ST model) or an auxiliary stand so that it is supported in an upright position, making sure it is secure. Note that the swingarm pivot must be slackened before removing the engine to allow expansion of the frame, so if you have a stand that locates in the pivot points, slacken the pivot before fitting the stand (see Step 19, 20 or 21 according to model). It is a good idea to hold the front

brake on by using a cable-tie or a rag tied around the throttle and brake lever. Work can be made easier by raising the machine to a suitable height on a hydraulic ramp.

**2** If the engine is dirty, particularly around its mountings, wash it thoroughly before starting any major dismantling work. This will make work much easier and rule out the possibility of caked on lumps of dirt falling into some vital component.

**3** Remove the seat (see Chapter 7), then remove the battery (see Chapter 8).

**4** Remove the fairing, fairing side panels and belly-pan, according to your model (see Chapter 7). Where a panel bolts to a mounting bracket on the engine, it is advisable to remove the bracket to prevent it becoming bent or damaged.

**5** Remove the fuel tank and the air filter housing (see Chapter 4).

**6** Drain the engine oil and coolant (see Chapter 1). Remove the oil cooler (see Section 20), and the radiator and the thermostat housing along with all the coolant hoses, noting their routing (see Chapter 3). It is advisable to tag the end of each hose using masking tape, then write the location of the hose on the tape. On Sprint models, disconnect the coolant temperature sensor wiring connector from the sensor on the left-hand side of the engine **(see illustration)**.

**7** Remove the exhaust system (Chapter 4).

**8** Make an alignment mark across the gearchange shaft end and the gearchange

linkage arm or gearchange lever (according to model) as an aid to installation, then unscrew the pinch bolt and slide the arm or lever off the shaft **(see illustration)**.

**9** Trace the wiring from the sidestand switch and disconnect it at the wiring connector. If required, remove the sidestand and its bracket (see Chapter 5).

**10** If required, remove the throttle bodies (see Chapter 4). The engine can be removed with them in place, though it is always best to remove them first to prevent the possibility of damage (see Chapter 4). Plug the intake manifold joints with clean rags to prevent anything dropping down them. If you are not removing the throttle bodies, detach the throttle cable from them (see Chapter 4).

**11** If required, remove the alternator (see Chapter 8). If it is not being removed, unscrew the mounting bolt securing the earth lead(s) and detach the lead(s) **(see illustration)**. Disconnect the wiring connector from the alternator **(see illustration)**. Pull back the rubber boot, then unscrew the nut and detach the lead from the end of the alternator.

**12** If required, remove the starter motor (see Chapter 8). If it is not being removed, pull back the rubber boot on the terminal, them unscrew the nut and detach the lead **(see illustration)**.

**13** Remove the front sprocket (see Chapter 5).

**14** Disconnect the crankshaft position sensor wiring connector **(see illustration)**. Where fitted, also detach the camshaft position sensor wiring connector from the sensor on the valve cover.

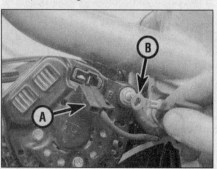

**5.11b  Disconnect the wiring connector (A), then unscrew the terminal nut and detach the lead (B)**

**5.12  Pull back the rubber boot and unscrew the nut (arrowed) securing the lead**

**5.14  Disconnect the crankshaft position sensor wiring connector**

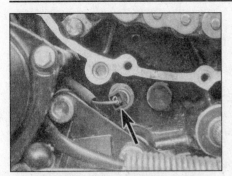

5.15 Disconnect the wiring connector from the neutral switch (arrowed)

5.17 Disconnect the wiring connector from the oil pressure switch (arrowed)

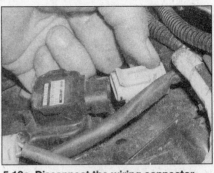

5.18a Disconnect the wiring connector . . .

**15** Detach the wire from the neutral switch **(see illustration)**.
**16** Detach the clutch cable from the release lever on the clutch cover (see Section 17).
**17** Detach the wire from the oil pressure switch **(see illustration)**.
**18** Disconnect the ignition coil/spark plug cap wiring connectors **(see illustration)**. Undo the screws securing the coils/caps to the valve cover and pull them off the spark plugs **(see illustrations)**.
**19** On Daytona, Speed Triple and Sprint ST models, remove the blanking cap from each end of the swingarm pivot. Counter-hold the pivot on the left-hand side and slacken the bolt on the right-hand side **(see illustration)**. Also slacken the bolt that secures the suspension linkage assembly to the frame **(see illustration)**.
**20** On Sprint RS models, remove the blanking cap from the right-hand end of the swingarm

5.18b . . . then undo the screws securing the coil to the valve cover . . .

pivot **(see illustration)**. Counter-hold the pivot on the right-hand end and slacken the nut on the left-hand end. Also slacken the bolt that secures the suspension linkage assembly to the frame **(see illustration)**.
**21** On Tiger models, remove the brake pedal

5.18c . . . and pull it off the spark plug

(see Chapter 5). Unscrew the bolts securing the footrest mounting plate, then detach it from the frame and support or tie it so that no strain is placed on the brake hose **(see illustration)**. Also unscrew the bolts securing the left-hand footrest bracket and remove it **(see illustration)**.

5.19a Slacken the swingarm pivot bolt (arrowed)

5.19b Slacken the suspension linkage-to-frame bolt (arrowed) – Sprint ST shown

5.20a Remove the blanking cap (arrowed) and slacken the pivot as described

5.20b Suspension linkage-to-frame bolt (arrowed)

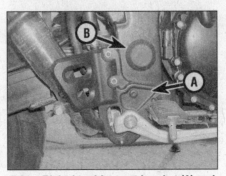

5.21a Right-hand footrest bracket (A) and swingarm pivot cap (B)

5.21b Left-hand footrest bracket (arrowed)

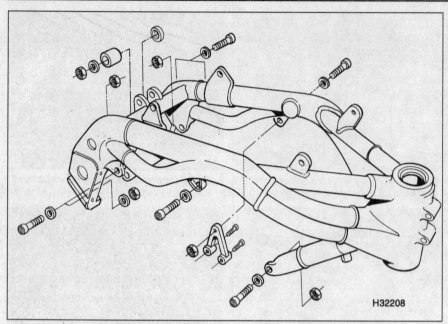

**5.23a Engine mounting details – Daytona and Speed Triple models**

Remove the blanking cap from each end of the swingarm pivot. Counter-hold the left-hand end of the pivot and slacken the bolt on the right-hand end.

**22** At this point, position an hydraulic jack under the engine with a block of wood between the jack head and sump. Make sure the jack is centrally positioned so the engine will not topple in any direction when the last mounting bolt is removed. Take the weight of the engine on the jack. Unless you are using a ramp with a front wheel clamp, also place a block of wood under the rear wheel to prevent the bike tilting back when the engine is removed. Check around the engine and frame to make sure that all wiring, cables and hoses that need to be disconnected have been disconnected, and that any remaining connected to the engine are not retained by any clips, guides or brackets connected to the frame. Check that any protruding mounting brackets will not get in the way and remove them if necessary.

**23** When removing the engine mounting bolts, retrieve all nuts, washers and spacers from the mountings and slip them back on the bolts in their correct order for safekeeping, noting carefully where each fits **(see illustrations)**. On Daytona, Speed .Triple and Tiger models, unscrew the bolts securing the engine mounting bracket to the frame and the engine on the left-hand side and remove the bracket, noting how it fits. On all models, slacken all the engine mounting bolts and nuts, then withdraw the mounting bolts from each side of the engine. On Tiger models, note which way round the exhaust system collector box brackets are fitted on the lower rear mounting bolts, and similarly note the radiator brackets on the front mounting bolts.

**24** Have an assistant steady the engine as it is lowered on the jack, and slip the drive chain off the output shaft. When it is clear of the frame lugs, move it to one side. Lift the engine off the jack and onto the work surface. On Tiger models, retrieve the chain rubbing block, noting how it fits.

> ⚠️ **Warning: The engine is heavy and may cause injury if it falls.**

### Installation

#### Daytona and Speed Triple models

**25** With the aid of an assistant place the engine on top of the jack and block of wood and carefully raise it into position in the frame, slipping the drive chain around the output shaft as you do so. Manoeuvre the engine as required so that all mounting holes align. Make sure no wires, cables or hoses become trapped between the engine and the frame.

**26** Fit the washers on the mounting bolts then install them in the frame, along with any spacers previously fitted, then fit the mounting

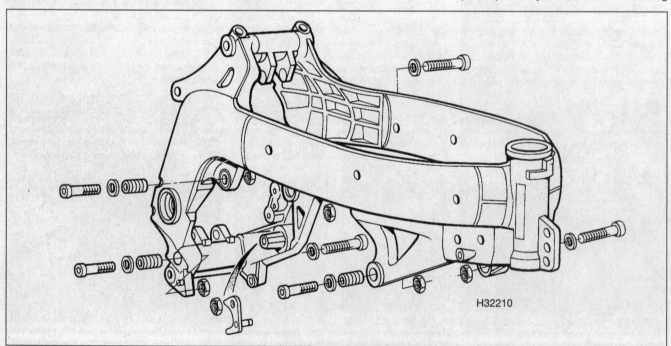

**5.23b Engine mounting details – Sprint models**

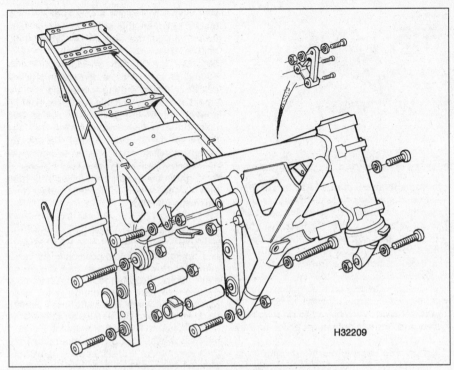

5.23c  Engine mounting details – Tiger models

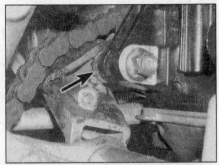

5.26a  Do not forget the spacer with the lower rear bolt on the left-hand side

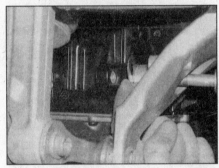

5.26b  Any spacers on the right-hand side fit between the engine and the frame

bolt nuts, where appropriate, and tighten them finger-tight **(see illustrations and 5.23a)**. Also fit the engine mounting bracket between the frame and the engine on the left-hand side and tighten its bolts finger-tight. Remove the jack from under the engine.

**27**  Unscrew the pivot bolt from the right-hand end of the swingarm pivot **(see illustration 5.19a)**. Now slacken both the locknut and the adjuster bolt, referring to Chapter 5 for details on the special tools required to do this. Now follow the correct tightening procedure as detailed below.

*Caution: The engine mounting bolts must be tightened in the correct sequence.*

*Failure to do so could leave the engine incorrectly aligned in the frame, placing undue stress on it, which could lead to severe damage.*

**28**  Tighten the engine mounting bracket-to-cylinder head bolts on the left-hand side to the torque setting specified at the beginning of the Chapter **(see illustration)**.

**29**  Tighten the left-hand front mounting bolt to the initial torque setting specified at the beginning of the Chapter.

**30**  Tighten the left-hand upper rear mounting bolt to the initial specified torque setting.

**31**  Tighten the left-hand lower rear mounting bolt to the initial specified torque setting.

**32**  Now check the gap between the engine and frame at all right-hand mounting points using a 1 mm feeler gauge. If any gap is found to be larger than 1 mm, insert a suitable washer to reduce the gap to below 1 mm. The Triumph Pt. No. for the correct washers is 3550220-T0301. **Note:** *If a washer is needed for the lower rear mounting bolt, then an identical washer must be fitted between the suspension linkage and the frame on the right-hand side – refer to Chapter 5 for removal of the linkage rods.*

**33**  Tighten the right-hand front mounting bolt to the initial specified torque setting **(see illustration)**.

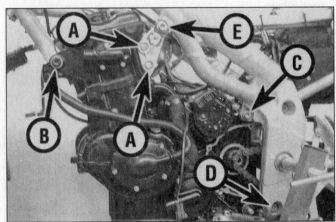

5.28  Mounting bracket-to-cylinder head bolts (A), front mounting bolt (B), upper rear mounting bolt (C), lower rear mounting bolt (D), bracket-to-frame bolt (E) – Daytona and Speed Triple models, left-hand side

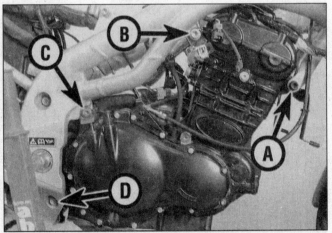

5.33  Front mounting bolt (A), middle mounting bolt (B), upper rear mounting bolt (C), lower rear mounting bolt (D) – Daytona and Speed Triple models, right-hand side

**34** Tighten the right-hand middle mounting bolt to the initial specified torque setting.
**35** Tighten the right-hand upper rear mounting bolt to the initial specified torque setting.
**36** Tighten the right-hand lower rear mounting bolt to the initial specified torque setting.
**37** Tighten the engine mounting bracket-to-frame bolt on the left-hand side to the initial specified torque setting (see illustration 5.28).
**38** With the exception of the engine mounting bracket-to-cylinder head bolts on the left-hand side, now tighten all the mounting bolts in the same sequence as above to the final torque setting specified at the beginning of the Chapter.
**39** Refer to Chapter 5 and tighten the swingarm adjuster bolt, lockring and pivot bolt as described, following the relevant Steps.
**40** Tighten the suspension linkage-to-frame bolt to the specified torque setting.

### Sprint models

**41** Using the Triumph special tool (Pt. No. T3880088) or a suitable peg spanner (which can be made by cutting four sections out of an old socket of a suitable size), unscrew the locknuts on the adjuster bolts at all right-hand mounting points (see illustration 5.23b). Now thread the adjuster bolts out of the frame until they no longer protrude on the inside.
**42** With the aid of an assistant place the engine on top of the jack and block of wood and carefully raise it into position in the frame, slipping the drive chain around the output shaft as you do. Manoeuvre the engine as required so that all mounting holes align. Make sure no wires, cables or hoses become trapped between the engine and the frame.
**43** Fit the washers on the left-hand mounting bolts then install them in the frame, along with any spacers previously fitted, then fit the mounting bolt nuts, where appropriate, and tighten them finger-tight (see illustration 5.23b).
**44** On ST models, unscrew the pivot bolt from the right-hand end of the swingarm pivot. On all models, slacken both the locknut

**TOOL TiP**

*A peg spanner can be made by cutting an old socket as shown – measure the width and depth of the slots in the locknut to determine the size of the castellations on the socket. If an old socket is not available, castellations can be welded onto a suitable nut.*

and the adjuster bolt on the right-hand side, referring to Chapter 5, Section 13, for details of the special tools required to do this. Now follow the correct tightening procedure as detailed below.
*Caution: The engine mounting bolts must be tightened in the correct sequence. Failure to do so could leave the engine incorrectly aligned in the frame, placing undue stress on it, which could lead to severe damage.*
**45** Tighten the left-hand upper rear mounting bolt to the torque setting specified at the beginning of the Chapter (see illustration).
**46** Tighten the left-hand front mounting bolt to the torque setting specified at the beginning of the Chapter.
**47** Tighten the left-hand lower rear mounting bolt to the specified torque setting.
**48** Tighten the three adjuster bolts on the right-hand side to the specified torque setting.
**49** Install the right-hand mounting bolts and tighten them to the specified torque setting, making sure that the adjuster bolts do not turn

with them – by making a couple of reference marks between the adjuster bolt and the frame you will be able to tell whether the adjuster bolts have moved.
**50** Using the Triumph special tool (Pt. No. T3880088) or a suitable peg spanner (which can be made by cutting four sections out of an old socket of a suitable size – see *Tool Tip above*), tighten the locknuts on the adjuster bolts to the specified torque setting.
**51** Refer to Chapter 5 and tighten the swingarm adjuster bolt, locknut and pivot bolt as described, following the relevant Steps.
**52** Tighten the suspension linkage-to-frame bolt to the specified torque setting (see illustration 5.20b).

### Tiger models

**53** With the aid of an assistant place the engine on top of the jack and block of wood and carefully raise it into position in the frame, slipping the drive chain around the output shaft as you do. Manoeuvre the engine as required so that all mounting holes align. Make sure no wires, cables or hoses become trapped between the engine and the frame. Do not forget to fit the chain rubbing block.
**54** Fit the washers on the mounting bolts then install them in the frame, along with the exhaust collector box and radiator brackets and any spacers previously fitted, then fit the mounting bolt nuts, where appropriate, and tighten them finger-tight (see illustration 5.23c). Also fit the engine mounting bracket between the frame and the engine on the left-hand side and tighten its bolts finger-tight. Remove the jack from under the engine.
*Caution: The engine mounting bolts must be tightened in the correct sequence. Failure to do so could leave the engine incorrectly aligned in the frame, placing undue stress on it, which could lead to severe damage.*
**55** Tighten the engine mounting bracket-to-cylinder head bolts on the left-hand side to the torque setting specified at the beginning of the Chapter (see illustration).

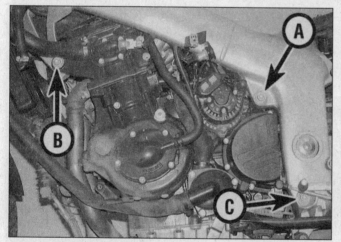

**5.45 Upper rear mounting bolt (A), front mounting bolt (B), lower rear mounting bolt (C) – Sprint models, left-hand side**

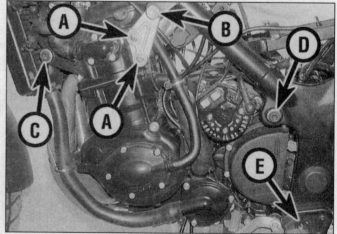

**5.55 Mounting bracket-to-cylinder head bolts (A), middle mounting bolt (B), front mounting bolt (C), upper rear mounting bolt (D), lower rear mounting bolt (E) – Tiger models, left-hand side**

**56** Tighten the left-hand middle mounting bolt to the torque setting specified at the beginning of the Chapter.
**57** Tighten the right-hand middle mounting bolt to the specified torque setting.
**58** Tighten the left-hand front mounting bolt to the initial specified torque setting.
**59** Tighten the left-hand upper rear mounting bolt to the specified torque setting.
**60** Tighten the left-hand lower rear mounting bolt to the specified torque setting.
**61** Tighten the right-hand front mounting bolt to the initial specified torque setting.
**62** Tighten the right-hand upper rear mounting bolt to the specified torque setting.
**63** Tighten the right-hand lower rear mounting bolt to the specified torque setting.
**64** Tighten the swingarm pivot bolt to the specified torque setting, then fit the blanking caps.

### All models

**65** The remainder of the installation procedure is a direct reversal of the removal sequence, noting the following points.
● Tighten all nuts and bolts to the specified torque settings (where given).
● Align the previously made mark on the gearchange linkage arm or lever with that on the gearchange shaft end.
● Make sure all wires, cables and hoses are correctly routed and connected, and secured by any clips or ties. Tighten the ignition coil/cap screws to the specified torque setting.
● Adjust the drive chain as described in Chapter 1.
● Use new gaskets on the exhaust pipe connections, and new O-rings on the coolant connections, where appropriate.
● Refill the engine with oil and coolant (see Chapter 1).
● Adjust the throttle and clutch cable freeplay (see Chapter 1).
● Adjust the drive chain slack (see Chapter 1).
● Start the engine and check that there are no oil or coolant leaks before installing the body panels.

### 6  Engine overhaul – general information

#### Disassembly

**1** Before disassembling the engine, thoroughly clean and degrease clean the external surfaces. This will prevent contamination of the engine internals, and will also make working a lot easier and cleaner. A high flash-point solvent, such as paraffin (kerosene) can be used, or better still, a proprietary engine degreaser such as Gunk. Use old paintbrushes and toothbrushes to work the solvent into the various recesses of the engine casings. Take care to exclude solvent or water from the electrical components and intake and exhaust ports.

**Warning: The use of petrol (gasoline) as a cleaning agent should be avoided due to the risk of fire.**

**2** When clean and dry, arrange the unit on the workbench, leaving a suitable clear area for working. Gather a selection of small containers and plastic bags so that parts can be grouped together in an easily identifiable manner. Some paper and a pen should be on hand to permit notes to be made and labels attached where necessary. A supply of clean rag is also required.
**3** Before commencing work, read through the appropriate section so that some idea of the necessary procedure can be gained. When removing various engine components it should be noted that great force is seldom required, unless specified. In many cases, a component's reluctance to be removed is indicative of an incorrect approach or removal method. If in any doubt, re-check with the text.
**4** An engine support stand can be made from short lengths of 2 x 4 inch wood bolted together into a rectangle to help support the engine if required **(see illustration)**, though the engine will sit nicely on the flat bottom of the sump, and there are two pegs at the front to keep it stable. The perimeter of the mount should be just big enough to accommodate the sump within it so that the engine rests on its crankcase.
**5** When disassembling the engine, keep 'mated' parts together (including gears, liners, pistons, connecting rods, valves, etc. that have been in contact with each other during engine operation). These 'mated' parts must be reused or renewed as an assembly.
**6** Engine/transmission disassembly should be done in the following general order with reference to the appropriate Sections.

*Remove the camshafts*
*Remove the cam chain/tensioner blade*
*Remove the cylinder head and cam chain guide blade*
*Remove the cylinder liners and pistons*
*Remove the clutch*
*Remove the alternator (see Chapter 8)*
*Remove the starter motor (see Chapter 8)*
*Remove the water pump (see Chapter 3)*
*Remove the sump*
*Separate the crankcase halves*
*Remove the crankshaft/connecting rods*
*Remove the balancer shaft*
*Remove the transmission shafts/gears*

**6.4  An engine support made from pieces of 2 x 4 inch wood**

*Remove the gearchange components*
*Remove the oil pump*
*Remove the alternator/starter drive*

#### Reassembly

**7** Reassembly is accomplished by reversing the general disassembly sequence.

### 7  Valve cover

**Note:** *The valve cover can be removed with the engine in the frame. If the engine has been removed, ignore the steps which do not apply.*

#### Removal

**1** Remove the seat and disconnect the battery negative lead.
**2** On Daytona and Sprint models, remove the fairing side panels (see Chapter 7).
**3** Remove the fuel tank and the airbox (see Chapter 4). On Tiger models, undo the screw securing the thermostat housing so that it can be moved aside when removing the valve cover – there is no need to drain the cooling system or detach any of the hoses **(see illustration)**.
**4** Disconnect the ignition coil/spark plug cap wiring connectors **(see illustration 5.18a)**. Undo the screws securing the coils/caps to the valve cover and pull them off the spark plugs **(see illustrations 5.18b and c)**.
**5** Unscrew the eight valve cover bolts evenly in a criss-cross pattern, starting at the centre and working outwards, and remove them with their seals, then lift the valve cover off the cylinder head **(see illustration)**. If the cover is

**7.3  Thermostat housing screw (arrowed) – Tiger models**

**7.5  Unscrew the cover bolts (arrowed) and lift the cover off the engine**

**7.9a Apply the sealant to the cutouts in the head**

**7.9b Make sure the gasket stays in place when fitting the cover**

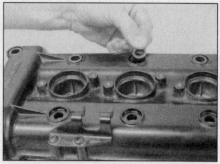

**7.9c Fit new bolt seals if necessary**

stuck, do not try to lever it off with a screwdriver. Tap it gently around the sides with a rubber hammer or block of wood to dislodge it.

### Installation

6 Examine the valve cover gasket for signs of damage or deterioration and fit a new one if necessary. Similarly check the rubber seals on the cover bolts for cracks, hardening and deterioration.

7 Clean the mating surfaces of the cylinder head and the valve cover with lacquer thinner, acetone or brake system cleaner. If a new gasket is being used, remove any traces of old glue or sealant.

8 Fit the gasket into the valve cover, making sure it locates correctly into the groove. Use a few dabs of grease to keep the gasket in place while the cover is fitted.

9 Apply a suitable silicone sealant to the cutouts in the cylinder head where the gasket half-circles fit **(see illustration)**. Position the valve cover on the cylinder head, making sure the gasket stays in place **(see illustration)**. Install the cover bolts, using new seals if necessary, and tighten them evenly in a criss-cross pattern, starting at the centre and working outwards, to the torque setting specified at the beginning of the Chapter – the two longer bolts are located at the cam chain end **(see illustration)**.

10 Install the remaining components in the reverse order of removal. Tighten the ignition

coil/cap screws to the specified torque setting.

### 8 Cam chain tensioner

### Removal

1 Remove the valve cover (see Section 7). On Daytona models, remove the belly-pan and the right-hand fairing side panel (see Chapter 7). On Sprint ST models, remove the belly-pan (see Chapter 7).

2 Drain the engine oil (see Chapter 1).

3 Remove the clutch cover, referring to the relevant Steps in Section 16. Using a ring spanner on the nut on the end of the crankshaft, rotate the crankshaft clockwise so that the T1 mark on the ignition timing rotor is aligned with the crankshaft position sensor pick-up **(see illustration 9.3a)**. In this position, the arrow marks on the cam sprockets should face inwards towards each other **(see illustration 9.3b)**. If they face away from each other, turn the crankshaft clockwise one full turn so that the T1 mark again aligns with the sensor – the arrows on the camshaft sprockets will now be facing towards each other.

4 When the tensioner is withdrawn from the cylinder block, the cam chain will be untensioned, and may jump a tooth on the intake cam sprocket. To prevent this, insert a

wedge between the tensioner blade and the crankcase to hold the blade in firm contact with the cam chain whilst the tensioner is removed.

5 Undo the large end bolt from the tensioner and withdraw the spring, noting that it will be under tension **(see illustration)**.

6 Remove the two mounting bolts and withdraw the tensioner **(see illustration)**. Discard its gasket as a new one must be used.

### Inspection

7 Examine the tensioner components for signs of wear or damage. Lift the catch on the tensioner body and move the plunger in and out – if it doesn't move smoothly and freely, replace the tensioner with a new one **(see illustration)**.

8 If the spring has sagged, the tensioner will not be able to take up chain play effectively. Measure the free length of the spring and compare to the specification. If the spring length has reduced significantly, the tensioner must be renewed.

### Installation

#### Method A

9 Lift the catch on the tensioner body and push the plunger fully inwards **(see illustration 8.7)**. Release the catch to lock the plunger in the retracted position.

10 Install the spring in the tensioner. Fit a new sealing washer to the end bolt and install the end bolt in the end of the spring **(see**

**8.5 Unscrew the bolt (arrowed) and withdraw the spring from the tensioner body**

**8.6 Unscrew the bolts (arrowed) and withdraw the tensioner body from the head**

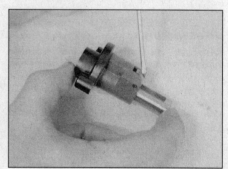

**8.7 Release the catch and check the plunger moves freely in and out**

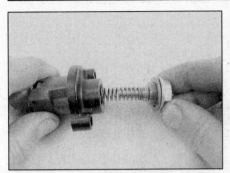

8.10a Fit the spring and end bolt into the tensioner . . .

8.10b . . . then turn the bolt anti-clockwise so that it threads into the plunger

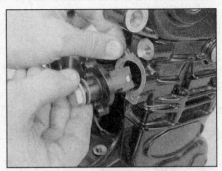

8.11a Install the tensioner assembly using a new gasket . . .

8.11b . . . and tighten the mounting bolts to the specified torque

8.12 Turn the end bolt clockwise as described to release the plunger, and tighten it to the specified torque

**illustration)**. Hold the tensioner body against the palm of your hand and compress the spring into the body so that the brass threaded ring on the end bolt contacts the end of the plunger; turn the end bolt **anti-clockwise** to thread the brass ring into the plunger **(see illustration)**. This will keep the plunger retracted even though it is under spring pressure. **Note:** *It may take several attempts to achieve this.*

**11** Check that the crankshaft is still aligned as described in Step 3. Slip a new gasket over the tensioner body and install the tensioner in the cylinder head **(see illustration)**. Secure it with the two mounting bolts, tightening them to the specified torque setting **(see illustration)**.

**12** Remove the wood wedge from the tensioner blade, making sure that the chain does not jump a tooth on the cam sprocket as you do. Screw the tensioner end bolt **clockwise** into the tensioner body **(see illustration)**; as you do this, the threaded brass section will thread itself out of the plunger, thereby releasing it, at the same time as the bolt threads will lock into the body. The tensioner ratchet will be heard to release and the plunger shoot out into contact with the tensioner blade as the brass ring releases the plunger. Tighten the end bolt to the specified torque setting.

**13** Check that the timing marks are correct (see Step 3). Rotate the engine several times and recheck the timing marks – if the cam chain has jumped whilst the tensioner was removed, reposition it as described in Section

9. Install the valve cover (see Section 7).
**14** Install the clutch cover (see Section 16, following the relevant Steps).
**15** Fill the engine to the correct level with oil (see *Daily (pre-ride) checks*).

## Method B

**16** Lift the catch on the tensioner body and push the plunger fully inwards **(see illustration 8.7)**. Release the catch to lock the plunger in the retracted position.
**17** Slip a new gasket over the tensioner body and install the tensioner in the cylinder head **(see illustration)**. Secure it with the mounting two bolts, tightening them to the specified torque setting **(see illustration 8.6)**.
**18** Remove the wood wedge from the tensioner blade, making sure that the chain does not jump a tooth on the cam sprocket as

you do. Using a slim rod inserted into the tensioner body, use finger pressure only to push the tensioner plunger in until it contacts the tensioner blade; the ratchet and catch will hold it in this position. Fit a new sealing washer onto the end bolt and install the spring and end bolt into the tensioner body **(see illustration)**. Tighten the end bolt to the specified torque setting.

**19** Check that the timing marks are correct (see Step 3). Rotate the engine several times and recheck the timing marks – if the cam chain has jumped whilst the tensioner was removed, reposition it as described in Section 9. Install the valve cover (see Section 7).

**20** Install the clutch cover (see Section 16, following the relevant Steps).

**21** Fill the engine to the correct level with oil (see Chapter 1).

## 9  Camshafts and followers

**Note:** *This procedure can be carried out with the engine in the frame.*

### Removal

**1** Remove the valve cover (see Section 7). On Daytona models, remove the belly-pan and the right-hand fairing side panel (see Chapter 7). On Sprint ST models, remove the belly-pan (see Chapter 7).

**2** Drain the engine oil (see Chapter 1).

**3** Remove the clutch cover, referring to the relevant Steps of Section 16. Using a ring

8.17 Install the tensioner using a new gasket

8.18 Fit the spring and end bolt into the tensioner

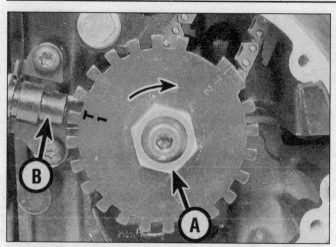

9.3a  Turn the crankshaft clockwise using the nut (A), until the T1 mark aligns with the sensor (B) as described

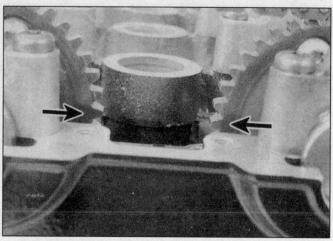

9.3b  The arrow on each sprocket must be facing in and be parallel with the head mating surface

spanner on the nut on the end of the crankshaft, rotate the crankshaft clockwise until the T1 mark on the ignition timing rotor aligns with the crankshaft position sensor pick-up (see illustration). In this position, the arrow marks on the camshaft sprockets will either be pointing inwards towards each other and be parallel with the top surface of the

9.5  Undo the screws (arrowed) and remove the guide

cylinder head, which is the position you want them in, or they will be pointing away from each other (see illustration). If they point away from each other, turn the crankshaft clockwise one full turn so that the T1 mark again aligns with the sensor – the arrows on the camshaft sprockets will now be pointing towards each other. Note: When the cam sprocket arrows are exactly parallel with the head, the centre of the crankshaft position sensor pick-up will be aligned either with the leading edge, centre or trailing edge of the T1 tooth on the rotor, depending on your model. If the timing is set up incorrectly, the sensor will not align with any part of the tooth.

4  Remove the cam chain tensioner (see Section 8).

5  Remove the four screws securing the cam chain upper guide and lift it off (see illustration).

6  Before disturbing the camshaft caps, check for identification markings scribed on their top surfaces. These markings ensure that the caps can be matched up to their original

journals on installation. The caps are numbered 1 to 6; the two outrigger caps on the cam chain end are denoted A and B (see illustration). If you can't see any markings, or they are unclear, make your own marks. Note that the numbered cap bolt holes are offset so that the caps can't be installed the wrong way round. The lettered caps on the outrigger journals are symmetrical, but have an arrow cast into them which must point forwards – mark your own arrow if one is not visible.

7  Working on one camshaft at a time, slacken all eight cap bolts evenly and a little at a time in a criss-cross sequence, slackening the bolts above any lobes that are pressing onto a valve last in the sequence so that the pressure from the open valves cannot cause the camshaft to bend (see illustration). Remove the bolts, then remove the caps (see illustration). Retrieve the dowels on each cap if they are loose – if they are not in the caps, they will be in the head.

Caution: A camshaft could break if the

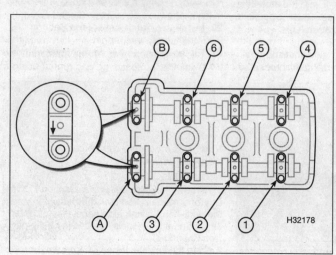

9.6  Camshaft cap identification markings

9.7a  Camshaft cap bolts (arrowed)

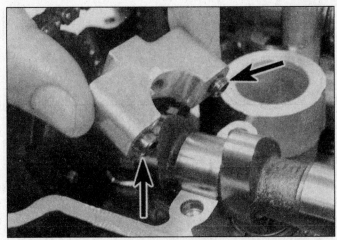

9.7b Lift the cap off its journal, noting the dowels (arrowed)

9.9a Lift the camshaft off the head and disengage it from the chain

9.9b Note the difference between the camshafts for identification

9.10 Lift each follower out of its bore – note the shim sitting in the top of the follower

*holder bolts are not slackened as described and the pressure from a depressed valve causes the shaft to bend. Also, if the holder does not come squarely away from the head, the holder is likely to break. If this happens the cylinder head must be renewed; the holders are matched to the head and cannot be obtained separately.*

**8** Lift the camshaft off the head and disengage it from the cam chain.

**9** Repeat the procedure for the other camshaft **(see illustration)**. The cam chain can be left to rest on its support bolt in the tunnel. Note that the camshafts are slightly different for identification purposes – the intake camshaft has a groove in its centre section, while the same section on the exhaust camshaft is plain **(see illustration)**.

**10** If the shims and followers are being removed from the cylinder head, obtain a container which is divided into twelve compartments, and label each compartment with the location of its corresponding valve in the cylinder head and whether it belongs with

an intake or an exhaust valve. If a container is not available, use labelled plastic bags (egg cartons also work very well!). Remove the cam follower of the valve in question **(see illustration)**. It is probably best to leave the shims in the followers for safekeeping.

## Inspection

**11** Inspect the cam bearing surfaces of the

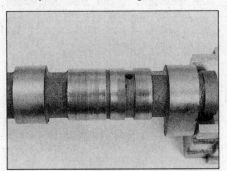

9.11a Inspect the bearing surfaces for scratches or wear

head and the caps **(see illustration)**. Look for score marks, deep scratches and evidence of spalling (a pitted appearance). Check the camshaft lobes for heat discoloration (blue appearance), score marks, chipped areas, flat spots and spalling **(see illustration)**.

**12** Check the amount of camshaft runout by supporting each end of the camshaft on V-blocks, and measuring any runout using a

9.11b Check the lobes of the camshaft for wear - here's an example of damage requiring camshaft repair or renewal

**9.15 Lay a strip of Plastigauge across each bearing journal, parallel with the camshaft centreline**

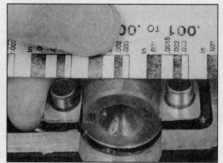

**9.17a Compare the width of the crushed Plastigauge to the scale printed on the Plastigauge container**

**9.17b Measure the cam bearing journals with a micrometer**

dial gauge. If the runout exceeds the specified limit the camshaft must be replaced with a new one.

**HAYNES HiNT** *Refer to Tools and Workshop Tips (Section 3) in the Reference section for details of how to read a micrometer and dial gauge.*

**13** Next, check the camshaft journal oil clearances, using a product called Plastigauge. Check each camshaft in turn rather than at the same time. The intake camshaft can be identified by its grooved centre section and the exhaust by its plain section **(see illustration 9.9b)**.
**14** Clean the camshafts, the bearing surfaces in the cylinder head and the caps with a clean, lint-free cloth, then lay the camshaft in place in the cylinder head – there is no need to engage the chain on the sprocket.
**15** Cut strips of Plastigauge and lay one piece on each bearing journal, parallel with the camshaft centreline **(see illustration)**. Make sure the camshaft cap dowels are installed then fit the caps in their proper positions (see Step 6) **(see illustration 9.7b and 9.6)**. Lubricate the threads of the cap bolts with clean engine oil, then fit them in the caps. Ensuring that the camshafts are not rotated at all, tighten all eight cap bolts evenly, a little at a time, in a criss-cross sequence, until the specified torque setting is reached.
**16** Now unscrew the bolts evenly, a little at a time, in a criss-cross sequence and carefully lift off the caps, again making sure the camshaft is not rotated.
**17** To determine the oil clearance, compare the crushed Plastigauge (at its widest point) on each journal to the scale printed on the Plastigauge container **(see illustration)**. Compare the results to this Chapter's Specifications. If the oil clearance is greater than specified, measure the diameter of the camshaft journal with a micrometer **(see illustration)**. If the journal diameter is less than the specified limit, replace the camshaft with a new one and recheck the clearance. If

the clearance is still too great, or if the camshaft journal is within its limit, replace the cylinder head and caps as a set with new ones – individual caps are not available. Note that if specialist measuring tools are available, the camshaft bearing bore inside diameter can be compared with the specified limit.

**HAYNES HiNT** *Before renewing the camshafts, cylinder head/caps because of damage, check with local machine shops specialising in motorcycle engine work. In the case of the camshafts, it may be possible for cam lobes to be welded, reground and hardened, at a cost far lower than that of a new camshaft. If the bearing surfaces in the head or holders are damaged, it may be possible for them to be bored out to accept bearing inserts. Due to the cost of new components it is recommended that all options are explored!*

**18** Repeat the oil clearance check on the other camshaft.
**19** Check the sprockets for wear, cracks and other damage, renewing them if necessary. If the sprockets are worn, the cam chain is also worn, and probably the sprocket on the crankshaft as well. If wear this severe is apparent, the cam chain and all sprockets should be renewed (see Section 10). Except in cases of oil starvation (and worn sprockets), the cam chain itself should

wear very little. If the chain has stretched excessively, which makes it difficult to maintain proper tension, or if it is stiff or the links are binding or kinking, replace it with a new one.
**20** The same design sprocket is used for each camshaft, but different hole positions are provided for fitting to the intake or exhaust camshaft. When fitted to the intake camshaft the holes next to the IN marking should be used, and those next to the EX marking for the exhaust camshaft **(see illustration)**. The sprocket bolts must have a drop of non-permanent thread locking compound applied to their threads and be tightened to the specified torque setting.
**21** Inspect the outer surfaces of the followers for evidence of scoring or other damage. If a follower is in poor condition, it is probable that the bore in which it works is also damaged. Measure the outside diameter of the followers and the inside diameter of the bores and compare the results to the limits in the Specifications at the beginning of this Chapter. If the bores are seriously out-of-round or tapered, the cylinder head and the followers must be renewed.

### Installation

**22** Lubricate each follower with engine oil and install each with its shim in the cylinder head **(see illustration)**. **Note:** *It is important that the followers and shims are returned to their original valves otherwise the valve clearances will be inaccurate.*

**9.20 This sprocket is fitted to the exhaust camshaft**

**9.22 Lubricate the followers and slip them into their bores**

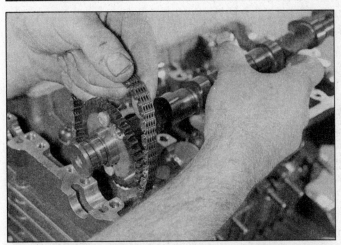

**9.25 Keeping the front run of the chain taut, lay the exhaust camshaft in the head, positioning it as described**

**9.26 Lay the intake shaft in the head, making sure the chain is taut between the sprockets**

**23** Check that the crankshaft is positioned as described in Step 3.

**24** Apply a smear of clean engine oil to the cylinder head camshaft bearing surfaces.

**25** Hook the cam chain up from its tunnel and make sure that it is engaged around the lower sprocket teeth on the crankshaft. Keeping the front run of the chain taut, lay the exhaust camshaft in position so that the arrow mark on its sprocket points rearwards and is parallel with the top mating surface of the cylinder head, then engage the chain on the sprocket teeth **(see illustration)**.

**26** Slip the intake camshaft through the cam chain so that the arrow mark on its sprocket points forwards and is parallel with the head **(see illustration)**. Engage the chain fully on the sprocket teeth, making sure that the chain is tight between the camshafts, with any slack lying in the rear run where it will later be taken up by the tensioner. Before proceeding, check that everything aligns as described in Step 3. If it doesn't, the valve timing is inaccurate, and the valves could contact the pistons when the engine is turned over.

**27** Oil the camshaft journals. Ensure that the camshaft cap dowels are installed and fit the caps in their proper positions (see Step 6) **(see illustration 9.7b and 9.6)**. Lubricate the threads of the cap bolts with clean engine oil, then fit them in the caps. Tighten all eight cap bolts evenly, a little at a time, in a criss-cross sequence, until the specified torque setting is reached **(see illustration)**. Repeat for the other camshaft. **Note:** *Be careful that the cam chain doesn't jump a tooth as the intake camshaft is tightened down* (see **Haynes Hint**).

**28** With all caps tightened down, check that the valve timing marks still align (see Step 3). If the chain has jumped a tooth, release the pressure on the tensioner blade (if applied), then slip the cam chain off the sprockets (there should be enough slack in the rear run to do this easily without having to displace the camshafts). Turn the camshaft(s) as required using a spanner on the cast hex until their alignment is correct **(see illustration)**. With the timing is set up correctly, check that each camshaft is not pinched by turning it a few degrees in each direction with a spanner on the hex.

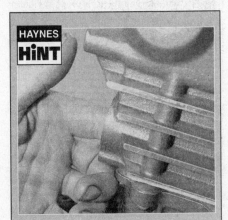

HAYNES HiNT

*Keep the cam chain taut all round by applying pressure to the tensioner blade via the tensioner hole – using a finger works well, though a wooden dowel is easier. Alternatively, place a wedge between the blade and the crankcase*

**9.27 Tighten the cap bolts to the specified torque setting**

**9.28 Slip the chain off the sprocket and turn the camshaft as required using a spanner on the cast hex**

9.29 Install the upper guide on the head

10.2a Unscrew the pivot bolt (arrowed) . . .

10.2b . . . and lift the tensioner blade out of the tunnel

29 Install the cam chain upper guide and tighten its screws to the specified torque setting (see illustration).
30 Install the cam chain tensioner (Section 8).
31 If the camshafts or any of the valve components have been renewed, or if you are unsure whether you have returned the shims to their original locations, check the valve clearances (see Chapter 1).
32 Install the clutch cover, referring to the relevant Steps of Section 16.
33 Install the valve cover (see Section 7).
34 Refill the engine with oil (see *Daily (pre-ride) checks*). On Daytona models, install the belly-pan and the right-hand fairing side panel (see Chapter 7). On Sprint ST models, install the belly-pan (see Chapter 7).

## 10 Cam chain and tensioner/guide blades

**Note:** *The cam chain and blades can be removed with the engine in the frame.*

### Cam chain tensioner blade

#### Removal

1 Remove the intake camshaft as described in Section 9.
2 Undo the tensioner blade pivot bolt from the right-hand side of the crankcase (see illustration). Retrieve the washer from between the blade and the crankcase as you withdraw the bolt, and the collar from the bolt hole if it doesn't come out with the bolt (see illustration 10.4). Lift the blade out of the back of the cam chain tunnel (see illustration).

10.4 Locate the inner washer between the blade and the crankcase

3 Check the tensioner blade for cracking and other damage, renewing it if necessary.

#### Installation

4 Slide the washer and collar onto the pivot bolt. Lower the tensioner blade down through the chain tunnel (see illustration 10.2b), then slip the bolt through the blade, locating the inner washer between the blade and the crankcase as you do (see illustration). Thread the bolt into the crankcase and tighten it to the torque setting specified at the beginning of the Chapter.
5 Install the intake camshaft (see Section 9).

### Cam chain guide blade

6 Remove the cylinder head (see Section 11).
7 Lift the blade out of the front of the cam chain tunnel, noting how it locates (see illustration).
8 Installation is the reverse of removal. Make

10.7 Lift the guide blade out of the tunnel

sure the blade locates correctly at the top and bottom (see illustrations).

### Cam chain upper guide

9 Remove the valve cover (see Section 7).
10 Remove the four screws securing the cam chain upper guide and lift off (see illustration 9.5).
11 Installation is the reverse of removal (see illustration 9.29).

### Cam chain and crankshaft sprocket

#### Removal

12 Remove the camshafts (see Section 9). To prevent the possibility of damage, remove the crankshaft position sensor (see Chapter 4).
13 Counterhold the engine turning hexagon on the crankshaft with a ring spanner and unscrew the Allen bolt from the centre (see illustration). Remove the hexagon and

10.8a Locate the lugs in the cutouts (arrows) . . .

10.8b . . . and make sure the blade hooks onto the crankcase correctly at the bottom

10.13a Counter-hold the hex and unscrew the bolt

10.13b Remove the hex . . .

10.13c . . . and the rotor, noting how they locate over the key

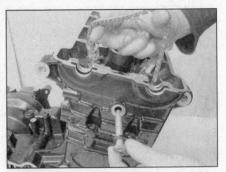

10.14 Unscrew and remove the support bolt . . .

10.15 . . . then disengage the chain from the crankshaft sprocket and lift it out of the tunnel

10.16a Slide the sprocket off the crankshaft, noting which way round it fits

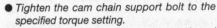

10.16b Remove the key for safekeeping if it is loose

ignition timing rotor from the crankshaft, noting how they locate over the square-section key **(see illustrations)**.

**14** Hold the cam chain and remove the support bolt from the centre of the right-hand side of the cylinder head **(see illustration)**.

**15** Slip the chain off the crankshaft sprocket and lift it out of the head **(see illustration)**.

**16** If required, slide the crankshaft sprocket off the crankshaft, noting how it is located by the key **(see illustration)**. Remove the key for safekeeping if it is loose **(see illustration)**.

### Inspection

**17** Inspect the sprocket for chipped or missing teeth. Check the cam chain for binding and obvious damage – inspect the chain plates for cracking and abrasion and inspect the inner plates for wear where they pass over the camshaft and crankshaft sprockets. Check for blue discolouration of the chain indicating excessive heat build-up.

Examine the chain pins and ensure none are loose. If the chain and sprocket show signs of extensive wear renew them as a set (including the camshaft sprockets).

**18** If there is any doubt about the condition of the chain, check it for stretch as follows. Hang the chain from a hook and attach a 13 kg (28 lb) weight to its lower end. Measure the length of 70 pins (from the centre of the 1st pin to the centre of the 70th pin) and compare the result to the service limit specified at the beginning of the Chapter. If the chain exceeds the service limit it must be replaced with a new one.

### Installation

**19** Installation is a reverse of the removal procedure, noting the following:
● *Locate the sprocket, timing rotor and hexagon on the crankshaft with the square-section key* **(see illustrations 10.16a, 13c and 13b)**. *Install the timing rotor with its marked side facing outwards.*

● *Tighten the cam chain support bolt to the specified torque setting.*
● *Apply a drop of non-permanent thread locking compound to the threads of the timing rotor Allen bolt and tighten it to the specified torque setting, counter-holding the hex as you do* **(see illustration)**.
● *Do not forget to install the crankshaft position sensor (see Chapter 4).*

### 11 Cylinder head removal and installation

**Caution: The engine must be completely cool before beginning this procedure or the cylinder head may become warped.**
**Note:** *This procedure can be performed with the engine in the frame. If the engine has already been removed, ignore the preliminary steps which don't apply. It will be necessary to support the engine under the sump during this procedure, therefore position the bike on its centrestand (Sprint ST) or on an auxiliary stand (all other models).*

### Removal

**1** Remove the fuel tank and airbox (see Chapter 4).
**2** Remove the radiator and thermostat housing (see Chapter 3). On Sprint models, disconnect the wire from the coolant temperature sender unit on the left-hand end of the cylinder head **(see illustration 5.6)**. On all models, slacken the clamp securing the coolant hose to the left-hand end of the cylinder head and detach the hose **(see illustration)**.

10.19 Tighten the Allen bolt to the specified torque

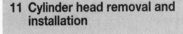

11.2 Slacken the clamp screw (arrowed) and detach the hose

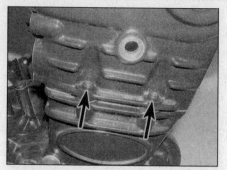

11.7 Remove the two screws (arrowed) from the right-hand end of the head

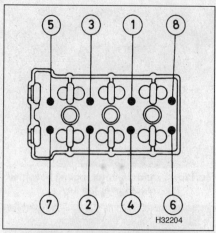

11.9 Cylinder head bolt TIGHTENING sequence

11.11 Carefully lift the head up off the engine

3 Remove the exhaust system (see Chapter 4).
4 Remove the throttle bodies (see Chapter 4).
5 Remove the camshafts and followers (see Section 9). Remove the cam chain support bolt from the centre of the right-hand side of the cylinder head (see illustration 10.14).
6 Unscrew the banjo bolt securing the external oil hose to the cylinder head and position the hose aside. Discard the sealing washers as new ones must be fitted on installation.
7 Remove the two screws from the right-hand end of the cylinder head-to-crankcase joint (see illustration).
8 Position a jack and wooden block under the sump, then refer to Section 5 and remove the cylinder head-to-frame bolts on each side. As they are withdrawn, take the weight of the engine on the jack so that no additional strain is placed on the engine's rear mountings.
9 Slacken the eight cylinder head bolts by

half a turn at a time in a **reverse** of the specified sequence shown (see illustration).
10 Tap around the joint faces of the cylinder head with a soft-faced mallet to free the head. Don't attempt to free the head by inserting a screwdriver between the head and cylinder block – you'll damage the sealing surfaces.
11 Carefully lift the head off the block, and remove it from the engine (see illustration). Recover the two dowels if they are loose.
12 Lift the cam chain guide blade from the front of the tunnel, noting how it locates (see illustration 10.7).
13 Whenever the cylinder head is disturbed it is possible that the seal between the liners and crankcase will be broken. Unfortunately there is

no easy way of telling whether this has occurred or not, and so the only way to be sure is to remove the liners and reseal them before installing the head, and Triumph specify this practice. On the model we stripped down, we found that the liners were in fact quite difficult to remove, and so the chances were that the seal remained intact. If the crankshaft is rotated at all with the head off, then the liners must be removed and resealed. If you feel certain that the seal has not broken, you can clamp them in place using suitable bolts, nuts and washers threaded into the head bolt holes as shown to prevent any movement (see illustration) – do not overtighten the clamps as the mating surface of the head could be indented, causing leakage and compression problems. However if you are in any doubt at all (and it is impossible to be 100% certain), it is essential that the liners are removed, otherwise coolant from the cylinder block water jacket will seep into the crankcase. Refer to Section 14 for liner removal and installation details.

## Installation

14 Fit and seal the liners in the cylinder block (see Section 14). If the liners were clamped in place, remove the clamps. Use a straight edge to check that the tops of the liners are level with the block sealing surface.
15 Locate the cam chain guide blade into the tunnel. Make sure the blade locates correctly at the top and bottom (see illustrations 10.8a and b).
16 Check that the cylinder head bolt holes in the block are clean and dry. Ensure both cylinder head and block mating surfaces are clean.
17 Fit the dowels to the block (if removed), then lay the new head gasket over the dowels and onto the head (see illustration).
18 Carefully lower the cylinder head onto the block (see illustration 11.11).
19 Clean the threads and under the heads of the cylinder head bolts. Lubricate the threads with clean engine oil, then wipe them with a lint-free cloth so that all excess oil is removed, but not so that they are completely dry. Install the cylinder head bolts and tighten them finger-tight only at this stage (see illustration).
20 Tighten the cylinder head bolts in the correct numerical sequence (see illustration 11.9) to the stage 1 torque setting (see illustration).

11.13 Assemble a bolt, nut and washers as shown to clamp the liners

11.17 Lay the new gasket on the head, locating it over the dowels (arrowed)

11.19 Install the bolts and tighten them finger-tight

11.20a Tighten the cylinder head bolts as described to the specified torque settings . . .

**11.20b . . . and then through the specified angle using a degree disc**

**11.22  Tighten the end screws to the specified torque**

**11.26  Use a new sealing washer on each side of the union**

Repeat to the stage 2 torque setting. Finally, attach a degree disc to the torque wrench and angle-tighten each bolt 90° following the same sequence **(see illustration)**.

**21**  Realign the engine mounting lugs with the frame, using pressure from the jack if necessary, and install the mounting bolts, washers and nuts, referring to Section 5 for model specific details. Tighten the bolts to the specified torque settings, following the procedure in section 5. Remove the jack.

**22**  Tighten the screws on the right-hand end of the cylinder head to the specified torque setting **(see illustration)**.

**23**  Lift the cam chain up the tunnel, using a piece of wire to hook it up if necessary, then install the support bolt and tighten it to the specified torque setting **(see illustration 10.14)**.

**24**  Install the followers and camshafts (see Section 9).

**25**  Install the valve cover (see Section 7).

**26**  Using new sealing washers on each side of the external oil hose union, install the hose on the engine and tighten the banjo bolt to the specified torque setting **(see illustration)**.

**27**  Push the coolant pipe onto its union on the cylinder head and tighten the clamp securely **(see illustration 11.2)**. On Sprint models, reconnect the coolant temperature sensor wire **(see illustration 5.6)**.

**28**  Install the throttle bodies, exhaust system radiator and thermostat housing, referring to the relevant Chapters.

**29**  Fill the cooling system (see Chapter 1).

**30**  Install the airbox and fuel tank (see Chapter 4).

## 12  Valves/valve seats/valve guides overhaul

**1**  Because of the complex nature of this job and the special tools and equipment required, most owners leave servicing of the valves, valve seats and valve guides to a professional. However, you can make an initial assessment of whether the valves are seating, and therefore sealing, correctly by pouring a small amount of solvent into each of the valve ports. If the solvent leaks past any valve into the combustion chamber area the valve is not seating and sealing correctly.

**2**  You can also remove the valves from the cylinder head, clean the components, check them for wear to assess the extent of the work needed, and, unless a valve service is required, grind in the valves (see Section 13). The head can then be reassembled.

**3**  A dealer service department will remove the valves and springs, renew the valves and guides, recut the valve seats, check and renew the valve springs, spring retainers and collets (as necessary), replace the valve seals with new ones and reassemble the valve components.

**4**  After the valve service has been performed, the head will be in like-new condition. When the head is returned, be sure to clean it again very thoroughly before installation on the engine to remove any metal particles or abrasive grit that may still be present from the valve service operations. Use compressed air, if available, to blow out all the holes and passages.

## 13  Cylinder head and valves overhaul

**1**  As mentioned in the previous section, valve seat recutting should be left to a Triumph dealer. However, disassembly, cleaning and inspection of the valves and related components can be done (if the necessary special tools are available) by the home mechanic. This way no expense is incurred if the inspection reveals that overhaul is not required at this time.

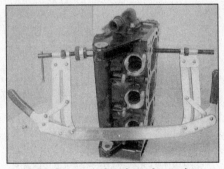

**13.6a  Compressing the valve springs using a valve spring compressor**

**2**  To disassemble the valve components without the risk of damaging them, a valve spring compressor is absolutely necessary. Make sure it is suitable for motorcycle work.

### Disassembly

**3**  Remove the followers and their shims if you haven't already done so (see Section 9). Store the components in such a way that they can be returned to their original locations without getting mixed up.

**4**  Carefully scrape all carbon deposits out of the combustion chamber area. A hand held wire brush or a piece of fine emery cloth can be used once the majority of deposits have been scraped away. Do not use a wire brush mounted in a drill motor, or one with extremely stiff bristles, as the head material is soft and may be eroded away or scratched by the wire brush.

**5**  Arrange to label and store the valves along with their related components so they can be kept separate and reinstalled in the same valve guides they are removed from (labelled plastic bags work well for this).

**6**  Compress the valve spring on the first valve with a spring compressor, then remove the collets from the valve assembly **(see illustrations)**. **Note:** *Take great care not to mark the follower bore with the spring compressor.* Do not compress the springs any more than is necessary. Carefully release the valve spring compressor, then remove the spring retainer and the springs and the valve from the head. If the valve binds in the guide (won't pull through), push it back into the head and deburr the area around the collet

**13.6b  Make sure the compressor is a good fit both on the top . . .**

**13.6c** ... and the bottom of the valve assembly

**13.6d Remove the collets with needle-nose pliers, tweezers, a magnet or a screwdriver with a dab of grease on it**

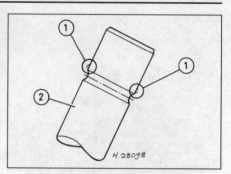

**13.6e If the valve stem (2) won't pull through the guide, deburr the area above the collet groove (1)**

groove with a very fine file or whetstone **(see illustration)**.

**7** Repeat the procedure for the other valves. Keep the parts for each valve together so they can be reinstalled in the same location.

**8** Pull the valve stem seals off the top of the valve guides with pliers and discard them (the old seals should never be reused) **(see illustration)**. Remove the spring seat – using a magnet is the easiest way to lift the seat off the head **(see illustration)**.

**9** Next, clean the cylinder head with solvent and dry it thoroughly. Compressed air will speed the drying process and ensure that all holes and recessed areas are clean. Clean any traces of old gasket material from the cylinder head. If a scraper is used, take care not to scratch or gouge the soft aluminium.

**HAYNES HiNT** *Refer to Tools and Workshop Tips (Section 7) for details of gasket removal methods.*

**10** Clean all of the valve springs, collets, retainers and spring seats with solvent and dry them thoroughly. Do the parts from one valve at a time so that no mixing of parts between valves occurs.

**11** Scrape off any deposits that may have formed on the valve, then use a motorised wire brush to remove deposits from the valve heads and stems. Again, make sure the valves do not get mixed up.

## Inspection

**12** Inspect the head very carefully for cracks and other damage. If cracks are found, a new head will be required. Check the cam bearing surfaces for wear and evidence of seizure. Check the camshafts for wear as well (see Section 9).

**13** Using a precision straight-edge and a feeler gauge, check the head gasket mating surface for warpage. Refer to *Tools and*

*Workshop Tips* (Section 3) in the Reference section for details of how to use the straight-edge. If the head is warped, but not excessively so, a specialist repair shop should be able to resurface it. If the head is excessively warped, replace it with a new one.

**14** Examine the valve seats in the combustion chamber. If they are pitted, cracked or burned, the head will require work beyond the scope of the home mechanic. Measure the valve seat width and compare it to this Chapter's Specifications **(see illustration)**. If it exceeds the service limit, or if it varies around its circumference, valve seat overhaul is required.

**15** Measure the valve stem diameter **(see illustration)**. Clean the valve guides to remove any carbon build-up, then measure the inside diameters of the guides (at both ends and the centre of the guide) with a small hole gauge and micrometer **(see illustrations)**. The guides are measured at the ends and at the centre to

**13.8a Pull the seal off the top of the guide ...**

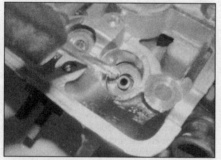

**13.8b ... then remove the spring seat**

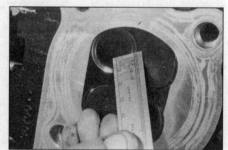

**13.14 Measure the valve seat width with a ruler (or for greater precision use a Vernier caliper)**

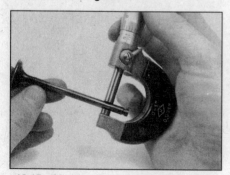

**13.15a Measure the valve stem diameter with a micrometer**

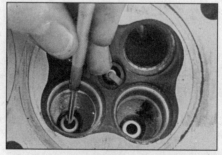

**13.15b Insert a small hole gauge into the valve guide and expand it so there's a slight drag when it's pulled out**

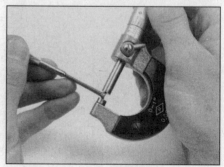

**13.15c Measure the small hole gauge with a micrometer**

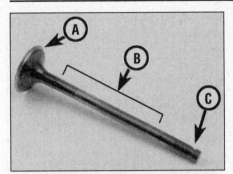

**13.16 Check the valve face (A), stem (B) and collet groove (C) for signs of wear and damage**

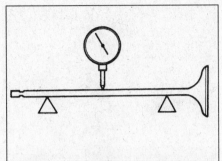

**13.17 Check the valve stem for runout using V-blocks and a dial gauge**

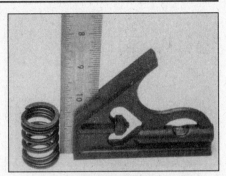

**13.18 Check the valve springs for squareness**

determine if they are worn in a bell-mouth pattern (more wear at the ends). Subtract the stem diameter from the valve guide diameter to obtain the valve stem-to-guide clearance. If the stem-to-guide clearance is greater than listed in this Chapter's Specifications, and fitting new valves will restore the clearance, renew the valves. If the guides are excessively worn, or worn unevenly, a new head will have to be fitted (see *Haynes Hint*, Section 9).

*Refer to Tools and Workshop Tips in the Reference Section for details on how to use a micrometer.*

**16** Carefully inspect each valve face, stem and collet groove area for cracks, pits and burned spots **(see illustration)**.
**17** Rotate the valve and check for any obvious indication that it is bent. Use V-blocks and a dial gauge if available **(see illustration)**. If the valve is bent, it must be replaced with a new one. Check the end of the stem for pitting and excessive wear. The presence of any of the above conditions indicates the need for valve servicing. The stem end can be ground down, provided that the amount of stem above the collet groove after grinding is sufficient.
**18** Check the end of each valve spring for wear and pitting. Measure the spring length with the specified load for the spring being measured (see Specifications) and compare it to that listed. If any spring compresses further than specified it has sagged and must be

replaced with a new one. Also place the spring upright on a flat surface and check it for bend by placing a ruler against it **(see illustration)**. If the bend in any spring is excessive, it must be replaced with a new one.
**19** Check the spring retainers and collets for obvious wear and cracks. Any questionable parts should not be reused, as extensive damage will occur in the event of failure during engine operation.
**20** If the inspection indicates that no overhaul work is required, the valve components can be reinstalled in the head.

### Reassembly

**21** Unless a valve service has been performed, before installing the valves in the head they should be ground in (lapped) to ensure a positive seal between the valves and seats. This procedure requires coarse and fine valve grinding compound and a valve grinding tool. If a grinding tool is not available, a piece of rubber or plastic hose can be slipped over the valve stem (after the valve has been installed in the guide) and used to turn the valve.
**22** Apply a small amount of coarse grinding compound to the valve face and some molybdenum disulphide oil (a 50/50 mixture of molybdenum disulphide grease and engine oil) to the valve stem, then slip the valve into the guide **(see illustration)**. **Note:** *Make sure each valve is installed in its correct guide and be careful not to get any grinding compound on the valve stem.*
**23** Attach the grinding tool (or hose) to the

valve and rotate the tool between the palms of your hands. Use a back-and-forth motion (as though rubbing your hands together) rather than a circular motion (i.e. so that the valve rotates alternately clockwise and anti-clockwise rather than in one direction only) **(see illustration)**. Lift the valve off the seat and turn it at regular intervals to distribute the grinding compound properly. Continue the grinding procedure until the valve face and seat contact area is of uniform and correct width and unbroken around the entire circumference of the valve face and seat **(see illustrations)**.
**24** Carefully remove the valve from the guide and wipe off all traces of grinding compound. Use solvent to clean the valve and wipe the seat area thoroughly with a solvent soaked cloth.

**13.22 Apply the lapping compound very sparingly, in small dabs, to the valve face only**

**13.23a Rotate the valve grinding tool back and forth between the palms of your hands**

**13.23b The valve face and seat should show a uniform unbroken ring . . .**

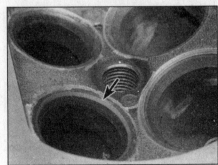

**13.23c . . . and the seat (arrowed) should be the specified width all the way round**

**13.26a Fit the spring seat . . .**

**13.26b . . . followed by the valve stem seal**

**13.26c Press the seal into position using a suitable deep socket**

**25** Repeat the procedure with fine valve grinding compound, then repeat the entire procedure for the remaining valves.

**26** Working on one valve at a time, lay the spring seat in place in the cylinder head **(see illustration)**. Fit a new valve stem seal onto the guide **(see illustration)**. Use an appropriate size deep socket to push the seal over the end of the valve guide until it is felt to clip into place **(see illustration)**. Don't twist or cock the seal, or it will not seal properly against the valve stem. Also, don't remove it again or it will be damaged. Note that there are different size seals for the intake and exhaust valves – make sure you have the correct size for the valve being installed (the intake valve seals are slightly smaller).

**27** Coat the valve stem with molybdenum disulphide oil (a 50/50 mixture of molybdenum disulphide grease and engine oil), then install it

into its guide, rotating it slowly to avoid damaging the seal **(see illustration)**. Check that the valve moves up and down freely in the guide. Install the inner spring, with its closer-wound coils facing down into the cylinder head, followed by the outer spring, also with its closer-wound coils facing down into the cylinder head **(see illustrations)**. Now fit the spring retainer, with its shouldered side facing down so that it fits into the top of the springs **(see illustration)**.

**28** Apply a small amount of grease to the inside of the collets – this will help to help hold them in place as the pressure is released from the spring **(see illustration)**. Compress the spring with the valve spring compressor and install the collets **(see illustration)**. When compressing the spring, do so only as far as is necessary to slip the collets into place. Make certain that the collets are securely locked in the retaining groove.

**29** Support the cylinder head on blocks so the valves can't contact the workbench top, then very gently tap the top of the valve stem to help seat the collets in the groove.

**30** Repeat the procedure for the remaining valves. Remember to keep the parts for each valve together and separate from the other valves so they can be reinstalled in the same location.

 **HAYNES HiNT** *Check for proper sealing of the valves by pouring a small amount of solvent into each of the valve ports. If the solvent leaks past any valve into the combustion chamber area the valve grinding operation on that valve should be repeated.*

**13.27a Lubricate the stem and slide the valve into its correct location**

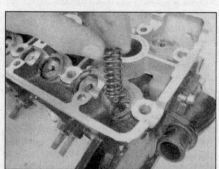

**13.27b Fit the inner valve spring . . .**

**13.27c . . . and the outer valve spring with their closer-wound coils facing down**

**13.27d . . . then fit the spring retainer**

**13.28a A small dab of grease will help to keep the collets in place on the valve while the spring is released**

**13.28b Compress the springs and install the collets, making sure they locate in the groove**

## 14 Cylinder liners

**Note:** *This procedure can be performed with the engine in the frame and with the pistons still in situ, following removal of the cylinder head. However to do this requires the use of a Triumph special tool, Part No. T3880315, to extract the liners. It may be possible to purchase a universal liner extractor from a good automotive tool supplier, though make sure it is suitable for engines below 1000cc. A suitable home-made tool can be used to release the liners, but as it uses the drawbolt principle it is necessary to remove the engine, separate the crankcase halves, then remove the crankshaft and connecting rods and pistons before it can be applied. If the liners are being removed as part of a complete engine overhaul and the engine is therefore removed anyway, then no extra work is involved, apart from making up the tool.*

### Removal

**1** If the Triumph special tool or a liner extractor is being used, just remove the cylinder head (see Section 11). Otherwise (see **Note** above), remove the engine from the frame, separate the crankcase halves, then remove the crankshaft and connecting rods and pistons, referring to the relevant Sections of this Chapter.

**2** Before removing the liners, mark the top edge of each liner at the front with a felt marker pen or similar, which will not damage the gasket surfaces. Indicate the cylinder number and front face of each liner.

**3** If the Triumph tool or a liner extractor is being used, turn the engine so that the piston in the liner being removed is at bottom dead centre (i.e. the bottom of its stroke). Gently draw each liner out of the cylinder block **(see illustration)**. The purpose of the extractor is to break the seal between the liner and the crankcase; once this has been achieved, the liner can be lifted out by hand. Do not attempt to lever the liners out because the gasket surfaces will be damaged. As each liner is removed, stuff the crankcase aperture with clean rag to cushion the piston and prevent anything falling into the crankcase.

**4** If the home-made drawbolt tool is being

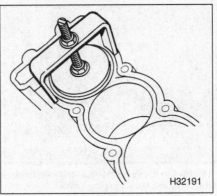

**14.3 Extracting a liner using the Triumph tool**

used (see **Tool Tip**), assemble the tool as shown. The bottom plate must be accurately fitted so that is bears on the bottom edge of the liner only – there must be no danger of it cocking sideways or slipping off the edge and scratching the inner surface of the liner **(see illustration)**. Also note that the bottom plate must locate inside the outside diameter of the liner and have no sharp edges that will score the block as the liner is drawn out. Tighten the top nut and gently draw the liner out of the cylinder block **(see illustration)**. Do not attempt to lever the liners out.

### Inspection

**5** Check the liner walls carefully for scratches and score marks. Using telescoping gauges and a micrometer (see Section 3 of *Tools and Workshop Tips*), check the dimensions of each cylinder to assess the amount of wear, taper and ovality. Measure near the top (but below the level of the top piston ring at TDC), centre and bottom (but above the level of the oil ring at BDC) of the bore, both parallel to and across the crankshaft axis **(see illustration)**. Compare the results to the specifications at the beginning of the Chapter. If the precision measuring tools are not available, take the crankcase to a Triumph dealer or specialist motorcycle repair shop for assessment and advice. If the liners are worn beyond the service limit, or badly scratched, scuffed or scored, replace them with new ones. The liners cannot be re-bored.

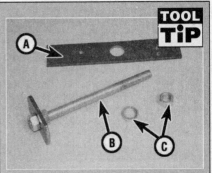

*Components of the home-made drawbolt tool; steel strap (A), drawbolt and bottom plate (B) and top nut and washer (C). The drawbolt tool can be made using a section of steel plate, accurately cut and chamfered so that it bears on the bottom edge of the liner, just inside the outside diameter of the liner. You will also need a length of flat steel bar of a suitable thickness, a length of threaded rod (15 mm diameter x 200 mm length), some washers and two nuts, and two pieces of wood (see illustration 14.4b). The thickness of the pieces of wood will determine by how much the liners can be extracted before they contact the flat steel bar, so make sure they are thick enough to allow the seal on the liner to be broken, and thereafter the liners can be removed by hand. Assemble the tool as described in Step 4.*

**6** Cast iron liners (as fitted to early models) can be honed to remove minor scratches and glazing, and to allow new piston rings to bed in. To perform the honing operation you will need the proper size flexible hone with fine stones (see Specialist Tools in *Tools and Workshop Tips* in the Reference section), or a bottle-brush type hone, plenty of light oil or honing oil, some clean rags and an electric drill motor. Note that the aluminium liners fitted to later models should not be honed.

**7** Securely hold the liner so that the bore is horizontal rather than vertical in a vice with soft jaws or cushioned with wooden blocks. Mount the hone in the drill motor, compress

**14.4a Make sure the bottom plate is accurately cut and fitted**

**14.4b Turn the top nut clockwise and draw the liner up until the seal is broken**

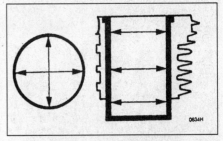

**14.7 Measure the cylinder bore in the directions shown with a telescoping gauge, then measure the gauge with a micrometer**

**14.12 Carefully fit the liner down over the piston, making sure the rings enter correctly**

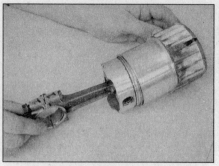

**14.15 Carefully feed the piston into the liner, making sure the rings enter correctly**

the stones and insert the hone into the cylinder. Thoroughly lubricate the cylinder, then turn on the drill and move the hone up and down in the cylinder at a pace which produces a fine cross-hatch pattern on the cylinder wall with the lines intersecting at an angle of approximately 60°. Be sure to use plenty of lubricant and do not take off any more material than is necessary to produce the desired effect. Do not withdraw the hone from the cylinder while it is still turning. Switch off the drill and continue to move it up and down in the cylinder until it has stopped turning, then compress the stones and withdraw the hone.

8 Wipe the oil from the cylinder and repeat the procedure on the other cylinder. Remember, do not take too much material from the cylinder wall. Wash the cylinders thoroughly with warm soapy water to remove all traces of the abrasive grit produced during the honing operation. After rinsing, dry the cylinders thoroughly and apply a thin coat of light, rust-preventative oil to all machined surfaces. If you do not have the equipment or desire to perform the honing operation, take the crankcase to a Triumph dealer or specialist motorcycle repair shop.

### Installation

**Note:** *If the crankcases were separated and the piston/connecting rod assemblies removed in order to remove the liners, you can either fit the piston/connecting rod assemblies into the liners before the liners are installed, then install them as an assembly (method 2) –*

**14.16 Apply the silicone sealant as shown . . .**

*or you can install the liners, then fit the piston/connecting rod assemblies into them afterwards (method 3).*

9 Remove all traces of old sealant from the mating surfaces of the liners and the crankcase. If the connecting rods and pistons are still in situ, this will be tricky because you must avoid old sealant dropping into the sump. Remove any rag from the crankcase and make sure the mating surfaces of the liner and crankcase are clean, oil-free and dry. Check that the piston rings are correctly positioned in relation to the front of the engine **(see illustration 15.27)**.

 **HAYNES HINT** *To ease entry of the pistons, carefully remove any ridge of carbon built up on the top of each liner bore using a scraper. If there is a pronounced wear ridge, remove it using a ridge reamer.*

### Method 1 – piston/connecting rod assemblies in situ

10 Apply a continuous bead of a suitable silicone sealant to the liner mating surface as shown, following any instructions on the sealant package regarding use **(see illustration 14.16)**.

11 Lubricate the bore surface of the liner with engine oil. Make sure that the No. 1 liner is matched with the No. 1 piston/connecting rod assembly and so on, and that it is installed with the previously made mark at the front

**14.17 . . . then fit the liner into the crankcase**

(see Step 2). Make sure that the piston is at top dead centre (i.e. at the top of its stroke).

12 Slip the liner over the piston, compressing each ring with your fingers as it enters the liner, and use a gentle rocking motion as the liner is pushed downwards **(see illustration)**. The liner has a chamfered lead-in to enable the pistons to be installed without the use of ring compressors. Press the liner fully down until it is felt to seat. Clamp the liner in place using suitable bolts, nuts and washers threaded into the head bolt holes as shown to prevent it lifting **(see illustration 11.13)** – do not overtighten the clamps as the mating surface of the head could be indented, causing leakage and compression problems.

13 Turn the crankshaft to position the next piston at TDC, then install the next liner in the same way. As the crankshaft is rotated, make sure that the installed liner does not lift off its seating. If this happens, the liner must be removed, cleaned and fresh sealant applied. Repeat the procedure for the third cylinder.

### Method 2 – piston/connecting rod assemblies removed

14 Lubricate the bore surface of the liner with engine oil. Make sure that the No. 1 piston/connecting rod assembly is matched with the No. 1 liner and so on, and that they are installed the correct way round – the arrow or dot on the piston crown must point to the front of the liner and the front of the engine, while the oil hole in the connecting rod must point to the rear of each.

15 Slip the piston into the liner, compressing each ring with your fingers as it enters, and use a gentle rocking motion as the liner is pushed downwards **(see illustration)**. The liner has a chamfered lead-in to enable the pistons to be installed without the use of ring compressors. Position the piston near the top of the liner.

16 Apply a continuous bead of a suitable silicone sealant to the liner mating surface as shown, following any instructions on the sealant package regarding use **(see illustration)**.

17 Fit the liner into the crankcase and press it down until it is felt to seat **(see illustration)**. Clamp the liner in place using suitable bolts, nuts and washers threaded into the head bolt holes as shown to prevent it lifting **(see illustration 11.13)** – do not overtighten the clamps as the mating surface of the head could be indented, causing leakage and compression problems.

18 Install the other liners in the same way. Note that if the cylinder head is being installed immediately, there is no need to clamp the individual liners in place.

### Method 3 – piston/connecting rod assemblies removed

19 Apply a continuous bead of a suitable silicone sealant to the liner mating surface as shown, following any instructions on the sealant package regarding use **(see illustration 14.16)**.

**14.22a  Carefully lower the connecting rod and piston into the liner . . .**

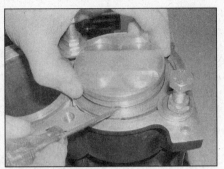

**14.22b  . . . feeding each ring in as you do**

**14.24  Check that the liners are all flush using a straight-edge**

**20**  Fit the liner into the crankcase and press it down until it is felt to seat. Clamp the liner in place using suitable bolts, nuts and washers threaded into the head bolt holes as shown to prevent it lifting **(see illustration 11.13)** – do not overtighten the clamps as the mating surface of the head could be indented, causing leakage and compression problems.
**21**  Lubricate the bore surface of the liner with engine oil. Make sure that the No. 1 piston/connecting rod assembly is matched with the No. 1 liner and so on, and that they are installed the correct way round – the arrow or dot on the piston crown must point to the front of the liner and the front of the engine, while the oil hole in the connecting rod must point to the rear of each.
**22**  Slip the piston into the liner, making sure the connecting rod does not scratch the

surface, then carefully compress and feed each piston ring into the liner until the piston crown is flush with the top **(see illustrations)**. If available, a piston ring compressor makes installation a lot easier.
**23**  Install the other liners in the same way.

### All methods

**24**  When all liners are installed, check that their top surfaces are all exactly level with the cylinder block using a precision straight-edge as shown **(see illustration)**.
**25**  Install the cylinder head as soon after installing the liners as possible to avoid crankshaft movement accidentally breaking the seals.
**26**  Install the remaining components in the reverse order of removal, referring to the relevant Sections of the Chapter.

## 15  Pistons and piston rings

**Note:** *This procedure can be performed with the engine in the frame.*

### Removal

**1**  Remove the cylinder head (see Section 11). If the engine is in the frame, also remove the cylinder liners (see Section 14). If the engine has been removed and the crankcases are being separated, it may not be necessary to remove the liners if you are 100% certain that the liner seals are intact (see Section 11, Step 13) – instead separate the connecting rods from the crankshaft and remove them with the pistons from the tops of the liners, then separate the pistons from the rods. If the liners, pistons and connecting rods are all being removed as part of a complete engine overhaul, choose the method you prefer, though it is easier to separate the pistons from the connecting rods after the rods themselves have been removed (see Section 24).
**2**  If the engine is not being fully disassembled, make sure that all apertures into the crankcase are well blocked with rag.
**3**  Before removing the pistons, use a felt marker pen to write the cylinder number on the crown of each piston. Also note the arrow or dot on each crown which points to the front of the engine – if the mark is not visible, make you own as the piston must be installed the correct way round **(see illustration)**. If the connecting rods have been removed, also note there is an oil hole in the rod which must face the rear of the engine.
**4**  Carefully prise out the circlip on one side of the piston using needle-nose pliers or a small flat-bladed screwdriver inserted into the notch **(see illustrations)**. Push the piston pin out from the other side to free the piston from the connecting rod **(see illustration)**. Remove the other circlip and discard them as new ones must be used. When the piston has been removed, install its pin back into its bore so that related parts do not get mixed up. If the connecting rods are still in the engine, rotate the crankshaft so that the best access is obtained for each piston. On the outer

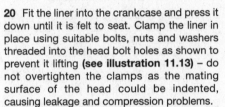

**15.3  The arrow on the piston must point to the front, and the oil hole in the connecting rod (arrowed) must face the rear**

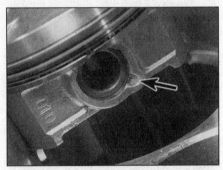

**15.4a  Use a small screwdriver or pointed instrument inserted in the notch (arrowed) . . .**

**15.4b  . . . to lever out the circlip**

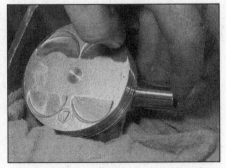

**15.4c  Withdraw the pin and remove the piston**

**15.6 Removing the piston rings using a ring removal and installation tool**

**15.12 Measure the piston ring-to-groove clearance with a feeler gauge**

**15.13 Measure the piston diameter with a micrometer at the specified distance from the bottom of the skirt**

pistons, the pins will have to be extracted inwards. Remember the importance of the rag in preventing dropped circlips from falling into the crankcase.

> **HAYNES HiNT**
> To prevent the circlip from pinging away, pass a rod or screwdriver, whose diameter is greater than the gap between the circlip ends, through the piston pin. This will trap the circlip if it springs out.

> **HAYNES HiNT**
> If a piston pin is a tight fit in the piston bosses, soak a rag in boiling water then wring it out and wrap it around the piston – this will expand the alloy piston sufficiently to release its grip of the pin. Alternatively purchase (or make up) a piston pin drawbolt tool – see 'Tools and Workshop Tips' in the Reference section.

### Inspection

#### Pistons

**5** Before the inspection process can be carried out, the pistons must be cleaned and the old piston rings removed.

**6** Using your thumbs or a piston ring removal and installation tool, carefully remove the rings from the pistons **(see illustration)**. Do not nick or gouge the pistons in the process. Carefully note which way up each ring fits and

in which groove as they must be installed in their original positions if being re-used. The upper surface of each ring should have a manufacturer's mark or letter at one end – if the mark on each ring is different, note which mark is for the top ring and which is for the second. The rings can also be distinguished by their different profiles **(see illustration 15.25a)**.

**7** Scrape all traces of carbon from the tops of the pistons. A hand-held wire brush or a piece of fine emery cloth can be used once most of the deposits have been scraped away. Do not, under any circumstances, use a wire brush mounted in a drill motor to remove deposits from the pistons; the piston material is soft and will be eroded away by the wire brush.

**8** Use a piston ring groove cleaning tool to remove any carbon deposits from the ring grooves. If a tool is not available, a piece broken off an old ring will do the job. Be very careful to remove only the carbon deposits. Do not remove any metal and do not nick or gouge the sides of the ring grooves.

**9** Once the deposits have been removed, clean the pistons with solvent and dry them thoroughly. Make sure the oil return holes below the oil ring groove are clear.

**10** Carefully inspect each piston for cracks around the skirt, at the pin bosses and at the ring lands. Normal piston wear appears as even, vertical wear on the thrust surfaces of the piston and slight looseness of the top ring in its groove. If the skirt is scored or scuffed, the engine may have been suffering from

overheating and/or abnormal combustion, which caused excessively high operating temperatures. The oil pump and cooling systems should be checked thoroughly.

**11** A hole in the piston crown, an extreme to be sure, is an indication that abnormal combustion (pre-ignition) was occurring. Burned areas at the edge of the piston crown are usually evidence of spark knock (detonation). If any of the above problems exist, the causes must be corrected or the damage will occur again.

**12** Measure the piston ring-to-groove clearance by laying a new piston ring in the ring groove and slipping a feeler blade in beside it **(see illustration)**. Check the clearance at three or four locations around the groove. If the clearance is greater than that specified, the piston is worn. Confirm this by measuring the piston ring groove width and comparing with the specification. **Note:** *Make sure you have the correct ring for the groove – the two compression rings can be identified by their profile* **(see illustration 15.25a)**.

**13** Measure the piston diameter 5 mm up from the bottom of the skirt and at 90° to the piston pin axis **(see illustration)**. If outside of the specified figure, the piston must be renewed.

**14** If the necessary measuring equipment is available, measure the connecting rod small-end bore diameter, the piston pin outside diameter and the inside diameter of the pin bore in the piston **(see illustrations)**. Renew any component that has worn beyond the specified limits.

**15.14a Measure the internal diameter of the small-end bore . . .**

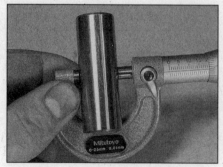

**15.14b . . . the external diameter of the pin . . .**

**15.14c . . . and the internal diameter of the bore in the piston**

**15.17 Measuring piston ring installed end gap**

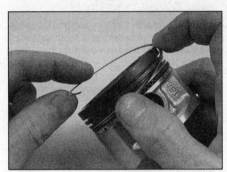

**15.23b . . . then fit the lower side rail and the upper side rail each side of it. The oil ring components must be installed by hand**

### Piston rings

**15** It is good practice to renew the piston rings when an engine is being overhauled. Before installing the new piston rings, the ring end gaps must be checked.

**16** Lay out the pistons and the new ring sets so the rings will be matched with the same piston and cylinder during the end gap measurement procedure and engine assembly.

**17** Insert the top ring into the top of the first liner and square it up with the cylinder walls by pushing it in with the top of the piston. The ring should be about 20 mm below the top edge of the liner. To measure the end gap, slip a feeler blade between the ends of the ring and compare the measurement to the Specification **(see illustration)**.

**15.19 Ring end gap can be enlarged by clamping a file in a vice and filing the ring ends**

**18** If the gap is larger or smaller than specified, double check to make sure that you have the correct rings before proceeding.

**19** If the gap is too small, it must be enlarged or the ring ends may come in contact with each other during engine operation, which can cause serious damage. The end gap can be increased by filing the ring ends very carefully with a fine file. When performing this operation, file only from the outside in **(see illustration)**.

**20** Excess end gap is not critical unless it is greater than 1 mm. Again, double check to make sure you have the correct rings for your engine and check that the bore is not worn.

**21** Repeat the procedure for each ring that will be installed in the first cylinder and for each ring in the remaining cylinders. Remember to keep the rings, pistons and cylinders matched up.

**22** Once the ring end gaps have been checked/corrected, the rings can be installed on the pistons.

**23** The oil control ring (lowest on the piston) is installed first. It is composed of three separate components. Slip the expander into the groove, then install the upper side rail **(see illustrations)**. Do not use a piston ring installation tool on the oil ring side rails as they may be damaged. Instead, place one end of the side rail into the groove between the expander and the ring land. Hold it firmly in place and slide a finger around the piston while pushing the rail into the groove. Next, install the lower side rail in the same manner.

**15.23a Fit the oil ring expander in its groove . . .**

**24** After the three oil ring components have been installed, check to make sure that both the upper and lower side rails can be turned smoothly in the ring groove.

**25** Install the second (middle) ring next. **Note:** *The second ring and top rings are slightly different in profile.* Make sure that the letter N near the end gap is facing up **(see illustration)**. Fit the ring into the middle groove on the piston. Either use your thumbs to hold the ring ends apart when installing the ring over the piston, or slip sections of old feeler gauge blades between the ring and piston to guide it into its groove **(see illustration)**, or use a ring removal/installation tool **(see illustration 15.6)**.

*Caution: Do not expand the ring any more than is necessary to slide it into place – the ring material is brittle and is easily broken if overstressed.*

**26** Finally, install the top ring in the same manner. The top ring can be distinguished from the second ring by its chamfer and chromed finish **(see illustration 15.25a)**. Make sure the letter N near the end gap is facing up.

**27** Correct positioning of the ring end gaps is important **(see illustration overleaf)**.

### Installation

**28** If the connecting rods have not been removed from the engine, stuff clean rag into the crankcase mouth to prevent any dropped circlips falling in (and see **Haynes Hint** above). Lubricate the connecting rod small-end bore with engine oil.

**29** Insert a new circlip in one side of the piston bore and install the piston on its rod so that the arrow or dot marking on its crown is facing forwards, and opposite to the oilway in the connecting rod **(see illustration 15.3)**. Push the piston pin fully into the piston and secure with a second new circlip – make sure the circlip is fully seated in its groove **(see illustrations 15.4c, b and a)**.

**30** Install the other pistons in the same way. If the connecting rods have not been removed from the engine, rotate the crankshaft to gain the best access.

**31** Check that the piston rings are still correctly positioned in relation to the front of the engine **(see illustration 15.27)**.

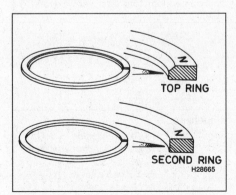

**15.25a The rings can be identified by their different profiles – the N mark must face up**

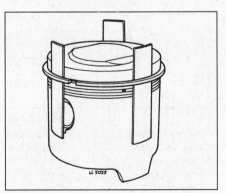

**15.25b Old pieces of feeler gauge blade can be used to guide the ring over the piston**

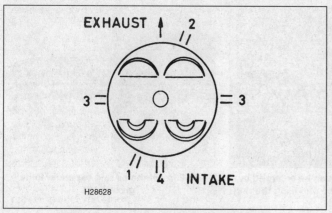

**15.27  Stagger the ring end gaps as shown**

1  Top ring end gap
2  Second (middle) ring end gap
3  Oil ring side rail end gaps
4  Oil ring expander ends

**32** Install all components and assemblies according to your removal procedure, referring to the relevant Sections of the Chapter.

## 16  Clutch overhaul

**Note:** This procedure can be performed with the engine in the frame. If the engine has already been removed, ignore the preliminary steps which don't apply.

### Removal

**1** On Daytona models, remove the belly-pan and the right-hand fairing side panel (see Chapter 7). On Sprint ST models, remove the belly-pan (see Chapter 7).

**2** Drain the engine oil (Chapter 1).

**3** Detach the clutch cable from the release lever on the clutch cover (see Section 17).

**4** Working in a criss-cross pattern, evenly slacken the clutch cover bolts, noting how the cable bracket is secured **(see illustration)**. Lift the cover away from the engine, being prepared to catch any residual oil that may be released as the cover is removed.

**5** Remove the gasket and discard it. Note the two locating dowels fitted to the crankcase and remove them for safe-keeping if they are loose.

**6** Remove the crankshaft position sensor (see Chapter 4). **Note:** If the clutch is being removed in preparation for separating the crankcase halves, remove the sensor complete with its mounting bracket as it bridges the halves. Otherwise, the sensor can be drawn out of its bracket, which avoids having to reset the air gap on installation (though it should be checked as a matter of course).

**7** Working in a criss-cross pattern, gradually slacken the clutch spring retaining bolts until spring pressure is released **(see illustrations)**. Remove the bolts, washers and

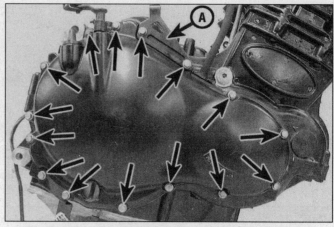

**16.4  Clutch cover bolts (arrowed) – note the cable bracket (A) secured by two of the bolts**

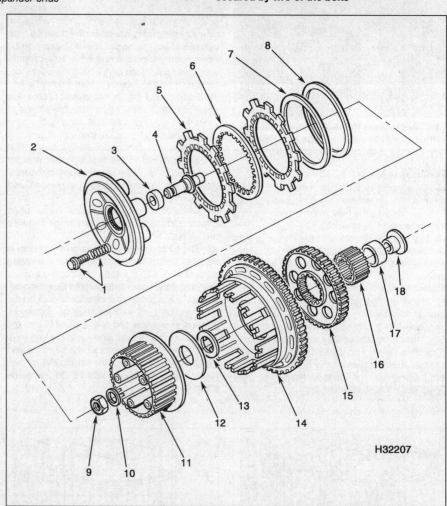

**16.7a  Clutch components**

1 Pressure plate bolts, washers and springs
2 Pressure plate
3 Bearing
4 Pull-rod
5 Friction plates
6 Plain plates
7 Anti-judder spring
8 Spring seat
9 Clutch nut
10 Washer
11 Clutch centre
12 Thrust washer
13 Shim
14 Clutch housing
15 Oil pump/alternator drive gear
16 Splined sleeve
17 Needle bearing
18 Shouldered sleeve

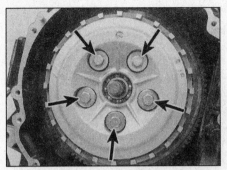

**16.7b  Unscrew the pressure plate bolts (arrowed) . . .**

**16.7c  . . . and draw the pressure plate off using the pull-rod**

**16.8a  Remove the clutch plates . . .**

**16.8b  . . . and the anti-judder spring and its seat**

springs, then lift out the clutch pressure plate complete with pull-rod end piece **(see illustration)**.

8  Grasp the complete set of clutch plates and remove them as a pack – you may have to hook the inner plates out using a piece of wire, otherwise remove them after the clutch centre has been removed **(see illustration)**. Similarly remove the anti-judder spring and spring seat, noting how they fit **(see illustration)**. Unless the plates are being renewed, keep them in their original order. Note that the outer and inner friction plates are different in colour to the rest, and that the tabs on the outer plate locate in the shallow slots in the housing, not in the deep slots with the rest of the plates.

9  The transmission input shaft must be locked to enable the clutch nut to be slackened. This can be done in several ways. If the engine is in the frame, engage 1st gear and have an assistant hold the rear brake on hard with the rear tyre in firm contact with the ground. Triumph market a service tool (Pt. No. 3880305) that can be located between the clutch centre and clutch housing to lock them together, although you still need to engage 1st gear and have an assistant hold the rear brake on. If the engine is out of the frame, a commercially available or home-made tool **(see Tool tip)** can be used to stop the clutch centre from turning whilst the nut is slackened. Unscrew the nut and remove the washer from the input shaft **(see illustrations)**. Discard the washer as a new one must be used on installation.

10  Slide the clutch centre off the input shaft, followed by the large thrust washer and the shim **(see illustrations 16.26a, 25b and 25a)**.

11  Slide the clutch housing off the shaft, using a small screwdriver to prevent the splined sleeve coming with it, and manoeuvre it out of the crankcase **(see illustrations)**.

12  Remove the oil pump/alternator drive gear, then slide the splined sleeve, the needle bearing and the shouldered sleeve off the shaft **(see illustrations 16.23b, 22b, 22a and 21)**.

### Inspection

13  After an extended period of service the clutch friction plates will wear and promote

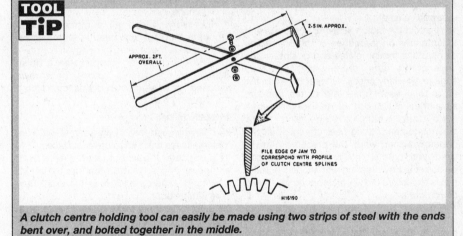

**TOOL TiP**

A clutch centre holding tool can easily be made using two strips of steel with the ends bent over, and bolted together in the middle.

**16.9a  Using a commercially available holding tool to hold the clutch**

**16.9b  Using the home-made holding tool to hold the clutch**

**16.11a  Draw the housing off the shaft as described . . .**

16.11b . . . and manoeuvre it out of the crankcase

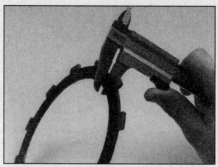

16.13 Measuring clutch friction plate thickness

16.14 Check the plain plates for warpage

16.17 Check the pressure plate and its bearing as described

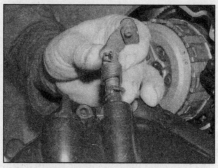

16.18a Check the release mechanism in the cover as described

clutch slip. Measure the thickness of each friction plate using a Vernier caliper (see illustration). If any plate has worn to or beyond the service limit given in the Specifications, the friction plates must be renewed as a set. If the plates are good, but the clutch has been slipping, it could be that the springs have sagged. Unfortunately Triumph provide no Specification for the spring free length, though it is worth taking yours to a Triumph dealer and asking them to compare them to new ones off the shelf. Replace the springs with new ones if necessary, or if in doubt.

14 The plain plates should not show any signs of excess heating (bluing). Check for warpage using a flat surface and feeler blades (see illustration). If any plate exceeds the maximum permissible amount of warpage, or

shows signs of bluing, all plain plates must be renewed as a set.

15 Inspect the clutch assembly for burrs and indentations on the edges of the protruding tangs of the friction plates and/or slots in the edge of the outer drum with which they engage. Similarly check for wear between the inner tongues of the plain plates and the slots in the clutch centre. Wear of this nature will cause clutch drag and slow disengagement during gear changes, as the plates will snag when the pressure plate is lifted. With care a small amount of wear can be corrected by dressing with a fine file, but if this is excessive the worn components should be renewed.

16 Inspect the input shaft end, the shouldered sleeve and the splined sleeve bearing surfaces for signs of wear and

damage. Similarly, check the condition of the needle roller bearing.

17 Check the pressure plate for signs of damage and its bearing for wear (see illustration). Ensure that the inner race of the bearing spins freely without any sign of notchiness. Push the bearing out of the pressure plate if renewal is required.

18 Check the clutch release mechanism in the clutch cover for smooth operation. If necessary, withdraw the shaft from the cover, noting the washer and how the return spring ends locate (see illustration). Check the condition of the oil seal and bearing, replacing them with new ones if necessary (see illustration). Check the pull-rod end and its locating cutout in the shaft for signs of wear and damage, and replace them with new ones if necessary. Clean all components and lubricate the seal and bearing with grease. Installation is the reverse of removal.

19 The clutch cover incorporates a noise damper. If necessary, remove the screws securing the noise damper plates, then lift out the damping pad.

### Installation

20 Remove all traces of gasket material from the crankcase and clutch cover surfaces.

21 Lubricate the shouldered sleeve with engine oil and slide it on the input shaft so that its shouldered end faces the crankcase (see illustration).

22 Lubricate the needle roller bearing with engine oil and slide it over the shouldered sleeve (see illustration). Now slide the

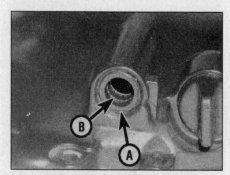

16.18b Check the oil seal (A) and bearing (B)

16.21 Slide the shouldered sleeve . . .

16.22a . . . the needle bearing . . .

16.22b . . . and the splined sleeve onto the shaft

16.23a Align the gear teeth at the bottom (arrow) . . .

16.23b . . . then slide the drive gear onto the shaft, making sure it engages correctly with both driven gears

splined sleeve over the bearing **(see illustration)**.

**23** The alternator driven gear has a backlash eliminator gear on its inside, which works by having one less tooth than the driven gear, and by using friction between the two gears to create a rolling cushion. In order for the large drive gear to mesh, the teeth on the driven gear and eliminator gear must be aligned at the bottom – this can be done using a screwdriver inserted between the teeth and used as a lever against the friction **(see illustration)**. Slide the oil pump/alternator drive gear, with its dished side facing the crankcase, onto the splined sleeve, meshing it with the oil pump driven gear and alternator driven gear **(see illustration)**.

**24** Slide the clutch housing onto the splined sleeve and engage the primary driven gear on the back of the housing with the primary drive gear on the crankshaft **(see illustration)**.

**25** Slide the shim and large thrustwasher over the input shaft **(see illustrations)**.

**26** Slide the clutch centre onto the input shaft splines, then install the new washer, with its OUT marking facing outwards, followed by the clutch nut **(see illustrations)**. Using the method employed on removal to lock the input shaft, tighten the nut to the specified torque setting **(see illustration)**. **Note:** *Check that the clutch centre rotates freely after tightening, but without any freeplay in it. If the centre is tight, fit a thicker shim between the thrust washer and the clutch housing. If there is freeplay, fit a thinner*

shim. Shims are available in 0.05 mm increments from 0.10 mm to 0.35 mm. Remove the clutch centre, thrust washer and shim, then measure the shim using a

micrometer to determine its thickness, and fit a replacement accordingly.

**27** Fit the anti-judder spring seat into the clutch centre, followed by the anti-judder

16.24 Slide the clutch housing onto the shaft . . .

16.25a . . . then fit the shim . . .

16.25b . . . and the thrust washer

16.26a Slide the clutch centre onto the shaft . . .

16.26b . . . then fit the washer with the OUT mark facing out

16.26c Thread the clutch nut onto the shaft . . .

16.26d . . . and tighten it to the specified torque

16.27 Fit the anti-judder spring so the outer edge is raised off the seat

16.28a Fit the dark inner friction plate . . .

16.28b . . . then a plain plate . . .

spring (see illustration 16.8b), fitting the spring so that its outer edge is raised off the spring seat (see illustration).
28 Coat each clutch plate with engine oil

16.28c . . . then a normal friction plate, and so on

16.29a Insert the pull-rod into the shaft . . .

prior to installation. Build up the clutch plates, starting with the inner friction plate that is darker in colour, then a plain plate and alternating normal friction and plain plates

16.28d Fit the dark outer friction plate tabs into the shallow slots in the housing

16.29b . . . then fit the pressure plate

until all but the last friction plate are installed (see illustrations). Fit the outer friction plate (also darker in colour), locating its tabs in the shallow slots, rather in the deep slots with the other friction plates (see illustration).
29 Insert the pull-rod into the end of the input shaft (see illustration). Fit the pressure plate over the pull-rod and onto the clutch, engaging the notches on its inner rim with the slots in the inside of the clutch centre (see illustration).
30 Install the springs, washers and bolts and tighten the bolts evenly in a criss-cross sequence to the specified torque setting (see illustration).
31 Install the crankshaft position sensor (see Chapter 4).
32 Insert the dowels in the crankcase. Place a new gasket on the crankcase, locating it over the dowels (see illustration). Install the cover, angling the release lever to the rear of the cover as shown (see illustrations). Tighten the cover bolts evenly in a criss-cross sequence to the specified torque setting, not forgetting to secure the cable bracket (see illustration 16.4). Push the release lever forwards and make sure it picks up the end of the pull-rod correctly – it should come up solid when it is pointing across the engine.
33 Attach the clutch cable to the release lever on the clutch cover (see Section 17).
34 Refill the engine with oil (see Daily (pre-ride) checks).
35 Where applicable, install the fairing side panels and belly-pan (see Chapter 7).

16.30 Fit the springs, washers and bolts, and tighten the bolts as described to the specified torque

16.32a Locate the gasket over the dowels (arrowed) . . .

16.32b . . . then install the cover

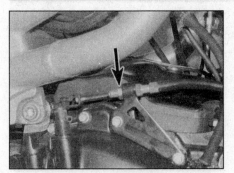

**17.2 Slacken the locknut (arrowed) and thread it off the adjuster**

**17.3a Release the cable end from the retainer . . .**

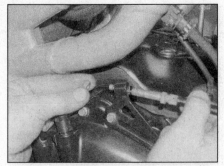

**17.3b . . . and draw the cable out of the bracket, feeding the locknut off the end**

## 17 Clutch cable

1 On Daytona models, remove the belly-pan and the right-hand fairing side panel (see Chapter 7). On Sprint ST models, remove the belly-pan (see Chapter 7). On Tiger models, remove the clutch lever (see Chapter 5) – this must be done to remove the handguard, which is secured by the same bolt.

2 Slacken the rear locknut securing the cable in the bracket on the engine and thread it off the cable (see illustration).

3 Slip the cable end out of the retainer, noting how it fits, then draw the cable out of the bracket, collecting the rear locknut as you do (see illustrations).

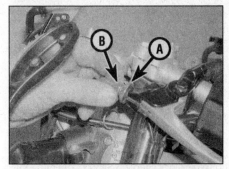

**17.4 Slacken the lockring (A) and set the adjuster (B) and lockring as described**

**17.5a Draw the outer cable end from the adjuster and slip the inner cable out via the slots . . .**

4 Fully slacken the adjuster lockring and screw the adjuster at the handlebar end of the cable fully in to the lever bracket, then turn the adjuster and lockring as required to align the slots with that in the lever bracket (see illustration).

5 Pull the outer cable end from the socket in the adjuster and release the inner cable from the lever (except Tiger models) (see illustrations). Remove the cable from the machine, noting its routing and any guides or clips.

> **HAYNES HiNT** *Before removing the cable from the bike, tape the lower end of the new cable to the upper end of the old cable. Slowly pull the lower end of the old cable out, guiding the new cable down into position. Using this method will ensure the cable is routed correctly.*

6 Installation is the reverse of removal. Apply grease to the cable ends. Make sure the cable is correctly routed. Make sure the cable lower end is properly located in the retainer on the release mechanism arm. Check the clutch release mechanism for smooth operation and any signs of wear or damage. Remove it for cleaning and re-greasing if required (see Section 16).

7 Adjust the clutch lever freeplay (see Chapter 1). Where applicable, install the fairing side panels and belly-pan (see Chapter 7).

**17.5b . . . then detach the inner cable end from the lever**

## 18 Sump and oil strainer

**Note:** *The sump can be removed with the engine in the frame. If work is being carried out with the engine removed ignore the steps which don't apply.*

### Removal

1 On Daytona and Sprint ST models, remove the belly-pan and the fairing side panels (see Chapter 7).

2 Drain the engine oil and remove the oil filter (see Chapter 1).

3 Remove the exhaust system (Chapter 4).

4 Unscrew the oil cooler hose banjo bolts and detach the hoses from the sump, noting which fits where (see illustration 20.3). Discard the sealing washers as new ones must be used.

5 Unscrew the sump bolts, slackening them evenly in a criss-cross sequence to prevent distortion (see illustration). Remove the sump and discard its gasket – a new one must be used. **Note:** *The internal oil pipe nozzle and gearbox oil feed nozzle locate in the sump –*

**18.5 Sump bolts (arrowed)**

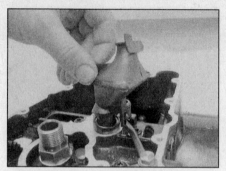

**18.6 Pull the strainer out of its socket**

**18.7a Pull the nozzle out of its socket, noting the O-rings**

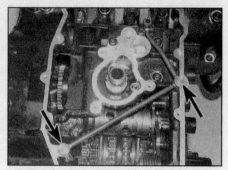

**18.7b Unscrew the banjo bolts (arrowed) and remove the pipe . . .**

they have O-rings and are a push fit. It is possible for them to stick in the sump – carefully ease them free with a long flat-bladed screwdriver rather than risk distorting them by pulling the sump off forcibly.

**6** Draw the oil strainer out of its socket, then remove the rubber seal (see illustration). Check the condition of the seal and discard it if it is damaged, distorted or deteriorated in any way. Clean the strainer in solvent and remove any debris caught in the gauze. Note that lots of metal caught in the strainer, or in the bottom of the sump, is indicative of engine wear that should be investigated.

**7** If required, remove the gearbox oil feed nozzle if required – it is a push fit in the crankcase (see illustration). Also if required, unscrew the banjo bolts securing the internal oil pipe and remove the pipe, noting how the

nozzle end locates in its seat (see illustrations). Discard the banjo bolt sealing washers as new ones must be used. Check the condition of the nozzle O-rings and discard them if they are damaged, distorted or deteriorated in any way.

### Installation

**8** Remove all traces of gasket material from the sump and crankcase mating surfaces.

**9** If removed, fit the gearbox oil feed nozzle into the crankcase, using new O-rings if necessary (see illustration 18.7a). Install the internal oil pipe using new sealing washers on each side of the unions, and tighten the banjo bolts to the specified torque setting (see illustration). Make sure the nozzle end locates in its seat, and fit a new O-ring to it if necessary (see illustration 18.7c).

**10** Fit the rubber seal for the strainer into its

socket in the crankcase, using a new one if necessary (see illustration). Fit the strainer into the seal (see illustration 18.6).

**11** Place a new gasket on the crankcase and install the sump (see illustrations); if the engine is in the frame, use a smear of grease on the gasket to hold it in place as the sump is installed. Install the bolts and tighten them evenly in a criss-cross sequence to the specified torque setting.

**12** Attach the oil cooler hoses using new sealing washers on each side of the unions, and tighten the banjo bolts to the specified torque setting (see illustration 20.7a).

**13** Install the exhaust system (see Chapter 4).

**14** Install a new oil filter, then fill the engine with the correct type and quantity of oil (see Chapter 1 and Daily (pre-ride) checks). Start the engine and check that there are no leaks.

**15** On Daytona and Sprint ST models, refit the belly-pan and the fairing side panels (see Chapter 7).

## 19 Oil pressure relief valve

### Removal

**1** Remove the engine from the frame and separate the crankcase halves (see Sections 5 and 21). Remove the selector forks, referring to the relevant Steps in Section 29.

**2** Use a socket on the relief valve hex and unscrew it from the crankcase – depending on

**18.7c . . . noting how the nozzle locates (arrowed)**

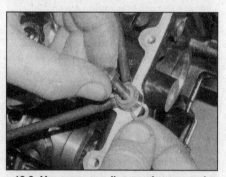

**18.9 Use a new sealing washer on each side of the union**

**18.10 Fit the strainer seal into the crankcase**

**18.11a Fit a new gasket . . .**

**18.11b . . . then install the sump**

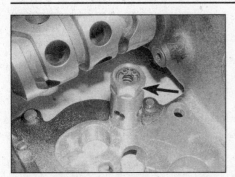

**19.2  Unscrew the valve using a socket on the hex (arrowed)**

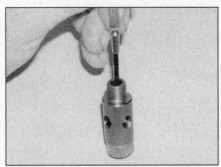

**19.3a  Push the plunger into the valve and check its action**

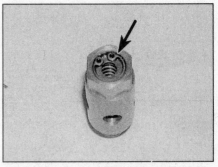

**19.3b  Remove the circlip (arrowed), noting it is under spring pressure**

your tools it may be necessary to remove the oil pump (see Section 30) to access the hex on the relief valve **(see illustration)**.

### Inspection

**3** Push the relief valve plunger into the valve body and check that it moves smoothly and freely against the spring pressure **(see illustration)**. If not, remove the circlip, noting that it is under spring pressure, and remove the spring seat, spring and plunger **(see illustration)**. Clean all the components in solvent and check them for scoring, wear or damage. If any is found, renew the relief valve – individual components are not available. Otherwise, coat the inside of the valve body and the plunger with clean engine oil, then insert the plunger, spring and spring seat and secure them with the circlip. Check the action of the valve plunger again – if it is still suspect, replace the valve with a new one.

### Installation

**4** Apply a drop of non-permanent thread locking compound to the pressure relief valve threads and tighten the valve to the specified torque setting **(see illustration)**.
**5** Install the remaining components and assemblies in a reverse of the removal procedure, referring to the relevant Sections.

## 20  Oil cooler

**Note:** *The oil cooler can be removed with the engine in the frame. If work is being carried*

out with the engine removed ignore the preliminary steps.

### Removal

**1** On Daytona and Sprint ST models, remove the belly-pan and the fairing side panels (see Chapter 7).
**2** Drain the engine oil (see Chapter 1). Keep the container below the sump to catch any residual oil in the cooler and hoses.
**3** To detach the hoses from the sump, unscrew the banjo bolts and detach the hoses, noting which fits where **(see illustration)**. Discard the sealing washers as new ones must be used.
**4** To detach the hoses from the cooler, counter-hold the large hex on the base of each union, then unscrew the banjo bolts and detach the hoses **(see illustration)**. Discard the sealing washers as new ones must be used.

**19.4  Install the valve and tighten it to the specified torque**

**5** To remove the cooler, first detach the hoses from either the sump or the cooler itself. Unscrew the nuts and/or bolts (according to model) securing the oil cooler, noting the arrangement of the collars and grommets **(see illustrations)**.
*Caution: Always counter-hold the hex on the oil cooler when slackening or tightening the banjo bolts or the cooler could be damaged.*
**6** Check the cooler for leaks and other damage. Check the cooler fins for mud, dirt and insects, which will impede the flow of air through it. If the fins are dirty, clean them using water or low pressure compressed air directed through from the rear face. If the fins are bent or distorted, straighten them carefully with a screwdriver. If the air flow is restricted by bent or damaged fins over more than 30% of the cooler's surface area, or if the cooler is leaking, replace it with a new one.

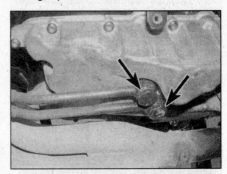

**20.3  Unscrew the banjo bolts (arrowed) and detach the hoses, noting the washers**

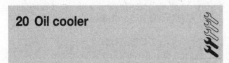

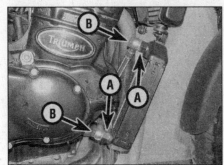

**20.4  Counter-hold the base hex (A), then unscrew the banjo bolt (B) – Tiger shown**

**20.5a  Cooler mounting bolts (arrowed) – Daytona models**

**20.5b  Cooler mounting bolts (arrowed) – Tiger models**

**20.7 Use a new sealing washer on each side of the union**

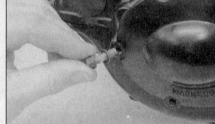

**21.3a Unscrew the bolts, noting the washer with the front one . . .**

**21.3b . . . and remove the cover**

## Installation

**7** Installation is a reverse of the removal procedure, noting the following:
● Use new sealing washers on each side of the banjo unions **(see illustration)**.
● Tighten the banjo bolts to the specified torque settings.
● Refill the engine with oil (see Chapter 1 and 'Daily (pre-ride) checks') and check that there are no leaks from the oil cooler hose connections when the engine is run.

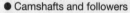

| 21 Crankcase separation and reassembly |
|---|

## Separation

**1** To access the crankshaft and connecting rods, bearings, balancer shaft, alternator/ starter clutch drive, starter clutch, oil pump and pressure relief valve, transmission shafts, gearchange mechanism and selector drum and forks, the crankcase must be split into two parts.
**2** To enable the crankcases to be separated, remove the engine from the frame (see Section 5) and remove the following components with reference to the relevant Sections.

● Camshafts and followers
● Cam chain and tensioner blade
● Cylinder head and cam chain guide blade*
● Cylinder liners and pistons*
● Clutch
● Sump
● Alternator and starter motor (Chapter 8)
*If the crankcase halves are being separated just to examine the transmission components, crankshaft, balancer shaft, oil pump or alternator/starter clutch drive, then there is no need to remove the cylinder head, liners and pistons. If a complete engine overhaul is planned, also remove the water pump (see Chapter 3), and the neutral and oil pressure switches (see Chapter 8).
**3** Unscrew the bolts securing the crankcase breather cover on the left-hand side of the crankcase and remove the cover, noting the washer with the front bolt **(see illustrations)**. Discard the gasket as a new one must be used. Note the two locating pins and remove them for safekeeping if loose. There is an oil seal in the cover, which, if it is in perfect condition and is being reused, must have a mandrel inserted in it immediately after the cover is removed **(see illustration)**. If not, the rim of the seal will distort and not reseal around the shaft on installation. This could result in high oil consumption. A suitable socket can be used as a mandrel. Otherwise,

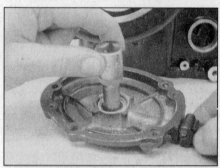

**21.3c A suitable socket can be used as a mandrel for the seal**

a new seal must be installed in the cover (see Step 28). Only remove the mandrel from the seal immediately before the cover is fitted to the engine. If required, undo the screws securing the breather disc and remove it from the end of the crankshaft **(see illustration)**.
**4** Unscrew the bolts securing the noise damper plate to the top of the crankcase and remove the plate, noting the washers, then remove the damper pad, noting how it fits **(see illustration)**.
**5** With the crankcase the right way up, slacken and remove all bolts from the upper crankcase half following the numbered sequence **(see**

**21.3d Undo the screws (arrowed) and remove the breather disc if required**

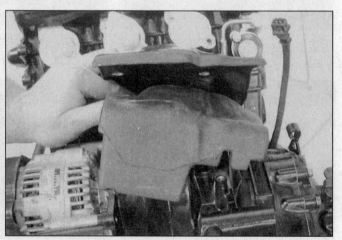

**21.4 Remove the damper plate and pad**

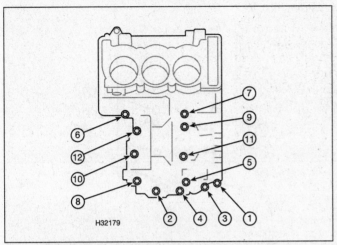

**21.5  Upper crankcase bolt slackening sequence**

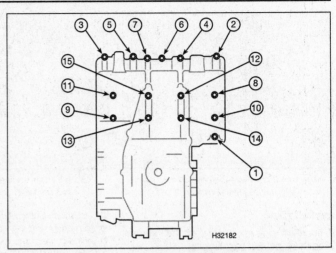

**21.6  Lower crankcase bolt slackening sequence**

**illustration). Note:** *As each bolt is removed, store it in its relative position in a cardboard template of the crankcase halves. This will ensure that all bolts are installed in the correct location on reassembly. Also, take note of any mounting brackets on the bolts and store them with the bolts to ensure correct reassembly.*

**6**  Turn the crankcase upside down. Again, following the numbered sequence, slacken and remove all bolts from the lower crankcase half **(see illustration). Note:** *As each bolt is removed, store it in its relative position in a cardboard template of the crankcase halves. This will ensure that all bolts are installed in the correct location on reassembly. Also, take note of any mounting brackets on the bolts and store them with the bolts to ensure correct reassembly.*

**7**  Carefully lift the lower crankcase half off the upper half, leaving the crankshaft, balancer shaft and transmission shafts in the upper half of the crankcase **(see illustration)**. As the lower half is lifted away take care not to dislodge or lose any main bearing shells. **Note:** *If the halves don't separate easily, make sure all fasteners have been removed. Don't lever between the crankcase mating surfaces or they will leak; initial separation can be achieved by tapping gently around the joint with a soft-faced mallet.*

**8**  Remove the three locating dowels if they

are loose – they could be in either crankcase half **(see illustration 21.12)**. Remove the O-ring from the oil passage joint **(see illustration 21.13)**. Check its condition and replace it with a new one if it is in any way damaged, deformed or deteriorated.

### Reassembly

**9**  Remove all traces of sealant from the crankcase mating surfaces.

**10**  Ensure that all components are in place in the upper and lower crankcase halves. If the transmission shafts have not been removed, check the condition of the oil seal on the left-hand end of the output shaft and replace it with a new one if it is damaged, deformed or deteriorated (see Section 27) – it is always good practice to renew this seal whenever the crankcases have been separated. Also note the instructions in Section 27 concerning applying thread lock to the transmission shaft bearing outer races. Check the position of the selector drum and forks and transmission shafts – make sure they're in the neutral position (i.e. the transmission shafts rotate independently of each other – see Section 29).

**11**  Lubricate the transmission shafts and crankshaft journals with clean engine oil, then use a rag soaked in high flash-point solvent to wipe over the mating surfaces of both halves to remove all traces of oil.

**21.7  Carefully lift the lower half off the upper half, noting how the selector forks locate in the transmission shafts**

**12**  If removed, fit the three locating dowels into one crankcase half **(see illustration)**.

**13**  Fit the O-ring onto the oil passage joint, using a new one if necessary **(see illustration)**.

**14**  Apply a small amount of suitable sealant to the indicated areas of the mating surface of one crankcase half **(see illustration)**.

**21.12  Make sure the dowels (arrowed) are installed**

**21.13  Fit the O-ring into the oil passage**

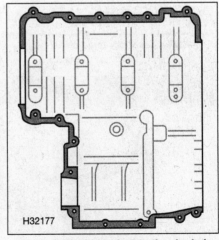

**21.14  Apply the sealant to the shaded areas shown**

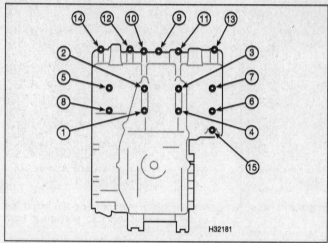

21.19 Lower crankcase bolt tightening sequence

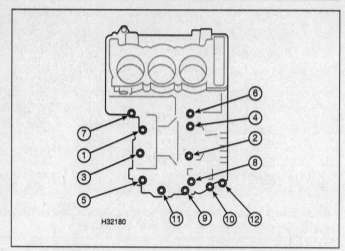

21.20 Upper crankcase bolt tightening sequence

*Caution: Take care not to apply an excessive amount of sealant, as it will ooze out when the case halves are assembled and may obstruct oil passages and prevent the bearings from seating.*

**15** Make sure that the main bearing shells are in position, then carefully guide the lower crankcase half onto the upper half **(see illustration 21.7)**. Make sure the selector forks engage with their respective slots in the transmission gears as the halves are joined.

**16** Check that the lower crankcase half is correctly seated and that all shafts are free to rotate. **Note:** *If the casings are not correctly seated, remove the lower crankcase half and*

investigate the problem. Do not attempt to pull them together using the crankcase bolts as the casing will crack and be ruined.

**17** Clean the threads of the lower crankcase bolts and insert them in their original locations, including any brackets. Secure all bolts finger-tight at this stage.

**18** Turn the crankcase over so that it is upright. Clean the threads of the upper crankcase bolts and install them in their original locations. Secure all bolts finger-tight at this stage.

*Caution: Note that two sizes of bolt are used, 6 mm and 8 mm. Care must be taken to distinguish between them during the*

tightening sequence, as the larger 8 mm bolts are set much tighter, and if a 6 mm bolt is mistaken for an 8 mm bolt, it may shear.

**19** Turn the crankcase over and tighten all lower crankcase bolts to 10 Nm, tightening them in the correct numbered sequence **(see illustration)**.

**20** Turn the crankcase over and tighten all upper crankcase bolts to 10 Nm, tightening them in the correct numbered sequence **(see illustration)**.

**21** Turn the crankcase over and tighten all lower crankcase bolts to 12 Nm, tightening them in the correct numbered sequence **(see illustration 21.19)**.

**22** Turn the crankcase over and tighten all upper crankcase bolts to 12 Nm, tightening them in the correct numbered sequence **(see illustration 21.20)**.

**23** Turn the crankcase over and tighten the 8 mm lower crankcase bolts to 28 Nm in the numerical sequence. The 8 mm bolts are the ones with the larger heads.

**24** Turn the crankcase over and tighten the 8 mm upper crankcase bolts to 28 Nm in the numerical sequence.

**25** With all crankcase fasteners tightened, check that the crankshaft and transmission shafts rotate smoothly and easily. If there are any signs of undue stiffness or of any other problem, the fault must be rectified before proceeding further.

**26** Install the noise damper pad and plate and tighten the bolts securely **(see illustration 21.4)**.

**27** Install all other removed assemblies in the reverse of the sequence in Step 2.

**28** If a new seal is being installed in the crankcase breather cover, prise the old seal out with a flat-bladed screwdriver **(see illustration)**. Two types of seal are available; if the new seal is supplied complete with a shaped mandrel, leave the mandrel in place while pressing the seal squarely into the cover so that it lies just below the face of the cover recess **(see illustrations)**. Only remove the

21.28a Lever out the old seal . . .

21.28b . . . then fit the new one, leaving the mandrel in place . . .

21.28c . . . and press or drive it squarely into place . . .

21.28d . . . setting it below the rim of its housing as shown

21.29a  Install the breather disc . . .

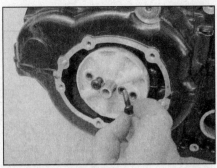

21.29b  . . . and tighten the screws to the specified torque

21.29c  Locate the new gasket over the pins (arrowed)

mandrel from the seal immediately before the cover is fitted to the engine. If the seal is supplied without a mandrel, press it into the cover as described ensuring that the lip faces into the cover.

29  If removed, install the breather disc on the end of the crankshaft, then apply a suitable non-permanent thread locking compound to the screws and tighten them to the specified torque setting **(see illustrations)**. If removed, fit the cover locating pins into the crankcase, then locate the new gasket onto them **(see illustration)**. Remove the mandrel from the seal in the cover, then install the cover, making sure it is correctly and squarely aligned so as not to distort the seal rim as it fits onto the shaft, and tighten the bolts **(see illustrations 21.3b and a)**.

*Caution: It is important that the seal is allowed 15 minutes to form on the shaft before the engine is turned from its present position – the breather will not operate correctly if this precaution is not observed. If care is not taken with installation, engine oil may leak past the seal and into the crankcase breather system.*

## 22  Crankcase inspection

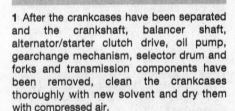

1  After the crankcases have been separated and the crankshaft, balancer shaft, alternator/starter clutch drive, oil pump, gearchange mechanism, selector drum and forks and transmission components have been removed, clean the crankcases thoroughly with new solvent and dry them with compressed air.

2  Remove the oil gallery plugs and blow through all oil passages with compressed air. Where fitted, replace the plug sealing washers with new ones.

3  Remove all traces of old gasket sealant from the mating surfaces. Minor damage to the surfaces can be cleaned up with a fine sharpening stone or grindstone.

*Caution: Be very careful not to nick or gouge the crankcase mating surfaces or leaks will result. Check both crankcase*

*halves very carefully for cracks and other damage.*

4  Small cracks or holes in aluminium castings may be repaired with an epoxy resin adhesive as a temporary measure. Permanent repairs can be effected by argon-arc welding, and only a specialist in this process is in a position to advise on the economy or practical aspect of such a repair. Alternatively you could try one of the low temperature aluminium welding kits available. If any damage is found that can't be repaired, renew the crankcase halves as a set.

5  Damaged threads can be economically reclaimed by using a diamond section wire insert, of the Helicoil type, which is easily fitted after drilling and re-tapping the affected thread.

6  Sheared studs or screws can usually be removed with screw extractors, which consist of a tapered, left thread screws of very hard steel. These are inserted into a pre-drilled hole in the stud, and usually succeed in dislodging the most stubborn stud or screw. If a problem arises which seems beyond your scope, it is worth consulting a professional engineering firm before condemning an otherwise sound casing. Many of these firms advertise regularly in the motorcycle press.

**HAYNES HiNT** *Refer to 'Tools and Workshop Tips' in the Reference section for details of how to install a thread insert and use a screw extractor.*

## 23  Main and connecting rod bearings – general information

1  Even though main and connecting rod bearings are generally renewed during the engine overhaul, the old bearings should be retained for close examination as they may reveal valuable information about the condition of the engine.

2  Bearing failure occurs mainly because of lack of lubrication, the presence of dirt or other foreign particles, overloading the engine and/or corrosion. Regardless of the cause of

bearing failure, it must be corrected before the engine is reassembled to prevent it from happening again.

3  When examining the bearings, remove the main bearings from the crankcase halves and the rod bearings from the connecting rods and caps and lay them out on a clean surface in the same general position as their location on the crankshaft journals. This will make it possible for you to match any noted bearing problems with the corresponding crankshaft journal.

4  Dirt and other foreign particles get into the engine in a variety of ways. It may be left in the engine during assembly or it may pass through filters or breathers. It may get into the oil and from there into the bearings. Metal chips from machining operations and normal engine wear are often present. Abrasives are sometimes left in engine components after reconditioning operations, especially when parts are not thoroughly cleaned using the proper cleaning methods. Whatever the source, these foreign objects often end up imbedded in the soft bearing material and are easily recognised. Large particles will not imbed in the bearing and will score or gouge the bearing and journal. The best prevention for this cause of bearing failure is to clean all parts thoroughly and keep everything spotlessly clean during engine reassembly. Frequent and regular oil and filter changes are also recommended.

5  Lack of lubrication or lubrication breakdown has a number of interrelated causes. Excessive heat (which thins the oil), overloading (which squeezes the oil from the bearing face) and oil leakage or throw off from excessive bearing clearances, worn oil pump or high engine speeds all contribute to lubrication breakdown. Blocked oil passages will also starve a bearing and destroy it. When lack of lubrication is the cause of bearing failure, the bearing material is wiped or extruded from the steel backing of the bearing. Temperatures may increase to the point where the steel backing and the journal turn blue from overheating.

6  Riding habits can have a definite effect on bearing life. Full throttle low speed operation, or labouring the engine, puts very high loads on bearings, which tend to squeeze out the oil

film. These loads cause the bearings to flex, which produces fine cracks in the bearing face (fatigue failure). Eventually the bearing material will loosen in pieces and tear away from the steel backing. Short trip riding leads to corrosion of bearings, as insufficient engine heat is produced to drive off the condensed water and corrosive gases produced. These products collect in the engine oil, forming acid and sludge. As the oil is carried to the engine bearings, the acid attacks and corrodes the bearing material.

**7** Incorrect bearing installation during engine assembly will lead to bearing failure as well. Tight fitting bearings which leave insufficient bearing oil clearances result in oil starvation. Dirt or foreign particles trapped behind a bearing insert result in high spots on the bearing which lead to failure.

**8** To avoid bearing problems, clean all parts thoroughly before reassembly, double check all bearing clearance measurements and lubricate the new bearings with clean engine oil during installation.

## 24 Connecting rods

**Note 1:** *There are a number of different ways in which the connecting rods can be removed, and your best approach will depend on what other work, if any, you are doing on the engine.*

● If the pistons have already been separated from the rods, then you can either remove the crankshaft with the rods still attached, and then separate them afterwards, or you can leave the crankshaft in situ, remove the rod caps and then remove the rods from the top of the crankcase (but bear in mind that if you need to tilt the crankcase at all to remove the rods from the top, then the crankshaft could fall out).

● If the pistons have not been separated from the rods, they cannot be removed along with the crankshaft as the pistons will not fit through. Remove the crankshaft, then remove the rod and piston assemblies from the top of the crankcase (do not leave the crankshaft in situ as the crankcase will have to be tilted to remove the rod and piston assemblies from the top). You will also have to make a decision regarding removal of the liners – they do not have to be removed unless you are separating the pistons from the rods before removing the rods. The pistons and rods can be removed together out of the top of the liners, and can be installed in the same way, but bear in mind the information given in Section 11, Step 13, and in Section 14, regarding the liners and their seals.

● If it makes no difference, we advise removing the crankshaft first, then drawing the rod and piston assemblies out of the top of the liners, then removing the liners. The rods can them be separated from the pistons.

**Note 2:** *The connecting rod bolts must be discarded and new ones used on installation – it is best to obtain the bolts in advance. The old bolts can however be used for the oil clearance check.*

### Removal

**1** Remove the engine from the frame (see Section 5) and separate the crankcase halves (see Section 21). If required (see **Note** above), remove the liners (see Section 14), then remove the pistons (see Section 15), and the crankshaft (see Section 25).

**2** Before separating the rods from the crankshaft, measure the side clearance on each rod with a feeler gauge **(see illustration)**. If the clearance on any rod is greater than the service limit listed in this Chapter's Specifications, replace that rod with a new one.

**3** Using paint or a felt marker pen, mark the relevant cylinder identity across the join between each connecting rod and cap. Note the oil hole in the rear of each connecting rod which must face to the rear of the engine, and the arrow on the piston which points to the front of the engine – these ensure that the cap and rod are fitted the correct way around on reassembly **(see illustration 15.3)**. Note that the number and letter already across the rod and cap indicate rod size and weight grade respectively, not cylinder number. If there is no arrow on the piston (apparently a number of engines were assembled without markings), mark or scribe your own as the piston must be installed the correct way round.

**4** Unscrew the connecting rod cap nuts and separate the cap and rod from the crankpin **(see illustration)**. If the cap appears stuck, tap it on one end with a hammer while pulling it. If it is in situ, lift the crankshaft out of the upper crankcase half, taking care not to dislodge the main bearing shells **(see illustration 25.3)**.

**5** If required (according to your chosen method), turn the crankcase on its side. Push each piston/connecting rod assembly up and remove it from the top of the liner, making sure the connecting rod does not mark the liner bore **(see illustration 14.22a)**.

**HAYNES HINT** *If required, to ease removal of the pistons from the tops of the liners, carefully remove any ridge of carbon built up on the top of each liner bore using a scraper. If there is a pronounced wear ridge, remove it using a ridge reamer.*

**Caution: Do not try to remove the piston/connecting rod from the bottom of the crankcase. The piston will not pass the crankcase main bearing webs.**

**6** Fit the relevant bearing shells (if removed), cap, and nuts and bolts on each piston/connecting rod assembly so that they are all kept together as a matched set.

**7** If required and not already done, separate the pistons from the connecting rods (see Section 15).

### Inspection

**8** Check the connecting rods for cracks and other obvious damage. Refer to Section 15, Step 14 and check the piston pin and connecting rod small-end bore dimensions for wear. Renew any components that are worn beyond the specified limit.

**9** Refer to Section 23 and examine the connecting rod bearing shells. If they are scored, badly scuffed or appear to have seized, new shells must be installed. Always renew the shells in the connecting rods as a set. If they are badly damaged, check the corresponding crankpin. Evidence of extreme heat, such as discoloration, indicates that lubrication failure has occurred. Be sure to thoroughly check the oil pump and pressure relief valve as well as all oil holes and passages before reassembling the engine.

**10** Have the rods checked for twist and bending by a Triumph dealer if you are in doubt about their straightness.

### Oil clearance check

**11** Whether new bearing shells are being fitted or the original ones are being re-used, the connecting rod bearing oil clearance should be checked prior to reassembly. Work on one rod at a time when checking the clearances.

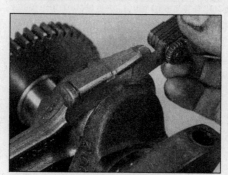

**24.2 Measure the connecting rod side clearance using a feeler gauge**

**24.4 Unscrew the nuts (arrowed) and pull the caps off the connecting rods**

**24.12  To remove a big-end bearing shell, push it sideways and lift it out**

**12** Remove the bearing shells from the rods and caps, keeping them in order **(see illustration)**. Clean the backs of the shells and the bearing locations in both the connecting rod and cap, and the crankpin journal.

**13** Press the bearing shells into their locations, ensuring that the tab on each shell engages the notch in the connecting rod/cap **(see illustration)**. Make sure the bearings are fitted in the correct locations and take care not to touch any shell's bearing surface with your fingers.

**14** Cut a length of the appropriate size Plastigauge (it should be slightly shorter than the width of the crankpin). Place a strand of Plastigauge on the crankpin journal for the rod being checked. Fit the rod onto its crankpin, then install the cap, making sure it is fitted the correct way around so the previously made markings align **(see illustration 24.26a and b)**. Note that the accuracy of this check is dependant on the rod not turning on the crankpin while it is installed and tightened – if it does, the Plastigauge will be disturbed and an inaccurate reading will result. Apply a smear of molybdenum disulphide grease to the bolt threads and to the underside of the nuts. Fit the nuts and tighten them first to the specified torque setting, and then by the specified angle using a degree disc, whilst ensuring that the connecting rod does not rotate **(see illustrations 24.26c, d and e)**. Slacken the cap nuts and remove the connecting rod caps, again taking great care not to rotate the crankshaft.

**24.15  Measure the crushed Plastigauge using the scale on the pack – be sure to use the correct one as both metric and imperial are included**

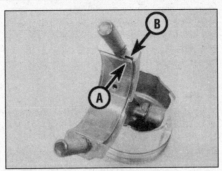

**24.13  Make sure the tab (A) locates in the notch (B)**

**15** Compare the width of the crushed Plastigauge on each crankpin to the scale printed on the Plastigauge envelope to obtain the connecting rod bearing oil clearance **(see illustration)**.

**16** On completion carefully scrape away all traces of the Plastigauge material from the crankpin and bearing shells using a fingernail or other object which is unlikely to score the shells.

**17** If the clearance is within the range listed in this Chapter's Specifications and the bearings are in perfect condition, they can be reused. If the clearance is not within the specified limits, the bearing shells may be the wrong grade (or excessively worn if the original shells are being reused). Before deciding that different grade shells are needed, make sure that no dirt or oil was trapped between the bearing shells and the connecting rod or cap when the clearance was measured. If the clearance is excessive, even with new shells (of the correct size), the crankpin is worn and the crankshaft should be renewed.

**18** Repeat the procedure for the remaining connecting rods.

**Bearing shell selection**

**19** The connecting rod big-end bearing oil clearance is controlled in production by selecting one of three grades of bearing shell. The grades are indicated by a colour-coding marked on the edge of each shell **(see illustration 25.19)**. New bearing inserts are selected as follows using the crankpin journal diameter and connecting rod size marking.

**20** Measure the crankpin journal diameter using a micrometer and record the result.

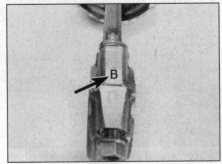

**24.20  Connecting rod size letter (arrowed)**

Inspect the connecting rod for its size marking, either the letter A or B **(see illustration)**.

**21** Match the rod marking with the measured journal diameter and select a new set of bearing shells using the following table.

| Con-rod marking | Crankpin journal diameter | Shell colour |
|---|---|---|
| A | 40.954 to 40.960 mm | White |
| A | 40.946 to 40.953 mm | Red |
| B | 40.954 to 40.960 mm | Red |
| B | 40.946 to 40.953 mm | Blue |

### Installation

**Note 1:** *There are a number of different ways in which the connecting rods can be installed, and your best approach will depend on what other work, if any, you are doing on the engine.*

● If the pistons have been separated from the rods and the crankshaft has been removed, then you can either fit the rods onto the crankshaft and then install the crankshaft, or you can install the crankshaft and then install the rods from the top of the crankcase (but bear in mind that if you need to tilt the crankcase at all to install the rods from the top, then the crankshaft could fall out).

● If the pistons have not been separated from the rods, the rod and piston assemblies cannot be installed attached to the crankshaft as the pistons will not fit through. Install the rod and piston assemblies from the top of the crankcase then install the crankshaft. You will also have to make a decision regarding installation of the liners, if they have been removed, as the rod and piston assemblies can be installed before them, with them or after them – see Section 14 for details.

● If it makes no difference, we advise fitting the pistons onto the rods first, then fitting the rod and piston assemblies into the liners, then installing the liners, followed by the crankshaft.

**Note 2:** *New connecting rod bolts and nuts must be used whenever the rods have been disassembled.*

**22** Remove the bearing shells from the rods and caps, keeping them in order **(see illustration 24.12)**. Clean the backs of the shells and the bearing locations in both the connecting rod and cap, and the crankpin journal. If new shells are being fitted, ensure that all traces of the protective grease are cleaned off using paraffin (kerosene). Wipe the shells, cap and rod dry with a clean lint free cloth.

**23** Press the bearing shells into their locations, ensuring that the tab on each shell engages the notch in the connecting rod/cap **(see illustration 24.13)**. Make sure the bearings are fitted in the correct locations and take care not to touch any shell's bearing surface with your fingers.

**24** Remove the old bolts from the rods and discard them, then fit the new ones – it will

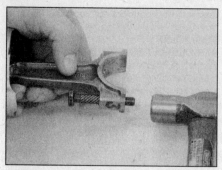

**24.24 Tap out the old bolts and install new ones**

**24.26a Fit the rod onto its correct crankpin . . .**

**24.26b . . . then fit the cap, making sure it is the correct way round**

**24.26c Fit the nuts . . .**

probably be necessary to tap the old bolts out using a hammer **(see illustration)**.

**25** Decide upon your installation procedure, then assemble the rods and pistons and/or install the liners and crankshaft as required, referring to the relevant Sections. **Note:** *When installing the connecting rods on the crankshaft, remember that the oil hole in the connecting rod must face to the rear of the engine, on the opposite side to the arrow on the piston crown which must point to the front of the engine* **(see illustration 15.3)**.

**26** Lubricate the shells with new engine oil. Fit the rod onto its crankpin, then install the cap, making sure it is fitted the correct way around so the previously made markings align **(see illustrations)**. Apply a smear of molybdenum disulphide grease to the bolt threads and to the underside of the nuts. Fit the nuts and tighten them finger-tight at this stage. Check to make sure that all components have been returned to their

original locations using the marks made on disassembly. Now tighten the nuts evenly, in two or three stages, first to the specified torque setting, and then by a further 120° using a degree disc **(see illustrations)**.

**HAYNES HiNT** *If a degree disc is not available, the angle can be determined by using the points on the connecting rod cap nut. There are six points on the nut, so the angle between each point is 60°. Select one point as a reference and mark it with paint or a marker. Now select the second point clockwise from it and mark its position on the connecting rod cap. Tighten the nut – when the mark on the first point aligns with the mark made on the connecting rod cap, it will have turned through 120°.*

**27** Check that the crankshaft is free to rotate easily, then install the other connecting rods in the same way. Check to make sure that all components have been returned to their original locations using the marks made on disassembly.

**28** Check that the rods rotate smoothly and freely on the crankpin. If there are any signs of roughness or tightness, remove the rods and re-check the bearing clearance. Sometimes tapping the bottom of the connecting rod cap will relieve tightness, but if in doubt, recheck the clearances.

**29** Reassemble the crankcase halves and the rest of the engine according to your removal procedure, referring to the relevant Sections.

## 25 Crankshaft and main bearings

### *Removal*

**1** Remove the engine from the frame (see Section 5) and separate the crankcase halves (see Section 21).

**2** Refer to Section 24 and separate the connecting rods from the crankpin (unless the pistons have been removed, in which case the rods can remain attached for now, and removed later if required). **Note:** *If no work is to be carried out on the piston/connecting rod assemblies there is no need to remove them from the bores (unless the liners have been removed), but push them up to the top of the bores so that their bottom ends are clear of the crankshaft.*

**3** Before removing the crankshaft, check the amount of end-float using a dial gauge. If it exceeds the limit specified, the crankshaft and/or the crankcases must be replaced with new ones. Lift the crankshaft out of the upper crankcase half, taking care not to dislodge the main bearing shells, then remove the cam chain if not already done **(see illustration)**.

**4** If required, remove the bearing shells from the crankcase halves by pushing their centres to the side, then lifting them out **(see illustration)**. Keep the shells in order.

**5** If required and not already done, undo the screws securing the breather disc and remove

**24.26d . . . and tighten them first to the specified torque . . .**

**24.26e . . . and then by the specified angle**

**25.3 Carefully lift the crankshaft out of the crankcase**

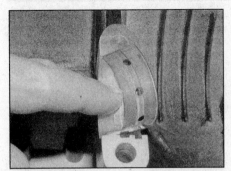

**25.4 To remove a main bearing shell, push it sideways and lift it out**

**25.11 Press each shell into place, locating the tab in the notch (arrowed)**

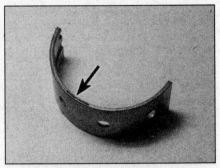

**25.19 The colour code is marked on the side of the shell (arrowed)**

it from the end of the crankshaft **(see illustration 21.3d)**.

## Inspection

**6** Clean the crankshaft with solvent, using a rifle-cleaning brush to scrub out the oil passages. If available, blow the crank dry with compressed air.

**7** Refer to Section 23 and examine the main bearing shells. If they are scored, badly scuffed or appear to have been seized, new bearings must be installed. Always renew the main bearings as a set. If they are badly damaged, check the corresponding crankshaft journal. Evidence of extreme heat, such as discoloration, indicates that lubrication failure has occurred. Be sure to thoroughly check the oil pump and pressure relief valve as well as all oil holes and passages before reassembling the engine.

**8** The crankshaft journals should be given a close visual examination, paying particular attention where damaged bearing shells have been discovered. If the journals are scored or pitted in any way a new crankshaft will be required. Note that oversize shells are not available, precluding the option of re-grinding the crankshaft.

### Oil clearance check

**9** Whether new bearing shells are being fitted or the original ones are being re-used, the main bearing oil clearance should be checked prior to reassembly.

**10** If not already done, remove the bearing shells from the crankcase halves by pushing their centres to the side, then lifting them out **(see illustration 25.4)**. Keep the shells in order. Clean the backs of the shells and the bearing locations in both the crankcase halves.

**11** Press the bearing shells back into their locations, ensuring that the tab on each shell engages in the notch **(see illustration)**. Make sure the bearings are fitted in the correct locations and take care not to touch any shell's bearing surface with your fingers.

**12** Ensure that the shells and crankshaft are clean and dry. Lay the crankshaft in position in the upper crankcase **(see illustration 25.3)**.

**13** Cut several lengths of the appropriate size Plastigauge (they should be slightly shorter than the width of the crankshaft journal). Place a strand of Plastigauge on each (cleaned) crankshaft journal.

**14** If removed, fit the three locating dowels into one crankcase half **(see illustration 21.12)**. Carefully guide the lower crankcase half onto the upper half. Make sure that the selector forks (if fitted) engage with their respective slots in the transmission gears as the halves are joined. Check that the lower crankcase half is correctly seated. **Note:** *If the casings are not correctly seated, remove the lower crankcase half and investigate the problem. Do not attempt to pull them together using the crankcase bolts as the casing will crack and be ruined.* Install the eight 8 mm lower crankcase bolts in their original locations and tighten them in the correct numerical sequence in three stages to the torque settings specified in Section 21 **(see illustration 21.19)**. Make sure that the crankshaft is not rotated as the bolts are tightened.

**15** Slacken and remove the crankcase bolts, working in a criss-cross pattern from the outside in, then carefully lift off the lower crankcase half, making sure the Plastigauge is not disturbed.

**16** Compare the width of the crushed Plastigauge on each crankshaft journal to the scale printed on the Plastigauge envelope to obtain the main bearing oil clearance **(see illustration 24.15)**.

**17** If the clearance is not within the specified limits, the bearing shells may be the wrong grade (or excessively worn if the original inserts are being reused). Before deciding that different grade shells are needed, make sure that no dirt or oil was trapped between the bearing shells and the crankcase halves when the clearance was measured. If the clearance is excessive, even with new shells (of the correct size), the crankshaft journal is worn and the crankshaft should be renewed.

**18** On completion carefully scrape away all traces of the Plastigauge material from the crankshaft journal and bearing shells; use a fingernail or other object which is unlikely to score them.

### Bearing shell selection

**19** The main bearing oil clearance is controlled in production by selecting one of four grades of bearing shell. The grades are indicated by a colour-coding marked on the edge of each shell **(see illustration)**. New bearing inserts are selected with reference to the following chart, having measured the crankshaft journal diameter and the crankcase bore diameter.

**20** Measure the diameter of each crankshaft journal with a micrometer and record the results. Assemble the crankcase halves with the shells and crankshaft removed, and tighten the 8 mm crankshaft journal bolts in the correct numerical sequence in three stages to the torque settings specified in Section 21. Now measure each crankshaft journal bore diameter using a bore gauge and micrometer and record the results. Refer to *Tools and Workshop Tips* in the Reference Section for details on how to use the measuring equipment.

| Crankcase bore dia. | Crankshaft journal dia. | Shell colour |
| --- | --- | --- |
| 41.118 to 41.126 mm | 37.969 to 37.976 mm | White |
| 41.118 to 41.126 mm | 37.960 to 37.968 mm | Red |
| 41.127 to 41.135 mm | 37.969 to 37.976 mm | Red |
| 41.127 to 41.135 mm | 37.960 to 37.968 mm | Blue |
| 41.136 to 41.144 mm | 37.969 to 37.976 mm | Blue |
| 41.136 to 41.144 mm | 37.960 to 37.968 mm | Green |

## Installation

**21** Clean the backs of the bearing shells and the bearing recesses in both crankcase halves. If new shells are being fitted, ensure that all traces of the protective grease are cleaned off using paraffin (kerosene). Wipe the shells and crankcase halves dry with a lint-free cloth.

**22** Press the bearing shells into their locations, ensuring that the tab on each shell engages in the notch **(see illustration 25.11)**. Make sure the bearings are fitted in the correct locations and take care not to touch any shell's bearing surface with your fingers. Lubricate all the shells with clean engine oil.

**23** Before installing the crankshaft, the

25.23a The eliminator gear tooth with the line (A) must be directly in front of the driven gear tooth with the dot (B) . . .

25.23b . . . use a screwdriver between the teeth as a lever to align them

25.23c As the dot on the driven gear will be covered, make some other dots on the tooth as a double-check

balancer shaft must be correctly aligned. The shaft driven gear has a backlash eliminator gear on its outside, which works by having one less tooth than the driven gear, and by using friction between the two gears to create a rolling cushion. First of all, align the tooth on the eliminator gear that is marked with a line with the tooth on the driven gear marked with a dot **(see illustration)** – this can be done using a screwdriver inserted between the teeth and used as a lever against the friction **(see illustration)**. Once they are aligned, make a mark on the top or side of the driven gear tooth – as the dot on the outside is now

25.24 Crankshaft drive gear and balancer shaft driven gear alignment marks

covered by the eliminator gear tooth, this serves as an easy way of double checking the alignment **(see illustration)**.

24 Identify the two teeth on the drive gear on the crankshaft marked with a dot – these two teeth must sit on each side of the marked and aligned teeth on the driven gear of the balancer shaft. Lower the crankshaft into position in the upper crankcase, engaging the teeth as described **(see illustration)**. Note: *If you turn the crankshaft through one full turn, you will notice that when the marked teeth on the crankshaft drive gear align with the lined tooth on the eliminator gear, the lined tooth on the eliminator gear no longer aligns with the marked tooth on the balancer shaft driven gear – do not be alarmed, this is correct, and happens because of the one tooth difference in the gears.*

25 Reassemble the crankcase halves and the rest of the engine according to your removal procedure, referring to the relevant Sections.

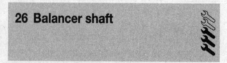

## 26 Balancer shaft

Note: *References to the right-hand and left-hand ends of the shaft are made as though the*

engine is the correct way up – remember that when the crankcases are split and the upper half is upside down, these references will appear to be the wrong way round.

### Removal

1 Remove the engine from the frame and separate the crankcase halves (see Sections 5 and 21).

2 Remove the crankshaft (see Section 25).

3 Before disturbing the balancer shaft holders, make some identification markings on their top surfaces to ensure that they can be installed on their original journals on installation, and the correct way round. Unscrew the holder bolts, noting the bearing retainer brackets where fitted (earlier models), and remove the holders **(see illustration)**.

4 Lift the shaft out of the crankcase **(see illustration)**, on later models noting the retaining ring for the left-hand bearing in the groove in the crankcase **(see illustration 26.8)**. Remove the ring for safekeeping. On all models, the ring for the other bearing comes away with the shaft, and is retained by the end cap.

### Inspection

5 Inspect the teeth of both gears for signs of wear or damage, and replace them with new

26.3 Unscrew the holder bolts (arrowed) and remove the holders . . .

26.4 . . . then lift the shaft out of the crankcase

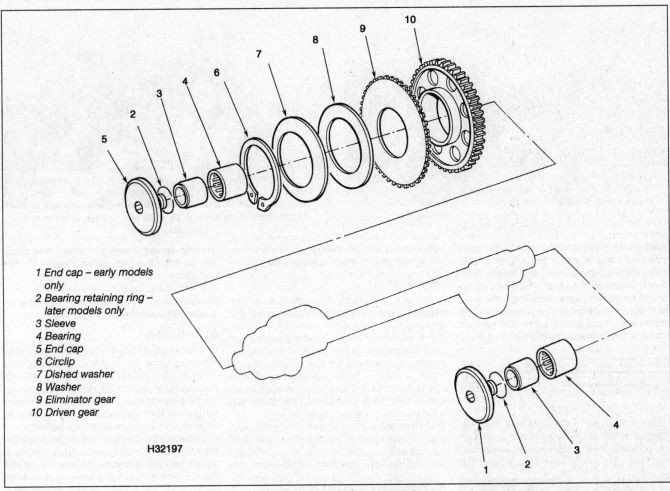

1 End cap – early models
   only
2 Bearing retaining ring –
   later models only
3 Sleeve
4 Bearing
5 End cap
6 Circlip
7 Dished washer
8 Washer
9 Eliminator gear
10 Driven gear

H32197

**26.5 Balancer shaft components**

ones if necessary. If damage is found, check
the teeth of the drive gear on the crankshaft.
The shaft can be disassembled if required – all
components are available individually **(see
illustration)**. On assembly, apply a suitable
non-permanent thread locking compound to
the end cap threads and tighten them to the
torque setting specified at the beginning of
the Chapter.
**6** Check the bearing on each end and replace
them with new ones if necessary.

## Installation

**7** Before installing the balancer shaft, refer to
Section 25, Step 23 and align the eliminator
gear with the driven gear as described.
**8** On later models, make sure the bearing
retainer ring is correctly positioned in the its
groove in the crankcase **(see illustration)**.
**9** Apply a bearing locking compound to the
bearing seats in the upper crankcase half only
**(see illustration)**.

**10** Lay the shaft in the crankcase, facing the
oil holes in the outer races of the bearings
away from the bearing locking compound
**(see illustration 26.4)**. Make sure the
retaining ring on the right-hand end locates in
its groove, and the ring for the left-hand
bearing is not dislodged from its groove **(see
illustration)**.
**11** Fit the shaft holders, making sure they are
the correct way round, on early models not
forgetting the bearing retainer brackets **(see**

**26.8  Make sure the retaining ring is fitted
in its groove**

**26.9  Apply the locking compound to the
cutouts for the bearings**

**26.10  Make sure the ring locates correctly
in its groove (arrowed)**

26.11a Install the holders, making sure the right-hand one locates correctly over the ring

26.11b Lubricate the bolt threads and tighten them to the specified torque

illustration). Lubricate the threads of the bolts with clean engine oil. Install the bolts, with their washers where fitted, and tighten them evenly to the torque setting specified at the beginning of the Chapter (see illustration).

12 Reassemble the crankcase halves and the rest of the engine according to your removal procedure, referring to the relevant Sections.

## 27 Transmission shaft removal and installation

**Note:** *References to the right-hand and left-hand ends of the shafts are made as though the engine is the correct way up – remember that when the crankcases are split and the*

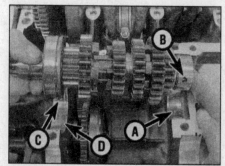

27.6 Locate the pin (A) in the hole (B) and the half-ring (C) in the groove (D)

27.7b Locate the pin in the hole . . .

*upper half is upside down, these references will appear to be the wrong way round.*

### Removal

1 Remove the engine from the frame and separate the crankcase halves (see Sections 5 and 21).

2 Lift the output shaft out of the crankcase (see illustration 27.7b). Remove the needle bearing locating pin for safekeeping if it is loose – it could be in the bearing or the crankcase. The ball bearing on the left-hand end of the shaft is located by a complete ring which remains loose on the shaft.

3 Lift the input shaft out of the crankcase (see illustration 27.6). Remove the ball bearing half ring retainer from the right-hand end and the dowel pin from the left-hand end

27.7a Fit a new oil seal on to the shaft

27.7c . . . and the ring and seal lip in the grooves

for safekeeping if they are loose – they could be in the bearing outer races or the crankcase.

4 If necessary, the transmission shafts can be disassembled and inspected for wear or damage as described in Section 28.

### Installation

5 If removed, fit the needle bearing locating pins into either the upper crankcase or the bearing outer races. Fit the input shaft ball bearing retainer into its slot in the bearing. Apply a smear of a suitable non-permanent thread locking compound to the bearing locations in the upper crankcase half only.

6 Install the input shaft, making sure the pin locates in its hole and the half ring locates in its groove (see illustration). Position the half ring in the ball bearing groove so that it will bridge both casing halves when reassembled.

7 If not already done, slip the old oil seal off the left-hand end of the output shaft and replace it with a new one (see illustration). Install the output shaft, making sure the pin locates in its hole, and the retaining ring and oil seal lip locate in their grooves (see illustrations).

8 Ensure that the gears of both shafts mesh correctly and that they're in the neutral position (i.e. the input shaft can be turned whilst the output shaft is held stationary).

9 Reassemble the crankcase halves and the rest of the engine according to your removal procedure, referring to the relevant Sections.

## 28 Transmission shaft overhaul

1 Remove the shafts from the crankcase as described in Section 27.

 **HAYNES HiNT** *When disassembling the transmission shafts, place the parts on a long rod or thread a wire through them to keep them in order and facing the proper direction.*

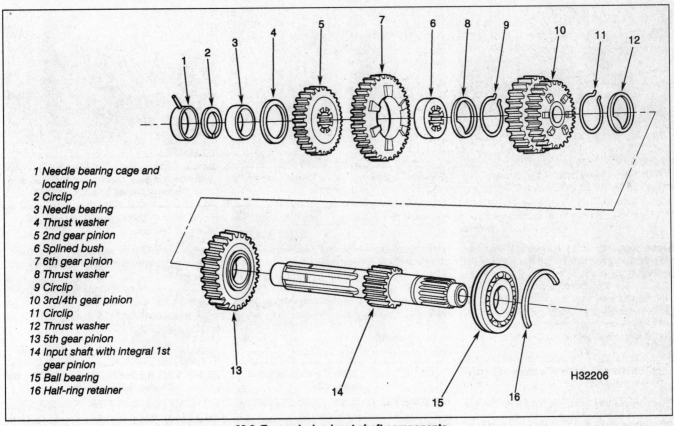

1 Needle bearing cage and
  locating pin
2 Circlip
3 Needle bearing
4 Thrust washer
5 2nd gear pinion
6 Splined bush
7 6th gear pinion
8 Thrust washer
9 Circlip
10 3rd/4th gear pinion
11 Circlip
12 Thrust washer
13 5th gear pinion
14 Input shaft with integral 1st
   gear pinion
15 Ball bearing
16 Half-ring retainer

H32206

**28.2 Transmission input shaft components**

## Input shaft disassembly

**2** Slide the needle roller bearing outer race off the left-hand end of the shaft (**see illustration and 28.17e**).
**3** Remove the circlip from the shaft end, then slide the needle roller bearing, the thrustwasher and the second gear pinion off the shaft (**see illustrations 28.17d, c, b and a**).
**4** Slide the 6th gear pinion and its bush off the shaft, followed by the thrust washer (**see illustrations 28.16b and a and 28.15c**).
**5** Remove the circlip securing the combined 3rd/4th gear pinion and slide it off the shaft (**see illustrations 28.15b and a**).
**6** Remove the circlip securing the 5th gear pinion, then slide the thrust washer and the pinion off the shaft (**see illustrations 28.14c, b and a**).

## Input shaft inspection

**7** Wash all of the components in clean solvent and dry them off.
**8** Check the gear teeth for cracking and other obvious damage. Check the 6th gear bush and the surface in the inner diameter of the gear for scoring or heat discoloration. If the gear or bush is damaged, renew it.
**9** Inspect the dogs and the dog holes in the gears for excessive wear. Renew the paired gears as a set if necessary.
**10** Measure the gearchange fork groove

width in the 3rd/4th gear pinion as described in Section 29.
**11** The shaft is unlikely to sustain damage unless the engine has seized, placing an unusually high loading on the transmission, or the machine has covered a very high mileage. Check the surface of the shaft, especially where a pinion turns on it, and renew the shaft if it has scored or picked up. Damage of any kind can only be cured by renewal.
**12** If the ball bearing requires renewal, a bearing puller will be required to extract the bearing from its shaft. Note the position of the locating groove in the outer race of the bearing prior to removing it and ensure that the new bearing is fitted with the groove in the same position. Pull the bearing off the shaft

and install the new bearing using a press. Replace the needle bearing with a new one if it is worn or damaged, or does not run freely.

## Input shaft reassembly

**13** During reassembly, always use new circlips. Lubricate the components with the correct grade of engine oil before assembling them.
**14** Slide on the 5th gear with its dogs facing away from the integral 1st gear pinion (**see illustration**). Install the thrustwasher and circlip, making sure that the circlip locates in the shaft groove (**see illustrations**).
**15** Install the combined 3rd/4th gear pinion so that the smaller (3rd) gear faces the 5th gear pinion and so that the oilway in the

**28.14a Slide the 5th gear on the shaft with its dogs away from the integral 1st gear**

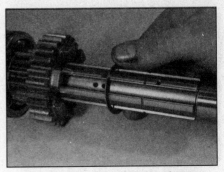

**28.14b Slide on the thrustwasher . . .**

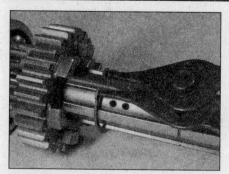

28.14c ... and then fit the circlip ...

28.14d ... making sure it locates correctly in its groove

28.15a Slide on the combined 3rd/4th gear with the 3rd gear facing the 5th gear, and aligning the oil holes (arrowed)

28.15b Fit the circlip into the groove ...

28.15c ... and slide the thrustwasher against it

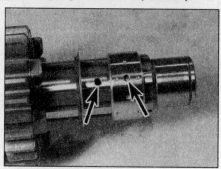

28.16a Slide the bush onto the shaft so the oil holes (arrowed) align ...

gearchange fork groove aligns with the two oilways in the shaft **(see illustration)**. Locate the circlip in the shaft groove and slide the thrustwasher on the shaft so that it abuts the circlip **(see illustrations)**.

16 Install the 6th gear pinion bush so that its oilway aligns with the shaft oilway, then slide on the 6th gear pinion with its dogs facing the 4th gear **(see illustrations)**.
17 Install the 2nd gear pinion with its stepped

side facing away from the 6th gear pinion **(see illustration)**. Slide on a thrustwasher and the needle roller bearing, then secure them with the circlip **(see illustrations)**. Slide the outer race over the bearing **(see illustration)**. The

28.16b ... then slide the 6th gear onto the bush

28.17a Install the 2nd gear with its stepped side facing away from the 6th gear

28.17b Slide the thrustwasher onto the shaft ...

28.17c ... followed by the needle bearing

28.17d Fit the circlip into the groove (arrowed) ...

28.17e ... then slide the outer race over the bearing

**28.17f  The assembled input shaft**

assembled input shaft should be as shown (see illustration).

## Output shaft disassembly

**18**  Slide the needle bearing outer race, bearing and thrustwasher off the right-hand end of the shaft (see illustrations 28.36c and b).
**19**  Make a paint mark on the outer face of the 1st gear pinion, then slide it off the shaft, followed by the 5th gear pinion (see illustrations 28.36a and 28.35).
**20**  Remove the circlip, then slide off the thrustwasher, 3rd gear pinion, bush, 4th gear pinion, bush and thrustwasher (see illustrations 28.34d, c, b and a, and 28.33c, b and a).
**21**  Remove the circlip and slide off the 6th gear pinion (see illustrations 28.32b and a).
**22**  Remove the circlip, then slide off the thrustwasher and the 2nd gear pinion (see illustrations 28.31c, b and a).
**23**  Moving to the left-hand end of the shaft, remove the oil seal and discard it (see illustration 27.7a), then remove the bearing retaining ring (see illustration 28.37c); a new seal must be installed on reassembly. If required, slide the sleeve off the shaft (see illustration 28.37b).

## Output shaft inspection

**24**  Wash all of the components in clean solvent and dry them off.
**25**  Check the gear teeth for cracking and other obvious damage. Check the 3rd and 4th gear bushes and the surface in the inner diameter of each gear for scoring or heat discoloration. If the gear or bush is damaged, renew it.
**26**  Inspect the dogs and the dog holes in the

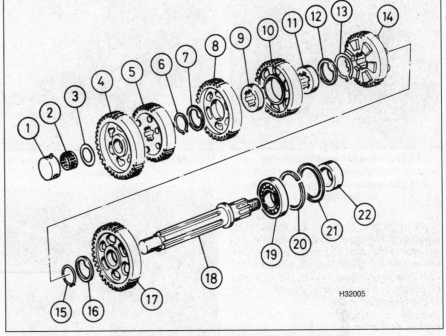

**28.18  Transmission output shaft components**

| | | |
|---|---|---|
| 1 Needle bearing outer race and locating pin | 8 3rd gear pinion | 16 Thrust washer |
| 2 Needle bearing | 9 3rd gear pinion bush | 17 2nd gear pinion |
| 3 Thrust washer | 10 4th gear pinion | 18 Output shaft |
| 4 1st gear pinion | 11 4th gear pinion bush | 19 Ball bearing |
| 5 5th gear pinion | 12 Thrust washer | 20 Bearing retaining ring |
| 6 Circlip | 13 Circlip | 21 Oil seal |
| 7 Thrust washer | 14 6th gear pinion | 22 Sleeve |
| | 15 Circlip | |

gears for excessive wear. Renew the paired gears as a set if necessary.
**27**  Measure the gearchange fork groove width in the 5th and 6th gear pinions (see Section 29).
**28**  The shaft is unlikely to sustain damage unless the engine has seized, placing an unusually high loading on the transmission, or the machine has covered a very high mileage. Check the surface of the shaft, especially where a pinion turns on it, and renew the shaft if it has scored or picked up. Damage of any kind can only be cured by renewal.
**29**  The ball bearing on the left-hand end of the shaft is a press fit. Refer to *Tools and*

*Workshop Tips* in the Reference Section for more information on bearing removal and installation methods. Replace the needle bearing with a new one if it is worn or damaged, or does not run freely.

## Output shaft reassembly

**30**  During reassembly, always use new circlips. Lubricate the components with engine oil before assembling them.
**31**  Slide the 2nd gear pinion on the shaft with its dished side facing away from the ball bearing (see illustration). Install a thrustwasher and secure with a circlip, making sure it seats in the shaft groove (see illustrations).

**28.31a  Fit the 2nd gear pinion with its dished side facing away from the bearing**

**28.31b  Slide on the thrust washer . . .**

**28.31c  . . . then fit the circlip, locating it in its groove (arrowed)**

28.32a Fit the 6th gear pinion with its selector fork groove facing away from the 2nd gear pinion, aligning the oil holes (arrowed)

28.32b Fit the circlip, locating it in its groove

28.33a Slide the thrust washer onto the shaft . . .

**32** Slide 6th gear pinion on the shaft with its gearchange fork groove facing away from the 2nd gear pinion, and so that the oilway in the fork groove aligns with the two oilways in the shaft **(see illustration)**. Secure the gear with the circlip, making sure it locates in the shaft groove **(see illustration)**.

**33** Slide a thrustwasher on the shaft, followed by the 4th gear pinion bush, aligning the bush oilway with the shaft oilway **(see illustrations)**. Slide 4th gear pinion on the shaft so that its stepped side faces away from the 6th gear pinion **(see illustration)**.

**34** Install the 3rd gear pinion bush so that its oilway aligns with the shaft oilway **(see illustration)**. Slide on the 3rd gear pinion so that its stepped side faces the 4th gear **(see illustration)**. Install a thrustwasher and retain

28.33b . . . followed by the 4th gear bush, aligning the oil holes (arrowed)

with a circlip, making sure it locates in the shaft groove **(see illustrations)**.
**35** Slide the 5th gear pinion on the shaft so that its gearchange fork groove faces the 3rd gear pinion and so that the oilway in the

28.33c Install the 4th gear pinion with its stepped centre facing away from the 6th gear

groove aligns with the two oilways in the shaft **(see illustration)**.
**36** Install the 1st gear pinion on the shaft, with the paint mark made on removal facing out **(see illustration)**. Install the thrustwasher,

28.34a Slide on the 3rd gear pinion bush, aligning the oil holes (arrowed) . . .

28.34b . . . then install the 3rd gear pinion with its stepped centre facing the 4th gear pinion

28.34c Slide the thrust washer onto the shaft . . .

28.34d . . . then fit the circlip, locating it in its groove

28.35 Install the 5th gear pinion with its selector fork groove facing the 3rd gear, aligning the oil holes

28.36a Install the 1st gear pinion . . .

28.36b . . . followed by the thrust washer . . .

28.36c . . . the needle bearing, and its outer race

28.37a  Fit the bearing . . .

28.37b . . . followed by the sleeve, with its chamfered side facing out

28.37c  Fit the locating ring onto the end of the shaft, then fit the oil seal

28.37d  The assembled output shaft

needle roller bearing and outer race **(see illustrations)**.

37  At the left end of the shaft, fit the bearing onto the shaft using a press, if removed and not already installed **(see illustration)**. Install the sleeve with its chamfered edge facing outwards then fit the bearing locating ring (the ring will float on the shaft until the countershaft is installed in the crankcase) **(see illustrations)**. Install a new oil seal over the sleeve with its marked side facing out **(see illustration 27.7a)**. The assembled output shaft should be as shown **(see illustration)**.

## 29 Gearchange mechanism

**Note:** *Access can be gained to the detent cam and stopper arms with the engine in the*

*frame and the clutch removed (see Section 16). All other operations require the crankcases to be separated.*

### Removal

1  Remove the engine from the frame and separate the crankcase halves (see Sections 5 and 21). The gearchange mechanism and selector drum and forks are all housed in the lower crankcase half.

2  Remove the screw and retaining plate from the left-hand side of the crankcase to free the selector fork shaft **(see illustration)**. Slide the rod out of the crankcase and lift each fork out as it clears the rod **(see illustrations 29.27e, d and c)**. Install the forks back on the rod the correct way round as a guide to reassembly.

3  Remove the oil pump and its middle gear assembly (see Section 30), and the pressure relief valve (see Section 19).

4  Unscrew the nuts securing the neutral and gear stopper arm assemblies in the right-hand side of the crankcase, then remove the outer washers, stopper arms (noting how the rollers locate in the detents in the cam), return springs and inner washers **(see illustration)**. Keep the components of each assembly separate to avoid their parts being interchanged – note that the neutral arm spring is a different colour for identification. **Note:** *If this is the only part of the mechanism that is being removed (see **Note** above), first remove the clutch (see Section 16). Now plug the aperture into the sump with rags to prevent the possibility of one of the washers or other components dropping into it – two of the washers involved are very small and are easy to drop.*

5  Remove the two screws which secure the pawl retainer plate to the crankcase **(see illustration)**. Rotate the plate clockwise, then

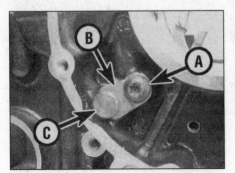

29.2  Undo the screw (A), remove the plate (B), and withdraw the shaft (C)

29.4  Unscrew the nuts (arrowed) and remove the stopper arm assemblies – note how they fit and keep the components for each assembly separate

29.5  Undo the screws (arrowed) and remove the plate as described

**29.6 Undo the screw (arrowed) and remove the detent cam**

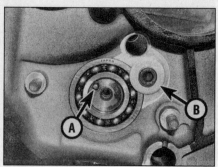

**29.7a Detent cam locating pin (A). Bearing retainer bolt and washer (B)**

**29.7b Remove the bearing, sliding the selector drum against it to dislodge it . . .**

slide it out to the rear of the drum and remove it, noting how it fits **(see illustration 29.22a)**.

**6** Remove the screw securing the detent cam to the right-hand end of the selector

drum and remove the cam, noting how it is located by a pin **(see illustration)**. Remove the pin for safekeeping if it is loose **(see illustration 29.7a)**.

**7** Remove the bolt and washer which retain the ball bearing in the right side of the crankcase **(see illustration)**. Push the bearing out from inside of the crankcase, using the selector drum to dislodge it, then lift the drum out of the crankcase, noting how it fits **(see illustrations)**.

**8** Remove the circlip and washer from the outer end of the gearchange shaft **(see illustration)**. If required, remove the circlip, spring guide and return spring from the inner end of the shaft, noting how the spring ends locate **(see illustration)**. Withdraw the shaft from the crankcase **(see illustration)**.

**9** If the pawl carrier requires removal from the left-hand end of the selector drum, remove the circlip and lift off the neutral disc. Drive out the roll pin in the shaft. Carefully withdraw the pawl carrier from the drum, taking care not to lose the spring-loaded pawls.

### Inspection

**10** Check the selector forks and shaft for wear and damage.

**11** Locate each selector fork in its corresponding gear groove and measure the gearchange fork-to-groove clearance using a feeler gauge **(see illustration)**. If the clearance is outside the maximum specified, measure the selector fork end widths and the groove in the gear using a Vernier caliper **(see illustrations)**. Renew any component which is worn beyond the service limit (see Specifications).

**12** Check the selector fork shaft for bending by rolling it along a flat surface. A bent shaft will cause difficulty in selecting gears and

**29.7c . . . then remove the drum, noting how it locates**

**29.8a Remove the circlip (arrowed) and the washer from the outer end of the shaft**

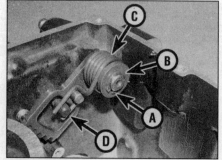

**29.8b If required, remove the circlip (A), spring guide (B) and spring (C), noting how the ends locate (D)**

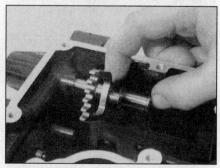

**29.8c Withdraw the shaft from the crankcase**

**29.11a Measure the fork-to-groove clearance using a feeler gauge**

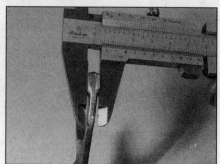

**29.11b If the clearance exceeds the limit, measure the thickness of the fork ends . . .**

**29.11c . . . and the width of the groove, and renew whichever component is worn**

**29.15a  Check the condition of the bearing (arrowed)**

**29.15b  Prise out the old oil seal . . .**

**29.15c  . . . and press in a new one so that it is flush with the housing**

make the gearchange action heavy. Replace the shaft with a new one if it is at all bent.

13  Inspect the selector drum grooves and selector fork guide pins for wear and damage. If they show signs of wear or damage the selector fork(s) and drum must be renewed.

14  Check that the selector drum bearing rotates freely and has no sign of freeplay between its inner and outer race. Renew the bearing if necessary.

15  Check the gearchange shaft for distortion and damage to the splines. If the shaft is bent you can attempt to straighten it, but if the splines are damaged it must be renewed. Slide the gearchange shaft into the crankcase and check that it turns smoothly and freely in its bore. If it feels rough, prise out the oil seal, then clean and lubricate the needle bearing and check it again **(see illustration)**. If it is still rough, replace the bearing with a new one – refer to *Tools and Workshop Tips* in the Reference Section for information on bearing check, removal and installation methods. Check the condition of the oil seal and look for signs of oil leakage from it. Replace it with a new one if necessary – prise out the old seal and press the new one into place **(see illustrations)**. If the seal is removed to access the bearing, use a new seal – the old one is likely to leak if it is reused.

16  Check the selector arm for cracks, distortion and wear of its teeth, and check for any corresponding wear on the teeth on the pawl carrier on the selector drum. Check the pawl assembly components for wear and damage. Also check the stopper arm rollers and the detents in the selector drum for any

**29.19a  Secure the shaft with the washer and circlip**

wear or damage, and make sure the rollers turn freely. Replace any components that are worn or damaged with new ones.

17  Inspect the shaft centralising spring and the stopper arm return springs for fatigue, wear or damage. If any faults are found, renew the components. Also check that the centralising spring locating pin in the crankcase is securely tightened. If it is loose, remove it and apply a non-permanent thread locking compound to its threads, then fit a new sealing washer and tighten it to the torque setting specified at the beginning of the Chapter.

### Installation

18  If the pawl assembly was disturbed, install the springs plungers and pawls in the carrier, then hold them compressed and insert the carrier in the end of the selector drum. Drift the roll pin into the hole in the shaft to retain the carrier. Fit the neutral disc over the drum

**29.19b  Fit the return spring and guide . . .**

end so that its cutout aligns with the roll pin. Secure the disc with the circlip.

19  Slide the gearchange shaft into the crankcase **(see illustration 29.8c)**. Fit the washer onto the outer end of the shaft, then secure the shaft with the circlip, making sure it is correctly located in its groove **(see illustration)**. If removed, fit the return spring and spring guide onto the inner end of the shaft and secure them with the circlip, making sure it locates correctly in its groove **(see illustrations)**. Make sure the return spring ends are correctly located **(see illustration)**.

20  Install the selector drum in the lower crankcase, locating its shaft end in the casing bore, and aligning the teeth on the selector arm with those on the pawl carrier **(see illustration 29.7c)** – it is important that the centre tooth on the pawl carrier locates between the 3rd and 4th teeth on the selector arm **(see illustration)**. Fit the ball bearing into

**29.19c  . . . and secure them with the circlip**

**29.19d  Make sure the spring ends are correctly located**

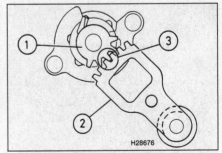

**29.20a  Make sure the centre tooth on the pawl carrier (1) locates between the central teeth (3) on the selector arm (2)**

**29.20b Secure the bearing with the washer and bolt**

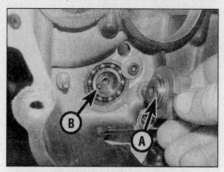

**29.21a Locate the hole (A) in the detent cam over the locating pin (B)**

**29.21b Secure the cam with its screw**

the right-hand side of the crankcase, noting that it must be installed from the outside **(see illustration 29.7b)**. Apply a suitable non-permanent thread locking compound to the threads of the bearing retainer bolt, then fit

the bolt with its washer and tighten it to the torque setting specified at the beginning of the Chapter **(see illustration)**.
**21** If removed, fit the detent cam locating pin into the selector drum **(see illustration 29.7a)**.

Install the cam, making sure the hole in the back of the cam fits over the locating pin **(see illustration)**. Apply a suitable non-permanent thread locking compound to the threads of the cam screw and tighten it to the torque setting specified at the beginning of the Chapter **(see illustration)**.
**22** Locate the pawl retainer plate around the pawls in the selector drum, then rotate it anti-clockwise to align its mounting holes with those in the crankcase **(see illustrations)**. Apply a suitable non-permanent thread locking compound to the threads of the screws and tighten them to the torque setting specified at the beginning of the Chapter.
**23** Rotate the selector drum so that the neutral switch plunger will be against the contact on the disc on the end of the drum **(see illustration)** – in this position the neutral detent in the detent cam is facing down and slightly back, roughly in the seven o'clock position. Fit the neutral stopper arm inner washer, then fit the spring, locating its straight end against the crankcase – in case you have muddled up the neutral and stopper arm assemblies, the spring for the neutral arm is painted white **(see illustrations)**. Fit the stopper arm, locating its lower edge in the bent end of the spring **(see illustration)**. Press the arm down against the spring, then locate the roller in the neutral detent in the cam and hold it there while you install the outer washer and nut **(see illustration)**. Tighten the nut to the specified torque setting.
**24** Build up the gear stopper arm assembly in the same way as the neutral arm. Note that in

**29.22a Fit the plate around the pawls as shown . . .**

**29.22b . . . then rotate it to the position shown and install the screws**

**29.23a Locate the neutral switch plunger against the contact on the disc (arrowed)**

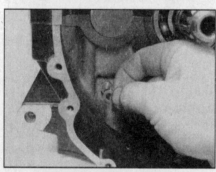

**29.23b Fit the inner washer . . .**

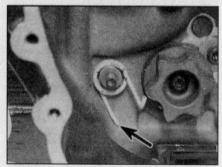

**29.23c . . . and the spring, locating the straight end against the crankcase (arrowed)**

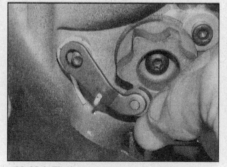

**29.23d Fit the stopper arm, locating it in the bent end of the spring**

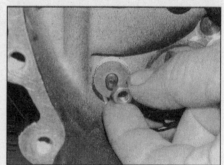

**29.23e Fit the outer washer and tighten the nut to the specified torque**

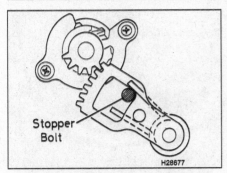

**29.26 Check that the pawl carrier teeth and the selector arm teeth remain engaged at the full extent of movement**

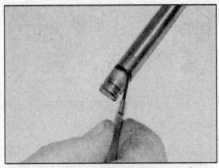

**29.27a Replace the O-ring with a new one if necessary**

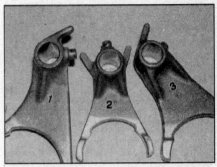

**29.27b The forks are numbered 1 to 3 from left to right, and the numbers must face the right-hand side of the engine**

the neutral position, the roller for the gear arm locates on the top of the flattened lobe. Check that the installed arms are located as shown **(see illustration 29.4)**.

**25** Install the oil pressure relief valve (see Section 19), and the oil pump and its middle gear assembly (see Section 30).

**26** Temporarily fit the gearchange lever onto the shaft end and rotate the selector drum fully in both directions. Check that when fully extended, the selector arm and pawl carrier teeth engage as shown **(see illustration)**. If the teeth do not engage correctly, check the pawl carrier and selector arm teeth for accurate alignment as described in Step 20.

**27** Check the condition of the O-ring on the selector fork shaft and replace it with a new one if it is damaged or deteriorated **(see illustration)**. The selector forks are marked 1, 2 and 3 from left to right to correspond with the cylinder numbers, and the numbers must face the right-hand side of the engine **(see illustration)**. Slide the selector fork shaft into its bore in the crankcase and engage the forks in turn on the shaft in the correct order and way round – locate the fork guide pins in the selector drum tracks **(see illustrations)**. Lock the shaft in position with the retaining plate, locating the cutout in the plate into the groove in the end of the shaft, and tighten the screw to the specified torque **(see illustration)**.

**28** Assemble the crankcase halves (see Section 21).

**29.27c Slide the shaft into the crankcase and through the No. 1 fork . . .**

**29.27e . . . and the No. 3 fork, and then into the other side of the crankcase. Locate the guide pin on each fork in its track**

**29.27d . . . then the No. 2 fork . . .**

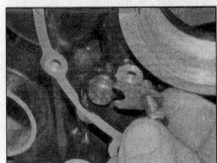

**29.27f Fit the retainer plate into the groove in the end of the shaft and secure it with the screw**

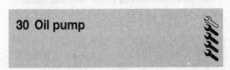

## 30 Oil pump

### Pressure check

**1** To check the oil pressure, a suitable gauge and adapter that screws into the oil pressure switch will be needed. Triumph do not list an adapter as a spare part, but it is worth checking with a dealer as to availability. Otherwise, remove the pressure switch (see Chapter 8), and take it to an accessory dealer to match it up – if you are buying a pressure gauge, it may well come with a range of adapters.

**2** Warm the engine up to normal operating

temperature then stop it. Remove the right-hand fairing side panel on Daytona and Sprint ST models (see Chapter 7).

**3** Remove the oil pressure switch (see Chapter 8) and screw the adapter in its place. Connect the gauge to the adapter.

**4** Start the engine and increase the engine speed to 5000 rpm whilst watching the gauge reading. The oil pressure should be similar to that given in the Specifications at the start of this Chapter.

**5** If the pressure is significantly lower than the standard, either the relief valve is stuck open, the oil pump is faulty, the oil pump pick-up strainer is blocked or there is other engine damage. Begin diagnosis by checking the oil pump pick-up strainer and relief valve (see Sections 18 and 19), then the oil pump. If

those items check out okay, chances are the bearing oil clearances are excessive and the engine needs to be overhauled.

**6** If the pressure is too high, the relief valve is stuck closed. To check it, see Section 19.

**7** Stop the engine and unscrew the gauge and adapter from the crankcase. Install the oil pressure switch (see Chapter 8).

**8** On Daytona and Sprint ST models install the fairing panel (see Chapter 7).

### Removal

**9** Remove the engine from the frame and separate the crankcase halves (see Sections 5 and 21).

**10** The oil pump is housed in the crankcase lower half. Remove the selector fork shaft and forks (see Section 29, Step 2).

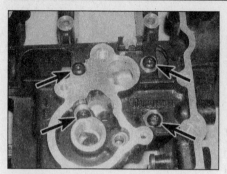

30.11a Undo the screws (arrowed) . . .

30.11b . . . and remove the oil pump

30.12a Counter-hold the gear and undo the screw . . .

11  Turn the oil pump so that the tab on the end of its shaft that locates into the water pump shaft is vertical. Remove the four screws from the underside of the crankcase and remove the oil pump from the top (see illustrations). Remove the pump locating dowels from the underside of the pump if they are loose (see illustration 30.21a).
12  If required, undo the screw and remove the washer securing the oil pump middle drive gear, then slide the gear off its shaft (see illustrations). Withdraw the middle driven gear from inside the crankcase (see illustration).

### Inspection

**Note:** *Individual internal parts are not available for the oil pump; if the checks described below indicate that the pump is worn, it must be renewed as a complete unit. The various drive gears are available individually.*
13  Counter-hold the oil pump driven gear, then undo the screw and remove the washer securing it on the pump shaft and slide it off.
14  Undo the four screws securing the pump cover and remove the cover. Remove the dowels for safekeeping if they are loose.
15  Measure the clearance between the inner rotor tip and the outer rotor tip with a feeler gauge (see illustration). Also measure the clearance between the outer rotor and the pump body (see illustration). Finally, lay a straight-edge across the rotors and pump body and measure the rotor end-float (gap between the rotors and pump body) with a feeler gauge (see illustration). If any of the results are outside the limits listed in this Chapter's Specifications, replace the pump with a new one.

16  Pick the inner and outer rotors out of the pump. Examine them for scoring and wear (see illustration).
17  Before reassembling the pump, make sure that all parts are clean. Have a supply of the correct grade of engine oil on hand to lubricate the rotors as they are installed. Install the outer rotor so that the side with the dot faces outwards.
18  If removed, fit the dowels into the pump, then locate the cover onto them and tighten the screws securely.
19  Inspect the oil pump drive gear, middle drive and driven gears, and the oil pump driven gear for signs of wear or damage, and replace them with new ones if necessary. Fit the oil pump driven gear onto the pump shaft, then fit the washer and tighten the screw to the torque setting specified at the beginning of the Chapter.

30.12b . . . then slide the gear off the shaft

30.12c Withdraw the middle gear from the crankcase

30.15a Measuring rotor tip clearance

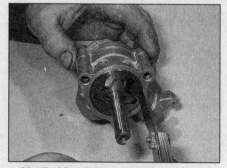

30.15b Measuring outer rotor-to-body clearance

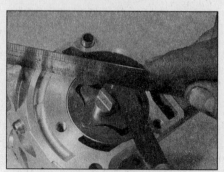

30.15c Measuring rotor end-float

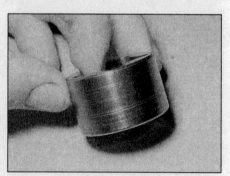

30.16 Look for scoring and wear, such as on this outer rotor

**30.20 The dished side of the washer faces out so the screw head sits in it**

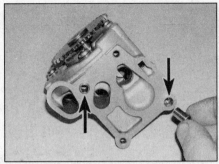

**30.21a Fit the dowels into the pump if removed (arrowed)**

**30.21b Apply a threadlock to the pump screws**

## Installation

**20** If removed, lubricate the middle gear shaft with clean oil and insert it in the crankcase **(see illustration 30.12c)**. Slide the drive gear onto the end of the shaft **(see illustration 30.12b)**, then fit the washer and tighten the screw to the torque setting specified at the beginning of the Chapter **(see illustration)**.

**21** Check that the pump driveshaft rotates freely. If removed, fit the two dowels in the underside of the pump **(see illustration)**. Install the oil pump in the crankcase, engaging the tab on the end of the shaft with the slot in the water pump shaft **(see illustration 30.11b)**. Apply a drop of non-permanent thread locking compound to the four retaining screws and tighten them to the specified torque setting **(see illustration)**.

**22** Install the selector forks and shaft (see Section 29, Step 27).

**23** Reassemble the crankcase halves (see Section 21).

---

### 31 Starter clutch and alternator driveshaft

**Note:** *While it is possible to remove the alternator drive shaft with the engine in the frame, it is a tricky operation that requires feeding a new shaft through the assembly at the same time as the old shaft is withdrawn. This is to prevent certain internal components*

*from falling out of position and to prevent others from dropping into the crankcase. It is possible for this to happen without you knowing it, and so it is not a procedure we advise. Besides which, it is very unlikely that you will ever to have to renew the drive shaft. To remove the starter clutch, which is a much more likely necessity, the engine must be removed and the crankcases split.*

### Starter clutch check

**1** If you suspect the starter clutch of being faulty, a simple check can be performed with the engine in the frame.

**2** Remove the starter motor (see Chapter 8).

**3** Using your finger inserted in the starter motor aperture, check that the starter idle/reduction gear turns freely anti-clockwise

**31.5 Remove the rubber dampers from the drive housing**

(as you look at it), and locks solid when turned clockwise. If not, remove the starter clutch for further investigation.

### Removal

**4** Remove the engine from the frame and separate the crankcase halves (see Sections 5 and 21). The alternator/starter clutch drive is housed in the upper crankcase half. Remove the transmission shafts (see Section 27).

**5** If not already done, remove the rubber dampers from the alternator drive housing **(see illustration)**.

**6** Counter-hold the drive shaft bolt (which also secures the alternator driven gear) and unscrew the drive housing nut **(see illustrations)**. Remove the nut, washer and the housing **(see illustrations)**. Withdraw the bolt and washer from the other side of the

**31.6a Counter-hold the bolt (arrowed) . . .**

**31.6b . . . and unscrew the nut (arrowed)**

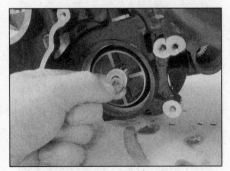

**31.6c Remove the nut and washer . . .**

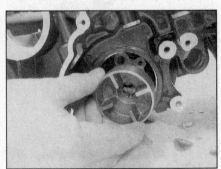

**31.6d . . . and slide the housing off the shaft**

31.6e Withdraw the bolt and remove the washer . . .

31.6f . . . and slide the gear off the shaft

31.7a Unscrew the bolts (arrowed) and remove the washers

31.7b Angle the shaft down and push it in to dislodge the bearing . . .

31.7c . . . then remove the bearing . . .

casing, the slide the driven gear off the shaft (see illustrations).

7 Unscrew the bolts and remove the ball bearing retaining washers from the alternator side (see illustration). Withdraw the driveshaft a little way from the right-hand side, then tilt it down and push it back in to displace the ball bearing in the alternator side (see illustration). Remove the bearing and the spacer, noting which way round it fits, then support the starter clutch and withdraw the shaft fully from the right-hand side (see illustrations). Lift the starter clutch out, then remove the splined spacer from the needle bearing if it didn't come out with the shaft (see illustration). Discard the drive shaft bolt and nut as Triumph specify new ones must be used.

8 If required, unscrew the bolt and remove the washer securing the starter idle/reduction gear shaft (see illustration). Support the idle/reduction gear and withdraw the shaft from the crankcase, using a small screwdriver inserted in it and levered against it to help draw it out, then remove the gear, noting which way round it fits (see illustration).

### Inspection

9 Hold the starter clutch body with the driven gear facing up, and check that the gear turns freely anti-clockwise (as you look at it), and locks solid when turned clockwise. If not, disassemble the starter clutch as follows for further investigation.

31.7d . . . and the spacer, noting which way round it fits

31.7e Withdraw the splined shaft and lift the starter clutch out

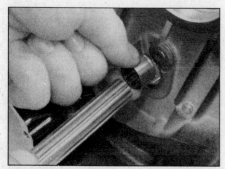

31.7f Remove the splined spacer from the needle bearing if it didn't come out with the shaft

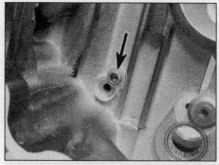

31.8a Unscrew the bolt (arrowed) and remove the washer . . .

31.8b . . . then withdraw the shaft and remove the idle/reduction gear

31.10a  Remove the circlip (arrowed) . . .

31.10b  . . . and the outer thrust washer

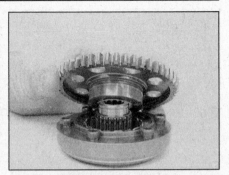

31.10c  Withdraw the driven gear from the hub as described . . .

**10** Remove the circlip securing the driven gear to the starter clutch and remove the outer thrustwasher **(see illustrations)**. Withdraw the gear from the clutch, rotating it anti-clockwise as you do so the sprags don't grip its hub **(see illustration)**. Withdraw the needle roller bearing and inner thrustwasher from the boss **(see illustrations)**.

**11** Examine the bearing surface of the starter driven gear hub and the condition of the sprags inside the clutch body. If the hub and sprags show signs of excessive wear or are damaged (and if problems have been experienced in starting the engine), replace the starter clutch assembly with a new one – the sprag assembly and driven gear are not available individually – the entire starter clutch must be renewed. Check that the six bolts securing the sprag assembly in the clutch body are all tight **(see illustration)**. If any are loose, remove them all, then apply a suitable

non-permanent thread locking compound to the threads and tighten them to the torque setting specified at the beginning of the Chapter **(see illustration)**.
**12** Fit the thrustwasher over the centre boss, followed by the needle roller bearing **(see illustrations 31.10e and d)**. Insert the driven gear hub in the starter clutch, rotating it anti-clockwise as you do to spread the sprags and allow it to enter **(see illustration 31.10c)**.
**13** Check the teeth of the various gears and renew the gears if any damage or excessive wear is found.
**14** Inspect the alternator cush drive rubbers. If compacted or deteriorated they should be renewed.
**15** Check the condition of the driveshaft splines and the corresponding splines on the spacer, the starter driven gear and alternator drive housing. Renew any components that are worn or damaged. Also check the

idle/reduction gear and its shaft for wear – fit the shaft into the gear and check for any freeplay between them.
**16** Check the condition of the ball and needle bearings for the driveshaft and replace them with new ones if necessary. Refer to *Tools and Workshop Tips* in the Reference Section for details of bearing checks. The needle bearing is secured by a screw and washer **(see illustration)**. Apply a non-permanent threadlock to the screw on installation and tighten it to the specified torque.

### Installation

**17** Lubricate the idle/reduction gear shaft with clean oil. Position the gear in the crankcase with its larger pinion against the side of the crankcase and slide the shaft fully into place from the outside of the crankcase **(see illustration)**. Apply a drop of non-permanent thread locking compound to the

31.10d  . . . then remove the needle bearing . . .

31.10e  . . . and the thrust washer

31.11a  Check that the bolts are tight

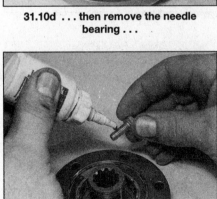

31.11b  If any are loose, remove them all and apply a thread-lock

31.16  Undo the screw and remove the washer to free the needle bearing

31.17  Position the gear in the crankcase and slide the shaft through

**31.19 Hold the other end of the shaft as you insert the bearing**

**31.20 Counter-hold the bolt and tighten the nut to the specified torque**

threads of the shaft retainer bolt, then install it with its washer and tighten it to the torque setting specified at the beginning of the Chapter **(see illustration 31.8a)**.

**18** Fit the splined spacer into the needle bearing **(see illustration 31.7f)**. Position the starter clutch in the crankcase as shown and locate it against the spacer to prevent it being pushed out, then slide the driveshaft through **(see illustration 31.7e)**.

**19** Fit the spacer onto the alternator end of the shaft with its notched side facing out **(see illustration 31.7d)**. Fit the ball bearing into its housing **(see illustration 31.7c)**, holding the other end of the shaft to prevent it being pushed out **(see illustration)**. Apply a suitable non-permanent threadlocking compound to the bearing retainer bolt threads, then install the bolts with their washers and tighten them to the specified torque **(see illustration 31.7a)**.

**20** Slide the alternator driven gear onto the right-hand end of the shaft **(see illustration 31.6f)**. Slide the alternator drive housing onto the left-hand end of the shaft **(see illustration 31.6d)**. Fit the washer onto the new long bolt, then slide the bolt through the driveshaft **(see illustration 31.6e)**. Fit the washer and a new nut onto the end of the bolt **(see illustration 31.6c)**, then counter-hold the bolt and tighten the nut to the specified torque setting **(see illustration)**.

**21** Install the transmission shafts (see Section 27) and reassemble the crankcase halves (see Section 21). When installing the alternator, do not forget to fit the rubber dampers **(see illustration 31.5)**.

## 32  Recommended running-in procedure

**1** Make sure the engine oil and coolant levels are correct (see *Daily (pre-ride) checks*).

**2** Make sure there is fuel in the tank.

**3** Start the engine and let it run at a moderately fast idle until it reaches normal operating temperature.

> ⚠ **Warning: If the oil pressure warning light doesn't go off, or it comes on while the engine is running, stop the engine immediately.**

**4** Check carefully that there are no oil leaks and make sure the transmission and controls, especially the brakes, function properly before road testing the machine.

**5** Upon completion of the road test, and after the engine has cooled down completely, recheck the valve clearances and check the engine oil and coolant levels (see *Daily (pre-ride) checks*).

>  **HAYNES HiNT** *If a lubrication failure is suspected, stop the engine immediately and try to find the cause. If an engine is run without oil, even for a short period of time, severe damage will occur.*

**6** Treat the machine gently for the first few miles to make sure oil has circulated throughout the engine and any new parts installed have started to seat.

**7** Even greater care is necessary if new pistons and liners or a new crankshaft has been installed. In the case of new pistons and liners, the bike will have to be run in as if when new. This means greater use of the transmission and a restraining hand on the throttle. There's no point in keeping to any set speed limit – it's the revs that are important. The main idea is to keep from labouring the engine and to gradually increase performance. It is best to vary engine and road speed as much as possible within the specified limits, so use the gearbox. These recommendations can be lessened to an extent when only a new crankshaft is installed. Experience is the best guide, since it's easy to tell when an engine is running freely. The table shows maximum engine speed limitations, which Triumph provide for new motorcycles, and this can be used as a guide. Full throttle should not be used until after the running-in period.

| Distance | Rev limit |
| --- | --- |
| Up to 100 miles (160 km) | 3500 rpm max |
| 100 to 300 miles (160 to 500 km) | 5000 rpm max |
| 300 to 600 miles (500 to 1000 km) | 6000 rpm max |
| 600 to 800 miles (1000 to 1300 km) | 7000 rpm max |
| 800 to 1000 miles (1300 to 1600 km) | 8000 rpm max |

# Chapter 2B
# Engine, clutch and transmission – 2002-on models

This chapter covers Daytona models from VIN 132513 to VIN 198874, Speed Triple models from VIN 141872 to VIN 210444, Sprint ST and RS models from VIN 139277 to VIN 208166 and Tiger 955 models

## Contents

## Degrees of difficulty

| | | | | |
|---|---|---|---|---|
| **Easy,** suitable for novice with little experience  | **Fairly easy,** suitable for beginner with some experience  | **Fairly difficult,** suitable for competent DIY mechanic 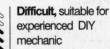 | **Difficult,** suitable for experienced DIY mechanic | **Very difficult,** suitable for expert DIY or professional |

## Specifications

### General

| | |
|---|---|
| Capacity ...................................................... | 955 cc |
| Bore ........................................................ | 79.0 mm |
| Stroke ...................................................... | 65.0 mm |
| Compression ratio | |
|    Daytona, Speed Triple and Sprint models ..................... | 11.2 to 1 |
|    Tiger models .............................................. | 11.6 to 1 |
| Cylinder numbering (from left side to right side of the bike) .......... | 1-2-3 |
| Firing order ................................................ | 1-2-3 |

## Camshafts, followers and camchain

| | |
|---|---|
| Camshaft runout | 0.05 mm max. |
| Camshaft end-float | |
|   Standard | 0.03 to 0.13 mm |
|   Maximum | 0.2 mm |
| Camshaft bearing oil clearance | |
|   Daytona, Speed Triple and Sprint models | 0.13 mm max. |
|   Tiger models | 0.12 mm max. |
| Camshaft journal diameter – all journals except outrigger | 22.93 to 22.96 mm |
| Camshaft journal diameter – outrigger journals (cam chain end) | 22.953 to 22.956 mm |
| Camshaft bearing bore diameter | 23.000 to 23.021 mm |
| Follower outside diameter | |
|   Daytona, Speed Triple and Sprint models | 28.476 to 28.490 mm |
|   Tiger models | 27.987 to 27.993 mm |
| Follower bore diameter | |
|   Daytona, Speed Triple and Sprint models | 28.515 to 28.535 mm |
|   Tiger models | 28.000 to 28.021 mm |
| Cam chain tensioner spring free length | 73.7 mm |
| Cam chain stretch limit | |
|   Daytona, Speed triple and Sprint models | 147.63 mm |
|   Tiger models | 442.90 mm |

## Valves, guides and springs

| | Standard | Service limit |
|---|---|---|
| Intake valve stem diameter | | |
|   Daytona, Speed Triple and Sprint models | 4.975 to 4.990 mm | 4.965 mm |
|   Tiger models | 5.475 to 5.490 mm | 5.470 mm |
| Exhaust valve stem diameter | | |
|   Daytona, Speed Triple and Sprint models | 4.955 to 4.990 mm | 4.945 mm |
|   Tiger models | 5.455 to 5.470 mm | 5.450 mm |
| Intake valve guide bore diameter | | |
|   Daytona, Speed Triple and Sprint models | 5.000 to 5.015 mm | 5.043 mm |
|   Tiger models | 5.500 to 5.515 mm | not available |
| Exhaust valve guide bore diameter | | |
|   Daytona, Speed Triple and Sprint models | 5.000 to 5.035 mm | 5.063 mm |
|   Tiger models | 5.500 to 5.515 mm | not available |
| Valve stem-to-guide clearance | | |
|   Daytona, Speed Triple and Sprint models | | |
|     Intake | 0.01 to 0.04 mm | |
|     Exhaust | 0.03 to 0.06 mm | |
|   Tiger models | Standard | Service limit |
|     Intake | 0.01 to 0.04 mm | 0.07 mm |
|     Exhaust | 0.03 to 0.06 mm | 0.09 mm |
| Valve face width | | |
|   Daytona, Speed Triple and Sprint models | 1.5 to 1.9 mm | |
|   Tiger models | 1.8 to 2.5 mm | |
| Intake valve seat width | Standard | Service limit |
|   Daytona, Speed Triple, Sprint and Tiger models | 0.9 to 1.1 mm | 1.5 mm |
|   Tiger models | 0.9 to 1.1 mm | 1.5 mm |
| Exhaust valve seat width | | |
|   Daytona, Speed Triple and Sprint models | 1.1 to 1.3 mm | 1.7 mm |
|   Tiger models | 0.9 to 1.1 mm | 1.5 mm |
| Valve spring length | | |
|   Daytona, Speed Triple and Sprint models | | |
|     Intake valve | | |
|       Inner spring | not less than 24.5 mm with 19 kg load | |
|       Outer spring | not less than 26.0 mm with 39 kg load | |
|     Exhaust valve | not less than 25.0 mm with 50 kg load | |
|   Tiger models (intake and exhaust) | | |
|     Inner spring | not less than 24.0 mm with 15 kg load | |
|     Outer spring | not less than 26.5 mm with 41 kg load | |

## Cylinder liners

| | Standard | Service limit |
|---|---|---|
| Cylinder liner ID | | |
|   Daytona models | 78.985 to 79.003 mm | 79.053 mm |
|   Speed Triple, Sprint and Tiger models | 79.030 to 79.050 mm | 79.10 mm |

## Lubrication system

| | Standard | Service limit |
|---|---|---|
| Oil pressure @ 5000 rpm | 40 psi (2.76 Bar) at 80°C oil temp. | |
| Oil pump rotor tip-to-outer rotor clearance | 0.15 mm | 0.20 mm |
| Oil pump outer rotor-to-body clearance | 0.15 to 0.22 mm | 0.35 mm |
| Oil pump rotor end-float | 0.02 to 0.07 mm | 0.10 mm |

## Pistons

Piston OD (measured 5 mm up from skirt, at 90° to piston pin axis)

| | Standard | Service limit |
|---|---|---|
| Daytona models | | |
| Cylinders 1, 2 and 3 | 78.970 to 78.980 mm | 78.930 mm |
| Speed Triple models | | |
| Cylinders 1 and 3 | 78.960 to 78.975 mm | 78.920 mm |
| Cylinder 2 | 78.960 to 78.970 mm | 78.920 mm |
| Sprint models | | |
| Cylinders 1, 2 and 3 | 78.960 to 78.970 mm | 78.920 mm |
| Tiger models | | |
| Cylinders 1 and 3 | 78.960 to 78.980 mm | 78.870 mm |
| Cylinder 2 | 78.960 to 78.970 mm | 78.860 mm |
| Piston pin bore diameter in piston | | |
| Daytona models | 16.993 to 17.001 mm | 17.029 mm |
| Speed Triple, Sprint and Tiger models | 19.002 to 19.008 mm | 19.036 mm |
| Piston pin diameter | | |
| Daytona models | 16.984 to 16.989 mm | 16.974 mm |
| Speed Triple, Sprint and Tiger models | 18.995 to 19.000 mm | 18.985 mm |
| Connecting rod small-end diameter | | |
| Daytona models | 17.005 to 17.018 mm | 17.028 mm |
| Speed Triple, Sprint and Tiger models | 19.016 to 19.034 mm | 19.050 mm |

## Piston rings

| | Standard | Service limit |
|---|---|---|
| Ring-to-groove clearance (top and second rings) | 0.02 to 0.06 mm | 0.075 mm |
| End gap (installed) | | |
| Daytona models | | |
| Top ring | 0.15 to 0.30 mm | 0.42 mm |
| Second ring | 0.30 to 0.45 mm | 0.60 mm |
| Oil control ring side rails | 0.20 to 0.70 mm | 0.90 mm |
| Speed Triple, Sprint and Tiger models | | |
| Top ring | 0.28 to 0.43 mm | 0.55 mm |
| Second ring | 0.43 to 0.58 mm | 0.73 mm |
| Oil control ring side rails | 0.33 to 0.83 mm | 1.03 mm |

## Connecting rods and bearings

| | Standard | Service limit |
|---|---|---|
| Connecting rod side clearance | 0.15 to 0.30 mm | 0.50 mm |
| Connecting rod big-end bearing oil clearance | 0.036 to 0.066 mm | 0.10 mm |
| Connecting rod big-end journal diameter | | |
| Daytona models | 34.984 to 35.000 mm | 34.960 mm |
| Speed Triple and Sprint models | 40.946 to 40.960 mm | 40.922 mm |
| Tiger models | 40.946 to 40.960 mm | 40.932 mm |

## Crankshaft and main bearings

| | Standard | Service limit |
|---|---|---|
| Main bearing oil clearance | | |
| Daytona, Speed Triple and Sprint models | 0.019 to 0.044 mm | 0.07 mm |
| Tiger models | 0.019 to 0.044 mm | 0.08 mm |
| Main bearing journal diameter | 37.960 to 37.976 mm | 37.936 mm |
| Crankshaft end-float | 0.05 to 0.20 mm | 0.40 mm |

## Clutch

Daytona, Speed Triple and Sprint models

Friction plates

Quantity ............................................... 10

| | Standard | Service limit |
|---|---|---|
| Thickness (inner and outer plate) | 3.80 mm | 3.60 mm |
| Thickness (all other plates) | 3.30 mm | 3.10 mm |

Plain plates

Quantity ............................................... 9

Warpage (service limit) ............................... 0.20 mm

Tiger models

Friction plates

Quantity ............................................... 9

Thickness

Standard ............................................ 3.80 to 4.60 mm

Service limit ........................................ 3.60 mm

Plain plates

Quantity ............................................... 8

Warpage (service limit) ............................... 0.20 mm

Clutch cable freeplay .................................... see Chapter 1

## Transmission

| | |
|---|---|
| Primary reduction ratio | 1.75 to 1 (105/60T) |
| Gear ratios (No. of teeth) | |
| First gear | 2.733 to 1 (41/15T) |
| Second gear | 1.947 to 1 (37/19T) |
| Third gear | 1.545 to 1 (34/22T) |
| Fourth gear | 1.291 to 1 (31/24T) |
| Fifth gear | 1.154 to 1 (30/26T) |
| Sixth gear | 1.074 to 1 (29/27T) |
| Final reduction ratio | |
| Daytona and Speed Triple models | |
| with single-sided swingarm | 2.333 to 1 (42/18T) |
| with double-sided swingarm | 2.316 to 1 (44/19T) |
| Sprint models | 2.263 to 1 (43/19T) |
| Tiger | 2.555 to 1 (46/18T) |
| Selector fork end width | |
| Standard | 5.8 to 5.9 mm |
| Service limit | 5.7 mm |
| Selector fork groove width in gears | |
| Standard | 6.0 to 6.1 mm |
| Service limit | 6.25 mm |
| Selector fork-to-groove clearance | 0.55 mm maximum |

## Torque settings

| | |
|---|---|
| Alternator rotor bolt | 105 Nm |
| Balancer shaft end cap | |
| Daytona, Speed Triple and Sprint models | 60 Nm |
| Tiger models | 40 Nm |
| Cam chain support bolt | 10 Nm |
| Cam chain tensioner end bolt | 23 Nm |
| Cam chain tensioner mounting bolts | 9 Nm |
| Cam chain tensioner blade pivot bolt | 18 Nm |
| Cam chain upper guide screws | 10 Nm |
| Camshaft cap and holder bolts | 10 Nm |
| Camshaft sprocket bolts | 15 Nm |
| Clutch centre nut | 105 Nm |
| Clutch pressure plate bolts | 10 Nm |
| Connecting rod cap nuts | |
| Daytona, Speed Triple and Sprint models | see Section 25 |
| Tiger models | 14 Nm + 120° (see text) |
| Crankcase 6 mm bolts (see text) | 12 Nm |
| Crankcase 8 mm bolts (see text) | 28 Nm |
| Cylinder head bolts | |
| Stage 1 | 20 Nm |
| Stage 2 | 27 Nm |
| Stage 3 | Angle-tighten 90° |
| Cylinder head-to-cylinder block screws | |
| Daytona, Speed Triple and Sprint models | 10 Nm |
| Tiger models | 12 Nm |
| Engine mounting bolts | |
| Daytona and Speed Triple models | |
| Engine mounting bracket-to-cylinder head bolts | 30 Nm |
| All other mounting bolts | 80 Nm |
| Swingarm spindle adjuster | 15 Nm |
| Swingarm spindle adjuster lock ring | 30 Nm |
| Swingarm pivot bolts (single-sided swingarm) | 60 Nm |
| Swingarm pivot bolt nut (twin-sided swingarm) | 110 Nm |
| Suspension linkage arm-to-frame bolt | 95 Nm |
| Sprint models | |
| Mounting bolts | 80 Nm |
| Adjuster bolts | 3 Nm |
| Adjuster bolt locknuts | 55 Nm |
| Swingarm spindle adjuster | 15 Nm |
| Swingarm spindle adjuster lock ring | 30 Nm |
| Swingarm pivot bolts (single-sided swingarm) | 60 Nm |
| Swingarm pivot bolt nut (twin-sided swingarm) | 110 Nm |
| Suspension linkage-to-frame bolt | 48 Nm |
| Tiger models | |
| Engine mounting bracket-to-cylinder head bolts | 30 Nm |
| All other mounting bolts | 80 Nm |
| Swingarm pivot bolt | 85 Nm |

## Torque settings (continued)

| | |
|---|---|
| Engine unit cover bolts | 9 Nm |
| External oil hose banjo bolts to cylinder head | 25 Nm |
| Gearchange mechanism centralising spring locating pin | 28 Nm |
| Internal oil pipe banjo bolts | 8 Nm |
| Oil cooler hose banjo bolts | 25 Nm |
| Oil cooler hose flange bolts (Daytona models) | 10 Nm |
| Oil pressure relief valve | 15 Nm |
| Oil pump driven gear bolt | 15 Nm |
| Oil pump mounting bolts | |
|     Daytona, Speed Triple and Sprint models | 14 Nm |
|     Tiger models | 12 Nm |
| Selector drum bearing retainer bolt | 12 Nm |
| Selector drum detent cam bolt | 12 Nm |
| Selector fork shaft retainer plate bolt | 12 Nm |
| Starter clutch bolt | 54 Nm |
| Stopper arm pivot bolt | 12 Nm |
| Sump bolts | 12 Nm |
| Timing inspection cap | 18 Nm |
| Transmission input shaft bearing retainer plate screws | 12 Nm |
| Valve cover bolts | 10 Nm |

## 1 General information

The engine/transmission is a water-cooled, in-line three-cylinder design, fitted across the frame. The twelve valves are operated by double overhead camshafts, chain driven off the right-hand end of the crankshaft. The pistons run in removable liners, surrounded by a water jacket. A single balancer shaft is driven directly off a gear on the right-hand end of the crankshaft.

The engine/transmission unit is constructed in aluminium alloy with the crankcase divided horizontally. The crankcase incorporates a wet sump, pressure fed lubrication system. An external oil feed pipe supplies oil to the cylinder head and cam components. The oil pump is chain driven off the back of the clutch housing and in turn drives the water pump.

The clutch is of the wet, multi-plate type and is gear driven off the crankshaft. The alternator is mounted on the left-hand end of the crankshaft.

The transmission is of the six-speed constant mesh type. Final drive to the rear wheel is by chain and sprockets.

Many of the bolts used on Triumph motorcycles are of the Torx type. Unless you are already equipped with a good range of Torx bits, you are advised to purchase a set before attempting work on the engine. Make sure you get bits that can be used in conjunction with a socket set so that a torque wrench can be applied – a Torx key set will not be adequate on its own, though will be a useful addition to the bits.

## 2 Operations possible with the engine in the frame

The components and assemblies listed below can be removed without having to remove the engine/transmission assembly from the frame. If however, a number of areas require attention at the same time, removal of the engine is recommended.

*Valve cover*
*Cam chain tensioner*
*Camshafts and followers*
*Cam chain and tensioner blade*
*Cylinder head (Tiger models only)*
*Cylinder liners and pistons (Tiger models only)*
*Starter motor*
*Starter clutch*
*Alternator*
*Water pump*
*Clutch*
*Gearchange detent cam and stopper arms*
*Oil pump*
*Oil cooler*
*Sump and oil strainer*
*Alternator*

## 3 Operations requiring engine removal

It is necessary to remove the engine/transmission assembly from the frame and separate the crankcase halves to gain access to the following components.

*Cylinder head (Daytona, Speed Triple and Sprint models)*
*Cylinder liners and pistons (Daytona, Speed Triple and Sprint models)*
*Connecting rod assemblies and bearings*
*Crankshaft and bearings*
*Balancer shaft*
*Transmission shafts*
*Gearchange selector drum and forks*
*Oil pressure relief valve*

## 4 Major engine repair – general note

1 It is not always easy to determine when or if an engine should be completely overhauled, as a number of factors must be considered.

2 High mileage is not necessarily an indication that an overhaul is needed, while low mileage, on the other hand, does not preclude the need for an overhaul. Frequency of servicing is probably the single most important consideration. An engine that has regular and frequent oil and filter changes, as well as other required maintenance, will most likely give many miles of reliable service. Conversely, a neglected engine, or one which has not been run in properly, may require an overhaul very early in its life.

3 Exhaust smoke and excessive oil consumption are both indications that piston rings and/or valve guides are in need of attention, although make sure that the fault is not due to oil leakage.

4 If the engine is making obvious knocking or rumbling noises, the connecting rod and/or main bearings are probably at fault.

**5** Loss of power, rough running, excessive valve train noise and high fuel consumption rates may also point to the need for an overhaul, especially if they are all present at the same time. If a complete tune-up does not remedy the situation, major mechanical work is the only solution.

**6** An engine overhaul generally involves restoring the internal parts to the specifications of a new engine. The piston rings and main and connecting rod bearings are usually renewed during a major overhaul. Generally the valve seats are reground, since they are usually in less than perfect condition at this point. The end result should be a like new engine that will give as many trouble-free miles as the original.

**7** Before beginning the engine overhaul, read through the related procedures to familiarise yourself with the scope and requirements of the job. Overhauling an engine is not all that difficult, but it is time consuming. Plan on the motorcycle being tied up for a minimum of two weeks. Check on the availability of parts and make sure that any necessary special tools, equipment and supplies are obtained in advance.

**8** Most work can be done with typical workshop hand tools, although a number of precision measuring tools are required for inspecting parts to determine if they must be renewed. Often a dealer will handle the inspection of parts and offer advice concerning reconditioning and renewal. As a general rule, time is the primary cost of an overhaul so it does not pay to install worn or substandard parts.

**9** As a final note, to ensure maximum life and minimum trouble from a rebuilt engine, everything must be assembled with care in a spotlessly clean environment.

| 5 | Engine removal and installation |
|---|---|

*Caution: The engine is very heavy. Engine removal and installation should be carried out with the aid of at least one assistant. Personal injury or damage could occur if the engine falls or is dropped. An hydraulic or mechanical floor jack should be used to support and lower or raise the engine if possible.*

### Removal

**1** Position the bike on its centrestand (ST model) or an auxiliary stand so that it is supported in an upright position, making sure it is secure. Note that the swingarm pivot must be slackened before removing the engine to allow expansion of the frame, so if you have a stand that locates in the pivot points, slacken the pivot before fitting the stand (see Step 26, 27 or 28 according to model). It is a good idea to hold the front brake on by using a cable-tie around the handlebar and brake lever. Work can be made easier by raising the machine to a suitable height on an hydraulic ramp.

**2** If the engine is dirty, particularly around its mountings, wash it thoroughly before starting

any major dismantling work. This will make work much easier and rule out the possibility of caked-on lumps of dirt falling into some vital component.

**3** Remove the seat (see Chapter 7), then remove the battery (see Chapter 8).

**4** Remove the fairing, fairing side panels and belly-pan, according to your model (see Chapter 7). Where a panel bolts to a mounting bracket on the engine, it is advisable to remove the bracket to prevent it becoming bent or damaged.

**5** Remove the fuel tank and the airbox (see Chapter 4).

**6** Drain the engine oil (see Chapter 1) and remove the oil cooler (see Section 21).

**7** Drain the coolant (see Chapter 1).

**8** On Tiger models, release the coolant sensor retaining clip and remove the sensor from the thermostat housing **(see illustration)**.

**9** Disconnect the horn wiring connector and remove the radiator and all the coolant hoses, noting their routing (see Chapter 3). It is advisable to tag the end of each hose using masking tape, then write the location of the hose on the tape.

**10** Remove the exhaust system (Chapter 4).

**11** Detach the clutch cable from the release lever on the clutch cover (see Section 18). On Daytona, Speed Triple and Sprint models, remove the air deflector shield, where fitted.

**12** Note the position of the punch mark or make an alignment mark across the gearchange shaft end and the gearchange linkage arm or gearchange lever (according to model) as an aid to installation, then unscrew the pinch bolt and slide the arm or lever off the shaft **(see illustration)**.

**13** Remove the front sprocket (see Chapter 5).

**14** On Tiger models, remove the brake pedal (see Chapter 5). Unscrew the bolts securing the footrest mounting plate, then detach it from the frame and support or tie it so that no strain is placed on the brake hose **(see illustration)**. Also unscrew the bolts securing the left-hand footrest bracket and remove it **(see illustration)**.

**15** Unclip the throttle position sensor wiring from the fuel rail and disconnect the connector **(see illustration)**. Release the

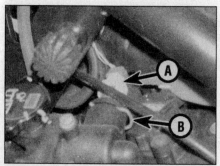

**5.8 Coolant temperature sensor (A) and retaining clip (B) – Tiger models**

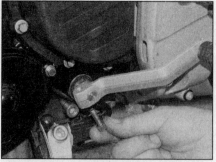

**5.12 Remove the gearchange lever as described**

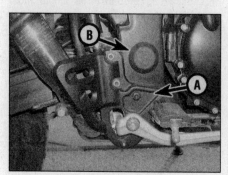

**5.14a Right-hand footrest bracket (A) and swingarm pivot cap (B)**

**5.14b Left-hand footrest bracket (arrowed)**

**5.15a Disconnect the throttle position sensor wiring connector**

**5.15b  Release the throttle body clamps (arrowed)**

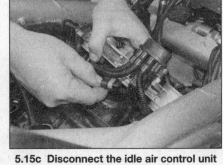

**5.15c  Disconnect the idle air control unit wiring connector . . .**

**5.15d  . . . and pull the hoses off their unions on the cylinder head**

clamps securing the throttle bodies and displace them **(see illustration)**. Disconnect the idle air control unit wiring connector and pull the vacuum hoses off the unions on the back of the cylinder head **(see illustrations)**. It is not necessary to detach the throttle cable(s) from the assembly. Plug the intake manifold joints with clean rags to prevent anything dropping inside.

**16** On Daytona, Speed Triple and Sprint models, unclip the wiring loom secured to the fuel rail and disconnect the individual injector wiring connectors **(see illustrations)**. Remove the bolts securing the fuel rail to its bracket, then ease the fuel rail and injectors away from the cylinder head and lift off the assembly.

**17** On Daytona, Speed Triple and Sprint models, either disconnect the coolant temperature sensor wiring connector from the sensor on the left-hand side of the engine, or trace the wiring to the connector and disconnect it **(see illustration)**.

**18** Trace the wiring from the top of the alternator cover and disconnect it at the connector **(see illustration)**.

**19** Trace the wiring from the sidestand switch and disconnect it at the wiring connector **(see illustration)**. If required, displace the water pump to access the sidestand mounting bolts (see Chapter 3). Remove the sidestand and its bracket (see Chapter 5).

**20** If required, disconnect the fuel injector, oil pressure and neutral switch sub loom wiring connector **(see illustration)**.

**5.16a  Release the wiring loom . . .**

**5.16b  . . . and disconnect the injector wiring connectors**

**5.17  Disconnect the coolant temperature sensor wiring connector**

**5.18  Disconnect the alternator wiring connector**

**21** If required, remove the starter motor (see Chapter 8). If it is not being removed, pull back the rubber boot on the terminal, them

unscrew the nut and detach the lead **(see illustration)**.

**22** Undo the bolt securing the earth lead to

**5.19  Disconnect the sidestand switch wiring connector**

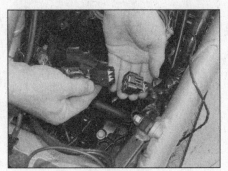

**5.20  Disconnect the sub-loom wiring connector**

**5.21  Pull back the rubber boot and unscrew the nut (arrowed) securing the lead**

5.22 Disconnect the earth lead (arrowed) from the crankcase

5.23 Location of the crankshaft position sensor

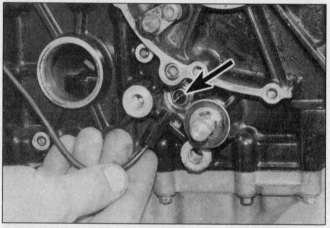

5.24a Detach the wire from the neutral switch (arrowed) . . .

5.24b . . . and the oil pressure switch (arrowed)

the top of the crankcase and disconnect it **(see illustration)**.

**23** Trace the wiring from the crankshaft position sensor on the left-hand side of the crankcase and disconnect it at the connector **(see illustration)**.

**24** If required, detach the wire from the neutral switch and the oil pressure switch **(see illustrations)**.

**25** Disconnect the ignition coil/spark plug cap wiring connectors **(see illustration)**.

**26** On Daytona, Speed Triple and Sprint models with single-sided swingarms, counter-hold the swingarm pivot bolt on the left-hand side and slacken the pivot bolt nut on the right-hand side. Also slacken the bolt that secures the suspension linkage assembly to the frame **(see illustration)**.

**27** On Daytona and Sprint RS models with double-sided swingarms, slacken the swingarm pivot nut on the left-hand side. Also slacken the bolt that secures the suspension linkage assembly to the frame **(see illustration)**.

**28** On Tiger models, remove the blanking cap from each end of the swingarm pivot. Counter-hold the left-hand end of the

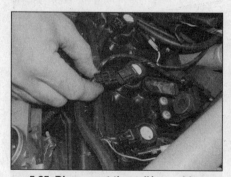

5.25 Disconnect the coil/cap wiring connectors

5.26 Slacken the suspension linkage-to-frame bolt (arrowed) – single-sided swingarm

5.27 Slacken the suspension linkage-to-frame bolt (arrowed) – double-sided swingarm

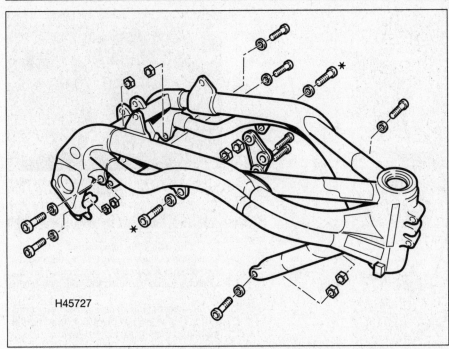

**5.31 Engine mounting details – Daytona and Speed Triple models**

*\* Speed triple only*

pivot and slacken the bolt on the right-hand end.

**29** At this point, position an hydraulic jack under the engine with a block of wood between the jack head and sump. Make sure the jack is centrally positioned so the engine will not topple in any direction when the last mounting bolt is removed. Take the weight of the engine on the jack. Unless you are using a ramp with a front wheel clamp, also place a block of wood under the rear wheel to prevent the bike tilting back when the engine is removed. Check that all wiring, cables and hoses are disconnected and clear of the engine.

**30** When removing the engine mounting bolts, retrieve all nuts, washers and spacers from the mountings and slip them back on the bolts in their correct order for safekeeping, noting carefully where each fits **(see illustrations 5.31, 5.32 and 5.33).**

**31** On Daytona and Speed Triple models, undo the bolts securing the frame-to-cylinder head mounting bracket on the left-hand side and remove the bracket, noting how it fits **(see illustration).** Have an assistant steady the engine and remove the remaining mounting bolts, then lower the engine on the jack and slip the drive chain off the output shaft. Manoeuvre the engine clear of the frame, then lift it off the jack and onto the

work surface. Slacken the swingarm spindle adjuster locknut on the right-hand side; either the Triumph special tool (Part No. T3880295) or a suitable peg spanner can be used. Slacken the swingarm spindle adjuster on the right-hand side; again either the Triumph special tool (Part No. T3880290) or a suitable peg spanner can be used.

**32** On Sprint models, remove the engine mounting adjuster locknuts on the right-hand side **(see illustration);** either the Triumph special tool (Part No. T3880088) or a suitable peg spanner can be used (see ***Tool Tip***). Have an assistant steady the engine and remove the mounting bolts, then lower the engine on the jack and slip the drive chain off the output shaft. Manoeuvre the engine clear of the frame, then lift it off the jack and onto the work surface. Slacken the engine mounting adjusters. Slacken the swingarm spindle adjuster locknut on the right-hand side using either the Triumph special tool (Part No. T3880295) or a suitable peg spanner. Slacken the swingarm spindle adjuster on the right-hand side, again using the Triumph special tool (Part No. T3880290) or a suitable peg spanner.

**33** On Tiger models, undo the bolts securing the frame-to-cylinder head mounting bracket on the left-hand side and remove the bracket, noting how it fits **(see illustration overleaf).** Now remove the lower rear engine mounting bolts, then remove all the other mounting bolts except the front bolts. Slacken the front mounting bolts. Have an assistant steady the engine, then lower the engine on the jack allowing it to pivot around the front mounting bolts. Slip the drive chain off the output shaft and retrieve the chain rubbing block, noting how it fits. Remove the front mounting bolts and manoeuvre the engine clear of the frame, then lift it off the jack and onto the work surface.

 *Warning: The engine is heavy and may cause injury if it falls.*

*A peg spanner can be made by cutting an old socket as shown – measure the width and depth of the slots in the locknut to determine the size of the castellations on the socket. If an old socket is not available, castellations can be welded onto a suitable nut.*

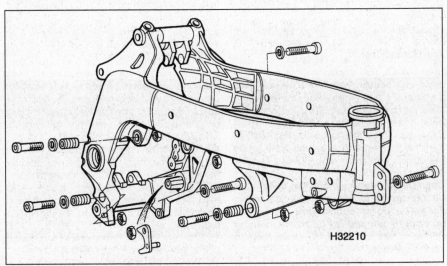

**5.32 Engine mounting details – Sprint models**

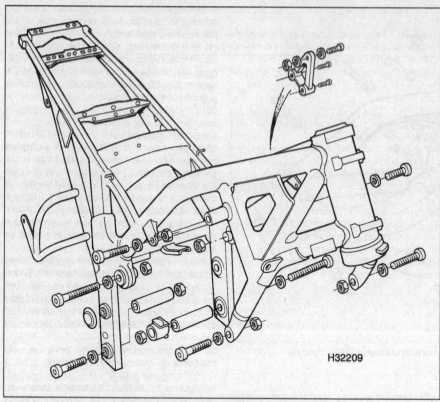

5.33 Engine mounting details – Tiger models

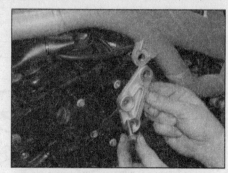

5.36 Install the cylinder head-to-frame bracket

## Installation

### Daytona and Speed Triple models

**34** With the aid of an assistant place the engine on top of the jack and block of wood and carefully raise it into position in the frame, slipping the drive chain around the output shaft as you do so. Manoeuvre the engine as required so that all mounting holes align. Make sure no wires, cables or hoses become trapped between the engine and the frame.

**35** Fit the washers on the mounting bolts then install them in the frame, along with any spacers previously fitted. **Note:** *Triumph specify that spacers must be fitted on the right-hand mounting bolts to eliminate gaps between the frame and the engine unit (see Step 39). On the machine photographed, a additional spacer was fitted between the frame and the engine unit on the left-hand lower rear mounting bolt.* Fit the mounting bolt nuts, where appropriate, and tighten them finger-tight **(see illustration 5.31)**. Remove the jack from under the engine. Now follow the correct tightening procedure as detailed below.

*Caution: The engine mounting bolts must be tightened in the correct sequence. Failure to do so could leave the engine incorrectly aligned in the frame, placing undue stress on it, which could lead to severe damage.*

**36** Fit the frame-to-cylinder head bracket on the left-hand side and tighten the two bracket-to-cylinder head bolts to the torque setting specified at the beginning of the Chapter **(see illustration)**. Note: *Do not tighten the bracket-to-frame bolt at this stage (see Step 42).*

**37** Tighten the left-hand front mounting bolt to the specified torque setting.

**38** Tighten the left-hand upper rear mounting bolt, then tighten the left-hand lower rear mounting bolt, to the specified torque setting.

**39** Check for gaps between the frame and the engine unit at all right-hand mounting locations – if spacers were fitted originally they should eliminate any gaps. However, if necessary, spacers are available in 0.5, 1.0, 1.5 and 2.0 mm thicknesses from Triumph dealers. Spacers must be fitted to avoid straining the frame when the mounting bolts are tightened. **Note:** *If a spacer is needed for the right-hand lower rear engine mounting bolt an equivalent sized spacer must be fitted on the bolt that secures the suspension linkage to the frame.*

**40** Tighten the right-hand front mounting bolt, then tighten the right-hand middle mounting bolt to the specified torque setting.

**41** Tighten the right-hand upper rear mounting bolt, then tighten the right-hand lower rear mounting bolt to the specified torque setting.

**42** Tighten the left-hand bracket-to frame bolt to the specified torque setting.

**43** Tighten the swingarm spindle adjuster, then tighten the adjuster locknut to the specified torque settings using the Triumph tool or suitable peg spanner.

**44** On models with single-sided swingarms, tighten the swingarm pivot bolts, then tighten the bolt that secures the suspension linkage assembly to the frame, to the specified torque settings.

**45** On models with double-sided swingarms, tighten the swingarm pivot nut, then tighten the bolt that secures the suspension linkage assembly to the frame, to the specified torque settings.

**46** The remainder of the installation procedure is a direct reversal of the removal sequence, noting the following points.

● Tighten all nuts and bolts to the specified torque settings (where given).

● Align the previously made mark on the gearchange linkage arm or lever with that on the gearchange shaft end.

● Make sure all wires, cables and hoses are correctly routed and connected, and secured by any clips or ties.

● Adjust the drive chain as described in Chapter 1.

● Use new gaskets on the exhaust pipe connections, and new O-rings and sealing washers on the coolant and oil connections, as appropriate.

● Refill the engine with oil and coolant (see Chapter 1).

● Adjust the throttle and clutch cable freeplay (see Chapter 1).

● Adjust the drive chain slack (see Chapter 1).

● Start the engine and check that there are no oil or coolant leaks before installing the body panels.

### Sprint models

**47** Thread the engine mounting adjusters out of the frame until they no longer protrude on the inside.

**48** With the aid of an assistant place the engine on top of the jack and block of wood and carefully raise it into position in the frame, slipping the drive chain around the output shaft as you do. Manoeuvre the engine as required so that all mounting holes align. Make sure no wires, cables or hoses become trapped between the engine and the frame. Now follow the correct procedure to install and tighten the mounting bolts as detailed below **(see illustration 5.32)**.

**Caution: The engine mounting bolts must be tightened in the correct sequence. Failure to do so could leave the engine incorrectly aligned in the frame, placing undue stress on it, which could lead to severe damage.**

49 Fit the washers on the left-hand mounting bolts then install them in the frame, together with any spacers previously fitted, then fit the mounting bolt nuts. Tighten the left-hand upper rear mounting bolt to the torque setting specified at the beginning of the Chapter, then tighten the lower rear and then the front mounting bolt to the specified torque setting.

50 Tighten the three engine mounting adjusters on the right-hand side to the specified torque setting using the Triumph tool or suitable peg spanner.

51 Install the right-hand mounting bolts and tighten them to the specified torque setting, making sure that the adjuster bolts do not turn with them – by making a couple of reference marks between the adjuster bolt and the frame you will be able to tell whether the adjuster bolts have moved.

52 Install the engine mounting adjuster locknuts and tighten them to the specified torque setting using the Triumph tool or suitable peg spanner.

53 Tighten the swingarm spindle adjuster, then tighten the adjuster locknut to the specified torque settings using the Triumph tool or suitable peg spanner.

54 On ST and RS models with single-sided swingarms, tighten the swingarm pivot bolts, then tighten the bolt that secures the suspension linkage assembly to the frame, to the specified torque settings.

55 On RS models with double-sided swingarms, tighten the swingarm pivot nut, then tighten the bolt that secures the suspension linkage assembly to the frame, to the specified torque settings.

56 Lower the jack and remove it.

57 The remainder of the installation procedure is a direct reversal of the removal sequence, noting the points in Step 46.

### Tiger models

58 With the aid of an assistant place the engine on top of the jack and block of wood and carefully raise it into position in the frame, slipping the drive chain around the output shaft as you do. When the front mounting bolt holes align, fit the washers on the front bolts and install them and tighten the nuts finger-tight. Continue to raise the engine until all the mounting holes align. Make sure no wires, cables or hoses become trapped between the engine and the frame. Do not forget to fit the chain rubbing block.

59 Fit the washers on the remaining mounting bolts then install them in the frame, along with any spacers previously fitted, then fit the mounting bolt nuts and tighten them finger-tight **(see illustration 5.33)**. Remove the jack from under the engine. Now follow

the correct tightening procedure as detailed below.

**Caution: The engine mounting bolts must be tightened in the correct sequence. Failure to do so could leave the engine incorrectly aligned in the frame, placing undue stress on it, which could lead to severe damage.**

60 Fit the frame-to-cylinder head bracket on the left-hand side and tighten the two bracket-to-cylinder head bolts to the torque setting specified at the beginning of the Chapter. **Note:** Do not tighten the bracket-to-frame bolt at this stage (see Step 62).

61 Tighten the left-hand front mounting bolt, then tighten the right-hand front mounting bolt to the specified torque setting.

62 Tighten the left-hand bracket-to frame bolt to the specified torque setting.

63 Tighten the left-hand upper rear and lower rear mounting bolts to the specified torque setting.

64 Tighten the right-hand middle mounting bolt, then tighten the right-hand upper rear mounting bolt and the right-hand lower rear mounting bolt to the specified torque setting.

65 Tighten the swingarm pivot bolt to the specified torque setting, then fit the blanking caps.

66 The remainder of the installation procedure is a direct reversal of the removal sequence, noting the points in Step 46.

---

## 6  Engine overhaul –
general information

### Disassembly

1 Before disassembling the engine, thoroughly clean and degrease clean the external surfaces. This will prevent contamination of the engine internals, and will also make working a lot easier and cleaner. A high flash-point solvent, such as paraffin (kerosene) can be used, or better still, a proprietary engine degreaser such as Gunk. Use old paintbrushes and toothbrushes to work the solvent into the various recesses of the engine casings. Take care to exclude solvent or water from the electrical components and intake and exhaust ports.

 **Warning: The use of petrol (gasoline) as a cleaning agent should be avoided due to the risk of fire.**

2 When clean and dry, arrange the unit on the workbench, leaving a suitable clear area for working. Gather a selection of small containers and plastic bags so that parts can be grouped together in an easily identifiable manner. Some paper and a pen should be on hand to permit notes to be made and labels attached where necessary. A supply of clean rag is also required.

3 Before commencing work, read through the appropriate section so that some idea of the necessary procedure can be gained. When removing various engine components it should be noted that great force is seldom required, unless specified. In many cases, a component's reluctance to be removed is indicative of an incorrect approach or removal method. If in any doubt, re-check with the text.

4 An engine support stand can be made from short lengths of 2 x 4 inch wood bolted together into a rectangle to help support the engine if required **(see illustration)**, though the engine will sit nicely on the flat bottom of the sump, and there are two pegs at the front to keep it stable. The perimeter of the mount should be just big enough to accommodate the sump within it so that the engine rests on its crankcase.

5 When disassembling the engine, keep 'mated' parts together (including gears, liners, pistons, connecting rods, valves, etc. that have been in contact with each other during engine operation). These 'mated' parts must be reused or renewed as an assembly.

6 Engine/transmission disassembly should be done in the following general order with reference to the appropriate Sections.

Remove the camshafts
Remove the cam chain/tensioner blade
Remove the cylinder head and cam chain guide blade
Remove the cylinder liners and pistons
Remove the starter motor (see Chapter 8)
Remove the clutch
Remove the oil pump
Remove the alternator (see Chapter 8)
Remove the starter motor (see Chapter 8)
Remove the water pump (see Chapter 3)
Remove the sump
Separate the crankcase halves
Remove the crankshaft/connecting rods
Remove the balancer shaft
Remove the transmission shafts/gears
Remove the gearchange components

### Reassembly

7 Reassembly is accomplished by reversing the general disassembly sequence.

**6.4 An engine support made from pieces of 2 x 4 inch wood**

## 7  Valve cover

**Note:** *The valve cover can be removed with the engine in the frame. If the engine has been removed, ignore the steps which do not apply.*

### Removal

**1** Remove the seat and disconnect the battery negative lead.

**2** On Daytona and Sprint models, remove the fairing side panels; on Speed Triple models, remove the radiator side panels if fitted (see Chapter 7).

**3** Remove the fuel tank and the airbox (see Chapter 4). On Tiger models, undo the screw securing the thermostat housing so that it can be moved aside when removing the valve cover – there is no need to drain the cooling system or detach any of the hoses **(see illustration)**.

**4** Disconnect the ignition coil/spark plug cap wiring connectors and pull the coils/caps off the spark plugs **(see illustration)**.

**5** On models fitted with secondary air injection, mark the air hoses to aid installation, then release the clips and pull the hoses off the unions on the reed valve covers, noting how they fit.

**6** Undo the screws securing the airbox front bracket and remove the bracket **(see illustration)**.

**7** Release the trim clips securing the air deflector where fitted. Detach the clutch cable from the release lever on the clutch cover (see Section 18). Pass the cable through the air deflector and lift off the deflector.

**8** On Daytona, Speed Triple and Sprint models, undo the valve cover bolts evenly, in the order shown **(see illustration)**. On Tiger models, undo the bolts evenly in a criss-cross pattern, starting at the centre and working outwards. Remove the bolts with their seals, then lift the valve cover off the cylinder head towards the left-hand side – where necessary, ease the coolant hoses to move the cover clear. **Note:** *If the cover is stuck, do not try to lever it off with a screwdriver. Tap it*

**7.3  Thermostat housing screw (arrowed) – Tiger models**

**7.4  Pull the coil/caps off the spark plugs**

**7.6  Remove the airbox front bracket (arrowed)**

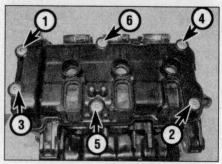

**7.8  Unscrew the cover bolts in the order shown**

*gently around the sides with a rubber hammer or block of wood to dislodge it.*

**9** On models fitted with secondary air injection, note the location of the dowels in the secondary air holes – they may remain in the head or come off with the cover. Remove them for safekeeping if they are loose.

### Installation

**10** Examine the valve cover gasket for signs of damage or deterioration and fit a new one if necessary. Check the seals on the cover bolts for cracks, hardening and deterioration and renew them if necessary. Similarly check the spark plug seals on Daytona, Speed triple and Sprint models.

**11** Clean the mating surfaces of the cylinder head and the valve cover with a suitable

solvent. If the original gasket is being used, remove any traces of old glue or sealant.

**12** On Daytona, Speed triple and Sprint models, fit the spark plug seals onto the camshaft holder **(see illustration)**.

**13** Fit the gasket into the valve cover, making sure it locates correctly into the groove. Use a few dabs of grease to keep the gasket in place while the cover is fitted. On models fitted with secondary air injection, fit the dowels in the secondary air holes in the cover.

**14** Apply a suitable silicone sealant to the corners of the cut-outs in the cylinder head where the gasket half-circles fit **(see illustration)**.

**15** Position the valve cover on the cylinder head, making sure the gasket stays in place **(see illustration)**. Install the cover bolts, using new seals if necessary – the two longer bolts

**7.12  Note the correct installation of the spark plug seals**

**7.14  Apply sealant to the half-circle cutouts in the head**

**7.15a  Make sure the gasket stays in place when fitting the cover**

**7.15b  Fit new bolt seals if necessary**

**8.2a  Remove the timing inspection cap . . .**

**8.2b  . . . noting the O-ring**

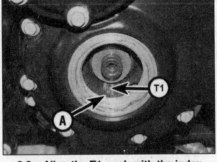

**8.3a  Align the T1 mark with the index mark (A)**

**8.3b  The arrow on each sprocket must be facing in and be parallel with the head mating surface**

are located at the cam chain end **(see illustration)**. Tighten the bolts evenly in the same order as for removal, to the torque setting specified at the beginning of the Chapter

**16** Install the remaining components in the reverse order of removal.

## 8  Cam chain tensioner

**Note:** *The cam chain tensioner can be removed with the engine in the frame. If the engine has been removed, ignore the steps which do not apply.*

### Removal

**1** Remove the valve cover (see Section 7).

**2** Unscrew the timing inspection cap from the right-hand crankcase cover **(see illustration)**. Note the cap O-ring – if it is damaged or deformed a new one must be fitted on reassembly **(see illustration)**.

**3** Using an Allen socket on the starter clutch nut, rotate the crankshaft clockwise until the T1 mark on the starter clutch is aligned with the index mark in the inspection hole **(see illustration)**. In this position, the No. 1 cylinder is at TDC and the arrow marks on the camshaft sprockets should face inwards towards each other **(see illustration)**. If they face away from each other, turn the crankshaft clockwise one full turn so that the T1 mark again aligns with the index mark – the arrows on the camshaft sprockets will now be facing towards each other.

**4** When the tensioner is withdrawn from the cylinder head, the cam chain will be untensioned, and may jump a tooth on the intake cam sprocket. To prevent this, insert a wedge, such as a large screwdriver, between the back of the tensioner blade and the crankcase to hold the blade in firm contact with the cam chain whilst the tensioner is removed. If the chain jumps the camshaft sprocket when the tensioner is removed, hold the camshaft with a spanner on the cast hexagon while realigning the chain **(see illustration)**.

**5** Undo the large end bolt from the tensioner and withdraw the spring, noting that it will be under tension **(see illustration)**. Note the sealing washer and discard it as a new one must be used.

**8.4  Use a spanner on the hexagons (arrowed) to realign the camshafts**

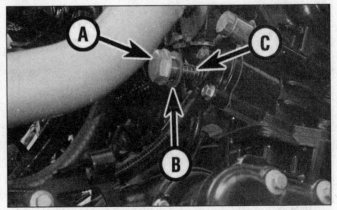

**8.5  Tensioner end bolt (A), sealing washer (B) and spring (C)**

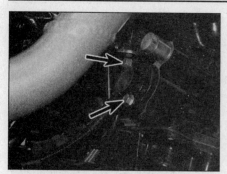

8.6a  Unscrew the bolts (arrowed) . . .

8.6b  . . . and withdraw the tensioner from the head

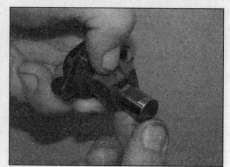

8.7  Release the catch and check the plunger moves freely in and out

**6** Remove the two mounting bolts and withdraw the tensioner **(see illustrations)**. Discard its gasket as a new one must be used.

### Inspection

**7** Examine the tensioner components for signs of wear or damage. Lift the catch on the tensioner body and move the plunger in and out – if it doesn't move smoothly and freely, replace the tensioner with a new one **(see illustration)**.

**8** If the spring has sagged, the tensioner will not be able to take up chain play effectively. Measure the free length of the spring and compare to the specification. If the spring length has reduced significantly, the tensioner must be renewed.

### Installation

**9** If a new tensioner is being fitted, it must be disassembled as follows prior to installation. The end bolt will not be fully tightened – turn the bolt clockwise until the plunger spring out, then undo the bolt and withdraw the spring.

**10** Lift the catch and push the plunger in until it engages with the first tooth on the plunger

ratchet in the fully retracted position. Fit a new gasket on the tensioner body, then install it in the cylinder head and tighten the mounting bolts to the specified torque setting.

**11** Using a slim rod inserted into the tensioner body, use finger pressure only to push the tensioner plunger in until it contacts the tensioner blade; the ratchet and catch will hold it in this position. Remove the wedge from the tensioner blade, making sure that the chain does not jump a tooth on the cam sprocket as you do.

**12** Fit a new sealing washer onto the end bolt and install the spring and end bolt into the tensioner body **(see illustration 8.5)**. Tighten the end bolt to the specified torque setting.

**13** Check that the tensioner plunger is correctly located in the middle of the tensioner blade when viewed from above.

**14** Rotate the engine several times and recheck the timing marks (see Step 3). If the cam chain has jumped whilst the tensioner was removed, reposition it as described in Section 9. Install the valve cover (see Section 7).

**15** Install the remaining components in the reverse order of removal.

## 9  Camshafts and followers

**Note:** *This procedure can be carried out with the engine in the frame.*

### Removal

#### Daytona, Speed Triple and Sprint models

**1** Remove the cam chain tensioner (see Section 8). Note that it is not necessary to wedge the cam chain tensioner blade.

**2** Remove the bolts securing the cam chain upper guide and lift it off **(see illustration)**.

**3** The camshaft caps and camshaft holder must be matched up to their original journals and fitted the same way round on installation. Check for identification markings scribed on the caps; if you can't see any markings, or they are unclear, make your own.

**4** Undo the remaining bolts securing the camshaft caps and remove them **(see illustration)**.

**5** Undo the camshaft holder bolts evenly, in

9.2  Undo the bolts (arrowed) and remove the guide

9.4  Remove the camshaft caps

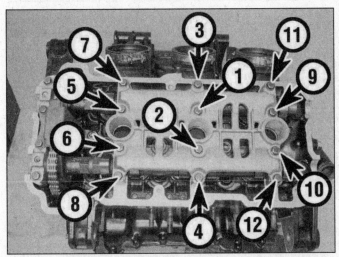

9.5a  Remove the bolts in the order shown

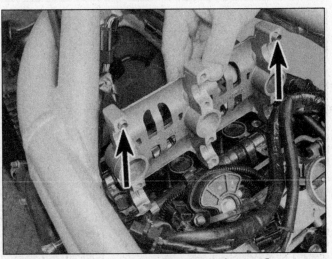

9.5b  Note the location of the dowels (arrowed) . . .

9.5c  . . . and the location of the O-rings

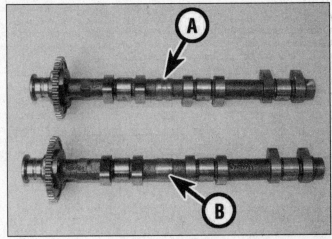

9.7  Intake camshaft has groove (A), exhaust camshaft is plain (B)

the order shown (see illustration). Remove the bolts, then lift the holder off. Note the location of the dowels and remove them for safekeeping if they are loose (see illustration). Note the location of the camshaft holder O-rings (see illustration).
Caution: A camshaft could break if the holder bolts are not slackened as described and the pressure from a depressed valve causes the shaft to bend. Also, if the holder does not come squarely away from the head, the holder is likely to break. If this happens the cylinder head must be renewed; the holders are matched to the head and cannot be obtained separately.
6  Lift the cam chain off the exhaust camshaft sprocket and remove the camshaft.
7  Repeat the procedure for the intake camshaft. The cam chain can be left to rest on its support bolt in the tunnel. Note that the camshafts are slightly different for identification purposes – the intake camshaft has a groove in its centre section, while the

same section on the exhaust camshaft is plain (see illustration).
8  If the followers and shims are being removed from the cylinder head, obtain a container which is divided into twelve compartments. Label each compartment with the location of its corresponding valve in the cylinder head and whether it belongs with an intake or an exhaust valve. If a container is not

available, use labelled plastic bags (egg cartons also work very well!). Remove the cam follower of the valve in question (see illustration). Retrieve the shim from either the inside of the follower or pick it out of the top of the valve using a magnet or a small screwdriver with a dab of grease on it (the shim will stick to the grease) (see illustration). Do not allow the shim to fall into the engine.

9.8a  Remove the cam follower . . .

9.8b  . . . and retrieve the shim (arrowed)

**9.10  Undo the bolts (arrowed) and remove the guide**

### Tiger models

**9** Remove the cam chain tensioner (see Section 8). Note that it is not necessary to wedge the cam chain tensioner blade.

**10** Remove the bolts securing the cam chain upper guide and lift it off **(see illustration)**.

**11** Before disturbing the camshaft caps, check for identification markings scribed on their top surfaces. These markings ensure that the caps can be matched up to their original journals on installation. The caps are numbered 1 to 6; the two outrigger caps on the cam chain end are marked A and B **(see illustration)**. If you can't see any markings, or they are unclear, make your own. Note that the numbered cap bolt holes are offset so that the caps can't be installed the wrong way round. The lettered caps on the outrigger journals are symmetrical, but have an arrow cast into them which must point forwards – mark your own arrow if one is not visible.

**12** Working on the intake camshaft first, slacken all eight cap bolts evenly and a little at a time in a criss-cross sequence, slackening the bolts above any lobes that are pressing onto a valve last in the sequence so that the pressure from the open valves cannot cause the camshaft to bend **(see illustration)**.

*Caution: A camshaft could bend under the pressure from a depressed valve if the cap bolts are not slackened as described. Also, if the cap does not come squarely away from the head, it is likely to break. If this happens the cylinder head must be renewed; the caps are matched to the head and cannot be obtained separately.*

**13** Repeat the procedure for the exhaust camshaft.

**14** Remove the bolts, then remove the caps **(see illustration)**. Retrieve the dowels on each cap if they are loose – if they are not in the caps, they will be in the head.

**15** Lift the cam chain off the exhaust camshaft sprocket and remove the camshaft.

**16** Repeat the procedure for the intake camshaft. The cam chain can be left to rest on its support bolt in the tunnel. Note that the camshafts are slightly different for identification purposes – the intake camshaft has a groove in its centre section, while the same section on the exhaust camshaft is plain **(see illustration 9.7)**.

**17** If the shims and followers are being removed from the cylinder head, obtain a container which is divided into twelve compartments, and label each compartment with the location of its corresponding valve in the cylinder head and whether it belongs with an intake or an exhaust valve. If a container is not available, use labelled plastic bags (egg cartons also work very well!). Remove the cam follower of the valve in question and leave the shim in the follower for safekeeping **(see illustration)**.

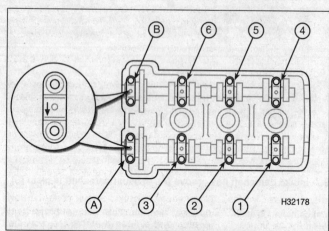

**9.11  Camshaft cap identification markings**

**9.12  Camshaft cap bolts (arrowed)**

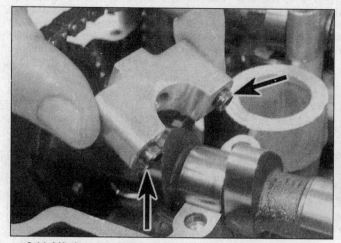

**9.14  Lift the cap off its journal, noting the dowels (arrowed)**

**9.17  Lift each follower out of its bore – note the shim sitting in the top of the follower**

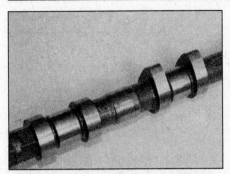

9.18a Inspect the bearing surfaces for scratches or wear

9.18b Check the lobes of the camshaft for wear - here's an example of damage requiring camshaft repair or renewal

9.22 Lay a strip of Plastigauge across each bearing journal, parallel with the camshaft centreline

### Inspection

18 Inspect the cam bearing surfaces of the cylinder head, caps and camshaft holder (see illustration). Look for score marks, deep scratches and evidence of spalling (a pitted appearance). Check the camshaft lobes for heat discoloration (blue appearance), score marks, chipped areas, flat spots and spalling (see illustration).

19 Check the amount of camshaft runout by supporting each end of the camshaft on V-blocks, and measuring any runout using a dial gauge. If the runout exceeds the specified limit the camshaft must be replaced with a new one.

**HAYNES HINT** *Refer to Tools and Workshop Tips (Section 3) in the Reference section for details of how to read a micrometer and dial gauge.*

20 Next, check the camshaft journal oil clearances, using a product called Plastigauge. Check each camshaft in turn rather than both at the same time.

21 Clean the camshaft journals, the bearing surfaces in the cylinder head and the caps and camshaft holder with a clean, lint-free cloth, then lay the camshaft in place in the cylinder head – there is no need to engage the chain on the sprocket. Ensure the camshaft is positioned as for removal (see Section 8, Step 3).

22 Cut strips of Plastigauge and lay one piece on each camshaft journal, parallel with

the camshaft centreline (see illustration). Make sure the dowels are installed then fit the caps and camshaft holder in their proper positions (see Step 3 or 11 as appropriate). Lubricate the threads of the cap/holder bolts with clean engine oil, then install them finger-tight. Ensuring that the camshafts are not rotated at all, tighten the bolts evenly, a little at a time, in the appropriate sequence, until the specified torque setting is reached – for Daytona, Speed Triple and Sprint models, follow the sequence in Step 5 and then tighten the cap bolts; for Tiger models, follow the sequence in Step 38.

23 Now unscrew the bolts evenly, a little at a time, in the appropriate sequence and carefully lift off the caps/holder, again making sure the camshaft is not rotated.

24 To determine the oil clearance, compare the crushed Plastigauge (at its widest point) on each journal to the scale printed on the Plastigauge container (see illustration). Compare the results to this Chapter's Specifications. If the oil clearance is greater than specified, measure the diameter of the camshaft journal with a micrometer (see illustration). If the journal diameter is less than the specified limit, replace the camshaft with a new one and recheck the clearance. If the clearance is still too great, or if the camshaft journal is within its limit, replace the cylinder head and caps/holder as a set with new ones – individual components are not available. Note that if specialist measuring tools are available, the camshaft bearing bore

inside diameter can be compared with the specified limit.

*Before renewing the camshafts, cylinder head/caps because of damage, check with local machine shops specialising in motorcycle engine work. In the case of the camshafts, it may be possible for cam lobes to be welded, reground and hardened, at a cost far lower than that of a new camshaft. If the bearing surfaces in the head or holders are damaged, it may be possible for them to be bored out to accept bearing inserts. Due to the cost of new components it is recommended that all options are explored!*

25 Repeat the oil clearance check on the other camshaft.

26 Check the camshaft sprockets for wear, cracks and other damage, renewing them if necessary. The same design sprocket is used for each camshaft, but different bolt hole positions are provided for fitting to the intake or exhaust camshaft. When fitted to the intake camshaft, the holes next to the IN marking should be used; for the exhaust camshaft, use the holes next to the EX markings (see illustration). Apply non-permanent thread locking compound to the sprocket bolt threads and tighten them to the specified torque setting.

27 If the sprockets are worn, it is likely the cam chain and sprocket on the crankshaft will be worn as well. Refer to Section 10 for details of how to check the cam chain for wear.

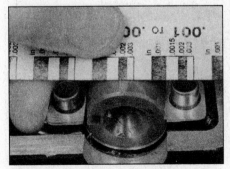

9.24a Compare the width of the crushed Plastigauge to the scale printed on the Plastigauge container

9.24b Measure the cam bearing journals with a micrometer

9.26 Bolt location on intake camshaft (A) and exhaust camshaft (B)

9.30 Install each shim (arrowed) on the top of the valve assembly

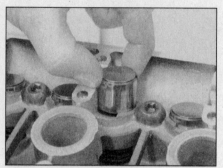

9.31 Lubricate the followers and slip them into their bores

9.33 Keeping the front run of the chain taut, install the exhaust camshaft with the arrow pointing rearwards

28 Inspect the outer surfaces of the followers for evidence of scoring or other damage. If a follower is in poor condition, it is probable that the bore in which it works is also damaged. Measure the outside diameter of the followers and the inside diameter of the bores and compare the results to the limits in the Specifications at the beginning of this Chapter. If the bores are seriously out-of-round or tapered, the cylinder head and the followers must be renewed.

Keep the cam chain taut all round by applying pressure to the tensioner blade via the tensioner hole – using a finger works well, though a wooden dowel is easier. Alternatively, place a wedge between the blade and the crankcase

### Installation

**Note:** *It is important that the followers and shims are returned to their original valves otherwise the valve clearances will be inaccurate.*

29 Make sure the bearing surfaces in the cylinder head, on the camshafts and in the caps and holders are clean, then liberally apply molybdenum disulphide oil (a 50/50 mixture of molybdenum disulphide grease and engine oil) to each of them. Also apply oil to the camshaft lobes and the followers.
30 On Daytona, Speed Triple and Sprint models, if removed, lubricate each shim and fit it into its recess on the top of the valve with the size marking facing up **(see illustration)**. **Note:** *On the machine photographed, some of the shims were not marked.* Check that the shims are correctly seated, then install the followers.
31 On Tiger models, if removed, install each follower, then fit each shim in the top of the follower with the size marking facing down **(see illustration)**. Check that the shims are correctly seated.
32 Check that the crankshaft is positioned as described in Section 8, Step 3.
33 Hook the cam chain up from its tunnel and make sure that it is engaged around the lower sprocket teeth on the crankshaft. Keeping the front run of the chain taut, lay the exhaust camshaft in position so that the arrow mark on its sprocket points rearwards and is parallel with the top mating surface of the

cylinder head, then engage the chain on the sprocket teeth **(see illustration)**.
34 Slip the intake camshaft through the cam chain so that the arrow mark on its sprocket points forwards and is parallel with the head **(see illustration)**. Engage the chain fully on the sprocket teeth, making sure that the chain is tight between the camshafts, with any slack lying in the rear run where it will be taken up by the tensioner. Check that the T1 mark on the starter clutch is still aligned with the index mark in the inspection hole.
35 Check the camshaft holder O-rings and renew them if they are crushed or damaged **(see illustration 9.5b)**. Ensure that the camshaft cap and holder dowels are installed and fit the caps/holder in their proper positions (see Step 3 or 11 as appropriate) **(see illustration)**. Lubricate the threads of the cap/holder bolts with clean engine oil, then fit them finger-tight. On Daytona, Speed Triple and Sprint models, don't forget to install the cam chain upper guide **(see illustration)**.
36 In order to prevent the cam chain jumping a tooth as the camshafts are tightened down, apply light pressure through the tensioner hole.
37 On Daytona, Speed Triple and Sprint models, tighten the camshaft holder bolts evenly, a little at a time, in the order shown in Step 5, until the specified torque setting is reached, then tighten the cap bolts.
38 On Tiger models, tighten the cap bolts evenly, a little at a time, in the order shown,

9.34 Lay the intake shaft in the head, making sure the chain is taut between the sprockets

9.35a Install the camshaft holder as noted on removal

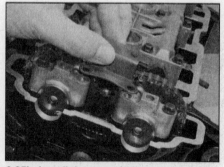

9.35b Install the cam chain upper guide as appropriate

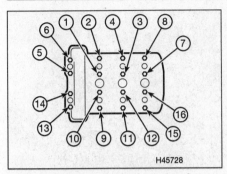

**9.38 Tighten the bolts in the order shown – Tiger models**

**9.40 Install the upper guide on the head – Tiger models**

until the specified torque setting is reached **(see illustration)**.

**39** With all bolts tightened down, check that the timing marks still align (see Section 8, Step 3). If the chain has jumped a tooth, release the pressure on the tensioner blade (if applied), then slip the cam chain off the sprockets (there should be enough slack in the rear run to do this easily without having to displace the camshafts). Turn the camshaft(s) as required using a spanner on the cast hex until their alignment is correct **(see illustration 8.4)**. With the timing is set up correctly, check that each camshaft is not pinched by turning it a few degrees in each direction with a spanner on the hex.

**40** On Tiger models, install the cam chain

upper guide and tighten its screws to the specified torque setting **(see illustration)**.

**41** Install the cam chain tensioner (Section 8).

**42** Check the valve clearances (see Chapter 1).

**43** Install the remaining components in the reverse order of removal.

## 10 Starter clutch

**Note:** *The starter clutch can be removed with the engine in the frame. If the engine has been removed, ignore the steps which do not apply.*

### Starter clutch check

**1** If you suspect the starter clutch of being faulty, a simple check can be performed as follows.

**2** On Daytona and Sprint models, first remove the right-hand fairing side panels and belly pan as applicable (see Chapter 7). On all models, undo the bolts and remove the starter cover **(see illustration)**.

**3** Using your finger, check that the starter idler gear turns freely anti-clockwise, and locks when turned clockwise. If not, remove the wave washer and plain washer and draw the idler gear and its bearing off the shaft **(see illustrations)**.

**4** Now check to see that the intermediate gear turns freely clockwise, and locks when turned anti-clockwise. If it does, it is likely the starter motor is faulty and should be removed for inspection (see Chapter 8). If not, remove the starter clutch for further investigation.

### Removal

**5** If not already done, follow Steps 2 and 3 and remove the starter idler gear and bearing.

**6** Withdraw the gear shaft and thrust washer **(see illustration)**.

**7** Remove the starter cover gasket and discard it as a new one must be used, then remove the dowels for safekeeping if they are loose **(see illustrations)**.

**8** Undo the bolts securing the right-hand crankcase cover, noting the sealing washer on the uppermost bolt, and lift off the cover

**10.2 Remove the starter cover**

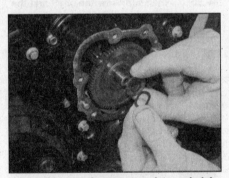

**10.3a Remove the wave washer and plain washer . . .**

**10.3b . . . the draw off the idler gear and its bearing**

**10.6 Withdraw the gear shaft and thrust washer**

**10.7a Remove the cover gasket . . .**

**10.7b . . . and the cover dowels (arrowed)**

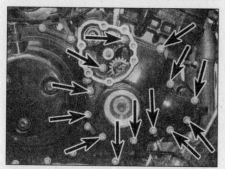

10.8a Undo the cover bolts (arrowed) . . .

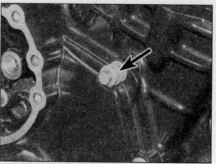

10.8b . . . noting the sealing washer (arrowed)

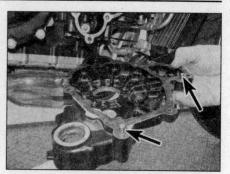

10.8c Note the location of the cover dowels (arrowed)

(see illustrations). Remove the cover gasket and discard it as a new one must be used, then remove the dowels for safekeeping if they are loose (see illustration).

9 Remove the wave washer from the end of the intermediate gear shaft, then withdraw the

shaft and the gear, noting which way round it fits (see illustrations).

10 To loosen the starter clutch bolt, the crankshaft must be locked to prevent it turning. Triumph provides a service tool (Part No. T3880017) to do this. Alternatively, a home-made

tool located in the holes on the face of the starter clutch can be used as shown (see illustration). If the engine is in the frame, engage 1st gear and have an assistant hold the rear brake on hard with the rear tyre in firm contact with the ground. Remove the bolt and washer and draw the starter clutch off, noting how the master spline locates on the shaft (see illustrations). Note the location of the thrust washer on the shaft.

### Inspection

11 Hold the starter clutch body and check that the gear turns freely anti-clockwise, and locks when turned clockwise (see illustration). If not, lift out the gear then lift out the needle roller bearing (see illustrations).

12 Examine the bearing surface of the gear hub and the condition of the sprags inside the clutch body. If the hub or sprags show signs of excessive wear or are damaged, replace them with new parts. Check the condition of the bearing rollers and renew the bearing if

10.9a Remove the wave washer . . .

10.9b . . . then withdraw the shaft and the intermediate gear

10.10a Using a home-made tool to hold the starter clutch

10.10b Remove the bolt and washer

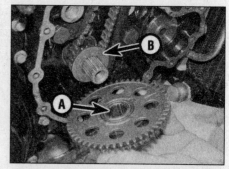

10.10c Draw off the starter clutch, noting the master spline (A) and thrust washer (B)

10.11a Starter clutch gear should turn freely anti-clockwise

10.11b Lift the gear . . .

10.11c . . . and the needle bearing out of the starter clutch body

necessary – refer to *Tools and Workshop Tips* in the Reference Section for details of bearing checks.

**13** Examine the teeth of the idler and intermediate gears and the corresponding teeth of the starter clutch gear and starter motor driveshaft. Renew the gears and/or starter motor if worn or chipped teeth are discovered on related gears. Also check the idler and intermediate gear shafts for damage, and check the idler gear needle roller bearing. Renew any components that are worn or damaged.

### Installation

**14** Clean all old gasket and sealant from the covers and crankcase. Clean any old thread locking compound off the threads of the starter clutch bolt.

**15** Lubricate the starter clutch sprags, the needle bearing and the hub of the starter clutch gear with clean engine oil. Install the bearing and then lower the gear into the clutch, rotating the gear clockwise as you do so to spread the sprags and allow the hub of the gear to enter **(see illustration 10.11c and b)**.

**16** If removed, install the thrust washer on the crankshaft, then align the master splines on the shaft and starter clutch and install the clutch assembly **(see illustration 10.10c)**.

**17** Apply a suitable non-permanent thread locking compound to the starter clutch bolt, then install the bolt and washer. Using the method employed on removal to stop the crankshaft from turning, tighten the bolt to the torque setting specified at the beginning of the Chapter.

**18** Lubricate the intermediate gear shaft with clean oil. Position the gear in the crankcase

and slide the shaft fully into place, then fit the wave washer **(see illustration 10.9b and a)**.

**19** If removed, install the crankcase cover dowels. Fit the new cover gasket, making sure it locates correctly onto the dowels, and install the cover **(see illustration 10.8c)**. Tighten the cover bolts to the torque setting specified at the beginning of the Chapter, ensuring a new sealing washer is installed on the uppermost bolt **(see illustration 10.8b)**.

**20** Install the idler gear shaft and thrust washer, then lubricate the needle bearing with clean engine oil and install the bearing and idler gear. Install the outer plain washer and wave washer.

**21** If removed, install the starter cover dowels. Fit the new cover gasket, making sure it locates correctly onto the dowels, and install the cover **(see illustration 10.2)**. Tighten the cover bolts to the specified torque setting.

**22** Install the remaining components in the reverse order of removal.

---

## 11 Cam chain and tensioner/guide blades

**Note:** *The cam chain and tensioner blade can be removed with the engine in the frame.*

### Cam chain upper guide

**1** Remove the valve cover (see Section 7).
**2** Remove the bolts securing the cam chain upper guide and lift off **(see illustration 9.2 or 9.10)**.
**3** Installation is the reverse of removal.

**11.6 Draw the sprocket off the crankshaft, noting which way round it fits**

**11.8 Lift the chain out of the engine**

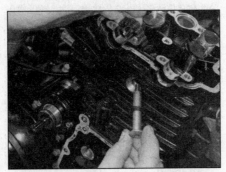

**11.7 Remove the cam chain support bolt**

**11.15a Note the washer (arrowed) behind the tensioner blade**

## Cam chain and crankshaft sprocket

### Removal

**4** Remove the camshafts (see Section 9).
**5** Remove the starter clutch and the crankshaft thrust washer (see Section 10).
**6** Lift the cam chain off the crankshaft sprocket and withdraw the sprocket, noting which way round it fits **(see illustration)**. Note how the master spline locates on the shaft.
**7** Hold the cam chain and remove the support bolt from the centre of the right-hand side of the cylinder head **(see illustration)**. Note the seal on the bolt and replace it with a new one if it is worn or damaged.
**8** Slip the chain off the crankshaft and lift it out **(see illustration)**.

### Inspection

**9** Check the cam chain for binding and obvious damage and renew it if necessary. Inspect the crankshaft and camshaft sprockets for worn, chipped or missing teeth. If the chain and sprockets show signs of extensive wear renew them as a set (including the camshaft sprockets).
**10** If the chain appears to be in good condition, check it for stretch as follows. Hang the chain from a hook and attach a 13 kg (28 lb) weight to its lower end.
**11** On Daytona, Speed Triple and Sprint models, measure the length of 24 pins (from the centre of the 1st pin to the centre of the 24th pin) and compare the result to the service limit specified at the beginning of the Chapter. If the chain exceeds the service limit it must be replaced with a new one.
**12** On Tiger models, measure the length of 70 pins (from the centre of the 1st pin to the centre of the 70th pin) and compare the result to the service limit specified at the beginning of the Chapter. If the chain exceeds the service limit it must be replaced with a new one.

### Installation

**13** Installation is a reverse of removal, noting the following:
● Hold the chain in position and tighten the cam chain support bolt to the specified torque setting.
● Align the master splines on the shaft and the crankshaft sprocket and ensure the sprocket is fitted the right way round.
● Do not forget to install the crankshaft thrust washer (see Section 10).

## Cam chain tensioner blade

### Removal

**14** Follow the procedure in Steps 4 to 8 and remove the cam chain.
**15** Undo the tensioner blade pivot bolt – retrieve the washer from between the blade and the crankcase as you withdraw the bolt **(see illustration)**. Manoeuvre the blade out of

**11.15b Manoeuvre the blade out from the cam chain tunnel**

**11.20a Remove the bolt and retrieve the inner washer . . .**

**11.20b . . . then lift out the guide blade**

the bottom of the cam chain tunnel **(see illustration)**. Note that on Tiger models, a collar is fitted in the hole in the blade.

**16** Check the tensioner blade for wear, cracking and other damage, and renew it if necessary.

### Installation

**17** Installation is the reverse of removal – don't forget to fit the washer on the pivot bolt between the blade and the crankcase. Tighten the pivot bolt to the specified torque setting.

### *Cam chain guide blade*

#### Removal

**18** The upper end of the cam chain guide blade locates in a slot in the front edge of the cam chain tunnel and is retained by the cylinder head – it cannot be removed unless the head is off (see Section 12).

**19** If not already done, follow the procedure in Steps 4 to 8 and remove the cam chain.

**20** Undo the guide blade pivot bolt – retrieve the washer from between the blade and the crankcase as you withdraw the bolt **(see illustration)**. Lift the blade out of the top of the cam chain tunnel, noting how it locates **(see illustration)**.

**21** Check the tensioner blade for wear, cracking and other damage, and renew it if necessary.

#### Installation

**22** Lower the tensioner blade down through the chain tunnel and ensure that it locates correctly in its slot.

**23** Don't forget to fit the washer on the pivot bolt between the blade and the crankcase. Tighten the pivot bolt to the specified torque setting.

**24** Install the remaining components in the reverse order of removal.

---

### 12 Cylinder head removal and installation

*Caution: The engine must be completely cool before beginning this procedure or the cylinder head may become warped.*

**Note 1:** *The cylinder head can be removed with the engine in the frame on Tiger models. On Daytona, Speed Triple and Sprint models, the engine must be removed from the frame.*

**Note 2:** *Whenever the cylinder head is disturbed it is possible that the seal between the bottom of the cylinder liners and crankcase will be broken. Unfortunately there is no easy way of telling whether this has occurred or not, and so the only way to be sure is to remove the liners and reseal them before installing the head. Triumph specifies this practice. Unless the crankcases are being split, a special tool will be required to remove the cylinder liners (see Section 15).*

### *Removal*

**1** To remove the cylinder head on Tiger models, follow the procedure in Chapter 2A,

Section 11. Note that on 955 cc engines, the same sequence should be used for the release and tightening of the cylinder head bolts. If required, the cylinder head can be removed with the engine in the frame.

**2** To remove the cylinder head on Daytona, Speed Triple and Sprint models, first remove the engine from the frame (see Section 5).

**3** Remove the camshafts and followers (see Section 9). Remove the cam chain support bolt from the right-hand side of the cylinder head **(see illustration 11.7)**.

**4** Unscrew the banjo bolt securing the external oil hose to the cylinder head and position the hose aside **(see illustration)**. Discard the sealing washers as new ones must be fitted on installation.

**5** Remove the two screws from the right-hand end of the cylinder head-to-crankcase joint **(see illustration)**.

**6** Slacken the eight cylinder head bolts by half a turn at a time in the specified sequence shown **(see illustration)**.

**7** Tap around the joint faces of the cylinder head with a soft-faced mallet to free the head. Don't attempt to free the head by inserting a screwdriver between the head and cylinder block – you'll damage the sealing surfaces.

**8** Carefully lift the head off the block, and

**12.4 Remove the banjo bolt (arrowed) and displace the oil hose**

**12.5 Remove the two screws (arrowed) from the right-hand end of the head**

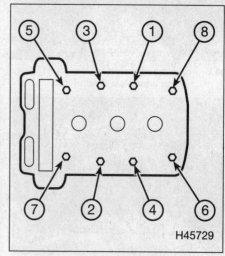

**12.6 Sequence for loosening and tightening the cylinder head bolts**

**12.8  Carefully lift the cylinder head up off the engine block**

remove it from the engine **(see illustration)**. Lift off the head gasket and recover the two dowels if they are loose.

**9**  If required, remove the cam chain guide blade **(see illustration 11.20b)**.

**10**  If the crankshaft is rotated at all with the head off, then the cylinder liners must be removed and resealed. If you feel certain that the seal has not broken, you can clamp the liners in place using suitable bolts, nuts and washers threaded into the head bolt holes as shown to prevent any movement **(see illustration)** – do not overtighten the clamps as the mating surface of the head could be indented, causing leakage and compression problems. However if you are in any doubt at all (and it is impossible to be 100% certain), it is essential that the liners are removed, otherwise coolant from the cylinder block water jacket will seep into the crankcase. Refer to Section 15 for liner removal and installation details.

**12.15a  Install the dowels (arrowed) . . .**

**12.19a  Tighten the cylinder head bolts as described to the specified torque settings . . .**

**12.10  Assemble a bolt, nut and washers as shown to clamp the liners**

**11**  Inspect the cylinder head gasket and the mating surfaces for signs of leakage, which could indicate that the head is distorted. If necessary, check the cylinder head with a straight-edge. Discard the old head gasket as a new one must be fitted on reassembly.

### Installation

**12**  Clean the mating surfaces of the cylinder head and block with a suitable solvent to remove all traces of old gasket. If a scraper is used, take care not to scratch or gouge the soft aluminium. Ensure none of the old gasket material falls into the crankcase.

 **HAYNES HiNT**  *Refer to Tools and Workshop Tips for details of gasket removal methods.*

**12.15b  . . . then fit the head gasket as described**

**12.19b  . . . and then through the specified angle using a degree disc**

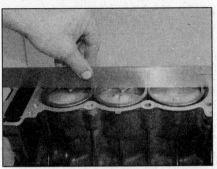

**12.14  Checking the sealing surface with a straight edge**

**13**  Check that the bolt holes in the block are clean and dry. Clean the threads of the head bolts and lubricate them with a smear of clean engine oil.

**14**  Fit and seal the liners in the cylinder block (see Section 15). If the liners were clamped in place, remove the clamps. Use a straight-edge to check that the tops of the liners are level with the block sealing surface **(see illustration)**.

**15**  If removed, install the two dowels in the block and fit the new head gasket **(see illustration)**. If one side of the gasket is marked TOP this should face uppermost. Check that the gasket locates over the dowels and that all the holes are correctly aligned **(see illustration)**.

**16**  If removed, install the cam chain guide blade in the front of the tunnel. Make sure the blade locates correctly in the slot at the top **(see illustration 11.20b)**.

**17**  Carefully lower the cylinder head onto the block.

**18**  Install the cylinder head bolts and tighten them finger-tight only at this stage.

**19**  Tighten the cylinder head bolts in the correct numerical sequence **(see illustration 12.6)** to the stage 1 torque setting **(see illustration)**. Repeat to the stage 2 torque setting. Finally, attach a degree disc to the torque wrench and angle-tighten each bolt 90° following the same sequence **(see illustration)**.

**20**  Tighten the screws on the right-hand end of the cylinder head to the specified torque setting **(see illustration 12.5)**.

**21**  Fit new sealing washers on each side of the external oil hose union, install the hose on the engine and tighten the banjo bolt to the specified torque setting **(see illustration 12.4)**.

**22**  Install the remaining components in the reverse order of removal.

### 13  Valves/valve seats/valve guides overhaul

**1**  Because of the complex nature of this job and the special tools and equipment required, most owners leave servicing of the valves, valve seats and valve guides to a professional. However, you can make an initial assessment of whether the valves are seating, and therefore sealing, correctly by pouring a small amount of solvent into each of the valve ports. If the solvent leaks past any valve into the combustion chamber area the valve is not seating and sealing correctly.

2 You can also remove the valves from the cylinder head, clean the components, check them for wear to assess the extent of the work needed, and, unless a valve service is required, grind in the valves (see Section 14). The head can then be reassembled.

3 A dealer service department will remove the valves and springs, renew the valves and recut the valve seats, check and renew the valve springs, spring retainers and collets (as necessary), replace the valve seals with new ones and reassemble the valve components.

4 After the valve service has been performed, the head will be in like-new condition. When the head is returned, be sure to clean it again very thoroughly before installation on the engine to remove any metal particles or abrasive grit that may still be present from the valve service operations. Use compressed air, if available, to blow out all the holes and passages.

### 14 Cylinder head and valves overhaul

1 As mentioned in the previous section, valve seat recutting should be left to a Triumph dealer. However, disassembly, cleaning and inspection of the valves and related components can be done (if the necessary special tools are available) by the home mechanic. Follow the procedure in Chapter 2A, Section 13, with reference to the Specifications at the beginning of this Chapter.

2 Note the following:
● *On Daytona, Speed Triple and Sprint models, inner and outer valve springs are fitted to intake valves only; exhaust valves have only one spring each.*
● *Intake and exhaust valve stem seals are the same size on all models.*

### 15 Cylinder liners

**Note 1:** *The cylinder liners can be removed with the pistons in situ, following removal of the cylinder head. However to do this requires the use of a Triumph special tool, Part No. T3880315, to extract the liners. It may be possible to purchase a universal liner extractor from a good automotive tool supplier, though make sure it is suitable for smaller engines (below 1000cc). A suitable home-made tool can be used to release the liners, but as it uses the drawbolt principle it is necessary to*

*remove the engine, separate the crankcase halves, then remove the crankshaft, connecting rods and pistons before it can be applied. If the liners are being removed as part of a complete engine overhaul and the engine is therefore removed anyway, then no extra work is involved, apart from making up the tool.*

**Note 2:** *On Tiger models, if required, the cylinder liners can be removed with the engine in the frame.*

### Removal

1 If the Triumph special tool or a liner extractor is being used, just remove the cylinder head (see Section 12). Otherwise, separate the crankcase halves, then remove the crankshaft, connecting rods and pistons, referring to the relevant Sections of this Chapter.

2 Before removing the liners, mark the top edge of each liner at the front with a felt marker pen or similar, which will not damage the gasket surfaces. Indicate the cylinder number and front face of each liner.

3 Follow the appropriate procedure in Chapter 2A, Section 14, Step 3 or 4 to remove the liners.

### Inspection

4 Check the liners carefully as described in Chapter 2A, Section 14. Compare the dimensions with the Specifications shown at the beginning of this Chapter.

5 Note that the cylinder liners may not be suitable for honing – check with a Triumph dealer first.

### Installation

6 Follow the appropriate procedure in Chapter 2A, Section 14, to install the liners.

7 Note that on Daytona models the connecting rods are symmetrical – install the piston/connecting rod assemblies with the dot on the piston crown facing the front of the engine.

### 16 Pistons and piston rings

**Note:** *On Tiger models, if required, the pistons and piston rings can be removed with the engine in the frame.*

### Removal

1 Remove the cylinder head (see Section 12).

2 If the crankcases have not been separated and a cylinder liner extractor is available, remove the cylinder liners (see Section 15). Make sure that all apertures into the crankcase are well blocked with clean rag.

3 If the engine has been removed and the crankcases are being separated, follow the procedure in Section 25 and separate the connecting rods from the crankshaft, then remove the rods with the pistons from the

tops of the liners.

4 Before removing the pistons, mark the cylinder number on the crown of each piston. Also note the arrow or dot on each crown which points to the front of the engine – if the mark is not visible, make you own as the piston must be installed the correct way round **(see illustration)**. If the connecting rods have been removed, also note which way round they are fitted – on Speed Triple, Sprint and Tiger models, the oil hole in the rod must face the rear of the engine.

5 Follow the procedure in Chapter 2A, Section 15, to remove, check and install the pistons and piston rings. Compare the dimensions with the Specifications shown at the beginning of this Chapter.

6 Note the following:
● *The piston ring end gap must not exceed the specified service limit.*
● *The second (middle) piston ring is marked 2N at one end.*
● *Ensure that the pistons are installed the correct way round (see Step 4).*

### 17 Clutch overhaul

**Note:** *This procedure can be performed with the engine in the frame. If the engine has already been removed, ignore the preliminary steps which don't apply.*

### Removal

1 On Daytona and Sprint models, first remove the right-hand fairing side panels and belly pan as applicable (see Chapter 7).

2 If required, drain the engine oil (Chapter 1).

3 Detach the clutch cable from the release mechanism arm on the clutch cover (see Section 18).

4 Follow the procedure in Section 10 and remove the right-hand crankcase cover to gain access to the right-hand clutch cover bolt.

5 Working in a criss-cross pattern, slacken the clutch cover bolts evenly, noting how the cable bracket is secured **(see illustrations)**. Lift the cover away from the engine, being prepared to catch any residual oil that may be

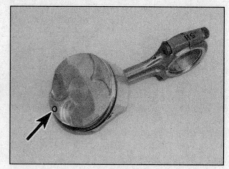

**16.4 Dot (arrowed) on the piston must face the front**

17.5a  Undo the clutch cover bolts (arrowed) . . .

17.5b  . . . noting how the cable bracket (arrowed) is secured . . .

17.5c  . . . and lift the cover off

17.7a  Remove the pressure plate bolts, washers and springs

17.7b  Lift out the pressure plate and pull-rod

17.8  Remove the anti-judder spring and its seat

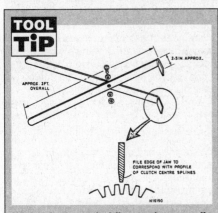

A clutch centre holding tool can easily be made using two strips of steel with the ends bent over, and bolted together in the middle.

released as the cover is removed (see illustration).

6  Remove the gasket and discard it. Note the two locating dowels fitted to the crankcase and remove them for safe-keeping if they are loose.

7  Working in a criss-cross pattern, gradually slacken the clutch spring retaining bolts until spring pressure is released, then remove the bolts, washers and springs (see illustration). Lift out the clutch pressure plate complete with pull-rod (see illustration).

8  Grasp the complete set of clutch plates and remove them as a pack – you may have to hook the inner plates out using a piece of wire. Unless the plates are being renewed, keep them in their original order. Note that the outer and inner friction plates are different in colour to the rest, and that the tabs on the outer plate locate in the shallow slots in the housing, not in the deep slots with the rest of the plates. Similarly remove

the anti-judder spring and spring seat, noting how they fit (see illustration).

9  The transmission input shaft must be locked to enable the clutch nut to be slackened. This can be done in several ways. If the engine is in the frame, engage 1st gear and have an assistant hold the rear brake on hard with the rear tyre in firm contact with the ground. Triumph service tool (Part No. T3880305) that can be located between the clutch centre and clutch housing to lock them together, although you still need to engage 1st gear and have an assistant hold the rear brake on. If the engine is out of the frame, a commercially available or home-made tool (see Tool tip) can be used to stop the clutch centre from turning whilst the nut is slackened. Unscrew the nut and remove the Belleville washer from the input shaft (see illustrations). Discard the washer as a new one must be used on installation.

17.9a  Using a commercially available tool to hold the clutch centre

17.9b  Remove the clutch centre nut . . .

17.9c  . . . and the Belleville washer

**17.11 Draw out the bearing sleeve as described . . .**

**17.12 . . . then slide out the clutch housing**

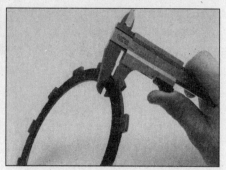

**17.13 Measuring clutch friction plate thickness**

**10** Slide the clutch centre off the input shaft, followed by the large thrust washer **(see illustrations 17.25b and a)**.

**11** Jiggle the clutch housing backwards and forwards to draw out the bearing sleeve noting which way round it fits, then support the housing and withdraw the sleeve **(see illustration)**.

**12** Slide the clutch housing off the shaft, noting how the primary driven gear on the back of the housing engages with the primary drive gear on the crankshaft, and manoeuvre it out of the crankcase **(see illustration)**. Note how the oil pump drive pegs locate in the holes around the centre of the clutch housing.

### Inspection

**13** After an extended period of service the clutch friction plates will wear and promote clutch slip. Measure the thickness of each friction plate using a Vernier caliper **(see illustration)**. If any plate has worn to or beyond the service limit given in the Specifications, the friction plates must be renewed as a set.

**14** If the plates are good, but the clutch has been slipping, it could be that the springs have sagged. As no specification is available for the spring free length, the only way to check them is to compare them with new ones. If the springs have sagged, renew them as a set.

**15** The plain plates should not show any signs of excess heating (bluing). Check for warpage using a flat surface and feeler blades **(see illustration)**. If any plate exceeds the maximum permissible amount of warpage, or shows signs of bluing, all plain plates must be renewed as a set.

**16** Inspect the clutch assembly for burrs and indentations on the edges of the protruding tangs of the friction plates and/or slots in the edge of the outer drum with which they engage **(see illustration)**. Similarly check for wear between the inner tongues of the plain plates and the slots in the clutch centre. Wear of this nature will cause clutch drag and slow disengagement during gear changes, as the plates will snag when the pressure plate is lifted. With care a small amount of wear can be corrected by dressing with a fine file, but if this is excessive the worn components should be renewed.

**17** Inspect the clutch housing needle bearing and the surface of the bearing sleeve **(see illustration)**. Check the springs in the clutch housing and check the teeth on the primary driven gear. If any components are worn of damaged, replace them with new ones. Note that if the needle bearing is worn or damaged, a new clutch housing must be fitted; the bearing is not available separately.

**18** Inspect the anti-judder spring and spring seat for wear. If the spring is flattened, renew the spring and seat as a set **(see illustration)**.

**19** Remove the pull-rod from the pressure plate bearing and check the plate for signs of damage and the bearing for wear **(see illustration)**. Ensure that the inner race of the bearing spins freely without any sign of notchiness. Push the bearing out of the pressure plate if renewal is required.

**20** Check the clutch release mechanism in the clutch cover for smooth operation. Note how the return spring ends locate, then

**17.15 Check the plain plates for warpage**

**17.16 Inspect the clutch assembly for wear and damage as described**

**17.17 Inspect the needle bearing (A) and the bearing sleeve (B)**

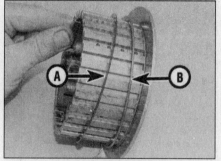

**17.18 Inspect the anti-judder spring (A) and spring seat (B)**

**17.19 Check the pressure plate bearing (arrowed) for wear**

**17.20a Note how the ends (arrowed) of the clutch release return spring locate ...**

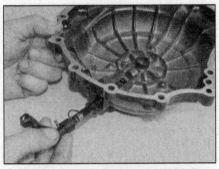

**17.20b ... then withdraw the shaft for inspection**

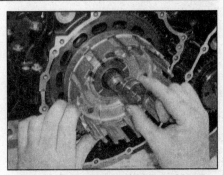

**17.24a Position the clutch housing as described then install the bearing sleeve**

withdraw the shaft from the cover and check it for wear **(see illustrations)**. The shaft oil seal and bearings are not available as separate items; if they are worn or damaged a new cover will have to be fitted.

21 Check the pull-rod end and its locating cutout in the shaft for signs of wear and damage, and replace them with new ones if necessary. Clean all components and lubricate the seal and bearings with grease prior to installation.

22 The clutch cover incorporates an outer cover retained by three screws. If necessary, remove the screws securing the cover and lift it off.

### Installation

23 Remove all traces of gasket material from the crankcase and clutch cover mating surfaces.

24 Lubricate the clutch housing bearing sleeve and the needle bearing with clean engine oil. Slide the clutch housing over the input shaft and manoeuvre it into the crankcase so that the primary driven gear engages with the primary drive gear on the crankshaft, then install the bearing sleeve with the grooved face outwards **(see illustration)**. If necessary, turn the oil pump driven sprocket until the holes on the clutch housing engage with the pegs on the oil pump drive sprocket **(see illustration)**.

25 Slide the large thrust washer over the input shaft, then slide the clutch centre onto the input shaft splines **(see illustrations)**.

26 Install the new Belleville washer with its OUT marking facing outwards, followed by the clutch nut **(see illustrations 17.9c and 9b)**. Using the method employed on removal to lock the input shaft, tighten the nut

to the specified torque setting. **Note:** *When the nut has been tightened, check that the clutch centre rotates freely with the transmission in neutral.*

27 Fit the anti-judder spring seat into the clutch centre, followed by the anti-judder spring, fitting the spring so that its outer edge is raised off the spring seat **(see illustration 17.18)**.

28 Coat each clutch plate with engine oil prior to installation. Build up the clutch plates, starting with the inner friction plate that is darker in colour, then a plain plate and alternating normal friction and plain plates until all but the last friction plate are installed **(see illustrations)**. Fit the outer friction plate (also darker in colour), locating its tabs in the shallow slots, rather in the deep slots with the other friction plates **(see illustration)**.

**17.24b Ensure that the oil pump drive sprocket pegs are engaged with the back of the clutch housing**

**17.25a Install the large thrust washer ...**

**17.25b ... and locate the clutch centre on the shaft splines**

**17.28a Fit the dark inner friction plate ...**

**17.28b ... then a plain plate**

**17.28c Fit the dark outer friction plate tabs into the shallow slots in the housing**

**29** Insert the pull-rod into the pressure plate, then install the pressure plate assembly, engaging the notches on its inner rim with the slots in the inside of the clutch centre (see illustration 17.7b).

**30** Install the springs, washers and bolts and tighten the bolts evenly in a criss-cross sequence to the specified torque setting (see illustration).

**31** If removed, install the release mechanism shaft and locate the spring ends as noted on removal (see illustrations 17.20b and 20a)

**32** Ensure that the dowels are in place in the crankcase, then install a new gasket, locating it over the dowels (see illustration). Install the cover, ensuring the release shaft engages with the pull rod (see illustration 17.5c).

**33** Install the cover bolts and tighten them evenly in a criss-cross sequence to the specified torque setting, not forgetting to secure the cable bracket (see illustrations 17.5a and 5b). Operate the release lever and make sure it picks up the end of the pull-rod correctly – it should come up solid when it is pointing across the engine.

**34** Attach the clutch cable to the release lever on the clutch cover and check the operation of the clutch (see Section 18).

**35** Install the right-hand crankcase cover and the starter cover (see Section 10).

**36** Refill or top-up the engine oil (see Daily (pre-ride) checks).

**37** If applicable, install the fairing side panels and belly pan (see Chapter 7).

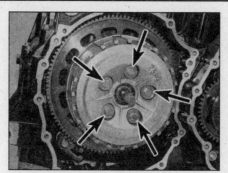

17.30 Tighten the bolts evenly in a criss-cross sequence

## 18 Clutch cable

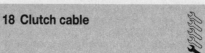

**1** On Daytona and Sprint models, first remove the right-hand fairing side panels and belly pan as applicable (see Chapter 7). On Tiger models, remove the left-hand handguard.

**2** Remove the fuel tank (see Chapter 4). On machines fitted with an air deflector underneath the airbox, remove the airbox – the clutch cable is routed through the air deflector (see Chapter 4).

**3** Slacken the locknuts securing the cable in the bracket on the clutch cover and thread the rear locknut off the adjuster (see illustration).

**4** Slip the cable end out of the retainer on the

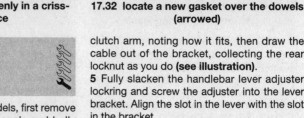

17.32 locate a new gasket over the dowels (arrowed)

clutch arm, noting how it fits, then draw the cable out of the bracket, collecting the rear locknut as you do (see illustration).

**5** Fully slacken the handlebar lever adjuster lockring and screw the adjuster into the lever bracket. Align the slot in the lever with the slot in the bracket.

**6** Pull the outer cable end from the socket in the adjuster and release the inner cable from the lever (see illustrations). Remove the cable from the machine, noting its routing and any guides or clips.

> **HAYNES HiNT**
> *Before removing the cable from the bike, tape the lower end of the new cable to the upper end of the old cable. Slowly pull the lower end of the old cable out, guiding the new cable down into position. Using this method will ensure the cable is routed correctly.*

**7** Installation is the reverse of removal. Apply grease to the cable ends. Make sure the cable is correctly routed. Make sure the cable lower end is properly located in the retainer on the release mechanism arm. Check the clutch release mechanism for smooth operation and any signs of wear or damage. Remove it for inspection if required (see Section 17).

**8** Adjust the clutch lever freeplay (see Chapter 1). Where applicable, install the body panels (see Chapter 7).

## 19 Sump and oil strainer

**Note:** *The sump can be removed with the engine in the frame. If work is being carried out with the engine removed ignore the steps which don't apply.*

### Removal

**1** On Daytona and Sprint models, remove the fairing side panels and belly-pan as applicable (see Chapter 7).

**2** Drain the engine oil and remove the oil filter (see Chapter 1).

**3** Remove the exhaust system (see Chapter 4).

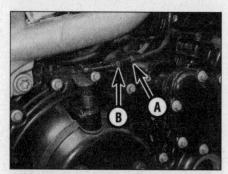

18.3 Slacken the front (A) and rear (B) locknuts

18.4 Release the cable from the clutch arm (arrowed) and draw it out of the bracket

18.6a Draw the outer cable end from the adjuster and slip the inner cable out via the slots . . .

18.6b . . . then detach the inner cable end from the lever

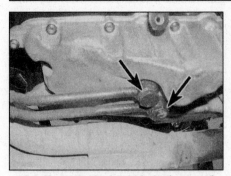

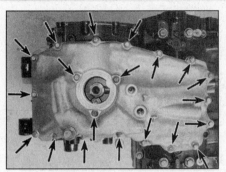

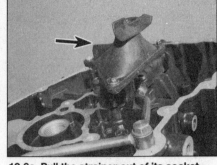

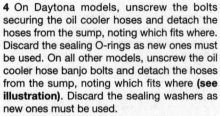

**19.4 Unscrew the banjo bolts (arrowed) and detach the hoses**

**19.5 Sump bolts (arrowed)**

**19.6a Pull the strainer out of its socket . . .**

**4** On Daytona models, unscrew the bolts securing the oil cooler hoses and detach the hoses from the sump, noting which fits where. Discard the sealing O-rings as new ones must be used. On all other models, unscrew the oil cooler hose banjo bolts and detach the hoses from the sump, noting which fits where **(see illustration)**. Discard the sealing washers as new ones must be used.

**5** Unscrew the sump bolts, slackening them evenly in a criss-cross sequence to prevent distortion **(see illustration)**. Remove the sump and discard its gasket – a new one must be used. **Note:** *The internal oil pipe nozzle and gearbox oil feed nozzle locate between the sump and the lower crankcase half – ease the sump off carefully to avoid distorting them.*

**6** Draw the oil strainer out of its socket, noting which way round it fits, then remove the rubber seal **(see illustrations)**. Check the condition of the seal and discard it if it is damaged, distorted or deteriorated in any way. Clean the strainer in solvent and remove any debris caught in the gauze. The presence of metal caught in the strainer, or in the bottom of the sump, is indicative of engine wear that should be investigated.

**7** If required, remove the gearbox oil feed nozzle – it is a push fit in the crankcase **(see illustration)**. Also if required, unscrew the banjo bolts securing the internal oil pipe and remove the pipe, noting how the nozzle end locates in its seat **(see illustrations)**. Discard the banjo bolt sealing washers as new ones

must be used. **Note:** *Triumph specify that washers should be fitted on both sides of each banjo union – on the engine photographed, washers were fitted under the heads of the banjo bolts only.* Check the condition of the nozzle O-rings and discard them if they are damaged, distorted or deteriorated in any way.

### Installation

**8** Remove all traces of gasket material from the sump and crankcase mating surfaces.

**9** If removed, fit the gearbox oil feed nozzle into the crankcase, using new O-rings if necessary **(see illustration 19.7a)**. Install the internal oil pipe using new sealing washers on the banjo bolts, and tighten the banjo bolts to the specified torque setting **(see illustration)**. Make sure the nozzle end locates in its seat,

and fit a new O-ring to it if necessary **(see illustration 19.7c)**.

**10** Fit the rubber seal for the strainer into its socket in the crankcase, using a new one if necessary **(see illustration 19.6b)**. Fit the strainer into the seal **(see illustration 19.6a)**.

**11** Place a new gasket on the crankcase and install the sump; if the engine is in the frame, use a smear of grease on the gasket to hold it in place as the sump is installed. Install the bolts and tighten them evenly in a criss-cross sequence to the specified torque setting **(see illustration 19.5)**.

**12** On Daytona models, attach the oil cooler hoses using new O-rings on the unions, and tighten the bolts to the specified torque setting. On all other models, attach the oil cooler hoses using new sealing washers on each side of the unions, and tighten the banjo

**19.6b . . . and pull out the rubber seal**

**19.7a Pull the gearbox oil feed nozzle out of its socket, noting the O-rings**

**19.7b Oil pipe is secured by two banjo bolts (arrowed)**

**19.7c Note how the nozzle end (arrowed) locates**

**19.9 Use new sealing washers on the oil pipe banjo bolts**

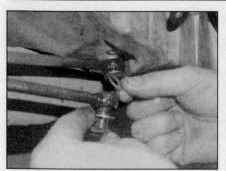

19.12 Use a new sealing washer on each side of the union

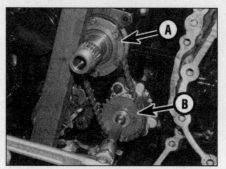

20.10 Lock the drive sprocket (A) as described then loosen the driven sprocket bolt (B)

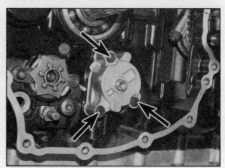

20.11 Remove the bolts (arrowed) securing the pump

bolts to the specified torque setting **(see illustration)**.

**13** Install the exhaust system (see Chapter 4).

**14** Install a new oil filter, then fill the engine with the correct type and quantity of oil (see Chapter 1 and *Daily (pre-ride) checks*). Start the engine and check that there are no leaks.

**15** On Daytona and Sprint models, install the body panels as applicable (see Chapter 7).

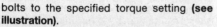

## 20 Oil pump and oil pressure relief valve

**Note:** *The oil pump can be removed with the engine in the frame, but removal of the pressure relief valve requires removal of the engine and separation of the crankcases.*

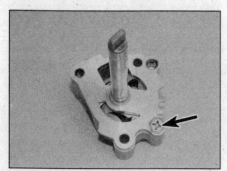

20.12a Remove the bolt (arrowed) . . .

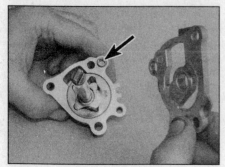

20.12b . . . and lift off the cover, noting the dowel (arrowed)

### Oil pressure check

**1** To check the oil pressure, a suitable gauge and adapter that screws into the oil pressure switch will be needed. Triumph do not list an adapter as a spare part, but it is worth checking with a dealer as to availability. Otherwise, remove the pressure switch (see Chapter 8), and take it to an accessory dealer to match it up – if you are buying a pressure gauge, it may well come with a range of adapters.

**2** Warm the engine up to normal operating temperature then stop it. Remove the fairing side panels on Daytona and Sprint models (see Chapter 7).

**3** Remove the oil pressure switch (see Chapter 8) and screw the adapter in its place. Connect the gauge to the adapter.

**4** Start the engine and increase the engine speed to 5000 rpm whilst watching the gauge reading. The oil pressure should be similar to that given in the Specifications at the start of this Chapter.

**5** If the pressure is significantly lower than the standard, the relief valve is stuck open, the oil pump is faulty, the oil pump pick-up strainer is blocked or there is other engine damage. Begin diagnosis by checking the oil pump pick-up strainer (see Section 19), then the oil pump. If those items check out okay, chances are the bearing oil clearances are excessive and the engine needs to be overhauled.

**6** If the pressure is too high, the relief valve is stuck closed. To check it, see Steps 22 to 24.

**7** Stop the engine and unscrew the gauge

and adapter from the crankcase. Install the oil pressure switch (see Chapter 8).

**8** If applicable, install the fairing panels (see Chapter 7).

### Oil pump

#### Removal

**9** Remove the clutch (see Section 17).

**10** The oil pump drive sprocket must be locked to enable the driven sprocket bolt to be slackened. Triumph provides a service tool to do this (Part No. T3880371). Alternatively, engage a length of bar between the pegs on the drive sprocket and secure it against the crankcase **(see illustration)**. Unscrew the bolt and remove the bolt and washer, then lift off the drive and driven sprockets, chain, drive sprocket needle bearing and sleeve as an assembly **(see illustration 20.19b)**.

**11** Remove the bolts securing the pump in the crankcase and withdraw the pump **(see illustrations)**.

#### Inspection

**Note:** *Individual internal parts are not available for the oil pump; if the checks described below indicate that the pump is worn, it must be renewed as a complete unit.*

**12** Undo the bolt securing the pump cover and remove the cover; remove the dowel for safekeeping if it is loose **(see illustrations)**.

**13** Measure the clearance between the inner rotor tip and the outer rotor tip with a feeler gauge **(see illustration)**. Also measure the clearance between the outer rotor and the pump body **(see illustration)**. Finally, lift out

20.13a Measuring rotor tip clearance

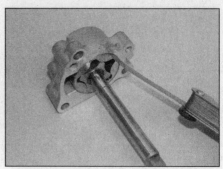

20.13b Measuring outer rotor-to-body clearance

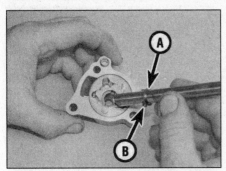

**20.13c Note the washer (A) and drive pin (B) on the pump shaft**

**20.13d Measuring rotor end float**

**20.14 look for scoring and wear, such as on this outer rotor**

the pump shaft, noting the location of the washer and inner rotor drive pin **(see illustration)**. Lay a straight-edge across the rotors and pump body and measure the rotor end-float (gap between the rotors and straight-edge) with a feeler gauge **(see illustration)**. If any of the results are outside the limits listed in this Chapter's Specifications, replace the pump with a new one.

**14** Lift the inner and outer rotors out of the pump, noting which way round they fit. Examine them for scoring and wear **(see illustration)**.

**15** Before reassembling the pump, make sure that all parts are clean. Have a supply of the correct grade of engine oil on hand to lubricate the rotors as they are installed. Ensure that the drive pin and washer are assembled on the pump shaft and that the shaft is fitted the right way round **(see illustration 20.13c)**.

**16** If removed, fit the dowel into the pump,

then install the cover and tighten the bolt securely.

**17** Inspect the oil pump drive and driven sprockets and chain for damage and wear and renew them as a set if necessary. Check the needle bearing and sleeve and renew them if they are worn or pitted **(see illustration)**.

### Installation

**18** Insert the pump shaft into the crankcase and ensure that the tab on the inner end of the shaft engages with the slot in the water pump drive; temporarily fit the driven sprocket onto the outer end of the shaft and rotate it until the tab is felt to engage and the back of the pump is directly in contact with the crankcase **(see illustration)**. Install the mounting bolts and tighten them to the torque setting specified at the beginning of the Chapter.

**19** Fit the sleeve, needle bearing and drive sprocket onto the end of the input shaft, then loop the chain over the drive sprocket. Fit the

driven sprocket into the chain, ensuring the side marked OUT is facing out, then slide the assembly in, ensuring the driven sprocket locates correctly on the oil pump shaft **(see illustrations)**.

**20** Install the driven sprocket bolt and washer, then using the method employed on removal to lock the drive sprocket, tighten the bolt to the specified torque setting.

**21** Install the clutch (see Section 17).

### Oil pressure relief valve

**22** The oil pressure relief valve is located in the lower crankcase half. Remove the engine from the frame and separate the crankcase halves to access the valve (see Sections 5 and 22).

**23** Refer to the relevant Steps in Section 30 and remove the gearchange forks and selector drum.

**24** Unscrew the valve from the crankcase, then follow the procedure in Chapter 2A, Section 19, to inspect and install the valve.

---

### 21  Oil cooler

**1** Follow the procedure in Chapter 2A, Section 20, to remove and install the oil cooler.

**2** Note the following:

● On Daytona models, the oil cooler hoses are retained by two bolts at each end and the hose unions are sealed with O-rings. Fit new O-rings on installation.

● Tighten the hose union bolts to the torque setting specified at the beginning of this Chapter.

---

### 22  Crankcase separation and reassembly

### Separation

**1** To access the crankshaft and connecting rods, bearings, balancer shaft, oil pressure relief valve, transmission shafts, gearchange selector drum and forks, the crankcase must be split into two parts.

**2** To enable the crankcases to be separated, remove the engine from the frame (see

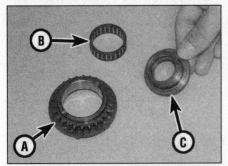

**20.17 Check the oil pump drive sprocket (A), needle bearing (B) and sleeve (C)**

**20.18 Ensure the tab (arrowed) engages with the water pump**

**20.19a Fit the drive sprocket assembly and chain onto the input shaft . . .**

**20.19b . . . then install the driven sprocket as described**

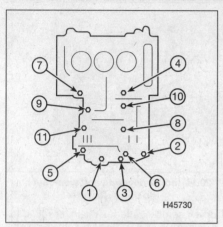

22.3  Upper crankcase bolt slackening sequence

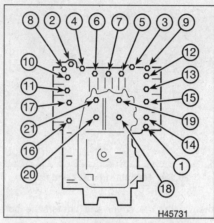

22.4  Lower crankcase bolt slackening sequence

22.5  Lift the lower crankcase half off carefully so as not to dislodge components

Section 5) and remove the following components with reference to the relevant Sections.

Camshafts and followers
Cam chain and tensioner blade
Cylinder head*
Cylinder liners and pistons*
Clutch
Alternator and starter motor (Chapter 8)
Sump

*If the crankcase halves are being separated just to examine the crankshaft, balancer shaft or transmission components, then there is no need to remove the cylinder head, liners and pistons. If a complete engine overhaul is planned, also remove the water pump (see Chapter 3), and the oil pump (see Section 20).

**3**  With the crankcase the right way up, slacken and remove all bolts from the upper crankcase half following the numbered sequence **(see illustration)**. **Note:** *As each bolt is removed, store it in its relative position in a cardboard template of the crankcase halves. This will ensure that all bolts are installed in the correct location on reassembly. Also, take note of any mounting brackets on the bolts and store them with the bolts to ensure correct reassembly.*

**4**  Turn the crankcase upside down. Again,

following the numbered sequence, slacken and remove all bolts from the lower crankcase half **(see illustration)**. **Note:** *As each bolt is removed, store it in its relative position in a cardboard template of the crankcase halves. This will ensure that all bolts are installed in the correct location on reassembly. Also, take note of any mounting brackets on the bolts and store them with the bolts to ensure correct reassembly.*

**5**  Carefully lift the lower crankcase half off the upper half, leaving the crankshaft, balancer shaft and transmission shafts in the upper half of the crankcase **(see illustration)**. As the lower half is lifted away take care not to dislodge or lose any main bearing shells. Note how the gear selector forks engage with their respective slots in the transmission gears. **Note:** *If the halves don't separate easily, make sure all fasteners have been removed. Don't lever between the crankcase mating surfaces or they will leak; initial separation can be achieved by tapping gently around the joint with a soft-faced mallet.*

**6**  Remove the three locating dowels if they are loose – they could be in either crankcase half. Remove the O-ring from the oil passage joint and discard it as a new one must be fitted **(see illustration)**.

### Reassembly

**7**  Remove all traces of sealant from the crankcase mating surfaces.

**8**  Ensure that all components are in place in the upper and lower crankcase halves. If the transmission shafts have not been removed, check the condition of the oil seal on the left-hand end of the output shaft and replace it with a new one if it is damaged, deformed or deteriorated (see Section 28) – it is always good practice to renew this seal whenever the crankcases have been separated. Also note the instructions in Section 28 concerning applying thread lock to the transmission shaft bearing outer races. Check the position of the selector drum and forks and transmission shafts – make sure they're in the neutral position (i.e. the transmission shafts rotate independently of each other – see Section 30).

**9**  Lubricate the transmission shafts and crankshaft journals with clean engine oil, then use a rag soaked in high flash-point solvent to wipe over the mating surfaces of both halves to remove all traces of oil.

**10**  If removed, fit the three locating dowels into the upper crankcase half.

**11**  Fit a new O-ring onto the oil passage joint **(see illustration 22.6)**.

**12**  Apply a small amount of suitable sealant to the indicated areas of the mating surface of one crankcase half **(see illustration)**.

22.6  Note the location of the oil passage O-ring

22.12  Apply sealant to the crankcase as shown

**Caution: Take care not to apply an excessive amount of sealant, as it will ooze out when the case halves are assembled and may obstruct oil passages and prevent the bearings from seating.**

**13** Make sure that the main bearing shells are in position, then carefully guide the lower crankcase half onto the upper half **(see illustration 22.5)**. Make sure the selector forks engage with their respective slots in the transmission gears as the halves are joined.

**14** Check that the lower crankcase half is correctly seated and that all shafts are free to rotate. **Note:** *If the casings are not correctly seated, remove the lower crankcase half and investigate the problem. Do not attempt to pull them together using the crankcase bolts as the casing will crack and be ruined.*

**15** Clean the threads of the lower crankcase bolts and insert them in their original locations, including any brackets. Secure all bolts finger-tight at this stage.

**16** Turn the crankcase over so that it is upright. Clean the threads of the upper crankcase bolts and install them in their original locations. Secure all bolts finger-tight at this stage. **Caution: Note that two sizes of bolt are used, 6 mm and 8 mm. Care must be taken to distinguish between them during the tightening sequence, as the larger 8 mm bolts are set much tighter, and if a 6 mm bolt is mistaken for an 8 mm bolt, it may shear.**

**17** Tighten the crankcase bolts as follows: turn the crankcase over and tighten all lower crankcase bolts to 12 Nm, tightening them in the correct numbered sequence **(see illustration)**. Now tighten all upper crankcase bolts to 12 Nm, tightening them in the correct numbered sequence **(see illustration)**.

**18** Now tighten the M8 size lower crankcase bolts (No. 1 to 14) to 28 Nm in the correct sequence **(see illustration 22.17a)**. Finally tighten the M8 size upper crankcase bolts (No. 1 to 8) to 28 Nm in the correct sequence **(see illustration 22.17b)**.

**19** With all crankcase fasteners tightened, check that the crankshaft and transmission shafts rotate smoothly and easily. If there are any signs of undue stiffness or of any other problem, the fault must be rectified before proceeding further.

**20** Install all other removed assemblies in the reverse of the sequence in Step 2.

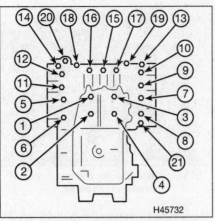

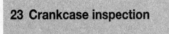

**22.17a  Lower crankcase bolt tightening sequence**

## 23 Crankcase inspection

**1** Follow the procedure in Chapter 2A, Section 22, to inspect the crankcases.

## 24 Main and connecting rod bearings – general information

**1** General information regarding inspection of the bearings and the possible causes of bearing failure can be found in Chapter 2A, Section 23.

## 25 Connecting rods

**Note 1:** *The connecting rod nuts and bolts must be discarded and new ones used on installation – it is best to obtain the new parts in advance. The old bolts can however be used for the oil clearance check.*

**Note 2:** *There are a number of different ways in which the connecting rods can be removed, and your best approach will depend on what other work, if any, you are doing on the engine.*
● *If the pistons have already been separated from the rods, then you can either remove*

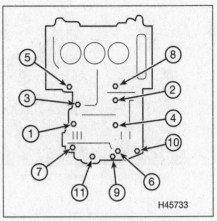

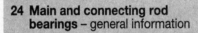

**22.17b  Upper crankcase bolt tightening sequence**

*the crankshaft with the rods still attached, and then separate them afterwards, or you can leave the crankshaft in situ, remove the rod caps and then remove the rods from the top of the crankcase.*
● *If the pistons have not been separated from the rods, they cannot be removed along with the crankshaft as the pistons will not fit through the crankcase main bearing webs. Remove the rod caps first, then remove the rod and piston assemblies from the top of the crankcase.*

**Note 3:** *If the crankshaft and transmission shafts are left in situ, take great care not to dislodge them when the rods/pistons are being removed.*

### Removal

**1** Remove the engine from the frame (see Section 5).

**2** Remove the cylinder head (see Section 12).

**3** If the Triumph special tool or a liner extractor is available, remove the cylinder liners (see Section 15), then remove the pistons (see Section 16).

**4** Separate the crankcase halves (see Section 22).

**5** Before separating the rods from the crankshaft, measure the side clearance on each rod with a feeler gauge **(see illustration)**. If the clearance on any rod is greater than the service limit listed in this Chapter's Specifications, replace that rod with a new one.

**6** Using paint or a marker pen, mark the relevant cylinder identity across the join between each connecting rod and cap – these ensure that the cap and rod are fitted correctly on reassembly. Cylinders are numbered 1 to 3, from the left to the right-hand side of the engine. **Note:** *The number and letter already across the rod and cap indicate rod size and weight grade respectively, not cylinder number.*

**7** Working on one connecting rod at a time, unscrew the connecting rod cap nuts and remove them **(see illustration)**.

**8** If the crankshaft and transmission shafts are being left in situ, lift the crankcase and support it with sufficient clearance for the rods or rod and piston assemblies to be removed through the top of the crankcase.

**9** Separate the cap, complete with the lower

**25.5  Measure the connecting rod side clearance using a feeler gauge**

**25.7  Working on one rod at a time, unscrew the cap nuts (arrowed) . . .**

25.9 .. and remove the connecting rod cap ...

25.10 ... then detach the rod from the crankpin (arrowed)

25.11 Keep the connecting rod assembly components together as a set

bearing shell, from the crankpin **(see illustration)**. If the cap appears stuck, tap it on one end with a hammer while pulling it.

10 Support the rod to prevent it marking the liner bore or block, and detach it, complete with the upper bearing shell, from the crankpin, then remove the rod or rod and piston assembly **(see illustration)**. Note on Speed Triple, Sprint and Tiger models, the oil hole in the rod which faces the rear of the engine.

**HAYNES HiNT** *If required, to ease removal of the pistons from the tops of the liners, carefully remove any ridge of carbon built up on the top of each liner bore using a scraper. If there is a pronounced wear ridge, remove it using a ridge reamer.*

**Caution: Do not try to remove the piston/connecting rod from the bottom of the crankcase. The piston will not pass the crankcase main bearing webs.**

11 Fit the relevant bearing shells (if removed), cap, nuts and bolts on each piston/ connecting rod assembly so that they are all kept together as a matched set **(see illustration)**.

12 If required and not already done, separate the pistons from the connecting rods (see Section 16).

### Inspection

13 Check the connecting rods for cracks and

other obvious damage. Refer to Section 16 and check the piston pin and connecting rod small-end bore dimensions for wear. Renew any components that are worn beyond the specified limit.

14 Refer to Section 24 and examine the connecting rod bearing shells. If they are scored, badly scuffed or appear to have seized, new shells must be installed. Always renew the shells in the connecting rods as a set. If they are badly damaged, check the corresponding crankpin. Evidence of extreme heat, such as discoloration, indicates that lubrication failure has occurred. Be sure to thoroughly check the oil pump and pressure relief valve as well as all oil holes and passages before reassembling the engine.

15 Have the rods checked for twist and bending by a Triumph dealer if you are in doubt about their straightness.

### Oil clearance check

16 Whether new bearing shells are being fitted or the original ones are being re-used, the connecting rod bearing oil clearance should be checked prior to reassembly. Work on one rod at a time when checking the clearances.

17 If it is in situ, lift the crankshaft out of the upper crankcase half, taking care not to dislodge the main bearing shells. Ensure that the crankshaft is securely supported on the work surface.

18 Remove the bearing shells from the rod and cap, keeping them in order **(see illustration)**. Clean the backs of the shells and

the bearing locations in both the connecting rod and cap, and the crankpin journal.

19 Press the bearing shells into their locations, ensuring that the tab on each shell engages the notch in the connecting rod/cap **(see illustration)**. Make sure the bearings are fitted in the correct locations and take care not to touch any shell's bearing surface with your fingers.

20 Cut a length of the appropriate size Plastigauge (it should be slightly shorter than the width of the crankpin). Place a strand of Plastigauge on the crankpin journal for the rod being checked. Fit the rod onto its crankpin, then install the cap, making sure it is fitted the correct way around so the previously made markings align. Note that the accuracy of this check is dependant on the rod not turning on the crankpin while it is installed and tightened – if it does, the Plastigauge will be disturbed and an inaccurate reading will result. Apply a smear of molybdenum disulphide grease to the bolt threads and to the underside of the nuts and install them finger-tight.

21 On Daytona, Speed Triple and Sprint models, tighten the nuts in five stages, using a torque wrench and a degree disc, as follows. First tighten the nuts to 22 Nm, then slacken them by 140°. Now tighten the nuts to 10 Nm, then to 14 Nm, and finally tighten them by 120° **(see illustrations)**.

22 On Tiger models, tighten the nuts in two stages, using a torque wrench and a degree disc, as follows. First tighten the nuts to 14 Nm, then tighten them by 120°.

23 Slacken the cap nuts and remove the

25.18 To remove a big-end bearing shell, push it sideways and lift it out

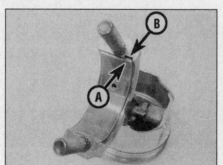

25.19 Make sure the tab (A) locates in the notch (B)

25.21a Tighten the nuts using a torque wrench ...

25.21b . . . and a degree disc as specified

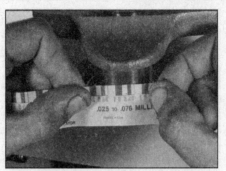

25.24 Measure the crushed Plastigauge using the appropriate scale on the pack

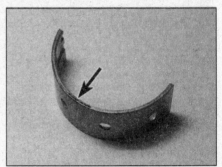

25.28 The colour code is marked on the side of the shell (arrowed)

connecting rod cap, again taking great care not to rotate the crankshaft.

24 Compare the width of the crushed Plastigauge on the crankpin to the scale printed on the Plastigauge envelope to obtain the connecting rod bearing oil clearance **(see illustration)**. Be sure to use the appropriate scale as both imperial and metric scales are shown.

25 On completion carefully scrape away all traces of the Plastigauge material from the crankpin and bearing shells using a fingernail or other object which will not score the bearing surfaces.

26 If the clearance is within the range listed in this Chapter's Specifications and the bearing shells are in perfect condition, they can be reused. If the clearance is beyond the specified service limit, first measure the diameter of the crankpin with a micrometer and compare the result with the Specifications at the beginning of this Chapter. If the journal diameter is larger than the service limit, new bearing shells can be fitted (see Steps 28 to 30). If the journal diameter is smaller than the service limit, the crankshaft must be renewed.

27 Repeat the procedure for the remaining connecting rods. If applicable, always renew all of the shells (on all three rods) at the same time.

### Bearing shell selection

28 The connecting rod big-end bearing oil clearance is controlled in production by selecting one of three grades of bearing shell. The grades are indicated by a colour-coding

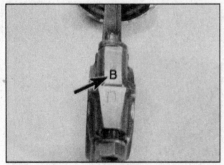

25.29 Typical connecting rod size marking (arrowed)

marked on the edge of each shell **(see illustration)**. New bearing shells are selected as follows using the crankpin journal diameter and connecting rod size marking.

29 Measure the crankpin journal diameter using a micrometer and record the result. Inspect the connecting rod for its size marking, either the letter A or B, or the number 4 or 5 **(see illustration)**.

30 Match the rod marking with the measured journal diameter and select a set of new bearing shells using the following tables.

### Daytona models

| Con-rod marking | Crankpin journal diameter | Shell colour |
|---|---|---|
| 5 | 34.992 to 35.000 mm | White |
| 5 | 34.984 to 34.991 mm | Red |
| 4 | 34.992 to 35.000 mm | Red |
| 4 | 34.984 to 34.991 mm | Blue |

### Speed Triple up to VIN 144667 and all Sprint and Tiger models

| Con-rod marking | Crankpin journal diameter | Shell colour |
|---|---|---|
| A | 40.954 to 40.960 mm | White |
| A | 40.946 to 40.953 mm | Red |
| B | 40.954 to 40.960 mm | Red |
| B | 40.946 to 40.953 mm | Blue |

### Speed Triple from VIN 144668

| Con-rod marking | Crankpin journal diameter | Shell colour |
|---|---|---|
| 5 | 40.954 to 40.960 mm | White |
| 5 | 40.946 to 40.953 mm | Red |
| 4 | 40.954 to 40.960 mm | Red |
| 4 | 40.946 to 40.953 mm | Blue |

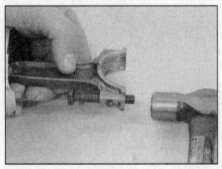

25.32 Tap out the old bolts and install new ones

### Installation

**Note 1:** *New connecting rod nuts and bolts* **must** *be used for final assembly.*

**Note 2:** *There are a number of different ways in which the connecting rods can be installed, and your best approach will depend on what other work, if any, you are doing on the engine.*

● *If the pistons have been separated from the rods and the crankshaft has been removed, then you can either fit the rods onto the crankshaft and then install the crankshaft, or you can install the crankshaft and then install the rods from the top of the crankcase.*

● *If the pistons have not been separated from the rods, the rod and piston assemblies cannot be installed attached to the crankshaft as the pistons will not fit through the crankcase main bearing webs. Install the rod and piston assemblies from the top of the crankcase then install the crankshaft. You will also have to make a decision regarding installation of the liners, if they have been removed, as the rod and piston assemblies can be installed before them, with them or after them – see Section 15 for details.*

● *If it makes no difference, we advise fitting the pistons onto the rods first, then fitting the rod and piston assemblies into the liners, then installing the liners. At this point the cylinder head can be installed to avoid the risk of disturbing the liner seal when installing the crankshaft.*

31 Remove the bearing shells from the rods and caps, keeping them in order **(see illustration 25.18)**. Clean the backs of the shells and the bearing locations in both the connecting rod and cap, and the crankpin journal. If new shells are being fitted, ensure that all traces of the protective grease are cleaned off using paraffin (kerosene). Wipe the shells, cap and rod dry with a clean lint free cloth.

32 Remove the old bolts from the rods and discard them, then fit the new ones – it will probably be necessary to tap the old bolts out using a hammer **(see illustration)**.

33 Press the bearing shells into their locations, ensuring that the tab on each shell engages the notch in the connecting rod/cap **(see illustration 25.19)**. Make sure the

bearings are fitted in the correct locations and take care not to touch any shell's bearing surface with your fingers.

**34** Decide upon your installation procedure, then assemble the rods, pistons, cylinder liners and crankshaft as required, referring to the relevant Sections. **Note:** *When installing the connecting rods on the crankshaft, refer to the previously made marks to ensure they are fitted in the correct positions (see Step 6). Remember that on Speed Triple, Sprint and Tiger models, the oil hole in the connecting rod must face to the rear of the engine, on the opposite side to the arrow or dot on the piston crown which must point to the front of the engine.*

**35** Lubricate the shells with new engine oil. Fit the rod onto its crankpin, then install the cap, making sure it is fitted the correct way around so the previously made markings align. Apply a smear of molybdenum disulphide grease to the bolt threads and to the underside of the nuts **(see illustration)**. Fit the nuts and tighten them finger-tight at this stage. Check to make sure that all components have been returned to their original locations using the marks made on disassembly. Now tighten the nuts to the specified settings as described in Steps 21 and 22.

 **HINT** *If a degree disc is not available, the angle can be determined by using the points on the connecting rod cap nut. There are six points on the nut, so the angle between each point is 60°. Select one point as a reference and mark it with paint or a marker. Now select the second point clockwise from it and mark its position on the connecting rod cap. Tighten the nut – when the mark on the first point aligns with the mark made on the connecting rod cap, it will have turned through 120°.*

**36** Install the other connecting rods in the same way. Check to make sure that all components have been returned to their original locations using the marks made on disassembly.

**37** Check that the crankshaft rotates freely and that the rods rotate smoothly and freely on the crankpins. If there are any signs of

**25.35 Lubricate the threads with molybdenum disulphide grease**

roughness or tightness, remove the rods and re-check the bearing clearance. Sometimes tapping the bottom of the connecting rod cap will relieve tightness, but if in doubt, recheck the clearances. **Note:** *If the cylinder liners have been installed, ensure appropriate measures have been taken to prevent them lifting off their seals when the crankshaft is rotated (see Section 15).*

**38** Reassemble the crankcase halves and the rest of the engine according to your removal procedure, referring to the relevant Sections.

## 26 Crankshaft and main bearings

### Removal

**1** Remove the engine from the frame (see Section 5) and separate the crankcase halves (see Section 22).

**2** Refer to Section 25 and separate the connecting rods from the crankshaft (unless the pistons have been removed, in which case the rods can remain attached for now, and removed later if required). **Note:** *If no work is to be carried out on the piston/connecting rod assemblies there is no need to remove them from the bores (unless the liners have been removed), but push them up to the top of the bores so that the big-ends are clear of the crankshaft.*

**3** Before removing the crankshaft, check the amount of end-float using a dial gauge. If it exceeds the limit specified, the crankshaft

and/or the crankcases must be replaced with new ones. Lift out the balancer shaft, noting how the shaft driven gear aligns with the gear on the crankshaft (see Section 27). Lift the crankshaft out of the upper crankcase half, taking care not to dislodge the main bearing shells **(see illustration)**.

**4** If required, remove the bearing shells from the crankcase halves by pushing their centres to the side, then lifting them out **(see illustration)**. Keep the shells in order.

### Inspection

**5** Clean the crankshaft with solvent. If available, blow the crank dry with compressed air.

**6** Refer to Section 24 and examine the main bearing shells. If they are scored, badly scuffed or appear to have been seized, new shells must be installed. Always renew the main bearings as a set. If they are badly damaged, check the corresponding crankshaft journals. Evidence of extreme heat, such as discoloration, indicates that lubrication failure has occurred. Be sure to thoroughly check the oil pump and pressure relief valve as well as all oil holes and passages before reassembling the engine.

**7** The crankshaft journals should be given a close visual examination, paying particular attention where damaged bearing shells have been discovered. If the journals are scored or pitted in any way a new crankshaft will be required. Note that oversize shells are not available, precluding the option of re-grinding the crankshaft.

### Oil clearance check

**8** Whether new bearing shells are being fitted or the original ones are being re-used, the main bearing oil clearance should be checked prior to reassembly.

**9** If not already done, remove the bearing shells from the crankcase halves by pushing their centres to the side, then lifting them out **(see illustration 26.4)**. Keep the shells in order. Clean the backs of the shells and their locations in both the crankcase halves.

**10** Press the bearing shells back into their locations, ensuring that the tab on each shell engages in the notch **(see illustration)**. Make sure the shells are fitted in the correct locations and take care not to touch any shell's bearing surface with your fingers.

**11** Ensure that the shells and crankshaft are

**26.3 Carefully lift the crankshaft out of the crankcase**

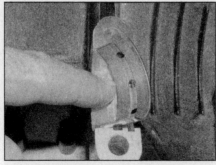
**26.4 To remove a main bearing shell, push it sideways and lift it out**

**26.10 Press each shell into place, locating the tab in the notch (arrowed)**

clean and dry. Lay the crankshaft in position in the upper crankcase.

**12** Cut several lengths of the appropriate size Plastigauge (they should be slightly shorter than the width of the crankshaft journal). Place a strand of Plastigauge on each (cleaned) crankshaft journal.

**13** If removed, fit the three locating dowels into the upper crankcase half. Carefully guide the lower crankcase half onto the upper half. Make sure that the selector forks (if fitted) engage with their respective slots in the transmission gears as the halves are joined. Check that the lower crankcase half is correctly seated. **Note:** *If the casings are not correctly seated, remove the lower crankcase half and investigate the problem. Do not attempt to pull them together using the crankcase bolts as the casing will crack and be ruined.* Install the eight 8 mm lower crankcase bolts in their original locations and tighten them in the correct numerical sequence in three stages to the torque settings specified in Section 22. Make sure that the crankshaft is not rotated as the bolts are tightened.

**14** Slacken and remove the crankcase bolts, working in a criss-cross pattern from the outside in, then carefully lift off the lower crankcase half, making sure the Plastigauge is not disturbed.

**15** Compare the width of the crushed Plastigauge on each crankshaft journal to the scale printed on the Plastigauge envelope to obtain the main bearing oil clearance **(see illustration 25.24).**

**16** On completion carefully scrape away all traces of the Plastigauge material from the journals and bearing shells using a fingernail or other object which will not score the bearing surfaces.

**17** If the clearance is within the range listed in this Chapter's Specifications and the bearing shells are in perfect condition, they can be reused. If the clearance is beyond the specified service limit, first measure the diameter of the crankshaft journals with a micrometer and compare the results with the Specifications at the beginning of this Chapter. If the journal diameters are larger than the service limit, new bearing shells can be fitted (see Steps 18 and 19). If the journal diameters are smaller than the service limit, the crankshaft must be renewed.

### Bearing shell selection

**18** The main bearing oil clearance is controlled in production by selecting one of four grades of bearing shell. The grades are indicated by a colour-coding marked on the edge of each shell **(see illustration 25.28)**. New bearing inserts are selected with reference to the following charts, having first measured the crankshaft journal diameter and the crankcase bore diameter.

**19** Measure the diameter of each crankshaft journal with a micrometer and record the results. Next, assemble the crankcase halves with the bearing shells and crankshaft removed, and tighten the 8 mm crankshaft journal bolts in the correct numerical sequence in three stages to the torque settings specified in Section 22.

Measure each crankshaft journal bore diameter using a bore gauge and micrometer and record the results. Refer to *Tools and Workshop Tips* in the Reference Section for details on how to use the measuring equipment.

#### Daytona, Speed Triple and Sprint models

| Crankcase bore dia. | Crankshaft journal dia. | Shell colour |
|---|---|---|
| 41.101 to 41.109 mm | 37.969 to 37.976 mm | White |
| 41.101 to 41.109 mm | 37.960 to 37.968 mm | Red |
| 41.110 to 41.118 mm | 37.969 to 37.976 mm | Red |
| 41.110 to 41.118 mm | 37.960 to 37.968 mm | Blue |
| 41.119 to 41.127 mm | 37.969 to 37.976 mm | Blue |
| 41.119 to 41.127 mm | 37.960 to 37.968 mm | Green |

#### Tiger models

| Crankcase bore dia. | Crankshaft journal dia. | Shell colour |
|---|---|---|
| 41.101 to 41.109 mm | 37.969 to 37.976 mm | White |
| 41.101 to 41.118 mm | 37.960 to 37.976 mm | Red |
| 41.110 to 41.127 mm | 37.960 to 37.976 mm | Blue |
| 41.119 to 41.127 mm | 37.960 to 37.968 mm | Green |

### Installation

**20** Clean the backs of the bearing shells and the bearing recesses in both crankcase halves. If new shells are being fitted, ensure that all traces of the protective grease are cleaned off using paraffin (kerosene). Wipe the shells and crankcase halves dry with a lint-free cloth.

**21** Press the bearing shells into their locations, ensuring that the tab on each shell engages in the notch **(see illustration 26.10)**. Make sure the bearings are fitted in the correct locations and take care not to touch any shell's bearing surface with your fingers. Lubricate all the shells with clean engine oil.

**22** Identify the two teeth on the crankshaft

**27.2 Balancer shaft driven gear and crankshaft drive gear alignment marks**

balancer drive gear marked with a dot – these two teeth must sit on each side of the marked and aligned teeth on the balancer shaft driven gear when it is installed. Lower the crankshaft into position in the upper crankcase, with the marked teeth facing forwards **(see illustration 26.3)**. Install the balancer shaft ensuring that it is correctly timed to the crankshaft (see Section 27).

**23** If removed, install the connecting rods, then reassemble the crankcase halves and the rest of the engine according to your removal procedure, referring to the relevant Sections.

### 27 Balancer shaft

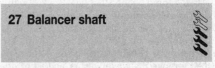

#### Removal

**1** Remove the engine from the frame and separate the crankcase halves (see Sections 5 and 22).

**2** The balancer shaft is gear driven off the right-hand end of the crankshaft – the crankshaft drive gear and the balancer shaft driven gear are marked so that precise timing of the two shafts can be achieved. The balancer shaft driven gear incorporates an outer spring-loaded backlash eliminator gear – rotate the crankshaft until the tooth marked with a line on the backlash eliminator gear aligns with the two teeth marked with dots on the crankshaft drive gear **(see illustration)**.

**3** Note how the circlips on the ends of the balancer shaft locate in the grooves in the crankcase, then lift out the balancer shaft **(see illustrations)**. Note that as the shaft is lifted

**27.3a Note the location of the circlip on the left . . .**

**27.3b . . . and right-hand end of the balancer shaft**

**27.4 Outer gear is marked with a line, inner gear with a dot**

**27.5a Remove the circlip . . .**

**27.5b . . . and the wave washer**

out the backlash eliminator gear will spring out of alignment.

### Inspection

**4** Inspect the teeth of both inner and outer driven gears for signs of wear or damage, and replace them with new ones if necessary. If damage is found, check the teeth of the drive gear on the crankshaft. Note that when the gears are not under tension (i.e. meshed with the crankshaft drive gear) the tooth on the outer gear marked with a line does not align with the tooth on the inner gear marked with a dot **(see illustration)**.

**5** The shaft can be disassembled if required – all components are available individually. Remove the circlip securing the outer gear, then remove the wave washer and lift off the gear, noting how the pin on the inside face

locates against one end of the backlash spring **(see illustrations)**. On assembly, ensure that the pins on the inner and outer gears are correctly located between the ends of the backlash spring.

**6** If required, hold the shaft in a soft-jawed vice and unscrew the right-hand end cap. Check the needle bearings on each end of the shaft and replace them with new ones if necessary. The bearings are secured by circlips; renew the circlips if the bearings have been removed. On assembly, apply a suitable non-permanent thread locking compound to the end cap threads and tighten the cap to the torque setting specified at the beginning of this Chapter.

**7** The balancer shaft is hollow and acts as a breather tube for the crankcase. Before reassembly, flush the tube with suitable

solvent and dry it with compressed air, if available.

### Installation

**8** Before installing the balancer shaft, ensure the two teeth on the crankshaft drive gear marked with dots are facing forwards.

**9** Align the tooth on the balancer shaft inner gear marked with a dot with the tooth on the outer gear marked with a line **(see illustration 27.4)**. To do this, first mark the top edge of the inner gear tooth with paint so that it can be identified when the two gears are aligned, then use two small screwdrivers inserted through the holes in the gears to draw the gears into position against the tension of the backlash spring **(see illustration)**. Lock the gears together; Triumph provides a special tool to do this (Part No. T3880016), or alternatively use a piece of crushed tube or similar between the gear teeth – note that when the balancer shaft is installed in the crankcase the locking tool must not interfere with the meshing of the driven and drive gears **(see illustration)**.

**10** Lubricate the needle bearings with clean engine oil, then lay the shaft in the crankcase, ensuring that the tooth marked with a line on the backlash eliminator gear is between the two teeth marked with dots on the crankshaft drive gear **(see illustration)**. If, necessary, rotate the shafts slightly to ensure that the gears are correctly aligned. Check that the circlips on the ends of the shaft are located in their grooves **(see illustrations 27.3a and 3b)**.

**11** Remove the locking tool and check that both the inner and outer balancer shaft driven gears are correctly aligned with the crankshaft drive gear – use the painted mark on the top edge of the inner driven gear to check its position.

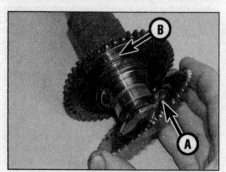

**27.5c Note how the pin (A) locates against the end of the backlash spring (B)**

**27.9a Align the marked gears (arrowed) as described**

⚠️ *Warning: If the balancer shaft and crankshaft gears are not correctly aligned, severe engine vibration will occur leading to damage to engine components.*

**12** Reassemble the crankcase halves and the rest of the engine according to your removal procedure, referring to the relevant Sections.

**27.9b . . . and lock them together**

**27.10 Ensure the gears are correctly aligned (arrow) when the shaft is installed**

28.2 Lift out the transmission output shaft

28.3 Remove the input shaft bearing retainer plate, noting the OUT mark (arrowed)

## 28 Transmission shaft removal and installation

### Removal

**1** Remove the engine from the frame and separate the crankcase halves (see Sections 5 and 22).

**2** Lift the output shaft out of the crankcase **(see illustration)**. Remove the needle bearing locating pin for safekeeping if it is loose – it could be in the bearing or the crankcase. The ball bearing on the left-hand end of the shaft is located by a complete ring which remains loose on the shaft.

**3** On Daytona and Sprint ST models from engine no. 148131, and Speed Triple, Sprint RS and Tiger models from engine no. 148007, undo the screws securing the input shaft bearing retainer plate and remove the plate **(see illustration)**.

**4** Lift the input shaft out of the crankcase **(see illustration)**.

**5** Where fitted, remove the ball bearing half ring retainer from the right-hand end of the input shaft. On all models, remove the dowel pin from the left-hand end for safekeeping if it is loose.

**6** If necessary, the transmission shafts can be disassembled and inspected for wear or damage as described in Section 29.

### Installation

**7** If removed, fit the needle bearing locating pins into either the upper crankcase or the bearing outer races. If fitted, install the input shaft ball bearing retainer into its slot in the bearing. Apply a smear of a suitable non-permanent thread locking compound to the bearing locations in the upper crankcase half only.

**8** Install the input shaft, making sure the pin locates in its hole and the half ring (if applicable) locates in its groove **(see illustration 28.4)**. Position the half ring in the ball bearing groove so that it will bridge both casing halves when reassembled. If applicable, apply a suitable non-permanent thread locking compound to the bearing retainer plate screws, then install the plate with the OUT mark facing out and tighten the screws to the torque setting specified at the beginning of the Chapter.

**9** If not already done, slip the old oil seal off the left-hand end of the output shaft and replace it with a new one **(see illustration)**.

Install the output shaft, making sure the pin locates in its hole, and the retaining ring and oil seal lip locate in their grooves **(see illustration)**.

**10** Ensure that the gears of both shafts mesh correctly and that they're in the neutral position i.e. the input shaft can be turned whilst the output shaft is held stationary **(see illustration)**.

**11** Reassemble the crankcase halves and the rest of the engine according to your removal procedure, referring to the relevant Sections.

28.4 Lift out the transmission input shaft, noting the location of the pin (arrowed)

28.9a Fit a new oil seal onto the output shaft

28.9b Note the grooves for the lip on the oil seal (A) and the bearing retaining ring (B)

28.10 Ensure the shafts and gears are correctly installed

1 Input shaft with integral 1st
  gear pinion
2 Needle bearing cage and
  locating pin
3 Needle bearing
4 Thrust washer
5 2nd gear pinion
6 Splined bush
7 6th gear pinion
8 Thrust washer
9 Circlip
10 3rd/4th gear pinion
11 Circlip
12 Thrust washer
13 5th gear pinion
14 Ball bearing
15 Half-ring retainer

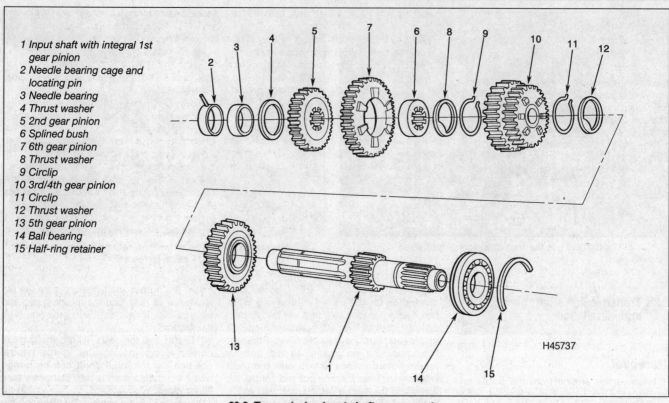

H45737

**29.3  Transmission input shaft components**

1 Needle bearing outer
  race and locating pin
2 Needle bearing
3 Thrust washer
4 1st gear pinion
5 5th gear pinion
6 Circlip
7 Thrust washer
8 3rd gear pinion
9 Bush
10 4th gear pinion
11 Thrust washer
12 Circlip
13 6th gear pinion
14 Circlip
15 Thrust washer
16 2nd gear pinion
17 Output shaft
18 Ball bearing
19 Bearing retaining ring
20 Oil seal
21 Sleeve

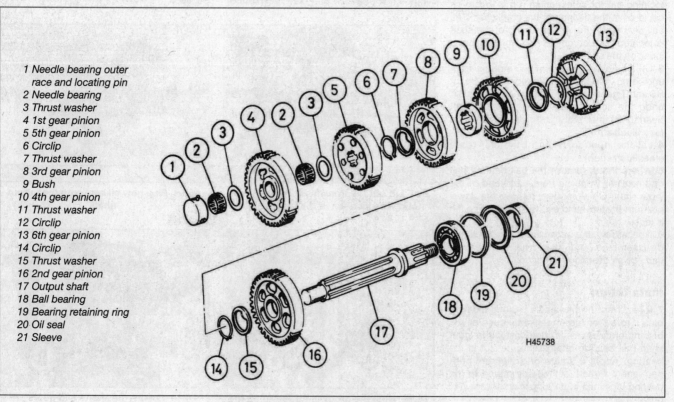

H45738

**29.4  Transmission output shaft components**

## 29 Transmission shaft overhaul

1 Remove the shafts from the crankcase as described in Section 28.
2 Follow the procedure in Chapter 2A, Section 28, to disassemble, inspect and reassemble the transmission shafts.
3 Note the following on the input shaft **(see illustration)**:
● *The needle bearing on the left-hand end of the shaft is not secured with a circlip.*
● *When the combined 3rd/4th gear pinion is installed, Triumph advise that the oilway in the pinion SHOULD NOT align with the oilway in the shaft.*
4 Note the following on the output shaft **(see illustration)**:
● *On the output shaft, the 1st gear pinion turns on a needle bearing – slide off the pinion then slide off the bearing and thrust washer .*
● *On the output shaft, there is no separate bush fitted for the 3rd gear pinion.*
● *When the 6th gear pinion is installed, Triumph advise that the oilway in the pinion*

*SHOULD NOT align with the oilway in the shaft.*
● *When the 5th gear pinion is installed, Triumph advise that the oilway in the pinion SHOULD NOT align with the oilway in the shaft.*

⚠️ **Warning: On the models covered in this Chapter, failure to install the 3rd/4th gear pinion, 6th gear pinion and 5th gear pinion as described will result in reduced engine oil pressure and gear lubrication, damage to engine components and possible engine seizure.**

## 30 Gearchange mechanism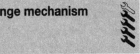

**Note:** *Access can be gained to the detent cam and stopper arms with the engine in the frame and the clutch removed (see Section 17). All other operations require the crankcases to be separated.*

### Removal

1 Remove the engine from the frame and

separate the crankcase halves (see Sections 5 and 22). The gearchange mechanism and selector drum and forks are all housed in the lower crankcase half.
2 Remove the E-clip and washer from the left-hand end of the gearchange shaft **(see illustration)**.
3 Working on the right-hand side of the engine, note how the gearchange shaft centralising spring ends fit on each side of the locating pin in the crankcase, and how the selector arm pawls engage with the pins on the gearchange cam **(see illustration)**. Withdraw the gearchange shaft from the crankcase, noting the thrust washer on the shaft **(see illustration)**.
4 Note how the stopper arm roller locates in the neutral detent on the gearchange cam **(see illustration)**. Undo the stopper arm pivot bolt and remove the bolt, stopper arm, washer and return spring in that order **(see illustration)**.
5 The selector forks are numbered 00, 01 and 02 from left to right, the numbers facing the right-hand side of the engine. If no numbers are visible, mark each fork for identification using paint or a felt pen and note which way round they fit, as an aid to

30.2 Remove the E-clip and washer

30.3a Centralising spring locating pin (A) and selector pawls (B)

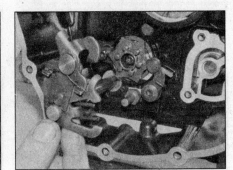

30.3b Withdraw the gearchange shaft

30.4a Gearchange cam (A) and stopper arm (B)

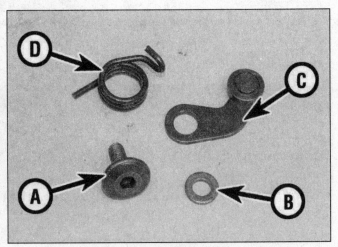

30.4b Pivot bolt (A), washer (B), stopper arm (C) and return spring (D)

30.5 Note the arrangement of the selector forks and how the guide pins locate in the selector drum (arrowed)

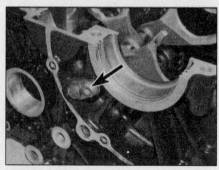

30.6a Selector fork shaft retainer screw (arrowed)

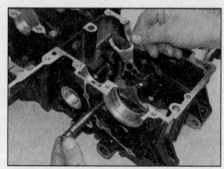

30.6b Support the forks and withdraw the shaft . . .

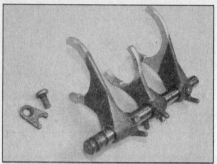

30.6c . . . then assemble the forks in the correct order on the shaft

30.7a Hold the selector drum and unscrew the centre bolt . . .

installation. Note how the guide pin on each fork locates in the groove in the selector drum (see illustration).

6 Undo the screw securing the selector fork shaft retainer and remove the retainer, noting how it fits (see illustration). Support the selector forks and withdraw the shaft from the left-hand side of the crankcase (see illustration). Once removed from the crankcase, slide the forks back onto the shaft in their correct order (see illustration). Note the O-ring on the shaft and replace it with a new one on assembly.

7 To remove the gearchange selector drum, first pass a steel rod or large screwdriver through the drum to hold it, then unscrew the centre bolt (see illustration). Remove the gearchange cam, noting how it is located by a pin, then remove the pin for safekeeping if it is loose (see illustrations).

8 Remove the bolt and retainer securing the selector drum bearing (see illustration). Push the bearing out from inside of the crankcase, using the selector drum to dislodge it, then lift the drum out of the crankcase, noting how it fits (see illustration).

### Inspection

9 Check the selector forks and shaft for wear and damage.

10 Locate each selector fork in its corresponding gear pinion groove and measure the fork-to-groove clearance using a feeler gauge (see illustration). If the

30.7b . . . then remove the gearchange cam . . .

30.7c . . . and withdraw the pin

30.8a Remove the bearing retainer . . .

30.8b . . . then remove the bearing and selector drum as described

30.10a Measure the fork-to-groove clearance using a feeler gauge

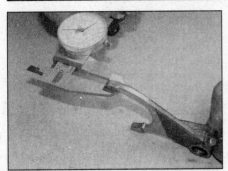

**30.10b Measuring the thickness of the fork ends . . .**

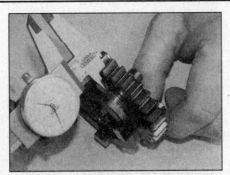

**30.10c . . . and the width of the fork groove in the gear pinion**

clearance is outside the service limit, measure the selector fork end widths and the groove in the gear using a Vernier caliper **(see illustrations)**. Renew any component which is worn beyond the service limit (see Specifications).

**11** Check the selector fork shaft for bending by rolling it along a flat surface. A bent shaft will cause difficulty in selecting gears and make the gearchange action heavy. Replace the shaft with a new one if necessary.

**12** Inspect the selector drum grooves and selector fork guide pins for wear and damage. If they show signs of wear or damage the selector fork(s) and drum must be renewed.

**13** Check that the selector drum bearing rotates freely and has no sign of freeplay between its inner and outer race. Renew the bearing if necessary.

**14** Check the gearchange shaft for distortion and damage to the splines. If the shaft is bent you can attempt to straighten it, but if the splines are damaged it must be renewed. Slide the shaft into the crankcase and check that it turns smoothly and freely in its bore. If it feels rough, prise out the oil seal, then clean and lubricate the needle bearing and check it again **(see illustration)**. If it is still rough, replace the bearing with a new one – refer to *Tools and Workshop Tips* in the Reference Section for information on bearing check, removal and installation methods. Check the condition of the oil seal and look for signs of oil leakage. Replace it with a new one if

necessary – prise out the old seal and press the new one into place. If the seal is removed to access the bearing, use a new seal – the old one is likely to leak if it is reused.

**15** Check the selector arm pawl assembly components for wear and damage and inspect the centralising spring for fatigue **(see illustration)**. The spring is retained by two circlips and can be renewed as an individual item. The pawl assembly is integral with the gearchange shaft. Also check that the centralising spring locating pin in the crankcase is securely tightened. If it is loose, remove it and apply a non-permanent thread locking compound to its threads, then tighten it to the torque setting specified at the beginning of this Chapter.

**16** Check the stopper arm roller and the detents in the gearchange cam for any wear or damage, and make sure the roller turns freely. Inspect the stopper arm return spring for fatigue. Replace any components that are worn or damaged with new ones.

### Installation

**17** Install the selector drum in the crankcase, then fit the bearing; apply a suitable non-permanent thread locking compound to the threads of the bearing retainer bolt, then install the bolt and retainer **(see illustration 30.8b and 8a)**. Tighten the bolt to the torque setting specified at the beginning of this Chapter.

**18** If removed, install the pin in the end of the

selector drum, then install the gearchange cam. Apply a suitable non-permanent thread locking compound to the threads of the centre bolt, then hold the drum as on removal and tighten the centre bolt to the specified torque setting.

**19** Assemble the stopper arm, return spring and washer on the pivot bolt. Apply a suitable non-permanent thread locking compound to the threads of the pivot bolt, then position the arm roller against the neutral detent on the cam and tighten the bolt to the specified torque setting.

**20** Check that the gearchange shaft centralising spring is properly positioned and that the circlips are in their grooves on the shaft, then slide the thrust washer onto the shaft. Lightly grease the inside of the gearchange shaft oil seal and slide the shaft into place from the right-hand side **(see illustration 30.3b)**.

**21** Lubricate the selector arm pawl assembly components with a 50/50 mixture of clean engine oil and molybdenum disulphide grease, then locate the selector arm pawls onto the pins on the selector cam and the ends of the centralising spring onto each side of the locating pin **(see illustration 30.3a)**.

**22** Install the washer onto the left-hand end of the gearchange shaft, then install the E-clip making sure it is correctly located in its groove **(see illustration 30.2)**.

**23** Fit a new O-ring onto the selector fork shaft, then slide the shaft into its bore in the crankcase and engage the forks in turn on the shaft in the correct order and way round (see Step 5). Locate the fork guide pins in the selector drum tracks **(see illustration 30.5)**.

**24** Install the selector fork shaft retainer, locating the cutout in the retainer into the groove in the end of the shaft, then apply a suitable non-permanent thread locking compound to the threads of the retainer bolt and tighten it to the specified torque setting.

**25** Assemble the crankcase halves (see Section 22).

## 31 Recommended running-in procedure

**1** Make sure the engine oil and coolant levels are correct (see *Daily (pre-ride) checks*).

**2** Make sure there is fuel in the tank.

**3** Start the engine and let it run at a moderately fast idle until it reaches normal operating temperature.

⚠️ *Warning: If the oil pressure warning light doesn't go off, or it comes on while the engine is running, stop the engine immediately.*

**4** Check carefully that there are no oil leaks and make sure the transmission and controls, especially the brakes, function properly before road testing the machine. Refer to Section 33 for the recommended running-in procedure.

**30.14 Check the condition of the gearchange shaft bearing (arrowed)**

**30.15 Selector arm pawl assembly and shaft centralising spring (arrowed)**

**5** Upon completion of the road test, and after the engine has cooled down completely, recheck the valve clearances and check the engine oil and coolant levels (see *Daily (pre-ride) checks*).

 **HAYNES HiNT** *If a lubrication failure is suspected, stop the engine immediately and try to find the cause. If an engine is run without oil, even for a short period of time, severe damage will occur.*

**6** Treat the machine gently for the first few miles to make sure oil has circulated throughout the engine and any new parts installed have started to seat.

**7** Even greater care is necessary if new pistons and liners or a new crankshaft has been installed. In the case of new pistons and liners, the bike will have to be run in as if when new. This means greater use of the transmission and a restraining hand on the throttle. There's no point in keeping to any set speed limit – it's the revs that are important. The main idea is to keep from labouring the engine and to gradually increase performance. It is best to vary engine and road speed as much as possible within the specified limits, so use the gearbox. These recommendations can be lessened to an extent when only a new crankshaft is installed. Experience is the best guide, since it's easy to tell when an engine is running freely. The table shows maximum engine speed limitations, which Triumph provide for new motorcycles, and this can be used as a guide. Full throttle should not be used until after the running-in period.

| Distance | Rev limit |
| --- | --- |
| Up to 100 miles (160 km) | 3500 rpm max |
| 100 to 300 miles (160 to 500 km) | 5000 rpm max |
| 300 to 600 miles (500 to 1000 km) | 6000 rpm max |
| 600 to 800 miles (1000 to 1300 km) | 7000 rpm max |
| 800 to 1000 miles (1300 to 1600 km) | 8000 rpm max |

# Chapter 3
# Cooling system

## Contents

## Degrees of difficulty

| **Easy,** suitable for novice with little experience  | **Fairly easy,** suitable for beginner with some experience  | **Fairly difficult,** suitable for competent DIY mechanic 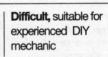 | **Difficult,** suitable for experienced DIY mechanic | **Very difficult,** suitable for expert DIY or professional  |
|---|---|---|---|---|

## Specifications

### Coolant
Mixture type and capacity .................................. see Chapter 1

### Radiator
Cap valve opening pressure ................................ 16.0 psi (1.1 Bar)

### Cooling fan
Cooling fan cut-in temperature
  1997 to 2001 models ..................................... 95°C
  2002-on models ........................................ 103°C

### Thermostat
Opening temperature ...................................... 85°C approx.

### Torque wrench settings
Coolant inlet union bolts .................................. 12 Nm
Coolant outlet union bolts ................................. 9 Nm
Radiator mounting bolts ................................... 9 Nm
Thermostat cover bolts
  1997 to 2001 Daytona and Speed Triple models .............. 7 Nm
  2002-on Daytona and Speed Triple models ................... 4 Nm
  1999 to 2001 Sprint models ............................... 7 Nm
  2002-on Sprint models .................................... 12 Nm
  Tiger models ............................................ 7 Nm
Water pump bolts ........................................ 10 Nm

## 1 General information

The cooling system uses a water/antifreeze coolant to carry away excess energy in the form of heat. The cylinders are surrounded by a water jacket from which the heated coolant is circulated by thermo-syphonic action in conjunction with a water pump. The water pump is driven by the oil pump. The hot coolant passes upwards to the thermostat and through to the radiator. The coolant then flows across the radiator core, where it is cooled by the passing air, to the water pump and back to the engine where the cycle is repeated.

A thermostat is fitted in the system to prevent the coolant flowing through the radiator when the engine is cold, therefore accelerating the speed at which the engine reaches normal operating temperature. A coolant temperature sensor transmits information to the engine management system. This information is used to help optimise the fuelling of the engine at all temperatures. The engine management system also controls the temperature gauge and the cooling fan, via a relay. Because the control side of these cooling system functions is integral with the engine management system, they are dealt with in Chapter 4. The function side of the cooling fan and relay are in this Chapter, while the function of the temperature gauge is in Chapter 8.

The complete cooling system is partially sealed and pressurised, the pressure being controlled by a valve contained in the spring-loaded radiator cap. By pressurising the coolant the boiling point is raised, preventing premature boiling in adverse conditions. The overflow pipe from the system is connected to a reservoir into which excess coolant is expelled under pressure. The discharged coolant automatically returns to the radiator when the engine cools.

 **Warning: Do not remove the pressure cap from the radiator when the engine is hot. Scalding hot coolant and steam may be blown out under pressure, which could cause serious injury. When the engine has cooled, place a thick rag, like a towel over the pressure cap; slowly rotate the cap anti-clockwise to the first stop. This procedure allows any residual pressure to escape. When the steam has stopped escaping, press down on the cap while turning it anti-clockwise and remove it. Do not allow antifreeze to come into contact with your skin or painted surfaces of the motorcycle. Rinse off any spills immediately with plenty of water. Antifreeze is highly toxic if ingested. Never leave antifreeze lying around in an open container or in puddles on the floor; children and pets are attracted by its sweet smell and may drink it. Check with the local authorities about disposing of used antifreeze. Many communities will have collection centres which will see that antifreeze is disposed of safely.**

**Caution: At all times use the specified type of antifreeze, and always mix it with distilled water in the correct proportion. The antifreeze contains corrosion inhibitors which are essential to avoid damage to the cooling system. A lack of these inhibitors could lead to a build-up of corrosion which would block the coolant passages, resulting in overheating and severe engine damage. Distilled water must be used as opposed to tap water to avoid a build-up of scale which would also block the passages.**

Many of the bolts used on Triumph motorcycles are of the Torx type. Unless you are already equipped with a good range of Torx bits, you are advised to obtain a set. Make sure you get bits that can be used in conjunction with a socket set so that a torque wrench can be applied – a Torx key set will not be adequate on its own, though will be useful in addition to the bits.

## 2 Radiator pressure cap

1 If problems such as overheating or loss of coolant occur, check the entire system as described in Chapter 1. The radiator cap opening pressure should be checked by a Triumph dealer with the special tester required for the job. If the cap is defective, replace it with a new one.

## 3 Coolant reservoir

### Removal

1 On Daytona and Speed Triple models, remove the seat (see Chapter 7). On Sprint models, remove the seat cowling (see Chapter 7). On Tiger models, remove the fairing (see Chapter 7).
2 Release the clamps securing the hoses to the unions on the reservoir and detach them, noting which fits where. Remove the reservoir – on Daytona and Speed Triple models, draw it out from under the frame cross-member; on Sprint models, remove the single bolt securing it to the frame **(see illustration)**; on Tiger models, remove the two bolts securing it to the fairing stay **(see illustration)**. Remove the filler cap and tip the contents into a suitable container.

### Installation

3 Installation is the reverse of removal. Make sure the hoses are correctly installed and secured with their clamps. On completion refill the reservoir (see *Daily (pre-ride) checks*).

## 4 Cooling fan and relay

### Cooling fan
#### Check

1 If the engine is overheating and the cooling fan isn't coming on, first check the fan fuse (see Chapter 8). On Daytona, Speed Triple, Sprint ST and Tiger models to VIN 89736, also check the fan relay as described below.
2 If the fuse and relay (where fitted) are good and the fan still does not come on, the fault could lie in either the cooling fan motor itself, or the relevant wiring and connectors. Test all the wiring and connections as described in Chapter 8, referring to the Wiring Diagram for your model.
3 To test the cooling fan motor, on Daytona and Sprint models, remove the fairing side panels (see Chapter 7). On all models, remove the fuel tank (see Chapter 4).
4 On all models, trace the wiring from the fan motor and disconnect it at the connector **(see illustration)**. Using a 12 volt battery and two jumper wires, connect the positive (+ve) battery lead to the blue/white or brown/pink wire terminal (depending on model) on the fan wiring connector and the negative (-ve) lead to the black, black/yellow or black/green wire terminal (depending on model). Once connected the fan should operate. If it does not, and the wiring is all good, then the fan motor is faulty. Replace the fan assembly with a new one – individual components are not available. If all tests so far have shown no problems, test the coolant temperature sensor and engine management system (see Chapter 4).

#### Renewal

 **Warning: The engine must be completely cool before carrying out this procedure.**

**3.2a Reservoir mounting bolt (arrowed) – Sprint models**

**3.2b Reservoir mounting bolts (arrowed) – Tiger models**

**4.4 Cooling fan wiring connector – Daytona shown**

4.5 Fan motor screws (arrowed)

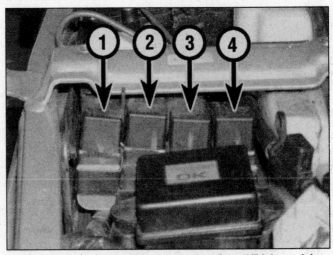

4.8a Cooling fan relay (2) – Daytona and Speed Triple models

**5** Remove the radiator (see Section 6). Undo the three screws securing the fan assembly to the radiator and remove it **(see illustration)**.
**6** Installation is the reverse of removal.

### Cooling fan relay – Daytona, Speed Triple, Sprint ST and Tiger models to VIN 89736

#### Check

**7** If the engine is overheating and the cooling fan isn't coming on, first check the fan fuse (see Chapter 8). If the fuse is blown, check the fan circuit for a short to earth (see the wiring diagrams at the end of this book).
**8** If the fuse is good, on Daytona, Speed Triple and Tiger models, remove both seats, and on Sprint ST models remove the seat cowling (see Chapter 7). Disconnect the relevant relay from its connector block **(see illustrations)** – on Sprint ST models, Triumph advise that the exact location of each relay is

subject to change, so it is impracticable to specify its exact position in the relay pack – identify the relay by the blue coloured tag around the wiring going into it. If the tag is missing, identify the relay by the colour of the wires going into it, referring to the *Wiring Diagrams* at the end of the Chapter.
**9** Set a multimeter to the ohms x 1 scale and its probes between the blue/black (No. 1) and blue/white (No. 8) wire terminals on the relay. Using a fully-charged 12 volt battery and two insulated jumper wires, connect the positive (+ve) terminal of the battery to the black/yellow (No. 4) wire terminal on the relay, and the negative (–ve) terminal to the brown/pink (No. 6) wire terminal on the relay. At this point the relay should be heard to click and the multimeter read 0 ohms (continuity). If this is the case the relay is proved good. If the relay does not click when battery voltage is applied and indicates no continuity (infinite resistance) across its terminals, it is faulty and

must be replaced with a new one. If the relay is good, test the fan motor (see Step 3).

#### Renewal

**10** Carefully disconnect the relevant relay from its connector block **(see illustration 4.8a, b or c)**.
**11** Plug the new relay into its connector.

---

**5  Thermostat and thermostat housing**

**1** The thermostat is automatic in operation and should give many years service without requiring attention. In the event of a failure, the valve will probably jam open, in which case the engine will take much longer than normal to warm up. Conversely, if the valve jams shut, the coolant will be unable to

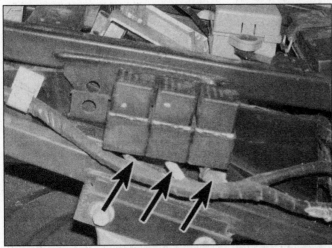

4.8b Relay pack – Sprint ST models. Identify the correct relay from the coloured identity tags (arrowed) – the cooling fan relay has a blue tag

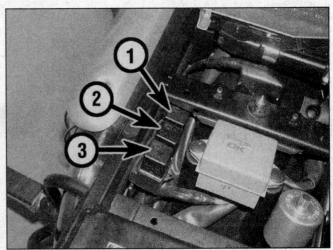

4.8c Cooling fan relay (1) – Tiger models

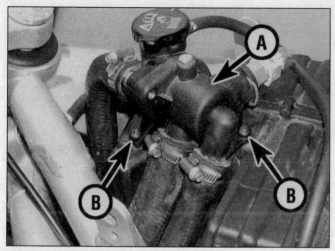

5.5a Thermostat housing (A) and mounting screws (B) – Daytona and Speed Triple models

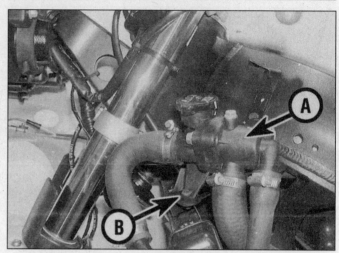

5.5b Thermostat housing (A) and mounting screw (B) – Sprint models

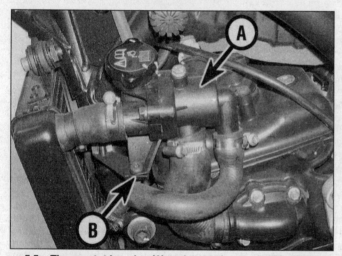

5.5c Thermostat housing (A) and mounting screw (B) – Tiger models

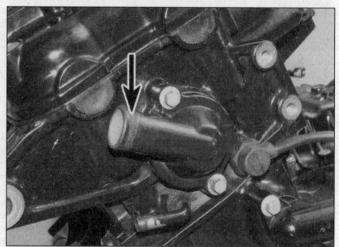

5.6a Detach the hose from the thermostat cover (arrowed)

circulate and the engine will overheat. Neither condition is acceptable, and the fault must be investigated promptly.

### *Removal*

#### Thermostat housing

**2** On 1997 to 2001 Daytona and Speed Triple models, and all Tiger models, remove the fuel tank (see Chapter 4). On 2002-on Daytona and Speed Triple models, and all Sprint models, remove the left-hand fairing side panel (see Chapter 7).

**3** Drain the cooling system (see Chapter 1).

**4** On 1997 to 2001 Daytona and Speed Triple models, and all Tiger models, either disconnect the coolant temperature sensor wiring connector, or remove the sensor from the housing (see Chapter 4).

**5** On 1997 to 2001 Daytona, Speed Triple and Sprint models, and all Tiger models, slacken the clamps securing the hoses to the thermostat housing and detach the hoses, noting which fits where **(see illustrations).**

Undo the screw(s) securing the housing and remove it, noting how it fits.

**6** On 2002-on Daytona, Speed Triple and Sprint models, slacken the clamp securing the hose to the thermostat cover and detach the hose. Undo the bolts securing the cover and remove it, noting the cover O-ring **(see illustrations).**

5.6b Remove the cover, noting the O-ring

### Thermostat

**7** Drain the cooling system (see Chapter 1).

**8** On 1997 to 2001 Daytona, Speed Triple and Sprint models, and all Tiger models, remove the thermostat housing if required (see above), then unscrew the bolts joining the thermostat housing and cover and separate them **(see illustration and 5.14c)**. Withdraw

5.8 Thermostat cover bolts (arrowed) – Daytona shown

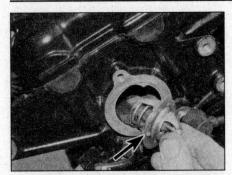

5.9 Withdraw the thermostat, noting the location of the jiggle-pin (arrowed)

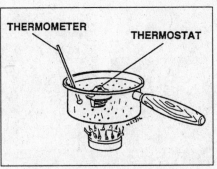

5.11 Thermostat testing set-up

5.14a Fit a new O-ring into the groove

the thermostat, noting how it fits **(see illustration 5.14b)**. Discard the O-ring as a new one must be used **(see illustration 5.14a)**.

9 On 2002-on Daytona, Speed Triple and Sprint models, remove the thermostat cover (see Step 6). Withdraw the thermostat, noting how it fits **(see illustration)**.

## Check

10 Examine the thermostat visually before carrying out the test. If it remains in the open position at room temperature, it should be replaced with a new one.

11 Suspend the thermostat by a piece of wire in a container of cold water. Place a thermometer in the water so that the bulb is close to the thermostat **(see illustration)**. Heat the water, noting the temperature when the thermostat opens, and compare the result with the specified opening temperature given at the beginning of the Chapter. If the thermostat opens at a different temperature, does not open at all, or is permanently open, it is faulty and must be replaced with a new one. **Note:** *In the event of thermostat failure, as an emergency measure only, it can be removed and the machine used without it. Take care when starting the engine from cold as it will take much longer than usual to warm up. Ensure that a new unit is installed as soon as possible.*

## Installation

### Thermostat housing

12 Installation is the reverse of removal. Make sure the hoses are pushed fully on to their unions and are secured by the clamps **(see illustrations 5.5a, b or c)**.

13 Refill the cooling system (see Chapter 1 and *Daily (pre-ride) checks*).

### Thermostat

14 On 1997 to 2001 Daytona, Speed Triple and Sprint models, and all Tiger models, fit a new O-ring into the groove in the housing **(see illustration)**. Fit the thermostat into the cover, locating the point of the thermostat in the socket in the cover **(see illustration)**. Join the housing and the cover, aligning the tabs on the thermostat with the slots in the housing, then install the bolts and tighten them to the torque setting specified at the beginning of the Chapter **(see illustration)**. Install the housing (see above).

15 On 2002-on Daytona, Speed Triple and Sprint models, install the thermostat with the jiggle-pin in the fully upright position **(see illustration)**. Fit a new O-ring in the cover, then install the cover and tighten the cover bolts to the specified torque setting **(see illustrations 5.6b and a)**

16 Install the remaining components, according to your model, referring to the relevant Chapter(s).

## 6 Radiator

## Removal

⚠️ **Warning: The engine must be completely cool before carrying out this procedure.**

1 On Daytona and Sprint models, remove the fairing side panels and belly-pan as applicable (see Chapter 7). On Speed Triple models, remove the radiator side panels if fitted (see Chapter 7). On all models, remove the fuel tank (see Chapter 4).

2 Drain the cooling system (see Chapter 1).

3 Trace the wiring from the fan motor and disconnect it at the connector **(see illustration 4.4)**.

4 On Sprint models, remove the screw securing the thermostat housing to the radiator **(see illustration 5.5b)**.

5 On 1997 to 2001 Daytona, Speed Triple and Sprint models, and all Tiger models, displace the oil cooler from its mountings and support it clear of the radiator (see Chapter 2A or 2B, as applicable) – there is no need to detach the hoses from the cooler.

6 On 2002-on Daytona, Speed Triple and Sprint models, remove the horn from the bracket on the left-hand side of the radiator (see Chapter 8). Where fitted, detach the air deflector shield from the top of the radiator.

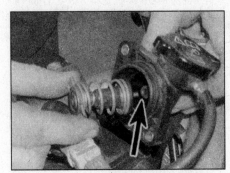

5.14b Locate the point in the socket (arrowed) . . .

5.14c . . . then join the housing, locating the thermostat tabs in the slots

5.15 Install the thermostat with the jiggle-pin in the upright position

6.7a Radiator hose clamps (arrowed) –
1997 to 2001 Daytona and Speed Triple
models

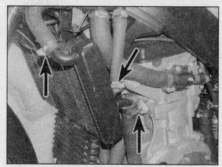

6.7b Radiator hose clamps (arrowed) –
1999 to 2001 Sprint models

6.7c Radiator hose clamps (arrowed) –
1999 to 2001 Tiger models

6.7d Location of the right-hand radiator
hose – 2002-on models

6.7e Location of the left-hand radiator
hoses – 2002-on models

**7** Slacken the clamps securing all the radiator hoses and detach them from the radiator, noting which fits where (see illustrations).

**8** Unscrew the bolts securing the radiator, noting the arrangement of the collars and rubber grommets, then lift the radiator off (see illustrations). On 1997 to 2001 Daytona, Speed Triple and Sprint models, and all Tiger models, note how the bottom mounting lugs fit their sockets (see illustration).

**9** If necessary, separate the cooling fan from the radiator (see Section 4).

**10** Check the radiator for signs of damage and clear any dirt or debris that might obstruct air flow and inhibit cooling. If the radiator fins are badly damaged or broken the radiator must be renewed. Also check the rubber mounting grommets, and replace them with new ones if necessary.

### Installation

**11** Installation is the reverse of removal, noting the following.

● Make sure the collars and grommets are correctly installed with the mounting bolts (see illustration 6.8d). Tighten the bolts to the torque setting specified at the beginning of the Chapter.

● Make sure that the wiring connector is correctly connected (see illustration 4.4).

● Ensure the coolant hoses are in good

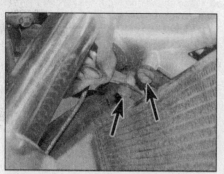

6.8a Radiator mounting bolts (arrowed) –
Daytona and Speed Triple models

6.8b Radiator mounting bolt (arrowed –
there is one on each side) – Sprint models

6.8c Radiator mounting bolts (arrowed) –
Tiger models

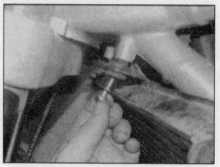

6.8d Note any collars, washers and
grommets

6.8e Lift the radiator so that the bottom
lugs clear their sockets (arrowed)

*condition (see Chapter 1), and are securely retained by their clamps, using new ones if necessary.*

- *On Sprint ST models, do not forget to secure the thermostat housing to the radiator (see illustration 5.5b).*
- *On completion refill the cooling system as described in Chapter 1 and 'Daily (pre-ride) checks'.*

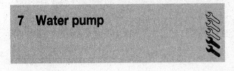

## 7 Water pump

### Check

**1** The water pump is located on the left-hand side of the engine.
**2** To prevent leakage of water from the cooling system to the lubrication system and vice versa, two seals are fitted on the pump shaft. The seal on the water pump side is of the mechanical type which bears on the rear face of the impeller. The second seal, which is mounted behind the mechanical seal is of the normal feathered lip type. On the bottom of the pump there is a drain hole **(see illustration)**. If either seal fails, the drain allows the coolant or oil to escape and prevents them mixing. However, neither seal is available as a separate item as the pump is sold as an assembly. Therefore, if on inspection the drainage hole shows signs of leakage, the pump must be removed and replaced with a new one.

**3** Remove the pump and lift off the cover (see Step 7), noting that the cooling system must first be drained. Wiggle the water pump impeller back-and-forth and in-and-out, and spin it by hand **(see illustration)**. If there is excessive movement, or the pump is noisy or rough when turned, remove the pump (see below) and check it, particularly the bearing, visually and mechanically. If any wear or damage is found, replace the pump with a new one – individual components are not available.

**4** Check the pump housing and cover, and the impeller and shaft for cracks, deformation and any other damage. Check that the shaft is straight – if it is bent, replace the pump with a new one. Also check for corrosion or a build-up of scale in the pump body and clean or renew the pump as necessary.

### Removal

**5** Drain the cooling system (see Chapter 1).

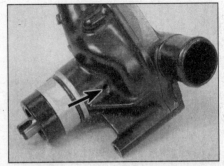

**7.2 Water pump drain hole (arrowed)**

**6** If you just want to remove the cover to inspect the pump, unscrew the three bolts and remove the cover (the hose can stay attached) **(see illustration)**.
**7** To remove the pump, slacken the clamps securing the coolant hoses to it and detach them, noting which fits where **(see illustration)**. Unscrew the lower and rear bolts only **(see illustration 7.6)** and draw the pump out of the engine **(see illustration)**. Note how the slot in the end of the pump shaft engages with the tab on the end of the oil pump shaft. Discard the O-ring as a new one must be used **(see illustration)**.

**7.3 Check the impeller (arrowed) as described**

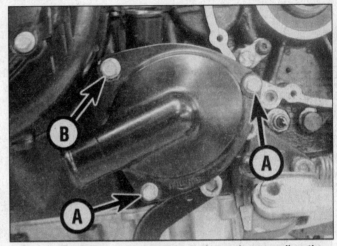

**7.6 The bolts (A) secure the pump to the engine as well as the cover, the bolt (B) just secures the cover**

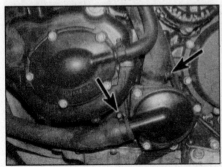

**7.7a Slacken the clamps (arrowed) and detach the hoses**

**7.7b Draw the pump out of the engine**

**7.7c Discard the O-ring**

7.8a Unscrew the remaining cover bolt . . .

7.8b . . . and remove it, noting the dowels (arrowed)

7.8c Discard the cover O-ring

**8** To remove the cover, unscrew the remaining bolt **(see illustration)**. It is possible that the dowels locating the cover have corroded, in which case the cover could be difficult to remove. Spray some penetrating oil around the joint and tap it with a soft-faced hammer to dislodge it – do not try to lever it off as the mating surfaces could be damaged, or the cover could crack. Remove the dowels if they are loose and discard the cover O-ring as a new one must be used **(see illustrations)**.

### Installation

**9** Installation is the reverse of removal, noting the following:
● *Fit new O-rings into the grooves in the cover and pump body* **(see illustrations 7.7c and 8c)**.
● *Fit the dowels into the cover if removed* **(see illustration 7.8b)**. *Clean the dowels and smear them with grease if they were corroded.*
● *Make sure the slot in the end of the pump shaft engages with the tab on the end of the oil pump shaft.*
● *Make sure the coolant hoses are pushed*

*fully onto their unions and are secured by their clamps* **(see illustration 7.7a)**.
● *Refill the cooling system (see Chapter 1 and 'Daily (pre-ride) checks').*

## 8 Coolant hoses, pipes and unions

### Removal

**1** Before removing a hose, pipe or union, drain the coolant (see Chapter 1).
**2** Use a screwdriver to slacken the larger-bore hose clamps, then slide them back along the hose and clear of the union spigot. The smaller-bore hoses are secured by spring clamps which can be expanded by squeezing their ears together with pliers.
**Caution: The radiator unions are fragile. Do not use excessive force when attempting to remove the hoses.**
**3** If a hose proves stubborn, release it by rotating it on its union before working it off. If all else fails, cut the hose with a sharp knife then slit it at each union so that it can be peeled off

in two pieces. Whilst this means renewing the hose, it is preferable to buying a new radiator.
**4** Remove the coolant pipes and the unions on the engine by detaching the hoses (see above), then unscrewing the retaining bolts **(see illustrations)**. Discard the gaskets as new ones must be used.

### Installation

**5** Slide the clamp onto the hose and then work it on to its respective union.

> **HAYNES HiNT**
> *If the hose is difficult to push on its union, it can be softened by soaking it in very hot water, or alternatively a little soapy water can be used as a lubricant.*

**6** Rotate the hose on its union to settle it in position before sliding the clamp into place and tightening it securely.
**7** If the water pipes or unions on the engine have been removed, fit new gaskets, then install them and tighten their mounting bolts to the torque setting specified at the beginning of the Chapter **(see illustration)**.

8.4a Coolant inlet union

8.4b Coolant outlet union

8.7 Always use a new gasket

# Chapter 4
# Engine management system (fuel and ignition)

## Contents

## Degrees of difficulty

| | | | | |
|---|---|---|---|---|
| **Easy,** suitable for novice with little experience  | **Fairly easy,** suitable for beginner with some experience  | **Fairly difficult,** suitable for competent DIY mechanic | **Difficult,** suitable for experienced DIY mechanic | **Very difficult,** suitable for expert DIY or professional |

## Specifications

### Fuel

Grade
  UK and Europe ........................................... Unleaded, minimum 95 RON (Research Octane Number)
  US .................................................. Unleaded, minimum 89 (R+M)/2 (CLC or AKI Octane rating)
Fuel tank capacity (including reserve)
  Daytona and Speed Triple
    1997 to 2001 models ................................. 18 litres
    2002-on models .................................... 22 litres
  Sprint
    1999 to 2001 models ................................. 21 litres
    2002-on models .................................... 19.5 litres
  Tiger models ....................................... 24 litres
Fuel quantity remaining when level warning light comes on
  Daytona and Speed Triple models
    1997 to 2001 models ................................. 3.5 litres
    2002-on models .................................... 4.0 litres
  Sprint models
    1999 to 2001 models ................................. 3.0 litres
    2002-on models .................................... 4.0 litres
  Tiger models ....................................... 3.5 litres

### Fuel injection system

Operating pressure .......................................... 40.0 to 47.0 psi (2.75 to 3.25 Bar) nominal
Idle speed ................................................ 1200 rpm
Idle air control valve stepper motor resistance ................... 47 to 59 ohms
Fuel injector resistance ...................................... 15.5 to 16.3 ohms
Purge valve resistance ...................................... 26.0 ohms

## Engine management system

Type

Daytona, Speed Triple, Sprint ST and Tiger models to VIN 89736 .. MC 2000 ECM

Daytona, Speed Triple, Sprint ST and Tiger models

from VIN 89737, and all Sprint RS models . . . . . . . . . . . . . . . . . MC 1000 ECM

Control sensors . . . . . . . . . . . . . . . . . . . . . . . . . . . . . . . . . . . . . . . .  Road speed and camshaft position (T509 and T595 only), intake air pressure, intake air temperature, coolant temperature, crankshaft position, throttle position and, where fitted, oxygen (lambda)

Sensor input voltage . . . . . . . . . . . . . . . . . . . . . . . . . . . . . . . . . . . .  4.5 to 5.5 V

Coolant temperature sensor resistance

Warm engine . . . . . . . . . . . . . . . . . . . . . . . . . . . . . . . . . . . . . . . .  200 to 400 ohms

Cold engine

20°C ambient . . . . . . . . . . . . . . . . . . . . . . . . . . . . . . . . . . . . .  2.35 to 2.65 K-ohms

10°C ambient . . . . . . . . . . . . . . . . . . . . . . . . . . . . . . . . . . . . .  3.60 to 4.00 K-ohms

0°C ambient . . . . . . . . . . . . . . . . . . . . . . . . . . . . . . . . . . . . .  5.60 to 6.25 K-ohms

Intake air temperature sensor resistance

30°C ambient . . . . . . . . . . . . . . . . . . . . . . . . . . . . . . . . . . . . . .  1.6 to 1.8 K-ohms

25°C ambient . . . . . . . . . . . . . . . . . . . . . . . . . . . . . . . . . . . . . .  1.9 to 2.2 K-ohms

20°C ambient . . . . . . . . . . . . . . . . . . . . . . . . . . . . . . . . . . . . . .  2.3 to 2.7 K-ohms

15°C ambient . . . . . . . . . . . . . . . . . . . . . . . . . . . . . . . . . . . . . .  2.9 to 3.3 K-ohms

10°C ambient . . . . . . . . . . . . . . . . . . . . . . . . . . . . . . . . . . . . . .  3.5 to 4.00 K-ohms

5°C ambient . . . . . . . . . . . . . . . . . . . . . . . . . . . . . . . . . . . . . .  4.4 to 4.9 K-ohms

0°C ambient . . . . . . . . . . . . . . . . . . . . . . . . . . . . . . . . . . . . . .  5.5 to 6.1 K-ohms

Coolant temperature gauge in-line resistor . . . . . . . . . . . . . . . . . . .  9.0 to 11.0 ohms

Tachometer in-line resistor . . . . . . . . . . . . . . . . . . . . . . . . . . . . . .  1.1 to 1.3 K-ohms

Fuel gauge in-line resistor (Sprint ST and Tiger) . . . . . . . . . . . . . . .  9.0 to 11.0 ohms

Oxygen (lambda) sensor heater resistance . . . . . . . . . . . . . . . . . . .  4.0 to 8.0 ohms

## Ignition system

Type . . . . . . . . . . . . . . . . . . . . . . . . . . . . . . . . . . . . . . . . . . . . . . .  Digital inductive

Firing order . . . . . . . . . . . . . . . . . . . . . . . . . . . . . . . . . . . . . . . . . .  1–2–3

Cylinder identification . . . . . . . . . . . . . . . . . . . . . . . . . . . . . . . . . . .  1–2–3, from left to right

Spark plugs . . . . . . . . . . . . . . . . . . . . . . . . . . . . . . . . . . . . . . . . . .  see Chapter 1

Ignition rev limiter

Daytona

1997 to 2001 models . . . . . . . . . . . . . . . . . . . . . . . . . . . . . . .  10,800 rpm

2002-on models . . . . . . . . . . . . . . . . . . . . . . . . . . . . . . . . . . .  11,500 rpm

Speed Triple models . . . . . . . . . . . . . . . . . . . . . . . . . . . . . . . . . .  9,700 rpm

Sprint

1999 to 2001 models . . . . . . . . . . . . . . . . . . . . . . . . . . . . . . . .  9,600 rpm

2002-on models . . . . . . . . . . . . . . . . . . . . . . . . . . . . . . . . . . .  9,700 rpm

Tiger

1999 to 2001 models . . . . . . . . . . . . . . . . . . . . . . . . . . . . . . . .  8,750 rpm

2002-on models . . . . . . . . . . . . . . . . . . . . . . . . . . . . . . . . . . .  9,500 rpm

Ignition coil/cap resistance . . . . . . . . . . . . . . . . . . . . . . . . . . . . . .  0.7 to 0.9 ohms

Crankshaft position sensor (pick-up coil) resistance

1997 to 2001 Daytona, Speed Triple and Sprint models,

and all Tiger models . . . . . . . . . . . . . . . . . . . . . . . . . . . . . . . . .  1.3 K-ohms ± 10% @ 20°C

2002-on Daytona, Speed Triple and Sprint models . . . . . . . . . . . .  0.56 K-ohms ± 10% @ 20°C

Crankshaft position sensor (pick-up coil) air gap

1997 to 2001 models . . . . . . . . . . . . . . . . . . . . . . . . . . . . . . . . .  0.8 to 1.2 mm

2002-on models . . . . . . . . . . . . . . . . . . . . . . . . . . . . . . . . . . . .  1.0 mm

## Torque settings

Camshaft position sensor screw (T509 and T595 models) . . . . . . . . .  10 Nm

Crankshaft position sensor . . . . . . . . . . . . . . . . . . . . . . . . . . . . . .  10 Nm

Exhaust collector box mounting bolts (1999 to 2001 Tiger models) . . .  3 Nm

Exhaust downpipe assembly nuts

1997 to 2001 Daytona, Speed Triple and Sprint models, all Tiger models

Initial setting . . . . . . . . . . . . . . . . . . . . . . . . . . . . . . . . . . . . . .  8 Nm

Final setting . . . . . . . . . . . . . . . . . . . . . . . . . . . . . . . . . . . . . . .  12 Nm

2002-on Daytona, Speed Triple and Sprint models . . . . . . . . . . . . .  19 Nm (see text)

Exhaust downpipe assembly rear mounting bolt . . . . . . . . . . . . . . . .  15 Nm

Exhaust downpipe to collector box clamp bolt (1999 to

2001 Tiger models) . . . . . . . . . . . . . . . . . . . . . . . . . . . . . . . . . . .  22 Nm

Exhaust silencer clamp bolt . . . . . . . . . . . . . . . . . . . . . . . . . . . . . .  22 Nm

## Torque settings (continued)

Exhaust silencer mounting bolt
  Daytona and Speed Triple
    1997 to 2001 models . . . . . . . . . . . . . . . . . . . . . . . . . . . . . . . . . . . . . 18 Nm
    2002-on models . . . . . . . . . . . . . . . . . . . . . . . . . . . . . . . . . . . . . . . . . . 27 Nm
  Sprint models . . . . . . . . . . . . . . . . . . . . . . . . . . . . . . . . . . . . . . . . . . . . . 15 Nm
  Tiger models . . . . . . . . . . . . . . . . . . . . . . . . . . . . . . . . . . . . . . . . . . . . . . 15 Nm
Fuel delivery hose union bolts (all other models) . . . . . . . . . . . . . . . . . 5 Nm
Fuel hose banjo bolts (Daytona to VIN 71698 and 885 cc Speed
  Triple models) . . . . . . . . . . . . . . . . . . . . . . . . . . . . . . . . . . . . . . . . . . . . 20 Nm
Fuel level sensor bolts . . . . . . . . . . . . . . . . . . . . . . . . . . . . . . . . . . . . . . . 5 Nm
Fuel pump mounting plate bolts
  1997 to 2001 models . . . . . . . . . . . . . . . . . . . . . . . . . . . . . . . . . . . . . . . 6 Nm
  2002-on models . . . . . . . . . . . . . . . . . . . . . . . . . . . . . . . . . . . . . . . . . . . 5 Nm
Fuel rail bolts
  1997 to 2001 Daytona, Speed Triple and Sprint models,
    and all Tiger models . . . . . . . . . . . . . . . . . . . . . . . . . . . . . . . . . . . . . . 5 Nm
  2002-on Daytona, Speed Triple and Sprint models . . . . . . . . . . . . . 6 Nm
Fuel tank mountings
  Daytona and Speed Triple
    1997 to 2001 models . . . . . . . . . . . . . . . . . . . . . . . . . . . . . . . . . . . . . 12 Nm
    2002-on models
      Front . . . . . . . . . . . . . . . . . . . . . . . . . . . . . . . . . . . . . . . . . . . . . . . . 8 Nm
      Rear . . . . . . . . . . . . . . . . . . . . . . . . . . . . . . . . . . . . . . . . . . . . . . . . . 5 Nm
  Sprint models
    Front . . . . . . . . . . . . . . . . . . . . . . . . . . . . . . . . . . . . . . . . . . . . . . . . . . 8 Nm
    Rear . . . . . . . . . . . . . . . . . . . . . . . . . . . . . . . . . . . . . . . . . . . . . . . . . . . 5 Nm
  Tiger
    1999 to 2001 models
      Front . . . . . . . . . . . . . . . . . . . . . . . . . . . . . . . . . . . . . . . . . . . . . . . . 8 Nm
      Rear . . . . . . . . . . . . . . . . . . . . . . . . . . . . . . . . . . . . . . . . . . . . . . . . . 9 Nm
    2002-on models . . . . . . . . . . . . . . . . . . . . . . . . . . . . . . . . . . . . . . . . . 9 Nm
Idle air control valve mounting screws . . . . . . . . . . . . . . . . . . . . . . . . . . 12 Nm
Speed sensor screw (T509 and T595 models) . . . . . . . . . . . . . . . . . . . . 9 Nm
Throttle body screws . . . . . . . . . . . . . . . . . . . . . . . . . . . . . . . . . . . . . . . . 12 Nm
Throttle position sensor screws . . . . . . . . . . . . . . . . . . . . . . . . . . . . . . . . 2 Nm

## 1  General information and precautions

### General information

All models are fitted with an electronic engine management system which controls both the fuel and ignition system functions. The system is controlled by an electronic control module, or ECM. The ECM receives information from various sensors around the motorcycle, which it uses to determine the optimum fuel requirements for the fuel injection system and the optimum timing for the ignition system for all engine speeds and loads. Two different systems have been used on the model range, though overall their function is very similar. Early Daytona, Speed Triple, Sprint ST and Tiger models have the MC 2000 ECM, while the later versions of those models and all Sprint RS models have the MC 1000 ECM. They are distinguishable by their different size and by their connectors – the MC 1000 ECM is smaller and has two connectors into it.

The sensors used are for road speed and camshaft position (T509 and T595 only),

intake air pressure, intake air temperature, coolant temperature, crankshaft position, and throttle position. In certain markets a Lambda sensor in the exhaust system provides information on the oxygen content of the exhaust gases. More information on the function of these sensors can be found later in this chapter.

The fuel system consists of the fuel tank, the fuel pump, the pressure regulator, the fuel hoses and throttle control cable, the fuel injectors and throttle bodies, and the air intake system. The fuel pump is housed inside the tank. There is an injector for each cylinder, housed in the throttle body. The low fuel warning circuit is operated by a level sensor inside the tank. Cold starting is controlled by the ECM which reacts to the information sent by the intake air temperature and pressure sensors, and the coolant temperature sensor, and adjusts the fuel requirements accordingly – there is no manual method (i.e. a choke) for assisting cold starting. Many of the fuel system service procedures are considered routine maintenance iterns and for that reason are included in Chapter 1.

The ignition system type is digital inductive, which due to its lack of mechanical parts is totally maintenance free. On all models, the coil

for each spark plug is incorporated in the spark plug cap. The system incorporates an electronic advance system controlled by the ECM, which reacts to the information sent to it from the various sensors to provide the spark at the optimum time. A rev limiter prevents the engine exceeding its maximum rpm. The system incorporates a safety interlock circuit which will cut the ignition if the sidestand is put down whilst the engine is running and in gear, or if a gear is selected whilst the engine is running and the sidestand is down. The tip-over sensor, as fitted to 2002-on Daytona, Speed Triple and Sprint models will cut the ignition if it detects that the machine has fallen over.

The engine management system has in-built diagnostic functions which record and store all data should a fault occur. Recorded faults can then be checked using Triumph's diagnostic tool, which reads the data and lists a code to indicate the exact fault. Should a fault occur, the malfunction indicator lamp (MIL) in the instrument cluster illuminates. If this happens, the management system switches itself into 'limp home' mode, so that in theory you should not be left stranded. Depending on the problem, it is possible that you will notice no difference in the running of the motorcycle.

Because of their nature, the individual system components can be checked but not repaired. If system troubles occur, and the faulty component can be isolated, the only cure for the problem is to replace the part with a new one. Keep in mind that most electrical parts, once purchased, cannot be returned. To avoid unnecessary expense, make very sure the faulty component has been positively identified before buying a new part.

Many of the bolts used on Triumph motorcycles are of the Torx type. Unless you are already equipped with a good range of Torx bits, you are advised to obtain a set. Make sure you get bits that can be used in conjunction with a socket set so that a torque wrench can be applied – a Torx key set will not be adequate on its own, though will be useful in addition to the bits.

### Precautions

⚠️ **Warning: Petrol (gasoline) is extremely flammable, so take extra precautions when you work on any part of the fuel system. Don't smoke or allow open flames or bare light bulbs near the work area, and don't work in a garage where a natural gas-type appliance is present. If you spill any fuel on your skin, rinse it off immediately with soap and water. When you perform any kind of work on the fuel system, wear safety glasses and have a fire extinguisher suitable for a class B type fire (flammable liquids) on hand.**

Always perform fuel-related procedures in a well-ventilated area to prevent a build-up of fumes.

Never work in a building containing a gas appliance with a pilot light, or any other form of naked flame. Ensure that there are no naked light bulbs or any sources of flame or sparks nearby.

Do not smoke (or allow anyone else to smoke) while in the vicinity of petrol (gasoline) or of components containing it. Remember the possible presence of vapour from these sources and move well clear before smoking.

Check all electrical equipment belonging to the house, garage or workshop where work is being undertaken (see the Safety first! section of this manual). Remember that certain electrical appliances such as drills, cutters etc. create sparks in the normal course of operation and must not be used near petrol (gasoline) or any component containing it. Again, remember the possible presence of fumes before using electrical equipment.

Always mop up any spilt fuel and safely dispose of the rag used.

Any stored fuel that is drained off during servicing work must be kept in sealed containers that are suitable for holding petrol (gasoline), and clearly marked as such; the containers themselves should be kept in a safe place. Note that this last point applies equally to the fuel tank if it is removed from the machine; also remember to keep its filler cap closed at all times.

Read the Safety first! section of this manual carefully before starting work.

Owners of machines used in the US, particularly California, should note that their machines must comply at all times with Federal or State legislation governing the permissible levels of noise and of pollutants such as unburnt hydrocarbons, carbon monoxide etc. that can be emitted by those machines. All vehicles offered for sale must comply with legislation in force at the date of manufacture and must not subsequently be altered in any way which will affect their emission of noise or of pollutants.

In practice, this means that adjustments may not be made to any part of the fuel, ignition or exhaust systems by anyone who is not authorised or mechanically qualified to do so, or who does not have the tools, equipment and data necessary to properly carry out the task. Also if any part of these systems is to be replaced it must be replaced with only genuine Triumph components or by components which are approved under the relevant legislation. The machine must never be used with any part of these systems removed, modified or damaged.

### 2 Fuel tank removal and installation

⚠️ **Warning: Refer to the precautions given in Section 1 before starting work.**

### Removal

#### Daytona and Speed Triple models

**1** Make sure the fuel cap is secure.
**2** On 1997 to 2001 models, remove the seats, the seat cowling and the fuel tank cover (see Chapter 7). On 2002-on models, remove the seats and the body side panels (see Chapter 7).
**3** Mark or tag each fuel hose with the location of its socket on the tank to prevent confusion on installation – the hoses must be fitted the same way round. **Note:** *From VIN 207555-on, only a single fuel feed hose is fitted.* The feed and return hose unions and the outlets from the tank are self-sealing, so there is no need to worry about fuel spillage when releasing them. Hold each hose union in turn and press the retaining clip in – the hose will spring out of its socket **(see illustration)**.
**4** Where fitted, release the clamp securing the hose to the fuel pressure regulator and detach the hose **(see illustration)**.
**5** On 1997 to 2001 models, unscrew the bolt securing the rear of the tank **(see illustration)**. Unscrew the bolt securing each tank support rubber at the front and remove them, noting how they fit **(see illustration)**. On 2002-on models, unscrew the bolt securing the rear of the tank and remove the bracket, noting how

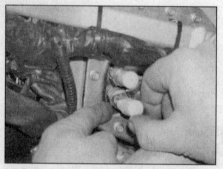

**2.3 Press the retaining clip in to release the fuel hose**

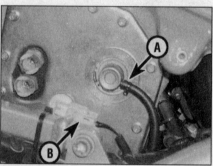

**2.4 Fuel pressure regulator hose (A), fuel pump wiring connector (B)**

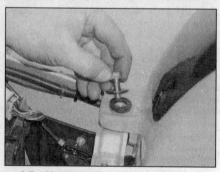

**2.5a Unscrew the bolt at the rear ...**

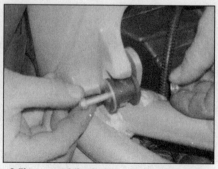

**2.5b ... and the bolt on each side at the front, noting how the rubber supports fit**

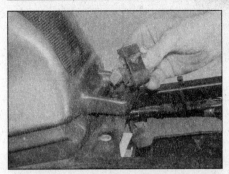

2.5c  Note how the rear fixing bracket fits

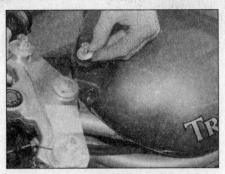

2.5d  Remove the bolt, washer and grommet at the front

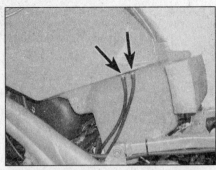

2.6  Detach the drain and breather hoses (arrowed), noting which fits where

it fits **(see illustration)**. Unscrew the bolt securing the tank at the front and remove the bolt, washer and rubber grommet, noting how they fit **(see illustration)**.

**6**  If required, raise the tank at the rear using a block of wood. Mark or tag the drain and breather hoses on the left-hand side of the tank so they can be installed on the correct union **(see illustration)**. Detach the hoses from the unions.

**7**  Disconnect the fuel pump wiring connector, then trace the wiring from the fuel level sensor on the underside of the tank and disconnect it at the connector **(see illustration)**.

**8**  Carefully lift the tank off the bike and remove it **(see illustration)**.

**9**  Discard the O-ring on each fuel hose union as new ones must be used **(see illustration)**. Inspect the tank support rubbers for signs of damage or deterioration and replace them with new ones if necessary.

### Sprint models

**10**  Make sure the fuel cap is secure.

**11**  Remove the seats and the seat cowling (see Chapter 7).

**12**  Mark or tag the drain and breather hoses on the right-hand side of the tank so they can be installed on the correct union **(see illustration)**. Detach the hoses from the unions.

2.7  Fuel pump connector (A) and level sensor wiring connector (B)

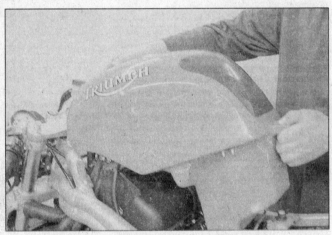

2.8  Carefully lift the tank off the frame and remove it

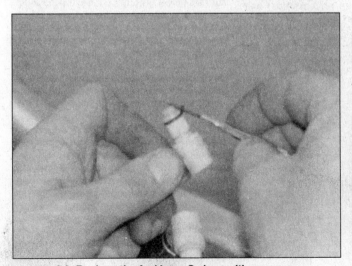

2.9  Replace the fuel hose O-rings with new ones

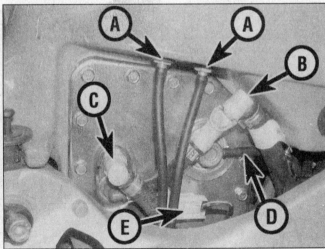

2.12  Drain and breather hoses (A), fuel feed hose (B) and return hose (C), fuel pressure regulator hose (D), fuel pump wiring connector (E)

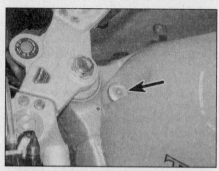

2.16a Front mounting screw (arrowed)

2.16b Rear mounting screws (arrowed)

2.21a Remove the screws (arrowed) and lift out the box . . .

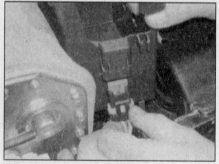

2.21b . . . releasing the main fuse from its housing

2.22a Undo the screws (arrowed) . . .

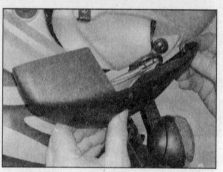

2.22b . . . and release the panel

13 Mark or tag each fuel hose with the location of its socket on the tank to prevent confusion on installation – the hoses must be fitted the same way round (see illustration 2.12). Note: *From VIN 207555-on, only a single fuel feed hose is fitted.* The feed and return hose unions and the outlets from the tank are self-sealing, so there is no need to worry about fuel spillage when releasing them. Hold each hose union in turn and press the retaining clip in – the hose will spring out of its socket. Release the feed hose from the socket that is on the short hose extension from the lower union on the tank – do not separate the short hose from the tank itself.

14 Where fitted, release the clamp securing the hose to the fuel pressure regulator and

detach the hose (see illustration 2.12).
15 Disconnect the fuel pump wiring connector (see illustration 2.12). Trace the wiring from the fuel level sensor on the underside of the tank and disconnect it at the connector.
16 Undo the screw securing the front of the tank, noting the arrangement of the washers, sleeve and rubber grommet (see illustration). Undo the screw securing each tank support rubber at the rear and remove them, noting how they fit (see illustration).
17 Carefully lift the tank off the bike and remove it.
18 Discard the O-ring on each fuel hose union as new ones must be used. Inspect the tank support rubbers for signs of damage or

deterioration and replace them with new ones if necessary.

**Tiger models**

19 Make sure the fuel cap is secure.
20 Remove the seat and the side panels (see Chapter 7), then remove the battery (see Chapter 8).
21 Undo the three screws securing the battery box and lift it out of the frame, releasing the main fuse holder from its housing on the left-hand end of the box as you do so (see illustrations).
22 Remove the two screws securing each turn signal panel to the fairing, then draw the panel away and disconnect the wiring connectors (see illustrations).
23 Remove the screws securing the right and left-hand tank infill panels and lift the panels off.
24 Mark or tag the drain and breather hoses on the left-hand side of the tank so they can be installed on the correct union, then detach the hoses from the unions; where fitted, release the clamp securing the hose to the fuel pressure regulator and detach the hose (see illustration).
25 Disconnect the fuel pump wiring connector (see illustration 2.24). Trace the wiring from the fuel level sensor on the underside of the tank and disconnect it at the connector (see illustration).
26 Mark or tag each fuel hose with the location of its socket on the tank to prevent confusion on installation – the hoses must be fitted the same way round (see illustration 2.24). Note: *From VIN 207447-on,*

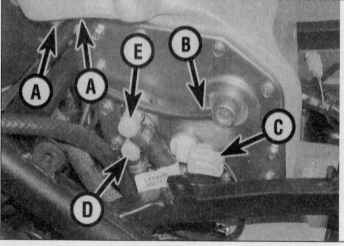

2.24 Drain and breather hoses (A), fuel pressure regulator hose (B), fuel pump wiring connector (C), fuel feed hose (D) and return hose (E)

**2.25 Disconnect the fuel level sensor wiring connector (arrowed)**

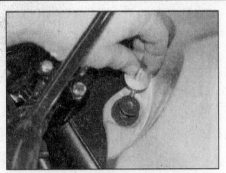

**2.27a Remove the front mounting screw . . .**

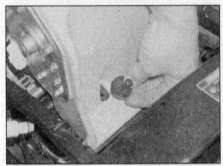

**2.27b . . . and the rear mounting screw . . .**

**2.28 . . . then carefully lift the tank off the frame and remove it**

*only a single fuel feed hose is fitted.* The feed and return hose unions and the outlets from the tank are self-sealing, so there is no need to worry about fuel spillage when releasing them. Hold each hose union in turn and press the retaining clip in – the hose will spring out of its socket.

**27** Undo the screw securing the front of the tank, noting the arrangement of the washers, sleeve and rubber grommet **(see illustration)**. Undo the screw securing the tank at the rear, again noting the arrangement **(see illustration)**.

**28** Make sure the handlebars are straight. Carefully lift the tank off the bike and remove it, noting how it locates onto the front support rubbers on each side of the frame **(see illustration)**.

**29** Discard the O-ring on each fuel hose union as new ones must be used. Inspect the tank support rubbers for signs of damage or

deterioration and replace them with new ones if necessary.

### Installation

**30** Installation is the reverse of removal, noting the following:

● *Check the condition of all the rubber grommets and supports and replace them with new ones if they are damaged, deformed or deteriorated.*
● *Fit a new O-ring onto each fuel hose union (see illustration 2.9).*
● *On Tiger models, make sure the handlebars are straight when installing the tank, and make sure the front support rubbers are in place, that they do not get knocked off, and locate correctly into the cut-outs in the tank.*
● *On Daytona, Speed Triple and Tiger models, fit the feed hose (which goes to the right-hand end of the fuel rail) into the bottom socket in the fuel pump mounting*

*plate, and fit the return hose (which comes from the left-hand end of the fuel rail) into the top socket (see illustration 2.3 or 2.24). Press each union into its socket until it is felt and heard to click into place.*
● *On Sprint models, fit the feed hose (which goes to the right-hand end of the fuel rail) into the socket on the end of the short hose extension from the union on the fuel pump mounting plate, and fit the return hose (which comes from the left-hand end of the fuel rail) into the socket on the plate (see illustration 2.12). Press each union into its socket until it is felt and heard to click into place.*
● *Tighten the fuel tank mounting bolts and/or screws to the torque settings specified at the beginning of the Chapter.*
● *Make sure the electrical connectors are secure.*
● *Before installing the body panels, switch the ignition ON and check that there are no leaks around the hose unions as the pump pressurises.*

### 3 Fuel tank cleaning and repair

**1** All repairs to the fuel tank should be carried out by a professional who has experience in this critical and potentially dangerous work. Even after cleaning and flushing of the fuel system, explosive fumes can remain and ignite during repair of the tank.

**2** If the fuel tank is removed from the bike, it should not be placed in an area where sparks or open flames could ignite the fumes coming out of the tank. Be especially careful inside garages where a natural gas-type appliance is located, because the pilot light could cause an explosion.

### 4 Airbox

### Removal

**1** Remove the fuel tank (see Section 2).

**2** On 1997 to 2001 Daytona and Speed Triple models, undo the screws securing the thermostat housing to the airbox and displace it – there is no need to drain the cooling system or detach any hoses or the wiring connector **(see illustration)**. Detach the intake ducts in the fairing from the ducts into the airbox. On models up to VIN 71698, unscrew the bolt securing the front of the airbox.

**3** On all models to VIN 89736, either disconnect the intake air pressure sensor wiring connector, or carefully pull the sensor out of the airbox **(see illustration)**. On models from VIN 89737, the sensor is housed in the ECM – disconnect the air hose to the sensor from the back of the airbox.

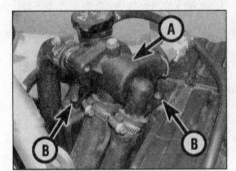

**4.2 Thermostat housing (A) and its mounting screws (B)**

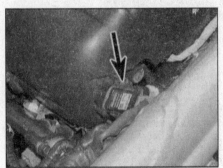

**4.3 Intake air pressure sensor (arrowed) – models to VIN 89736**

**4.5a  Intake air temperature sensor (arrowed) is located on the side ...**

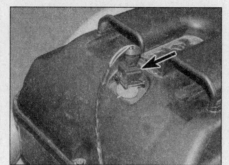

**4.5b  ... or on the top of the airbox**

**4.6a  Disconnect the breather ...**

**4** On models fitted with secondary air injection, release the clips securing the hoses to the control valve on the front of the airbox and trace the wiring from the valve and disconnect it at the connector.

**5** Disconnect the intake air temperature sensor wiring connector **(see illustrations)**.

**6** Working around the airbox, disconnect the various drain and breather hoses from their unions on the airbox, noting which fits where – mark or tag the hoses if required. If any are inaccessible with the airbox in situ, disconnect them as you lift the box off the throttle bodies **(see illustrations)**.

**7** On Sprint and Tiger models, and 2002-on Daytona and Speed Triple models, undo the screws securing the back of the airbox to the bracket **(see illustration)**.

**8** On Daytona and Speed Triple models up to VIN 71698, slacken the clamp screws securing the airbox to the throttle bodies. On all other models, spring clamps are used which are self releasing. Lift up the rear of the box to release it from the throttle bodies, then draw it back and remove it – on all models except Daytona and Speed Triple up to VIN 71698, note how the hook on the front of the box locates **(see illustrations)**. On Daytona models, you will have to manoeuvre the intake ducts on the front of the airbox or they catch on the frame. Block the throttle bodies with a clean rag to prevent anything falling in.

## Installation

**9** Installation is the reverse of removal, noting the following:

● *Do not forget to remove the rag from the throttle bodies.*

● *On Daytona and Speed Triple models up to VIN 71698, make sure the clamp screws are positioned so they will be accessible for tightening.*

**4.6b  ... and drain hoses and tag them**

**4.7  Undo the screws (arrowed)**

**4.8a  Lift airbox at rear to release it from throttle bodies**

**4.8b  Note how the hook (arrowed) locates**

● *On all models except Daytona and Speed Triple up to VIN 71698, make sure the hook on the front of the box locates correctly (see illustration 4.8).*

● *Make sure the airbox locates correctly onto the throttle bodies, and that the self gripping spring clamps seat correctly – if necessary, on 2002-on models, remove the air filter to check.*

● *Make sure all hoses and wiring connectors are correctly and securely attached.*

---

## 5  Fuel pump and relay

⚠ **Warning: Refer to the precautions given in Section 1 before starting work.**

## Check

**1** The fuel pump is located inside the fuel tank. The relay is fitted to Daytona, Speed Triple, Sprint ST and Tiger models up to VIN 89736, and is not fitted to Sprint RS models.

**2** The fuel pump runs for a few seconds when the ignition is switched ON, then cuts out when the system is up to operating pressure, until the engine is started. If you can't hear anything, first check the fuse (see Chapter 8), then check the wiring and wiring connectors in the fuel pump and relay circuit, referring to the Wiring Diagrams at the end of Chapter 8. Next, check the relay (see Step 4). If they are all good, remove the pump (see below) and check the internal connections.

**3** If the pump still does not work, using a fully charged 12 volt battery and two insulated jumper wires, briefly touch the jumper wires to the pump wiring connector terminals. The pump should operate. If the pump does not operate, replace it with a new one. The pump is controlled by the ECM, so if the pump, relay (where fitted) and wiring are all good, it is possible the ECM is faulty. Refer to Section 13 for further information.

**4** To check the relay, remove the seats on Daytona and Speed Triple models, the seat cowling on Sprint ST models, and the seat on Tiger models (see Chapter 7). Disconnect the relevant relay from its connector block **(see**

**5.4a Fuel pump relay (3) – Daytona and Speed Triple**

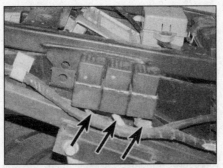

**5.4b Relay identification tags (arrowed) – Sprint ST**

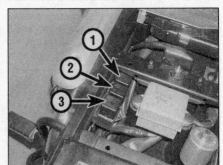

**5.4c Fuel pump relay (2) – Tiger**

**illustrations)** – on Sprint ST models Triumph advise that the exact location of each relay is subject to change, so it is impracticable to specify its exact position in the relay pack – identify the relay by its white coloured tag around the wiring going into it. If the tag is missing, identify the relay by the colour of the wires going into it, referring to the *Wiring Diagrams* at the end of the Chapter.

**5** Set a multimeter to the ohms x 1 scale and connect its probes between the purple (or purple/green) (terminal No. 1) and purple/white (No. 8) wire terminals on the relay. Using a fully-charged 12 volt battery and two insulated jumper wires, connect the positive (+ve) terminal of the battery to the green/red (No. 6) wire terminal on the relay, and the negative (–ve) terminal to the black/purple (No. 4) wire terminal on the relay. At this point the relay should be heard to click

and the multimeter read 0 ohms (continuity). If this is the case the relay is proved good. If the relay does not click when battery voltage is applied and indicates no continuity (infinite resistance) across its terminals, it is faulty and must be replaced with a new one.

**6** If the pump operates but is thought to be delivering an insufficient amount of fuel, first check that the fuel tank breather hose is unobstructed, that all fuel hoses are in good condition and not pinched or trapped. Remove the pump (see below) and check that the fuel strainer and filter are not blocked. Also check the fuel rail and injectors for blockages. If all is good, check the fuel pressure and the pressure regulator (see Section 6).

### Removal

**7** Make sure the ignition is switched

OFF. Remove the fuel tank and drain it (see Section 2).

**8** Unscrew the bolts securing the fuel pump mounting plate to the tank, then withdraw the pump assembly **(see illustrations)**. Discard the gasket as a new one must be used **(see illustration)**.

**9** If a new fuel pump is being installed, release the fuel pipe link piece from its clamp (where fitted), then release the clamp securing the hose to the pump and detach it **(see illustration)**. Disconnect the wiring connector from the pump. Release the fuel pump clamp and remove the pump, taking care not to damage the strainer, and noting how it fits.

### Installation

**10** Installation is the reverse of removal, noting the following:
- *Check the condition of the strainer and/or filter on the fuel pump and clean or renew as required (see Chapter 1).*
- *Make sure the wires are correctly and securely fitted to the pump.*
- *Install the pump assembly using a new gasket and tighten the mounting plate bolts evenly and a little at a time in a criss-cross pattern to the torque setting specified at the beginning of the Chapter* **(see illustrations 5.8c, b and a).**
- *On completion, start the engine and check carefully that there is no leakage from around the pump mounting plate and from the hose connections.*

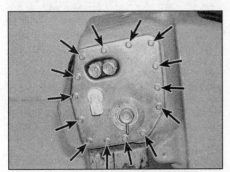

**5.8a Unscrew the bolts (arrowed) . . .**

**5.8b . . . and remove the pump assembly**

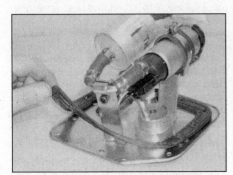

**5.8c Discard the old gasket as a new one must be used**

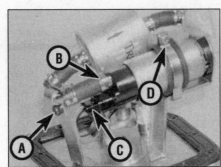

**5.9 Link pipe clamp bolt (A), hose clamp (B), wiring connector (C), pump clamp screw (D)**

**6  Fuel pressure and pressure regulator**

⚠ *Warning: Refer to the precautions given in Section 1 before starting work.*

### Fuel pressure check

**1** To check the fuel pressure, the Triumph gauge (Pt. No. T3880048) is needed. The gauge comes fitted with the special unions required to fit into the fuel hose sockets in the fuel tank. A commercial pressure gauge will not be of any use.

**2** Make sure the ignition switch is in the OFF position. Remove the appropriate body panels according to your models to gain access to the fuel feed hose union on the tank (see Section 2). Do not remove the tank.

**3** Detach the fuel feed hose from the bottom socket on the fuel pump mounting plate on Daytona, Speed Triple and Tiger models, and from the short hose extension coming from the bottom union on Sprint models – to release the hose, hold the union and press the retaining clip in – the hose will spring out of its socket **(see illustrations 2.3 and 2.12 or 2.24)**. Note: *On Daytona, Speed Triple and Sprint models from VIN 207555-on, and Tiger models from VIN 207447-on, only a single fuel feed hose is fitted.*

**4** Fit the union on the end of the hose coming from the gauge into the socket on the tank (or on the end of the extension on Sprint models), then fit the fuel feed hose union into the socket on the gauge. Press each union into its socket until it is felt and heard to click into place.

**5** Turn the ignition switch ON and check the pressure reading on the gauge. The pressure should be as specified at the beginning of the Chapter.

**6** Turn the ignition OFF and remove the gauge, then fit the fuel feed hose back into its socket.

**7** If the pressure is too low, either the pressure regulator is stuck open, the fuel pump is faulty, the strainer or filter is blocked, or there is a leak in the system, probably from a hose joint.

**8** If the pressure is too high, either the feed or return hose is pinched or clogged, the regulator is stuck closed or the fuel pump check valve is faulty.

**9** Refer to the relevant Sections of this Chapter and Chapter 1 and check the possible problems according to whether the pressure was too low or too high. Triumph provide no test procedure for the pressure regulator. However, if it is stuck open, it will be possible to blow through it with a low pressure air source. If it is stuck closed, then a high pressure air source with a gauge can be used to check the pressure at which it does open, if at all. Alternatively, substitute the suspect one with a known good one and repeat the fuel pressure check.

### Pressure regulator – check and renewal

**10** Make sure the ignition is switched OFF. Remove the fuel tank and drain it (see Section 2).

**11** On Daytona, Speed Triple and Sprint models up to VIN 207554, and Tiger models up to VIN 207446, remove the large circlip holding the regulator in the fuel pump mounting plate and draw it out **(see illustration)**. Discard the O-rings and circlip as new ones must be used.

**12** On Daytona, Speed Triple and Sprint models from VIN 207555-on, and Tiger

models from VIN 207447-on, the regulator is located inside the tank. Follow the procedure in Section 5 and remove the fuel pump assembly from the tank. Release the clip securing the hose from the fuel filter to the regulator and detach the hose, then detach the regulator from the pump mounting plate. Note the O-ring on the regulator union.

**13** Triumph provide no test data or procedure for checking the operation of the regulator, but it is safe to assume that if you apply more than the maximum operating pressure specified to the inlet on the regulator, and it doesn't open and allow a flow out of the outlet, then it is faulty. Similarly, if it opens and allows a flow out before the minimum operating pressure is reached, then it is faulty. You will have to devise a method of applying the pressure in a controlled and measurable way to the inlet – using air pressure is probably easier than using a fluid. If a known good regulator is available, it is probably best to substitute that for the suspect one and see if the fault is cured.

**14** Fit new O-ring(s) onto the regulator and smear them with petroleum jelly (e.g. Vaseline).

**15** On Daytona, Speed Triple and Sprint models up to VIN 207554, and Tiger models up to VIN 207446, press the regulator into its socket and secure it with a new circlip.

**16** On Daytona, Speed Triple and Sprint models from VIN 207555-on, and Tiger models from VIN 207447-on, connect the hose to the regulator and secure it with the clip. Press the regulator into its socket and secure it with the mounting screws. Follow the procedure in Section 5 and install the pump assembly in the tank.

**17** Install the fuel tank (see Section 2).

## 7 Fuel level sensor

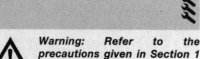

⚠️ **Warning:** *Refer to the precautions given in Section 1 before starting work.*

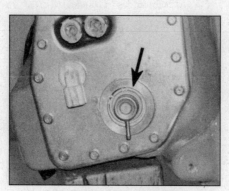

**6.11 Fuel pressure regulator (arrowed)**

### Check

**1** If the low fuel level warning light fails to come on, first check the bulb in the instrument cluster (see Chapter 8), then check the wiring and connectors between the sensor and the instrument cluster for continuity, referring to the wiring diagrams at the end of Chapter 8.

**2** On Sprint ST and Tiger models, if the fuel level gauge fails to work, first check the fuse (see Chapter 8), then check the wiring and connectors between the sensor and the instrument cluster for continuity, referring to the wiring diagrams at the end of Chapter 8. If they are good, check that the resistance value of the in-line resistor(s) going into the fuel gauge are as specified on the wiring diagrams at the end of Chapter 8, using the diagrams to determine the correct connections. **Note:** *Triumph advise that in some cases, fuel level sensor faults have been corrected by fitting a new earth (ground) wire connection to the sensor. Disconnect the sensor wiring connector and substitute the existing earth (ground) wire on the loom side of the connector with a separate wire – connect this new wire either directly to the battery negative (-ve) terminal or to the engine earth (ground) terminal.*

**3** Triumph provide no test data or procedure for checking the operation of the sensor, but it is safe to assume that if you connect an ohmmeter to the sensor wiring connector, then as the float in the sensor moves up and down the resistance will change – in the case of Sprint ST and Tiger models with a fuel gauge, the resistance should change gradually as the float moves, while in the case of other models with only a warning light, there should be infinite resistance when the float is at the top of the sensor, and little or no resistance when it is at the bottom. To perform this test you will have to start with an empty fuel tank, then gradually fill it while watching the reading on the ohmmeter. Remove the appropriate body panels according to your models to gain access to the sensor wiring connector (see Section 2). Do not remove the tank. If the sensor does not behave as described, or if you are in any doubt, take it to Triumph dealer for further assessment.

**4** On Daytona models from VIN 132513-on, Speed Triple models from VIN 141872-on, all Sprint models, Tiger 885 cc models from VIN 71699-on, and all Tiger 955 cc models, a new float can be fitted to the sensor – Triumph advise that incorrect fuel level readings and stuck fuel level needles may be resolved by fitting a new float (see below).

### Removal

**5** Make sure the ignition is switched OFF. Remove the fuel tank and drain it (see Section 2). Turn the tank upside down and rest it on some clean rag.

**6** Unscrew the sensor itself, or the bolts

securing it to the tank, according to your model, and withdraw the sensor from the tank **(see illustrations)**. Discard the sealing washer or gasket as a new one must be used.

**7** If appropriate (see Step 4), release the tabs at the top of the sensor tube assembly and lift off the cap. Slide out the old float, noting how it fits. **Note:** *Be prepared to catch any residual fuel in the sensor assembly.* Insert the new float into the tube, ensuring that the small magnet on the float faces towards the bottom. Install the cap and ensure that the tabs lock correctly. Tilt the sensor tube slowly and check that the float slides freely up and down.

### Installation

**8** Installation is the reverse of removal, noting the following:

● *Install the sensor using a new sealing washer or gasket. Where the sensor is secured by four bolts, tighten them to the torque setting specified at the beginning of the Chapter. Where the sensor itself threads into the tank, tighten it securely, but do not overtighten it as the threads could be damaged* **(see illustration 7.6a or b).**

● *On completion, start the engine and check carefully that there is no leakage from around the pump mounting plate and from the hose connections.*

## 8  Throttle body removal, cleaning, inspection and installation

⚠ *Warning:  Refer  to  the precautions given in Section 1 before starting work.*

### 1997 to 2001 Daytona, Speed Triple, and Sprint models and all Tiger models

#### Removal

**Note:** *A gasket is fitted between the throttle bodies and the cylinder head – a new one must used on installation so it is wise to obtain it in advance. Note that the gasket design differs between 885 and 995 cc engines, so be sure to obtain the correct one for your machine. The gasket on 955 cc engines is identifiable by the small hole in the portion of gasket that protrudes from the left-hand side of the No. 1 cylinder throttle body* **(see illustration 8.12).**

**1** The throttle bodies can be removed with the fuel rail and injectors attached if required, or you can remove them beforehand or afterwards (see Section 9). If you are going to separate the assembly at any stage, first disconnect the fuel pump wiring connector (see Section 5), then turn the engine over on the starter for a few seconds – this reduces the pressure in the fuel rail and so prevents the fuel from being sprayed everywhere when the rail is removed or the hoses are detached.

**2** Remove the fuel tank and the airbox (see Sections 2 and 4).

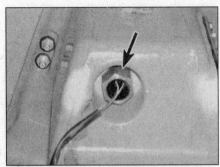

**7.6a  Fuel level sensor (arrowed) – Daytona and Speed Triple models**

**3** On Daytona and Speed Triple models to VIN 71843, mark or tag the idle air control valve hoses with the identity of the throttle body they attach to, then detach them from their unions. On all other models the valve is removed with the throttle bodies. If you want to remove it first, or afterwards, refer to Section 16 for details.

**4** Disconnect the wiring connector on each fuel injector, then release the wiring from any clips or ties on the fuel rail, noting where they fit and which wires are held **(see illustration)**. Disconnect the throttle position sensor wiring connector **(see illustration)**.

**5** Detach the throttle cable from the throttle bodies (see Section 10).

**6** Using a socket extension, undo the screws securing the throttle body assembly to the cylinder head, on Daytona and Speed Triple models to VIN 71843 noting how the idle air control valve bracket is secured by one of the

**8.4a  Disconnect the injector wiring connectors (arrowed) . . .**

**8.6a  Undo the screws (arrowed) . . .**

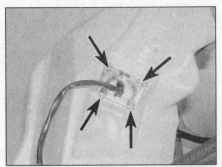

**7.6b  Fuel level sensor mounting bolts (arrowed) – Sprint and Tiger models**

screws **(see illustration)**. Lift the throttle body assembly off the engine, and on Daytona and Speed Triple models from VIN 71844-on, and on all other models, disconnect the idle air control valve wiring connector when it is accessible **(see illustration)**. Discard the gasket as a new one must be used. Note the locating dowels and remove them for safekeeping if they are loose. Block the intake tracts with clean rag to prevent anything falling in. Clean all traces of old gasket material from the throttle bodies and cylinder head. Do not remove the throttle position sensor from the throttle bodies unless you know it is faulty and are replacing it with a new one, or unless you are replacing the throttle bodies with new ones. If you do remove it, it has to be set up using the Triumph diagnostic tool. There is no alternative, unless you want to run the risk of having the bike running incorrectly. Refer to

**8.4b  . . . and the throttle position sensor wiring connector (arrowed)**

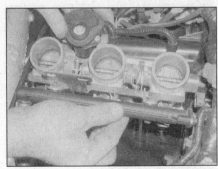

**8.6b  . . . and remove the throttle body assembly**

**8.7 Make sure the throttle linkage and springs are clean and operate smoothly**

**8.12 Make sure the dowels (arrowed) are installed, and use a new gasket**

**8.15 Disconnect the throttle position sensor wiring connector**

the engine management section for further information.

## Cleaning

*Caution: Use only a dedicated spray cleaner (such as a carburettor and injector cleaner) for throttle body cleaning.*

7 Spray the cleaner over the throttle bodies to remove any dirt and grime, paying particular attention to the throttle linkage assembly and springs in between each body (see illustration). Use a nylon brush if required, but be careful not to embed dirt particles into the springs as this could cause the throttles to stick.

## Inspection

8 Check the throttle bodies for cracks or any other damage which may result in air getting in. Also check for any signs of fuel leakage from the joints between the injectors, the fuel rail and the throttle bodies (refer to Section 9 to remove them).

9 Check that the throttle butterflies move smoothly and freely in the bodies, and make sure that the inside of each body is completely clean.

10 Check that the throttle cable cam moves smoothly and freely, taking into account spring pressure. Clean any grit and dirt from around the cams. Check all the springs for signs of damage and distortion.

11 Do not attempt to separate the throttle bodies. If a body or the linkage assembly is damaged, the whole assembly must be renewed as individual components are not available.

## Installation

12 Installation is the reverse of removal, noting the following:
● Do not forget to remove the rag from the intake tracts. Install the throttle bodies using a new gasket, and make sure that the dowels are installed and the gasket and

bodies locate correctly onto them **(see illustration)**.
● Tighten the throttle body screws to the torque setting specified at the beginning of the Chapter, not forgetting to secure the idle air control valve on Daytona and Speed Triple models to VIN 71843.
● Make sure all the wiring connectors are reconnected. Secure the wiring to the fuel rail in the same way as before.
● On Daytona and Speed Triple models to VIN 71843, connect each idle air control valve hose to its union on the correct throttle body as noted on removal.
● Check the operation of the throttle cable and adjust it as necessary (see Chapter 1).
● Check throttle body synchronisation and adjust as necessary (see Chapter 1).

## 2002-on models Daytona, Speed Triple, and Sprint models
### Removal

13 The throttle body unit and the fuel rail and injectors assembly are separate items that can be removed independently of each other. If you are going to remove the fuel rail and injectors at any stage, first disconnect the fuel pump wiring connector (see Section 5), then turn the engine over on the starter for a few seconds – this reduces the pressure in the fuel rail and so prevents the fuel from being sprayed everywhere when the rail is removed or the hoses are detached.

14 Remove the fuel tank and the airbox (see Sections 2 and 4). Remove the fairing side panels as required according to your model (see Chapter 7).

15 Unclip the throttle position sensor wiring from the fuel rail and disconnect the connector **(see illustration)**.

16 Release the clamps securing the throttle body assembly and ease the assembly off the intake stubs **(see illustration)**.

17 Disconnect the idle air control unit wiring connector and pull the hoses off the unions on the back of the cylinder head **(see illustrations)**. Tag the hoses with the identity of the cylinder they attach to.

18 Note how the throttle opening and closing cables locate on the cam, then slacken the locknuts securing the outer cables in the bracket and lift them off; disconnect the inner cable ends from the cam **(see illustration)**.

**8.16 Throttle body assembly is secured by three clamps (arrowed)**

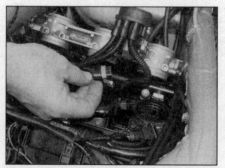

**8.17a Disconnect the idle air control unit wiring connector . . .**

**8.17b . . . and pull the hoses off the unions on the cylinder head**

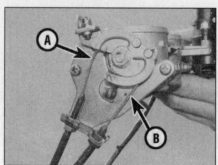

**8.18 Throttle opening (A) and closing (B) cables**

**19** Remove the throttle body unit and plug the intake stubs with clean rags to prevent anything dropping inside. Note the location of the clamps on the stubs to aid reassembly **(see illustration)**.

**20** If required, undo the bolts securing the idle air control valve to the throttle body unit and lift it off (see Section 16).

**21** Do not remove the throttle position sensor from the throttle bodies unless you know it is faulty and are replacing it with a new one, or unless you are replacing the throttle bodies with new ones. If you do remove it, it has to be set up using the Triumph diagnostic tool. There is no alternative, unless you want to run the risk of having the bike running incorrectly. Refer to the engine management section for further information.

### Cleaning

*Caution: Use only a dedicated spray cleaner (such as a carburettor and injector cleaner) for throttle body cleaning.*

**22** Spray the cleaner over the throttle bodies to remove any dirt and grime, paying particular attention to the throttle cam assembly and spring **(see illustration 8.18)**. Use a nylon brush if required, but be careful not to embed dirt particles into the cam assembly as this could cause the throttles to stick. Ensure no dirt is lodged in the locations for the throttle body synchronising screws **(see illustration)**. Note that the screws may be locked with sealant – do not remove this unnecessarily. Take great care not to disturb the screw settings (see Chapter 1, Section 17 for synchronisation details).

### Inspection

**23** Check the throttle bodies for cracks or any other damage which may result in air getting in.

**24** Check that the throttle butterflies move smoothly and freely in the bodies, and make sure that the inside of each body is completely clean.

**25** Check that the throttle cable cam moves smoothly and freely, taking into account spring pressure. Clean any grit and dirt from around the cam. Check the spring for signs of damage and distortion.

**26** If a body or the butterfly linkage assembly is damaged, the whole assembly must be renewed as individual components are not available.

### Installation

**27** Installation is the reverse of removal, noting the following:
● Do not forget to remove the rag from the intake stubs.
● Ensure that the throttle bodies are fully engaged with the intake stubs before tightening the clamps.
● Connect each idle air control valve hose to its union on the cylinder head as noted on removal.
● Make sure all the wiring connectors are

**8.19  Note how each clamp fits over the tab on the intake stub**

reconnected. Secure the wiring to the fuel rail in the same way as before.
● Check the operation of the throttle cable and adjust it as necessary (see Chapter 1).
● Check throttle synchronisation and adjust as necessary (see Chapter 1).

## 9  Fuel rail and injectors

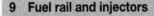

!  *Warning: Refer to the precautions given in Section 1 before proceeding.*

### 1997 to 2001 Daytona, Speed Triple, and Sprint models and all Tiger models

### Removal

**1** Before removing the fuel rail and injectors, disconnect the fuel pump wiring connector (see Section 5), then turn the engine over on the starter for a few seconds – this reduces the pressure in the fuel rail and so prevents the fuel from being sprayed everywhere when the rail is removed or the hoses are detached. If the throttle bodies have already been removed, ignore any steps which do not apply.

**2** Remove the fuel tank and the airbox (see Sections 2 and 4). If required, remove the throttle bodies (see Section 8), but note that the rail and injectors can be separated from them, leaving them in situ.

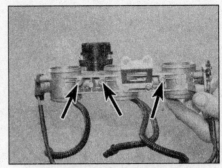

**8.22  Location of the throttle body synchronising screws (arrowed)**

**3** Disconnect the wiring connector on each fuel injector, then release the wiring from any clips or ties on the fuel rail, noting where they fit and which wires are held **(see illustration 8.4a)**.

**4** If required, disconnect the fuel hoses from the fuel rail. On Daytona models to VIN 71698 and 885 cc Speed Triple models, the hoses are secured by banjo fittings which use a sealing washer on each side of the union. All other models have the feed hose secured by two bolts and sealed by an O-ring, while the return hose slips over a union and is held by a clamp **(see illustration)**.

**5** Unscrew the bolts securing the fuel rail to the bracket and lift the rail off the throttle bodies, bringing the injectors with the rail **(see illustrations)**.

**6** To separate the injectors from the fuel rail,

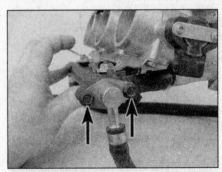

**9.4  Fuel feed hose union bolts (arrowed)**

**9.5a  Unscrew the bolts (arrowed) . . .**

**9.5b  . . . and carefully remove the fuel rail with the injectors attached**

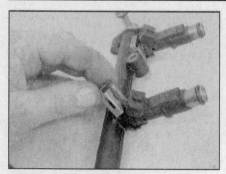

9.6a Release the clip . . .

9.6b . . . and carefully pull the injector out of the rail

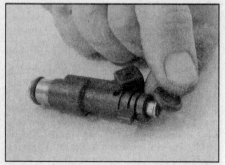

9.9 Fit a new O-ring onto each end of the injector

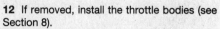

release the clip and carefully pull the injector out of the fuel rail (see illustrations). Discard the injector O-rings as new ones must be used.

7 Modern fuels contain detergents which should keep the rail injectors clean and free of gum or varnish from residue fuel. Clean the rail in a dedicated cleaner and blow it through with compressed air. If an injector is suspected of being blocked, flush it through with injector cleaner.

8 If an injector is clean but its performance is suspect, test its resistance as follows. Using an ohmmeter or multimeter set to the ohms x 1 scale, measure the resistance between the terminals in the injector wiring connector. The resistance should be as specified at the beginning of the Chapter. If not, the injector is faulty and must be replaced with a new one.

## Installation

9 Fit new O-rings onto each injector (see illustration). Push the injector into the fuel rail, making sure you do not turn it whilst doing so, and that it is properly seated (see illustration 9.6b). Secure the injector with its clip (see illustration 9.6a).

10 Fit the fuel rail and injectors onto the throttle bodies, making sure each injector seats correctly (see illustration 9.5b). Install the fuel rail bolts and tighten them to the specified torque setting (see illustration 9.5a).

11 If removed, install the fuel hoses, using new sealing washers and O-rings where fitted, and tighten the banjo bolts or union bolts to the torque setting specified at the beginning of the Chapter (see illustration 9.4). Use a new clamp on the return hose on later models.

12 If removed, install the throttle bodies (see Section 8).

13 Connect the injector wiring connectors and secure the wiring on the rail as noted on removal (see illustration 8.4a).

14 Install the airbox and the fuel tank (see Sections 4 and 2).

## 2002-on Daytona, Speed Triple, and Sprint models

### Removal

15 Before removing the fuel rail and injectors, disconnect the fuel pump wiring connector (see Section 5), then turn the engine over on the starter for a few seconds – this reduces the pressure in the fuel rail and so prevents the fuel from being sprayed everywhere when the rail is removed or the hoses are detached. If the throttle body unit has already been removed, ignore any steps which do not apply.

16 Remove the fuel tank and the airbox (see Sections 2 and 4). Remove the fairing side panels as required according to your model (see Chapter 7). If required, remove the throttle body unit (see Section 8).

17 Unclip the wiring loom secured to the fuel rail and disconnect the individual injector wiring connectors (see illustrations).

18 Remove the bolts securing the fuel rail to its bracket, then ease the fuel rail and injectors away from the cylinder head and lift off the assembly (see illustrations).

19 To separate the injectors from the fuel rail, release the clip and carefully pull the injector out of the fuel rail (see illustrations 9.6a and b). Discard the injector O-rings as new ones must be used.

20 If required, disconnect the fuel hoses from the fuel rail. The feed hose is secured by two bolts and sealed by an O-ring, while the return hose slips over a union and is held by a clamp (see illustration 9.4). Note: On models from VIN 207555 only a single fuel feed hose is fitted.

21 Modern fuels contain detergents which should keep the rail injectors clean and free of gum or varnish from residue fuel. Clean the rail in a dedicated cleaner and blow it through with compressed air. If an injector is suspected of being blocked, flush it through

9.17a Release the wiring from the fuel rail . . .

9.17b . . . and disconnect the injector connectors

9.18a Unscrew the bolts (arrowed) . . .

9.18b . . . and carefully remove the fuel rail with the injectors attached

**9.24 Align the fuel injectors and ensure they seat correctly**

with injector cleaner. If an injector is clean but its performance is suspect, follow the procedure in Step 8 and test its resistance.

## Installation

22 If removed, install the fuel hoses, using a new O-ring on the fuel feed union. Tighten the union bolts to the torque setting specified at the beginning of the Chapter (see illustration 9.4). Use a new clamp on the return hose, where fitted.
23 Fit new O-rings onto each injector (see illustration 9.9). Push the injector into the fuel rail, making sure you do not turn it whilst doing so, and that it is properly seated (see illustration 9.6b). Secure the injector with its clip (see illustration 9.6a).
24 Fit the fuel rail and injector assembly onto the cylinder head, making sure each injector seats correctly (see illustration).

25 Install the fuel rail bolts and tighten them to the specified torque setting (see illustration 9.18a).
26 Connect the injector wiring connectors and secure the wiring on the rail as noted on removal (see illustration 9.17b).
27 If removed, install the throttle bodies (see Section 8).
28 Install the remaining components in the reverse order of removal.

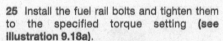

## 10 Throttle cable removal and installation

⚠️ *Warning: Refer to the precautions given in Section 1 before proceeding.*

### 1997 to 2001 Daytona, Speed Triple, and Sprint models and all Tiger models

#### Removal

1 Remove the fuel tank and the airbox (see Sections 2 and 4).
2 Slacken the top locknut securing the cable in its bracket on the throttle bodies and thread it off the top (see illustration). Rotate the throttle cam to the fully open position using your fingers and hold it there, then draw the outer cable out of its bracket and detach the inner cable from the throttle cam (see illustrations).

3 On Daytona, Speed Triple and Sprint RS models, pull the rubber boot off the throttle pulley housing on the handlebars and remove the housing screws (see illustration). Separate the halves and free the cable elbow from the housing, then detach the inner cable end from the pulley, noting how it all fits (see illustrations).
4 On Sprint ST and Tiger models, remove the right-hand switch housing screws on the handlebar and separate the halves. Free the cable elbow from the housing and detach the inner cable end from the pulley, noting how it all fits.
5 Remove the cable from the machine noting its correct routing.

#### Installation

6 Installation is the reverse of removal. If necessary, lubricate the cable (see Chapter 1). Make sure the cable is correctly routed – it must not interfere with any other component and should not be kinked or bent sharply. Lubricate the end of each inner cable with multi-purpose grease.
7 Adjust the cable as described in Chapter 1, Section 5. Turn the handlebars back and forth to make sure the cable doesn't cause the steering to bind.
8 Install the airbox and the fuel tank (see Sections 4 and 2).
9 Start the engine and check that the engine speed does not rise as the handlebars are turned. If it does, correct the problem before riding the motorcycle.

**10.2a Thread the top nut (arrowed) off the cable . . .**

**10.2b . . . then free the outer cable from the bracket . . .**

**10.2c . . . and detach the inner cable end from the cam**

**10.3a Pull back the rubber boot, then undo the screws (arrowed)**

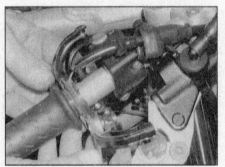

**10.3b Separate the housing halves and detach the cable elbow . . .**

**10.3c . . . then free the cable end from the throttle pulley**

10.11 Throttle cables are secured in the bracket by locknuts (arrowed)

11.2 Carefully unhook the springs

### 2002-on Daytona, Speed Triple, and Sprint models

#### Removal

**10** Remove the fuel tank and the airbox (see Sections 2 and 4). Remove the fairing side panels as required according to your model (see Chapter 7). If required, to gain access to the throttle cable bracket on the right-hand end of the throttle body unit, displace the throttle body unit (see Section 8).

**11** Slacken the locknuts securing the opening and closing cables in the bracket and thread them off the adjusters **(see illustration)**. Draw the outer cables out of the bracket and detach the inner cable ends from the throttle cam **(see illustration 8.18)**.

**12** Pull the rubber boot off the throttle pulley housing on the handlebars and remove the housing screws **(see illustration 10.3a)**. Separate the halves and free the cable elbow from the housing, then detach the inner cable end from the pulley, noting how it all fits **(see illustrations 10.3b and c)**.

**13** Remove the cable from the machine noting its correct routing.

#### Installation

**14** Installation is the reverse of removal. If necessary, lubricate the cable (see Chapter 1). Make sure the cable is correctly routed – it must not interfere with any other component and should not be kinked or bent sharply.

Lubricate the end of each inner cable with multi-purpose grease.

**15** Adjust the cable as described in Chapter 1, Section 5. Turn the handlebars back and forth to make sure the cable doesn't cause the steering to bind.

**16** Install the remaining components in the reverse order of removal.

**17** Start the engine and check that the engine speed does not rise as the handlebars are turned. If it does, correct the problem before riding the motorcycle.

## 11 Exhaust system

> **Warning: If the engine has been running the exhaust system will be very hot. Allow the system to cool before carrying out any work.**

**Note:** *The exhaust system on all models can be removed as one piece if required, but unless you have an assistant it is awkward to manoeuvre and support the system while simultaneously removing or installing bolts and nuts. To prevent the possibility of damage, remove the individual sections in turn as described.*

### 1997 to 2001 Daytona and Speed Triple models

#### Silencer

**1** On Daytona models, remove the belly pan (see Chapter 7).

**2** Carefully release the springs holding the silencer in the downpipe assembly **(see illustration)**.

**3** Unscrew and remove the nut on the inside of the footrest bracket, then support the silencer and withdraw the bolt, noting the washer and the arrangement of the collars **(see illustration)**. Draw the silencer out of the downpipe assembly **(see illustration)**. Remove the collars, and on Daytona models to VIN 71698 and T509 Speed Triple models the rubber bushes for safekeeping if required **(see illustration)**.

**4** Installation is the reverse of removal. Use new springs if the old ones have stretched or weakened. On Daytona models to VIN 71698 and T509 Speed Triple models, check the condition of the rubber bushes and replace them with new ones if hardened or cracked. Tighten the silencer mounting bolt to the torque setting specified at the beginning of the Chapter. Run the engine and check that there are no leaks.

#### Downpipe assembly

**5** On Daytona models, remove the fairing side panels and the belly pan (see Chapter 7). On all models, remove the silencer (see above).

**6** Drain the cooling system (see Chapter 1), then remove the radiator (see Chapter 3).

**7** Unscrew the six downpipe assembly nuts from the cylinder head **(see illustration)**.

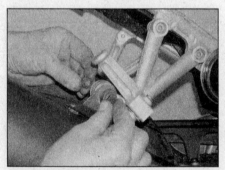

11.3a Unscrew the nut and withdraw the bolt . . .

11.3b . . . and remove the silencer

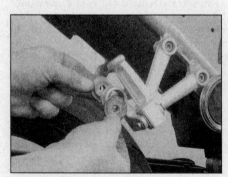

11.3c Remove the collars for safekeeping if loose

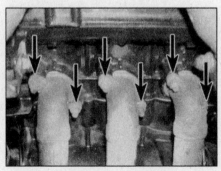

11.7a Unscrew the nuts (arrowed) . . .

**11.7b ... and remove the downpipe assembly**

**11.9 Smear the gaskets with grease to stop them falling out**

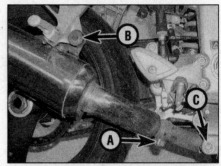

**11.15 Silencer clamp bolt (A), silencer mounting bolt (B), downpipe assembly rear mounting bolt (C) – ST shown**

Draw the downpipes out of the cylinder head and remove them **(see illustration)**.

**8** Remove the gasket from each port in the cylinder head and discard them as new ones must be fitted **(see illustration 11.9)**.

**9** Apply a smear of grease to the new gaskets to keep them in place and fit one into each of the cylinder head ports **(see illustration)**.

**10** Manoeuvre the assembly into position so that the head of each downpipe is located in its port in the cylinder head, then fit the downpipe nuts and tighten them first to the initial torque setting specified at the beginning of the Chapter, then to the final torque setting **(see illustrations 11.7b and a)**.

**11** Install the silencer (see above).

**12** Install the radiator (see Chapter 3) and fill the cooling system (see Chapter 1 and *Daily (pre-ride) checks*).

**13** Run the engine and check that there are no leaks from the exhaust system. On Daytona models install the body panels.

### *1999 to 2001 Sprint models*

#### Silencer

**14** On ST models, remove the belly pan (see Chapter 7).

**15** Slacken the clamp bolt securing the silencer in the downpipe assembly **(see illustration)**.

**16** Unscrew and remove the nut on the inside of the footrest bracket, then support the silencer and withdraw the bolt, noting the arrangement of the collars **(see illustration 11.15)**. Draw the silencer out of the downpipe

assembly. Remove the collars and the rubber bushes for safekeeping if required.

**17** Installation is the reverse of removal. Check the condition of the rubber bushes and replace them with new ones if hardened or cracked. Tighten the silencer mounting bolt to the torque setting specified at the beginning of the Chapter, then tighten the clamp bolt to the specified torque. Run the engine and check that there are no leaks from the exhaust system.

#### Downpipe assembly

**Note:** *The downpipe assembly on German and US California market models incorporates a catalytic converter at the 4-into-1 joint. Take care when handling the downpipe assembly, not to strike or drop it because the delicate catalytic converter element could be damaged.*

**18** Remove the fairing side panels and on ST models the belly pan (see Chapter 7). Remove the silencer (see above).

**19** Drain the cooling system (see Chapter 1), then remove the radiator (see Chapter 3). On German market models, disconnect the Lambda (oxygen) sensor wiring connector.

**20** Unscrew the bolt securing the rear of the downpipe assembly to the frame, noting the arrangement of the collars and rubber bushes **(see illustration 11.15)**.

**21** Unscrew the six downpipe assembly nuts from the cylinder head **(see illustration 11.7a)**. Draw the downpipes out of the cylinder head and remove them **(see illustration 11.7b)**.

**22** Remove the gasket from each port in the

cylinder head and discard them as new ones must be fitted **(see illustration 11.9)**. Remove the collars and bushes from the rear mounting for safekeeping if required. Check the condition of the rubber bushes and replace them with new ones if hardened or cracked.

**23** Apply a smear of grease to the new gaskets to keep them in place and fit one into each of the cylinder head ports **(see illustration 11.9)**. If removed, fit the bushes and collars into the rear mounting.

**24** Manoeuvre the assembly into position so that the head of each downpipe is located in its port in the cylinder head, then install the rear mounting bolt, but do not yet tighten it **(see illustration 11.15)**. Fit the downpipe nuts and tighten them first to the initial torque setting specified at the beginning of the Chapter, then to the final torque setting **(see illustrations 11.7b and a)**. Now tighten the rear mounting bolt to the specified torque. On German market models, do not forget to connect the Lambda sensor wiring connector.

**25** Install the silencer (see above).

**26** Install the radiator (see Chapter 3) and fill the cooling system (see Chapter 1 and *Daily (pre-ride) checks*).

**27** Run the engine and check that there are no leaks from the exhaust system before installing the body panels.

### *1999 to 2001 Tiger models*

#### Silencer

**28** Slacken the clamp bolt securing the silencer in the collector box **(see illustration)**.

**29** Unscrew and remove the nut on the inside of the footrest bracket, then support the silencer and withdraw the bolt, noting the arrangement of the washers, collar and bush **(see illustration)**. Draw the silencer out of the collector box. Remove the collar and the rubber bush for safekeeping if required.

**30** Installation is the reverse of removal. Check the condition of the rubber washer and bush and replace them with new ones if hardened or cracked. Tighten the silencer mounting bolt to the torque setting specified at the beginning of the Chapter, then tighten the clamp bolt to the specified torque. Run the engine and check the system for leaks.

**11.28 Slacken the clamp bolt (arrowed) ...**

**11.29 ... then unscrew the mounting bolt (arrowed) and remove the silencer**

11.32 Slacken the clamp bolt (arrowed) . . .

11.33 . . . then unscrew the mounting bolts (arrowed) and remove the collector box

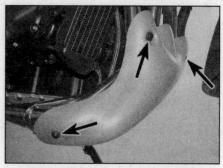

11.37 Undo the screws (arrowed) and remove the guard if required

## Collector box

**Note:** *The collector box on German and US California market models incorporates a catalytic converter. Take care when handling the collector box, not to strike or drop it because the delicate catalytic converter element could be damaged.*

**31** Remove the silencer (see above). Disconnect the Lambda (oxygen) sensor wiring connector – German market models.

**32** Slacken the clamp bolt securing the collector box to the downpipe assembly **(see illustration)**.

**33** Unscrew the collector box mounting bolts, then draw the box off the downpipe assembly **(see illustration)**. Remove the rubber bushes for safekeeping if required.

**34** Installation is the reverse of removal. Check the condition of the rubber bushes and replace them with new ones if hardened or cracked. Tighten the mounting bolts to the torque setting specified at the beginning of the Chapter, then tighten the clamp bolt to the specified torque. On German market models do not forget to connect the Lambda sensor wiring connector. Run the engine and check that there are no leaks from the exhaust system.

### Downpipe assembly

**35** Remove the silencer and the collector box (see above).

**36** Drain the cooling system (see Chapter 1), then remove the radiator (see Chapter 3).

**37** If required, undo the screws securing the exhaust guard and remove it **(see illustration)**.

**38** Unscrew the six downpipe assembly nuts from the cylinder head **(see illustration 11.7a)**. Draw the downpipes out of the cylinder head and remove them **(see illustration 11.7b)**.

**39** Remove the gasket from each port in the cylinder head and discard them as new ones must be fitted **(see illustration 11.9)**. Remove the collars and bushes from the rear mounting for safekeeping if required. Check the condition of the rubber bushes and replace them with new ones if hardened or cracked.

**40** Apply a smear of grease to the new gaskets to keep them in place and fit one into each of the cylinder head ports **(see illustration 11.9)**. If removed, fit the bushes and collars into the rear mounting.

**41** Manoeuvre the assembly into position so that the head of each downpipe is located in its port in the cylinder head, then fit the downpipe nuts and tighten them first to the initial torque setting specified at the beginning of the Chapter, then to the final torque setting **(see illustrations 11.7b and a)**.

**42** Install the collector box and silencer (see above). If removed, fit the exhaust guard **(see illustration 11.37)**.

**43** Install the radiator (see Chapter 3) and fill the cooling system (see Chapter 1 and *Daily (pre-ride) checks*).

**44** Run the engine and check that there are no leaks from the exhaust system.

## 2002-on all models

### Silencer

**45** Release the clamp securing the silencer in the downpipe assembly **(see illustration)**.

**46** Unscrew and remove the nut on the inside of the footrest bracket (inside of frame on Tiger models), then support the silencer and withdraw the bolt, noting the washer and the arrangement of the collars **(see illustration)**. Draw the silencer out of the downpipe assembly **(see illustration)**.

**47** Installation is the reverse of removal. Where fitted, check the condition of the rubber bushes and replace them with new ones if hardened or cracked. Tighten the silencer mounting bolt and the clamp bolt to the torque settings specified at the beginning of the Chapter. Run the engine and check that there are no leaks.

### Downpipe assembly

**48** On Daytona models remove the fairing side panels and on Sprint ST models remove the fairing side panels and belly pan (see Chapter 7). On Tiger models remove the sump guard (see Chapter 7).

**49** On all models, remove the silencer (see above).

**50** On all models, remove the oil cooler (see Chapter 2B, Section 21).

**51** On Daytona, Speed Triple and Sprint models, drain the cooling system (see Chapter 1), then remove the radiator (see Chapter 3).

11.45 Slacken the silencer clamp bolt

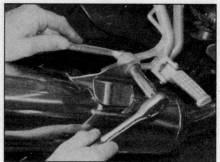

11.46a Remove the nut and bolt on the footrest bracket . . .

11.46b . . . and draw the silencer off

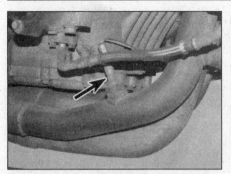

11.52a  Trace the wire from the oxygen sensor (arrowed) . . .

11.52b  . . . to the left-hand side of the bike and disconnect it

11.54  Remove the rear mounting bolt (arrowed)

**52** Trace the wiring from the oxygen sensor and disconnect it at the connector **(see illustrations)**.

**53** Unscrew and remove the six downpipe assembly nuts from the cylinder head **(see illustration 11.7a)**.

**54** Unscrew the bolt securing the rear of the downpipe assembly to the frame, noting the arrangement of the collars and rubber bushes **(see illustration)**. Support the downpipe assembly and withdraw the bolt, then draw the downpipes out of the cylinder head and remove them **(see illustration 11.7b)**.

**55** Remove the gasket from each port in the cylinder head and discard them as new ones must be fitted **(see illustration)**. Remove the collars and bushes from the rear mounting for safekeeping if required. Check the condition of the rubber bushes and replace them with new ones if hardened or cracked.

**56** Before installation, apply a smear of grease to the new gaskets to keep them in place and fit one into each of the cylinder head ports **(see illustration 11.55)**.

**57** Manoeuvre the assembly into position so that the head of each downpipe is located in its port in the cylinder head, then fit the downpipe nuts and tighten them finger-tight. Ensure that all the collars and bushes are in place, then install the rear downpipe nut and bolt finger-tight.

**58** Working from left to right, first tighten the upper downpipe assembly nuts to the torque setting specified at the beginning of the Chapter, then tighten the lower nuts to the specified torque setting **(see illustration)**. Finally retighten the upper downpipe assembly nuts to the specified torque setting.

**59** Tighten the rear downpipe fixing bolt to the specified torque setting.

**60** Reconnect the oxygen sensor wiring connector and ensure the wire is secured clear of the exhaust system.

**61** On Daytona, Speed Triple and Sprint models, install the radiator (see Chapter 3) and fill the cooling system (see Chapter 1).

**62** On all models, install the oil cooler (see Chapter 2B, Section 21).

**63** On all models, install the silencer (see above).

11.55  Always fit new gaskets in the exhaust ports

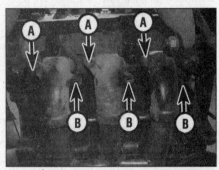

11.58  Tighten the upper (A) and lower (B) nuts as described

**64** Run the engine and check that there are no leaks from the exhaust system. Install the body panels according to your model (see Chapter 7).

## 12  Ignition coils/caps

**Warning: The energy levels in electronic systems can be very high. On no account should the ignition be switched on whilst the plugs or plug caps are being held. Shocks from the HT circuit can be most unpleasant. Secondly, it is vital that the**

engine is not turned over or run with any of the plug caps removed, and that the plugs are soundly earthed (grounded) when the system is checked for sparking. The ignition system components can be seriously damaged if the HT circuit becomes isolated.

**1** Before testing the coils, check that the spark plugs are in good condition and that the electrode gap is correct (see Chapter 1).

**2** If not already done, remove the fuel tank and the airbox (see Sections 2 and 4).

**3** Working on one coil/cap at a time, disconnect the wiring connector **(see illustration)**. On 1997 to 2001 models, undo the Torx screw securing the coil/cap to the valve cover **(see illustration)**.

**4** Pull the coil/cap off the spark plug **(see**

12.3a  Disconnect the wiring connector . . .

12.3b  . . . then undo the screws where fitted . . .

**12.4 . . . and pull the coil/cap off the spark plug**

illustration). Reconnect the wiring connector. Connect the cap to a new spark plug and lay the plug on the engine with the threads contacting the engine. If necessary, hold the spark plug with an insulated tool. Do not hold the plug against an engine cover that is magnesium coated as the coating could be damaged.

 **Warning: Do not remove any of the spark plugs from the engine to perform this check – atomised fuel being pumped out of the open spark plug hole could ignite, causing severe injury!**

5 Check that the kill switch is in the RUN position and the transmission is in neutral, then turn the ignition switch ON and turn the engine over on the starter motor. If the system is in good condition a regular, fat blue spark should be evident at the plug electrodes. If the spark appears thin or yellowish, or is non-existent, further investigation will be necessary. Turn the ignition OFF. Repeat the check for the other coils/caps.

6 The ignition system must be able to produce a spark which is capable of jumping a particular size gap. Triumph provide no specification, but a healthy system should produce a spark capable of jumping at least 6 mm. A simple testing tool can be made to test the minimum gap across which the spark will jump (see **Tool Tip**) or alternatively it is possible to buy an ignition spark gap tester tool and some of these tools are adjustable to alter the spark gap.

7 Connect the coil/cap to the protruding

**12.7 Connect the tester as shown – when the engine is cranked sparks should jump the gap between the nails**

*A simple spark gap testing tool can be made from a block of wood, a large alligator clip and two nails, one of which is fashioned so that the spark plug cap can be connected to its end. Make sure the gap between the two nail ends is the same as specified.*

electrode on the test tool, and clip the tool to a good earth (ground) on the engine or frame (see illustration). Check that the kill switch is in the RUN position, turn the ignition switch ON and turn the engine over on the starter motor. If the system is in good condition a regular, fat blue spark should be seen to jump the gap between the nail ends. Repeat the test for the other coil/caps. If the test results are good the entire ignition system can be considered good. If the spark appears thin or yellowish, or is non-existent, further investigation is necessary.

8 Using an ohmmeter or multimeter set to the ohms x 1 scale, measure the resistance between the terminals on the coil/cap (see illustration). The resistance should be as specified at the beginning of the Chapter. If not, the coil is faulty and must be replaced with a new one; the coil is a sealed unit and cannot therefore be repaired.

9 If the coils/caps and spark plugs are good, then there is a fault elsewhere in the system. The likely faults are listed below, starting with the most probable source of failure. Work through the list systematically, referring to the subsequent sections for full details of the necessary checks and tests. **Note:** *Before checking the following items ensure that the*

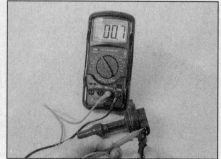

**12.8 To test the coil resistance, connect the meter as shown**

battery is fully charged and that all fuses are in good condition.

● *Loose, corroded or damaged wiring connections, broken or shorted wiring between any of the component parts of the ignition system (see Chapter 8).*
● *Faulty spark plug, dirty, worn or corroded plug electrodes, or incorrect gap between electrodes.*
● *Faulty ignition (main) switch or engine kill switch (see Chapter 8).*
● *Faulty clutch, neutral or sidestand switch (see Chapter 8).*
● *Faulty crankshaft position sensor, incorrect air gap, or damaged rotor.*
● *Faulty ECM.*

10 If the above checks don't reveal the cause of the problem, have the engine management system tested by a Triumph dealer. Triumph produce a diagnostic tool which can perform a complete analysis of the engine management system. Refer to Sections 1 and 13 for more information.

**13 Engine management system and ECM fault finding**

 **Warning: Refer to the precautions given in Section 1 before starting work.**

1 For a general description of the system, see Section 1.

### Diagnostic tool and fault codes

2 To diagnose the exact cause of a failure in the system, the Triumph diagnostic tool, specifically designed for this system, is essential. Hence if a problem occurs, the motorcycle should be taken to a Triumph dealer.

3 The engine management system has in-built diagnostic functions which record and store all data should a fault occur. Recorded faults can then be checked using Triumph's diagnostic tool, which reads the data and lists a code to indicate the exact fault. Should a fault occur, the malfunction indicator lamp (MIL) in the instrument cluster illuminates. If this happens, the management system switches itself into 'limp home' mode, so that in theory you should not be left stranded. Depending on the problem, it is possible that you will notice no difference in the running of the motorcycle.

4 In order to diagnose the problem and to turn the MIL off, the diagnostic tool is essential. Take your machine to a Triumph dealer and have them check the system – it should not take them long. Note that this task is impracticable for the DIY mechanic, not only because the diagnostic tool would be prohibitively expensive, but because an authorisation code is required to operate it and the codes are only available to Triumph dealers. For information, the diagnostic tool plugs into a main wiring harness at a

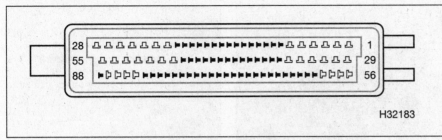

**13.7a  MC 2000 ECM wiring connector pin identification**

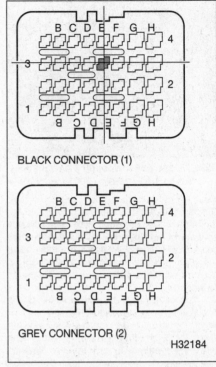

BLACK CONNECTOR (1)

GREY CONNECTOR (2)

H32184

**13.7b  MC 1000 ECM wiring connector pin identification**

connection point under the rider's seat on the right-hand side of the frame

**5** It is possible to perform certain tests and checks to identify a particular fault, but the difficulty is knowing in which part of the system the fault has occurred, and therefore where to start checking. Further details on the functions of and checks that can be made to the individual sensors and components and the wiring between them are detailed below and in the following Sections.

### Fault tracing

**6** If a fault is indicated, first check the wiring and connectors to and from the ECM (electronic control module) and the various sensors and all their related components. It may be that a connector is dirty or corroded or has come loose – a dirty or corroded terminal or connector will affect the resistance in that circuit, which will upset the information going to the ECM, and therefore affect the decisions it makes in controlling the system. Triumph recommends that the ECM and main wiring loom connector pins are lightly coated with petroleum jelly (e.g. Vaseline) to deter corrosion.

**7** A wire could be pinched and is shorting out – a continuity test of all wires from connector to connector will locate this. Albeit a fiddly and laborious task, the only way to determine any wiring faults is to systematically work through the Wiring Diagrams at the end of Chapter 8 and test each individual wire and

connector for continuity – all wires are colour-coded. The Wiring Diagrams show the terminal identification for each wire on the ECM – match these to the terminals on the ECM connector(s) when making the tests **(see illustrations)**.

**8** Two different systems have been used on the model range, though overall their function is very similar. Early Daytona, Speed Triple, Sprint ST and Tiger models have the MC 2000 ECM, while the later versions of those models and all Sprint RS models have the MC 1000 ECM. They are distinguishable by their different size and by their connectors – the MC 1000 ECM is smaller and has two connectors into it. When making continuity checks, isolate the wire being tested by disconnecting the wiring connectors at each end. To release the MC 2000 ECM wiring connector, pull the retaining clip up **(see illustration)**. To release the MC 1000 ECM wiring connectors, press in the locking tab and rotate the clamping ring until a click is felt **(see illustration)**. Note that when identifying a terminal on the MC 1000 ECM, the first number given on the wiring diagram indicates the relevant connector – number 1 is the black connector, number 2 is the grey connector. The letter and number given afterwards are like grid references for the terminals – in the illustration 13.7b, the highlighted terminal is 1/E3.

**9** Some of the circuits in the system have in-line resistors, which are also shown with their resistance value in the Wiring Diagrams. If you

are testing a circuit with an in-line resistor, set the meter to the appropriate range, and make sure the reading obtained is correct for the value of the resistor.

### 14 ECM power relay, ignition relay and tip-over sensor

**Note:** Before disconnecting the relay, make sure the ignition is switched OFF, then remove the seat(s) (see Chapter 7) and disconnect the battery (see Chapter 8).

**13.8a  Releasing the connector on MC 2000 ECM**

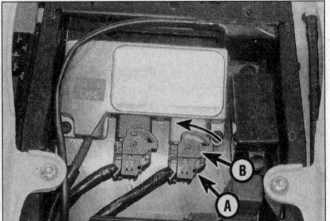

**13.8b  To release MC 1000 ECM connectors, press in the tab (A), then turn the locking ring (B) as shown until it is free**

**14.2a ECM power relay (4) – Daytona and Speed Triple 1997 to 2001 models**

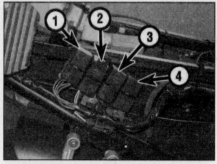

**14.2b ECM power relay (4) – Daytona and Speed Triple 2002-on models**

**14.2c Relay identification tags (arrowed) – Sprint ST to VIN 89736**

### ECM power relay

1 The ECM has its own power relay which is designed to provide a steady voltage supply to the ECM. The ECM holds the relay open after the ignition is switched off to enable it perform various power-down functions, such as writing data to the memory, referencing the position of the idle air control valve, and if necessary, running the cooling fan.

2 To check the relay, remove the seats on 1997 to 2001 Daytona and Speed Triple models; the seat cowling on 2002-on Daytona and Speed Triple models and Sprint ST models to VIN 89736; the seat on all other Sprint ST models and RS models; and the seat on Tiger models (see Chapter 7). Disconnect the relay from its connector block (see illustrations) – on Sprint ST models to VIN 89736 Triumph advise that the exact location of each relay is subject to change, so it is impracticable to specify its exact position in the relay pack – identify the relay by the red coloured tag around the wiring going into it. If the tag is missing, identify the relay by the colour of the wires going into it, referring to the Wiring Diagrams at the end of the Chapter. Test according to the applicable procedure:

### Daytona, Speed Triple and Tiger up to VIN 89736

3 Set an ohmmeter or multimeter to the ohms x 1 scale and connect its probes between the purple (terminal No. 1) and brown/pink (No. 8) wire terminals on the relay. Using a fully-charged 12 volt battery and two insulated jumper wires, connect the positive

(+ve) terminal of the battery to the purple (No. 6) wire terminal on the relay, and the negative (–ve) terminal to the yellow/brown (No. 4) wire terminal on the relay.

4 At this point the relay should be heard to click and the multimeter read 0 ohms (continuity). If this is the case the relay is proved good. If the relay does not click when battery voltage is applied and indicates no continuity (infinite resistance) across its terminals, it is faulty and must be replaced with a new one.

### Daytona, Speed Triple and Tiger from VIN 89737, all Sprint models

5 Set an ohmmeter or multimeter to the ohms x 1 scale and connect its probes between the brown (terminal No. 1) and brown/pink (No. 8) wire terminals on the relay. Using a fully-charged 12 volt battery and two insulated jumper wires, connect the positive (+ve) terminal of the battery to the brown (No. 6) wire terminal on the relay, and the negative (–ve) terminal to the yellow/brown (No. 4) wire terminal on the relay.

6 At this point the relay should be heard to click and the multimeter read 0 ohms (continuity). If this is the case the relay is proved good. If the relay does not click when battery voltage is applied and indicates no continuity (infinite resistance) across its terminals, it is faulty and must be replaced with a new one.

### Ignition relay and tip-over sensor

7 2002-on Daytona, Speed Triple and Sprint

models are fitted with an ignition relay and tip-over sensor. Refer to Chapter 8, Section 17 for location and basic test details for the relay.

## 15 Sensors

**Note:** Before disconnecting the wiring connector from any sensor, make sure the ignition is switched OFF, then remove the seat(s) (see Chapter 7) and disconnect the battery (see Chapter 8).

### Camshaft position sensor (Daytona and Speed Triple models to VIN 67207 only)

#### Function

1 The sensor reads the position of the camshaft and how fast it is turning. This information is used by the ECM to determine which cylinder is on its ignition stroke and when it should fire.

#### Removal and installation

2 The camshaft position sensor is located in the valve cover. Make sure the ignition is switched OFF. Remove the airbox (see Section 4). Disconnect the sensor wiring connector, then undo the screw and remove the sensor. Check the condition of the seal in the valve cover and replace it with a new one if it is damaged or deteriorated. On installation, tighten the sensor screw to the torque setting specified at the beginning of the Chapter.

### Speed sensor (Daytona and Speed Triple models to VIN 67207 only)

#### Function

3 The sensor reads the rotational speed of the rear wheel. This information is used by the ECM in conjunction with engine speed information to determine which gear the bike is in, and controls fuelling and ignition accordingly. The information also helps to determine the idle air control valve setting.

**14.2d ECM power relay (arrowed) – Sprint ST (VIN 89737-on) and Sprint RS**

**14.2e ECM power relay (3) – Tiger**

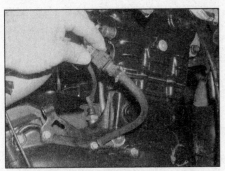

**15.7 Disconnect the wiring connector**

**15.8a Measuring the air gap with a feeler gauge**

**15.8b Loosen the screws (arrowed) to adjust the air gap**

### Removal and installation

**4** The speed sensor is located by the rear wheel. Make sure the ignition is switched OFF. Disconnect the sensor wiring connector, then undo the screw and remove the sensor. On installation, tighten the sensor screw to the torque setting specified at the beginning of the Chapter.

## Crankshaft position sensor

### Function

**5** The sensor reads the position of the crankshaft and how fast it is turning; this information is used by the ECM to determine which cylinder is on its ignition stroke and when it should fire. The ECM combines engine speed with information from other sensors to determine fuelling and ignition requirements.

### Test, removal and installation – 1997 to 2001 models

**6** The crankshaft position sensor is located on the right-hand end of the crankshaft. Remove the right-hand fairing side panel and the belly pan for access, according to your model (see Chapter 7).

**7** To check the sensor resistance, first make sure the ignition is switched OFF, then trace the wiring from the sensor and disconnect it at the connector **(see illustration)**. Using an ohmmeter or multimeter set to the K-ohms scale, measure the resistance between the terminals on the sensor side of the connector. If the result is as specified, check that there is no continuity between each terminal and earth (ground).

**8** Remove the clutch cover (see Chapter 2). Inspect the sensor and the sensor triggers on the timing rotor for damage. Turn the crankshaft using a spanner or socket on the large hex on the timing rotor so that one of the triggers on the rotor is directly aligned with the sensor pick-up. Use a feeler gauge to measure the air gap between the sensor and the trigger and compare the result with the Specifications at the beginning of the Chapter **(see illustration)**. If necessary, loosen the sensor screws and adjust the air gap, then

**15.10a Remove the mounting screws . . .**

tighten the screws, making sure the sensor does not move **(see illustration)**.

**9** If the sensor is faulty, replace it with a new one.

**10** To remove the sensor, remove the screws and free the wiring grommet from its cut-out **(see illustrations)**.

**11** Install the sensor and secure it with the screws, but do not fully tighten them yet – leave them loose enough to allow positional adjustment of the sensor (see Step 8).

**12** Fit the wiring grommet into its cut-out and reconnect the wiring connector **(see illustrations 15.10b and 15.7)**, then install the clutch cover (see Chapter 2).

### Test, removal and installation – 2002-on models

**13** The crankshaft position sensor is located on the left-hand side of the crankcase (see

**15.10b . . . then free the wiring grommet**

illustration). Remove the left-hand fairing side panel and the belly pan for access, according to your model (see Chapter 7).

**14** To check the sensor resistance, first make sure the ignition is switched OFF, then trace the wiring from the sensor and disconnect it at the connector, then follow the procedure in Step 7.

**15** Remove the alternator cover (see Chapter 8). Inspect the sensor and the sensor triggers on the back of the alternator rotor for damage **(see illustration)**. Use a feeler gauge to measure the air gap between the sensor and the triggers and compare the result with the Specifications at the beginning of the Chapter. The air gap is not adjustable.

**16** If the sensor is faulty, replace it with a new one.

**17** Undo the screw securing the sensor and draw the sensor and its mounting plate out of

**15.13 Location of the crankshaft position sensor**

**15.15 Sensor triggers are located on the back of the alternator rotor**

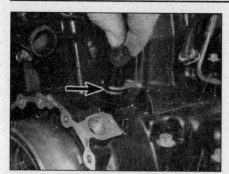

15.17 Remove the sensor, noting the O-ring (arrowed)

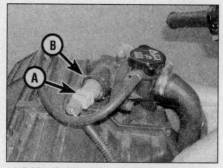

15.28a Coolant temperature sensor (A) and its retaining clip (B) – Daytona and Speed Triple

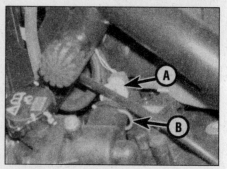

15.28b Coolant temperature sensor (A) and its retaining clip (B) – Tiger

the crankcase (see illustration). Discard the O-ring as a new one must be fitted.

18 Fit the mounting plate in the slot in the sensor body, then install the sensor in the crankcase with a new O-ring and tighten the fixing screw securely. Reconnect the wiring connector.

19 Install the alternator cover (see Chapter 8).

### Intake air pressure sensor

#### Function

20 The sensor reads the pressure of the air in the airbox and from this calculates atmospheric (barometric) pressure (i.e. air density). The ECM combines this with other information to determine engine load and adjusts fuelling requirements accordingly.

#### Removal and installation

21 On models to VIN 89736, the sensor is located in the right-hand side of the airbox at the back (see illustration 4.3a). On all later models, the sensor is housed within the ECM itself and is connected to the airbox via a tube, and therefore cannot itself be removed. On models to VIN 89736, make sure the ignition is switched OFF. Remove the fuel tank (see Section 2). Disconnect the wiring connector from the sensor and carefully pull it out of the airbox. Installation is the reverse of removal.

### Intake air temperature sensor

#### Function

22 The sensor reads the temperature of the air in the airbox. As changes in temperature affect air density, the ECM uses the information to determine fuelling requirements.

#### Test, removal and installation

23 On 1997 to 2001 Daytona, Speed Triple and Sprint models, and all Tiger models, the sensor is located in the right-hand side of the airbox at the front (see illustration 4.5a). On 2002-on Daytona, Speed Triple and Sprint models, the sensor is located on the top of the airbox at the back (see illustration 4.5b).

24 Make sure the ignition is switched OFF. Remove the fuel tank (see Section 2).

25 To test the sensor resistance, disconnect the wiring connector and measure the resistance between the sensor terminals using an ohmmeter or multimeter set to the K-ohms scale. If the result is not as specified, the sensor is faulty.

26 To remove the sensor, unscrew it from the airbox. Installation is the reverse of removal.

### Engine coolant temperature sensor

#### Function

27 The sensor reads the temperature of the engine coolant, and the ECM uses the information to determine fuelling requirements, particularly for hot and cold starting.

#### Test, removal and installation

28 On 1997 to 2001 Daytona and Speed Triple models, and all Tiger models, the sensor is located in the thermostat housing; on 1999 to 2001 Sprint models the sensor is located in the coolant union on the left-hand side of the cylinder head; on 2002-on Daytona, Speed Triple and Sprint models the sensor is located in the left-hand side of the cylinder head (see illustrations).

29 Make sure the ignition is switched OFF. To access the sensor, remove the fuel tank (see Section 2) or the left-hand fairing side panel (see Chapter 7) as applicable to your model.

30 To test the sensor resistance, disconnect the wiring connector and measure the resistance between the sensor terminals using an ohmmeter or multimeter set to the K-ohms scale. If the result is not as specified, the sensor is faulty.

31 To remove and install the sensor, first drain the cooling system (see Chapter 1).

32 On 1997 to 2001 Daytona and Speed Triple models, and all Tiger models, pull out the sensor retaining clip and withdraw the sensor. Discard the O-ring as a new one must be used. Fit a new O-ring onto the sensor, then push it into the thermostat housing until it is seated and secure it with the retaining clip, making sure It locates correctly around the sensor.

33 On 1999 to 2001 Sprint models, unscrew the sensor from the union. Discard the sealing washer as a new one must be used. Fit a new sealing washer onto the sensor, then thread it into the coolant union and tighten it securely.

34 On 2002-on Daytona, Speed Triple and Sprint models, unscrew the sensor from the cylinder head. Discard the sealing washer as a new one must be used. Fit a new sealing washer onto the sensor, then thread it into the coolant union and tighten it securely.

35 On all models, reconnect the wiring connector, then fill the cooling system (see Chapter 1).

36 Install the remaining components in the reverse order of removal.

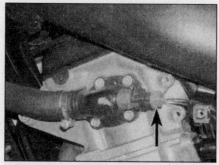

15.28c Coolant temperature sensor (arrowed) – Sprint

15.28d Coolant temperature sensor (arrowed) – 2002-on Daytona, Speed Triple and Sprint

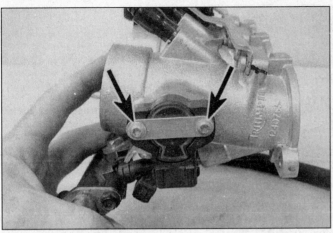

15.39 Throttle position sensor screws (arrowed)

15.43 Location of the throttle position sensor (arrowed)

## Throttle position sensor

### Function

**37** The sensor reads the amount of throttle being used, and the ECM uses this in conjunction with the information from other sensors to determine fuelling and ignition requirements.

### Removal and installation – 1997 to 2001 Daytona, Speed Triple and Sprint models, and all Tiger models

**38** The sensor is located on the right-hand end of the throttle bodies. Do not remove the throttle position sensor unless you know it is faulty and are replacing it with a new one, or unless you are replacing the throttle bodies with new ones. If you do remove it, it has to be set up using the Triumph diagnostic tool. There is no alternative, unless you want to run the risk of having the bike running incorrectly.

**39** Remove the throttle bodies (see Section 8). Undo the screws securing the sensor and remove the retaining plate, then draw the sensor off the end of the throttle shaft **(see illustration)**.

**40** Locate the sensor onto the end of the throttle shaft, aligning it so the D-shaped end of the shaft fits into the sensor. Fit the retaining plate and tighten the screws to the torque setting specified at the beginning of the Chapter.

**41** Install the throttle bodies (see Section 8).

15.49 Oxygen sensor (arrowed) – 2002-on location shown

The sensor must now be set up correctly using the Triumph diagnostic tool.

### Removal and installation – 2002-on Daytona, Speed Triple and Sprint models

**42** The sensor is located on the left-hand end of the throttle bodies. Do not remove the throttle position sensor unless you know it is faulty and are replacing it with a new one, or unless you are replacing the throttle bodies with new ones. If you do remove it, it has to be set up using the Triumph diagnostic tool. There is no alternative, unless you want to run the risk of having the bike running incorrectly.

**43** Remove the throttle bodies (see Section 8). Undo the screws securing the sensor, then draw the sensor off the end of the throttle shaft noting the position of the O-ring **(see illustration)**.

**44** Locate the sensor onto the end of the throttle shaft, aligning it so the D-shaped end of the shaft fits into the sensor. Tighten the screws to the torque setting specified at the beginning of the Chapter.

**45** Install the throttle bodies (see Section 8). The sensor must now be set up correctly using the Triumph diagnostic tool.

## Oxygen (lambda) sensor

### Function

**46** The sensor measures oxygen left in the unburnt exhaust gases and generates a signal voltage which is fed back to the ECM. In this way the ECM can correct the mixture supplied to the engine to ensure that the oxygen content of the exhaust gases remains within a narrow range and suitable for the operation of the catalytic converter. This type of system is called closed-loop control. **Note:** *The oxygen sensor is fitted on 1999 to 2001 German and US California market Sprint and Tiger models and on all-market 2002-on Daytona, Speed Triple, Sprint and Tiger models.*

### Test, removal and installation

**47** On 1999 to 2001 Sprint models, the sensor is located at the 4-into-1 junction in the exhaust downpipes, at the point where the catalytic

converter is housed; on ST models remove the belly pan for access (see Chapter 7). On 1999 to 2001 Tiger models, the sensor is located on the top surface of the exhaust collector box. On all 2002-on models, the sensor is located in the right-hand exhaust pipe below the crankcase; for access, remove the right-hand fairing side panel or belly pan as required according to your model (see Chapter 7).

**48** To test the sensor heater resistance, first make sure the ignition is switched OFF. Trace the wiring from the sensor to the connector and disconnect it. Measure the resistance between the white and brown/pink wire terminals (terminals 3 and 4) in the sensor side of the connector using an ohmmeter or multimeter set to the ohms x 1 scale. If the result is not as specified, the sensor is faulty.

**49** To remove the sensor, unscrew it from the exhaust system – the sensor and catalytic converter are fragile so care must be taken not to apply undue force **(see illustration)**. If the sensor is difficult to unscrew or the area around it is badly corroded, apply a penetrating fluid. When installing the sensor, apply copper grease to the sensor threads and fit a new sealing washer – it is essential to have an air-tight joint at this point.

## 16 Idle air control valve

**Note:** *Before disconnecting the valve, make sure the ignition is switched OFF, then remove the seat(s) (see Chapter 7) and disconnect the battery (see Chapter 8).*

### Check

**1** The idle air control valve is actuated by the ECM and set according to information received by the ECM from the various sensors. The valve is used to control the engine idle speed, to adjust the air supply on engine overrun, to correct for altitude, and for cold starting. The idle speed cannot be adjusted manually.

**16.3 Location of the idle air control valve (arrowed)**

**16.7 Idle air control valve screws (arrowed)**

2 The ECM actuates a stepper motor which moves a plunger in and out of the valve to vary the amount it is open. The operation of the valve can only be checked using the Triumph diagnostic tool. However, if a fault in the valve is suspected it is worth checking the wiring connector for loose, corroded or damaged terminals, and the wiring between the valve and the ECM for continuity, referring to the wiring diagrams at the end of Chapter 8 for details. Also check that the hoses are securely connected between the valve and the stubs on the cylinder head. Check the stepper motor resistance (see Step 4).

3 The valve is mounted either adjacent to, or on, the throttle body assembly **(see illustration)**. To gain access, remove the fuel tank and the airbox (see Sections 2 and 4).

4 To test the stepper motor resistance, first make sure the ignition is switched OFF. Disconnect the control valve wiring connector. First measure the resistance between the orange/green and green/grey wire terminals in the sensor side of the connector using an ohmmeter or multimeter set to the ohms x 10 scale. Next, measure the resistance between the pink/blue and orange/white wire terminals in the sensor side of the connector. If either of the results is not as specified, the stepper motor is faulty.

### Renewal

5 Disconnect the idle air control valve hoses from their unions on the valve – mark each hose according to the union it attaches to so that it can be correctly installed later **(see illustration 8.17b)**. If not already done, disconnect the valve wiring connector **(see illustration 8.17a)**.

6 On Daytona and Speed Triple models to VIN 71843, unscrew the throttle body bolt that secures the idle air control valve bracket, then remove the valve.

7 On all other models, undo the two screws securing the valve to the throttle bodies and remove the valve **(see illustration)**.

8 If required, undo the screws securing the stepper motor to the valve body and separate them. Check the condition of the O-ring and replace it with a new one if necessary.

9 Installation is the reverse of removal. Make sure the hoses and wiring connector are securely attached. Tighten the mounting screws to the torque setting specified at the beginning of the Chapter.

### 17 EVAP system – California market models

1 This system prevents the escape of fuel vapour into the atmosphere by storing it in a charcoal-filled canister located on the frame right-hand side at the rear **(see illustrations)**.

2 When the engine is stopped, fuel vapour from the tank is directed into the canister where it is absorbed and stored whilst the motorcycle is standing. When the engine is started, the purge control valve opens, thus drawing vapours which are stored in the canister into the throttle bodies to be burned during the normal combustion process.

3 The tank vent pipe also incorporates a roll-over valve which closes and prevents any fuel from escaping through it in the event of the bike falling over. The tank filler cap has a one-way valve which allows air into the tank as the volume of fuel decreases, but prevents any fuel vapour from escaping.

4 The system is not adjustable and can be properly tested only by a Triumph dealer, as the diagnostic tool is required. However the

**17.1a EVAP system – Daytona and Speed Triple models to VIN 71843**

1 Vent pipe from fuel tank
2 Roll-over valve
3 Pressure control valve
4 One-way valve
5 Canister
6 Purge control valve
7 Idle air control valve

H32215

owner can check that all the hoses are in good condition and are securely connected at each end. Renew any hoses that are cracked, split or generally deteriorated.

## 18 Catalytic converter

### General information

**1** The catalytic converter minimises the level of exhaust pollutants released into the atmosphere. It consists of a canister containing a fine mesh impregnated with a catalyst material, over which the hot exhaust gases pass. The catalyst speeds up the oxidation of harmful carbon monoxide, unburned hydrocarbons and soot, effectively reducing the quantity of harmful products released into the atmosphere via the exhaust gases.

**2** On 1999 to 2001 Tiger models the catalytic converter is housed in the exhaust collector box. On all other models, the catalytic converter is housed in the exhaust downpipe assembly.

**3** On 1999 to 2001 German and California market models the catalytic converter operates in an open loop system with no oxygen (lambda) sensor. On all other models it operates under closed-loop control with a Lambda sensor feeding back gas oxygen content information to the ECM; information on the Lambda sensor can be found in Section 15.

### Precautions

**4** The catalytic converter is a reliable and simple device which needs no maintenance in itself, but there are some precautions the owner should note if the converter is to function properly for its full service life.

● DO NOT use leaded or lead replacement petrol (gasoline) – the additives will coat the precious metals, reducing their converting efficiency and will eventually destroy the catalytic converter.

● Always keep the ignition and fuel systems well-maintained in accordance with the

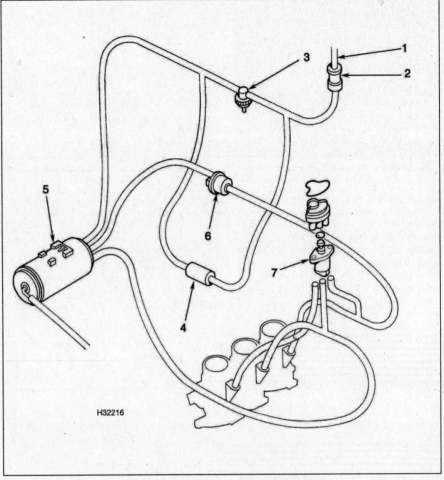

**17.1b  EVAP system – all other models**

| | |
|---|---|
| 1  Vent pipe from fuel tank | 5  Canister |
| 2  Roll-over valve | 6  Purge control valve |
| 3  Pressure control valve | 7  Idle air control valve |
| 4  One-way valve | |

manufacturer's schedule – if the fuel/air mixture is suspected of being incorrect have it checked on an exhaust gas analyser.

● If the engine develops a misfire, do not ride the bike at all (or at least as little as possible) until the fault is cured.

● DO NOT use fuel or engine oil additives –

these may contain substances harmful to the catalytic converter.

● DO NOT continue to use the bike if the engine burns oil to the extent of leaving a visible trail of blue smoke.

● Remember that the catalytic converter is FRAGILE – do not strike it with tools during servicing work.

# Chapter 5
# Frame, suspension and final drive

## Contents

## Degrees of difficulty

| Easy, suitable for novice with little experience  | Fairly easy, suitable for beginner with some experience  | Fairly difficult, suitable for competent DIY mechanic | Difficult, suitable for experienced DIY mechanic | Very difficult, suitable for expert DIY or professional |
|---|---|---|---|---|

## Specifications

### Front forks

Fork oil type
  Daytona and Speed Triple models ........................... Showa SS8 or equivalent
  Sprint models
    1999 to 2001 models ................................ Showa SS8 or equivalent
    2002-on models ..................................... SAE 10W
  Tiger models ............................................. Kayaba G10 or equivalent
Fork oil capacity
  Daytona and Speed Triple models
    1997 to 2001 models ................................ 589 cc
    2002-on models ..................................... 586 cc
  Sprint models ........................................... 459 cc
  Tiger models
    1999 to 2001 models ................................ 682 cc
    2002-on models ..................................... 720 cc
Fork oil level*
  Daytona and Speed Triple models
    1997 to 2001 models ................................ 76 mm
    2002-on models ..................................... 78 mm
  Sprint models ........................................... 145 mm
  Tiger models
    1999 to 2001 models ................................ 119 mm
    2002-on models ..................................... 107 mm

*Oil level is measured from the top of the tube with the fork spring removed and the leg fully compressed.

## Final drive

| | |
|---|---|
| Chain size | 530 |
| No. of links | |
| Daytona models to VIN 89736 | 108 |
| Daytona models from VIN 89737 – 132512 (except German models) | 106 |
| Daytona models from VIN 89737 – 132512 (German models) | 108 |
| Daytona models from VIN 132513 | 106 |
| Speed Triple | |
| 1997 to 2001 models | 108 |
| 2002-on models | 106 |
| Sprint models | 108 |
| Tiger models | |
| 1999 to 2001 models | 116 |
| 2002-on models | 114 |

## Torque wrench settings

| | |
|---|---|
| Centrestand pivots – Sprint ST models | 36 Nm |
| Chainguard mounting bolts | |
| Daytona and Speed Triple models | |
| Single-sided swingarm | 7 Nm |
| Twin-sided swingarm | 9 Nm |
| Sprint ST models | 4.5 Nm |
| Sprint RS models | 7 Nm |
| Tiger models | 7 Nm |
| Footrest (front) holder bolts – Daytona and Speed Triple models | |
| 1997 to 2001 models | 40 Nm |
| 2002-on models | 80 Nm |
| Footrest (rear) holder nuts – Tiger models | 42 Nm |
| Footrest bracket bolts | |
| Daytona and Speed Triple models | |
| Front | 30 Nm |
| Rear | 27 Nm |
| Sprint | |
| 1999 to 2001 models (front and rear | 30 Nm |
| 2002-on models (front and rear) | 27 Nm |
| Tiger | |
| Left-hand side | 15 Nm |
| Right-hand side | 27 Nm |
| Fork clamp bolts (top yoke) | 20 Nm |
| Fork damper rod Allen bolt | |
| Daytona and Speed Triple models | 35 Nm |
| Sprint and Tiger models | 25 Nm |
| Fork top bolt | |
| Daytona and Speed Triple models | 22 Nm |
| Sprint and Tiger models | 30 Nm |
| Front brake lever pivot bolt | |
| Daytona, Speed Triple and Sprint models | 1 Nm |
| Tiger models | 6 Nm |
| Front brake lever pivot bolt locknut | 6 Nm |
| Front sprocket nut | 132 Nm |
| Gearchange lever pivot bolt | |
| Sprint 1999 to 2001 models | 27 Nm |
| Sprint 2002-on models | 22 Nm |
| Handlebar clamp bolts | |
| Daytona and Speed Triple models with separate handlebars | |
| 6 mm bolts (up to VIN 47600 and from VIN 49061 to 49165) | 20 Nm |
| 8 mm bolts (from VIN 47601 to 63315 except VIN 49061to 49165) | 25 Nm |
| 8 mm bolts (from VIN 63316) | 35 Nm |
| Handlebar clamp bolts | |
| Sprint 1999 to 2001 models | 22 Nm |
| Sprint 2002-on models | 26 Nm |
| Handlebar holder clamp bolts | |
| Speed Triple models (with one-piece handlebars) | 22 Nm |
| Tiger models | 26 Nm |
| Handlebar positioning bolts | |
| Sprint 1999 to 2001 models | 22 Nm |
| Sprint 2002-on models | 26 Nm |
| Handlebar retaining bolts | |
| Daytona and Speed Triple models with separate handlebars | |
| (from VIN 105633) | 11 Nm |

Rear brake pedal pivot bolt
  Sprint 1999 to 2001 models . . . . . . . . . . . . . . . . . . . . . . . . . . . . . . . . .  27 Nm
  Sprint 2002-on models . . . . . . . . . . . . . . . . . . . . . . . . . . . . . . . . . . . . . .  22 Nm
  Tiger models . . . . . . . . . . . . . . . . . . . . . . . . . . . . . . . . . . . . . . . . . . . . . .  27 Nm
Rear master cylinder mounting bolts
  Daytona and Speed Triple models
    1997 to 2001 models . . . . . . . . . . . . . . . . . . . . . . . . . . . . . . . . . . . .  30 Nm
    2002-on models . . . . . . . . . . . . . . . . . . . . . . . . . . . . . . . . . . . . . . . .  18 Nm
  Sprint and Tiger models . . . . . . . . . . . . . . . . . . . . . . . . . . . . . . . . . . .  27 Nm
Rear shock absorber
  Daytona with single-sided swingarm and Speed Triple models
    Upper mounting . . . . . . . . . . . . . . . . . . . . . . . . . . . . . . . . . . . . . . . .  48 Nm
    Lower mounting . . . . . . . . . . . . . . . . . . . . . . . . . . . . . . . . . . . . . . . .  100 Nm
  Daytona with twin-sided swingarm
    Upper and lower mountings . . . . . . . . . . . . . . . . . . . . . . . . . . . . . .  48 Nm
  Sprint models – upper and lower mountings . . . . . . . . . . . . . . . . . .  48 Nm
  Tiger models
    Upper mounting . . . . . . . . . . . . . . . . . . . . . . . . . . . . . . . . . . . . . . . .  95 Nm
    Lower mounting . . . . . . . . . . . . . . . . . . . . . . . . . . . . . . . . . . . . . . . .  48 Nm
Rear sprocket nuts
  Daytona and Speed Triple 1997 to 2001 models . . . . . . . . . . . . . . .  33 Nm
  Daytona and Speed Triple 2002-on single-sided swingarm models .  33 Nm
  Daytona and Speed Triple 2002-on twin-sided swingarm models . .  55 Nm
  Sprint ST and RS models with single-sided swingarm . . . . . . . . . . .  33 Nm
  Sprint RS models with twin-sided swingarm . . . . . . . . . . . . . . . . . .  55 Nm
  Tiger models . . . . . . . . . . . . . . . . . . . . . . . . . . . . . . . . . . . . . . . . . . . .  85 Nm
Rear suspension linkage
  Daytona with single-sided swingarm and Speed Triple models
    Linkage arm-to-swingarm . . . . . . . . . . . . . . . . . . . . . . . . . . . . . . . .  48 Nm
    Linkage rods-to-frame . . . . . . . . . . . . . . . . . . . . . . . . . . . . . . . . . .  95 Nm
  Daytona with twin-sided swingarm
    Linkage rods-to-swingarm . . . . . . . . . . . . . . . . . . . . . . . . . . . . . . .  48 Nm
    Linkage rods-to-linkage arm . . . . . . . . . . . . . . . . . . . . . . . . . . . . .  65 Nm
    Linkage arm-to-frame . . . . . . . . . . . . . . . . . . . . . . . . . . . . . . . . . .  95 Nm
  Sprint models – all mountings . . . . . . . . . . . . . . . . . . . . . . . . . . . . .  48 Nm
Sidestand bracket bolts . . . . . . . . . . . . . . . . . . . . . . . . . . . . . . . . . . . . .  40 Nm
Sidestand pivot . . . . . . . . . . . . . . . . . . . . . . . . . . . . . . . . . . . . . . . . . . . .  20 Nm
Sprocket coupling nut – Daytona, Speed Triple, Sprint ST models
  and Sprint RS models with single-sided swingarm . . . . . . . . . . . . .  146 Nm
Steering head bearing adjuster locknut . . . . . . . . . . . . . . . . . . . . . . . .  40 Nm
Steering stem nut
  Daytona 1997 to 2001 models . . . . . . . . . . . . . . . . . . . . . . . . . . . . .  40 Nm
  Daytona 2002 to early 2004 models . . . . . . . . . . . . . . . . . . . . . . . . .  65 Nm
  Daytona 2004-on models . . . . . . . . . . . . . . . . . . . . . . . . . . . . . . . . .  90 Nm
  Speed Triple models (up to VIN 172426, inc. 173398 to 173815) . . .  40 Nm
  Speed Triple models (from VIN 172427, except 173398 to 173815) .  65 Nm
  Sprint and Tiger models . . . . . . . . . . . . . . . . . . . . . . . . . . . . . . . . . . .  65 Nm
Swingarm
  Daytona and Speed Triple 1997 to 2001 models
    Adjuster bolt . . . . . . . . . . . . . . . . . . . . . . . . . . . . . . . . . . . . . . . . . .  18 Nm
    Adjuster bolt locknut . . . . . . . . . . . . . . . . . . . . . . . . . . . . . . . . . . .  32 Nm
    Pivot . . . . . . . . . . . . . . . . . . . . . . . . . . . . . . . . . . . . . . . . . . . . . . . .  60 Nm
  Daytona and Speed Triple 2002-on models
    Single-sided swingarm
      Adjuster bolt . . . . . . . . . . . . . . . . . . . . . . . . . . . . . . . . . . . . . . . .  15 Nm
      Adjuster bolt locknut . . . . . . . . . . . . . . . . . . . . . . . . . . . . . . . . .  30 Nm
      Pivot . . . . . . . . . . . . . . . . . . . . . . . . . . . . . . . . . . . . . . . . . . . . . .  60 Nm
    Twin-sided swingarm
      Adjuster bolt . . . . . . . . . . . . . . . . . . . . . . . . . . . . . . . . . . . . . . . .  15 Nm
      Adjuster bolt locknut . . . . . . . . . . . . . . . . . . . . . . . . . . . . . . . . .  30 Nm
      Pivot bolt nut . . . . . . . . . . . . . . . . . . . . . . . . . . . . . . . . . . . . . . .  110 Nm
  Sprint ST and RS models with single-sided swingarm
    Adjuster bolt . . . . . . . . . . . . . . . . . . . . . . . . . . . . . . . . . . . . . . . . . .  15 Nm
    Adjuster bolt locknut . . . . . . . . . . . . . . . . . . . . . . . . . . . . . . . . . . .  30 Nm
    Pivot . . . . . . . . . . . . . . . . . . . . . . . . . . . . . . . . . . . . . . . . . . . . . . . .  60 Nm
  Sprint RS models with twin-sided swingarm
    Adjuster bolt . . . . . . . . . . . . . . . . . . . . . . . . . . . . . . . . . . . . . . . . . .  15 Nm
    Adjuster bolt locknut . . . . . . . . . . . . . . . . . . . . . . . . . . . . . . . . . . .  30 Nm
    Pivot bolt nut . . . . . . . . . . . . . . . . . . . . . . . . . . . . . . . . . . . . . . . . .  110 Nm
  Tiger models – pivot bolt . . . . . . . . . . . . . . . . . . . . . . . . . . . . . . . . . .  85 Nm

## 1 General information

Daytona and Speed Triple models have a twin spar oval-section aluminium tube frame. Sprint models have a twin spar box-section aluminium frame. Tiger models have a twin spar steel tube frame. All frames use the engine as a stressed member.

Front suspension is by a pair of oil-damped telescopic forks. Daytona and Speed Triple models have a cartridge-type damper, and the forks are adjustable for spring pre-load and both rebound and compression damping. Sprint models have a conventional damper system, and the forks are adjustable for spring pre-load only. Tiger models have a conventional damper system, but the forks are not adjustable.

At the rear, an aluminium alloy swingarm acts on a single shock absorber via a three-way linkage. Daytona, Speed Triple and Sprint ST models, and Sprint RS models from VIN 161318 have a single-sided swingarm; Sprint RS models up to VIN 161317 and all Tiger models have the conventional, twin-sided type – certain Daytona and Speed Triple models have also been supplied with twin-sided swingarms. On Daytona and Speed Triple models the shock absorber is adjustable for both rebound and compression damping. On Sprint and Tiger models the shock absorber is adjustable for spring pre-load and rebound damping.

The drive to the rear wheel is by chain and sprockets.

Many of the bolts used on Triumph motorcycles are of the Torx type. Unless you are already equipped with a good range of Torx bits, you are advised to obtain a set. Make sure you buy bits that can be used in conjunction with a socket set so that a torque wrench can be applied – a Torx key set will not be adequate on its own, though will be useful in addition to the bits.

## 2 Frame

1 The frame should not require attention unless accident damage has occurred. In most cases, frame renewal is the only satisfactory remedy for such damage. A few frame specialists have the jigs and other equipment necessary for straightening the frame to the required standard of accuracy, but even then there is no simple way of assessing to what extent the frame may have been over stressed.
2 After the machine has accumulated a lot of miles, the frame should be examined closely for signs of cracking or splitting at the welded joints. Loose engine mounting bolts can cause ovaling or fracturing of the mounts themselves. Minor damage can often be repaired by welding, depending on the extent and nature of the damage, but this is a task for an expert.
3 Remember that a frame which is out of alignment will cause handling problems. If misalignment is suspected as the result of an accident, it will be necessary to strip the machine completely so the frame can be thoroughly checked.

## 3 Footrests, brake pedal and gearchange lever

### *Footrests*

1 Remove the E-clip from the bottom of the footrest pivot pin, then withdraw the pivot pin and remove the footrest (see illustration). On the front footrests, note the fitting of the return spring. On the rear footrests, note the fitting of the detent plate (except Tiger models), detent ball and spring, and take care that they do not spring out when removing the footrest.
2 On Sprint and Tiger models, the rider's footrest rubbers, and on Tiger models the passenger rubbers, can be renewed if required – they are secured to the footrest by two screws or bolts (see illustrations).
3 Installation is the reverse of removal.

### *Brake pedal*
### Removal

4 Unhook the brake pedal return spring and the brake light switch spring.
5 Remove the retaining clip from the clevis pin securing the brake pedal to the master cylinder pushrod (see illustrations). Remove the clevis pin and separate the pedal from the pushrod.
6 On Daytona models up to VIN 186150 and all Speed Triple models, the footrest holder acts as the pedal pivot, and the holder is secured from the back of the footrest bracket by a bolt (see illustration). Unscrew the bolt, then draw the footrest holder out of the

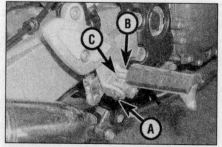

3.1 Remove the E-clip (A) and withdraw the pivot pin (B), noting the return spring (C) on the front footrests

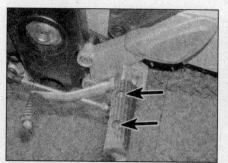

3.2a Footrest rubber screws (arrowed) – Sprint models

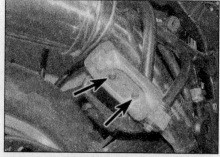

3.2b Footrest rubber screws (arrowed) – Tiger models

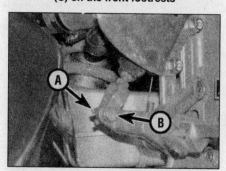

3.5a Remove the retaining clip (A) and withdraw the clevis pin (B)

3.5b On Tiger models, access to the clevis (arrowed) is restricted

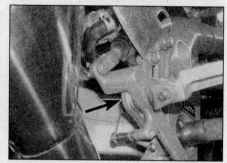

3.6a The footrest holder bolt is on the inside of the bracket (arrowed)

**3.6b Rear brake master cylinder bolts (arrowed)**

**3.8 Brake pedal pivot bolt (arrowed)**

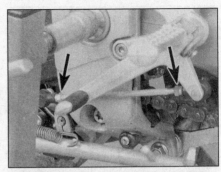

**3.10a Slacken the locknuts (arrowed), then thread the rod out of the lever and arm**

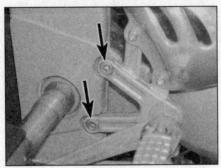

**3.10b Footrest bracket bolts (arrowed)**

**3.11 Remove the pinch bolt and pull the lever off the shaft**

bracket and slide the pedal off it. If you don't have the correct tools to access the bolt with the bracket in situ, unscrew the bolts securing the master cylinder to the bracket and displace it (there is no need to detach the hoses), then unscrew the bolts securing the bracket to the frame **(see illustration)**. On Daytona models from VIN 186151, a separate pivot bolt is fitted on the back of the footrest bracket. Unscrew the bolt and remove the pedal.

**7** On Sprint models, the pivot bolt is on the back of the footrest bracket. Unscrew the bolt and remove the pedal. If you don't have the correct tools to access the bolt with the bracket in situ, unscrew the bolts securing the master cylinder to the bracket and displace it (there is no need to detach the hoses), then unscrew the bolts securing the bracket to the frame.

**8** On Tiger models, unscrew the pivot bolt and remove the pedal **(see illustration)**.

### Installation

**9** Installation is the reverse of removal, noting the following:
● *Apply grease to the brake pedal pivot.*
● *Use a new split pin on the clevis pin securing the brake pedal to the master cylinder pushrod.*
● *Where removed, tighten the footrest holder bolts, footrest bracket bolts and master cylinder mounting bolts to the torque settings specified at the beginning of the Chapter, according to model.*
● *Check the operation of the rear brake light switch (see Chapter 1, Section 10).*

### *Gearchange lever*

#### Removal

**10** On 1997 to 2001 Daytona and Speed Triple models, slacken the gearchange lever linkage rod locknuts, then unscrew the rod and separate it from the lever and the arm (the rod is reverse-threaded on one end and so will simultaneously unscrew from both lever and arm when turned in the one direction) **(see illustration)**. Note how far the rod is threaded into the lever and arm as this determines the height of the lever relative to the footrest. The footrest holder acts as the lever pivot, and the holder is secured from the

back of the footrest bracket by a bolt. Unscrew the footrest bracket mounting bolts and remove the bracket **(see illustration)**. Unscrew the footrest holder bolt, then draw the holder out of the bracket and slide the lever off it.

**11** On 2002-on Daytona and Speed Triple models, make an alignment mark across the gearchange shaft end and the gearchange lever as an aid to installation, then unscrew the pinch bolt and slide the lever off the shaft **(see illustration)**. On Daytona models from VIN 210262, slacken the gearchange lever linkage rod locknuts, then unscrew the rod and separate it from the lever and the arm (the rod is reverse-threaded on one end and so will simultaneously unscrew from both lever and arm when turned in the one direction). Note how far the rod is threaded into the lever and arm as this determines the height of the lever relative to the footrest. Unscrew the lever pivot bolt and remove the lever.

**12** On Sprint models, slacken the gearchange lever linkage rod locknuts, then unscrew the rod and separate it from the lever and the arm (the rod is reverse-threaded on one end and so will simultaneously unscrew from both lever and arm when turned in the one direction) **(see illustration)**. Note how far the rod is threaded into the lever and arm as this determines the height of the lever relative to the footrest. Unscrew the lever pivot bolt and remove the lever.

**13** On Tiger models, make an alignment mark across the gearchange shaft end and the gearchange lever as an aid to installation, then unscrew the pinch bolt and slide the lever off the shaft **(see illustration)**.

### Installation

**14** Installation is the reverse of removal, noting the following:
● *Apply grease to the gear lever pivot.*
● *On 1997 to 2001 Daytona and Speed Triple*

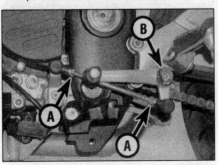

**3.12 Gearchange linkage rod locknuts (A), lever pivot bolt (B) – Sprint models**

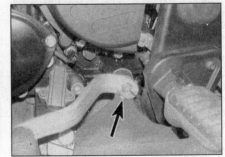

**3.13 Gearchange lever pinch bolt (arrowed) – Tiger models**

**4.3 Sidestand pivot bolt (arrowed) – Daytona shown**

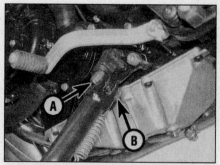

**4.4 On Tiger models, counter-hold the pivot bolt (A) and unscrew the nut (B)**

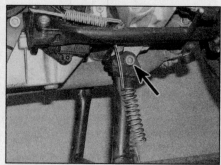

**4.9 Centrestand pivot bolt (arrowed)**

models, tighten the footrest holder bolt and footrest bracket bolts to the torque settings specified at the beginning of the Chapter. On Sprint models, tighten the pivot bolt to the specified torque setting.

● If applicable, adjust the gear lever height as required by screwing the linkage rod in or out of the lever and arm. Tighten the locknuts securely.

## 4 Sidestand and centrestand

### Sidestand

**1** Support the motorcycle securely in an upright position using an auxiliary stand, or on Sprint ST models the centrestand.
**2** Unhook the stand springs.
**3** On Daytona, Speed Triple and Sprint models, unscrew the pivot bolt and remove the stand, noting how it locates against the switch plunger **(see illustration)**.
**4** On Tiger models, counter-hold the pivot bolt and unscrew the nut on the inside of the bracket **(see illustration)**. Remove the pivot bolt and the stand, noting how it locates against the switch plunger.
**5** On installation apply grease to the pivot and to the contact surfaces of the stand and bracket. Apply a suitable non-permanent thread locking compound to the bolt threads. Reconnect the sidestand springs. Check that the springs hold the stand securely up when not in use – an accident is almost certain to occur if the stand extends while the machine is in motion.
**6** Check the operation of the sidestand switch (see Chapter 8).

### Centrestand (Sprint ST models)

**7** Support the motorcycle on its sidestand.
**8** Unhook the stand springs.
**9** Counter-hold the pivot bolts and unscrew the nuts on the inside **(see illustration)**. Withdraw the bolts and remove the stand, noting the washers and collars.
**10** On installation apply grease to the pivot bolts and collars and to the contact surfaces of the stand and bracket. Reconnect the

springs and check that they hold the stand securely up when not in use – an accident is almost certain to occur if the stand extends while the machine is in motion.

## 5 Handlebars and levers

### Handlebars

#### Removal

**Note:** The handlebars can be displaced from the forks or top yoke without having to remove the lever or switch assemblies.

**1** Where fitted, remove the fairing (see Chapter 7). **Note:** The fairing can remain on the bike if required, though it is advisable to remove it to prevent the possibility of damaging it.
**2** On the right-hand side, displace the front brake master cylinder and reservoir (see Chapter 6). There is no need to disconnect the hydraulic hose. Keep the reservoir upright to prevent possible fluid leakage and make sure no strain is placed on the hydraulic hose. Displace the handlebar switch housing, and on models with the throttle cable located in the housing, detach the cable (see Chapters 4 and 8). There is no need to disconnect the loom wiring connector. On models with a separate throttle cable housing, displace it from the handlebar (see Chapter 4). There is no need to detach the throttle cable from the

throttle bodies. Where applicable and if required, remove the rear view mirror (see Chapter 7). On Speed Triple and Tiger models, release the wiring and cable from any ties on the handlebars.
**3** On the left-hand side, unscrew the two bolts securing the clutch lever bracket to the handlebar and displace it **(see illustration)**. There is no need to detach the clutch cable. Either remove the clutch switch (see Chapter 8), or support the bracket so that no strain is placed on its wiring. Displace the handlebar switch (see Chapter 8). There is no need to disconnect the loom wiring connector. Where applicable and if required, remove the rear view mirror (see Chapter 7). On Speed Triple and Tiger models, release the wiring and cable from any ties on the handlebars.
**4** If required, unscrew the handlebar end-weight bolts and remove them from the ends of the handlebars. Slide the throttle twistgrip off the right-hand bar. Remove the grip from the left-hand bar – it may be necessary to slit it open using a sharp blade as may have been glued in place, though a screwdriver between the grip and the handlebar and some aerosol lubricant directed into the grip will usually work. Depending on your removal method and its success, a new grip may be required on assembly.
**5** On Daytona and Speed Triple models with separate handlebars, check on the underside of the handlebar brackets for the location of a retaining bolt **(see illustration)**. Retaining bolts are fitted from VIN 105633. If fitted, remove the retaining bolts. On all models,

**5.3 Clutch lever bracket clamp bolts (arrowed)**

**5.5a Location of the handlebar retaining bolt (arrowed)**

5.5b  Slacken the handlebar clamp bolt (arrowed) on each side and move the bars down

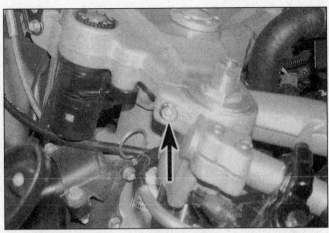

5.5c  Slacken the fork clamp bolt (arrowed) on each side

slacken the handlebar clamp bolts **(see illustration)**. On models up to VIN 105632, a pin in the handlebar bracket locates in a hole in the underside of the top yoke – slide the handlebars down the forks until the pins are clear of the holes. On all models, twist the bars round until the fork clamp bolts in the top yoke are accessible and slacken the clamp bolts **(see illustration)**. Unscrew the steering stem nut and remove it – this requires the use of a special Triumph tool (Pt. No. T3880300), or a suitable equivalent **(see illustration)**. Gently ease the top yoke up off the fork tubes and position it clear, using a rag to protect the tank or other components **(see illustration)**. Ease the handlebar up and off the fork **(see illustration)**. Note how the pin on the handlebar holder locates in the hole in the underside of the top yoke.

6 On Sprint models with separate handlebars, remove the blanking caps from the heads of the handlebar positioning bolts using a small flat-bladed screwdriver, then unscrew the bolts **(see illustrations)**. Slacken

5.5d  Unscrew the steering stem nut, using either the Triumph tool shown or a suitable equivalent

5.5e  Ease the yoke up off the forks and position it clear . . .

5.5f  . . . then slide the handlebar up off the fork

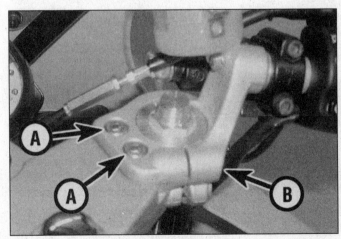

5.6a  Handlebar positioning bolts (A), handlebar clamp bolt (B) – RS models

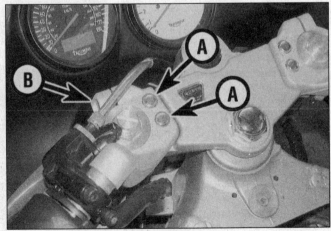

5.6b  Handlebar positioning bolts (A), handlebar clamp bolt (B) – ST models

5.7 Handlebar holder clamp bolts (arrowed) – Tiger shown

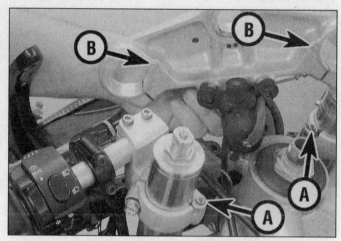

5.8 Locate the pins (A) in the holes (B)

the handlebar clamp bolt, then ease the handlebar up and off the fork.

**7** On Sprint models with one piece handlebars, and on Tiger models, unscrew the handlebar holder clamp bolts, then remove the clamps and the handlebars **(see illustration)**.

### Installation

**8** Installation is the reverse of removal, noting the following.

● On Daytona and Speed Triple models with separate handlebars, tighten the steering stem nut, fork clamp bolts, handlebar clamp bolts and, where fitted, handlebar retaining bolts, to the torque settings

specified at the beginning of the Chapter, in that order. Don't forget to locate the pins on the handlebar holders into the holes in the underside of the top yoke **(see illustration)** if applicable. **Note:** *If only one handlebar has been removed, slacken the clamp bolt securing the other handlebar before tightening the steering stem nut, then tighten it along with the other as described.*

● *On Sprint models, tighten the handlebar positioning bolts before the clamp bolts, and tighten the bolts to the torque settings specified at the beginning of the Chapter. Fit the blanking caps into the tops of the positioning bolts.*

● *On Sprint models with one-piece handlebars, and on Tiger models, make sure the handlebars are central in the holders, and align the punch mark in the front of the handlebar with the mating surface of the holder. Tighten the holder clamp bolts to the torque setting specified at the beginning of the Chapter, making sure the holders are evenly set front and rear.*

● *Apply some rubber adhesive to the left-hand bar before fitting the grip. Apply some grease to the right-hand bar before sliding on the throttle twistgrip.*

● *Refer to the relevant Chapters as directed for the installation of the handlebar mounted assemblies. Align the slit in the clutch lever bracket with the punch mark on the handlebar.*

● *Adjust throttle and clutch cable freeplay (see Chapter 1).*

● *Check the operation of the switches, the throttle, the front brake and the clutch before taking the machine on the road.*

### Clutch lever

**9** Slacken the clutch cable adjuster lockring and thread the adjuster fully into the bracket to provide maximum freeplay in the cable **(see illustration)**. Unscrew the lever pivot bolt locknut, then unscrew the pivot bolt and remove the lever, detaching the cable nipple as you do so **(see illustration)**. On Tiger models, note how the handguard is located by the bolt, and note the flanged sleeve **(see illustration)**.

**10** Installation is the reverse of removal. Apply grease to the pivot bolt shaft and the contact areas between the lever and its bracket, and to the clutch cable nipple. Adjust the clutch cable freeplay (see Chapter 1).

### Front brake lever

**11** Unscrew the lever pivot bolt locknut, then unscrew the pivot bolt and remove the lever **(see illustration)**. On Tiger models, note how the handguard is located by the bolt, and note the flanged sleeve.

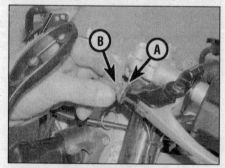

5.9a Slacken the lockring (A) and thread the adjuster (B) fully in

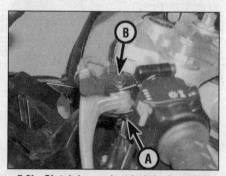

5.9b Clutch lever pivot bolt locknut (A), pivot bolt (B)

5.9c On Tiger models, note the fitting of the handguard

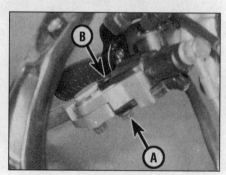

5.11 Brake lever pivot bolt locknut (A), pivot bolt (B)

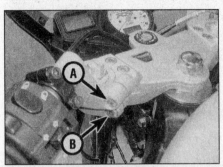

6.6a Handlebar clamp bolt (A), fork clamp bolt (B) – RS models

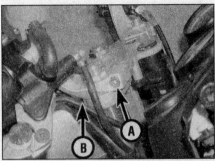

6.6b Handlebar clamp bolt (A), fork clamp bolt (B) – ST models

6.6c Fork clamp bolts (arrowed) – Tiger models

**12** Installation is the reverse of removal. Apply grease to the pivot bolt shaft and the contact areas between the lever and its bracket. Tighten the pivot bolt and its locknut to the torque settings specified at the beginning of the Chapter.

## 6 Fork removal and installation

### Removal

*Caution: Although not strictly necessary, and where applicable, before removing the forks it is recommended that the fairing side panels and/or fairing are removed (see Chapter 7). This will prevent accidental damage to the paintwork should a tool slip.*

**1** Where applicable and if required, remove the fairing and the fairing side panels (see Chapter 7).

**2** Displace the front brake calipers (see Chapter 6). There is no need to disconnect the hydraulic hoses.

**3** Remove the front wheel (see Chapter 6).

**4** Remove the front mudguard (see Chapter 7).

**5** Work on each fork individually. Note the routing of the various cables and hoses around the forks, and release any cable ties that secure them.

**6** On Daytona and Speed Triple models with separate handlebars, slacken the handlebar clamp bolt and the fork clamp bolt in the top yoke (**see illustrations 5.5b and c**). On Sprint models, slacken the handlebar clamp bolt and the fork clamp bolt in the top yoke (**see illustrations**). On Tiger models, slacken the fork clamp bolts in the top yoke (**see illustration**).

**7** If the forks are to be overhauled, or if the fork oil is being changed, slacken the fork top bolt now whilst it is still clamped in the yokes.

**8** Note the alignment of the tops of the fork tube with the top yoke. Slacken but do not remove the fork clamp bolt(s) in the bottom yoke (**see illustrations**). Remove the fork by twisting it and pulling it downwards; on Daytona and Speed Triple models with separate handlebars, support the handlebars as you do so (**see illustration**). Note which fork fits on which side.

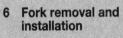 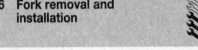

> **HAYNES HINT** *If the fork legs are seized in the yokes, spray the area with penetrating oil and allow time for it to soak in before trying again.*

### Installation

**9** Remove all traces of corrosion from the fork tubes and the yokes. Slide the fork up through the bottom yoke, and the handlebar on Daytona and Speed Triple models (with separate handlebars), and up into the top yoke, making sure the wiring, cables and hoses are the correct side of the fork as noted on removal (**see illustration 6.8d**). On Sprint models, make sure that the fork with the threaded section for the axle fits on the right, and the fork with the axle clamp bolts fits on the left. Check that the amount of protrusion

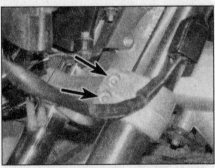

6.8a Bottom yoke fork clamp bolts (arrowed) – Daytona and Speed Triple models

6.8c Bottom yoke fork clamp bolts (arrowed) – Tiger models

of the fork tube above the top yoke is as noted on removal and equal on both sides – the joint between the fork top bolt and the top of the fork tube should be flush with the top surface of the top yoke on Daytona, Speed Triple and Tiger models, and flush with the top of the handlebar holder on Sprint models.

**10** Tighten the fork clamp bolts in the bottom yoke to the torque setting specified at the beginning of the Chapter (**see illustration 6.8a, b or c**). If the fork leg has been dismantled or if the fork oil has been changed, tighten the fork top bolt to the specified torque setting. Now tighten the fork clamp bolt in the top yoke, and the handlebar clamp bolt where applicable, to the specified torque settings (**see illustrations 5.5b and c, or 6.6a, b or c**).

**11** Install the front wheel (see Chapter 6), the front mudguard (see Chapter 7), and the brake calipers (see Chapter 6).

6.8b Bottom yoke fork clamp bolt (arrowed) – Sprint models

6.8d Slide the fork down and out of the yokes, collecting the handlebar where applicable

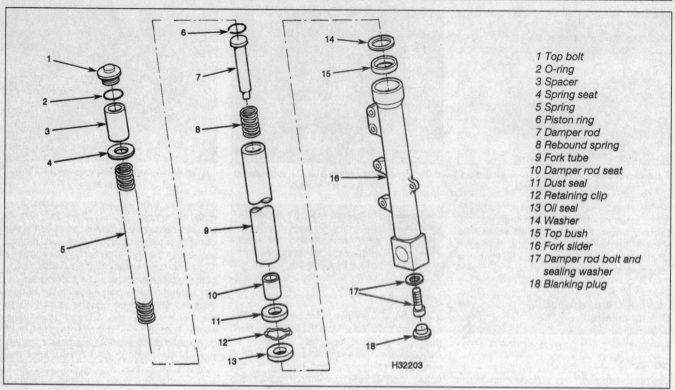

1 Top bolt
2 O-ring
3 Spacer
4 Spring seat
5 Spring
6 Piston ring
7 Damper rod
8 Rebound spring
9 Fork tube
10 Damper rod seat
11 Dust seal
12 Retaining clip
13 Oil seal
14 Washer
15 Top bush
16 Fork slider
17 Damper rod bolt and
   sealing washer
18 Blanking plug

H32203

**7.1a  Front fork components – Sprint models**

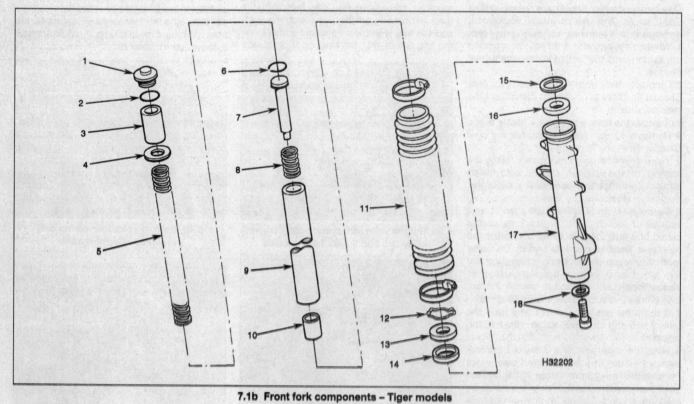

**7.1b  Front fork components – Tiger models**

| 1 Top bolt | 5 Spring | 9 Fork tube | 13 Dust seal | 17 Fork slider |
| 2 O-ring | 6 Piston ring | 10 Damper rod seat | 14 Oil seal | 18 Damper rod bolt and |
| 3 Spacer | 7 Damper rod | 11 Gaiter | 15 Washer | sealing washer |
| 4 Spring seat | 8 Rebound spring | 12 Retaining clip | 16 Top bush | |

**12** Where removed, install the fairing and the fairing side panels (see Chapter 7).
**13** Check the operation of the front forks and brakes before taking the machine out on the road.

## 7  Fork overhaul

### Sprint and Tiger models
#### Disassembly

**1** Remove the forks (see Section 6). Always dismantle the fork legs separately to avoid interchanging parts and thus causing an accelerated rate of wear. Store all components in separate, clearly marked containers **(see illustrations)**. Unless you are just changing the oil, on Sprint models remove the fork guard from the top of the slider, noting how it locates, and the blanking plug from the base of the slider **(see illustrations 7.30b and c)**, and on Tiger models remove the rubber gaiter.
**2** If required (for full overhaul), compress the fork tube in the slider so that the spring exerts maximum pressure on the damper rod head, then have an assistant slacken the damper rod bolt in the base of the fork slider **(see illustration)**. Do not remove the bolt at this stage. If an assistant is not available, clamp the brake caliper mounting lugs in a soft-jawed vice to support the fork. If the bolt turns without coming loose, it is turning the damper rod with it – use an air wrench if available, or wait until the fork is dismantled so the rod can be held.
**3** If the fork top bolt was not slackened with the fork in situ, carefully clamp the tube in a vice equipped with soft jaws, taking care not to overtighten the clamp or score the surface, and slacken the top bolt.
**4** Unscrew the fork top bolt from the top of the fork tube **(see illustration 7.27)**.

⚠ *Warning: The fork spring is pressing on the fork top bolt with considerable pressure. Unscrew the bolt very carefully, keeping a downward pressure on it and release it slowly as it is likely to spring clear. It is advisable to wear some form of eye and face protection when carrying out this operation, and it is best to use a ratchet-type tool (see Tool Tip on page 5•16).*

**5** Slide the fork tube down into the slider and withdraw the spacer, spring seat and the spring from the tube **(see illustrations 7.26c, b and a)**.
**6** Invert the fork leg over a suitable container and pump the fork vigorously to expel as much fork oil as possible. **Note:** *If you are only changing the oil and carrying out no other work on the fork, ignore the following Steps and proceed to Step 25, though it is always worth checking through Steps 14 to 18.*
**7** If required (for full disassembly), remove the previously slackened damper rod bolt and its

**7.2 Slacken the damper rod bolt**

**7.9a Prise out the dust seal using a flat-bladed screwdriver**

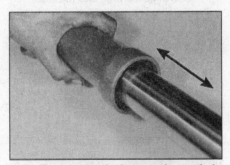
**7.11 To separate the inner and outer fork tubes, pull them apart firmly several times – the slide-hammer effect will pull the tubes apart**

copper sealing washer from the bottom of the slider **(see illustration 7.2)**. Discard the sealing washer as a new one must be used on reassembly. If the damper rod bolt was not slackened before dismantling the fork, pass a long metal bar or length of wood doweling down through the fork tube and press it hard into the damper rod head to counter-hold it. A suitable sized nut threaded or welded onto the end of a metal bar is best, as the top of the damper rod is hex shaped for just that purpose.
**8** Invert the fork and withdraw the damper rod from inside the fork tube **(see illustration)**. Remove the rebound spring from the damper rod.
**9** On Sprint models, carefully prise out the dust seal from the top of the slider to gain access to the oil seal retaining clip **(see illustration)**. Discard the dust seal as a new one must be used. Carefully remove the

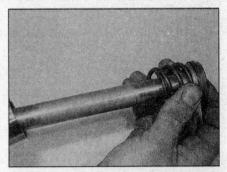
**7.8 Withdraw the damper rod and rebound spring from the tube**

**7.9b Prise out the retaining clip using a flat-bladed screwdriver**

**7.12 The oil seal (1), washer (2), and top bush (3) will come out with the fork tube**

retaining clip, taking care not to scratch the surface of the tube **(see illustration)**.
**10** On Tiger models, carefully remove the seal retaining clip, taking care not to scratch the surface of the tube, then prise the dust seal out from the top of the slider **(see illustration 7.9b)**.
**11** To separate the tube from the slider it is necessary to displace the top bush and oil seal. The bottom bush should not pass through the top bush, and this can be used to good effect. Push the tube gently inwards until it stops against the damper rod seat. Take care not to do this forcibly or the seat may be damaged. Then pull the tube sharply outwards until the bottom bush strikes the top bush. Repeat this operation until the top bush and seal are tapped out of the slider **(see illustration)**.
**12** With the tube removed, slide off the oil seal and its washer, noting which way up they fit **(see illustration)**. Discard the oil seal as a

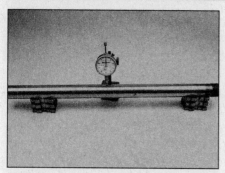

**7.15 Check the fork tube for runout using V-blocks and a dial gauge**

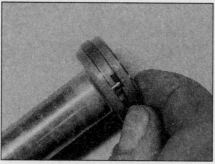

**7.18 Damper rod piston ring**

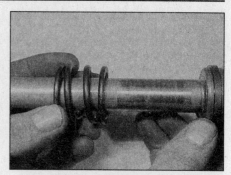

**7.19a Slide the rebound spring onto the damper rod**

new one must be used. The top bush can then also be slid off its upper end.

*Caution: Do not try to remove the bottom bush from the tube. The bush is not an individual component – it is integral with the tube.*

**13** Tip the damper rod seat out of the slider, noting which way up it fits.

### Inspection

**14** Clean all parts in solvent and blow them dry with compressed air, if available. Check the fork tube for score marks, scratches, flaking of the chrome finish and excessive or abnormal wear. Look for dents in the tube and renew the tube in both forks if any are found. Check the fork seal seat for nicks, gouges and scratches. If damage is evident, leaks will occur. Also check the oil seal washer for damage or distortion and replace it if necessary.

**15** Check the fork tube for runout using V-blocks and a dial gauge, or have it done by

a dealer **(see illustration)**. If the tube is bent, replace it with a new one.

 **Warning: If the tube is bent, it should not be straightened; replace it with a new one.**

**16** Check the spring for cracks and other damage. Compare the spring from one fork with the other. If a spring is defective or has sagged, replace the springs in both forks with new ones. Never replace only one spring. Also check the rebound spring.

**17** Examine the working surfaces of the two bushes; if worn or scuffed they must be replaced with new ones. Only the top bush is available separately – if the bottom bush is worn, replace the whole fork tube with a new one.

**18** Check the damper rod and its piston ring for damage and wear, and replace them if necessary **(see illustration)**. Do not remove the ring from the piston unless it is being

renewed. Triumph specify that a new one should be used as a matter of course.

### Reassembly

**19** If removed, fit the piston ring into the groove in the damper rod head, using a new one if necessary **(see illustration 7.18)**. Slide the rebound spring onto the rod **(see illustration)**. Insert the damper rod into the fork tube and slide it into place so that it projects fully from the bottom of the tube, then fit the seat on the bottom of the damper rod **(see illustration)**.

**20** Oil the fork tube and bottom bush with the specified fork oil and insert the assembly into the slider **(see illustration)**. Fit a new copper sealing washer onto the damper rod bolt and apply a few drops of a suitable non-permanent thread locking compound, then install the bolt into the bottom of the slider **(see illustration)**. Tighten the bolt to the specified torque setting. If the damper rod rotates inside the tube, press a long metal bar or length of wood doweling hard into the damper rod head to counter-hold it. A suitable sized nut threaded or welded onto the end of a metal bar is best, as the top of the damper rod is hex shaped for just that purpose. Otherwise, wait until the fork is fully reassembled before tightening the bolt.

**21** Push the fork tube fully into the slider, then oil the top bush and slide it down over the tube **(see illustration)**. Press the bush squarely into its recess in the slider as far as possible, then install the oil seal washer **(see illustration)**. Either use the Triumph service tool (Pt. No. 3880080-T0301) or a suitable piece of tubing to

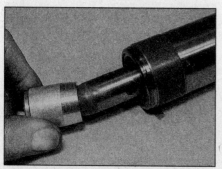

**7.19b Fit the seat onto the bottom of the rod**

**7.20a Slide the tube into the slider**

**7.20b Apply a thread locking compound to the damper rod bolt and use a new sealing washer**

**7.21a Install the top bush . . .**

**7.21b . . . followed by the washer**

**7.22 Make sure the oil seal is the correct way up**

**7.23a Install the retaining clip . . .**

**7.23b . . . followed by the dust seal**

tap the bush fully into place; the tubing must be slightly larger in diameter than the fork tube and slightly smaller in diameter than the bush recess in the slider. Take care not to scratch the fork tube during this operation; it is best to make sure that the fork tube is pushed fully into the slider so that any accidental scratching is confined to the area above the oil seal.

22 When the bush is seated fully and squarely in its recess in the slider, (remove the washer to check, wipe the recess clean, then reinstall the washer), install the new oil seal. Smear the seal's lips with fork oil and slide it over the tube so that its markings face upwards and drive the seal into place as described in Step 21 until it seats on the washer **(see illustration)**.

 **HAYNES HINT** *Place the old oil seal on top of the new one to protect it when driving the seal into place.*

**7.25a Pour the oil into the top of the tube**

**7.25b Measure the oil level with the fork held vertical**

23 On Sprint models, once the seal is correctly seated (the groove for the retaining clip should be fully exposed), fit the retaining clip, making sure it locates correctly in its groove **(see illustration)**. Lubricate the lips of the new dust seal then slide it down the fork tube and press it into position **(see illustration)**.

24 On Tiger models, lubricate the lips of the new dust seal then slide it down the fork tube and press it into position. Once the seal is correctly seated (the groove for the retaining clip should be fully exposed), fit the retaining clip, making sure it locates correctly in its groove **(see illustration 7.23a)**.

25 Slowly pour in the specified quantity of the specified grade of fork oil and pump the fork at least ten times to distribute it evenly **(see illustration)**; the oil level should also be measured and adjustment made by adding or subtracting oil. Fully compress the fork tube into the slider and measure the fork oil level from the top of the tube **(see illustration)**. Add or subtract fork oil until it is at the level specified at the beginning of the Chapter.

26 Clamp the slider in a soft-jawed vice using the brake caliper mounting lugs, taking care not to overtighten and damage them. Pull the fork tube out of the slider as far as possible then install the spring, with its closer-spaced coils at the bottom on Sprint models, and at the top on Tiger models **(see illustration)**. Fit the spring seat and the spacer **(see illustrations)**.

27 Fit a new O-ring to the fork top bolt and thread the bolt into the fork tube **(see illustration)**.

⚠ *Warning: It will be necessary to compress the spring by pressing it down using the top bolt to engage the threads of the top bolt with the fork tube. This is a potentially dangerous operation and should be performed with care, using an assistant if necessary. Wipe off any excess oil before starting to prevent the possibility of slipping.*

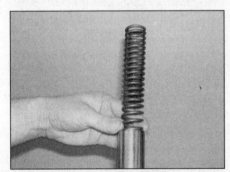

**7.26a Install the spring . . .**

**7.26b . . . the spring seat . . .**

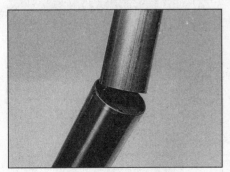

**7.26c . . . and the spacer**

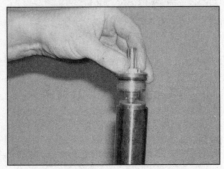

**7.27 Thread the top bolt into the tube**

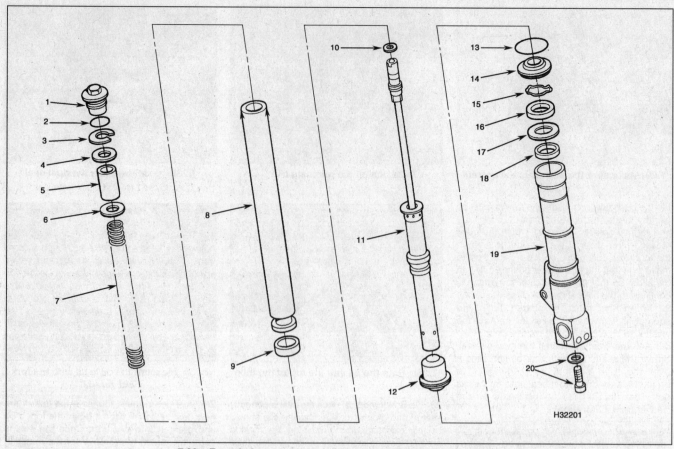

**7.30a  Front fork components – Daytona and Speed Triple models**

1 Top bolt
2 O-ring
3 Slotted spring collar
4 Upper spring seat
5 Spacer
6 Lower spring seat

7 Spring
8 Fork slider
9 Bottom bush
10 O-ring
11 Damper cartridge

12 Damper rod seat
13 O-ring
14 Dust seal
15 Retaining clip
16 Oil seal

17 Washer
18 Top bush
19 Fork tube
20 Damper rod bolt and
    sealing washer

Keep the fork tube fully extended whilst pressing on the spring. Screw the top bolt carefully into the fork tube making sure it is not cross-threaded. **Note:** *The top bolt can be tightened to the specified torque setting at this stage if the tube is held between the padded jaws of a vice, but do not risk distorting the tube by doing so. A better method is to tighten the top bolt when the fork has been installed in the bike and is securely held in the bottom yoke.*

**28** If the damper rod bolt requires tightening (see Step 20), clamp the fork slider between the padded jaws of a vice, then have an assistant compress the tube into the slider so that maximum spring pressure is placed on the damper rod head and tighten the damper rod bolt to the specified torque setting **(see illustration 7.31)**.

**29** If removed, on Sprint models fit the fork guard and blanking plug **(see illustrations 7.30b and c)**, and on Tiger models fit the rubber gaiter. Install the forks (see Section 6). Check the operation of the forks before taking

the bike on the road. Set the spring preload adjuster as required on Sprint models (see Section 12).

## Daytona and Speed Triple models

### Disassembly

**30** Remove the forks (see Section 6). Always dismantle the fork legs separately to avoid

interchanging parts and thus causing an accelerated rate of wear. Store all components in separate, clearly marked containers **(see illustration)**. Unless you are just changing the oil, remove the fork guard from the top of the slider, noting how it locates, and the blanking plug from the base of the slider **(see illustrations)**.

**31** If required (for full disassembly), compress the fork tube in the slider so that

**7.30b  Remove the fork guard . . .**

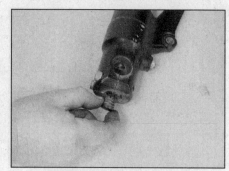

**7.30c  . . . and the blanking plug**

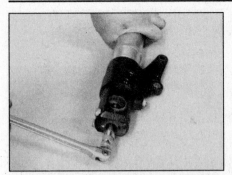

**7.31 Slacken the damper cartridge bolt**

**7.33 Unscrew the top bolt . . .**

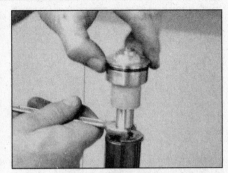

**7.34 . . . then counter-hold the nut and thread the top bolt off the adjuster**

the spring exerts maximum pressure on the damper cartridge head, then have an assistant slacken the damper cartridge bolt in the base of the fork slider **(see illustration)**. Do not remove the bolt at this stage. If an assistant is not available, clamp the brake caliper mounting lugs in a soft-jawed vice to support the fork. If the bolt turns without coming loose, it is turning the cartridge with it – use an air wrench if available, or wait until the fork is disassembled so the cartridge can be held.

**32** If the fork top bolt was not slackened with the fork in situ, carefully clamp the fork tube in a vice equipped with soft jaws, taking care not to overtighten or score its surface, and slacken the top bolt.

**33** Now unscrew the fork top bolt from the top of the fork tube **(see illustration)**. The bolt will remain threaded on the pre-load adjuster.

**34** Carefully clamp the fork slider in a vice and slide the fork tube down into the slider a little way (wrap a rag around the top of the tube to minimise oil spillage) while, with the aid of an assistant if necessary, keeping the damper rod fully extended. Note the amount of protrusion of the pre-load adjuster above the top of the top bolt – there are lines to indicate this. Counter-hold the nut on the base of the preload adjuster and thread the fork top bolt off the damper rod **(see illustration)**.

**35** Remove the slotted spring collar by slipping it out to the side **(see illustration)**, then remove the washer, the spacer, the spring seat and the spring **(see illustrations)**.

**36** Invert the fork leg over a suitable container and pump the fork and damper rod vigorously to expel as much fork oil as possible. **Note:** *If you are only changing the oil and carrying out no other work on the fork, ignore the following Steps and proceed to Step 55, though it is always worth checking through Steps 44 to 48.*

**37** If required (for full overhaul), remove the previously slackened damper cartridge bolt and its copper sealing washer from the bottom of the slider **(see illustration 7.31)**. Discard the sealing washer as a new one must be used on reassembly.

**38** Invert the fork and withdraw the damper cartridge from inside the fork tube **(see illustration 7.49)**.

**39** Carefully prise out the dust seal from the top of the slider to gain access to the oil seal retaining clip **(see illustration 7.9a)**. Discard the dust seal as a new one must be used.

**40** Carefully remove the retaining clip, taking

care not to scratch the surface of the tube **(see illustration 7.9b)**.

**41** To separate the tube from the slider it is necessary to displace the top bush and oil seal. The bottom bush should not pass through the top bush, and this can be used to good effect. Push the tube gently inwards until it stops against the damper rod seat. Take care not to do this forcibly or the seat may be damaged. Then pull the tube sharply outwards until the bottom bush strikes the top bush. Repeat this operation until the top bush and seal are tapped out of the slider **(see illustration 7.11)**.

**42** With the tube removed, slide off the oil seal, washer and top bush, noting which way up they fit **(see illustration 7.12)**. Discard the oil seal as a new one must be used.

*Caution: Do not remove the bottom bush from the tube unless it is to be replaced.*

**43** If required, tip the damper rod seat out of the slider, noting which way up it fits – you

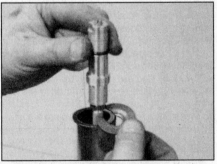

**7.35a Remove the slotted spring collar . . .**

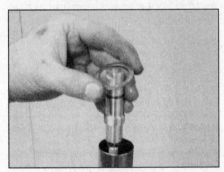

**7.35b . . . the washer . . .**

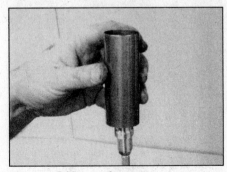

**7.35c . . . the spacer . . .**

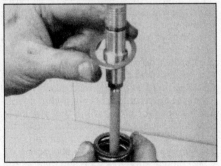

**7.35d . . . the spring seat . . .**

**7.35e . . . and the spring**

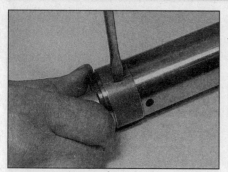

**7.47 Prise off the bottom bush using a flat-bladed screwdriver**

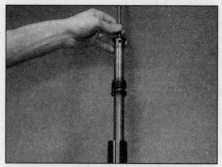

**7.49 Slide the damper cartridge into the tube**

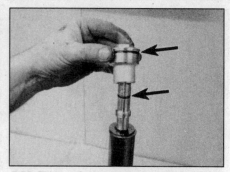

**7.58 Fit new O-rings onto the top bolt and adjuster, then thread the bolt onto the adjuster**

may have to dislodge it by pushing it up from the bottom via the Allen bolt hole. Discard the O-ring as a new one must be used.

### Inspection

**44** Clean all parts in solvent and blow them dry with compressed air, if available. Check the fork tube for score marks, scratches, flaking of the chrome finish and excessive or abnormal wear. Look for dents in the tube and replace the tube in both forks if any are found. Check the fork seal seat for nicks, gouges and scratches. If damage is evident, leaks will occur. Also check the oil seal washer for damage or distortion and replace it if necessary.
**45** Check the fork tube for runout using V-blocks and a dial gauge, or have it done by a dealer **(see illustration 7.15)**. If the tube is bent, replace it with a new one.

 *Warning: If the tube is bent, it should not be straightened; replace it with a new one.*

**46** Check the spring for cracks and other damage. Compare the spring from one fork with the other. If a spring is defective or has sagged, replace the springs in both forks with new ones. Never replace only one spring.
**47** Examine the working surfaces of the two bushes; if worn or scuffed they must be renewed. To remove the bottom bush from the fork tube, prise it apart at the slit using a flat-bladed screwdriver and slide it off **(see illustration)**. Make sure the new one seats properly.
**48** Check the damper cartridge for damage and wear, and renew it if necessary. Holding the outside of the damper, pump the rod in and out of the damper. If the rod does not move smoothly in the damper it must be renewed.

### Reassembly

**49** Insert the damper cartridge into the fork tube and slide it into place so that it projects fully from the bottom of the tube **(see illustration)**. If the damper rod seat was removed, fit a new O-ring onto it, then fit it onto the bottom of the damper rod.
**50** Oil the fork tube and bottom bush with the specified fork oil and insert the assembly into the slider **(see illustration 7.20a)**. Fit a new copper sealing washer onto the damper cartridge bolt and apply a few drops of a

suitable non-permanent thread locking compound, then fit the bolt into the bottom of the slider **(see illustration 7.20b)**. Tighten the bolt to the specified torque setting. If the damper cartridge rotates inside the tube, wait until the fork is fully reassembled before tightening the bolt.
**51** Push the fork tube fully into the slider, then oil the top bush and slide it down over the tube **(see illustration 7.21a)**. Press the bush squarely into its recess in the slider as far as possible, then install the oil seal washer with its flat side facing up **(see illustration 7.21b)**. Either use the Triumph service tool (Pt. No. 3880285) or a suitable piece of tubing to tap the bush fully into place; the tubing must be slightly larger in diameter than the fork tube and slightly smaller in diameter than the bush recess in the slider. Take care not to scratch the fork tube during this operation; it is best to make sure that the fork tube is pushed fully into the slider so that any accidental scratching is confined to the area above the oil seal.
**52** When the bush is seated fully and squarely in its recess in the slider (remove the washer to check, wipe the recess clean, then reinstall the washer), install the new oil seal **(see illustration 7.22)**. Smear the seal's lips with fork oil and slide it over the tube so that its markings face upwards and drive the seal into place as described in Step 51 until the retaining clip groove is visible above the seal.

> **HAYNES HiNT** *Place the old oil seal on top of the new one to protect it when driving the seal into place.*

**53** Once the seal is correctly seated, fit the retaining clip, making sure it is correctly located in its groove **(see illustration 7.23a)**.
**54** Lubricate the lips of the new dust seal then slide it down the fork tube and press it into position **(see illustration 7.23b)**.
**55** Slowly pour in the specified quantity of the specified grade of fork oil and pump the fork and damper rod at least ten times each to distribute it evenly **(see illustration 7.25a)**; the oil level should also be measured and adjustment made by adding or subtracting oil. Fully compress the fork tube and damper rod

into the slider and measure the fork oil level from the top of the tube **(see illustration 7.25b)**. Add or subtract fork oil until it is at the level specified at the beginning of the Chapter.
**56** Clamp the slider in a vice via the brake caliper mounting lugs, taking care not to overtighten and damage them. Pull the fork tube and damper rod out of the slider as far as possible then install the spring with its closer-wound coils at the bottom **(see illustration 7.35e)**. Install the spring seat, the spacer and the washer **(see illustrations 7.35d, c and b)**.
**57** Slide the slotted spring collar into position between the upper spring seat and the nut on the base of the pre-load adjuster **(see illustration 7.35a)**.
**58** Fit new O-rings onto the pre-load adjuster and fork top bolt **(see illustration)**. Thread the top bolt onto the pre-load adjuster, using a spanner on the nut on the base of the adjuster to prevent it from turning, and set it so that the amount of protrusion of the adjuster above the top of the top bolt is roughly as noted on removal **(see illustration 7.34)**.
**59** Withdraw the tube fully from the slider and carefully screw the top bolt into the tube making sure it is not cross-threaded **(see illustration)**. **Note:** *The top bolt can be tightened to the specified torque setting at this*

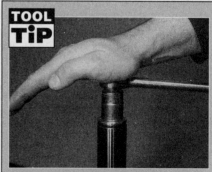

**TOOL TiP**

*Use a ratchet-type tool when installing the fork top bolt. This makes it unnecessary to remove the tool from the bolt whilst threading it in, thus making it easier to maintain a downward pressure on the spring.*

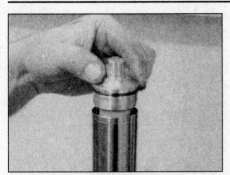

**7.59 Thread the top bolt into the tube**

*stage if the tube is held between the padded jaws of a vice, but do not risk distorting the tube by doing so. A better method is to tighten the top bolt when the fork leg has been installed and is securely held in the yokes.*
**60** If the damper cartridge bolt requires tightening (see Step 50), clamp the fork slider between the padded jaws of a vice, then have an assistant compress the tube into the slider so that maximum spring pressure is placed on the damper cartridge head and tighten the bolt to the specified torque setting **(see illustration 7.31)**.
**61** If removed, fit the fork guard and blanking plug **(see illustrations 7.30b and c)**. Install the forks (see Section 6). Set the spring preload and damping adjusters as required (see Section 12).

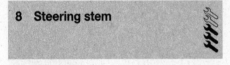

## 8  Steering stem

### Removal

**1** Remove the fairing and the fairing side panels (see Chapter 7). It is also advisable to remove the fuel tank to avoid the possibility of scratching it (see Chapter 4).
**2** Remove the front forks (see Section 6).
**3** Displace any assemblies from the bottom yoke (horn, brake hose guides, etc).
**4** If the top yoke is being removed from the bike rather than just being displaced, trace the wiring from the ignition switch and disconnect it at the connector. Release the wiring from any ties.
**5** On Speed Triple models with one-piece handlebars, and on Sprint and Tiger models, displace the handlebars from the top yoke (see Section 5). Secure the handlebar assemblies so that the master cylinder is upright, making sure there is no strain on the hoses, cables or wiring.
**6** Unscrew the steering stem nut and remove it along with its washer, where fitted. On Daytona and Speed Triple models, this requires the use of a special Triumph tool (Part No. T3880300), or a suitable equivalent to engage the drillings in the nut **(see illustration 5.5d)**. Lift the top yoke up off the

steering stem and position it clear, using a rag to protect the tank or other components.
**7** On Daytona and Speed Triple models, check to see if there is a bearing adjuster nut, or adjuster nut and locknut (2004-on year models). If there is only an adjuster nut, support the bottom yoke, then unscrew the adjuster nut and remove the bearing cover. Gently lower the bottom yoke and steering stem out of the frame. On models with an adjuster nut and locknut, unscrew the locknut first and remove the tabbed washer, then support the bottom yoke and unscrew the adjuster nut. Remove the bearing cover and gently lower the bottom yoke and steering stem out of the frame.
**8** On Sprint models, support the bottom yoke, then unscrew the bearing adjuster nut and gently lower the bottom yoke and steering stem out of the frame.
**9** On Tiger models, unscrew the bearing adjuster locknut. Support the bottom yoke, then unscrew the adjuster nut and gently lower the bottom yoke and steering stem out of the frame.
**10** Remove all traces of old grease from the bearings and races and check them for wear or damage as described in Section 9. **Note:** *Do not attempt to remove the races from the steering head or the steering stem unless they are to be replaced with new ones.*

### Installation

**11** Smear a liberal quantity of lithium-based grease (see Chapter 1 Specifications) onto the lower bearing race in the steering head. Work grease well into the lower bearing and, if the upper bearing is unsealed, also work some grease into that.
**12** Carefully lift the steering stem/bottom yoke up through the steering head. On Daytona and Speed Triple models, install the bearing cover.
**13** Thread the adjuster nut onto the steering stem and adjust the bearings as described in Chapter 1. On Daytona and Speed Triple models, if applicable, fit the tabbed washer and locknut and tighten the locknut to the torque setting specified at the beginning of the Chapter. On Tiger models, fit the adjuster locknut and tighten it against the adjuster nut while counter-holding it – it is important the adjuster nut does not turn with the locknut.
**14** Fit the top yoke onto the steering stem, then install the washer (where fitted) and steering stem nut and tighten it finger-tight. Temporarily install one of the forks to align the top and bottom yokes, and secure it by tightening the bottom yoke clamp bolts only.
**15** Tighten the steering stem nut to the torque setting specified at the beginning of the Chapter; on Daytona, Speed Triple and Sprint models with no adjuster nut locknut, counter-hold the adjuster nut to prevent it turning as you do so.
**16** Install the remaining components in a reverse of the removal procedure, referring to the relevant Sections or Chapters, and to the

torque settings specified at the beginning of the Chapter.
**17** Carry out a check of the steering head bearing freeplay as described in Chapter 1, and if necessary re-adjust.

## 9  Steering head bearing overhaul

### Inspection

**1** Remove the steering stem (see Section 8). A caged ball bearing is fitted in the top of the steering head, and a taper roller bearing is on the bottom of the steering stem. The bearing outer races are an interference fit in the steering head. Pick the caged ball bearing out of the top of the steering head.
**2** Remove all traces of old grease from the bearings and races and check them for wear or damage, referring to *Tools and Workshop Tips* in the Reference Section for information on bearing checks.
**3** The bearing outer races in the steering head should be polished and free from indentations. Inspect the bearing balls (upper bearing) or rollers (lower bearing) for signs of wear, damage or discoloration, and examine their cage for signs of cracks or splits. Spin the bearings by hand. They should spin freely and smoothly. If there are any signs of wear on any of the above components both upper and lower bearing assemblies should be renewed as a set, complete with new outer races. Only remove the outer races in the steering head and the lower bearing from the steering stem if they need to be renewed – do not re-use them once they have been removed.

### Renewal

**4** Pick the caged ball bearing out of the top of the steering head.
**5** The bearing outer races are an interference fit in the steering head and can be tapped from position with a suitable drift located on the rim of the race **(see illustration)**. Move the drift around the rim so that the race is driven out squarely. It may prove advantageous to

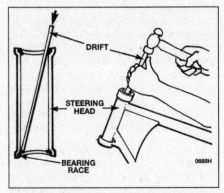

**9.5 Drive the outer races from the steering head using a drift located as shown**

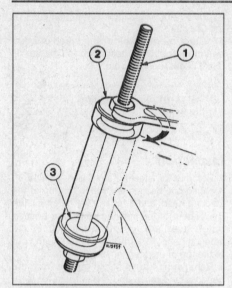

**9.7 Drawbolt arrangement for fitting steering stem bearing races**

1   Long bolt or threaded bar
2   Thick washer
3   Guide for lower race

curve the end of the drift slightly to improve access.

**6** Alternatively, the races can be removed using a slide-hammer type bearing extractor – these can often be hired from tool shops.

**7** The new outer races can be pressed into the steering head using a drawbolt arrangement **(see illustration)**, or by using a large diameter tubular drift. Ensure that the drawbolt washer or drift (as applicable) bears only on the outer edge of the race and does not contact the working surface.

  *Installation of new bearing outer races is made much easier if they are left overnight in the freezer. This causes it to contract slightly making it a looser fit. Alternatively, use a freeze spray.*

**8** The tapered roller bearing should only be removed from the steering stem if a new one is being fitted. To remove the race from the steering stem, use two screwdrivers placed on opposite sides of the race to work it free, using blocks of wood to improve leverage and protect the yoke, or tap under it using a cold chisel. If the race is firmly in place it will be necessary to use a puller **(see illustration)**. Take the steering stem to a Triumph dealer if required.

**9** Fit the new bearing onto the steering stem. A length of tubing with an internal diameter slightly larger than the steering stem will be needed to tap the new race into position **(see illustration)**.

**10** Install the steering stem (see Section 8).

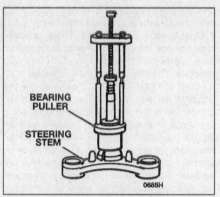

**9.8  It is best to remove the inner race using a puller**

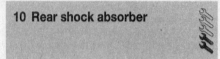

**10  Rear shock absorber**

### Removal

**1** Support the motorcycle securely in an upright position using the centrestand (Sprint ST only) or an auxiliary stand. Position a support under the rear wheel so that it does not drop when the shock absorber is removed, but also making sure that the weight of the machine is off the rear suspension so that the shock is not compressed.

### Daytona and Speed Triple models

**2** Remove the seat cowling (see Chapter 7). Also remove the exhaust silencer (see

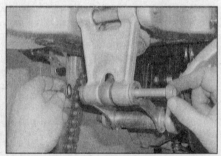

**10.3a  Unscrew the nut and withdraw the bolt securing the shock to the linkage assembly**

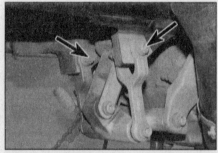

**10.4a  Unscrew the nuts and withdraw the bolts (arrowed) securing the linkage rods to the swingarm**

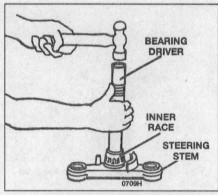

**9.9  Drive the new bearing on using a suitable driver or a length of pipe**

Chapter 4), and if required for best access, the rear wheel (see Chapter 6).

**3** On models with a single-sided swingarm, unscrew the nut and withdraw the bolt securing the bottom of the shock absorber to the linkage rods and arm **(see illustration)**. Pivot the rods down off the arm, then draw the bottom of the shock out of the arm, noting the two spacers and the seals – the seals may come out with the spacers, or they could remain in the shock **(see illustration)**.

**4** On models with a twin-sided swingarm, unscrew the nuts and withdraw the bolts securing the tops of the linkage rods to the swingarm **(see illustration)**. Pivot the rods down. Unscrew the nut and withdraw the bolt securing the bottom of the shock absorber to the linkage arm, then pivot the linkage assembly down **(see illustration)**.

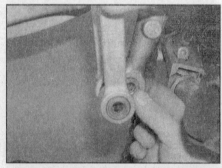

**10.3b  Swing the linkage rods down and slip the shock out of the arm**

**10.4b  Remove the bolt securing the bottom of the shock to the linkage arm**

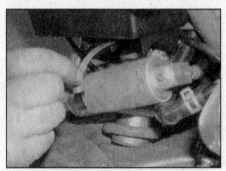

**10.5 Release the reservoir clamp**

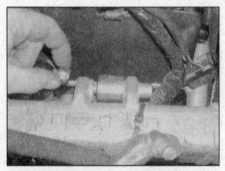

**10.6a Unscrew the nut and withdraw the upper mounting bolt . . .**

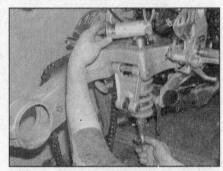

**10.6b . . . then manoeuvre the shock down and out as described**

**5** Fully undo the remote reservoir clamp screw and release the clamp **(see illustration)**.

**6** Unscrew the nut on the shock absorber upper mounting bolt, then support the shock absorber and withdraw the bolt **(see illustration)**. Lower the shock out of the frame, twisting it anti-clockwise as you do to help feed the reservoir and hose round into the hole in the swingarm **(see illustration)**.

### Sprint models

**7** Remove the seat (see Chapter 7), and the fuel tank (see Chapter 4).

**8** Unscrew the nut and withdraw the bolt securing the bottom of the shock absorber to the linkage plates **(see illustration)**.

**9** Unscrew the nut on the shock absorber

upper mounting bolt, then support the shock absorber and withdraw the bolt **(see illustration)**. Lift the shock out of the frame.

### Tiger models

**Note:** *The lower mounting for the shock absorber contains an uncaged needle roller bearing, which means that once the shock is removed, or more likely as you are removing it, the rollers are likely to drop out. With luck, the grease lubricating the rollers will retain them in the shock, but be prepared to watch where any of them drop. Clear the work area underneath the shock and place a clean rag or paper down to catch any rollers that escape.*

**10** Remove the seat and the side panels (see Chapter 7). Also remove the exhaust silencer

and collector box (see Chapter 4), and the battery (see Chapter 8). Undo the three screws securing the battery box and lift it out of the frame, releasing the main fuse holder from its housing on the left-hand end of the box **(see illustrations)**.

**11** Unscrew the bolts securing the remote pre-load adjuster and displace it **(see illustration)**.

**12** Remove the blanking plugs from the swingarm to access the shock absorber lower mounting bolt **(see illustration)**. Unscrew the nut and withdraw the bolt, noting the washers. Using a suitable brass or aluminium drift, carefully drive the spacer out of the swingarm.

**13** Unscrew the nut on the shock absorber upper mounting bolt, then support the shock absorber and withdraw the bolt **(see**

**10.8 Lower mounting bolt (arrowed) – Sprint models**

**10.9 Upper mounting bolt (arrowed) – Sprint models**

**10.10a Remove the screws (arrowed) and lift out the box . . .**

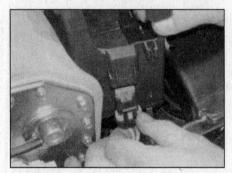

**10.10b . . . releasing the main fuse from its housing**

**10.11 Pre-load adjuster (A) and its mounting screws (B)**

**10.12 Remove the blanking plugs to access the lower bolt**

10.13 Upper mounting bolt nut (arrowed)

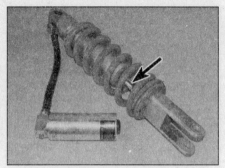

10.14 Look for cracks, pitting and oil leakage on the damper rod (arrowed)

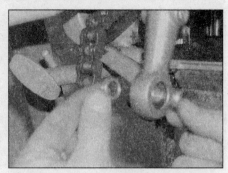

10.19 Do not forget to fit the spacers into the shock

illustration). Manoeuvre the shock and remote adjuster out of the frame via the battery box space, watching all the time for any of the rollers dropping out of the lower mounting – cup the mounting with your hand if possible.

### Inspection

14 Inspect the shock absorber for obvious physical damage and the coil spring for looseness, cracks or signs of fatigue.; inspect the damper rod for signs of bending, pitting and oil leakage (see illustration).

15 Inspect the pivot hardware at the top and bottom of the shock for wear or damage. Triumph do not list any bearings or bushes as being available separately, however it is worth first checking with a bearing or suspension specialist, rather than having to fit a new shock.

16 On Daytona, Speed Triple and Sprint models, check the reservoir for damage, cracks or leakage. On Tiger models, check the remote pre-load adjuster for damage.

17 Replacement parts for the shock absorber are not available from Triumph. If it is worn or damaged, it must be replaced with a new one, although it is worth first seeking the advice of a suspension specialist.

### Installation

18 Installation is the reverse of removal. Apply molybdenum disulphide or lithium-based grease to the shock absorber and linkage pivot points. On 1997 to 2001 Daytona and Speed Triple models, fit the shock so the rebound damping adjuster is on the left-hand side. On 2002-on Daytona and Speed Triple models, and all Sprint and Tiger models, fit the shock so the rebound damping adjuster is on the right-hand side.

19 On Daytona and Speed Triple models with a single-sided swingarm, fit the seals (if removed) onto the shouldered section of the spacers, then fit the spacers into the lower mounting and hold them there as you fit it into the linkage arm (see illustration).

20 On Tiger models, pack the rollers in the lower mounting with grease to hold them in place. Make sure all are installed, and that none become dislodged as you install the spacer.

21 Install the bolts and nuts finger-tight only until all components are in position, then tighten the nuts to the torque settings specified at the beginning of the Chapter.

Check the operation of the rear suspension before taking the machine on the road.

### 11 Rear suspension linkage

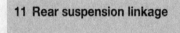

### Removal

1 Support the motorcycle securely in an upright position using the centrestand (Sprint ST only) or an auxiliary stand. Position a support under the rear wheel so that it does not drop when the shock absorber lower mounting bolt is removed, but also making sure that the weight of the machine is off the rear suspension so that the shock is not compressed.

2 Remove the exhaust system (see Chapter 4).

### Daytona and Speed Triple models with single-sided swingarm

3 Unscrew the nut and withdraw the bolt securing the bottom of the shock absorber to the linkage rods and arm (see illustration 10.3a). Pivot the rods down off the arm, then draw the bottom of the shock out of the arm, noting the two spacers and the seals – the seals may come out with the spacers, or they could remain in the shock (see illustration 10.3b).

4 Unscrew the nut and withdraw the bolt securing the linkage arm to the swingarm. Feed the bearing sleeve out of the swingarm and remove the linkage arm, noting which way round it fits (see illustration). If the sleeve is stuck, thread an M14 bolt with 1.5

mm thread pitch into its right-hand end and draw it out by pulling on the bolt head with pliers.

5 Unscrew the nut and withdraw bolt securing the linkage rods to the frame, noting the washers and remove the rods, noting which way round they fit (see illustration 11.4).

### Daytona models with twin-sided swingarm

6 Unscrew the nuts and withdraw the bolts securing the tops of the linkage rods to the swingarm (see illustration 10.4a). Pivot the rods down. Unscrew the nut and withdraw the bolt securing the bottom of the shock absorber to the linkage arm, then pivot the linkage assembly down (see illustrations 10.4b).

7 Unscrew the nut and withdraw bolt securing the linkage arm to the frame, then lift off the linkage assembly. Note the arrangement of washers and thrust washers on the bolt and fit them onto the bolt in the correct order to aid reassembly.

8 Mark the linkage arms so that they can be fitted in their original positions, then unscrew the nut and withdraw bolt securing the linkage rods to the linkage arm and separate the assembly.

### Sprint models

9 Unscrew the nut and withdraw the bolt securing the bottom of the shock absorber to the linkage plates (see illustration 10.8).

10 Unscrew the nut and withdraw the bolt securing the linkage plates to the linkage arm and detach the arm (see illustrations).

11 Unscrew the nut and withdraw the bolt securing the linkage plates to the swingarm

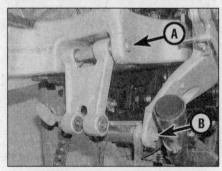

11.4 Linkage arm-to-swingarm bolt (A), linkage rods-to-frame bolt (B)

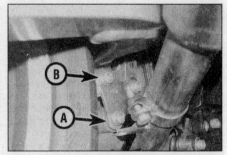

11.10a Linkage plate-to-linkage arm bolt (A), linkage plate-to-swingarm bolt (B) – RS models

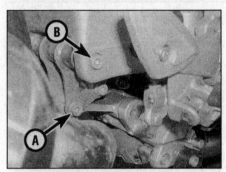

**11.10b  Linkage plate-to-linkage arm bolt (A), linkage plate-to-swingarm bolt (B) – ST models**

**11.12  Linkage arm-to-frame bolt (arrowed)**

(see illustration 11.10a or b). On ST models and RS models with single-sided swingarms, feed the bearing sleeve out of the swingarm and remove the plates, noting which way round they fit. If the sleeve is stuck, thread an M14 bolt with 1.5 mm thread pitch into its right-hand end and draw it out by pulling on the bolt head with pliers.

12  Unscrew the nut and withdraw the bolt securing the linkage arm to the frame and remove the arm, noting which way round it fits (see illustration).

### Inspection

13  Withdraw the bearing spacers, noting which fits where (see illustrations). Lever the grease seals out. On Sprint RS models with twin-sided swingarms, the linkage plate spacers, seals and bearings are in the mount in the swingarm. Thoroughly clean all components, removing all traces of dirt, corrosion and grease.

14  Inspect all components closely, looking for obvious signs of wear such as heavy scoring, or for damage such as cracks or distortion. Slip each spacer back into its bearing and check that there is not an excessive amount of freeplay between the two components. Renew any components as required.

15  Check the condition of the needle roller bearings. Refer to *Tools and Workshop Tips* (Section 5) in the Reference section for more information on bearings.

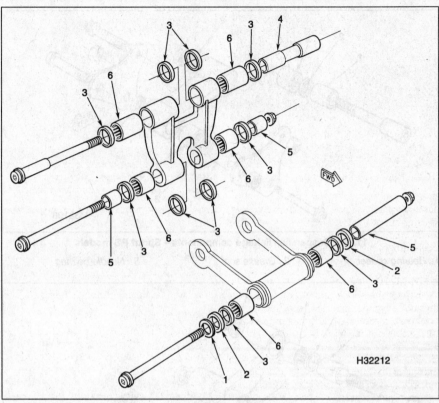

**11.13a  Suspension linkage components – single-sided swingarm Daytona and Speed Triple models**

| | | |
|---|---|---|
| 1  Washer | 3  Grease seal | 5  Bearing spacer |
| 2  Thrust washer | 4  Bearing sleeve | 6  Needle bearing |

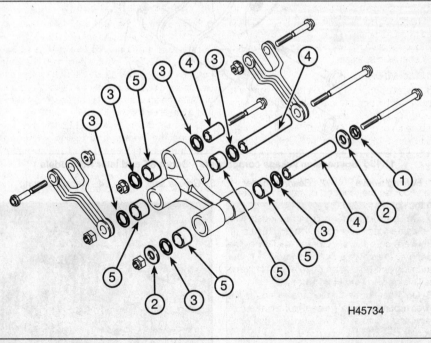

**11.13b  Suspension linkage components – twin-sided swingarm Daytona models**

| | | |
|---|---|---|
| 1  Washer | 3  Grease seal | 5  Needle bearing |
| 2  Thrust washer | 4  Bearing sleeve | |

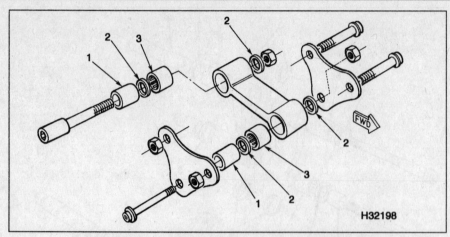

**11.13c Suspension linkage components – Sprint RS models**

| | | |
|---|---|---|
| 1 Bearing spacer | 2 Grease seal | 3 Needle bearing |

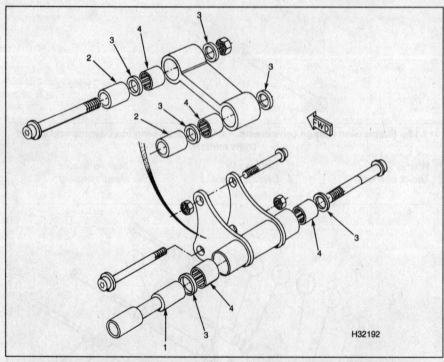

**11.13d Suspension linkage components – Sprint ST and later RS models**

| | | | |
|---|---|---|---|
| 1 Bearing sleeve | 2 Bearing spacer | 3 Grease seal | 4 Needle bearing |

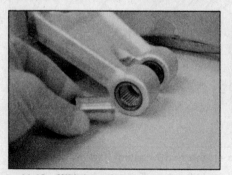

**11.13e Withdraw the spacers from the needle bearings**

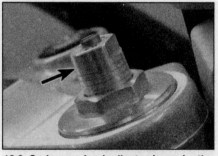

**12.2 Spring pre-load adjuster (arrow) – the amount of pre-load is indicated by the lines – Daytona/Speed Triple**

**16** Worn bearings can be drifted out of their bores, but note that removal will destroy them; new bearings should be obtained before work commences. The new bearings should be pressed or drawn into their bores rather than driven into position. In the absence of a press, a suitable drawbolt tool can be made up as described in *Tools and Workshop Tips* (Section 5) in the Reference section.
**17** Lubricate the needle roller bearings and the spacers with grease and install the spacers.
**18** Check the condition of the grease seals and renew them if they are damaged or deteriorated. Press the seals squarely into place.

### Installation

**19** Installation is the reverse of removal, noting the following:
● *Apply grease to the pivot points, and to the long bearing sleeve on Daytona, Speed Triple and Sprint ST models.*
● *Note that on Sprint RS models with twin-sided swingarms, each linkage plate is marked to show the swingarm mounts (S/ARM) and shock absorber mounts (RSU) so they cannot be installed the wrong way round – these marks must face the right-hand side. On Sprint ST models, the right-hand linkage plate is marked ↑UP – the arrow must point upwards.*
● *Install the bolts and nuts finger-tight only until all components are in position, then tighten the nuts to the torque settings specified at the beginning of the Chapter.*
● *Check the operation of the rear suspension before taking the machine on the road.*

### 12 Suspension adjustment

**Note:** *Refer to the owners handbook supplied with the machine for recommended front and rear suspension settings to suit loading.*

### Front forks

**1** On Daytona and Speed Triple models the forks are adjustable for spring pre-load and both rebound and compression damping. On Sprint models the forks are adjustable for spring pre-load only. On Tiger models the forks are not adjustable.

#### Daytona and Speed Triple models

**2 Spring pre-load** is adjusted using a suitable spanner on the adjuster flats on the top of each fork **(see illustration)**. The amount of pre-load is indicated by lines on the adjuster. The standard position is with the 5th line just visible above the top bolt hex. Turn the adjuster clockwise to increase pre-load and anti-clockwise to decrease it. Always make sure both adjusters are set equally.
**3 Rebound damping** is adjusted using a screwdriver in the slot in the adjuster protruding from the pre-load adjuster **(see**

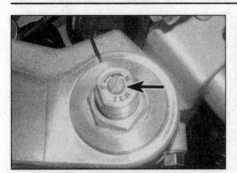

**12.3 Rebound damping adjuster – Daytona/Speed Triple**

**12.4 Compression damping adjuster – Daytona/Speed Triple**

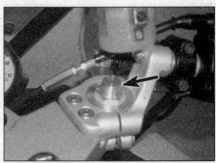

**12.5 Spring preload adjuster – Sprint**

illustration). The amount of damping is indicated by the number of turns out from the fully screwed-in position. The standard position is one turn out. Turn the adjuster clockwise to increase damping and anti-clockwise to decrease it. To establish the current setting, turn the adjuster in (clockwise) until it stops, counting the number of turns, then reset it as required by turning it out. Always make sure both adjusters are set equally.

**4 Compression damping** is adjusted using a screwdriver in the slot in the adjuster on the base of each fork (see illustration). The amount of damping is indicated by the number of turns out from the fully screwed-in position. The standard position is one turn out. Turn the adjuster clockwise to increase damping and anti-clockwise to decrease it. To establish the current setting, turn the adjuster in (clockwise) until it stops, counting the number of turns, then reset it as required by turning it out. Always make sure both adjusters are set equally.

### Sprint models

**5 Spring pre-load** is adjusted using a screwdriver in the slot in the top of the adjuster on the top of each fork (see illustration). The amount of pre-load is indicated by the amount of protrusion of the adjuster above the top bolt hex. The standard position is with 10 mm visible above the top bolt hex. Turn the adjuster clockwise to increase pre-load and anti-clockwise to decrease it. Always make sure both adjusters are set equally.

### *Rear shock absorber*

**6** On Daytona and Speed Triple models the shock absorber is adjustable for both rebound and compression damping – note that although the shock does have an adjustable upper spring seat, Triumph state that the pre-load should not be adjusted, though if you are unhappy with the pre-set position, it may be worth seeking advice from a Triumph dealer or a suspension specialist. On Sprint and Tiger models the shock absorber is adjustable for spring pre-load and rebound damping.

### Daytona and Speed Triple models

**7 Rebound damping** is adjusted using a screwdriver in the slot in the adjuster on the base of the shock absorber – on single-sided

swingarm models the adjuster is on the left-hand side and on twin-sided swingarm models the adjuster is on the right-hand side (see illustration). The amount of damping is indicated by the number of turns out from the fully screwed-in position. The standard position is one and a half turns out. Turn the adjuster clockwise to increase damping and anti-clockwise to decrease it. To establish the current setting, turn the adjuster in (clockwise) until it stops, counting the number of turns, then reset it as required by turning it out.

**8 Compression damping** is adjusted using a screwdriver in the slot in the adjuster on the remote reservoir (see illustration). The amount of damping is indicated by the number of turns out from the fully screwed-in position. The standard position is one and a half turns out. Turn the adjuster clockwise to increase damping and anti-clockwise to decrease it. To establish the current setting, turn the adjuster in (clockwise) until it stops,

counting the number of turns, then reset it as required by turning it out.

### Sprint models

**9 Spring pre-load** is adjusted using a screwdriver in the slot in the adjuster on the top of the shock absorber on the left-hand side, and access is via the hole in the frame – remove the blanking plug from the hole (see illustration). The amount of pre-load is indicated by the number of turns out from the fully screwed-in position. The standard position is twelve turns out. Turn the adjuster clockwise to increase pre-load and anti-clockwise to decrease it. To establish the current setting, turn the adjuster in (clockwise) until it stops, counting the number of turns, then reset it as required by turning it out.

**10 Rebound damping** is adjusted using a screwdriver in the slot in the adjuster on the base of the shock absorber on the right-hand side (see illustration). The amount of

**12.7 Rebound damping adjuster – Daytona/Speed Triple**

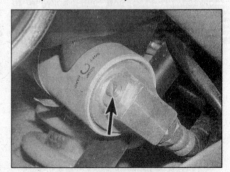

**12.8 Compression damping adjuster – Daytona/Speed Triple**

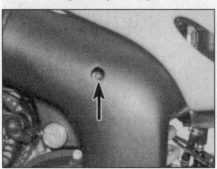

**12.9 Spring pre-load adjuster (arrowed) – Sprint**

**12.10 Rebound damping adjuster – Sprint**

**12.12  Rebound damping adjuster – Tiger**

**13.2  Remove the cover to free the hose from the chainguard**

**13.7  Unscrew and remove the pivot bolt (arrowed)**

damping is indicated by the number of turns out from the fully screwed-in position. The standard position is one and a half turns out. Turn the adjuster clockwise to increase damping and anti-clockwise to decrease it. To establish the current setting, turn the adjuster in (clockwise) until it stops, counting the number of turns, then reset it as required by turning it out.

### Tiger models

**11 Spring pre-load** is adjusted using a suitable spanner to turn the hex on the top of the remote adjuster **(see illustration 10.11)** – remove the rider's seat to access the adjuster (see Chapter 7). There are five positions. Position 1 is the softest setting, position 2 is the standard, position 5 is the hardest. Turn the adjuster hex as required to align the lower edge of the adjuster cover with the setting required. Turn the adjuster clockwise to increase pre-load and anti-clockwise to decrease it.

**12 Rebound damping** is adjusted using a screwdriver in the slot in the adjuster on the base of the shock absorber on the right-hand side **(see illustration)**. The amount of damping is indicated by the number of clicks out from the fully screwed-in position. The standard position is six clicks out. Turn the adjuster clockwise to increase damping and anti-clockwise to decrease it. To establish the current setting, turn the adjuster in (clockwise) until it stops, counting the number of clicks, then reset it as required by turning it out.

### 13  Swingarm removal and installation

#### Removal

**Note:** *Before removing the swingarm, it is advisable to perform the rear suspension checks described in Chapter 1 to assess the extent of any wear. On models with a single-sided swingarm, if you want to remove the rear sprocket, disc and axle assembly from the swingarm, do so before removing the swingarm so the rear brake can be used to stop the assembly turning while slackening the hub nut (see Chapter 6).*

#### Daytona, Speed Triple, Sprint ST and RS models – single-sided swingarm

**1** Remove the exhaust silencer (see Chapter 4), the rear wheel (see Chapter 6), and the shock absorber (see Section 10). On early models, remove the speed sensor (see Chapter 4, Section 15).

**2** Unscrew the brake hose cover bolts from the chainguard on the swingarm and free the hose **(see illustration)**. If required, unscrew the bolts securing the chainguard to the swingarm and remove it, noting how it fits.

**3** Unscrew the bolt securing the brake hose guide to the swingarm. Displace the rear brake caliper from the disc (see Chapter 6) –

there is no need to disconnect the hose. Feed the brake caliper over the swingarm and position it clear, making sure no strain is placed on the hose.

**4** If the sprocket has not been removed, fully slacken the drive chain (see Chapter 1). Disengage the chain from the rear sprocket – if there is not enough slack, you will have to remove the front sprocket (see Section 16).

**5** On Sprint models, and if required on Daytona and Speed Triple models, unscrew the nut and withdraw the bolt securing the linkage plates (Sprint) or linkage arm (Daytona and Speed Triple) to the swingarm, referring to Section 11 for details and illustrations. On Sprint models, swing the plates down off the swingarm.

**6** Before removing the swingarm it is advisable to re-check for play in the bearings (see Chapter 1). Any problems which may have been overlooked with the other suspension components attached to the frame are highlighted with them loose.

**7** Counter-hold the left-hand end of the swingarm pivot, and unscrew the bolt from the right-hand end **(see illustration)**.

**8** Using the Triumph special tool (Pt. No. T3880295) or a suitable peg spanner (which can be made by cutting two sections out of an old socket of a suitable size – see **Tool Tip**), unscrew the locknut on the adjuster bolt on the right-hand side **(see illustration)**. Using the Triumph special tool (Pt. No. T3880290) or a suitable peg spanner, now thread the adjuster bolt out of the frame until it no longer protrudes on the inside **(see illustration)**.

**13.8a  Unscrew the locknut (arrowed) – the Triumph special tool is shown here**

**13.8b  Unscrew the adjuster bolt (arrowed) – a peg spanner fabricated from a socket is shown**

 **TOOL TiP**  *Peg spanners can be made by cutting old sockets as shown in photo 13.8b – measure the width and depth of the slots in the locknut and adjuster bolt to determine the size of the castellations on the socket. If an old socket is not available, castellations can be welded onto a suitable nut.*

**9** Support the swingarm, then withdraw the pivot from the left-hand side and remove the

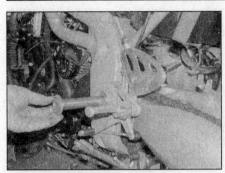

**13.9a Withdraw the pivot and remove the swingarm**

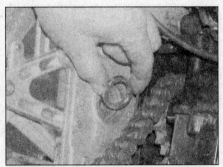

**13.9b Retrieve the spacer from the frame**

**13.13 Remove the chainguard**

swingarm **(see illustration)**. Knock the pivot through using a drift if required. Remove the spacer from the inside of the frame on the left-hand side **(see illustration)**.

**10** Remove the chain slider from the front of the swingarm if necessary, noting how it fits. If it is badly worn or damaged, it should be replaced with a new one.

**11** Inspect all components for wear or damage as described in Section 14.

### Daytona and Sprint RS models – twin-sided swingarm

**12** Remove the exhaust silencer (see Chapter 4), the rear wheel (see Chapter 6), and the shock absorber (see Section 10).

**13** If required, unscrew the bolts securing the chainguard to the swingarm and remove it, noting how it fits **(see illustration)**.

**14** Unscrew the bolt securing the brake hose guide to the swingarm. Displace the rear brake caliper from the disc (see Chapter 6) – there is no need to disconnect the hose. Position the brake caliper clear, making sure no strain is placed on the hose. On 2002 Daytona models, unclip the brake hose and displace the caliper, noting how the caliper bracket locates on the swingarm **(see illustrations)**. Unscrew the bolts securing the rear hugger and remove it (see Chapter 7, Section 7).

**15** Unscrew the nut and withdraw the bolt securing the linkage plates to the swingarm, referring to Section 11 for details and illustrations. Swing the plates down off the swingarm.

**16** Before removing the swingarm it is advisable to re-check for play in the bearings (see Chapter 1). Any problems which may have been overlooked with the other suspension components attached to the frame are highlighted with them loose.

**17** Remove the blanking cap from the right-hand end of the swingarm pivot. Counter-hold the pivot bolt and unscrew the nut from the left-hand end.

**18** Using the Triumph special tool (Pt. No. T3880295) or a suitable peg spanner (which can be made by cutting two sections out of an old socket of a suitable size – see **Tool Tip** above), unscrew the locknut on the adjuster bolt on the right-hand side **(see**

illustration 13.8a). Using the Triumph special tool (Pt. No. T3880290) or a suitable peg spanner, now thread the adjuster bolt out of the frame until it no longer protrudes on the inside **(see illustration 13.8b)**.

**19** Support the swingarm, then withdraw the pivot bolt from the right-hand side and remove the swingarm. Knock the bolt through using a drift if required. Remove the spacer from the inside of the frame on the left-hand side.

**20** Remove the chain slider from the front of the swingarm if necessary, noting how it fits. If it is badly worn or damaged, it should be replaced with a new one.

**21** Inspect all components for wear or damage as described in Section 14.

### Tiger models

**22** Remove the exhaust silencer (see Chapter 4), the rear wheel (see Chapter 6), and the shock absorber lower mounting bolt (see Section 10, bearing in mind the information given regarding the bearing). Swing the bottom of the shock rearwards so it is clear of the swingarm.

**23** If required, unscrew the bolts securing the chainguard to the swingarm and remove it, noting how it fits.

**24** Unscrew the bolt securing the brake hose guide to the swingarm. Position the brake caliper clear, making sure no strain is placed on the hose.

**25** Before removing the swingarm it is advisable to re-check for play in the bearings (see Chapter 1). Any problems which may have been overlooked with the other

suspension components attached to the frame are highlighted with them loose.

**26** Remove the blanking caps on each end of the swingarm pivot. Counter-hold the left-hand end of the pivot and unscrew the bolt from the right-hand end.

**27** Support the swingarm, then withdraw the pivot from the left-hand side and remove the swingarm. Knock the pivot through using a drift if required. Note the position of any spacers fitted between the swingarm and the inside of the frame and remove them for safekeeping.

**28** Remove the chain slider from the front of the swingarm if necessary, noting how it fits. If it is badly worn or damaged, it should be replaced with a new one.

**29** Inspect all components for wear or damage as described in Section 14.

## *Installation*

### Daytona, Speed Triple, Sprint ST and RS models – single-sided swingarm

**30** If not already done, remove the bearing spacers and lubricate the bearings, spacers and swingarm pivot with grease **(see illustration 14.4a)**. If removed, install the chain slider and tighten the bolts securely.

**31** Fit the spacer into its recess in the inside of the frame on the left-hand side – a smear of grease will help keep it in place **(see illustration 13.9b)**.

**32** Offer up the swingarm and have an assistant hold it in place, making sure the chain is looped around it and the spacer

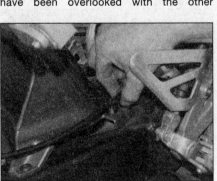

**13.14a Unclip the brake hose**

**13.14b Caliper bracket locates on lug (arrowed) on swingarm**

**13.32 Do not forget to loop the chain around the swingarm when installing it**

**13.33a Tighten the adjuster bolt to the specified torque . . .**

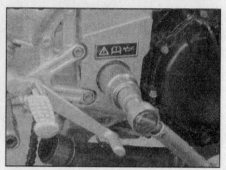

**13.33b . . . then fit the locknut and tighten that to the specified torque**

remains in place (**see illustration**). Slide the pivot through from the left-hand side (**see illustration 13.9a**).

**33** Using the Triumph special tool (Pt. No. T3880290) or a suitable peg spanner (see **Tool Tip**) (**see illustration 13.8b**), tighten the adjuster bolt to the torque setting specified at the beginning of the Chapter (**see illustration**). Make some reference marks between the adjuster bolt and the frame – these are used to check that the adjuster bolt turns no further when the locknut is tightened. Fit the locknut (**see illustration**), then tighten it to the specified torque using the Triumph special tool (Pt. No. T3880295) or a suitable peg spanner (**see illustration 13.8a**). Check that the adjuster bolt hasn't turned – if it has, repeat the tightening procedure.

**34** Fit the bolt into the right-hand end of the pivot (**see illustration**). Counter-hold the pivot and tighten the right-hand bolt to the specified torque (**see illustration**).

**35** Install all remaining components and assemblies in a reverse of the removal procedure, referring to the relevant Sections and Chapters where necessary. When fitting the brake hose guide, position it so the hose is vertical to allow for some forward movement in the caliper bracket, otherwise the end of the bracket could press into the hose and distort or kink it, which would lead to poor performance of the rear brake.

**36** Check and adjust the drive chain slack (see Chapter 1). Check the operation of the rear suspension and brake before taking the machine on the road.

### Daytona and Sprint RS models – twin-sided swingarm

**37** If not already done, remove the bearing spacers and lubricate the bearings, spacers and swingarm pivot with grease (**see illustration 14.4b**). If removed, install the chain slider.

**38** Fit the spacer into its recess in the inside of the frame on the left-hand side – a smear of grease will help keep it in place.

**39** Offer up the swingarm and have an assistant hold it in place, making sure the chain is looped around it and the spacer remains in place. Slide the pivot bolt through from the right-hand side.

**40** Using the Triumph special tool (Pt. No. T3880290) or a suitable peg spanner (see **Tool Tip**), tighten the adjuster bolt to the torque setting specified at the beginning of the Chapter. Make some reference marks between the adjuster bolt and the frame – these are used to check that the adjuster bolt turns no further when the locknut is tightened. Fit the locknut, then tighten it to the specified torque using the Triumph special tool (Pt. No. T3880295) or a suitable peg spanner. Check that the adjuster bolt hasn't turned – if it has repeat the tightening procedure.

**41** Fit the nut onto the left-hand end of the pivot bolt. Counter-hold the bolt on the right-hand end and tighten the nut to the specified torque.

**42** Install all remaining components and assemblies in a reverse of the removal procedure, referring to the relevant Sections and Chapters where necessary.

**43** Check and adjust the drive chain slack (see Chapter 1). Check the operation of the rear suspension and brake before taking the machine on the road.

### Tiger models

**44** If not already done, remove the bearing spacers and lubricate the bearings, spacers and swingarm pivot with grease (**see illustration 14.4c**). If removed, install the chain slider.

**45** Fit the spacers into their recesses in the inside of the frame – a smear of grease will help keep them in place.

**46** Offer up the swingarm and have an assistant hold it in place, making sure the chain is looped around it and the spacers remain in place. Slide the pivot through from the left-hand side.

**47** Fit the bolt into the right-hand end of the pivot. Counter-hold the pivot on the left-hand end and tighten the bolt to the specified torque.

**48** Install all remaining components and assemblies in a reverse of the removal procedure, referring to the relevant Sections and Chapters where necessary.

**49** Check and adjust the drive chain slack (see Chapter 1). Check the operation of the rear suspension and brake before taking the machine on the road.

### 14 Swingarm bearings

### *Inspection*

**1** Thoroughly clean the swingarm, removing all traces of dirt, corrosion and grease.

**2** Inspect all components closely, looking for obvious signs of wear such as heavy scoring, and cracks or distortion due to accident damage. Check the bearings for roughness, looseness and any other damage, referring to *Tools and Workshop Tips* (Section 5) in the Reference section. Any damaged or worn component must be renewed.

**3** Check the swingarm pivot/pivot bolt for straightness by rolling it on a flat surface such as a piece of plate glass (first wipe off all old grease and remove any corrosion using wire

**13.34a Install the pivot bolt . . .**

**13.34b . . . and tighten it to the specified torque**

wool). If the equipment is available, place the pivot in V-blocks and measure the runout using a dial gauge. If the pivot is bent, replace it with a new one.

### Bearing renewal

**4** On Daytona, Speed Triple and Sprint models, remove the needle bearing spacer from the left-hand side, then lever out the grease seal. Also remove the seal from the right-hand side, then remove the circlip securing the ball bearing(s) – Daytona and Sprint RS models with twin-sided swingarms, and 2005-on Tiger models, have two ball bearings in the right-hand side **(see illustrations)**. On 1999 to 2004 Tiger models, remove the bearing spacer on each side, then lever out the grease seals – there is a needle bearing in each side **(see illustration overleaf)**.

**5** Refer to *Tools and Workshop Tips* (Section 5) in the Reference section for more information on bearing checks and renewal methods. Needle bearings can be drawn or drifted out of their bores, but note that removal will make them unusable; new bearings should be obtained before work commences. Pass a long drift with a hooked end through one side of the swingarm and locate it on the inner edge of the bearing on the other side. Tap the drift around the bearing's inner edge to ensure that it leaves its bore squarely. Use the same method to extract ball bearings. If available, a slide-hammer with knife-edged bearing puller can be used, and is better than using a drift, to extract the bearings.

**6** The new bearings should be pressed or drawn into their bores rather than driven into position. In the absence of a press, a suitable

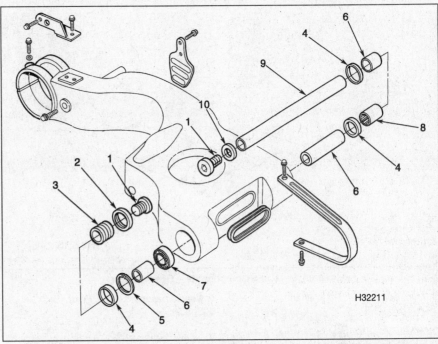

**14.4a  Single-sided swingarm components – Daytona, Speed Triple, Sprint ST and RS models**

| | | |
|---|---|---|
| 1 Pivot bolt | 4 Grease seal | 7 Ball bearing | 9 Pivot |
| 2 Locknut | 5 Circlip | 8 Needle bearing | 10 Washer |
| 3 Adjuster bolt | 6 Spacer | | |

drawbolt arrangement can be made up as described in *Tools and Workshop Tips* (Section 5) in the Reference section. Lubricate the bearings, spacers and seal lips with the recommended grease (see Chapter 1 Specifications) on installation.

### 15 Drive chain removal, cleaning and installation

**Note:** *If the drive chain fitted is an endless chain, which means it cannot be split, you must remove the swingarm. If the drive chain fitted has a riveted-type soft (joining) link, it can be disassembled using one of several commercially-available chain cutting/staking tools. Such chains can be recognised by the soft link side plate's identification marks (and usually its different colour), as well as by the riveted ends of the link's two pins which look as if they have been deeply centre-punched, instead of peened over as with all the other pins.*

### Endless chain

**1** Remove the front sprocket cover (see Section 16). Note that if the front sprocket is being removed, the nut should be slackened before removing the swingarm, so that the rear brake can be used so stop the sprocket turning (see Section 16).

**2** Remove the swingarm (see Section 13). Slip the chain off the front sprocket and remove it from the bike.

**3** If the chain is excessively dirty, soak it in kerosene (paraffin) for approximately five or six minutes, then clean it using a soft brush.

**4** Installation is the reverse of removal. On completion adjust and lubricate the chain following the procedures described in Chapter 1.

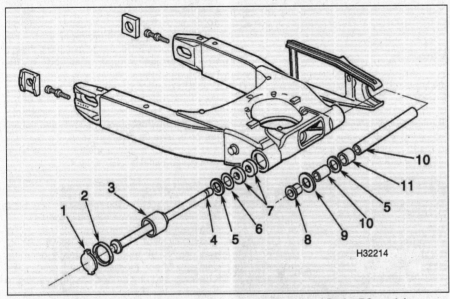

**14.4b  Twin-sided swingarm components – Daytona and Sprint RS models**

| | | |
|---|---|---|
| 1 Blanking cap | 5 Grease seal | 9 Washer |
| 2 Locknut | 6 Circlip | 10 Spacer |
| 3 Adjuster bolt | 7 Ball bearing | 11 Needle bearing |
| 4 Pivot bolt | 8 Nut | |

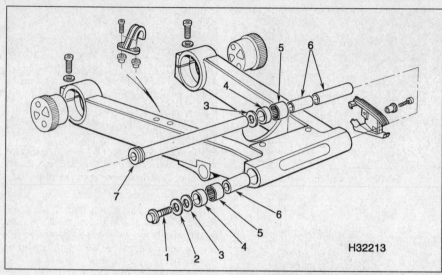

**14.4c Swingarm components – Tiger models**

| | | |
|---|---|---|
| 1 *Pivot bolt* | 3 *Shim* | 5 *Needle bearing* | 7 *Pivot* |
| 2 *Washer* | 4 *Grease seal* | 6 *Spacer* | |

*Caution: Don't use gasoline (petrol), solvent or other cleaning fluids which might damage its internal sealing properties. Don't use high-pressure water. Remove the chain, wipe it off, then blow dry it with compressed air immediately. The entire process shouldn't take longer than ten minutes – if it does, the O-rings in the chain rollers could be damaged.*

### Split chain with soft link

**5** Remove the front sprocket cover (see Section 16).

**6** Locate the soft link in a suitable position to work on by rotating the back wheel.

**7** Slacken the drive chain as described in Chapter 1.

**8** The chain can be separated at the soft link using a chain breaker tool and the soft link withdrawn to split the chain. Refer to Section 8 'Chains' of *Tools and Workshop Tips* in the Reference section at the end of this manual for details of how to use the tool and how to rivet the new soft link securely. Note that it is essential to use a new soft link when re-joining the chain. Never install a clip-type master link.

**9** After riveting, check the soft link and pin ends for any signs of cracking. If there is any evidence of cracking, the soft link, O-rings and side plate must be renewed. Measure the diameter of the riveted pin ends in two directions and check that each pin has been evenly riveted.

**10** Install the sprocket cover (see Section 16).

**11** On completion, adjust and lubricate the chain following the procedures described in Chapter 1.

### 16 Sprockets

### Check

**1** On Daytona and Sprint ST models, remove the left-hand fairing side panel (see Chapter 7).

**2** Unscrew the bolts securing the front sprocket cover and remove the cover **(see illustration)**. If access to the bottom bolt is restricted by the gearchange linkage arm, move the gearchange lever up or down to move the arm out of the way.

**3** Check the wear pattern on both sprockets **(see illustration 2.4 in Chapter 1)**. Whenever the sprockets are inspected the drive chain should also be inspected. If the sprocket teeth are worn excessively, or you are fitting a new chain, renew the chain and sprockets as a set.

**4** Adjust and lubricate the chain following the procedures described in Chapter 1.

### Front sprocket

**Note:** *Slacken the front sprocket nut before disengaging the chain from the rear sprocket so the rear brake can be used to prevent the front sprocket turning.*

**5** On Daytona and Sprint ST models, remove the left-hand fairing side panel (see Chapter 7).

**6** Unscrew the bolts securing the front sprocket cover and remove the cover **(see illustration 16.2)**. If access to the bottom bolt is restricted by the gearchange linkage arm, move the gearchange lever up or down to move the arm out of the way.

**7** Bend down the tab(s) on the sprocket nut lockwasher **(see illustration)**. Have an assistant apply the rear brake hard, then unscrew the nut and remove the washer. Discard the washer as a new one should be used. Refer to Chapter 1 and adjust the chain so that it is fully slack.

**8** If the sprocket is not being replaced with a new one, mark the outside with a scratch or dab of paint so that it can be installed the same way round. Slide the sprocket and chain off the shaft and slip the sprocket out of the chain **(see illustration)**. If there is not enough slack in the chain to remove the sprocket, disengage the chain from the rear wheel.

**9** Engage the new sprocket with the chain and slide it on the shaft **(see illustration 16.8)**. Take up the slack in the chain (see Chapter 1).

**10** Slide on the new lockwasher, locating it onto the splines **(see illustration)**. Fit the nut with its shouldered side facing in and tighten it to the torque setting specified at the beginning of the Chapter, applying the rear brake to prevent the sprocket from turning **(see illustrations)**. Bend up the tabs of the lockwasher against the nut **(see illustration)**.

**11** Install the front sprocket cover and tighten the bolts **(see illustration 16.2)**. On Daytona and Sprint ST models, install the left-hand fairing side panel (see Chapter 7).

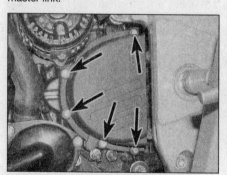

**16.2 Sprocket cover bolts (arrowed)**

**16.7 Bend back the lockwasher tab(s) then unscrew the nut and remove the washer**

**16.8 Slide the sprocket off the shaft and remove it**

16.10a Fit the new lockwasher . . .

16.10b . . . and the nut . . .

16.10c . . . and tighten it to the specified torque

16.10d Bend the tabs up against the nut

## Rear sprocket – models with single-sided swingarm

12 Refer to Chapter 1 and adjust the chain so that it is fully slack. Disengage the chain from the rear sprocket.

13 Have an assistant apply the rear brake,

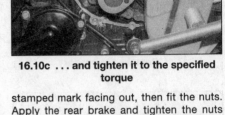

16.13 Counter-hold the bolts (arrowed) if they turn with the nuts

then unscrew the nuts securing the sprocket to the coupling – counter-hold the bolt heads on the inside of the coupling if they turn (see illustration). Remove the sprocket, noting which way round it fits.

14 Fit the sprocket onto the coupling with the

stamped mark facing out, then fit the nuts. Apply the rear brake and tighten the nuts evenly and in a criss-cross sequence to the torque setting specified at the beginning of the Chapter.

15 Fit the chain around the sprocket, then adjust and lubricate the chain following the procedures described in Chapter 1.

## Rear sprocket – models with twin-sided swingarm

16 Remove the rear wheel (see Chapter 6).

17 Unscrew the nuts securing the sprocket to the coupling. Remove the sprocket, noting which way round it fits.

18 Fit the sprocket onto the coupling with the stamped mark facing out, then fit the nuts. Tighten the nuts evenly and in a criss-cross sequence to the torque setting specified at the beginning of the Chapter.

19 Install the rear wheel (see Chapter 6).

## 17 Rear sprocket coupling/rubber dampers

1 On models with a single-sided swingarm, unscrew the bolts securing the chainguards and remove them. Have an assistant apply the rear brake hard, then slacken the sprocket coupling nut (see illustration). Slacken the drive chain adjuster clamp bolt (see illustration). Remove the coupling nut and its washer, noting which way round it fits, then slide the sprocket coupling off the axle and disengage it from the chain (see illustrations).

17.1a Apply the rear brake and slacken the nut (arrowed)

17.1b Slacken the clamp bolt (arrowed)

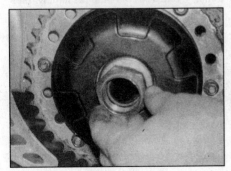

17.1c Remove the nut . . .

17.1d . . . and the dished washer, noting which way round it fits

17.1e Slide the sprocket coupling off the axle and disengage the chain

17.1f Remove the spacer . . .

17.1g . . . and the thrust washer if required

17.1h Lift the driven hub out of the coupling

17.1i Remove the spacer for safekeeping

17.2 Lift out the sprocket coupling

17.4a Check the rubber dampers in the sprocket coupling . . .

17.4b . . . or in the hub as applicable

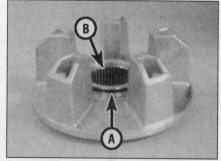

17.5 Check the O-ring (A) and the splines (B)

17.7 Stake the rim of the nut against the cutout in the shaft

Note the shouldered spacer in the outside of the coupling and the thrust washer in the hub assembly and remove them for safekeeping if required (see illustrations). Lift the driven hub out of the coupling, leaving the rubber dampers in position (see illustration). Note the spacer and remove it for safekeeping if required (see illustration). Note that Triumph specify to use a new sprocket coupling nut on installation.

2 On models with a twin-sided swingarm, remove the rear wheel (see Chapter 6). Lift the sprocket coupling out of the wheel, leaving the rubber dampers in position (see illustration).

3 Check the coupling for cracks or any obvious signs of damage.

4 Lift the rubber damper segments from the sprocket coupling or wheel hub as applicable, and check them for cracks, hardening and general deterioration (see illustrations). Renew the rubber dampers as a set if necessary.

5 On models with a single-sided swingarm, check the condition of the O-ring on the driven hub and replace it with a new one if necessary (see illustration). Also check the splines in the hub and on the shaft for signs of wear or damage.

6 Checking and replacement procedures for the sprocket coupling/hub assembly bearings are described in Chapter 6.

7 Installation is the reverse of removal. On

models with a single-sided swingarm, do not forget to fit the spacer inside the sprocket coupling (see illustration 17.1i), the shouldered spacer in the outside of the coupling (see illustration 17.1f), and the thrust washer in the hub assembly (see illustration 17.1g). Fit the dished washer so that its outer rim is against the spacer and the inner rim is raised off it (see illustration 17.1d). Tighten the coupling nut to the torque setting specified at the beginning of the Chapter, using the rear brake or a suitable holding tool on the brake disc to prevent the coupling turning. Stake the rim of the nut into the cutout in the end of the axle (see illustration).

# Chapter 6
# Brakes, wheels and tyres

## Contents

## Degrees of difficulty

| | | | | |
|---|---|---|---|---|
| **Easy,** suitable for novice with little experience  | **Fairly easy,** suitable for beginner with some experience  | **Fairly difficult,** suitable for competent DIY mechanic 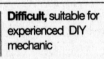 | **Difficult,** suitable for experienced DIY mechanic | **Very difficult,** suitable for expert DIY or professional |

## Specifications

### Brakes – Daytona, Speed Triple and Sprint models

| | |
|---|---|
| Brake fluid type | DOT 4 |
| Brake pad minimum thickness | 1.5 mm |
| Front caliper piston OD | |
|    Large bore | 33.96 mm |
|    Small bore | 30.23 mm |
| Front disc thickness | |
|    Standard | 4.0 mm |
|    Service limit | 3.5 mm |
| Front disc maximum runout | 0.3 mm |
| Front master cylinder bore ID | 14.0 mm |
| Rear caliper piston OD | |
|    Single-sided swingarm type | 27.0 mm |
|    Twin-sided swingarm type | 38.18 mm |
| Rear disc thickness | |
|    Standard | 5.0 mm |
|    Service limit | 4.5 mm |
| Rear disc maximum runout | 0.3 mm |
| Rear master cylinder bore ID | 14.0 mm |

### Brakes – Tiger models

| | |
|---|---|
| Brake fluid type | DOT 4 |
| Brake pad minimum thickness | 1.5 mm |
| Front caliper piston OD | 27.0 mm |
| Front disc thickness | |
|    Standard | 5.0 mm |
|    Service limit | 4.5 mm |
| Front disc maximum runout | 0.3 mm |
| Front master cylinder bore ID | 12.7 mm |
| Rear caliper piston OD | 27.0 mm |
| Rear disc thickness | |
|    Standard | 6.0 mm |
|    Service limit | 5.5 mm |
| Rear disc maximum runout | 0.3 mm |
| Rear master cylinder bore ID | 14.0 mm |

## Wheels

Runout (max) – axial (side-to-side) and radial (out-of round)
Daytona, Speed Triple and Sprint models ..................... 0.5 mm
Tiger models ....................................................... 1.0 mm

## Tyres

Tyre pressures ..................................................... see *Daily (pre-ride) checks*

| Tyre sizes* | Front | Rear |
|---|---|---|
| Speed Triple models ........................................... | 120/70-17 | 190/50-17 |
| Daytona models | | |
| 2002 model with twin-sided swingarm ..................... | 120/70-17 | 180/55-17 |
| All other models ............................................... | 120/70-17 | 190/50-17 |
| Sprint models .................................................. | 120/70-17 | 180/55-17 |
| Tiger models ................................................... | 110/80-19 | 150/70-17 |

*Refer to the owners handbook, the tyre information label on the swingarm, or your Triumph dealer or a tyre specialist for approved tyre brands and ratings.

## Torque wrench settings

Brake bleed valves
Daytona, Speed Triple and Sprint models ..................... 7 Nm
Tiger models ....................................................... 5 Nm
Brake hose banjo bolts .............................................. 25 Nm
Brake pad retaining pins
Daytona and Speed Triple models
Front
1997 to 2001 models ...................................... 25 Nm
2002-on models ............................................. 20 Nm
Rear
Single-sided swingarm ................................... 20 Nm
Twin-sided swingarm ..................................... 17 Nm
Sprint models (front and rear) ................................ 20 Nm
Tiger models (front and rear) ................................. 18 Nm
Front brake caliper mounting bolts
Daytona, Speed Triple and Sprint models ..................... 40 Nm
Tiger models ....................................................... 28 Nm
Front brake disc bolts .............................................. 22 Nm
Front brake master cylinder clamp bolts ....................... 15 Nm
Front wheel axle bolt – Daytona and Speed Triple
1997 to 2001 models .......................................... 60 Nm
2002-on models ................................................. 65 Nm
Front wheel axle – Sprint models ................................ 61 Nm
Front wheel axle nut – Tiger models ............................ 60 Nm
Front wheel axle clamp bolts – Daytona, Speed Triple and
Sprint models ..................................................... 20 Nm
Rear brake caliper mounting bolts
Daytona models
Single-sided swingarm ................................... 40 Nm
Twin-sided swingarm
M8 bolt ..................................................... 20 Nm
M12 bolt ................................................... 29 Nm
Speed Triple and Sprint models ............................. 40 Nm
Tiger models ....................................................... 28 Nm
Rear brake caliper carrier peg – Daytona (with single-sided swingarm),
Speed Triple and Sprint ST models ........................ 40 Nm
Rear brake disc bolts .............................................. 22 Nm
Rear brake light switch – Sprint and Tiger models
1999 to 2001 models .......................................... 25 Nm
2002-on models ................................................. 15 Nm
Rear brake master cylinder mounting bolts
Daytona and Speed Triple models
1997 to 2001 models ...................................... 30 Nm
2002-on models ............................................. 18 Nm
Sprint and Tiger models ....................................... 27 Nm
Rear wheel axle bolt – Tiger models ............................ 85 Nm
Rear wheel axle nut
Daytona, Speed Triple and Sprint models
Single-sided swingarm ................................... 146 Nm
Twin-sided swingarm ..................................... 110 Nm
Sprocket coupling nut – Daytona, Speed Triple, Sprint ST
and Sprint RS models with single-sided swingarm .............. 146 Nm

## 1  General information

All Daytona, Speed Triple and Sprint models, and 2005 Tiger models, are fitted with cast alloy wheels designed for tubeless tyres only. 1999 to 2004 Tiger models have wire spoked wheels which require the use of tubed tyres.

Both front and rear brakes are hydraulically operated disc brakes. On Daytona, Speed Triple and Sprint models, the front brakes have twin opposed-piston calipers; a single- or twin-piston sliding caliper is used at the rear. On Tiger models, both front and rear brakes have twin piston sliding calipers.

*Caution: Disc brake components rarely require disassembly. Do not disassemble components unless absolutely necessary. If an hydraulic brake line is loosened, the system must be thoroughly bled. Do not use solvents on internal brake components. Solvents will cause the seals to swell and distort. Use only clean brake fluid or denatured alcohol for cleaning. Use care when working with brake fluid as it can injure your eyes and it will damage painted surfaces and plastic parts.*

Many of the bolts used on Triumph motorcycles are of the Torx type. Unless you are already equipped with a good range of Torx bits, you are advised to obtain a set. Make sure you get bits that can be used in conjunction with a socket set so that a torque wrench can be applied – a Torx key set will not be adequate on its own, though will be useful in addition to the bits.

## 2  Brake pad renewal

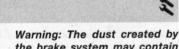

⚠️ *Warning: The dust created by the brake system may contain asbestos, which is harmful to your health. Never blow it out with compressed air and don't inhale any of it. An approved filtering mask should be worn when working on the brakes.*

### Daytona, Speed Triple and Sprint models

#### Front

**1** If new pads are being installed, displace the calipers from the discs (see Section 3) – this makes it easier to push the pistons back into the caliper to allow for the extra thickness of new pads. If you do this, slacken the pad retaining pin before displacing the caliper, but only by a very small amount (just to break the seal) as there is a split pin in the end of it (see

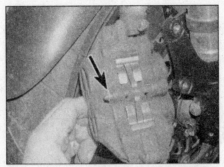

**2.2a  Remove the split pin (arrowed) . . .**

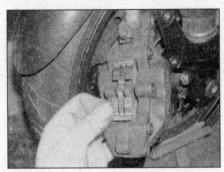

**2.2c  Remove the pad spring . . .**

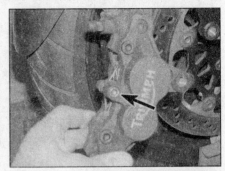

**2.2b  . . . then unscrew the pad pin (arrowed)**

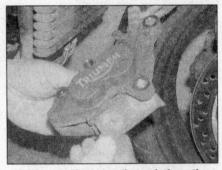

**2.2d  . . . and remove the pads from the caliper**

Step 2). Otherwise, the pads can be removed with the caliper in situ.

**2** Remove the split pin from the inner end of the pad retaining pin **(see illustration)**. Unscrew and withdraw the pad pin, noting how it fits through the pad spring, then remove the pad spring **(see illustrations)**. Withdraw the pads from the caliper **(see illustration)**.

**3** Inspect the surface of each pad for contamination and check that the friction material has not worn beyond its service limit (see Chapter 1, Section 9). If either pad is worn down to or beyond the service limit wear indicator, is fouled with oil or grease, or is heavily scored or damaged by dirt and debris, both pads in each caliper must be renewed. Note that it is not possible to degrease the friction material; if the pads are contaminated in any way new ones must be fitted.

**4** If the pads are in good condition clean them carefully, using a fine wire brush which is completely free of oil and grease, to remove all traces of road dirt and corrosion. Using a pointed instrument, clean out the groove in the friction material and dig out any embedded particles of foreign matter. Spray with a dedicated brake cleaner to remove any dust.

**5** Check the condition of the brake disc (see Section 4).

**6** Remove all traces of corrosion from the pad pin. Check it for signs of damage and renew it if necessary.

**7** If new pads are being installed, push the pistons as far back into the caliper as possible using hand pressure or a piece of wood as

leverage. This will displace brake fluid back into the reservoir, so it may be necessary to remove the fluid reservoir cap, plate and diaphragm and siphon out some fluid (depending on how much fluid was in there in the first place and how far the pistons have to be pushed in). If the pistons are difficult to push back, attach a length of clear hose to the bleed valve and place the open end in a suitable container, then open the valve and try again. Take great care not to draw any air into the system. If in doubt, bleed the brakes afterwards (see Section 10).

**8** Lightly smear the backs of the pads and the shank of the pad pin with copper-based grease, making sure that none gets on the front or sides of the pads.

**9** Insert the pads into the caliper so that the friction material on each pad faces the other **(see illustration)**. Fit the pad spring onto the pads, making sure it is the correct way up

**2.9a  Install the pads**

2.9b Press down on the spring and insert the pad pin

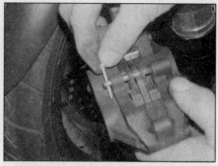

2.9c Secure the pad pin with a new split pin

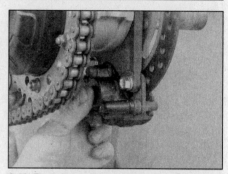

2.13 Push the caliper against the disc so the pistons are pressed back into the caliper

(see illustration 2.2c). Slide the pad retaining pin through the hole in the outer pad, then press down on the pad spring and slide the pin over the spring and through the hole in the inner pad (see illustration). Tighten the pin to the torque setting specified at the beginning of the Chapter. Fit a new split pin into the end of the retaining pin and bend its ends round to secure it (see illustration).

10 If displaced, install the calipers (see Section 3). Top up the master cylinder reservoir if necessary (see *Daily (pre-ride) checks*), and refit the diaphragm, plate and reservoir cap.

11 Operate the brake lever several times to bring the pads into contact with the disc. Check the operation of the brake before riding the motorcycle.

**Rear**

12 On Daytona, Speed Triple, Sprint ST models and Sprint RS models with single-sided swingarms, remove the rear wheel (see Section 14). Note: *Although the caliper can be displaced and the pads removed with the wheel in situ, access to the caliper mounting bolts is restricted, and there is little clearance between the wheel and the caliper when removing it – it is too easy to scratch the wheel, so it is best to remove it. On Sprint RS models and Daytona models with twin-sided swingarms, remove the exhaust silencer for best access to the pad retaining pins and caliper mounting bolts, if required (see Chapter 4).*

13 If new pads are being fitted, to allow for the increased friction material thickness of new pads, push the brake caliper against the disc so that the pistons are forced back into the caliper (see illustration). This will displace brake fluid back into the reservoir, so it may be necessary to remove the master cylinder

reservoir cover and diaphragm and siphon out some fluid. If the pistons are difficult to push back, attach a length of clear hose to the bleed valve and place the open end in a suitable container, then open the valve and try again. Take great care not to draw any air into the system. If in doubt, bleed the brakes afterwards (see Section 10).

14 On all models except 2002 Daytona models, slacken the pad retaining pins, but do not yet remove them (see illustrations). Displace the caliper from the disc (see Section 6). Press down on the bottom of the pads and withdraw the retaining pins (see illustration). Remove the outer pad, noting how it hooks against the pin on the caliper bracket, then remove the inner pad, noting how it fits in the bracket (see illustrations). Note how the pad spring is fitted and remove it if required (see illustration).

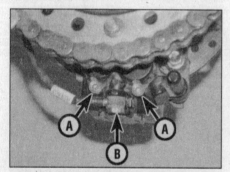

2.14a Pad retaining pins (A), brake hose banjo bolt (B) – Daytona, Speed Triple and Sprint ST

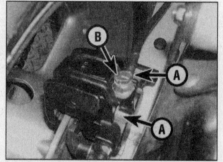

2.14b Pad retaining pins (A), brake hose banjo bolt (B) – Sprint RS

2.14c Withdraw the pad pins . . .

2.14d . . . then remove the outer pad, noting how it locates . . .

2.14e . . . and the inner pad

2.14f Remove the pad spring if required, noting how it fits

2.15a Remove the plug . . .

2.15b . . . then slacken the retaining pin

2.15c Remove the caliper mounting bolt . . .

2.15d . . . and pivot the caliper up

2.15e Remove the pad retaining pin . . .

2.15f . . . and remove the pads from the caliper

**15** On 2002 Daytona models, unscrew the pad retaining pin plug, then slacken the retaining pin **(see illustrations)**. Remove the rear caliper mounting bolt and pivot the caliper up **(see illustrations)**. Remove the retaining pin and withdraw the pads from the caliper **(see illustrations)**.

**16** Refer to Steps 3, 4, 5, and 6 above and inspect the pads and caliper components.

**17** On all models except the 2002 Daytona, check that the caliper body is able to slide freely on the slider pins on the bracket. Separate the bracket from the caliper by sliding them apart **(see illustration)**. Clean off all traces of corrosion and hardened grease. Check the rubber boots in the caliper. If they are damaged or deteriorated, they should be replaced with new ones (but check with a Triumph dealer as they do not list them as being available separately). Apply a smear of copper or silicone based grease to the slider pins. Slide the bracket back onto the caliper. If removed, fit the pad spring into the caliper **(see illustration 2.14f)**, making sure it is correctly located **(see illustration)**. Fit the inner pad into the caliper **(see illustration 2.14e)** and locate its ends against the bracket **(see illustration)**. Fit the outer pad, locating the cutout around the pin on the bracket **(see illustration 2.14d)**. Press the pads against the spring and slide the pad retaining pins through **(see illustration)**. Make sure the pins pass through the holes in each pad. Tighten the pad retaining pins to the torque setting specified at the beginning of the Chapter (this can be done after installing

the caliper if required). Install the caliper (see Section 6). If not done earlier, now tighten the retaining pins to the torque setting specified at the beginning of the Chapter **(see illustration 2.14a and b)**. Install the rear wheel if applicable (see Section 14).

**18** On 2002 Daytona models, remove the front mounting bolt and displace the caliper

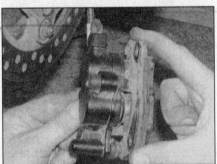

2.17a Slide the bracket out of the caliper

2.17b Make sure the spring locates correctly in the caliper

2.17c Make sure the inner pad locates correctly

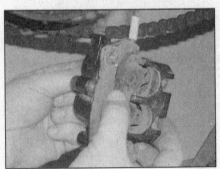

2.17d Press down on the pads and insert the pins

**2.18a Remove the front caliper mounting bolt**

**2.18b Location of the pad spring (arrowed)**

**2.18c Location of the spring on the caliper bracket**

from the disc **(see illustration)**. Note how the pad spring is fitted in the caliper and remove it if required **(see illustration)**. Note the location of the spring on the caliper bracket and remove it if required **(see illustration)**. Clean off all traces of corrosion and hardened grease from the caliper mounting bolts. Clean the inside of the caliper with brake system cleaner. Check the rubber boots in the caliper and the caliper bracket; if damaged or deteriorated they should be replaced with new ones (the boots, internal spacers and mounting bolts are listed as an overhaul kit). Apply a smear of copper or silicone-based grease to the mounting bolts. If removed, fit the springs into the caliper and onto the caliper bracket, then install the caliper onto the disc and secure it with the front mounting bolt **(see illustration 2.18a)**. Install the pads in the caliper, making sure they are correctly located on either side of the disc with the friction material facing the disc, then press them into the caliper against the spring and

install the retaining pin **(see illustrations 2.15e)**. Pivot the caliper down and install the rear mounting bolt. Tighten the mounting bolts and the retaining pin to the torque setting specified at the beginning of the Chapter. Install the pad retaining pin plug.
**19** Top up the master cylinder reservoir if necessary (see *Daily (pre-ride) checks*).
**20** Operate the brake pedal several times to bring the pads into contact with the disc. Check the operation of the brake before riding the motorcycle.

### Tiger models

**Note:** *To renew the rear brake pads on 2005 Tiger models, follow the procedure for Sprint RS models with twin-sided swingarms*
**21** If new pads are being fitted, to allow for the increased friction material thickness of new pads, push the brake caliper against the disc so that the pistons are forced back into the caliper. This will displace brake fluid back into the reservoir, so it may be necessary to remove

the master cylinder reservoir cover and diaphragm and siphon out some fluid. If the pistons are difficult to push back, attach a length of clear hose to the bleed valve and place the open end in a suitable container, then open the valve and try again. Take great care not to draw any air into the system. If in doubt, bleed the brakes afterwards (see Section 10).
**22** Unscrew the pad retaining pin plug and the pad retaining pin, then remove the pads **(see illustrations)**. Note how the pad spring is fitted.
**23** Refer to Steps 3, 4, 5, and 6 above and inspect the pads and caliper components.
**24** Check that the caliper body is able to slide freely on the slider pins on the bracket. If it doesn't, displace the caliper (see Section 6).
**25** Separate the bracket from the caliper by sliding them apart **(see illustration)**. Clean off all traces of corrosion and hardened grease. Check the rubber boots in the caliper. If they are damaged or deteriorated, they should be replaced with new ones (but check with a Triumph dealer as they do not list them as being available separately). Apply a smear of copper or silicone-based grease to the slider pins. Slide the bracket back onto the caliper.
**26** Make sure the pad spring is correctly positioned in the caliper. Insert the pads into the caliper so that the friction material faces the disc **(see illustration)**, then press the pads up against the spring and slide the pad retaining pin through **(see illustration 2.22b)**. Make sure the pin passes through the hole in each pad, and the pad ends locate correctly. Tighten the pad retaining pin to the torque setting specified at the beginning of the Chapter. Install the pad pin plug **(see illustration 2.22a)**.

**2.22a Unscrew the plug . . .**

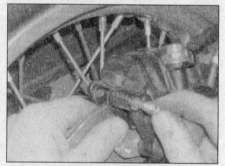

**2.22b . . . then unscrew and withdraw the pin . . .**

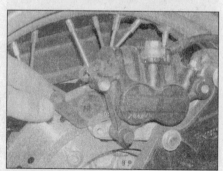

**2.22c . . . and remove the pads**

**2.25 Slide the bracket out of the caliper**

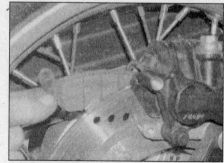

**2.26 Slide the pads into the caliper**

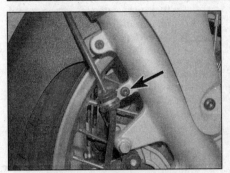

**3.4 Unscrew the bolt (arrowed) and displace the hose guide**

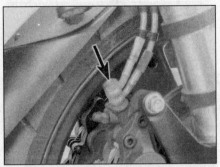

**3.5a Brake hose banjo bolt (arrowed) – note the two hoses on the right-hand caliper**

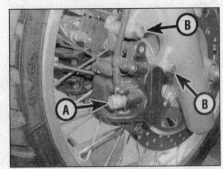

**3.5b Brake hose banjo bolt (A), caliper mounting bolts (B) – Tiger models**

**3.6a Unscrew the bolts (arrowed) . . .**

**3.6b . . . and slide the caliper off the disc**

27 Top up the master cylinder reservoir if necessary (see *Daily (pre-ride) checks*).

28 Operate the brake lever or pedal several times to bring the pads into contact with the disc. Check the operation of the brake before riding the motorcycle.

## 3 Front brake calipers

⚠️ **Warning: If a caliper indicates the need for an overhaul (usually due to leaking fluid or sticky operation), all old brake fluid should be flushed from the system. Also, the dust created by the brake system may contain asbestos, which is harmful to your health. Never blow it out with compressed air and don't inhale any of it. An approved filtering mask should be worn when working on the brakes. Do not, under any circumstances, use petroleum-based solvents to clean brake parts. Use the specified clean brake fluid, dedicated brake cleaner or denatured alcohol only, as described.**

1 If the caliper is leaking fluid, or the brake pads are wearing unevenly due to a sticky or seized piston (first check that this is not due to misalignment of the caliper on the disc), or if the brake lever produces a firm feel when the brake is applied but the brakes are no good, and the hydraulic hoses and the master cylinder are all in good condition, then the caliper must be overhauled.

2 Before disassembling the caliper, read through the entire procedure and make sure that you have a new seal kit. Also, you will need some new DOT 4 brake fluid and some clean rags.

*Caution: Disassembly, overhaul and reassembly of the caliper must be done in a spotlessly clean work area to avoid contamination and possible failure of the brake hydraulic system components.*

### Removal

3 If the calipers are being overhauled, remove the brake pads (see Section 2). If the calipers are just being displaced or removed, the pads can be left in place.

4 On Tiger models, unscrew the bolt securing

the brake hose guide to the front fork and displace it (see illustration).

5 If the calipers are just being displaced and not completely removed or overhauled, do not disconnect the brake hose(s). If the calipers are being completely removed or overhauled, remove the brake hose banjo bolt and detach

the hose(s), noting the alignment with the caliper (see illustrations). Plug the hose end(s) or wrap a plastic bag tightly around to minimise fluid loss and prevent dirt entering the system. Discard the sealing washers as new ones must be used on installation. **Note:** *If you are planning to overhaul the caliper and*

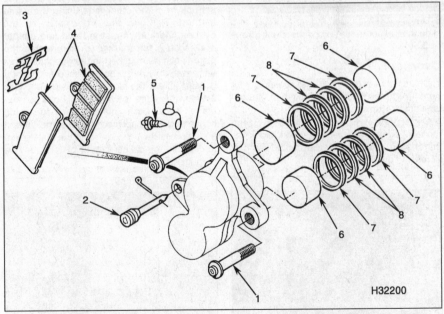

**3.7a Front brake caliper components – Daytona, Speed Triple and Sprint models**

1 Mounting bolts
2 Pad retaining pin and split pin
3 Pad spring
4 Brake pads
5 Bleed valve
6 Piston
7 Piston seal
8 Dust seal

H32200

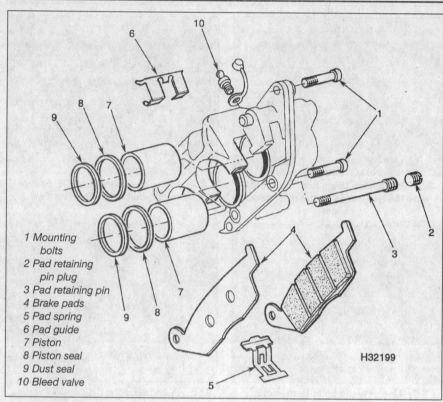

1 Mounting
  bolts
2 Pad retaining
  pin plug
3 Pad retaining pin
4 Brake pads
5 Pad spring
6 Pad guide
7 Piston
8 Piston seal
9 Dust seal
10 Bleed valve

H32199

**3.7b Front brake caliper components – Tiger models**

**Warning: Never place your fingers in front of the pistons in an attempt to catch or protect them when applying compressed air, as serious injury could result.**

**Caution: Do not try to remove the pistons by levering them out, or by using pliers or any other grips. On Daytona, Speed Triple and Sprint models, do not attempt to separate the caliper body halves.**

**9** On Tiger models, separate the bracket from the caliper by sliding them apart **(see illustration 2.26)**. Remove the pad spring from the caliper noting how it fits **(see illustration 6.8)**. Displace the pistons either by pumping them out by operating the front brake lever, or by easing them out using compressed air. Mark each piston head and caliper body with a felt marker to ensure that the pistons can be matched to their original bores on reassembly. If the compressed air method is used, direct the air into the fluid inlet. Use only low pressure to ease the pistons out and make sure both pistons are displaced at the same time. If the air pressure is too high and the pistons are forced out, the caliper and/or pistons may be damaged.

**10** Using a wooden or plastic tool, remove the dust seals from the caliper bores, noting which way round they fit **(see illustration)**. Discard them as new ones must be used on installation. If a metal tool is being used, take great care not to mark the caliper bores.

**11** Remove and discard the piston seals in the same way.

**12** Clean the pistons and bores with clean brake fluid of the specified type. If compressed air is available, use it to dry the parts thoroughly (make sure it's filtered and unlubricated).

**Caution: Do not, under any circumstances, use a petroleum-based solvent to clean brake parts.**

**13** Inspect the caliper bores and pistons for signs of corrosion, nicks and burrs and loss of plating. If surface defects are present, the caliper assembly must be renewed. If the caliper is in bad shape the master cylinder should also be checked.

**14** On Daytona, Speed Triple and Sprint models, note that two sizes of bore and piston are used (see Specifications), and care must therefore be taken to ensure that the correct size seals are fitted to the correct bores. Lubricate the new piston seals with clean brake fluid and install them in the lower grooves in the caliper bores, making sure their wider side is fitted outermost **(see illustration)**. Lubricate the new dust seals with clean brake fluid and install them in the upper grooves in the caliper bores, again making sure the wider side fits outermost.

**15** On Tiger models lubricate the new piston seals with clean brake fluid and install them in the lower grooves in the caliper bores. Lubricate the new dust seals with clean brake fluid and install them in the upper grooves in the caliper bores.

don't have a source of compressed air to blow out the pistons, just loosen the banjo bolt at this stage and retighten it lightly. The bike's hydraulic system can then be used to force the pistons out of the body once the pads have been removed. Disconnect the hose once the pistons have been sufficiently displaced.

**6** Unscrew the caliper mounting bolts and slide the caliper off the disc **(see illustrations or 3.5b)**.

## Overhaul

**7** Clean the exterior of the caliper with denatured alcohol or brake system cleaner **(see illustrations)**.

**8** On Daytona, Speed Triple and Sprint models, using a flat piece of wood, block the pistons on one side of the caliper in their bores and displace the opposite pistons either

by pumping them out by operating the front brake lever, or by easing them out using compressed air. Remove the seals (see Steps 10 and 11) from the bore of the displaced pistons, then reinstall the pistons and block them using the wood. Now displace the pistons from the other side using the same method. Remove the wood and all the pistons. Mark each piston head and caliper body with a felt marker to ensure that the pistons can be matched to their original bores on reassembly. If the compressed air method is used, direct the air into the fluid inlet. Use only low pressure to ease the pistons out and make sure both pistons on the side concerned are displaced at the same time. If the air pressure is too high and the pistons are forced out, the caliper and/or pistons may be damaged.

**3.10 Use a plastic or wooden tool (such as a pencil) to remove the seals**

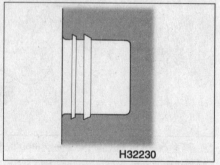

H32230

**3.14 Caliper seal orientation – Daytona, Speed Triple and Sprint models**

**3.21 Slide the caliper onto the disc and install the mounting bolts**

16 Lubricate the pistons with clean brake fluid and install them closed-end first into the caliper bores. Using your thumbs, push the pistons all the way in, making sure they enter the bore squarely without dislodging the seals.

17 On Tiger models, check that the caliper body is able to slide freely on the slider pins on the bracket. Separate the bracket from the caliper by sliding them apart (see illustration 2.26). Clean off all traces of corrosion and hardened grease. Check the rubber boots in the caliper. If they are damaged or deteriorated, they should be replaced with new ones (but check with a Triumph dealer as they do not list them as being available separately). Apply a smear of copper or silicone based grease to the slider pins. Slide the bracket back onto the caliper. Fit the pad spring back into the caliper, making sure it locates correctly (see illustration 6.8).

### Installation

18 On Tiger models, if not already done, carry out the checks in Step 17.

19 If necessary, push the pistons a little way back into the caliper using hand pressure or a piece of wood as leverage.

20 If removed, install the brake pads (see Section 2).

21 Slide the caliper onto the brake disc, making sure the pads sit squarely each side of the disc (see illustration). Install the caliper mounting bolts and tighten them to the torque setting specified at the beginning of the Chapter. If necessary and not already done,

tighten the pad retaining pin(s) to the specified torque setting.

22 If removed, connect the brake hose(s) to the caliper, using new sealing washers on each side of the union(s). Align the hose(s) as noted on removal (see illustration 3.5a or b). Tighten the banjo bolt to the torque setting specified at the beginning of the Chapter.

23 On Tiger models, fit the brake hose guide onto the front fork and tighten the bolt securely (see illustration 3.4).

24 Top up the master cylinder reservoir with DOT 4 brake fluid (see *Daily (pre-ride) checks*) and bleed the hydraulic system as described in Section 10. Check for leaks and thoroughly test the operation of the brake before riding the motorcycle.

---

## 4 Front brake discs

### Inspection

1 Visually inspect the surface of the disc for score marks and other damage. Light scratches are normal after use and won't affect brake operation, but deep grooves and heavy score marks will reduce braking efficiency and accelerate pad wear. If a disc is badly grooved it must be machined or a new one fitted.

2 To check disc runout, position the bike on an auxiliary stand and support it so that the front wheel is raised off the ground. Mount a dial gauge to a fork leg, with the plunger on the gauge touching the surface of the disc about 10 mm (1/2 in) from the outer edge (see illustration). Rotate the wheel and watch the gauge needle, comparing the reading with the limit listed in the Specifications at the beginning of the Chapter. If the runout is greater than the service limit, check the wheel bearings for play (see Chapter 1). If the bearings are worn, install new ones (see Section 15) and repeat this check. If the disc runout is still excessive, a new one will have to be fitted, although machining by an engineer may be possible.

3 The disc must not be machined or allowed

to wear down to a thickness less than the service limit as listed in this Chapter's Specifications. The thickness of the disc can be checked with a micrometer or any other measuring tool (see illustration). If the thickness of the disc is less than the service limit, a new one must be fitted. Note: *Even if only one disc needs to be renewed, Triumph specify that they must be renewed as a pair. They also specify that the disc bolts should only be used once, so get new ones in advance.*

### Removal

4 Remove the wheel (see Section 13).
Caution: *Do not lay the wheel down and allow it to rest on the disc – the disc could become warped. Set the wheel on wood blocks so the disc doesn't support the weight of the wheel.*

5 Mark the relationship of the discs to the wheel, so they can be installed in the same position (unless you are fitting new discs). Also mark the discs according to their side – this is especially important on Daytona, Speed Triple and Sprint models as the discs are different. If you are installing new discs, match them to the old ones so they can be installed correctly.

6 Unscrew the disc retaining bolts, loosening them evenly and a little at a time in a criss-cross pattern to avoid distorting the disc, then remove the disc from the wheel (see illustration). Discard the bolts as Triumph specify that new ones should be used.

### Installation

7 Before installing the disc, make sure there is no dirt or corrosion where the disc seats on the hub, particularly right in the angle of the seat, as this will not allow the disc to sit flat when it is bolted down and it will appear to be warped when checked or when using the front brake.

8 Mount the disc on the wheel making sure it is the correct way round, and on Daytona, Speed Triple and Sprint models, on the correct side (see Step 5). Align the previously applied matchmarks (if you're reinstalling the original disc).

9 Install new bolts and tighten them evenly and a little at a time in a criss-cross pattern to

**4.2 Set up a dial gauge with the probe contacting the brake disc, then rotate the wheel to check for runout**

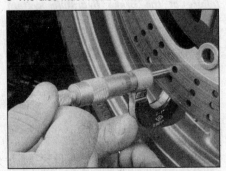

**4.3 Using a micrometer to measure disc thickness**

**4.6 Unscrew the bolts (arrowed) and remove the disc**

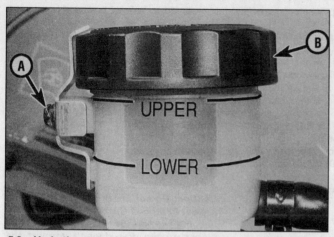

5.3a Undo the screw (A) and remove the clamp, then slacken the cap (B)

5.3b Slacken the reservoir cover screws

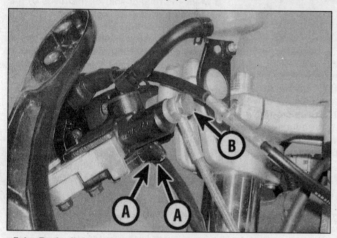

5.4a Brake light switch wiring connectors (A), brake hose banjo bolt (B) – Daytona shown

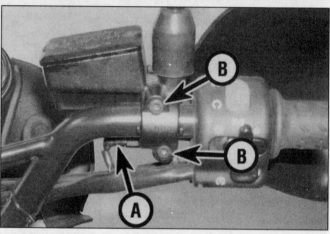

5.4b Brake light switch wiring connectors (A), master cylinder clamp bolts (B) – Tiger models

the torque setting specified at the beginning of the Chapter (see illustration 4.6). Clean off all grease from the brake disc using acetone or brake system cleaner. If a new brake disc has been installed, remove any protective coating from its working surfaces.

10 Install the front wheel (see Section 13).

11 Operate the brake lever several times to bring the pads into contact with the disc. Check the operation of the brake carefully before riding the bike.

## 5 Front brake master cylinder

1 If the master cylinder is leaking fluid, or if the lever does not produce a firm feel when the brake is applied, and bleeding the brakes does not help (see Section 10), and the hydraulic hoses and the brake calipers are all in good condition, then master cylinder overhaul is recommended.

2 Before disassembling the master cylinder, read through the entire procedure and make sure that you have the correct rebuild kit.

Also, you will need some new DOT 4 brake fluid, some clean rags and internal circlip pliers. Note: *To prevent damage to the paintwork from spilled brake fluid, always cover the fuel tank and surrounding areas when working on the master cylinder.*
Caution: *Disassembly, overhaul and reassembly of the brake master cylinder must be done in a spotlessly clean work area to avoid contamination and possible failure of the brake hydraulic system components.*

### Removal

3 On Daytona, Speed Triple and Sprint models, remove the reservoir cap clamp and partially unscrew the cap (see illustration). On Tiger models, slacken the reservoir cover screws, but do not yet remove them (see illustration).

4 Disconnect the brake light switch wiring connectors (see illustrations).

5 If the master cylinder is being overhauled, remove the front brake lever (see Chapter 5). If it is just being displaced it can remain in situ.

6 If the master cylinder is being completely removed or overhauled, place some rags

under and around it, then unscrew the brake hose banjo bolt and separate the hose from the master cylinder, noting its alignment (see illustration or 5.4a). Discard the sealing washers as they must be replaced with new ones. Wrap the end of the hose in a clean rag and suspend it in an upright position or bend it down carefully and place the open end in a clean container. The objective is to prevent excessive loss of brake fluid, fluid spills and system contamination. Also wrap a rag

5.6 Brake hose banjo bolt (arrowed) – Tiger models

**5.7 Reservoir mounting bolt (arrowed) – Sprint shown**

**5.8 Front brake master cylinder clamp bolts (arrowed) – Daytona shown**

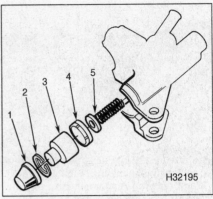

H32195

**5.11a Front master cylinder components – Daytona, Speed Triple and Sprint models**

1 Rubber boot     4 Cup
2 Circlip     5 Spring
3 Piston

around the master cylinder fluid outlet. If the master cylinder is just being displaced and not completely removed or overhauled, do not disconnect the brake hose.

**7** On Daytona, Speed Triple and Sprint models, unscrew the bolt securing the reservoir to its mounting bracket **(see illustration)**. Temporarily support the reservoir upright.

**8** Unscrew the master cylinder clamp bolts, then lift the master cylinder and reservoir away from the handlebar **(see illustration or 5.4b)**.

**9** On Daytona, Speed Triple and Sprint models, remove the reservoir cap, the diaphragm plate and the rubber diaphragm. On Tiger models, remove the reservoir cover and the rubber diaphragm. Drain the brake fluid from the reservoir into a suitable container. On Daytona, Speed Triple and Sprint models, release the clamp securing the reservoir hose to the union on the master cylinder, then detach the hose. Wipe any remaining fluid out of the reservoir with a clean rag.

**10** If required, remove the screw securing the brake light switch to the underside of the master cylinder and remove the switch.

*Caution: Do not tip the master cylinder upside down or brake fluid will run out.*

## Overhaul

**11** Carefully remove the dust boot from the master cylinder, noting how it locates **(see illustrations)**.

**12** Using circlip pliers, remove the circlip and slide out the piston assembly and the spring, noting how they fit **(see illustration)**. If they are difficult to remove, apply low pressure compressed air to the fluid outlet. Lay the parts out in the proper order to prevent confusion during reassembly.

**13** Clean all parts with clean brake fluid. If compressed air is available, use it to dry the parts thoroughly (make sure it's filtered and unlubricated).

*Caution: Do not, under any circumstances, use a petroleum-based solvent to clean brake parts.*

**14** Check the master cylinder bore for corrosion, scratches, nicks and score marks. If damage or wear is evident, the master

cylinder must be replaced with a new one. If the master cylinder is in poor condition, then the calipers should be checked as well. Check that the fluid inlet and outlet ports in the master cylinder are clear.

**15** The dust boot, circlip, piston assembly and spring are included in the rebuild kit. Use all of the new parts, regardless of the apparent condition of the old ones. Fit them according to the layout of the old piston assembly **(see illustration 5.11a or b)**.

**16** Fit the spring into the master cylinder.

**17** Lubricate the piston assembly with clean brake fluid. Fit the assembly into the master cylinder, making sure it is the correct way round. Make sure the lips on the cup do not turn inside out when they are slipped into the

bore. Depress the piston and install the new circlip, making sure that it locates in the groove **(see illustration 5.12)**.

**18** Install the rubber dust boot, making sure the lip is seated correctly in the groove **(see illustration 5.11c)**.

**19** Inspect the reservoir rubber diaphragm and renew it if it is damaged or deteriorated. On Daytona, Speed Triple and Sprint models, inspect the reservoir hose for cracks or splits and renew if necessary.

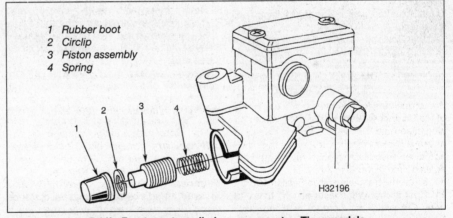

1 Rubber boot
2 Circlip
3 Piston assembly
4 Spring

H32196

**5.11b Front master cylinder components – Tiger models**

**5.11c Remove the rubber boot from the end of the master cylinder piston . . .**

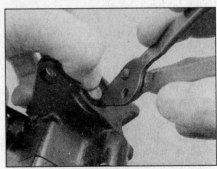

**5.12 . . . then depress the piston and remove the circlip using a pair of internal circlip pliers**

**5.21 Align the mating surfaces of the clamp with the punchmark (arrowed) on the handlebar**

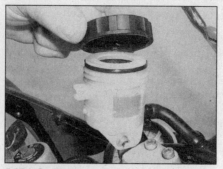

**5.27a On Daytona, Speed Triple and Sprint models, fit the diaphragm, plate and cap and secure them with the clamp**

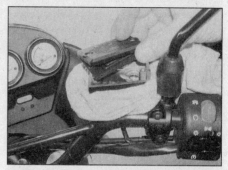

**5.27b On Tiger models, fit the diaphragm and cover and secure them with the screws**

## Installation

**20** If removed, fit the brake light switch onto the underside of the master cylinder.

**21** Attach the master cylinder to the handlebar and fit the clamp with its 'UP' mark facing up, aligning the top mating surfaces of the clamp with the punchmark on the handlebar **(see illustration)**. Tighten the upper bolt first, then the lower bolt to the torque setting specified at the beginning of the Chapter.

**22** If detached, connect the brake hose to the master cylinder, using new sealing washers on each side of the union, and aligning the hose as noted on removal **(see illustration 5.4a or 5.6)**. Tighten the banjo bolt to the torque setting specified at the beginning of the Chapter.

**23** If removed, install the brake lever (see Chapter 5).

**24** On Daytona, Speed Triple and Sprint models, mount the reservoir and tighten the bolt securely **(see illustration 5.7)**. Connect the reservoir hose to the union on the master cylinder and secure it with the clamp.

**25** Connect the brake light switch wiring connectors **(see illustration 5.4a or b)**.

**26** Fill the fluid reservoir with new DOT 4 brake fluid as described in *Daily (pre-ride) checks*. Refer to Section 10 of this Chapter and bleed the air from the system.

**27** Fit the rubber diaphragm, making sure it is correctly seated, the diaphragm plate (except Tiger models) and the cap or cover onto the master cylinder reservoir, then fit the cap clamp or tighten the cover screws, according to model **(see illustrations)**.

**28** Check the operation of the front brake before riding the motorcycle.

---

## 6   Rear brake caliper

⚠️ **Warning: If a caliper indicates the need for an overhaul (usually due to leaking fluid or sticky operation), all old brake fluid should be flushed from the system. Also, the dust created by the brake system may contain asbestos, which is harmful to your health.**

*Never blow it out with compressed air and don't inhale any of it. An approved filtering mask should be worn when working on the brakes. Do not, under any circumstances, use petroleum-based solvents to clean brake parts. Use the specified clean brake fluid, dedicated brake cleaner or denatured alcohol only, as described.*

**1** If the caliper is leaking fluid, or the brake pads are wearing unevenly due to a sticky or seized piston (first check that this is not due to misalignment of the caliper on the disc), or if the brake pedal produces a firm feel when the brake is applied but the brakes are no good, and the hydraulic hoses and the master cylinder are all in good condition, then the caliper must be overhauled.

**2** Before disassembling the caliper, read through the entire procedure and make sure that you have a new seal kit. Also, you will need some new DOT 4 brake fluid and some clean rags.

*Caution: Disassembly, overhaul and reassembly of the caliper must be done in a spotlessly clean work area to avoid contamination and possible failure of the brake hydraulic system components.*

### All models except 2002 Daytona models

#### Removal

**3** On Daytona, Speed Triple, Sprint ST models and Sprint RS models with single-sided swingarms, remove the rear wheel (see Section 14). **Note:** *Although the caliper can be*

**6.5 Brake hose banjo bolt (arrowed) – Tiger models**

*displaced and the pads removed with the wheel in situ, access to the caliper mounting bolts is restricted, and there is little clearance between the wheel and the caliper when removing it – it is too easy to scratch the wheel, so it is best to remove it.* On Sprint RS models with a twin-sided swingarm, remove the exhaust silencer for best access to the pad retaining pins and caliper mounting bolts, if required (see Chapter 4).

**4** If the caliper is being overhauled, remove the brake pads (see Section 2). If the caliper is just being displaced or removed, the pads can be left in place.

**5** If the caliper is just being displaced and not completely removed or overhauled, do not disconnect the brake hose. If the caliper is being completely removed or overhauled, remove the brake hose banjo bolt and detach the hose, noting the alignment with the caliper **(see illustration or 2.14a or b)**. Plug the hose end or wrap a plastic bag tightly around to minimise fluid loss and prevent dirt entering the system. Discard the sealing washers as new ones must be used on installation. **Note:** *If you are planning to overhaul the caliper and don't have a source of compressed air to blow out the pistons, just loosen the banjo bolt at this stage and retighten it lightly. The bike's hydraulic system can then be used to force the pistons out of the body once the pads have been removed. Disconnect the hose once the pistons have been sufficiently displaced.*

**6** Unscrew the caliper mounting bolts and slide the caliper off the disc **(see illustrations)**.

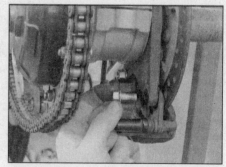

**6.6a On Daytona, Speed Triple and Sprint ST, unscrew the mounting bolts . . .**

**6.6b . . . and slide the caliper off the disc**

**6.6c  Caliper mounting bolts (arrowed) –
Sprint RS models**

**6.6d  Removing the caliper – Tiger models**

## Overhaul

**7** Clean the exterior of the caliper with denatured alcohol or brake system cleaner **(see illustration)**.

**8** Separate the bracket from the caliper by sliding them apart **(see illustration 2.17a or 2.25)**. On Tiger models, and if not already done on all other models, remove the pad spring from the caliper, noting how it fits **(see illustration or 2.14f)**. Displace the pistons either by pumping them out by operating the brake pedal, or by easing them out using compressed air. Mark each piston head and caliper body with a felt marker to ensure that the pistons can be matched to their original bores on reassembly. If the compressed air method is used, direct the air into the fluid inlet. Use only low pressure to ease the pistons out and make sure both pistons are displaced at the same time. If the air pressure is too high and the pistons are forced out, the caliper and/or pistons may be damaged.

⚠ **Warning: Never place your fingers in front of the pistons in an attempt to catch or protect them when applying compressed air, as serious injury could result.**
*Caution: Do not try to remove the pistons by levering them out, or by using pliers or any other grips.*

**9** Using a wooden or plastic tool, remove the dust seals from the caliper bores, noting which way round they fit **(see illustration 3.10)**. Discard them as new ones must be used on installation. If a metal tool is being used, take great care not to mark the caliper bores.

**10** Remove and discard the piston seals in the same way.

**11** Clean the pistons and bores with clean brake fluid of the specified type. If compressed air is available, use it to dry the parts thoroughly (make sure it's filtered and unlubricated).

*Caution: Do not, under any circumstances, use a petroleum-based solvent to clean brake parts.*

**12** Inspect the caliper bores and pistons for signs of corrosion, nicks and burrs and loss of plating. If surface defects are present, the caliper assembly must be renewed. If the caliper is in bad shape the master cylinder should also be checked.

**13** Lubricate the new piston seals with clean brake fluid and install them in the lower grooves in the caliper bores.

**14** Lubricate the new dust seals with clean brake fluid and install them in the upper grooves in the caliper bores.

**15** Lubricate the pistons with clean brake

fluid and install them closed-end first into the caliper bores. Using your thumbs, push the pistons all the way in, making sure they enter the bore squarely without dislodging the seals.

**16** Check that the caliper body is able to slide freely on the slider pins on the bracket. Clean off all traces of corrosion and hardened grease. Check the rubber boots in the caliper. If they are damaged or deteriorated, they should be replaced with new ones (but check with a Triumph dealer as they do not list them as being available separately). Apply a smear of copper or silicone based grease to the slider pins. Slide the bracket back onto the caliper.

**17** Fit the pad spring back into the caliper, making sure it locates correctly **(see illustrations 2.14f and 2.17b)**.

## Installation

**18** If not already done, carry out the checks in Step 16.

**19** If necessary, push the pistons a little way back into the caliper using hand pressure or a piece of wood as leverage.

**20** If removed, install the brake pads (see Section 2).

**21** Slide the caliper onto the brake disc, making sure the pads sit squarely each side of the disc **(see illustrations 6.6b, or 6.6d)**. Install the caliper mounting bolts and tighten them to the torque setting specified at the beginning of the Chapter.

**22** If removed, connect the brake hose to the caliper, using new sealing washers on each side of the union. Align the hose as noted on removal **(see illustration 2.14b or 6.5)**.

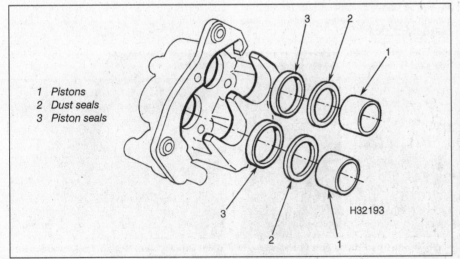

1  Pistons
2  Dust seals
3  Piston seals

H32193

**6.7  Rear brake caliper components**

**6.8  Pad spring (arrowed) – Tiger models**

**6.27 Note the alignment of the union (arrowed) with the caliper**

Tighten the banjo bolt to the torque setting specified at the beginning of the Chapter.

23 On Daytona, Speed Triple and Sprint ST models, install the rear wheel if removed (see Section 14). On Sprint RS models, install the exhaust silencer if removed (see Chapter 4).

24 Top up the master cylinder reservoir with DOT 4 brake fluid (see *Daily (pre-ride) checks*) and bleed the hydraulic system as described in Section 10. Check that there are no leaks and thoroughly test the operation of the brake before riding the motorcycle.

### 2002 Daytona models

#### Removal

25 Remove the exhaust silencer for best access to the pad retaining pin and caliper mounting bolts, if required (see Chapter 4).

26 If the caliper is being overhauled, remove the brake pads (see Section 2). If the caliper is just being displaced or removed, the pads can be left in place.

27 If the caliper is just being displaced and not completely removed or overhauled, do not disconnect the brake hose. If the caliper is being completely removed or overhauled, remove the brake hose banjo bolt and detach the hose, noting the alignment of the union with the caliper **(see illustration)**. Plug the hose end or wrap a plastic bag tightly around to minimise fluid loss and prevent dirt entering the system. Discard the sealing washers as

new ones must be used on installation. **Note:** *If you are planning to overhaul the caliper and don't have a source of compressed air to blow out the piston, just loosen the banjo bolt at this stage and retighten it lightly. The bike's hydraulic system can then be used to force the piston out of the body once the pads have been removed. Disconnect the hose once the piston has been sufficiently displaced.*

28 Unscrew the caliper mounting bolts and slide the caliper off the disc **(see illustration 2.18a)**.

#### Overhaul

29 Remove the pad spring from the caliper, noting how it fits **(see illustration or 2.18b)**.

30 Clean the exterior of the caliper with denatured alcohol or brake system cleaner.

31 Displace the piston either by pumping it out by operating the brake pedal, or by easing it out using compressed air. If the compressed air method is used, direct the air into the fluid inlet. Use only low pressure to ease the piston out – if the air pressure is too high and the piston is forced out, the caliper and/or piston may be damaged.

⚠ **Warning: Never place your fingers in front of the piston in an attempt to catch or protect it when applying compressed air, as serious injury could result.**
**Caution: Do not try to remove the piston by levering it out, or by using pliers or any other grips.**

32 Follow the procedure in Steps 9 to 15 to inspect the caliper bore and piston and to install new piston and dust seals.

33 Clean off all traces of corrosion and hardened grease from the caliper mounting bolts. Check the rubber boots in the caliper and the caliper bracket. If they are damaged or deteriorated, they should be replaced with new ones (the boots, internal spacers and mounting bolts are listed as an overhaul kit). Apply a smear of copper or silicone based grease to the mounting bolts.

34 Fit the pad spring back into the caliper, making sure it locates correctly **(see illustration 2.18b)**.

35 If necessary, push the piston a little way back into the caliper using hand pressure or a piece of wood as leverage.

36 Install the caliper onto the disc and install the pads in the caliper (see Section 2). Tighten the mounting bolts and the pad retaining pin to the torque setting specified at the beginning of the Chapter. Install the pad retaining pin plug.

37 If removed, connect the brake hose to the caliper, using new sealing washers on each side of the union. Align the hose as noted on removal **(see illustration 6.27)**. Tighten the banjo bolt to the torque setting specified at the beginning of the Chapter.

38 Top up the master cylinder reservoir with DOT 4 brake fluid (see *Daily (pre-ride) checks*) and bleed the hydraulic system as described in Section 10. Check that there are no leaks and thoroughly test the operation of the brake before riding the motorcycle.

39 Install the exhaust silencer if removed (see Chapter 4).

---

### 7  Rear brake disc

#### Inspection

1 Refer to Section 4 of this Chapter, noting that the dial gauge should be attached to the swingarm.

#### Removal

2 Remove the rear wheel (see Section 14).

3 On Daytona, Speed Triple, Sprint ST models and Sprint RS models with a single-sided swingarm, unscrew the bolts securing the chainguards and remove them. Have an assistant apply the rear brake hard, then slacken the sprocket coupling nut **(see illustration)**. Displace the rear caliper (see Section 6). Slacken the drive chain adjuster clamp bolt **(see illustration)**. Remove the coupling nut and its washer, noting which way round it fits, then slide the sprocket coupling off the axle and disengage it from the chain

**7.3a  Apply the rear brake and slacken the nut (arrowed)**

**7.3b  Slacken the clamp bolt (arrowed)**

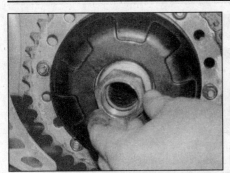

7.3c  Remove the nut . . .

7.3d  . . . and the dished washer, noting which way round it fits

7.3e  Slide the sprocket coupling off the axle and disengage the chain

7.3f  Remove the spacer for safekeeping if required

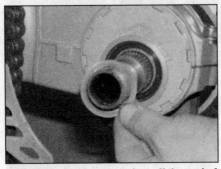

7.3g  Slide the thrust washer off the end of the axle . . .

7.3h  . . . then draw the axle/disc carrier out of the hub

(see illustrations). Note the shouldered spacer in the outside of the coupling and remove it for safekeeping if required (see illustration). Slide the thrust washer off the end of the axle, then draw the axle/disc carrier out of the hub, noting which way round it fits (see illustrations). Note that Triumph specify to use a new sprocket coupling nut on installation.

**4** On all models, mark the relationship of the disc to the carrier or wheel, and note which side of the carrier the disc sits on, so it can be installed in the same position (unless you are fitting a new disc).

**5** Unscrew the disc retaining bolts, loosening them evenly and a little at a time in a criss-cross pattern to avoid distorting the disc, then remove the disc from the carrier or wheel (see illustration). On Daytona, Speed Triple, Sprint ST models and Sprint RS models with a single-sided swingarm, you may have to counter-hold the nuts. Discard the bolts as Triumph specify that new ones should be used.

### Installation

**6** Before installing the disc, make sure there is no dirt or corrosion where the disc seats on the hub, particularly right in the angle of the seat, as this will not allow the disc to sit flat when it is bolted down and it will appear to be warped when checked or when using the rear brake.

**7** Mount the disc on the carrier or wheel making sure it is the correct way round, and on Daytona, Speed Triple and Sprint models, on the correct side (see illustration 7.5). Align the previously applied matchmarks (if you're reinstalling the original disc).

**8** Install new bolts (on Daytona, Speed Triple, Sprint ST models and Sprint RS models with a single-sided swingarm the nuts can be reused), then tighten them evenly and a little at a time in a criss-cross pattern to the torque setting specified at the beginning of the Chapter. Clean off all grease from the brake disc using acetone or brake system cleaner. If a new

brake disc has been installed, remove any protective coating from its working surfaces.

**9** On Daytona, Speed Triple, Sprint ST models and Sprint RS models with a single-sided swingarm, slide the axle/disc carrier fully into the hub, making sure it is the correct way round (see illustration 7.3h). Fit the shouldered spacer into the outside of the sprocket coupling if removed (see illustration 7.3f). Slide the thrust washer onto the axle (see illustration 7.3g). Fit the sprocket coupling into the chain and slide it onto the axle (see illustration). Fit the dished washer so that its outer rim is against the spacer and the inner rim is raised off it, then fit the nut and tighten it finger-tight (see illustrations 7.3d and c). Install the brake caliper (see Section 6). Tighten the coupling nut to the torque setting specified at the beginning of the Chapter, applying the rear brake to prevent the coupling turning. Stake the rim of the nut into the cutout in the end of the axle (see illustration).

7.5  Rear disc bolts (arrowed) – Daytona, Speed Triple and Sprint ST models

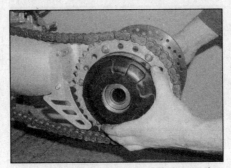

7.9a  Slide the sprocket coupling onto the axle

7.9b  Stake the rim of the nut against the detent in the axle

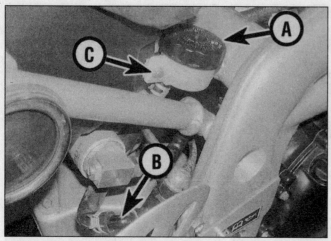

8.4a Reservoir cap (A), hose union (B) and reservoir bolt (C) – Daytona

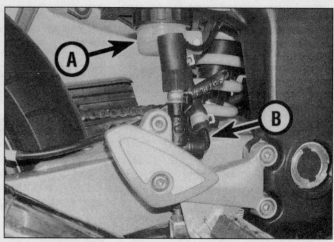

8.4b Reservoir (A) and hose union (B) – Sprint

**10** Install the rear wheel (see Section 14). Refer to Chapter 1 and adjust the drive chain slack.

**11** Operate the brake pedal several times to bring the pads into contact with the disc. Check the operation of the brake carefully before riding the motorcycle.

## 8 Rear brake master cylinder

**1** If the master cylinder is leaking fluid, or if the pedal does not produce a firm feel when the brake is applied, and bleeding the brake does not help (see Section 10), and the hydraulic hose and brake caliper are in good condition, then master cylinder overhaul is recommended.

**2** Before disassembling the master cylinder, read through the entire procedure and make sure that you obtain any replacement parts required. Also, you will need some new DOT 4 brake fluid, some clean rags and internal circlip pliers. **Note:** *To prevent damage to the paintwork from spilled brake fluid, always cover the surrounding components when working on the master cylinder.*
**Caution: Disassembly, overhaul and reassembly of the brake master cylinder must be done in a spotlessly clean work**

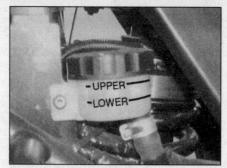

8.4c Reservoir . . .

8.4d . . . and hose union (arrowed) – Tiger

*area to avoid contamination and possible failure of the brake hydraulic system components.*

### Removal

**3** On Daytona, Speed Triple and Sprint models, remove the seat cowling, and on Tiger models remove the right-hand side panel (see Chapter 7).

**4** Place some rags around the master cylinder and prepare a small container to hold some brake fluid. Remove the reservoir cap, diaphragm plate and diaphragm **(see illustrations)**. Release the clamp securing the reservoir hose to the union on the master cylinder and detach the hose, pinching its end

as you do to retain the fluid, then place the end in the container and allow the reservoir to drain. Refit the diaphragm, plate and cap.

**5** Remove the bolt securing the reservoir to the frame and remove it, being prepared to catch any drops from the end of the hose.

**6** Remove the retaining clip from the clevis pin securing the master cylinder pushrod to the brake pedal **(see illustrations)**. Withdraw the clevis pin and separate the pushrod from the pedal.

**7** On Sprint and Tiger models, displace the rubber boot from the top of the master cylinder and detach the brake light switch wiring connectors **(see illustration)**.

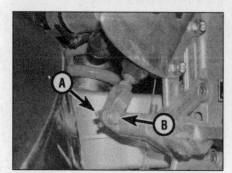

8.6a Remove the retaining clip (A) and slide out the clevis pin (B)

8.6b On Tiger models, access to the clevis (arrowed) is restricted

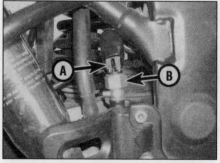

8.7 Brake light switch wiring connectors (A), brake light switch (B) – Tiger shown

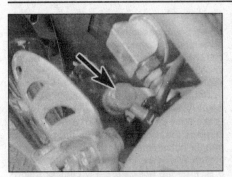

**8.8a Note the alignment of the hose before removing the banjo bolt (arrowed) or switch**

**8.8b On Sprint models, note how the hose butts against the lug (arrowed)**

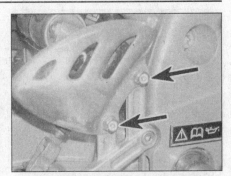

**8.9a Master cylinder mounting bolts (arrowed) – Daytona and Speed Triple**

**8.9b Master cylinder mounting bolts (arrowed) – Sprint**

**8.9c Master cylinder mounting bolts (arrowed) – Tiger**

**8.10 Hold the clevis and slacken the locknut**

**8** Unscrew the brake hose banjo bolt or brake light switch and separate the brake hose from the master cylinder, noting its alignment **(see illustrations)**. Discard the two sealing washers as they must be replaced with new ones. Wrap the end of the hose in a clean rag and suspend the hose in an upright position or bend it down carefully and place the open end in a clean container. The objective is to prevent excessive loss of brake fluid, fluid spills and system contamination.

**9** Unscrew the two bolts securing the master cylinder to the footrest bracket and remove the master cylinder, on Daytona and Speed Triple models noting how the bottom bolt secures the brake light switch, and that there is an equivalent spacer with the top bolt, both fitting between the cylinder and the footrest bracket, and also how the bolts secure the heel guard **(see illustrations)**.

### Overhaul

**10** If required, mark the position of the clevis locknut on the pushrod, then slacken the locknut and thread the clevis and nut off the pushrod **(see illustration)**.

**11** Dislodge the rubber dust boot from the base of the master cylinder to reveal the pushrod retaining circlip **(see illustration)**.

**12** Depress the pushrod and, using circlip pliers, remove the circlip **(see illustration)**. Slide out the pushrod, piston assembly and spring **(see illustration)**. If they are difficult to remove, apply low pressure compressed air to the fluid outlet. Lay the parts out in the proper order to prevent confusion during reassembly.

**13** Clean all of the parts with clean brake fluid.

*Caution: Do not, under any circumstances, use a petroleum-based solvent to clean*

*brake parts. If compressed air is available, use it to dry the parts thoroughly (make sure it's filtered and unlubricated).*

**14** Check the master cylinder bore for corrosion, scratches, nicks and score marks. If damage is evident, the master cylinder must be replaced with a new one. If the master cylinder is in poor condition, then the caliper should be checked as well.

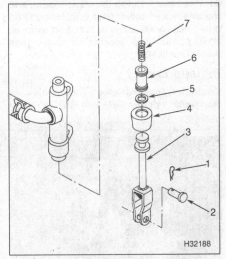

**8.12b Rear master cylinder components**

| | |
|---|---|
| 1 Retaining clip | 5 Circlip |
| 2 Clevis pin | 6 Piston assembly |
| 3 Push rod | 7 Spring |
| 4 Rubber boot | |

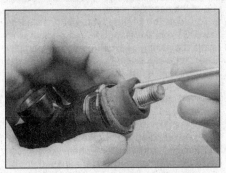

**8.11 Remove the dust boot from the bottom of the master cylinder**

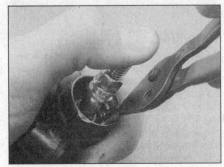

**8.12a Depress the pushrod and remove the circlip**

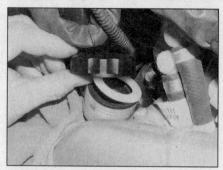

**8.28 Fit the diaphragm, plate and cap**

15 Inspect the reservoir hose for cracks or splits and replace it with a new one if necessary. If required, remove the circlip securing the hose union to the master cylinder and pull the union out. Discard the O-ring as a new one must be used.

16 Install a new piston and spring, regardless of the apparent condition of the old ones. Fit them according to the layout of the old piston assembly **(see illustration 8.12b)**.

17 Fit the spring into the master cylinder.

18 Lubricate the piston assembly with clean brake fluid. Fit the assembly into the master cylinder, making sure it is the correct way round. Make sure the lips on the cup do not turn inside out when they are slipped into the bore.

19 Fit the new rubber boot onto the rod and locate the lower rim in its groove. Install and depress the pushrod, then fit a new circlip, making sure it is properly seated in the groove **(see illustration 8.12a)**. Fit the inner rim of the boot into the groove in the master cylinder **(see illustration 8.11)**.

20 If removed, fit a new reservoir hose union O-ring, then push the union into the master cylinder and secure it with the circlip.

21 If removed, thread the clevis locknut and the clevis onto the master cylinder pushrod end. Position the clevis as noted on removal, then tighten the locknut securely **(see illustration 8.10)**.

### Installation

22 On Daytona and Speed Triple models, fit the master cylinder bolts into the heel guard

**9.4 Remove the banjo bolt and separate the hose from the caliper; there is a sealing washer on each side of the fitting**

and locate it on the footrest bracket. Fit the brake light switch onto the lower bolt, aligning it correctly, and the equivalent spacer onto the top bolt. Locate the master cylinder and tighten the bolts to the torque setting specified at the beginning of the Chapter **(see illustration 8.9a)**.

23 On Sprint and Tiger models, fit the master cylinder onto the footrest bracket and tighten its mounting bolts to the torque setting specified at the beginning of the Chapter **(see illustration 8.9b or 8.9c)**.

24 Connect the brake hose to the master cylinder, using new sealing washers on each side of the union, and aligning the hose as noted on removal **(see illustration 8.8a and b)**. Tighten the banjo bolt or brake light switch to the torque setting specified at the beginning of the Chapter. On Sprint and Tiger models, connect the brake light switch wiring connectors, then fit the rubber boot over them **(see illustration 8.7)**.

25 Install the reservoir and secure it with the bolt. Ensure that the hose is correctly routed, then connect it to the union on the master cylinder and secure it with the clamp **(see illustration 8.4a, 8.4b or 8.4c and d)**. Check that the hose is secure and clamped at the reservoir end as well. If the clamps have weakened, use new ones.

26 Align the brake pedal with the master cylinder pushrod clevis, then slide in the clevis pin and secure it with the retaining clip **(see illustration 8.6a or b)**.

27 Fill the fluid reservoir with new DOT 4 brake fluid (see *Daily (pre-ride) checks*) and bleed the system following the procedure in Section 10.

28 Fit the rubber diaphragm, making sure it is correctly seated, the diaphragm plate and the cap onto the master cylinder reservoir **(see illustration)**.

29 On Daytona, Speed Triple and Sprint models, install the seat cowling, and on Tiger models install the right-hand side panel (see Chapter 7).

30 Check the operation of the brake carefully before riding the motorcycle.

## 9 Brake hoses and unions

### Inspection

1 Brake hose condition should be checked regularly and the hoses renewed at the specified interval (see Chapter 1).

2 Twist and flex the hoses while looking for cracks, bulges and seeping fluid. Check extra carefully around the areas where the hoses connect with the banjo fittings, as these are common areas for hose failure.

3 Check the banjo union fittings connected to the brake hoses. If the union fittings are rusted, scratched or cracked, fit new hoses.

### Renewal

4 The brake hoses have banjo union fittings on each end. Cover the surrounding area with plenty of rags and unscrew the banjo bolt at each end of the hose or pipe, noting its alignment **(see illustration)**. Note that on Sprint and Tiger models, the hose from the rear brake master cylinder is secured by the brake light switch instead of a banjo bolt – displace the rubber boot from the top of the master cylinder and detach the brake light switch wiring connectors **(see illustration 8.7)**. Free the hose from any clips or guides and remove it, noting its routing. Discard the sealing washers on the hose unions.

5 Position the new hose, making sure it isn't twisted or otherwise strained, and abut the tab on the hose union with the lug on the component casting, where present. Otherwise align the hose as noted on removal. Install the hose banjo bolts using new sealing washers on both sides of the unions. Tighten the banjo bolts (or brake light switch) to the torque setting specified at the beginning of this Chapter. Make sure the hoses are correctly aligned and routed clear of all moving components.

6 Flush the old brake fluid from the system, refill with new DOT 4 brake fluid (see *Daily (pre-ride) checks*) and bleed the air from the system (see Section 10). Check the operation of the brakes carefully before riding the motorcycle.

## 10 Brake bleeding and fluid change

### Air bleeding

1 Bleeding the brakes is simply the process of removing all the air bubbles from the brake fluid reservoirs, the hoses and the brake calipers. Bleeding is necessary whenever a brake system hydraulic connection is loosened, when a component or hose is replaced or renewed, or when the master cylinder or caliper is overhauled. Leaks in the system may also allow air to enter, but leaking brake fluid will reveal their presence and warn you of the need for repair.

2 To bleed the brakes, you will need some new DOT 4 brake fluid, a length of clear vinyl or plastic tubing, a small container partially filled with clean brake fluid, some rags and a ring spanner to fit the brake caliper bleed valves.

3 Cover the fuel tank and other painted components to prevent damage in the event that brake fluid is spilled.

4 When bleeding the brakes, look for any 'high spots' in the system where air bubbles could become trapped and eliminate them by displacing the component and positioning it where bubbles are less likely to get trapped.

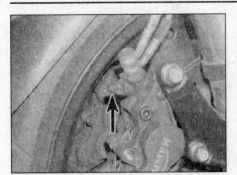

**10.6a Front brake caliper bleed valve (arrowed) – Daytona, Speed Triple and Sprint models**

**10.6b Rear brake caliper bleed valve (arrowed) – Tiger models**

**10.6c To bleed the brakes, you need a spanner, a short section of clear tubing, and a clear container half-filled with brake fluid**

Wiggling or tapping any such spots will help to dislodge any bubbles already trapped.

**5** Remove the reservoir cap clamp where fitted, cap or cover, diaphragm plate (where fitted) and diaphragm **(see illustrations 5.27a or b (front) or 8.28 (rear))**. Slowly pump the brake lever or pedal a few times, until no air bubbles can be seen floating up from the holes in the bottom of the reservoir. This bleeds the air from the master cylinder end of the line. Loosely refit the reservoir cap or cover.

**6** Pull the dust cap off the bleed valve **(see illustrations)**. Attach one end of the clear vinyl or plastic tubing to the bleed valve and submerge the other end in the brake fluid in the container **(see illustration)**.

**7** Remove the reservoir cap and check the fluid level. Do not allow the fluid level to drop below the lower mark during the bleeding process.

**8** Carefully pump the brake lever or pedal three or four times and hold it in (front) or down (rear) while opening the caliper bleed valve. When the valve is opened, brake fluid will flow out of the caliper into the clear tubing and the lever will move toward the handlebar or the pedal will move down.

**9** Retighten the bleed valve, then release the brake lever or pedal gradually. Repeat the process until no air bubbles are visible in the brake fluid leaving the caliper, or if the fluid is being changed until new fluid is coming out, and the lever or pedal is firm when applied. On completion, disconnect the bleeding equipment, then tighten the bleed valve to the torque setting specified at the beginning of the Chapter and install the dust cap.

**HAYNES HINT** *Old brake fluid is invariably much darker in colour than new fluid, making it easy to see when all old fluid has been expelled from the system.*

**10** Install the diaphragm, plate (where fitted) and cap or cover. Wipe up any spilled brake fluid and check the entire system for leaks.

**HAYNES HINT** *If it's not possible to produce a firm feel to the lever or pedal the fluid may be aerated. Let the brake fluid in the system stabilise for a few hours and then repeat the procedure when the tiny bubbles in the system have settled out.*

### Fluid change

**11** Changing the brake fluid is a similar process to bleeding the brakes and requires the same materials plus a suitable tool for siphoning the fluid out of the hydraulic reservoir. Also ensure that the container is large enough to take all the old fluid when it is flushed out of the system.

**12** Follow Steps 3, 4 and 6 above, then remove the reservoir cap clamp where fitted, cap or cover, diaphragm plate (where fitted) and diaphragm and siphon the old fluid out of the reservoir. Fill the reservoir with new brake fluid, then follow Step 8.

**13** Retighten the bleed valve, then release the brake lever or pedal gradually. Keep the reservoir topped-up with new fluid to above the LOWER level at all times or air may enter the system and greatly increase the length of the task. Repeat the process until new fluid can be seen emerging from the bleed valve.

**14** Disconnect the hose, tighten the bleed valve to the specified torque and install the dust cap.

**15** Top-up the reservoir, install the diaphragm, plate (where fitted) and cap or cover, wipe up any spilled brake fluid and check the entire system for leaks.

**16** Check the operation of the brakes before riding the motorcycle.

### 11 Wheel inspection and repair

**1** In order to carry out a proper inspection of the wheels, it is necessary to support the bike upright so that the wheel being inspected is raised off the ground. Position the motorcycle on an auxiliary stand. Clean the wheels thoroughly to remove mud and dirt that may interfere with the inspection procedure or mask defects. Make a general check of the wheels (see Chapter 1) and tyres (see *Daily (pre-ride) checks*).

**2** Attach a dial gauge to the fork or the swingarm and position its tip against the side of the rim **(see illustration)**. Spin the wheel slowly and check the axial (side-to-side) runout of the rim. In order to accurately check radial (out of round) runout with the dial gauge, the wheel would have to be removed from the machine, and the tyre from the wheel. With the axle clamped in a vice and the dial gauge positioned on the top of the rim, the wheel can be rotated to check the runout.

**3** An easier, though slightly less accurate, method is to attach a stiff wire pointer to the fork or the swingarm and position the end a fraction of an inch from the wheel (where the wheel and tyre join). If the wheel is true, the distance from the pointer to the rim will be constant as the wheel is rotated. **Note:** *If*

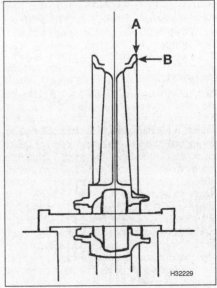

**11.2 Check the wheel for radial (out-of-round) runout (A) and axial (side-to-side) runout (B)**

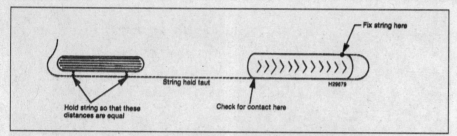

**12.5 Wheel alignment check using string**

*wheel runout is excessive, check the wheel bearings very carefully before renewing the wheel.*

**4** The wheels should also be visually inspected for cracks, flat spots on the rim and other damage. On cast wheels, look very closely for dents in the area where the tyre bead contacts the rim. Dents in this area may prevent complete sealing of the tyre against the rim, which leads to deflation of the tyre over a period of time. If damage is evident, or if runout in either direction is excessive, the wheel will have to be replaced with a new one. Never attempt to repair a damaged cast alloy wheel.

**5** On spoked wheels (1999 to 2004 Tiger models), check for loose or broken spokes as described in Chapter 1, Section 12. Spoke renewal and tensioning must be carried out by a wheel building specialist.

## 12 Wheel alignment check

**1** Misalignment of the wheels, which may be due to a cocked rear wheel or a bent frame or fork yokes, can cause strange and possibly serious handling problems. If the frame or yokes are at fault, repair by a frame specialist or replacement with new parts are the only alternatives.

**2** To check the alignment you will need an assistant, a length of string or a perfectly straight piece of wood and a ruler. A plumb bob or other suitable weight will also be required.

**3** In order to make a proper check of the wheels it is necessary to support the bike in an upright position, using an auxiliary stand (or on its centrestand – Sprint ST). Measure the width of both tyres at their widest points. Subtract the smaller measurement from the larger measurement, then divide the difference by two. The result is the amount of offset that should exist between the front and rear tyres on both sides.

**4** If a string is used, have your assistant hold one end of it about halfway between the floor and the rear axle, touching the rear sidewall of the tyre.

**5** Run the other end of the string forward and pull it tight so that it is roughly parallel to the floor **(see illustration)**. Slowly bring the string

into contact with the front sidewall of the rear tyre, then turn the front wheel until it is parallel with the string. Measure the distance from the front tyre sidewall to the string.

**6** Repeat the procedure on the other side of the motorcycle. The distance from the front tyre sidewall to the string should be equal on both sides.

**7** As previously mentioned, a perfectly straight length of wood or metal bar may be substituted for the string **(see illustration)**. The procedure is the same.

**8** On Sprint RS models with a twin-sided swingarm, 2002 Daytona models and all Tiger models, if the distance between the string and tyre is greater on one side, or if the rear wheel appears to be cocked, refer to Chapter 1, Section 1 and check that the chain adjuster markings coincide on each side of the swingarm.

**9** If the front-to-back alignment is correct, the wheels still may be out of alignment vertically.

**10** Using a plumb bob, or other suitable weight, and a length of string, check the rear wheel to make sure it is vertical. To do this, hold the string against the tyre upper sidewall and allow the weight to settle just off the floor. When the string touches both the upper and lower tyre sidewalls and is perfectly straight, the wheel is vertical. If it is not, place thin spacers under one leg of the stand until it is.

**11** Once the rear wheel is vertical, check the front wheel in the same manner. If both wheels are not perfectly vertical, the frame and/or major suspension components are bent.

## 13 Front wheel

### Removal

**1** On Daytona and Sprint ST models, remove the belly-pan where fitted (see Chapter 7). Put the motorcycle on the centrestand (Sprint ST), or on an auxiliary stand and support it under the crankcase so that the front wheel is off the ground. Always make sure the motorcycle is properly supported.

**2** Displace the front brake calipers (see Section 3). Support the calipers with a piece of wire or a bungee cord so that no strain is placed on the hydraulic hoses. There is no

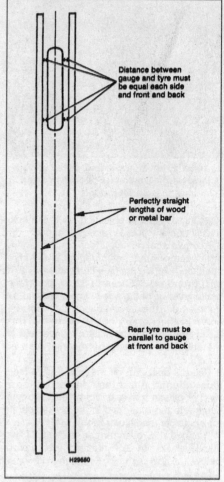

**12.7 Wheel alignment check using a straight-edge**

need to disconnect the hoses from the calipers. **Note:** *Do not operate the front brake lever with the calipers removed.*

**3** On 1997 to 2001 Daytona and Speed Triple models, if required, remove the screw securing the speedometer cable in the drive housing on the right-hand side of the wheel and detach the cable, but note that it can remain attached to the housing if you don't need to completely remove it for any reason **(see illustration)**. Unscrew the axle bolt from

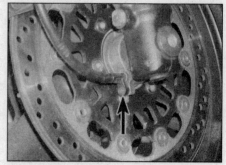

**13.3a Remove the screw and detach the cable if required**

**13.3b On 1997 to 2001 Daytona and Speed Triple models, unscrew the axle bolt (A), then the clamp bolts (B) on each fork**

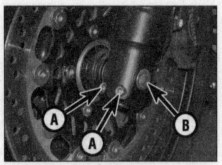

**13.4 On 2002-on Daytona and Speed Triple models, slacken the clamp bolts (A) on each fork, then unscrew the axle (B)**

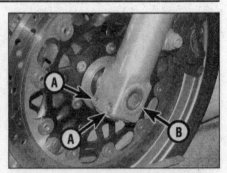

**13.5 On Sprint models, slacken the clamp bolts (A), then unscrew the axle (B)**

the right-hand end of the axle, then slacken the axle clamp bolts on the bottom of each fork (see illustration).

**4** On 2002-on Daytona and Speed Triple models, slacken the axle clamp bolts on the bottom of each fork, then unscrew the axle (see illustration).

**5** On Sprint models, slacken the axle clamp bolts on the bottom of the left-hand fork, then unscrew the axle (see illustration).

**6** On Tiger models, slacken the nut on the right-hand end of the axle and remove the washer (see illustration).

**7** Support the wheel, then withdraw the axle from the left-hand side and lower it to the ground (see illustrations). Use a drift to drive out the axle if required. Roll the wheel out from between the forks.

**8** Remove the speedometer drive housing from the right-hand side of the wheel on 1997 to 2001 Daytona and Speed Triple models and all Sprint models, and from the left-hand side on 2002-on Daytona and Speed Triple models and all Tiger models, noting how it fits (see illustration 13.12a). Remove the spacer from the opposite side of the wheel (see illustration 13.12b).

*Caution: Don't lay the wheel down and allow it to rest on a disc – the disc could become warped. Set the wheel on wood blocks so the disc doesn't support the weight of the wheel, or keep it upright.*

**9** Check the axle for straightness by rolling it on a flat surface such as a piece of plate glass (first wipe off all old grease and remove any corrosion using wire wool). If the equipment is

available, place the axle in V-blocks and check for runout using a dial gauge. If the axle is bent, replace it with a new one.

**10** Check the condition of the wheel bearings (see Section 15).

### Installation

**11** Apply lithium-based grease to the lips of the bearing seals, to the speedometer drive gear in the housing, to the axle and to the spacer. **Note:** *Triumph advise applying a smear of copper grease in the areas where the axle is retained in the fork bottoms.*

**12** Manoeuvre the wheel into position. Fit the speedometer drive housing as noted on removal (see Step 8), locating the cutouts in the drive gear in the housing over the tabs on the driveplate in the wheel (see illustration). Align the housing so that the cable or wiring exits backwards. Fit the spacer into the opposite side of the wheel (see illustration).

**13.7a Support the wheel and withdraw the axle**

**13.6 On Tiger models, unscrew the axle nut (arrowed)**

**13** Lift the wheel into place between the forks, making sure the spacer and drive housing remain in position, and locating the drive housing correctly against the fork (see illustration). Slide the axle in from the left-hand side (see illustration 13.7a).

**13.7b On Daytona and Speed Triple models, slide a screwdriver or bar through the hole in the end of the axle as a handle**

**13.12a Fit the drive housing, locating the cutouts (A) over the tabs (B) . . .**

**13.12b . . . and fit the wheel spacer**

**13.13 Make sure the drive housing locates correctly against the fork (arrowed)**

13.14a Install the axle bolt . . .

13.14b . . . and tighten it to the specified torque

### Removal

**Daytona, Speed Triple and Sprint ST models, and Sprint RS models with a single-sided swingarm**

**1** Support the motorcycle securely in an upright position using the centrestand (Sprint ST only) or an auxiliary stand.

**2** Remove the exhaust silencer (see Chapter 4).

**3** Remove the wheel nut retaining clip (see illustration). Unscrew the wheel nut and remove the dished washer, the plain washer and the conical spacer, noting how they fit (see illustrations) – prevent the wheel from turning either by applying the rear brake hard, or by counter-holding the sprocket coupling nut on the other side (see illustration 14.11). Draw the wheel off the axle and remove it (see illustration).

**4** Check the hub bearings and sprocket coupling bearing (see Section 15). **Note:** *Triumph recommend that the tightness of the rear brake caliper carrier peg is checked whenever the rear wheel is removed (see illustration 15.40). Ensure the peg is tightened to the specified torque setting.*

**All Tiger models, 2002 Daytona models and Sprint RS models with a twin-sided swingarm**

**5** Support the motorcycle securely in an upright position using an auxiliary stand.

**6** Refer to Chapter 1 and slacken the drive chain. Displace the rear brake caliper (see Section 6). Make sure no strain is placed on the hydraulic hose. There is no need to disconnect the hose from the caliper. **Note:** *Do not operate the brake pedal with the caliper removed.*

**7** On Daytona, Sprint RS and 2005 (from VIN 198875) Tiger models, unscrew the axle nut and remove the washer, then remove the adjustment position marker from the left-hand end of the axle (see illustration). Support the wheel then withdraw the axle along with the

**14** On 1997 to 2001 Daytona and Speed Triple models, install the axle bolt and tighten it to the torque setting specified at the beginning of the Chapter (see illustrations). Move the bike off its stand and pump the forks a few times. Now tighten the axle clamp bolts on the bottom of each fork to the specified torque setting (see illustration 13.3b). If removed, fit the speedometer cable into the drive housing and secure it with the screw (see illustration 13.3a).

**15** On 2002-on Daytona and Speed Triple models, tighten the axle to the torque setting specified at the beginning of the Chapter. Move the bike off its stand and pump the forks a few times. Now tighten the axle clamp bolts on the bottom of each fork to the specified torque setting (see illustration 13.4).

**16** On Sprint models, tighten the axle to the torque setting specified at the beginning of the Chapter (see illustration 13.5). Move the

bike off its stand and pump the forks a few times. Now tighten the axle clamp bolts on the bottom of the left-hand fork to the specified torque setting.

**17** On Tiger models, fit the washer and nut onto the end of the axle and tighten the nut finger-tight only (see illustration 13.6). Move the bike off the stand and pump the forks a few times. Now tighten the nut to the torque setting specified at the beginning of the Chapter.

**18** On all models, wipe any excess grease off the axle and around the fork bottoms.

**19** Install the brake calipers, making sure the pads sit squarely on each side of the discs (see Section 3).

**20** On Daytona and Sprint ST models, install the belly-pan if applicable (see Chapter 7).

**21** Apply the front brake a few times to bring the pads back into contact with the discs. Check for correct operation of the front brake before riding the motorcycle.

14.3a Remove the retaining clip . . .

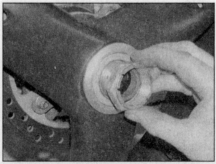

14.3b . . . then unscrew the nut . . .

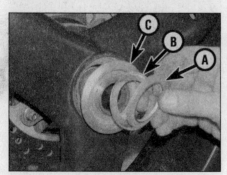

14.3c . . . remove the dished washer (A), plain washer (B) and conical spacer (C) . . .

14.3d . . . and draw the wheel off the axle

14.7a Unscrew the axle nut (arrowed) and remove the washer and adjustment position marker

**14.7b Withdraw the axle (arrowed), noting how its head locates in the adjustment marker**

right-hand adjustment position marker and lower the wheel to the ground **(see illustration)**. Disengage the chain from the sprocket and remove the wheel from between the swingarm ends. Note how the caliper bracket locates between the wheel and the swingarm and remove it **(see illustration)**. Remove the plain spacer from the left-hand side of the wheel and the shouldered spacer from the right-hand side for safekeeping if required.

*If you are working outside or on a dirty floor, tie the chain to the rear sub-frame, or lay some paper or rag on the ground for the chain to rest on, to prevent any dust and grit sticking to it.*

**8** On 1999 to 2004 Tiger models, remove the axle retaining clip from each side **(see illustration)**. Unscrew the axle bolt on the right-hand side and remove the washer. Support the wheel then withdraw the axle from the left-hand side and lower the wheel to the ground. Disengage the chain from the sprocket and remove the wheel from between the swingarm ends. Note how the caliper bracket locates between the wheel and the swingarm. Remove the plain spacer from the left-hand side of the wheel and the shouldered spacer from the right-hand side for safekeeping if required. Also note that there is a shouldered spacer in the caliper bracket – if you remove the bracket, note which way round it fits.

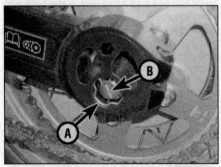

**14.8 Retaining clip (A), axle head (B) – Tiger models**

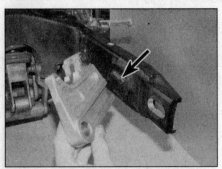

**14.7c Caliper bracket locates on lug (arrowed) on swingarm**

**9** Check the axle for straightness by rolling it on a flat surface such as a piece of plate glass (first wipe off all old grease and remove any corrosion using wire wool). If the equipment is available, place the axle in V-blocks and check for runout using a dial gauge. If the axle is bent, replace it with a new one.
**10** Check the wheel bearings and sprocket coupling bearings (see Section 15).

### Installation

#### Daytona, Speed Triple and Sprint ST models, and Sprint RS models with a single-sided swingarm

**11** Slide the wheel onto the axle, then fit the conical spacer, the plain washer and the dished washer **(see illustration 14.3d and c)** – fit the dished washer so that its outer rim sits on the plain washer and the inner rim is raised off it. Fit the wheel nut and tighten it to the torque setting specified at the beginning of the Chapter **(see illustration 14.3b)** – prevent the wheel from turning either by applying the rear brake hard, or by counter-holding the sprocket coupling nut on the other side **(see illustration)**. Fit the wheel nut retaining clip **(see illustration 14.3a)**.
**12** Install the exhaust silencer (see Chapter 4).

#### All Tiger models, 2002 Daytona models and Sprint RS models with a twin-sided swingarm

**13** Apply a thin coat of lithium-based grease to the lips of each grease seal, and also to the spacers and the axle.

**14.11 Tighten the wheel nut to the specified torque**

**14** If removed, fit the plain spacer into the left-hand side of the wheel and the shouldered spacer into the right-hand side.
**15** On Daytona, Sprint RS and 2005 Tiger models, fit the brake caliper bracket onto the swingarm, locating the lug on the swingarm in the groove in the bracket **(see illustration 14.7c)**. Slide the right-hand adjustment position marker (the one with the raised sections, which must face out) onto the axle. Manoeuvre the wheel into place between the ends of the swingarm and engage the drive chain with the sprocket. Lift the wheel into position, making sure the caliper bracket and the spacers remain in place, and slide the axle, with the adjustment marker, through from the right-hand side. Make sure it passes through the caliper bracket. Align the flats on the axle head between the raised sections on the adjustment marker, and make sure the raised sections are vertical, not horizontal **(see illustration 14.7b)**. Check that everything is correctly aligned, then fit the left-hand adjustment position marker with the chamfered edges along the top and bottom. Fit the washer and the axle nut **(see illustration 14.7a)**. Adjust the chain slack as described in Chapter 1, then tighten the axle nut to the torque setting specified at the beginning of the Chapter.
**16** On 1999 to 2004 Tiger models, check that the spacer is in position in the brake caliper bracket. Manoeuvre the wheel into place between the ends of the swingarm and engage the drive chain with the sprocket. Lift the wheel into position, making sure the caliper bracket and the spacers remain in place, and slide the axle through from the left-hand side. Make sure it passes through the caliper bracket. Check that everything is correctly aligned, then fit the axle bolt with its washer into the right-hand end and tighten it to the torque setting specified at the beginning of the Chapter, counter-holding the axle head if it turns **(see illustration 14.8)**. Fit the axle retaining clips, making sure they locate in their grooves. Adjust the chain slack as described in Chapter 1.
**17** Install the brake caliper, making sure the pads sit squarely on each side of the disc (see Section 6).
**18** Operate the brake pedal several times to bring the pads into contact with the disc. Check the operation of the rear brake carefully before riding the bike.

### 15 Wheel, sprocket coupling and hub bearings

### Front wheel bearings

**Note:** *Always renew the wheel bearings in pairs, never individually. Avoid using a high pressure cleaner on the wheel bearing area.*
**1** Remove the wheel (see Section 13). A caged ball bearing is fitted in each side of the wheel.

15.3  Lever out the grease seals

15.4  Remove the speedometer drive plate

15.5  Remove the circlip as described

2  Set the wheel on blocks so as not to allow the weight of the wheel to rest on either brake disc.

3  Lever out the grease seal on each side of the wheel using a large flat-bladed screwdriver, taking care not to damage the rim **(see illustration)**. Discard the seals if they are damaged or have deteriorated.

 *Position a piece of wood against the wheel to prevent the screwdriver shaft damaging it when levering the grease seal out.*

4  Remove the speedometer drive plate from the right-hand side of the wheel on 1997 to 2001 Daytona and Speed Triple models and all Sprint models, and from the left-hand side on 2002-on Daytona and Speed Triple models

15.6a  Knock out the bearings using a drift . . .

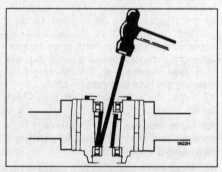

15.6b  . . . locating it as shown

and all Tiger models, noting how it fits **(see illustration)**.

5  Remove the circlip from the left-hand side of the wheel on 1997 to 2001 Daytona, Speed Triple and all Sprint models, and from the right-hand side on 2002-on Daytona and Speed Triple models and all Tiger models **(see illustration)**. Discard the circlip if it is weakened or deformed and obtain a new one.

6  Using a metal rod (preferably a brass drift punch) inserted through the centre of one bearing, tap evenly around the inner race of the other bearing to drive it from the hub **(see illustrations)**. The bearing spacer will also come out. Turn the wheel over so that the remaining bearing faces down. Drive the bearing out of the wheel using the same technique.

7  If the bearings are of the unsealed type or are only sealed on one side, clean them with a high flash-point solvent (one which won't

leave any residue) and blow them dry with compressed air (don't let the bearings spin as you dry them). Apply a few drops of oil to the bearing. **Note:** *If the bearing is sealed on both sides don't attempt to clean it.*

 *Refer to Tools and Workshop Tips (Section 5) for more information about bearings.*

8  Hold the outer race of the bearing and rotate the inner race – if the bearing doesn't turn smoothly, has rough spots or is noisy, replace it with a new one. If the bearing is good and can be re-used, wash it in solvent once again and dry it, then pack the bearing with the recommended grease (see Chapter 1 Specifications).

9  Thoroughly clean the hub area of the wheel.

10  On 1997 to 2001 Daytona and Speed Triple models and all Sprint models, install the left-hand bearing into its recess in the hub, with the marked or sealed side facing outwards. Using the old bearing (if new ones are being fitted), a bearing driver or a socket large enough to contact the outer race of the bearing, drive it in until it's completely seated **(see illustration)**. Turn the wheel over and install the bearing spacer, then drive the right-hand bearing into place as described above. Install the speedometer drive plate, locating the tabs on the drive plate rim in the cutouts in the hub **(see illustration 15.4)**. Install the new right-hand seal **(see illustration)**.

11  On 2002-on Daytona and Speed Triple models and all Tiger models, install the right-hand bearing into its recess in the hub, with the marked or sealed side facing outwards. Using the old bearing (if new ones are being fitted), a bearing driver or a socket large enough to contact the outer race of the bearing, drive it in until it's completely seated **(see illustration 15.10a)**. Secure the bearing with the circlip, making sure it locates in its groove **(see illustration 15.5)**. Apply a smear of grease to the lips of the new seal, then press it into the wheel, using a seal or bearing driver, a suitable socket or a piece of wood **(see illustration 15.10b)**. Turn the wheel over and install the bearing spacer, then drive the left-hand bearing into place as described

15.10a  A socket can be used to drive in the bearing

15.10b  Fit the grease seal and tap it into place

15.15 Lever out the grease seal (arrowed)

15.23a Remove the spacer from inside the coupling – single-sided swingarm type shown

15.23b Remove the spacer from inside the coupling – twin-sided swingarm type shown

above. Install the speedometer drive plate, locating the tabs on the drive plate rim in the cutouts in the hub **(see illustration 15.4)**. Install the new left-hand seal.

**12** Clean off all grease from the brake discs using acetone or brake system cleaner then install the wheel (see Section 13).

### Rear wheel bearings

#### All Tiger models, 2002 Daytona models and Sprint RS models with a twin-sided swingarm

**13** Remove the rear wheel (see Section 14). Lift the sprocket coupling out of the wheel, noting how it fits. A caged ball bearing is fitted in each side of the wheel.

**14** Set the wheel on wood blocks with the disc (right-hand side) facing up.

**15** Lever out the grease seal on the right-hand side of the wheel using a large flat-bladed screwdriver, taking care not to damage the rim of the hub **(see Haynes Hint above) (see illustration)**. Discard the seal if it is damaged or deteriorated. Remove the circlip securing the right-hand bearing. Discard the circlip if it is weakened or deformed and obtain a new one.

**16** Using a metal rod (preferably a brass drift punch) inserted through the centre of the right-hand bearing, tap evenly around the inner race of the left-hand bearing to drive it from the hub. The bearing spacer will also come out.

**17** Turn the wheel over so that the right-hand bearing faces down. Drive the bearing out of the wheel using the same technique as above.

**18** Refer to Steps 7 and 8 above and check the bearings.

**19** Thoroughly clean the hub area of the wheel.

**20** Install the right-hand bearing into its recess in the hub, with the marked or sealed side facing outwards. Using the old bearing (if new ones are being fitted), a bearing driver or a socket large enough to contact the outer race of the bearing, drive it in until it's completely seated **(see illustration 15.10a)**. Secure the bearing with the circlip, making sure it locates in its groove **(see illustration 15.5)**. Apply a smear of grease to the lips of the new seal, then press it into the wheel, using a seal or bearing driver, a suitable socket or a piece of wood **(see illustration 15.10b)**.

**21** Turn the wheel over and install the bearing spacer. Drive the other bearing into place as described above.

**22** Clean off all grease from the brake disc using acetone or brake system cleaner. Install the sprocket coupling assembly. Install the wheel (see Section 14).

### Sprocket coupling bearing

**23** On Daytona, Speed Triple, Sprint ST and Sprint RS models with a single-sided swingarm, remove the rear sprocket coupling (see Chapter 5, Section 17). On Daytona, Sprint RS and Tiger models with a twin-sided swingarm, remove the rear wheel (see Section 14), then lift the sprocket coupling out of the wheel, noting how it fits. On all models, remove the spacer from inside the coupling **(see illustrations)**.

**24** Using a large flat-bladed screwdriver lever out the grease seal from the outside of the coupling, taking care not to damage the rim of

15.24a Lever out the grease seal – single-sided swingarm type shown

15.25 Drive the bearing out from the inside

the coupling **(see Haynes Hint above) (see illustrations)**. Discard the seal if it is damaged or deteriorated. On Daytona and Sprint RS models with a twin-sided swingarm, remove the circlip from the coupling. Discard it if it has weakened or is deformed and obtain a new one.

**25** Support the coupling on blocks of wood and drive the bearing out from the inside using a bearing driver or socket **(see illustration)**.

**26** Refer to Steps 7 and 8 above and check the bearing.

**27** Thoroughly clean the bearing recess in the coupling then fit the bearing from the outside of the coupling, with the marked or sealed side facing out. Using the old bearing (if a new one is being fitted), a bearing driver or a socket large enough to contact the outer race of the bearing, drive it in until it is completely seated **(see illustration)**. On Daytona and Sprint RS models with a twin-

15.24b Lever out the grease seal (arrowed) – twin-sided swingarm type shown

15.27 A socket can be used to drive in the bearing

15.28 Press or drive the seal into the coupling

15.34a Remove the circlip . . .

15.34b . . . and the caliper carrier . . .

sided swingarm, secure the bearing with the circlip, making sure it locates in its groove.

**28** Apply a smear of grease to the lips of the new seal, and press it into the coupling, using a seal or bearing driver or a suitable socket if necessary **(see illustration)**.

**29** Check the sprocket coupling/rubber dampers (see Chapter 5, Section 17).

**30** On Tiger models, check the condition of the hub O-ring and replace it with a new one if necessary.

**31** On Daytona, Speed Triple, Sprint ST and Sprint RS models with a single-sided swingarm, install the rear sprocket coupling (see Chapter 5, Section 17).

**32** On Daytona, Sprint RS and Tiger models with a twin-sided swingarm, fit the sprocket coupling into the wheel, then install the wheel (see Section 14).

### Rear hub assembly bearings

#### Daytona, Speed Triple, Sprint ST and Sprint RS models with single-sided swingarms

**33** Remove the rear axle/brake disc carrier (see Section 7).

**34** Remove the large circlip on the inner (right-hand) end of the hub and slide off the brake caliper carrier, noting how it locates on

the swingarm **(see illustrations)**. Draw the hub assembly out of the swingarm **(see illustration)**.

**35** The hub assembly houses a caged ball bearing in the left-hand side and a needle roller bearing in the right-hand side. Triumph specify that the bearings are a press-fit, and so require special tools for removal and installation. They suggest that if the bearings are worn and need renewing, it is easier to renew the hub assembly as a unit with the bearings already installed. However, the bearings are listed individually – you will have to check on the relative cost, both in money and time.

**36** Refer to *Tools and Workshop Tips* in the Reference Section at the back of this manual and check the bearings.

**37** Using a large flat-bladed screwdriver lever out the grease seal from the right-hand end of the hub, taking care not to damage the rim of the hub **(see Haynes Hint above)**. Discard the seal if it is damaged or deteriorated. Remove the circlips from the outer ends of the hub. Discard them if they have weakened or are deformed and fit new ones on reassembly.

**38** Support the hub on blocks of wood and press or drive out the left-hand caged ball bearing from the inside, referring to *Tools and Workshop Tips* in the Reference Section for

more information on removal methods. Turn the hub over and press out the needle roller bearing. If the bearings are too tight, take the hub to a workshop equipped with an hydraulic press. A third circlip and a grease seal are fitted behind the needle bearing.

**39** Thoroughly clean the bearing recesses in the hub. Install the new bearings, seals and circlips in a reverse of the removal procedure. Apply a smear of grease to the lips of the new seals and to the needle bearing.

**40** Check that the brake caliper carrier peg is tightened to the specified torque setting. Slide the hub assembly into the swingarm **(see illustration 15.34c)**. Fit the brake caliper carrier onto the hub, locating its slot over the peg on the swingarm as shown, and secure it with the circlip **(see illustration)**.

**41** Install the rear axle/brake disc carrier (see Section 7).

### 16 Tyre information and fitting

### *General information*

**1** 1999 to 2004 Tiger models have tubed tyres due to their spoke wheel design. All

15.34c . . . then withdraw the hub assembly from the swingarm

15.40 Locate the slot in the carrier over the peg (arrowed)

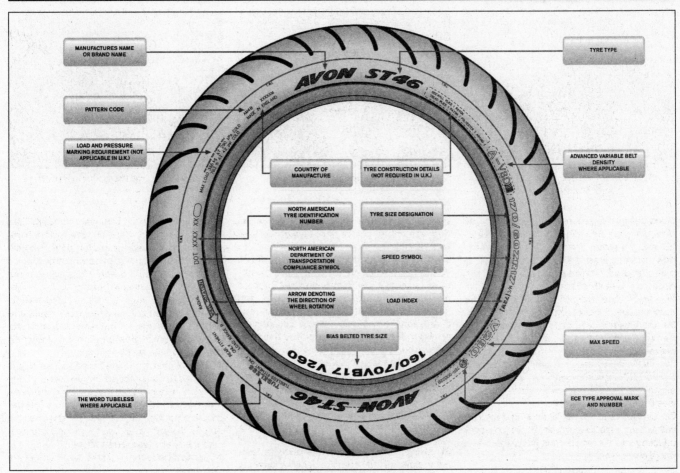

**16.3  Common tyre sidewall markings**

other models are fitted with tubeless tyres. Tyre sizes are given in the Specifications at the beginning of this Chapter.

**2** Refer to the Daily (pre-ride) checks listed at the beginning of this manual for tyre maintenance.

### Fitting new tyres

**3** When selecting new tyres, refer to the tyre information label on the swingarm and the tyre options listed in the owners handbook. Ensure that front and rear tyre types are compatible,

the correct size and correct speed rating; if necessary seek advice from a Triumph dealer or tyre fitting specialist **(see illustration)**.

**4** It is recommended that tyres are fitted by a motorcycle tyre specialist rather than attempted in the home workshop. This is particularly relevant in the case of tubeless tyres because the force required to break the seal between the wheel rim and tyre bead is substantial, and is usually beyond the capabilities of an individual working with

normal tyre levers. Additionally, the specialist will be able to balance the wheels after tyre fitting.

**5** Note that punctured tubeless tyres can in some cases be repaired. Seek the advice of a Triumph dealer or a motorcycle tyre fitting specialist concerning tyre repairs. In the case of tubed tyres (1999 to 2004 Tiger models) always fit a new inner tube if a puncture occurs and ensure that the item which caused the puncture is not still held in the tyre tread.

# Chapter 7
# Bodywork

## Contents

## Degrees of difficulty

| **Easy,** suitable for novice with little experience |  | **Fairly easy,** suitable for beginner with some experience | | **Fairly difficult,** suitable for competent DIY mechanic |  | **Difficult,** suitable for experienced DIY mechanic | | **Very difficult,** suitable for expert DIY or professional |  |

## Specifications

### Torque wrench settings

| | |
|---|---|
| Grab-rail mounting bolts – Sprint models ...................... | 27 Nm |
| Luggage rack bolts – Tiger models | |
| Front bolts (M8) ............................................ | 27 Nm |
| Rear bolts (M6) ............................................. | 10 Nm |
| Mirror mounting nuts – Daytona, Speed Triple and Sprint models .... | 9 Nm |
| Rear hugger mounting screws ............................... | 9 Nm |
| Sump guard bolts – 955 Tiger models ........................ | 7 Nm |

### 1 General information

This Chapter covers the procedures necessary to remove and install the body parts. Since many service and repair operations on these motorcycles require the removal of the body parts, the procedures are grouped here and referred to from other Chapters.

In the case of damage to the body parts, it is usually necessary to remove the broken component and replace it with a new (or used) one. The material that the body panels are composed of doesn't lend itself to conventional repair techniques. There are however some shops that specialise in 'plastic welding', so it may be worthwhile seeking the advice of one of these specialists before scrapping an expensive component. There are also DIY kits available for making small repairs.

When attempting to remove any body panel, first study it closely, noting any fasteners and associated fittings, to be sure of returning everything to its correct place on installation. In some cases the aid of an assistant will be required when removing panels, to help avoid the risk of damage to paintwork. Once the evident fasteners have been removed, try to withdraw the panel as described but DO NOT FORCE IT – if it will not release, check that all fasteners have been removed and try again. Where a panel engages another by means of tabs, be careful not to break the tab or its mating slot or to damage the paintwork. Remember that a few moments of patience at this stage will save you a lot of money in replacing broken fairing panels! To undo quick-release fasteners, turn them 90° anti-clockwise.

Many of the bolts used on the motorcycle are of the Torx type. Unless you are already equipped with a good range of Torx bits, you are advised to purchase a set. Make sure you get bits that can be used in conjunction with a socket set so that a torque wrench can be applied – a Torx key set will not be adequate on its own, though will be useful in addition to the bits.

When installing a body panel, first study it closely, noting any fasteners and associated fittings removed with it, to be sure of returning everything to its correct place. Check that all fasteners and damping/rubber mounts are in good condition; any of these must be replaced with new ones if faulty before the panel is reassembled. Check also that all mounting brackets are straight and repair or renew them if necessary before attempting to install the panel. Where assistance was required to remove a panel, make sure your assistant is on hand to install it. To install quick-release fasteners, turn them 90° clockwise.

Tighten the fasteners securely, but be careful not to overtighten any of them or the panel may break (not always immediately) due to the uneven stress.

2.1a Turn the key and lift the rear of the seat . . .

2.1b . . . then draw it backwards, noting how the tab (arrowed) locates

2.1c Location of the tabs on 2002-on models

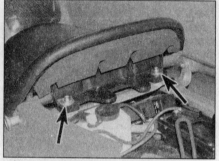

2.1d Remove the bolt on each rear corner – 1997 to 2001 models

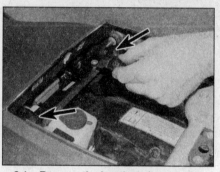

2.1e Remove the brackets (arrowed) – 2002-on models

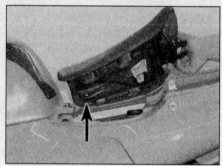

2.1f Lift the rear of the seat and draw it back, noting how the tab (arrowed) locates

## 2 Seats

### Removal

**1** On Daytona and Speed Triple models, to remove the passenger seat, insert the ignition key into the seat lock located on the left-hand side of the bike, and turn it anti-clockwise to unlock the seat **(see illustration)**. Lift up the rear of the seat and draw it backwards, noting how the tab at the front locates **(see illustrations)**. To remove the rider's seat, first remove the passenger seat. On 1997 to 2001 models, unscrew the two bolts securing the rear of the seat **(see illustration)**; on 2002-on models, unscrew the two bolts securing the brackets and remove the brackets **(see illustration)**. Draw the seat back, noting how the tab at the front locates under the tank bracket **(see illustration)**.

**2** On Sprint models, insert the ignition key into the seat lock located on the left-hand side of the bike, and turn it anti-clockwise to unlock the seat **(see illustration)**. Lift up the rear of the seat and draw it backwards, noting how the tab at the front locates **(see illustration)**.

**3** On Tiger models, to remove the passenger seat, insert the ignition key into the seat lock located on the left-hand side of the bike, and turn it anti-clockwise to unlock the seat **(see illustration)**. Lift up the rear of the seat and

2.2a Turn the key and lift the rear of the seat . . .

draw it backwards, noting how the hooks at the front locate under the frame cross-member **(see illustration)**. To remove the rider's seat,

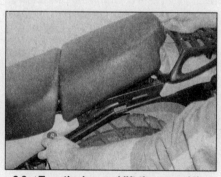

2.3a Turn the key and lift the rear of the seat . . .

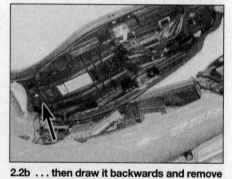

2.2b . . . then draw it backwards and remove it, noting how the tab (arrowed) locates

first remove the passenger seat. Pull back the latch release ring at the rear of the seat, then lift the seat and draw it backwards, noting how

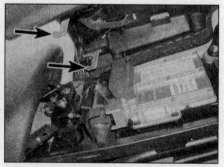

2.3b . . . then draw it backwards and remove it, noting how the hooks (arrowed) locate

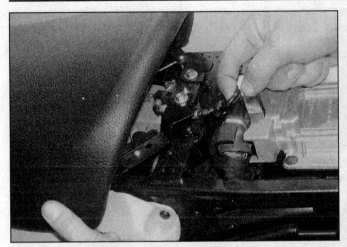

2.3c  Pull back on the release ring . . .

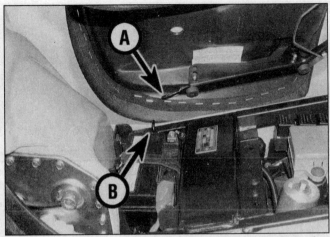

2.3d  . . . then lift the rear of the seat and draw it back, noting how the tab (A) on each side locates under the hook (B) on each frame rail

the tabs locate under the hooks on the frame rails **(see illustrations)**.

## *Installation*

**4** Installation is the reverse of removal. Push down on the seat to engage the latch.

### 3   Fairing and body panels

## *Daytona models*

### Seat cowling

**1** Remove the seats (see Section 2).
**2** On 1997 to 2001 models, disconnect the tail light assembly wiring connector **(see illustration)**. Remove the eight screws securing the seat cowling, noting the washers, then carefully draw it back and off the bike **(see illustrations)**.
**3** On 2002-on models, undo the screws and remove the left and right-hand body side panels – note how the peg on the back of each panel locates in the grommet in the frame **(see illustrations)**. Remove the six screws securing the seat cowling, noting the washers on the middle pair of screws **(see illustrations)**. Release the trim clips securing

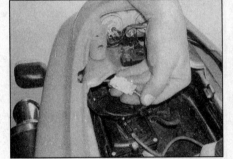

3.2a  Disconnect the tail light wiring connector

3.2b  Undo the screws (arrowed) . . .

3.2c  . . . and carefully draw the cowling back

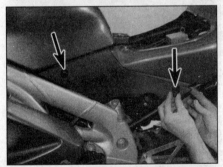

3.3a  Undo the screws (arrowed) and lift off the panel . . .

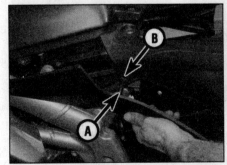

3.3b  . . . note how the peg (A) locates in the grommet (B)

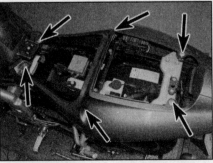

3.3c  Undo the screws (arrowed) . . .

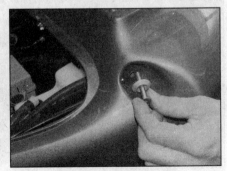

3.3d  . . . noting the washers

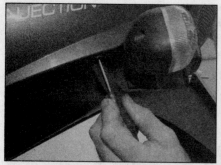

3.3e Press the centre of the trim clip in . . .

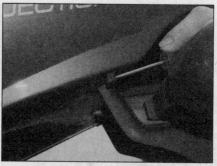

3.3f . . . then draw the clip out

3.3g Ease the cowling off carefully

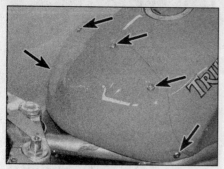

3.5a Undo the screws (arrowed) . . .

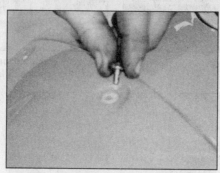

3.5b . . . noting the nylon washers . . .

3.5c . . . and remove the cover

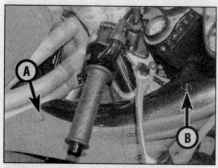

3.7a Release the fastener (A) and undo the screw (B) . . .

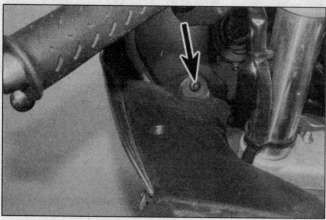

3.7b . . . and remove the trim panel

**4** Installation is the reverse of removal. On 1997 to 2001 models, check the tail and brake lights after connecting the wiring.

### Fuel tank cover – 1997 to 2001 models

**5** Remove the five screws securing the cover, noting the washers, then carefully lift it off the tank (see illustrations).

**6** Installation is the reverse of removal.

### Cockpit trim panels

**7** On 1997 to 2001 models, release the quick-release fastener and undo the normal screw securing the trim panel and remove it, noting how it fits (see illustrations).

**8** On 2002-on models, remove the appropriate fairing side panel first (see Step 13). Undo the screw securing the trim panel to the back of the headlight assembly and lift it out (see illustrations).

the underside rear of the cowling to the mudguard – press the centre of the clip in, them draw the clip out from the cowling (see illustrations). Ease the rear of the cowling up off the tail light surround and lift it off (see illustration).

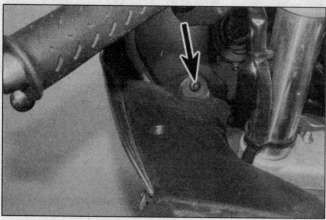

3.8a Remove the screw (arrowed) . . .

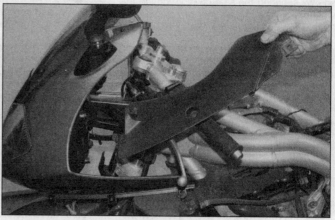

3.8b . . . and lift out the trim panel

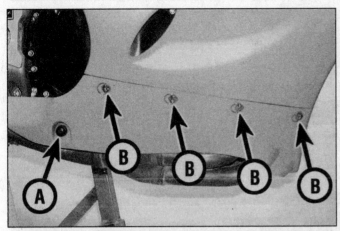

3.10a Unscrew the bolt (A) and release the fasteners (B) . . .

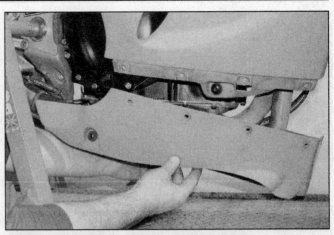

3.10b . . . and remove the belly pan

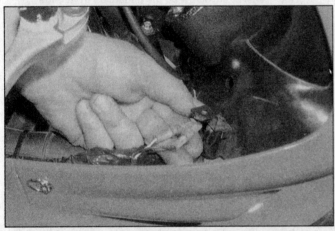

3.12a Disconnect the turn signal wiring connectors

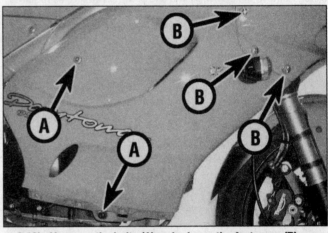

3.12b Unscrew the bolts (A) and release the fasteners (B) . . .

**9** Installation is the reverse of removal. Make sure the panel locates correctly with the fairing and fairing side panel.

## Belly pan – 1997 to 2001 models

**10** Unscrew the bolt securing each side of the belly pan **(see illustration)**. Support the belly pan, then release the four quick-release fasteners on each side and carefully lower the belly pan off the fairing side panels **(see illustration)**.

**11** Installation is the reverse of removal.

## Fairing side panels

**12** On 1997 to 2001 models, remove the cockpit trim panel (see Step 7), then disconnect the turn signal wiring connectors **(see illustration)**. Remove the belly pan (see Step 10). Unscrew the bolts securing the side and bottom of the panel, then support the panel and release the three quick-release fasteners securing the panel to the fairing **(see illustration)**. Carefully draw the panel away, noting how it engages with the fairing along its front edge **(see illustration)**.

**13** On 2002-on models, remove the screw securing the side panel to the cockpit trim panel **(see illustration)**. Remove the screw

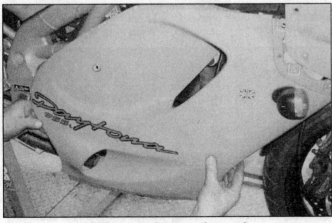

3.12c . . . and remove the panel

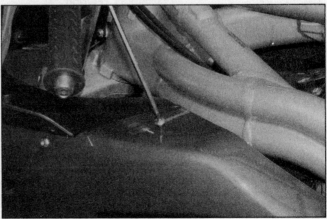

3.13a Remove the screw on the top edge of the side panel

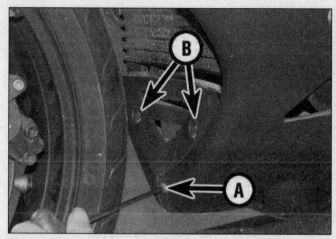

3.13b Remove the screw (A) and one of the screws (B) as required

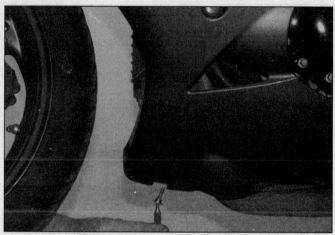

3.13c Remove the screw on the underside front edge

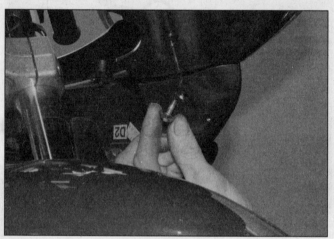

3.13d Remove the screw on the upper inside front edge

3.13e Remove the bolts (arrowed)

joining the left and right-hand panels at the lower front edge, one of the front infill panel screws (left or right-hand as required) and the joining screw on the front underside **(see illustrations)**. Remove the screw joining the upper inside front edge of the panel to the fairing **(see illustration)**. Unscrew the three bolts securing the panel to the fairing, then support the panel and unscrew the three bolts securing the side and bottom of the panel **(see illustration)**. Carefully draw the panel away, noting how it engages with the fairing, and disconnect the turn signal wiring connectors **(see illustration)**.

14 Installation is the reverse of removal. Make sure the panel locates correctly with the fairing. Check the turn signals after connecting the wiring.

**Fairing**

15 On 1997 to 2001 models, remove the cockpit trim panels (see Step 7), and the mirrors (see Section 4). Remove the screw in the top of each air intake **(see illustration)**. Release the three quick-release fasteners securing the fairing to the side panel **(see illustration 3.12b)**. Ease the fairing forward off the headlights, detaching the air ducts as you do so **(see illustration)**. When it becomes accessible, either elease the sidelight bulbholder (applicable markets) by turning it a quarter turn anti-clockwise, or disconnect its wiring connector

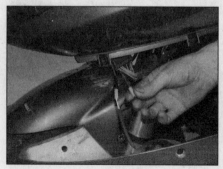

3.13f Disconnect the turn signal wiring connectors

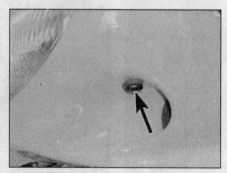

3.15a Undo the screw (arrowed) on each side

3.15b Detach the air intake ducts (arrowed) from the fairing

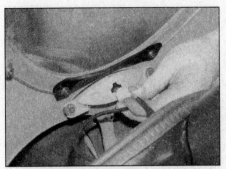

3.15c Release the sidelight bulbholder . . .

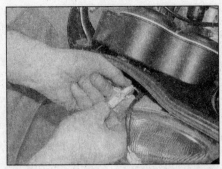

3.15d . . . and disconnect the LED if fitted

3.15e Draw the fairing off the bike

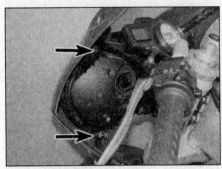

3.16a Remove the screws (arrowed) on each side . . .

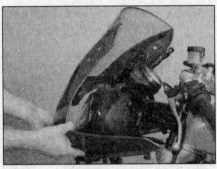

3.16b . . . and draw the fairing off the bike

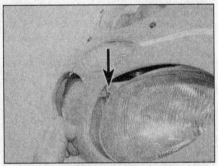

3.17 Locate the peg on the fairing in the hole (arrowed)

(see illustration). Also, if fitted, disconnect the alarm system LED wiring connector (see illustration). Carefully draw the fairing forwards and remove it (see illustration).

16 On 2002-on models, first remove both fairing side panels (see Step 13). Remove the cockpit trim panels (see Step 8). Remove the mirrors (see Section 4). Undo the two screws on each side securing the headlight assembly to the inside of the fairing, then carefully draw the fairing forwards and remove it (see illustrations).

17 Installation is the reverse of removal. On 1997 to 2001 models, don't forget to fit the sidelight bulbholder and connect the alarm LED, where fitted. Make sure the air ducts locate correctly onto the fairing (see illustration 3.15b), and the peg on the inside

of the fairing at the front locates into the hole in the headlight assembly (see illustration).

### Speed Triple models

#### Seat cowling

18 Remove the seats (see Section 2). On 1997 to 2001 models, follow the procedure in Step 2 to remove the seat cowling. Installation is the reverse of removal. Check the tail and brake lights after connecting the wiring.

19 On 2002-on models, follow the procedure in Step 3 to remove the seat cowling. Installation is the reverse of removal.

#### Fuel tank cover

20 On 1997 to 2001 models, follow the procedure in Step 5 to remove the fuel tank cover. Installation is the reverse of removal.

#### Radiator cowling

21 The radiator cowling is a two-piece assembly. Undo the quick-release fastener securing the top edge of the cowling (see illustration). Trace the wiring from the appropriate front turn indicator and disconnect it at the connector (see illustration). Pull back the boot on the indicator stem and undo the nut securing the indicator to the bracket on the radiator, then draw the indicator wiring through the bracket and lift the indicator and cowling off (see illustration).

22 Installation is the reverse of removal. Check the turn indicators after connecting the wiring.

#### Fly screen

23 The fly screen is secured by four screws

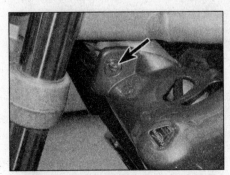

3.21a Undo the quick-release fastener (arrowed)

3.21b Disconnect the wiring connector

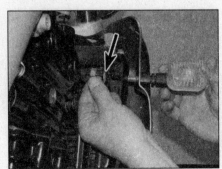

3.21c Indicator is secured to the bracket (arrowed)

**3.23a Fly screen is secured by screws (arrowed)**

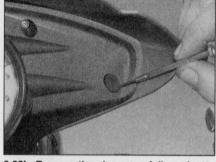

**3.23b Remove the plugs carefully and note where they fit**

**3.23c Draw the screen off carefully to avoid damaging the locating pegs**

(see illustration). Prise out the plugs to access the screws – remove the plugs carefully and note where they fit as they are

shaped to match the contour of the trim panel (see illustrations). Undo the mounting screws and draw the fly screen off, noting

how the pegs locate in the instrument cluster bracket (see illustration). Pull the trim panel forward and disconnect the instrument cluster wiring connector, then lift the trim panel off (see illustration).
24 Installation is the reverse of removal. Ensure that the instrument cluster wiring connector is securely connected.

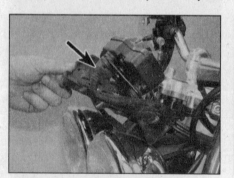

**3.23d Disconnect the wiring connector (arrowed) and remove the trim panel**

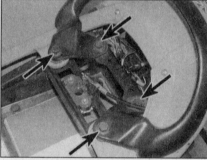

**3.25a Unscrew the bolts (arrowed) . . .**

### Sprint ST models
#### Seat cowling

25 Remove the seat (see Section 2). Unscrew the four bolts securing the grab-rail and remove it (see illustrations).
26 Disconnect the tail light assembly wiring connector (see illustration). Remove the screws securing the seat cowling, noting the washers, then carefully pull the sides away at the front to release the two pegs on each side from their grommets (see illustrations). Carefully draw the seat cowling back and off the bike (see illustration).
27 Installation is the reverse of removal. Tighten the grab-rail bolts to the torque settings specified at the beginning of the Chapter. Check the tail and brake lights after connecting the wiring.

#### Fairing side panels

28 If required, remove the screws securing the inner panel to the side panel and remove it, noting how it fits – the side panels can be removed with the inner panels in place, but it

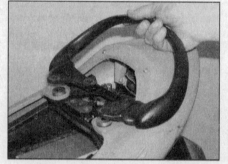

**3.25b . . . and remove the grab-rail**

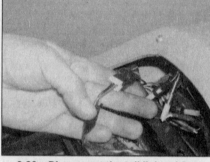

**3.26a Disconnect the tail light wiring connector**

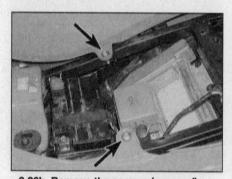

**3.26b Remove the screws (arrowed) . . .**

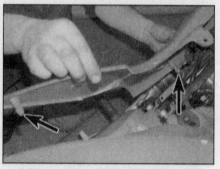

**3.26c . . . then pull the sides away to release the pegs (arrowed) . . .**

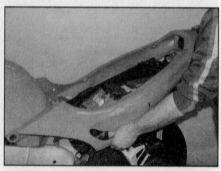

**3.26d . . . and remove the seat cowling**

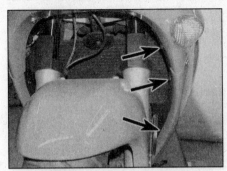

**3.28a Undo the screws (arrowed) . . .**

**3.28b . . . and remove the inner panel**

**3.29a Remove the screws (arrowed) . . .**

is easier if they are removed first **(see illustrations)**.

**29** Remove the screws securing the side panel, then carefully draw it away, noting how it engages with the fairing along its front edge and the belly panel along its lower edge **(see illustrations)**.

**30** Installation is the reverse of removal. Make sure the panel locates correctly with the fairing and belly pan.

### Belly pan

**31** Remove the fairing side panels (see Steps 28 and 29).

**32** Unscrew the bolts securing each side of the belly pan and carefully lower it **(see illustration)**.

**33** Installation is the reverse of removal.

### Fairing

**34** Remove the fairing side panels (see Steps 28 and 29). Remove mirrors (see Section 4).

**35** Remove the two bottom screws securing the windshield **(see illustration)**.

**36** Remove the remaining screws securing the fairing.

**37** Ease the fairing forward off the headlights, noting how the pegs locate **(see illustration)**. When it becomes accessible, either release the sidelight bulbholder (applicable markets) by turning it a quarter turn anti-clockwise, or disconnect its wiring connector and disconnect the turn signal wiring connectors **(see illustrations)**. Also, if fitted, disconnect the alarm system LED wiring connector.

**38** Installation is the reverse of removal. Do

not forget to connect the sidelight, alarm system LED (if fitted), and turn signal wiring connectors.

### Sprint RS models

### Seat cowling

**39** Remove the seat (see Section 2).

**40** Follow the procedure in steps 25 to 26 to remove the seat cowling. Installation is the reverse of removal. Check the tail and brake lights after connecting the wiring.

### Fairing side panels

**41** Remove the screws securing the side panel, then carefully draw it away, noting how it engages with the fairing along its front edge,

**3.29b . . . and remove the side panel**

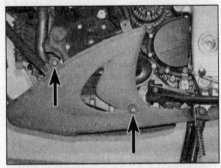

**3.32 Unscrew the two bolts (arrowed) from each side and remove the belly pan**

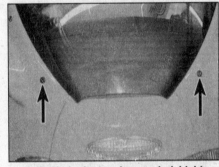

**3.35 Undo the two lower windshield screws (arrowed)**

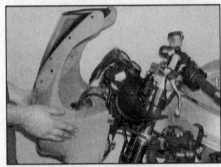

**3.37a Ease the fairing off the headlights . . .**

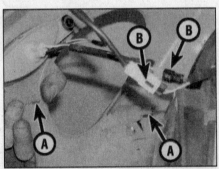

**3.37b . . . noting how the pegs (A) locate. Disconnect the sidelight and LED wiring connectors (B) . . .**

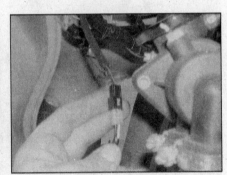

**3.37c . . . and the turn signal wiring connectors**

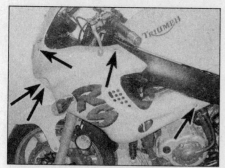

3.41a Undo the screws (arrowed) . . .

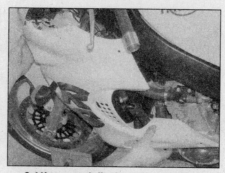

3.41b . . . and displace the panel . . .

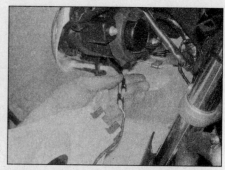

3.41c . . . then disconnect the turn signal wiring connectors

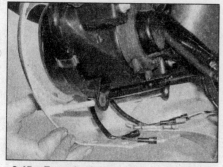

3.45a Ease the fairing off the headlights, noting how the pegs locate

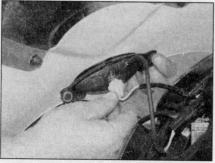

3.45b Release the sidelight bulbholder . . .

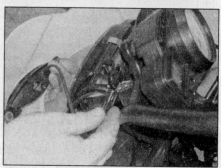

3.45c . . . and disconnect the LED if fitted

and disconnect the turn signal wiring connectors **(see illustrations)**.

**42** Installation is the reverse of removal. Make sure the panel locates correctly with the fairing. Check the turn signals after connecting the wiring.

### Fairing

**43** Remove the mirrors (see Section 4).

**44** Remove the screws securing the fairing to each fairing side panel **(see illustration 3.41a)**.

**45** Ease the fairing forward off the headlights, noting how the pegs locate in the grommets

under the headlight **(see illustration)**. When it becomes accessible, either release the sidelight bulbholder (applicable markets) by turning it a quarter turn anti-clockwise, or disconnect its wiring connector **(see illustration)**. Also, if fitted, disconnect the alarm system LED wiring connector **(see illustration)**.

**46** Carefully draw the fairing forwards and remove it, noting how it engages with the side panels.

**47** Installation is the reverse of removal. Do not forget to fit the sidelight bulbholder and connect the alarm LED where fitted.

### Tiger models

#### Side panels

**48** Remove the seats (see Section 2).

**49** To remove the right-hand side panel, undo the two screws securing the trim panel to the fuel tank and remove it, noting how the tab at the front engages **(see illustration)**. Undo the two screws securing the side panel, then carefully draw it away to release the central peg from its grommet **(see illustration)**.

**50** To remove the left-hand side panel, undo the screw securing the trim panel to the fuel

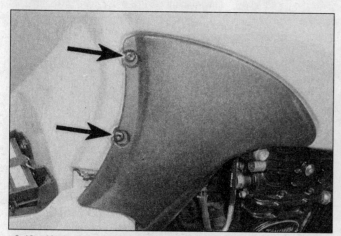

3.49a Undo the screws (arrowed) and remove the trim panel . . .

3.49b . . . then undo the side panel screws and draw it away to release the peg from its grommet (arrowed)

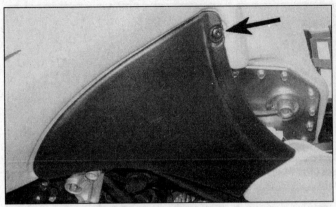

3.50a Undo the screw (arrowed) . . .

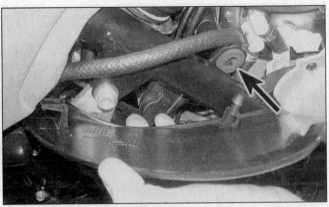

3.50b . . . and draw the panel away to release the peg from its grommet (arrowed), noting how the tab at the front locates

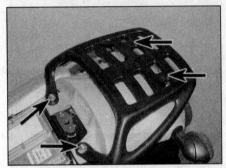

3.52 Luggage rack/tail light cover mounting bolts (arrowed)

3.54a Undo the screws (arrowed) . . .

3.54b . . . then displace the panel and disconnect the wiring connectors

tank, then carefully draw it away to release the peg from its grommet and remove it, noting how the tab at the front engages **(see illustrations)**. Undo the two screws securing the side panel, then carefully draw it away to release the central peg from its grommet **(see illustration 3.49b)**.

51 Installation is the reverse of removal.

### Luggage rack and tail light cover

52 Prise out the blanking caps from the rear mountings **(see illustration)**. Unscrew the four bolts securing the rack and cover – leave the rear bolts loose in situ. Lift the rack and

cover away together, noting the spacers for the rear mounts and the rubber washers on all mountings. Separate them if required.

53 Installation is the reverse of removal. Make sure the large rubber washers are fitted between the rack and the cover at the front, and the small ones are fitted between the spacers and the cover at the back. Tighten the mounting bolts to the torque settings specified at the beginning of the Chapter.

### Fairing

54 Remove the two screws securing each turn signal panel, then draw the panel away

and disconnect the wiring connectors **(see illustrations)**.

55 Remove the mirrors (see Section 4). Remove the windshield (see Section 5).

56 Remove the two screws at the front of the fairing and the screw on each side at the bottom **(see illustration)**. Ease the fairing forward off the headlights and remove it **(see illustration)**.

57 Installation is the reverse of removal.

### Belly pan

58 The belly pan is secured to the frame by three screws which pass through grommets and spacers set in the belly pan.

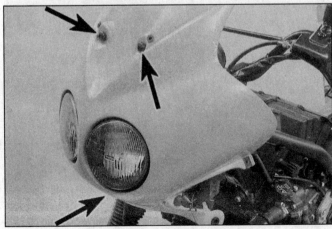

3.56a Undo the screws (arrowed) . . .

3.56b . . . and remove the fairing

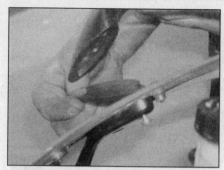

**4.1 Unscrew the bolts and remove the mirror and its rubber pad**

**4.2a Remove the plugs (arrowed) and undo the nuts . . .**

**4.2b . . . then lift off the mirror**

## 4 Mirrors

### Removal

**1** On 1997 to 2001 Daytona models, unscrew the bolts on the inside of the fairing and remove the mirror along with its rubber insulator pad **(see illustration)**.
**2** On 2002-on Daytona models, remove the plugs, then unscrew the two nuts on the inside of the fairing and remove the mirror along with its rubber insulator pad **(see illustrations)**.
**3** On Speed Triple and Tiger models, lift the rubber cover off the base of the mirror, then unscrew it from its mount.
**4** On Sprint ST models, undo the screws securing the cockpit trim panels and remove the panels **(see illustrations)**. Pull back the rubber boot from the base of the mirror, then unscrew the two nuts on the inside, counterholding the bolts **(see illustration)**. Remove the mirror along with its rubber insulator pad.
**5** On Sprint RS models, unscrew the two nuts on the inside of the fairing and remove the mirror along with its rubber insulator pad **(see illustration)**.

**4.4a Undo the screws (arrowed) . . .**

### Installation

**6** Installation is the reverse of removal. Tighten the mounting nuts to the torque setting specified at the beginning of the Chapter.

## 5 Windshield

### Removal

**1** Remove the screws securing the windshield to the fairing and remove the windshield, noting how it fits. Make sure none of the

**4.4b . . . and remove the trim panel**

rubber wellnuts drop out of the fairing, and check that they are all in good condition.

### Installation

**2** Installation is the reverse of removal. Do not overtighten the screws.

## 6 Front mudguard

### Removal

**1** On Daytona and Speed Triple models, displace the left-hand brake caliper (see

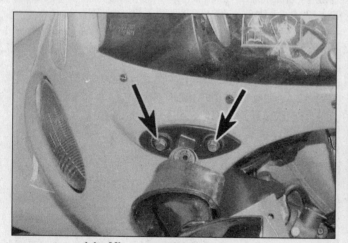

**4.4c Mirror mounting bolts (arrowed)**

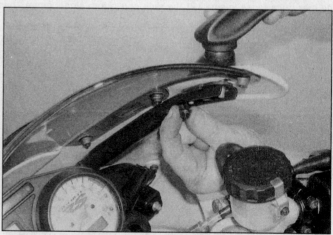

**4.5 Unscrew the nuts on the inside and remove the mirror**

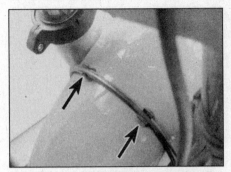

**6.1a Release the brake hose from the clips (arrowed)**

**6.1b If applicable, undo the screw (arrowed) and detach the cable**

**6.1c Unscrew the bolts (arrowed) . . .**

Chapter 6), then release the brake hose from its clips on the top of the mudguard (**see illustration**). On 1997 to 2001 models, remove the screw securing the speedometer cable to the drive housing on the front wheel and detach it, then draw it out of its guide on the mudguard (**see illustration**). Unscrew the two bolts securing each side of the mudguard, then draw it forwards and off the bike (**see illustrations**).

**2** On Sprint and Tiger models, displace the left-hand brake caliper (see Chapter 6), then release the brake hose from its clips on the top of the mudguard (**see illustration**). Remove all the screws securing each section of the front mudguard to the other and to the forks, then separate the sections and remove them, noting how they fit together.

### *Installation*

**3** Installation is the reverse of removal.

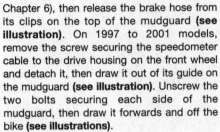

**6.1d . . . and remove the mudguard**

**6.2 Release the brake hose from the clips (A), then remove the screws (B) on each side**

**2** To remove the hugger, first remove the screws securing the chainguard and lift it off (**see illustration**).

**3** Release the rear brake hose from its clip, then undo the two screws securing the right-hand side of the hugger to the swingarm and lift the hugger off (**see illustrations**).

### *Installation*

**4** Installation is the reverse of removal. Tighten the mounting screws to the torque settings specified at the beginning of the Chapter. Don't forget to secure the brake hose in its clip.

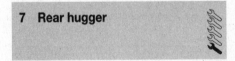

**7.2 Remove the chainguard**

## 7 Rear hugger

### *Removal*

**1** A rear hugger is fitted to 2002 Daytona models with a twin-sided swingarm.

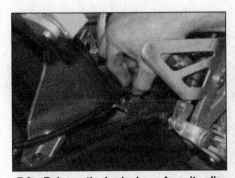

**7.3a Release the brake hose from its clip**

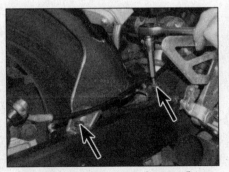

**7.3b Remove the screws (arrowed) . . .**

**7.3c . . . and lift the hugger off**

# Chapter 8
## Electrical system

## Contents

## Degrees of difficulty

| Easy, suitable for novice with little experience | | Fairly easy, suitable for beginner with some experience | | Fairly difficult, suitable for competent DIY mechanic | | Difficult, suitable for experienced DIY mechanic | | Very difficult, suitable for expert DIY or professional | |
|---|---|---|---|---|---|---|---|---|---|
| |  | |  | |  | |  | | |

## Specifications

### Battery
Capacity
T595 Daytona and T509 Speed Triple ...................... 12V, 14Ah
All other models ........................................ 12V, 12Ah
Type
T595 Daytona and T509 Speed Triple ..................... Yuasa YB14L-A2
All other models ........................................ GS GTX14-BS
Current leakage ......................................... 1 mA (max)
Charging rate ........................................... 1.4A (max)
Charging time (flat battery)
T595 Daytona and T509 Speed Triple ..................... 15 to 20 hours
All other models ........................................ 5 hours

### Starter motor brushes
Minimum length
1997 to 2001 models .................................... 8 mm
2002-on models ......................................... not available

## Alternator

Nominal output
    1997 to 2001 Daytona, Speed Triple and Sprint models . . . . . . . . . .   40A
    2002-on Daytona, Speed Triple and Sprint models . . . . . . . . . . . . .   25A
    All Tiger models . . . . . . . . . . . . . . . . . . . . . . . . . . . . . . . . . . . . . . .   40A

## Fuse

Ratings . . . . . . . . . . . . . . . . . . . . . . . . . . . . . . . . . . . . . . . . . . . . . . . . . . .   refer to the information on the inside of the fusebox lid

## Bulbs

Headlight . . . . . . . . . . . . . . . . . . . . . . . . . . . . . . . . . . . . . . . . . . . . . . . . .   12V 60/55W H4
Brake/tail light . . . . . . . . . . . . . . . . . . . . . . . . . . . . . . . . . . . . . . . . . . . . .   12V 21/5W
Turn signal light . . . . . . . . . . . . . . . . . . . . . . . . . . . . . . . . . . . . . . . . . . . .   12V 10W

## Torque wrench settings

Coolant inlet union screws . . . . . . . . . . . . . . . . . . . . . . . . . . . . . . . . . .   12 Nm
Oil pressure switch . . . . . . . . . . . . . . . . . . . . . . . . . . . . . . . . . . . . . . . .   13 Nm
Neutral switch . . . . . . . . . . . . . . . . . . . . . . . . . . . . . . . . . . . . . . . . . . . .   10 Nm
Rear brake light switch – Sprint and Tiger models
    1999 to 2001 models . . . . . . . . . . . . . . . . . . . . . . . . . . . . . . . . . . . .   25 Nm
    2002-on models . . . . . . . . . . . . . . . . . . . . . . . . . . . . . . . . . . . . . . . .   15 Nm
Sidestand bracket mounting bolts . . . . . . . . . . . . . . . . . . . . . . . . . . .   40 Nm
Starter motor mounting bolts . . . . . . . . . . . . . . . . . . . . . . . . . . . . . . .   10 Nm
Alternator mounting bolts (1997 to 2001 models) . . . . . . . . . . . . . . .   20 Nm
Alternator cover bolts (2002-on models) . . . . . . . . . . . . . . . . . . . . . .   9 Nm
Alternator rotor bolt (2002-on models) . . . . . . . . . . . . . . . . . . . . . . .   105 Nm
Alternator stator mounting bolts (2002-on models) . . . . . . . . . . . . . .   12 Nm

## 1 General information

All models have a 12 volt electrical system charged by a three-phase alternator. On 1997 to 2001 models, the alternator is mounted externally behind the cylinder block and has an integral regulator/rectifier. On 2002-on models, the alternator rotor is mounted on the left-hand end of the crankshaft and the stator is located inside the left-hand engine cover; the regulator/rectifier is mounted on the frame.

The regulator maintains the charging system output within the specified range to prevent overcharging, and the rectifier converts the ac (alternating current) output of the alternator to dc (direct current) to power the lights and other components and to charge the battery.

The starter motor is mounted on the top of the crankcase. The starting system includes the motor, the battery, the relay and the various wires and switches.

**Note:** *Keep in mind that electrical parts, once purchased, cannot be returned. To avoid unnecessary expense, make very sure the faulty component has been positively identified before buying a replacement part.*

Many of the bolts used on Triumph motorcycles are of the Torx type. Unless you are already equipped with a good range of Torx bits, you are advised to obtain a set. Make sure you get bits that can be used in conjunction with a socket set so that a torque wrench can be applied – a Torx key set will not be adequate on its own, though will be useful in addition to the bits.

## 2 Electrical system fault finding

*Warning: To prevent the risk of short circuits, the ignition (main) switch must always be OFF and the battery negative (–ve) terminal should be disconnected before any of the bike's other electrical components are disturbed. Don't forget to reconnect the terminal securely once work is finished or if battery power is needed for circuit testing.*

1 A typical electrical circuit consists of an electrical component, the switches, relays, etc. related to that component and the wiring and connectors that hook the component to both the battery and the frame. To aid in locating a problem in any electrical circuit, refer to the *Wiring Diagrams* at the end of this Chapter.

2 Before tackling any troublesome electrical circuit, first study the wiring diagram (see end of Chapter) thoroughly to get a complete picture of what makes up that individual circuit. Trouble spots, for instance, can often be narrowed down by noting if other components related to that circuit are operating properly or not. If several components or circuits fail at one time, chances are the fault lies in the fuse or earth (ground) connection, as several circuits are often routed through the same fuse and earth (ground) connections.

3 Electrical problems often stem from simple causes, such as loose or corroded connections or a blown fuse. Prior to any electrical fault finding, always visually check the condition of the fuse, wires and connections in the problem circuit. Intermittent failures can be especially frustrating, since you can't always duplicate the failure when it's convenient to test. In such situations, a good practice is to clean all connections in the affected circuit, whether or not they appear to be good. All of the connections and wires should also be wiggled to check for looseness which can cause intermittent failure.

4 If testing instruments are going to be utilised, use the wiring diagram to plan where you will make the necessary connections in order to accurately pinpoint the trouble spot.

5 The basic tools needed for electrical fault finding include a battery and bulb test circuit, a continuity tester, a test light, and a jumper wires. A multimeter capable of reading volts, ohms and amps is also very useful as an alternative to the above, and is necessary for performing more extensive tests and checks.

*Refer to Fault Finding Equipment in the Reference section for details of how to use electrical test equipment.*

## 3 Battery removal and installation

*Caution: Be extremely careful when handling or working around the battery. The electrolyte is very caustic and an explosive gas (hydrogen) is given off when the battery is charging.*

3.2a  Disconnect the negative terminal first (A), then the positive (B) – Daytona shown

3.2b  Unhook the strap . . .

## Removal and installation

1  Remove the seat(s) (see Chapter 7).

2  Unscrew the negative (–ve) terminal bolt first and disconnect the lead from the battery (see illustration). Lift up the insulating cover to access the positive (+ve) terminal, then unscrew the bolt and disconnect the lead. Release the battery strap and remove the battery from the bike, on T595 and T509 models disconnecting the breather hose from its union as you do (see illustrations).

3  On installation, clean the battery terminals and lead ends with a wire brush or knife and emery paper. Reconnect the leads, connecting the positive (+ve) terminal first.

4  Install the seat(s) (see Chapter 7).

> **HAYNES HINT**
> *Battery corrosion can be kept to a minimum by applying a layer of petroleum jelly or dielectric grease (available as a spray) to the terminals after the cables have been connected.*

## Inspection and maintenance

5  T595 Daytona and T509 Speed Triple models are fitted with a standard battery which requires regular checks of the electrolyte level (see Chapter 1), as well as the checks detailed below. Note that Triumph supply a conversion kit for these models to enable them to use the maintenance-free battery used on later models.

6  The battery fitted on all other models is of the maintenance-free (sealed) type, therefore requiring no specific maintenance. However, the following checks should still be regularly performed.

7  Check the battery terminals and leads for tightness and corrosion. If corrosion is evident, unscrew the terminal bolts and disconnect the leads from the battery, disconnecting the negative (–ve) terminal first, and clean the terminals and lead ends with a wire brush or knife and emery paper. Reconnect the leads, connecting the negative (–ve) terminal last, and apply a thin coat of petroleum jelly or dielectric grease to the connections to slow further corrosion.

8  The battery case should be kept clean to prevent current leakage, which can discharge the battery over a period of time (especially when it sits unused). Wash the outside of the case with a solution of baking soda and water. Rinse the battery thoroughly, then dry it.

9  Look for cracks in the case and renew the battery if any are found. If acid has been spilled on the frame or battery box, neutralise it with a baking soda and water solution, dry it thoroughly, then touch up any damaged paint.

10  If the motorcycle sits unused for long periods of time, disconnect the leads from the battery terminals, negative (–ve) terminal first. Refer to Section 4 and charge the battery once every month to six weeks.

11  The condition of the battery can be assessed by measuring the voltage present at the battery terminals. Connect the voltmeter positive (+ve) probe to the battery positive (+ve) terminal, and the negative (–ve) probe to the battery negative (–ve) terminal. When fully charged there should be 12.8 volts (or more) present. If the voltage falls below 12.3 volts the battery must be removed, disconnecting the negative (–ve) terminal first, and recharged as described in Section 4.

## 4  Battery charging

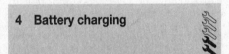

**Caution: Be extremely careful when handling or working around the battery. The electrolyte is very caustic and an explosive gas (hydrogen) is given off when the battery is charging.**

1  Remove the battery (see Section 3).

2  Connect the charger to the battery, making sure that the positive (+ve) lead on the charger is connected to the positive (+ve) terminal on the battery, and the negative (–ve) lead is connected to the negative (–ve) terminal. The battery should be charged at the specified rate for the specified time if it is completely

3.2c  . . . and remove the battery

flat, or until the voltage across the terminals reaches 12.8V (allow the battery to stabilise for 30 minutes after charging before taking a voltage reading). Exceeding this can cause the battery to overheat, buckling the plates and rendering it useless. Few owners will have access to an expensive current controlled charger, so if a normal domestic charger is used check that after a possible initial peak, the charge rate falls to a safe level (see illustration). If the battery becomes hot during charging **stop**. Further charging will cause damage. **Note:** *In emergencies, the maintenance-free type battery can be charged*

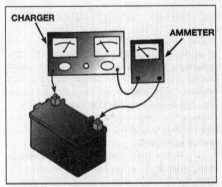

4.2  If the charger doesn't have an ammeter built in, connect one in series as shown. DO NOT connect the ammeter between the battery terminals or it will be ruined

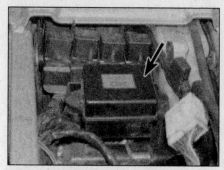

**5.1a Fusebox (arrowed) – Daytona and Speed Triple models**

**5.1b Fusebox (arrowed) – Sprint models**

**5.1c Fusebox (arrowed) – Tiger models**

**5.1d Main fuse – Tiger models**

at a higher rate of around 3.0 to 6.0 amps for a period of 1 hour maximum. However, this is not recommended and the low amp charge is by far the safer method of charging the battery.

3 If the recharged battery discharges rapidly when left disconnected it is likely that an internal short caused by physical damage or sulphation has occurred. A new battery will be required. A sound battery will tend to lose its charge at about 1% per day.

4 Install the battery (see Section 3).

5 If the motorcycle sits unused for long periods of time, charge the battery once every month to six weeks and leave it disconnected.

## 5  Fuses

1 The electrical system is protected by fuses of different ratings. All fuses (with the exception of the main fuse on 2000 to 2001 Sprint models and all Tiger models) are housed in the fusebox, which is located under the rider's seat **(see illustrations)**. On 2000 to 2001 Sprint models and all Tiger models the main fuse is contained in a holder in the loom **(see illustration)**.

2 To access the fuses, remove the seat(s) (see Chapter 7) and unclip the fusebox lid **(see illustration)**. The identity, location and rating of each fuse is marked on the inside of the lid.

3 The fuses can be removed and checked visually. If you can't pull the fuse out with your

fingertips, use a suitable pair of pliers. A blown fuse is easily identified by a break in the element **(see illustration)**, or can be tested for continuity using an ohmmeter or continuity tester – if there is no continuity, it has blown. Each fuse is clearly marked with its rating and must only be replaced by a fuse of the same rating. If a spare fuse is used, always replace it with a new one so that a spare of each rating is carried on the bike at all times.

⚠️ **Warning: Never put in a fuse of a higher rating or bridge the terminals with any other substitute, however temporary it may be. Serious damage may be done to the circuit, or a fire may start.**

4 If a fuse blows, be sure to check the wiring circuit very carefully for evidence of a short-circuit. Look for bare wires and chafed, melted or burned insulation. If the fuse is

**5.2 Unclip the lid to access the fusebox fuses – the identity, location and rating of each fuse is marked in the lid**

renewed before the cause is located, the new fuse will blow immediately.

5 Occasionally a fuse will blow or cause an open-circuit for no obvious reason. Corrosion of the fuse ends and fusebox terminals may occur and cause poor fuse contact. If this happens, remove the corrosion with a wire brush or emery paper, then spray the fuse end and terminals with electrical contact cleaner.

## 6  Lighting system check

1 The battery provides power for operation of the headlight, tail light, brake light, turn signals and instrument cluster lights. If none of the lights operate, always check battery voltage before proceeding. Low battery voltage indicates either a faulty battery or a defective charging system. Refer to Section 3 for battery checks and Sections 29 and 30 for charging system tests. Also, check the condition of the fuses (see Section 5). When checking for a blown filament in a bulb, it is advisable to back up a visual check with a continuity test of the filament as it is not always apparent that a bulb has blown. When testing for continuity, remember that on tail light and turn signal bulbs it is often the metal body of the bulb which is the earth (ground).

**Note:** *During 2002 Triumph discontinued fitting light switches and machines for all markets were equipped with permanently operating lights as follows: Daytona 955i, Speed Triple 955i, Sprint ST and RS models from VIN 171873, Tiger 955 from VIN 168574. The headlight cut-out relay turns the lights off during the engine starting procedure to ensure full battery power for starting.*

### Headlight

2 If the headlights fail to work, check the bulb(s) and the bulb terminals and wiring connector first (see Section 7), then the circuit fuses (see Section 5). If they are all good, check for battery voltage at the relevant (hi or low beam) supply wire terminal on the headlight wiring connector, with the ignition switch and light switch (where fitted) ON, and

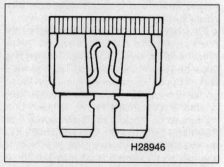

H28946

**5.3 A blown fuse can be identified by a break in its element**

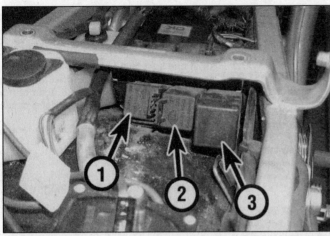

**6.4a  Main beam relay (1), dip beam relay (2), turn signal relay (3) – 1997 to 2001 Daytona and Speed Triple models**

**6.4b  Main beam relay (1), dip beam relay (2), headlight cut-out relay (3), main power relay (4) – 2002-on Daytona and Speed Triple models**

**6.4c  Relay pack – Sprint ST models. Identify the correct relay from the coloured identity tags (arrowed)**

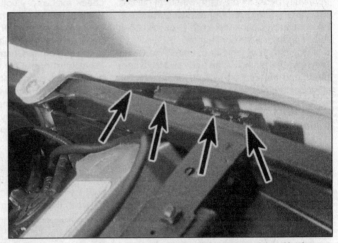

**6.4d  Relay pack (arrowed) – Sprint RS models. Identify the correct relay from the coloured identity tags**

the dip beam/main beam switch set appropriately, referring to the *Wiring Diagrams* at the end of the Chapter to identify the wiring for your model. If voltage is present, check for continuity between the earth wire terminal and the battery negative (-ve) terminal. If there is no continuity, check the earth (ground) circuit for an open or poor connection.

**3** If no voltage is indicated, check the wiring between the headlight, relays, light switches (where fitted) and the ignition switch, then check the switches themselves.

**4** To access the headlight relays, remove the seats on 1997 to 2001 Daytona and Speed Triple models; remove the seat cowling on 2002-on Daytona and Speed Triple models and all Sprint RS models; remove the fairing on all Sprint ST and Tiger models (see Chapter 7). Disconnect the relevant relay from its connector block **(see illustrations)** – on Sprint and Tiger models, Triumph advise that the exact location of each relay is subject to change, so it is impracticable to specify its exact position in the relay pack – identify the relay by the coloured tag around the wiring going into it. On 1999 Sprint ST models, the

main beam relay tag is black, and the dip beam relay tag is white. On 2000-on Sprint ST models, Sprint RS models and Tiger models, the main beam relay tag is red, and the dip beam relay tag is white. If the tag is missing, identify the relay by the colour of the wires going into it, referring to the *Wiring Diagrams* at the end of the Chapter.

**5** The easiest way to test the relays is by substituting the suspect one with a known good one – if the low beam is not working and the hi beam is, swap the relays and see if the problem follows.

**6** The relays should have terminal identification numbers and a small circuit diagram marked on their underside – use this and the appropriate wiring diagram at the end of this Chapter to identify the activating power in and out terminals, and the main power in and out terminals that provide the power to the lights. Using an ohmmeter or continuity tester, connect the positive (+ve) probe to the relay's main power in terminal, and the negative (–ve) probe to the relay's main power out terminal. There should be no continuity. Leaving the meter connected, and using a

fully charged 12 volt battery and two insulated jumper wires, connect the positive (+ve) terminal of the battery to the activating power in terminal, and the negative (–ve) terminal to

**6.4e  Relay pack – Tiger models. Identify the correct relay from the coloured identity tags (arrowed)**

the activating power out terminal. At this point the relay should close and the multimeter read 0 ohms (continuity) – there should be an audible click as the relay closes.

### Tail light

7 If the tail light fails to work, check the bulb(s) and the bulb terminals and wiring connector first (see Section 9), then the circuit fuses (see Section 5). If they are all good, check for battery voltage at the supply wire terminal on the tail light wiring connector, with the ignition switch and light switch (where fitted) ON, referring to the *Wiring Diagrams* at the end of the Chapter to identify the wiring for your model. Also check for continuity between the wiring connector terminals on the tail light side of the wiring connector and the corresponding terminals in the bulbholder. If voltage and continuity are present, check for continuity between the earth wire terminal and the battery negative (-ve) terminal. If there is no continuity, check the earth (ground) circuit for an open or poor connection.

8 If no voltage is indicated, check the wiring between the tail light, the light switch (where fitted) and the ignition switch, then check the switches themselves.

### Sidelight (applicable markets)

9 If the sidelight fails to work, check the bulb and the bulb terminals and wiring connectors first (see Section 7), then the circuit fuses. If they are all good, check for battery voltage at the supply wire terminal on the sidelight wiring connector, with the ignition switch and light switch (where fitted) ON, referring to the *Wiring*

Diagrams at the end of the Chapter to identify the wiring for your model. Also check for continuity between the wiring connector terminals on the tail light side of the wiring connector and the corresponding terminals in the bulbholder. If voltage and continuity are present, check for continuity between the earth wire terminal and the battery negative (-ve) terminal. If there is no continuity, check the earth (ground) circuit for an open or poor connection.

10 If no voltage is indicated, check the wiring between the sidelight, the light switch (where fitted) and the ignition switch, then check the switches themselves.

### Brake light

11 If the brake light fails to work, check the bulb(s) and the bulb terminals and wiring connector first (see Section 9), then the circuit fuses (see Section 5). If they are all good, check for battery voltage at the supply wire terminal on the tail light wiring connector, with the ignition switch ON, and the brake lever or pedal applied, referring to the *Wiring Diagrams* at the end of the Chapter to identify the wiring for your model. Also check for continuity between the wiring connector terminals on the tail light side of the wiring connector and the corresponding terminals in the bulbholder. If voltage and continuity are present, check for continuity between the earth wire terminal and the battery negative (-ve) terminal. If there is no continuity, check the earth (ground) circuit for an open or poor connection.

12 If no voltage is indicated, check the brake light switches (see Section 14), then the wiring between the tail light and the switches.

### Instrument and warning lights

13 See Section 16.

### Turn signal lights

14 If one light fails to work, check the bulb and the bulb terminals first, then the wiring connectors (see Section 12). If none of the turn signals work, first check the signal circuit fuse (see Section 5).

15 If the fuse is good, see Section 11 for the turn signal circuit check.

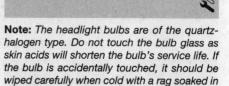

**7  Headlight bulb and sidelight bulb**

**Note:** *The headlight bulbs are of the quartz-halogen type. Do not touch the bulb glass as skin acids will shorten the bulb's service life. If the bulb is accidentally touched, it should be wiped carefully when cold with a rag soaked in methylated spirit and dried before fitting.*

⚠ **Warning: Allow the bulb time to cool before removing it if the headlight has just been on.**

### Headlight

1 On 1997 to 2001 Daytona models, and all Sprint ST and Tiger models, you have to remove the headlight assembly to get decent access to the bulbs (see Section 8). On Sprint RS models, remove the fairing side panel(s) for best access, although small hands might be able to reach the bulb assembly without removing the panels.

2 On Speed Triple models, slacken the headlight rim clamp screw, then support the headlight and remove the rim. Carefully draw the light unit out of the shell, noting how it fits. Release the bulbholder from the light unit.

3 On Sprint RS models, remove the headlight connector cover, then disconnect the wiring connector **(see illustration)**. On 2002-on Daytona models, disconnect the wiring connector **(see illustration)**.

4 On all models, remove the rubber dust cover, noting how it fits **(see illustration)**. Release the bulb retaining clip, noting how it fits, then remove the bulb **(see illustrations)**.

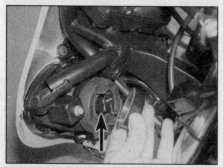

**7.3a  Remove the cover and disconnect the wiring connector (arrowed)**

**7.3b  On 2002-on Daytona models, disconnect the wiring connector**

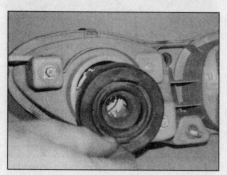

**7.4a  Remove the rubber cover, noting how it fits . . .**

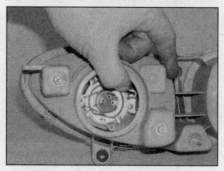

**7.4b  . . . then release the clip . . .**

**7.4c  . . . and remove the bulb**

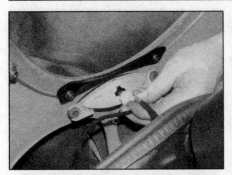

7.9a  Release the bulbholder from the sidelight

7.9b  On 2002-on Daytona models, pull the bulbholder out

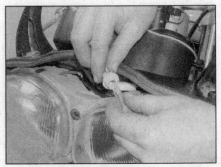

7.12  Carefully pull the bulb out of the holder

5 Fit the new bulb, bearing in mind the information in the **Note** above. Make sure the tabs on the bulb fit correctly in the slots in the bulb housing, and secure it in position with the retaining clip.

6 Install the dust cover, making sure it is correctly seated and with the 'TOP' mark at the top, and connect the wiring connector.

7 Install or reassemble the headlight and fairing panel(s) as required. Check the operation of the headlight.

 **HAYNES HiNT** *Always use a paper towel or dry cloth when handling new bulbs to prevent injury if the bulb should break and to increase bulb life.*

### Sidelight

8 On Daytona, Sprint and Tiger models, remove the fairing (see Chapter 7).

9 On 1997 to 2001 Daytona models and all Sprint models, if not already done, release the bulbholder from the sidelight by turning it a quarter turn anti-clockwise **(see illustration)**. On 2002-on Daytona models, pull the bulbholder out of the headlight assembly **(see illustration)**.

10 On Speed Triple models, slacken the headlight rim clamp screw, then support the

headlight and remove the rim. Carefully draw the light unit out of the shell, noting how it fits. Release the bulbholder from the light unit.

11 On Tiger models, remove the headlight assembly for best access to the bulbholders, though you might be able to get at them if you have small hands – they are located in the back of each light unit. Release the bulbholder from the unit.

12 Carefully pull the bulb out of the holder and install the new bulb **(see illustration)**.

13 Install or reassemble the headlight and fairing as required. Check the operation of the sidelight.

8.2a  On Daytona models, unscrew the nut on the underside . . .

### 8  Headlight assembly

### *Removal*

1 On Daytona, Sprint and Tiger models, remove the fairing (see Chapter 7).

2 On 1997 to 2001 Daytona models and all Sprint models, remove the three nuts (Daytona) or two screws and nut (Sprint) securing the headlight assembly, then displace it from its mounts, noting how it fits, and disconnect the wiring connectors **(see illustrations)**. On 1997 to 2001 Daytona

8.2b  . . . and the nut on each end . . .

8.2c  . . . then displace the headlight . . .

8.2d  . . . and disconnect the wiring connectors

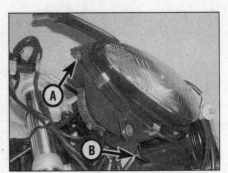

8.2e  On Sprint models, there is a screw on each end (A), and a nut on the underside (B)

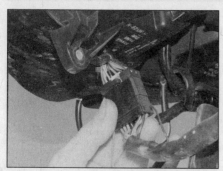

**8.3a Disconnect the headlight unit wiring connectors**

**8.3b Remove the screws and lift off the headlight unit**

**8.6 Headlight mounting bolts (arrowed) – Tiger models**

models, access to the lower nut is restricted by the horn – displace it if required (see Section 25).

3 On 2002-on Daytona models, disconnect the headlight and sidelight wiring connectors, then detach the wiring loom from the clips on the underside of the headlight unit **(see illustration)**. Remove the four screws securing the headlight assembly, then displace it from its mounts, noting how it fits **(see illustration)**.

4 On all Daytona and Sprint models, if required, remove the headlight bulbs (see Section 7). Check the condition of the rubber grommets on each mounting and replace them with new ones if damaged, deformed or deteriorated – note that the grommets for the lower mountings could fall out, so remove them for safekeeping if they are loose.

5 On Speed Triple models, trace the wiring

from the headlights and disconnect it at the connectors. Support the headlight assembly, then unscrew the two clamp bolts and remove the clamp and the headlights. To remove an individual light, disconnect its wiring connector, then unscrew the bolt securing it to the central mounting piece and remove the light.

6 On Tiger models, unscrew the three bolts securing the headlight assembly, then displace it from its mounts, noting how it fits, and disconnect the wiring connectors **(see illustration)**. If required, remove the headlight bulbs (see Section 7). If required, the lights can be separated from the casing – all components are available individually.

### Installation

7 Installation is the reverse of removal. Make sure all the wiring is correctly connected and

secured. Check the operation of the headlight and sidelight. Check the headlight aim (see Chapter 1).

## 9  Brake/tail and licence plate bulbs

### Brake/tail lights

1 On 1997 to 2001 Daytona and Speed Triple models and all Sprint models, remove the passenger seat (see Chapter 7). On 2002-on Daytona and Speed Triple models, remove the seat cowling (see Chapter 7). Turn the bulbholder anti-clockwise and withdraw it from the tail light **(see illustration)**. Push the bulb into the holder and twist it anti-clockwise to remove it **(see illustration)**.

2 On Tiger models, undo the screws securing the tail light lens and remove the lens **(see illustrations)**. Push the bulb into the holder and twist it anti-clockwise to remove it **(see illustration)**.

3 Check the socket terminals for corrosion and clean them if necessary. Line up the pins of the new bulb with the slots in the socket, then push the bulb in and turn it clockwise until it locks into place. **Note:** *The pins on the bulb are offset so it can only be installed one way. It is a good idea to use a paper towel or dry cloth when handling the new bulb to prevent injury if the bulb should break and to increase bulb life.*

4 On Daytona, Speed Triple and Sprint

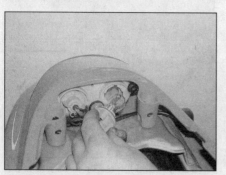

**9.1a Release the bulbholder from the tail light . . .**

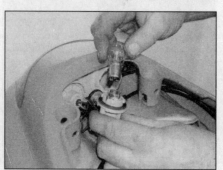

**9.1b . . . then release the bulb from the holder**

**9.2a Undo the screws (arrowed) . . .**

**9.2b . . . and remove the lens**

**9.2c Push the bulb in and twist it anti-clockwise to release it**

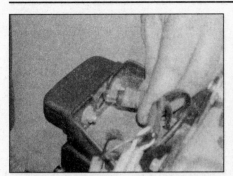

**9.6a Ease the bulbholder from the back of the light unit ...**

**9.6b ... and pull the bulb out of the holder**

**9.6c Access to the licence plate bulb – 2002-on Daytona and Speed Triple models**

models, fit the bulbholder into the tail light and turn it clockwise to secure it **(see illustration 9.1a)**. Install the seat or seat cowling as applicable (see Chapter 7).

**5** On Tiger models, fit the tail light lens and secure it with the screws, taking care not to overtighten them as it is easy to strip the threads or crack the lens.

### *Licence plate light*

**6** On Daytona and Speed Triple models, to replace the licence plate bulb, first remove the seat cowling (see Chapter 7). On 1997 to 2001 models, then ease the bulbholder out of the back of the licence plate light, and pull the bulb out of the holder **(see illustrations)**. On 2002-on models, remove the tail light assembly and tail light surround (see Section 10). Ease the bulbholder out of the back of the licence plate light, and pull the bulb out of the holder **(see illustration)**.

**7** On Sprint and Tiger models, there is no separate licence plate bulb – the licence plate is illuminated by the tail light bulbs.

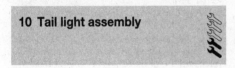

### 10 Tail light assembly

### *Removal*

**1** Remove the passenger seat (see Chapter 7). On Tiger models, remove the luggage rack and tail light cover (see Chapter 7).

**2** On 1997 to 2001 Daytona and Speed Triple

models and all Sprint models, either remove the bulbholders **(see illustration 9.1a)**, or disconnect the tail light assembly wiring connector **(see illustrations)**.

**3** On 1997 to 2001 Daytona and Speed Triple models, unscrew the two bolts securing the tail light, accessing them via the holes in the seat cowling rear mounts, and noting how the brackets locate **(see illustration)**. Withdraw the tail light from the back of the cowling.

**4** On 2002-on Daytona and Speed Triple models, remove the seat cowling (see Chapter 7). Remove the bulbholders, then unscrew the four nuts securing the tail light and withdraw it from its bracket **(see illustration)**.

**5** On Sprint models, for best access to the tail light nuts, remove the seat cowling (see Chapter 7), though with small hands and a small spanner you can access them in situ. Unscrew the four nuts securing the tail light

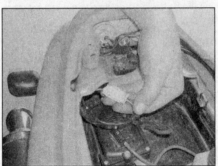

**10.2a Tail light wiring connector – Daytona and Speed Triple models**

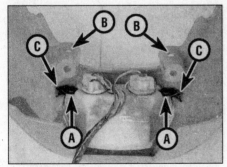

**10.3 Unscrew the bolts (A) via the holes (B), noting how the brackets (C) locate**

and withdraw it from the seat cowling **(see illustration)**.

**6** On Tiger models, unscrew the two nuts securing the tail light and remove it from the back of the bike.

### *Installation*

**7** Installation is the reverse of removal. Check the operation of the tail light and the brake light.

### 11 Turn signal circuit check and relay

**1** Most turn signal problems are the result of a burned out bulb or corroded socket. This is especially true when the turn signals function properly in one direction, but fail to flash in the other direction. Check the bulbs and the

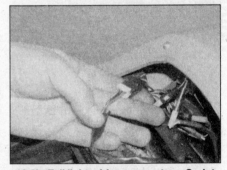

**10.2b Tail light wiring connector – Sprint models**

**10.4 Tail light assembly nuts – 2002-on Daytona and Speed Triple models**

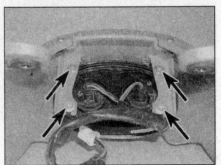

**10.5 Tail light assembly nuts – Sprint models**

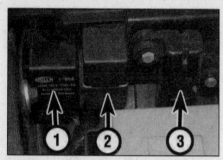

**11.3 Turn signal relay (1), ignition relay (2), tip-over sensor (3) – 2002-on Daytona and Speed Triple models**

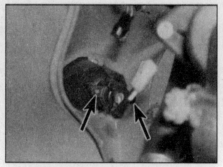

**12.2 Undo the screws (arrowed) and remove the bulbholder**

**12.5 Remove the screw and detach the lens . . .**

sockets (see Section 12) and the wiring connectors. Also, check the signal circuit fuse (see Section 5) and the switch (see Section 20).

2 The battery provides power for operation of the turn signal lights, so if they do not operate, also check the battery voltage. Low battery voltage indicates either a faulty battery or a defective charging system. Refer to Section 3 for battery checks and Sections 30 and 31 for charging system tests.

3 If the bulbs, sockets, connectors, fuse, switch and battery are good, check the turn signal relay. Remove the seats on Daytona and Speed Triple models, the seat cowling on Sprint RS models, and the fairing on Sprint ST and Tiger models (see Chapter 7). Disconnect the relevant relay from its connector block **(see illustration 6.4a, c, d or e)**; on 2002-on Daytona and Speed Triple models the turn signal relay is located under the rider's seat **(see illustration)**. Note that on Sprint and Tiger models, Triumph advise that the exact location of each relay is subject to change, so it is impracticable to specify its exact position in the relay pack – identify the relay by the coloured tag around the wiring going into it. On 1999 Sprint ST models, the turn signal relay tag is red. On 2000-on Sprint ST models, Sprint RS models and Tiger models, the relay tag is blue. If the tag is missing, identify the relay by the colour of the wires going into it, referring to the *Wiring Diagrams* at the end of the Chapter. Triumph do not provide any specific test data for the relay itself, so the easiest way to test it is by substituting the suspect one with a known good one. You can however test the wiring to and from the relay as follows.

4 Check for voltage at the orange/green wire

in the relay wiring connector with the ignition ON. If no voltage is present, using the appropriate wiring diagram at the end of this Chapter check the wiring between the relay and the fusebox, and then to the ignition (main) switch. If voltage was present, first check for continuity to earth in the black or black/green wire, then check for voltage at the light green/brown wire with the ignition ON, and with the switch turned to either LEFT or RIGHT. If no voltage is present, replace the relay with a new one. If voltage was present, check the wiring between the relay, turn signal switch and turn signal lights for continuity. Turn the ignition OFF when the check is complete.

## 12 Turn signal bulbs

### *Front turn signals – Sprint ST models*

1 Remove the fairing side panel (see Chapter 7).

2 If required, disconnect the turn signal wiring connector. Undo the screws securing the bulbholder to the lens assembly and withdraw the bulbholder **(see illustration)**.

3 Push the bulb into the holder and twist it anti-clockwise to remove it. Check the socket terminals for corrosion and clean them if necessary. Line up the pins of the new bulb with the slots in the socket, then push the bulb in and turn it clockwise until it locks into place.

4 Fit the holder onto the lens, and secure it with the screws. Do not overtighten the screw as the threads could be damaged.

### *All turn signals – all other models*

5 Remove the screw securing the turn signal lens and remove the lens, noting how it fits **(see illustration)**.

6 Push the bulb into the holder and twist it anti-clockwise to remove it **(see illustration)**. Check the socket terminals for corrosion and clean them if necessary. Line up the pins of the new bulb with the slots in the socket, then push the bulb in and turn it clockwise until it locks into place.

7 Fit the lens onto the holder, making sure the tab locates correctly **(see illustration)**. Do not overtighten the screw as the lens or threads could be damaged.

## 13 Turn signal assemblies

### *Front*

#### Removal

1 On Daytona models, remove the fairing side panel (see Chapter 7). Unscrew the nut securing the turn signal to the inside of the panel and withdraw it from the outside, taking care not to snag the wiring, and noting the arrangement of the washer, plate and rubber block **(see illustration)**.

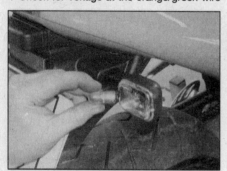

**12.6 . . . and remove the bulb**

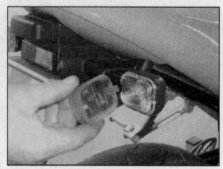

**12.7 Make sure the tab locates correctly when fitting the lens**

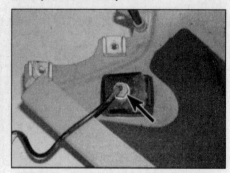

**13.1 Front turn signal nut (arrowed) – Daytona**

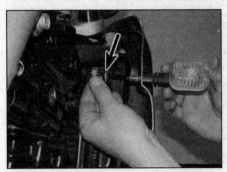

**13.2 Indicator is secured to the bracket (arrowed)**

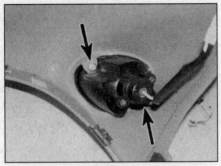

**13.3 Front turn signal screws (arrowed) – Sprint ST**

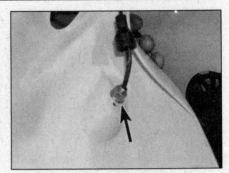

**13.4 Front turn signal nut (arrowed) – Sprint RS**

**2** On Speed Triple models, disconnect the wiring connectors. Pull the rubber boot off the turn signal mount, then unscrew the nut, noting the arrangement of the washers, and withdraw the turn signal from the bracket, taking care not to snag the wiring **(see illustration)**.

**3** On Sprint ST models, remove the fairing side panel, and if required for best access, the fairing (see Chapter 7). Disconnect the turn signal wiring connector. Undo the screws securing the turn signal to the fairing and withdraw it, noting how it fits **(see illustration)**.

**4** On Sprint RS models, remove the fairing side panel (see Chapter 7). Pull the rubber boot off the turn signal mount, then draw the boot off the wiring **(see illustration)**. Unscrew the nut, noting the arrangement of the washers, and withdraw the turn signal from

the bracket, taking care not to snag the wiring.

**5** On Tiger models, remove the two screws securing each turn signal panel, then draw it away and disconnect the wiring connectors **(see illustrations)**. Unscrew the nut on the inside, counter holding the screw on the outside, then withdraw the turn signal, taking care not to snag the wiring **(see illustration)**.

### Installation

**6** Installation is the reverse of removal. Make sure the wiring is correctly routed and securely connected. Check the operation of the turn signals.

## Rear
### Removal

**7** On Daytona and Speed Triple models, remove the seat cowling (see Chapter 7). On

Sprint models, remove the seat (see Chapter 7). On Tiger models, remove the luggage rack and tail light cover (see Chapter 7).

**8** Trace the wiring back from the turn signal and disconnect it at the connectors **(see illustration)**. Release the wiring from any clips and feed it through to the turn signal.

**9** On Daytona, Speed Triple and Sprint models, unscrew the nut securing the turn signal to the inside of the mudguard, then remove the washers, noting their arrangement, and remove the mounting plate where fitted **(see illustration)**. Remove the turn signal from the mudguard, taking care not to snag the wiring as you pull it through.

**10** On Tiger models, undo the screw securing the turn signal to the outside of the mudguard. Remove the turn signal from the mudguard, taking care not to snag the wiring as you pull it through.

### Installation

**11** Installation is the reverse of removal. Make sure the wiring is correctly routed and securely connected. Check the operation of the turn signals.

**14 Brake light switches**

## Circuit check

**1** Before checking the switches, check the brake light circuit (see Section 6, Step 11).

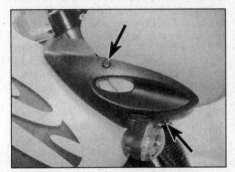

**13.5a Undo the screws (arrowed) . . .**

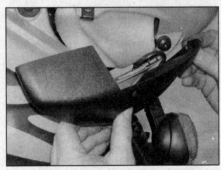

**13.5b . . . and displace the panel**

**13.5c Turn signal nut (arrowed) – Tiger**

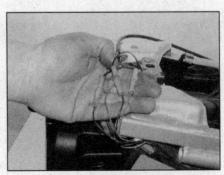

**13.8 Rear turn signal wiring connectors – Daytona shown**

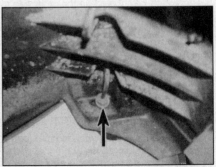

**13.9 The turn signal is secured by a nut (arrowed) on the inside of the mudguard**

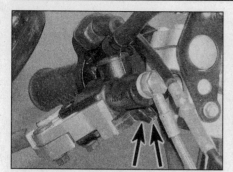

14.2 Front brake switch wiring connectors (arrowed)

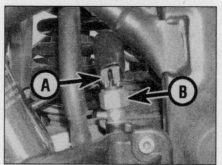

14.3 Rear brake light switch wiring connectors (A), rear brake light switch (B) – Tiger shown

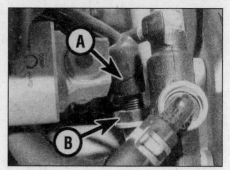

14.9 Rear brake light switch (A) and adjuster nut (B) – Daytona and Speed Triple

2 The front brake light switch is mounted on the underside of the brake master cylinder. Disconnect the wiring connectors from the switch (see illustration). Using a continuity tester, connect the probes to the terminals of the switch. With the brake lever at rest, there should be no continuity. With the brake lever applied, there should be continuity. If the switch does not behave as described, replace it with a new one.

3 The rear brake light switch is mounted on the right-hand side, above the brake pedal. On Daytona and Speed Triple models, trace the wiring from the switch and disconnect it at the connector. On Sprint and Tiger models, pull the rubber boot off the switch and disconnect the wiring connectors (see illustration). Using a continuity tester, connect the probes to the terminals on the wiring connector or the switch, according to model. With the brake pedal at rest, there should be no continuity. With the brake pedal applied, there should be continuity. If the switch does not behave as described, replace it with a new one.

4 If the switches are good, check for voltage at the orange/green wire terminal on the connector with the ignition switch ON – there should be battery voltage. If there's no voltage present, check the wiring between the switch and the ignition switch (see the *Wiring Diagrams* at the end of this Chapter).

### Switch renewal

#### Front brake light switch

5 The switch is mounted on the underside of the brake master cylinder. Disconnect the wiring connectors from the switch (see illustration 14.2).

6 Remove the single screw securing the switch to the bottom of the master cylinder and remove the switch.

7 Installation is the reverse of removal. The switch isn't adjustable.

#### Rear brake light switch

8 The rear brake light switch is mounted on the right-hand side, above the brake pedal. On Daytona and Speed Triple models, trace the wiring from the switch and disconnect it at the connector. Free the wiring from any clips

or ties and feed it through to the switch. On Sprint and Tiger models, pull the rubber boot off the switch and disconnect the wiring connectors (see illustration 14.3).

9 On Daytona and Speed Triple models, detach the lower end of the switch spring from the brake pedal. Unscrew and remove the switch from the adjuster nut in the bracket (see illustration).

10 On Sprint and Tiger models, have some rag handy to catch any fluid spills, then unscrew the brake light switch and separate the brake hose from the master cylinder, noting its alignment. Discard the two sealing washers as they must be replaced with new ones. Wrap the end of the hose in a clean rag and suspend the hose in an upright position or bend it down carefully and place the open end in a clean container. The objective is to prevent excessive loss of brake fluid, fluid spills and system contamination.

11 On Daytona and Speed Triple models, installation is the reverse of removal. Make sure the brake light is activated just before the rear brake pedal takes effect. If adjustment is necessary, hold the switch and turn the adjuster nut on the switch body until the brake light is activated when required (see illustration 14.9).

12 On Sprint and Tiger models, connect the brake hose to the master cylinder, using new sealing washers on each side of the union, and aligning the hose as noted on removal (see illustration 14.3). Tighten brake light switch to the torque setting specified at the

15.3 Inspect the speedometer wire (arrowed) for damage

beginning of the Chapter. Connect the brake light switch wiring connectors, then fit the rubber boot over them.

### 15 Instrument cluster removal and installation

### Check

1 Triumph provide no specific test data for the instruments themselves. Check that the wiring connectors are securely connected both to the instrument cluster and at the other end of the wiring to the source. Check all wires for continuity from pin to pin, referring to the wiring diagrams at the end of the Chapter. Note that on all models except 2002-on Daytona and Speed Triples, there are in-line resistors for the tachometer and temperature gauge, and on Sprint ST and Tiger models the fuel gauge – refer to Chapter 4 for test details.

2 Check that all earth wires have a good connection. If all the wiring is good, it is possible that there are faults in the sensors or electronic control module (ECM) of the engine management system which provide much of the information to the instruments. Refer to Chapter 4 for details. If all checks point at faulty instruments rather than wiring or engine management system, take the instrument cluster to a Triumph dealer for further assessment. Individual components are available for 1997 to 2001 Daytona and Speed Triple models, and all Sprint ST and Tiger models. If any of the warning lights or instrument lights fail, refer to Section 16.

3 Note that if the speedometer is not working on 1997 to 2001 Daytona and Speed Triple models, the most likely cause is a broken cable, which should be checked first. Remove the headlight to access the knurled ring securing the cable to the instrument cluster (see Section 8) (see illustration 15.4b). The cable is secured to the drive gear on the wheel by a single screw (see Chapter 6, Section 13). On all other models, inspect the wire between the front wheel and the instrument cluster for damage (see illustration).

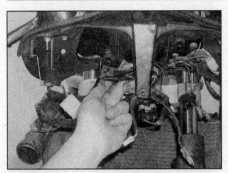

**15.4a Disconnect the wiring connectors . . .**

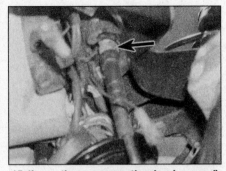

**15.4b . . . then unscrew the ring (arrowed) and detach the cable**

**15.4c Undo the screws (arrowed) . . .**

**15.4d . . . and remove the instruments**

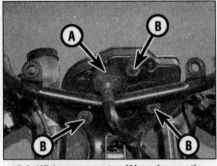

**15.6 Wiring connector (A) and mounting bolts (B)**

**15.7 Disconnect the multi-pin wiring connector**

## Removal

**4** On 1997 to 2001 Daytona models, remove the fairing (see Chapter 7), then remove the headlight (see Section 8). Disconnect the instrument cluster wiring connectors **(see illustration)**. Unscrew the knurled ring securing the speedometer cable and detach it **(see illustration)**. Remove the screws securing the instrument cluster and lift it off the bracket **(see illustrations)**.

**5** On 1997 to 2001 Speed Triple models, disconnect the instrument cluster wiring connectors. Unscrew the knurled ring securing the speedometer cable and detach it. Remove the screws securing the instrument cluster and lift it off the bracket, turning the handlebars as required to access the screws.

**6** On 2002-on Daytona models, remove the fairing (see Chapter 7), then remove the

headlight (see Section 8). Pull back the rubber cover and disconnect the instrument cluster multi-pin wiring connector, then unscrew the bolts securing the cluster to the bracket and lift it off **(see illustration)**.

**7** On 2002-on Speed Triple models, where fitted, remove the fly screen and trim panel (see Chapter 7, Section 3). Alternatively, unscrew the two bolts securing the lower cover and lift it off. If not already done, pull back the rubber cover and disconnect the multi-pin wiring connector **(see illustration)**. Unscrew the bolts securing the cluster to the bracket and lift it off.

**8** On Sprint ST models, remove the fairing (see Chapter 7). Unscrew the nuts securing the instrument cluster and lift it off the bracket, then disconnect the wiring connectors and remove the cluster **(see illustration)**.

**9** On Sprint RS models, remove the fairing (see Chapter 7). Pull back the rubber cover and disconnect the wiring connector from the instrument cluster **(see illustration)**. Remove the screws securing the cluster and lift it off the stay **(see illustration)**.

**10** On Tiger models, remove the fairing (see Chapter 7), then remove the headlight (see Section 8). Unscrew the nuts securing the instrument cluster and lift it off the bracket, then disconnect the wiring connectors and remove the cluster.

## Installation

**11** Installation is the reverse of removal. Check all the rubber mounting grommets for cracks and deterioration and replace them with new ones if necessary. Make sure the instruments are installed with all washers, collars and grommets previously installed.

**15.8 Instrument cluster nuts (arrowed) – Sprint ST**

**15.9a Pull back the rubber cover and disconnect the wiring connector**

**15.9b Undo the screws (arrowed) and remove the instruments**

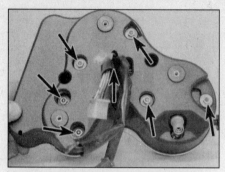

16.1a Unscrew the nuts (arrowed) . . .

16.1b . . . and remove the grommets . . .

16.1c . . . then undo the three screws (arrowed) . . .

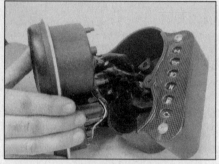

16.1d . . . and lift the instruments out of the casing

16.1e Pull out the bulbholder . . .

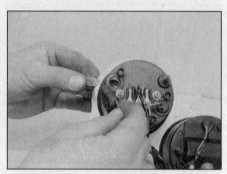

16.1f . . . and renew the bulb

## 16 Instrument and warning light bulbs

**1** On 1997 to 2001 Daytona and Speed Triple models, remove the instrument cluster (see Section 15). To replace instrument illumination bulbs, unscrew the six nuts on the back of the cluster and remove the rubber grommets, then undo the three screws on the front of the cluster **(see illustrations)**. Lift the instrument assembly out of the casing **(see illustration)**. Pull the relevant bulbholder out of the instrument, then pull the bulb out of the holder

and install a new one **(see illustrations)**. To replace warning light bulbs, remove the instrument assembly from the housing as described above, then lift the warning light assembly out **(see illustration)**. Pull the relevant bulbholder out of the assembly, then pull the bulb out of the holder and install a new one **(see illustration)**.

**2** On 2002-on Daytona and Speed Triple models, and all Sprint RS models, remove the instrument cluster (see Section 15). Undo the five screws on the back of the cluster and separate the two halves of the casing. Twist the relevant bulbholder anti-clockwise to release it, then pull out the bulb and replace it with a new one.

**3** On Sprint ST models, remove the fairing (see Chapter 7). Some of the instrument illumination bulbs are accessible without removing anything else **(see illustration)**. For others, and for the warning light bulbs, undo the screws securing the shroud and remove it. If there are any you can't get at, either displace the headlight or the instrument cluster to access them (see Section 8 or 15). Pull the relevant bulbholder out of the assembly, then pull the bulb out of the holder and install a new one.

**4** On Tiger models, remove the fairing (see Chapter 7). Some of the instrument illumination bulbs and all of the warning light bulbs are accessible without removing

16.1g Lift out the warning light assembly . . .

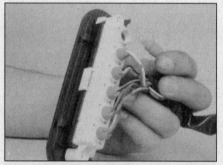

16.1h . . . then pull out the bulbholder to access the bulb

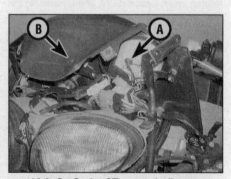

16.3 On Sprint ST, some bulbs are accessible (A), otherwise remove the shroud (B) or displace the cluster

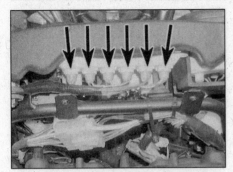

**16.4 Warning light bulbs – Tiger models**

anything else **(see illustration)**. For others, displace the instrument cluster to access them (see Section 15), and if necessary displace the instrument itself from its mount. Pull the relevant bulbholder out of the assembly, then pull the bulb out of the holder and install a new one.

## 17 Relays

### General information

**Note:** *Changes to relay location and application are given below where known. If you are in any doubt regarding the quantity, function and location of any relays, refer to your Triumph dealer.*

### Daytona and Speed Triple

**1** On 1997 to 2001 models, all the relays are housed under the seats **(see illustration 6.4a)**.
**2** From 2002-on, the ECM power relay, headlight cut-out relay, dip beam and main beam relays were housed behind the seat cowling on the right-hand side and the ignition relay and turn signal relay are housed under the rider's seat, next to the ECM and tip-over sensor **(see illustrations 6.4b and 11.3)**.

### Sprint ST

**3** On models up to VIN 89736 models, the headlight and turn signal relays are housed behind the fairing, and the engine management relays (ECM power, cooling fan and fuel pump) are housed behind the seat cowling on the right-hand side.
**4** From VIN 89737 to 139276, the ECM power relay was under the seat, and the headlight and turn signal relays were behind the fairing **(see illustration 6.4c)** – the fuel pump and cooling fan relays were discontinued.
**5** From 2002-on, the ECM power relay and ignition relay are located under the seat, next to the tip-over sensor and ECM. The turn signal and headlight relays (main beam, dip beam and cut-out) are mounted to the sub-frame behind the fairing on the right-hand side. Note that the relay locations are subject to change – use the relay tags for identification if necessary.

### Sprint RS

**6** On early models, the ECM power relay is under the seat, and the headlight and turn signal relays are behind the seat cowling on the right-hand side **(see illustration 6.4d)**. Fuel pump and cooling fan relays are not fitted.
**7** From 2002-on, the ECM power relay and ignition relay are located under the seat, next to the tip-over sensor and ECM. The turn signal and headlight relays (main beam, dip beam and cut-out) are mounted to the rear sub-frame on the right-hand side; remove the seat cowling to access them. Note that the relay locations are subject to change – use the relay tags for identification if necessary.

### Tiger

**8** The ECM power relay is under the seat, along with the cooling fan and fuel pump relays to VIN 89736. From VIN 89737-on the fuel pump and cooling fan relays are no longer fitted. The headlight and turn signal relays are behind the fairing **(see illustration 6.4e)**.
**9** From 2002-on, the headlight cut-out relay was housed behind the fairing.

### Check and renewal

**10** To check the relays, remove the seats, seat cowling and/or the fairing, according to your model as outlined above. On Sprint and Tiger models, Triumph advise that the exact location of each relay is subject to change, so it is impracticable to specify its exact position in the relay pack – identify the relay by the coloured tag around the wiring going into it.
**11** On 1999 Sprint ST models, the main beam relay tag is black, the dip beam relay tag is white, the turn signal relay tag is red, the headlight cut-out relay (lights-on models only) tag is blue, the cooling fan relay tag is blue, the fuel pump relay tag is white and the ECM relay tag is red. If the tag is missing, identify the relay by the colour of the wires going into it, referring to the *Wiring Diagrams* at the end of the Chapter.
**12** On 2000 to 2001 Sprint ST models, Sprint RS models and Tiger models, the main beam relay tag is red, and the dip beam relay tag is white, the turn signal relay tag is red on Sprint and blue on Tiger, the headlight cut-out relay (lights-on models only) tag is yellow on Sprint, and on Tiger models there is no tag. If the tag is missing, identify the relay by the colour of the wires going into it, referring to the *Wiring Diagrams* at the end of the Chapter.
**13** On 2002-on Sprint ST and RS models, the main beam relay tag is red, and the dip beam relay tag is white, the turn signal relay tag is blue and the headlight cut-out relay tag is yellow.
**14** Triumph do not provide any specific test data for the relays, so the best way to test it is by substituting the suspect one with a known good one – if the low beam is not working and the hi beam is, swap the relays and see if the problem follows. The cooling fan relay, where fitted, is covered in Chapter 3. The headlight

relays are covered in Section 6 of this Chapter. The ECM and fuel pump relays (where fitted) are covered in Chapter 4.
**15** The relays should have terminal identification numbers and a small circuit diagram marked on their underside – use this to identify the activating power in and out terminals, and the main power in and out terminals that provide the power to the appropriate electrical component. Using an ohmmeter or continuity tester, connect the positive (+ve) probe to the relay's main power in terminal, and the negative (–ve) probe to the relay's main power out terminal. There should be no continuity. Leaving the meter connected, and using a fully charged 12 volt battery and two insulated jumper wires, connect the positive (+ve) terminal of the battery to the activating power in terminal, and the negative (-ve) terminal to the activating power out terminal. At this point the relay should close and the multimeter read 0 ohms (continuity) – there should be an audible click as the relay closes.
**16** If you are replacing a relay, first disconnect the battery negative (-ve) terminal. The relays have terminals on their underside which plug directly into sockets – simply pull the relay out of its socket, and fit the new one in.

## 18 Ignition (main) switch

**Warning: To prevent the risk of short circuits, remove the seat(s) and disconnect the battery negative (–ve) lead before making any ignition (main) switch checks.**

### Check

**1** Trace the ignition (main) switch wiring back from the base of the switch and disconnect it at the connector, removing the fairing, fairing side panels or fuel tank as required by your model. Make the checks on the switch side of the connector.
**2** Using an ohmmeter or a continuity tester, check the continuity of the connector terminal pairs (see the *Wiring Diagrams* at the end of this Chapter). Continuity should exist between the terminals connected by a solid line on the diagram when the switch key is turned to the indicated position.
**3** If the switch fails any of the tests, replace it with a new one.

### Removal

**4** Trace the ignition (main) switch wiring back from the base of the switch and disconnect it at the connector, removing the fairing, fairing side panels or fuel tank as required by your model (it is advisable to remove them anyway to prevent the possibility of damage should a tool slip when removing the top yoke.
**5** On Speed Triple models with one-piece handlebars, and on Sprint and Tiger models, displace the handlebars from the top yoke

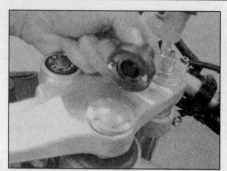

**18.6a Unscrew the steering stem nut . . .**

**18.6b . . . and draw the yoke up off the forks**

**18.7 Ignition switch bolts (arrowed)**

(see Chapter 5). Secure the handlebar assemblies so that the master cylinder is upright, making sure there is no strain on the hoses, cables or wiring. On all models, slacken the fork clamp bolts in the top yoke – on Daytona and Speed Triple models with separate handlebars, to access the clamp bolts, slacken the handlebar clamp bolts, then slide the handlebars down the forks until the locating pins are clear of the holes in the underside of the yoke, and twist them round until the fork clamp bolts in the top yoke are accessible.

6 Unscrew the steering stem nut and remove it along with its washer, where fitted. On Daytona and Speed Triple models, this requires the use of a special Triumph tool (Pt. No. T3880300), or a suitable equivalent **(see illustration)**. Lift the top yoke up off the steering stem and position it clear, using a rag to protect the tank and other components **(see illustration)**.

7 Two shear-head bolts mount the ignition switch to the underside of the top yoke **(see illustration)**. The heads of the bolts must be driven round using a suitable punch or drift, or drilled off, before the switch can be removed. Mount the yoke in a vice equipped with soft jaws and padded out with rags to do this. Remove the bolts and withdraw the switch from the top yoke.

### Installation

8 Installation is the reverse of removal. Obtain new shear-head bolts and tighten them until their heads shear off. Make sure wiring

connectors are securely connected and correctly routed. Tighten the steering stem nut, the fork clamp bolts, the handlebar bolts, in that order, to the torque settings specified at the beginning of Chapter 5, and refer to Sections 5 and 8 in that Chapter for procedural details and illustrations.

## 19 Handlebar switches check

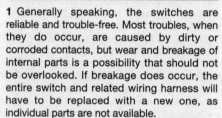

1 Generally speaking, the switches are reliable and trouble-free. Most troubles, when they do occur, are caused by dirty or corroded contacts, but wear and breakage of internal parts is a possibility that should not be overlooked. If breakage does occur, the entire switch and related wiring harness will have to be replaced with a new one, as individual parts are not available.
2 The switches can be checked for continuity using an ohmmeter or a continuity test light.
3 Trace the wiring harness of the switch in question back to its connectors and disconnect them, removing the fairing, fairing side panels or fuel tank as required by your model.
4 Check for continuity between the terminals of the switch harness with the switch in the various positions (i.e. switch off – no continuity, switch on – continuity) – see the *Wiring Diagrams* at the end of this Chapter.
5 If the continuity check indicates a problem exists, refer to Section 20, remove the switch and spray the switch contacts with electrical

contact cleaner. If they are accessible, the contacts can be scraped clean with a knife or polished with crocus cloth. If switch components are damaged or broken, it should be obvious when the switch is disassembled.

## 20 Handlebar switches removal and installation

### Removal

1 If the switch is to be removed from the bike, rather than just displaced from the handlebar, trace the wiring harness of the switch in question back to its connectors and disconnect them, removing the fairing, fairing side panels or fuel tank as required by your model. Work back along the harness, freeing it from all the relevant clips and ties, noting its correct routing.
2 Disconnect the wiring connectors from the front brake light switch if removing the right-hand switch **(see illustration 14.2)**.
3 Unscrew the handlebar switch screws (either on the back or the underside of the switch) and free the switch from the handlebar by separating the halves **(see illustrations)**. On Sprint ST and Tiger models, when removing the right-hand switch, detach the throttle cable, noting how it fits – refer to Chapter 4, Section 10 for details.

### Installation

4 Installation is the reverse of removal. Make sure the locating pin in the switch housing locates in the hole in the handlebar. Make sure the wiring connectors are correctly routed and securely connected.

## 21 Neutral switch

### Check

1 If the neutral light fails to come on, first check the circuit fuse (see Section 5) and the bulb in the instrument cluster (see Section 16).

**20.3a Right-hand switch housing screws (arrowed) – Daytona shown**

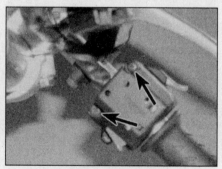

**20.3b Left-hand switch housing screws (arrowed) – Daytona shown**

21.2 Disconnect the wiring connector (arrowed) from the switch

21.4 Neutral switch (arrowed)

**2** The switch is located on the left-hand side of the engine just below the front sprocket cover. Disconnect the wiring connector from the switch **(see illustration)**.

**3** With the connector disconnected and the ignition switched ON, the neutral light should be out. If not, the wire between the connector and instrument cluster must be earthed (grounded) at some point.

**4** Check for continuity between the terminal on the switch and the crankcase. With the transmission in neutral, there should be continuity. With the transmission in gear, there should be no continuity. If there is no continuity when in neutral, remove the switch (see below), and check that the contact plunger is not damaged or seized in the switch body **(see illustration)**.

**5** If the continuity tests prove the switch is good, check for voltage (ignition ON) at the terminal on the wiring connector. If there's no voltage present, check the wire between the switch and the bulb, and if that is good, check for voltage in the other wire to the bulb (see the *Wiring Diagrams* at the end of this Chapter).

### Removal

**6** The switch is on the left-hand side of the engine just below the front sprocket cover. On Daytona models, remove the belly pan or left-hand fairing side panel as appropriate (see Chapter 7). Drain the engine oil (see Chapter 1).

**7** Disconnect the wiring connector from the switch **(see illustration 21.2)**.

**8** Unscrew the switch and withdraw it from

the casing **(see illustration 21.4)**. Discard the sealing washer as a new one should be used.

### Installation

**9** Install the switch using a new sealing washer and tighten it securely.

**10** Connect the wiring connector. Check the operation of the neutral light. Fill the engine with the correct quantity of oil (see Chapter 1 and *Daily (pre-ride) checks*). On Daytona, install the belly pan or fairing side panel (see Chapter 7).

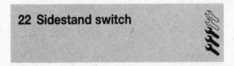

## 22 Sidestand switch

### Check

**1** The sidestand switch is mounted on the sidestand bracket **(see illustration 22.8b)**. The switch is part of the safety circuit which prevents or stops the engine running if the transmission is in gear whilst the sidestand is down, and prevents the engine from starting if the transmission is in gear unless the sidestand is up, and unless the clutch is pulled in. Before checking the electrical circuit, check the fuse (see Section 5).

**2** Trace the wiring from the switch and disconnect it at the connector, removing the fairing side panels or fuel tank as required by your model.

**3** Check the operation of the switch using an

ohmmeter or continuity test light. Connect the meter probes to the terminals on the switch side of the connector. With the sidestand up there should be continuity (zero resistance) between the terminals, and with the stand down there should be no continuity (infinite resistance).

**4** If the switch does not perform as expected, it is defective and must be renewed.

**5** If the switch is good, check the other components in the starter circuit as described in the relevant sections of this Chapter. If all components are good, check the wiring between the various components (see the *Wiring Diagrams* at the end of this Chapter).

### Renewal

**6** The sidestand switch is mounted on the sidestand bracket. Trace the wiring from the switch and disconnect it at the connector, removing the fairing, fairing side panels or fuel tank as required by your model. Work back along the switch wiring, freeing it from any relevant retaining clips and ties, noting its correct routing.

**7** On Daytona, Speed Triple and Sprint models, first displace the water pump to gain access to the sidestand bracket bolts (see Chapter 3, Section 7). Unscrew the bolts securing the sidestand bracket to the crankcase and displace it **(see illustration)**.

**8** On all models, undo the screws or bolts securing the switch and remove the switch, noting how it fits **(see illustrations)**.

22.7 Unscrew the bolts (arrowed) and remove the sidestand assembly

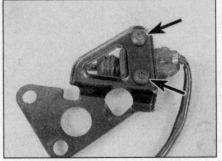

22.8a Sidestand switch screws (arrowed) – Daytona, Speed Triple and Sprint

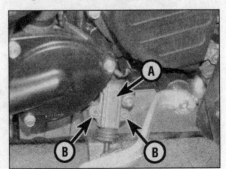

22.8b Sidestand switch (A) and its mounting bolts (B) – Tiger

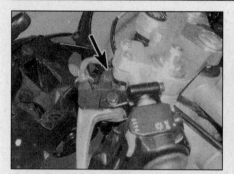

**23.1 Clutch switch (arrowed)**

**23.5 Release the clip and withdraw the switch**

**24.2a Location of the horn – 2002-on Daytona and Speed Triple models**

**9** Fit the new switch and tighten the screws or bolts securely. On Daytona, Speed Triple and Sprint models, install the sidestand assembly and tighten the bolts securely **(see illustration 22.7)**.

**10** Make sure the wiring is correctly routed up to the connector and retained by all the necessary clips and ties. Reconnect the wiring connector and check the operation of the sidestand switch.

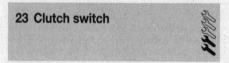

## 23 Clutch switch

### Check

**1** The clutch switch is mounted in the clutch lever bracket **(see illustration)**. The switch is part of the safety circuit which prevents or stops the engine running if the transmission is in gear whilst the sidestand is down, and prevents the engine from starting if the transmission is in gear unless the sidestand is up and the clutch lever is pulled in. The switch isn't adjustable.

**2** To check the switch, trace the wiring from the switch and disconnect it at the connector. Connect the probes of an ohmmeter or a continuity tester to the two terminals on the switch side of the connector. With the clutch lever pulled in, continuity should be indicated.

With the clutch lever out, no continuity (infinite resistance) should be indicated.

**3** If the switch is good, turn the ignition on and check that there is voltage at one of the terminals on the loom side of the connector, and check that the other terminal has continuity with earth (ground). If not check the wiring. Otherwise, check the other components in the starter circuit as described in the relevant sections of this Chapter, and check the wiring between the various components (see the *Wiring Diagrams* at the end of this Chapter).

### Renewal

**4** The clutch switch is mounted in the clutch lever bracket **(see illustration 23.1)**.

**5** Trace the wiring from the switch and disconnect it at the connector. Use a small screwdriver to release the clip on the underside of the switch and pull it out of the clutch lever bracket **(see illustration)**.

**6** Installation is the reverse of removal.

## 24 Horn

### Check

**1** If the horn doesn't work, first check the circuit fuse (see Section 5) and the battery (see Section 3).

**2** The horn is mounted on the instrument/headlight bracket on 1997 to 2001 Daytona models **(see illustration 8.2a)**, below the radiator on 2002-on Daytona and Speed Triple models, and on the bottom yoke on all other models **(see illustrations)**. If required, remove the fairing for best access (see Chapter 7).

**3** Unplug the wiring connectors from the horn. Using two jumper wires, apply battery voltage directly to the terminals on the horn. If the horn sounds, check the button in the switch housing (see Section 19) and the wiring between the switch housing and the horn (see *Wiring Diagrams* at the end of this Chapter).

**4** If the horn doesn't sound, replace it with a new one.

### Renewal

**5** The horn is mounted on the instrument/headlight bracket on 1997 to 2001 Daytona models, below the radiator on 2002-on Daytona and Speed Triple models, and on the bottom yoke on all other models **(see illustrations 8.2a, 24.2a, b or c)**. Remove the fairing for best access (see Chapter 7).

**6** Unplug the wiring connectors from the horn. Unscrew the bolt(s) securing the horn and remove it from the bike.

**7** Install the horn and securely tighten the bolt(s). Connect the wiring connectors to the horn. Install the fairing (see Chapter 7).

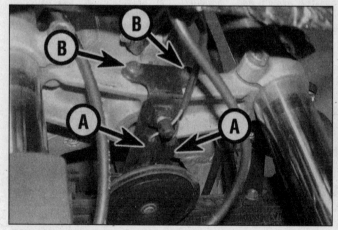

**24.2b Horn wiring connectors (A) and mounting bolts (B) – Sprint models**

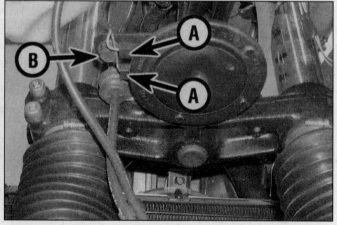

**24.2c Horn wiring connectors (A) and mounting bolt (B) – Tiger models**

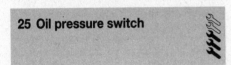

**25.3 Oil pressure switch wiring connector (arrowed)**

**25.8 Unscrew the switch, noting the sealing washers and how the oil hose is secured**

## 25 Oil pressure switch

### Check

1 The oil pressure warning light should come on when the ignition (main) switch is turned ON and extinguish a few seconds after the engine is started; on Sprint RS models, the low oil pressure symbol should flash. If the oil pressure warning light comes on whilst the engine is running, stop the engine immediately and carry out an oil level check (see *Daily (pre-ride) checks*), and if the level is correct, an oil pressure check (see Chapter 2).

2 If the oil pressure warning light does not come on when the ignition is turned on, first check the bulb (see Section 16) and circuit fuse (see Section 5).

3 The oil pressure switch is screwed into the top of the crankcase on the right-hand side **(see illustration)**. On Daytona and Sprint ST models remove the right-hand fairing side panel for access (see Chapter 7). To check the switch, pull the wiring connector off the switch. With the ignition switched ON, earth (ground) the wire on the crankcase and check that the warning light comes on. If the light comes on, the switch is proven defective and must be replaced with a new one.

4 If the light still does not come on, check for voltage at the wire terminal. If there is no voltage present, check the wiring between the switch, the instrument cluster and ECM for continuity (see the *wiring diagrams* at the end of this Chapter).

5 If the warning light comes on whilst the engine is running, yet the oil pressure is satisfactory, remove the wire from the oil pressure switch. With the wire detached and the ignition switched ON the light should be out. If it is illuminated, the wire between the switch and instrument cluster must be earthed (grounded) at some point. If the wiring is good, the switch must be assumed faulty and renewed.

### Removal

6 On Daytona and Sprint ST models remove the right-hand fairing side panel for access (see Chapter 7).

7 Pull the wiring connector off the switch. **(see illustration 25.3)**.

8 Unscrew the oil pressure switch, noting how it also secures the oil hose, and withdraw it from the crankcase **(see illustration)**. Be prepared to catch any residual oil from the pipe. Discard the sealing washers as new ones should be used.

### Installation

9 Install the switch using new sealing washers on each side of the oil hose union and tighten it to the torque setting specified at the beginning of the Chapter **(see illustration 25.8)**. Attach the wiring connector **(see illustration 25.3)**.

10 Run the engine and check that the switch operates correctly without leakage.

11 On Daytona and Sprint ST models install the right-hand fairing side panel (see Chapter 7).

## 26 Starter solenoid

### Check

1 If the starter circuit is faulty, first check the main fuse (see Section 5).

2 To check the starter solenoid, first trace the lead from the top of the starter motor to the solenoid, removing the seat(s) or seat cowling as required by your model (see Chapter 7). The starter motor is mounted on the crankcase, behind the cylinder block. Note that the exact location of the solenoid is subject to change,

so it is impracticable to specify its exact position **(see illustrations)**.

3 Lift the rubber terminal cover and unscrew the nut securing the starter motor lead to the solenoid; position the lead away from the terminal. With the ignition switch ON, the engine kill switch in the RUN position, and the transmission in neutral, press the starter switch. The solenoid should be heard to click. If the solenoid doesn't click, switch the ignition OFF and remove the solenoid as described below; then test it as follows.

4 Set a multimeter to the ohms x 1 scale and connect it across the solenoid's starter motor and battery lead terminals. Using a fully-charged 12 volt battery and two insulated jumper wires, connect the positive (+ve) terminal of the battery to the white/red wire terminal on the solenoid, and the negative (−ve) terminal to the black/pink wire terminal. At this point the solenoid should be heard to click and the multimeter read 0 ohms (continuity). If this is the case the solenoid is proved good. If the solenoid does not click when battery voltage is applied and indicates no continuity (infinite resistance) across its terminals, it is faulty and must be replaced with a new one.

5 If the solenoid is good, check for battery voltage at the white/red wire terminal on the loom side of the wiring connector when the starter button is pressed. If voltage is present, check the other components in the starter circuit as described in the relevant sections of this Chapter. If no voltage was present, check the wiring between the various components (see *Wiring Diagrams* at the end of this Chapter).

### Renewal

6 Remove the seat(s) and body panels as required by your model (see Chapter 7). Disconnect the battery negative (−ve) lead before removing the solenoid.

7 Lift the rubber terminal covers, then unscrew the two nuts securing the starter motor and battery leads and detach them, noting which fits where **(see illustrations 26.2a and b)**. Disconnect the solenoid wiring connectors, displacing the solenoid from its mount to access them if required. Remove the solenoid with its rubber sleeve from its mounting lug on the frame.

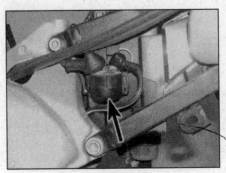

**26.2a Starter solenoid (arrowed) – Sprint models**

**26.2b Starter solenoid (arrowed) – Tiger models**

27.2a Slacken the clamp screw and detach the hose from the union

27.2b Undo the screws (arrowed) and remove the union

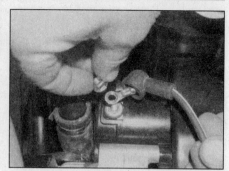

27.3 Lift the rubber cover, then unscrew the nut and detach the lead

8 Installation is the reverse of removal. Make sure the terminal nuts are securely tightened. Connect the negative (–ve) lead last when reconnecting the battery.

## 27 Starter motor removal and installation

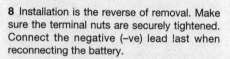

### Removal

1 The starter motor is mounted on the crankcase, behind the cylinder block. Remove the seat(s) and body panels as required by your model to gain access (see Chapter 7). Disconnect the battery negative (–ve) lead.
2 On 1997 to 2001 models, drain the cooling system (see Chapter 1). Slacken the clamp securing the coolant hose to the inlet union on the engine and detach the hose (see illustration). Undo the screws securing the union and remove it (see illustration). Discard the gasket as a new one must be used.
3 On all models peel back the rubber terminal cover and unscrew the nut securing the lead to the starter motor (see illustration). Detach the lead.
4 Unscrew the two bolts securing the starter motor (see illustrations). Draw the starter motor out of the crankcase and remove it (see illustrations).
5 Remove the O-ring on the end of the starter motor and discard it as a new one must be used.

### Installation

6 Fit a new O-ring onto the end of the starter motor, making sure it is seated in its groove, and smear it with grease (see illustration).

7 Manoeuvre the motor into position and slide it into the crankcase (see illustration 27.4c or d). Ensure that the starter motor teeth mesh correctly with those of the starter idle/reduction gear. Install the mounting bolts and tighten them to the torque setting specified at the beginning of the Chapter (see illustration 27.4a or b).
8 Connect the lead to the starter motor and secure it with the nut (see illustration 27.3). Make sure the rubber cover is correctly seated over the terminal.
9 On 1997 to 2001 models, remove all traces of old gasket from the mating surfaces of the coolant union and the engine. Install the union using a new gasket smeared on both sides with a suitable sealant, and tighten the screws to the specified torque setting (see illustration). Fit the hose onto the union and tighten the clamp to secure it (see illustration 27.2a). Fill the cooling system (see Chapter 1).

27.4a Unscrew the bolts – 1997 to 2001 models

27.4b Unscrew the bolts – 2002-on models

27.4c Remove the starter motor – 1997 to 2001 models

27.4d Remove the starter motor – 2002-on models

27.6 Fit a new O-ring and smear it with grease

27.9 Install the union using a new gasket

**28.3 Unscrew the two long bolts, noting the O-rings fitted on them**

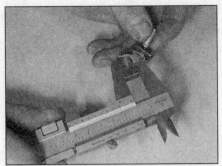

**28.8 Measuring brush length – replace brushes if they are worn beyond service limit**

**28.10 Inspect the commutator segments for wear and test as described in the text**

**10** Connect the battery negative (–ve) lead and install the seat(s) and body panels as required (see Chapter 7).

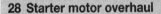
## 28 Starter motor overhaul

### Disassembly

**1** Remove the starter motor (see Section 27).
**2** Make some alignment marks between the housing and both end covers.
**3** Unscrew the two long bolts, then remove the rear cover from the motor, noting how it locates **(see illustration)**. Discard the O-ring as a new one should be used.
**4** Wrap insulating tape around the teeth of the starter motor gear – this will protect the oil seal from damage as the front cover is removed. Remove the front cover from the motor along with its O-ring, and discard the O-ring.
**5** Withdraw the armature from the housing.
**6** Unscrew the nut from the terminal bolt and remove the insulating washer and the O-ring **(see illustrations 28.14d, c and b)**. Withdraw the terminal bolt and brushplate assembly from the housing **(see illustration 28.14a)**.
**7** Lift the brush springs and slide the brushes out from their holders.

### Inspection

**Note:** *No replacement parts are available from Triumph for the starter motor. If the following checks indicate a worn or faulty internal component, seek the advice of a Triumph dealer or auto electrical specialist before buying a new starter motor.*
**8** The parts of the starter motor that are most likely to wear are the brushes. On 1997 to 2001 models, measure the length of the brushes and compare the results to the service limit in this Chapter's Specifications **(see illustration)**. If the brushes are not worn excessively, nor cracked, chipped, or otherwise damaged, they may be re-used.
**9** Inspect the commutator for scoring, scratches and discoloration. The commutator can be cleaned and polished with crocus cloth, but do not use sandpaper or emery paper. After cleaning, wipe away any residue with a cloth soaked in electrical system cleaner or denatured alcohol.
**10** Using an ohmmeter or a continuity test light, check for continuity between the commutator bars **(see illustration)**. Continuity should exist between each bar and all of the others. Also, check for continuity between the commutator bars and the armature shaft. There should be no continuity (infinite resistance) between the commutator and the shaft. If the checks indicate otherwise, the armature is defective.
**11** Check for continuity between the brushplate brush and the brushplate itself, and between the terminal bolt brush and the terminal bolt itself. There should be continuity in both cases.

**12** Check the starter gear for worn, cracked, chipped and broken teeth. If the gear is damaged or worn, renew the starter motor.
**13** Inspect the end covers for signs of cracks or wear. Inspect the magnets in the main housing and the housing itself for cracks.

### Reassembly

**14** Ensure that the rubber insulating seat is in place on the terminal bolt, then insert the bolt through the rear cover **(see illustration)**. Fit the O-ring and the insulating washer and secure them in place with the nut **(see illustrations)**.
**15** Lift the brush springs on the brushplate and slide the brushes back into position in their holders, then install the brushplate assembly in the rear cover making sure its tab is correctly located in the slot in the cover

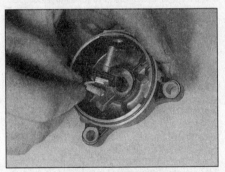

**28.14a  Install the terminal bolt . . .**

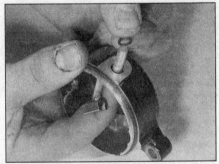

**28.14b  . . . then fit the O-ring . . .**

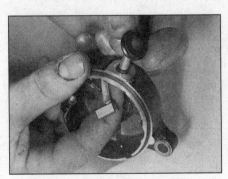

**28.14c  . . . the insulating washer . . .**

**28.14d  . . . and the terminal nut**

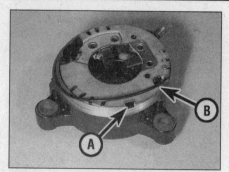

**28.15 Align the brushplate tab with the slot in the cover (A) and fit the cover O-ring (B)**

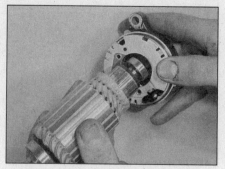

**28.16 Fit the armature into the rear cover . . .**

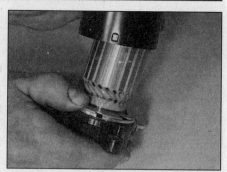

**28.17a . . . and fit the main housing over the armature . . .**

**(see illustration)**. Make sure the O-ring is fitted to the cover.

**16** Insert the armature into the rear end cover taking care not to damage the brushes **(see illustration)**. As it is inserted, locate the brushes on the commutator bars. Check that each brush is securely pressed against the commutator by its spring and is free to move easily in its holder.

**17** Fit the main housing over the armature, aligning the marks made on removal **(see illustrations)**.

**18** Fit the O-ring to the front end cover and carefully slide the cover into position, aligning the marks made on removal **(see illustration)**. Remove any protective tape from the gear teeth.

**19** Check the marks made on removal are correctly aligned then fit the long bolts and tighten them securely **(see illustration 28.3)**.

**20** Install the starter motor (see Section 27).

### 29 Charging system testing – general information and precautions

**1** If the performance of the charging system is suspect, the system as a whole should be checked first, followed by testing of the individual components. **Note:** *Before beginning the checks, make sure the battery is fully charged and that all system connections are clean and tight.*

**2** Checking the output of the charging system and the performance of the various components within the charging system

requires the use of a multimeter (with voltage, current and resistance checking facilities), though a simple voltmeter will at least be able to tell what if any voltage is being put out.

**3** When making the checks, follow the procedures carefully to prevent incorrect connections or short circuits, as irreparable damage to electrical system components may result if short circuits occur.

**4** If a multimeter is not available, the job of checking the charging system should be left to a Triumph dealer or automotive electrician.

### 30 Charging system leakage and output tests

**1** If the charging system of the machine is thought to be faulty, remove the seat(s) (see Chapter 7) and perform the following checks.

### Leakage test

*Caution: Always connect an ammeter in series, never in parallel with the battery, otherwise it will be damaged. Do not turn the ignition ON or operate the starter motor when the ammeter is connected – a sudden surge in current will blow the meter's fuse.*

**2** Turn the ignition switch OFF and disconnect the lead from the battery negative (–ve) terminal.

**3** Set the multimeter to the Amps function and connect its negative (–ve) probe to the battery negative (–ve) terminal, and positive (+ve) probe to the disconnected negative (–ve)

lead **(see illustration)**. Always set the meter to a high amps range initially and then bring it down to the mA (milli Amps) range; if there is a high current flow in the circuit it may blow the meter's fuse.

**4** No current flow should be indicated. If current leakage is indicated (generally greater than 1 mA), there is a short circuit in the wiring, although if an alarm is fitted remember to take its current draw into account. Using the wiring diagrams at the end of this Chapter, systematically disconnect individual electrical components, checking the meter each time until the source is identified.

**5** If no leakage is indicated, disconnect the meter and connect the negative (–ve) lead to the battery, tightening it securely.

### Output test

**6** Start the engine and warm it up to normal operating temperature.

**7** To check the regulated voltage output, allow the engine to idle and connect a multimeter set to the 0 to 20 volts DC scale (voltmeter) across the terminals of the battery (positive (+ve) lead to battery positive (+ve) terminal, negative (–ve) lead to battery negative (–ve) terminal). Slowly increase the engine speed briefly to around 5000 rpm and note the reading obtained. Triumph provide no data on the specific output of their charging system, but the regulated voltage should be around 13.5 to 15.0V. If the voltage is outside these limits, check the alternator/regulator/rectifier (see Section 31).

**28.17b . . . aligning the marks made on removal (arrowed)**

**28.18 Fit the front cover, again aligning the marks made on removal (arrowed)**

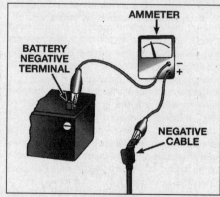

**30.3 Checking the charging system leakage rate – connect the ammeter as shown**

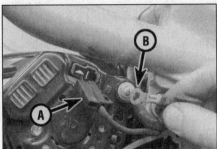

**31.3  Disconnect the wiring connector (A) and the earth lead (B)**

**31.4a  Unscrew the bolts (arrowed) . . .**

**31.4b  . . . and remove the alternator**

### 31 Alternator/regulator/rectifier

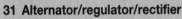

## 1997 to 2001 models

### Removal

**1** The alternator is mounted on the crankcase, behind the cylinder block. Remove the seat(s), and on Daytona and Sprint models the left-hand fairing side panel, then on Sprint ST remove the belly pan (see Chapter 7).

Disconnect the battery negative (–ve) lead.
**2** Drain the cooling system (see Chapter 1). Slacken the clamp securing the coolant hose to the inlet union on the engine and detach the hose **(see illustration 27.2a)**.
**3** Disconnect the alternator wiring connector, then pull the rubber boot off the earth terminal, unscrew the nut and detach the earth lead **(see illustration)**.
**4** Unscrew the three alternator mounting bolts, noting the earth lead(s) secured by the rear bolt **(see illustration)**. Withdraw the alternator from the engine, leaving the shock absorber rubbers in the driveshaft housing **(see illustration)**. Discard the alternator O-ring as a new one should be used.

### Testing

**Note:** *No replacement parts are available from Triumph for the alternator. If the following checks indicate a worn or faulty internal component, seek the advice of a Triumph dealer or auto electrical specialist before buying a new alternator.*
**5** The following checks can be made without removing the alternator from the engine, although the alternator wiring must first be disconnected as described in Step 3.
**6** Undo the three screws securing the alternator end cover, and the nut on the earth terminal, noting the sleeve, and remove the cover **(see illustrations)**.
**7** Remove the two screws securing the brush holder and remove the holder, noting how the brushes locate **(see illustrations)**. Inspect the holder for any signs of damage. Measure the brush lengths (i.e. the amount of brush extending from the holder) **(see illustration)**. Triumph provide no minimum length specification, but generally on this type of alternator around 4.0 to 5.0 mm is common.
**8** Whilst the brush holder is removed, clean the slip rings with a rag moistened with solvent **(see illustration)**. If they are badly

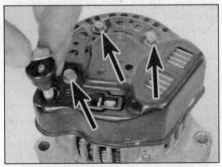

**31.6a  Remove the terminal nut and sleeve, then undo the screws (arrowed) . . .**

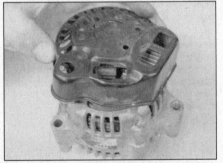

**31.6b  . . . and remove the cover**

**31.7a  Undo the screws (arrowed) . . .**

**31.7b  . . . and remove the brush holder**

**31.7c  Check the length and condition of the brushes as described**

**31.8  Check the condition of the slip rings (arrowed) and clean them up if necessary**

31.13 Fit the rubber dampers into the housing

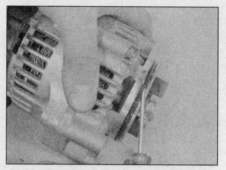

31.14 Fit a new O-ring onto the alternator

31.15 Do not forget to secure the earth lead(s) with the rear bolt

marked, tidy them up with very fine emery cloth.

**9** Triumph provide no test data for the regulator and rectifier, which are integral with the alternator. If the charging system tests in the previous section indicate a fault, take the unit to a Triumph dealer for further assessment.

**10** Check the condition of the rubber dampers in the drive housing and renew them if they are hardened, compacted or damaged.

**11** Further testing of the alternator components should be left to a Triumph dealer or auto electrician. This also applies to removal of the rotor and bearing renewal.

### Installation

**12** If not already done, install the brush holder, making sure the brushes locate correctly against the slip rings, and secure it with the screws (see illustrations 31.7b and a). Fit the end cover and secure it with the three screws, then fit the sleeve and terminal nut (see illustration 31.6b and a).

**13** If removed, fit the rubber dampers into the housing, using a smear of grease to secure them in place if necessary (see illustration).

**14** Fit a new O-ring onto the alternator and smear it with oil (see illustration).

**15** Install the alternator and fit the mounting bolts (see illustration 31.4b), not forgetting to connect the earth lead(s) with the rear bolt (see illustration). Tighten the bolts to the torque setting specified at the beginning of the Chapter.

**16** Fit the hose onto the union and tighten the clamp to secure it (see illustration 27.2a). Fill the cooling system (see Chapter 1).

**17** Reconnect the alternator wiring connector,

31.20 Trace the alternator wiring (arrowed) to the connector

then attach the earth lead and secure it with the nut (see illustration 31.3). Fit the rubber boot over the terminal.

**18** Connect the battery negative (–ve) lead and install the seat(s), and on Daytona and Sprint models the fairing panels (see Chapter 7).

### 2002-on models – alternator

**19** The alternator rotor is mounted on the left-hand end of the crankshaft and the stator is located inside the left-hand engine cover. Remove the seat(s), and on Daytona and Sprint models the left-hand fairing side panel, then on Sprint ST remove the belly pan for access (see Chapter 7).

### Testing

**Note:** *Triumph provides no test data for the alternator. If the output test in Section 30 indicates a fault, the following general check may help to isolate the problem.*

**20** Disconnect the battery negative (–ve) lead. Trace the alternator wiring from the left-

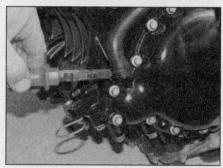

31.24 Release the clip and disconnect the breather hose

hand engine cover and disconnect it at the connector (see illustration).

**21** Using a multimeter set to the ohms scale, connect the meter probes to one pair of terminals at a time on the alternator side of the wiring connector and measure the resistance between the terminals. Make a note of the three readings obtained. Now check for continuity between each terminal and ground (earth).

**22** If the stator coil windings are in good condition the three readings should be within a consistent range and there should be no continuity (infinite resistance) between any of the terminals and ground (earth). If not, the alternator stator coil assembly is probably faulty and should be taken to a Triumph dealer for further assessment. **Note:** *Before condemning the stator coils, check the fault is not due to damaged wiring between the connector and coils.*

### Removal

**23** Disconnect the battery negative (–ve) lead. Trace the alternator wiring from the left-hand engine cover and disconnect it at the connector (see illustration 31.20). Free the wiring from any clips or ties and feed it through to the cover.

**24** Release the clip securing the breather hose to the front of the cover and disconnect the hose (see illustration).

**25** Working in a criss-cross pattern, evenly slacken the engine cover bolts and remove them (see illustration).

**26** Draw the cover off, being prepared to catch any residual oil that may be released as the cover is removed (see illustration).

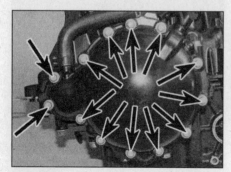

31.25 Remove the alternator cover bolts . . .

31.26a . . . and draw the cover off

31.26b  Note the locating pins (arrowed)

31.27  Insert a suitable mandrel into the seal to preserve its shape

31.28a  Using a holding strap to enable the rotor bolt to be slackened

31.28b  Remove the bolt and washer

31.29  Using a puller to remove the alternator rotor

31.30  Remove the Woodruff key (arrowed) if it is loose

Discard the gasket as a new one must be used. Note the three locating pins and remove them for safekeeping if loose **(see illustration)**.

**27** There is an oil seal in the cover, which, if it is in perfect condition and is being reused, must have a mandrel inserted in it immediately after the cover is removed **(see illustration)**. If this is not done, the rim of the seal will distort and not reseal around the balancer shaft on installation. A suitable socket can be used as a mandrel, otherwise a new seal must be fitted before reassembly (see Step 32). Only remove the mandrel from the seal immediately before the cover is fitted to the engine.

**28** To remove the rotor bolt it is necessary to stop the crankshaft from turning. Triumph produces a Service Tool (Part No. T3880375)

to do this. If a rotor holding strap or tool is not available, and the engine is in the frame, place the transmission in gear and have an assistant apply the rear brake. Alternatively, a large spanner can be applied to the two flats machined into the boss in the rotor. Unscrew the bolt and remove the bolt and washer **(see illustrations)**.

**29** To remove the rotor from the crankshaft taper it is necessary to use a rotor puller. Triumph produces a service tool (Part No. T3880365) to do this. If using the Triumph tool, insert the thrust pad into the end of the crankshaft, then install the rotor puller fully onto the centre of the rotor. Hold the puller with a large spanner to stop it the crankshaft turning, then turn the puller centre bolt clockwise until the rotor is displaced.

Alternatively, a commercially available tool can be used **(see illustration)**.

**30** Lift off the rotor, noting the location of the Woodruff key in the crankshaft – remove the key for safekeeping if it is loose **(see illustration)**.

**31** To remove the stator from the cover, unscrew the bolts securing the stator, and the bolt securing the wiring clamp, then remove the assembly, noting how the wiring grommet fits **(see illustration)**.

**32** If required, prise the old oil seal out of the cover with a flat-bladed screwdriver **(see illustration)**. The new seal is supplied complete with a shaped mandrel – leave the mandrel in place while pressing the seal squarely all the way into the cover **(see illustration)**. Only remove the mandrel from

31.31  Remove the bolts (arrowed) securing the stator

31.32a  Lever out the old seal . . .

31.32b  . . . and press the new one in all the way

**31.33 Align the wiring grommet with the cut-out in the cover**

**31.34 Align the slot with the Woodruff key (arrowed)**

**31.41 Location of the regulator/rectifier – Daytona and Speed Triple models shown**

the seal immediately before the cover is fitted to the engine **(see illustration 31.27)**.

### Installation

**33** Apply a suitable sealant to the stator wiring grommet, then install the stator into the cover, aligning the grommet with the cut-out in the cover **(see illustration)**. Install the stator and wiring clamp bolts and tighten them to the specified torque setting **(see illustration 31.31)**.

**34** Clean the tapered end of the crankshaft and the corresponding mating surface on the inside of the rotor with a suitable solvent. If removed, install the Woodruff key in its slot in the crankshaft **(see illustration 31.30)**. Make sure that no metal objects have attached themselves to the magnet on the inside of the rotor, then align the slot on the inside of the rotor boss with the Woodruff key and slide the rotor onto the shaft **(see illustration)**.

**35** Install the rotor bolt with its washer and tighten it to the torque setting specified at the beginning of this Chapter, using the method

employed on removal to prevent the rotor from turning.

**36** If removed, fit the cover locating pins into the crankcase, then locate the new gasket onto them **(see illustration 31.26b)**. Remove the mandrel from the seal in the cover, then install the cover, making sure it is correctly and squarely aligned so as not to distort the seal rim as it fits onto the balancer shaft. Tighten the bolts evenly in a criss-cross pattern **(see illustration 31.25)**.

**37** Feed the alternator wiring back to its connector, making sure it is correctly routed and secured by any clips or ties, and reconnect it.

**38** Connect the breather hose to the union on the cover and secure it with the clip **(see illustration 31.24)**.

**39** Check the engine oil level (see *Daily (pre-ride) checks*) .

**40** Connect the battery negative (–ve) lead and install the seat(s), and on Daytona and Sprint models the fairing panels (see Chapter 7).

### *2002-on models – regulator/rectifier*

**Note:** *Triumph provides no test data for the regulator/rectifier. If the output test in Section 30 indicates a fault, take the unit to a Triumph dealer for further assessment.*

**41** On Daytona and Speed Triple models, the regulator/rectifier is mounted on the right-hand side of the frame behind the seat cowling **(see illustration)**. On Sprint models, the regulator/rectifier is mounted inside the frame on the right-hand side of the rear shock absorber. On Tiger models, the regulator/rectifier is mounted on the left-hand side to the rear of the fuel tank. Remove the body panels as required for access (see Chapter 7).

**42** To remove the regulator/rectifier, first trace the wiring to the connector and disconnect it. Undo the two bolts securing the regulator/rectifier to the frame and lift it off.

**43** Installation is the reverse of removal.

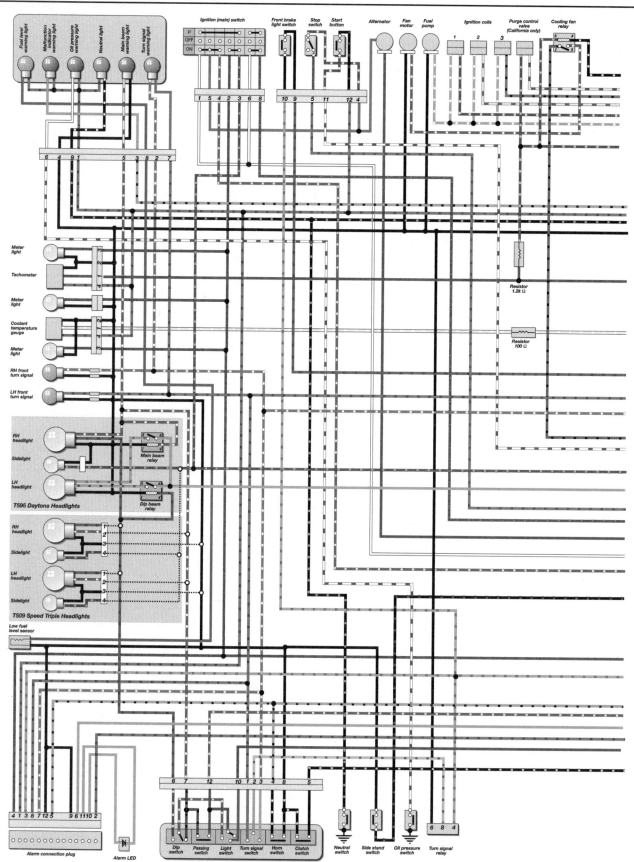

T509 Speed Triple and T595 Daytona

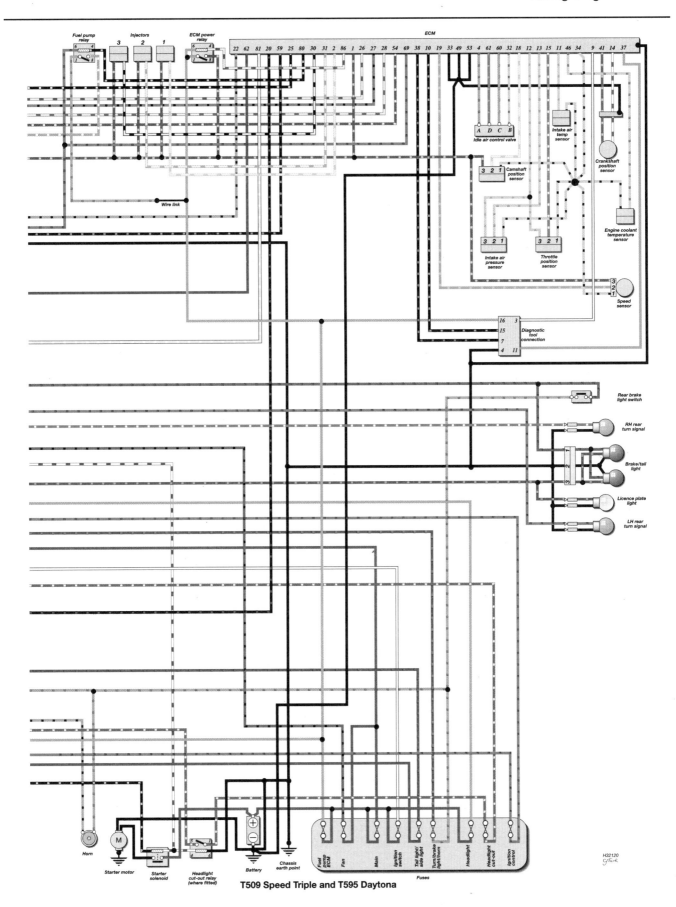

**T509 Speed Triple and T595 Daytona**

H32120

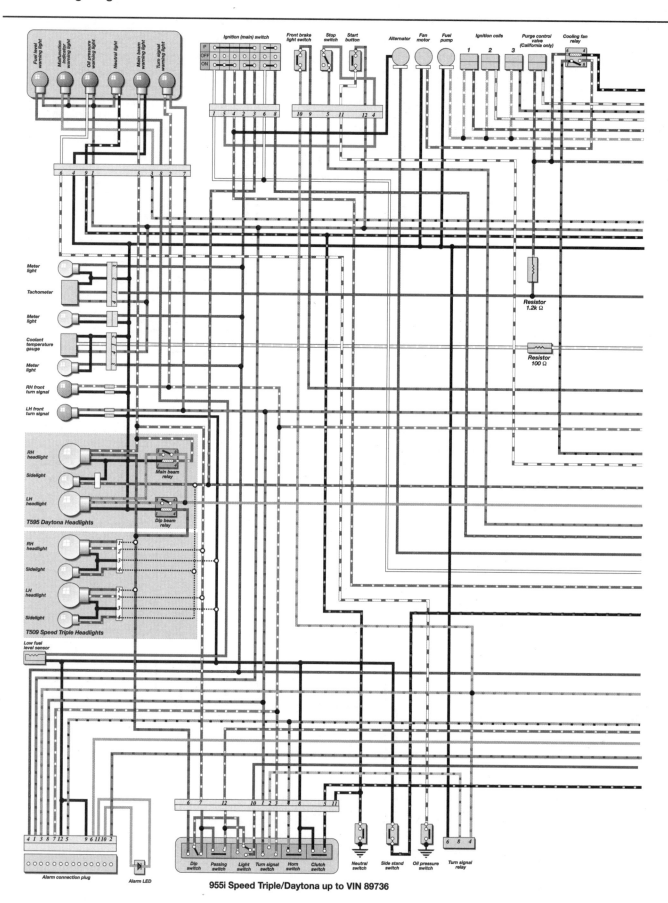

**955i Speed Triple/Daytona up to VIN 89736**

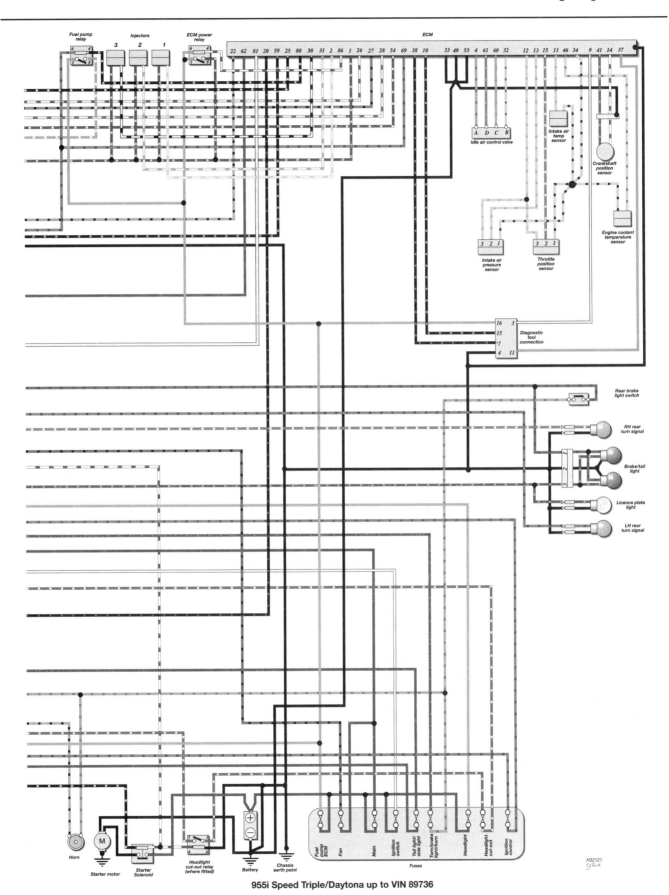

955i Speed Triple/Daytona up to VIN 89736

H32121

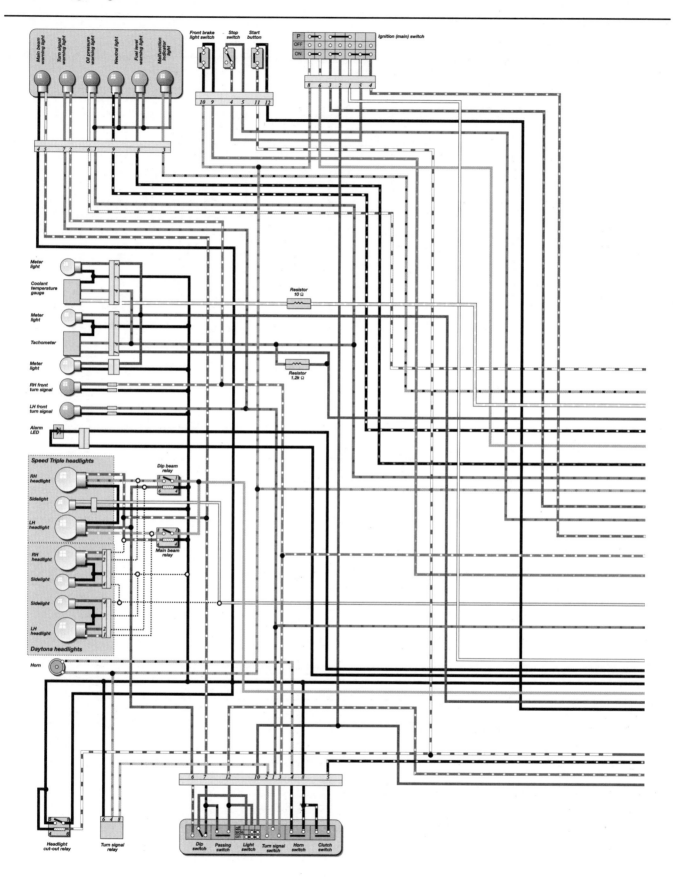

**955i Speed Triple/Daytona from VIN 89737 to 2001**

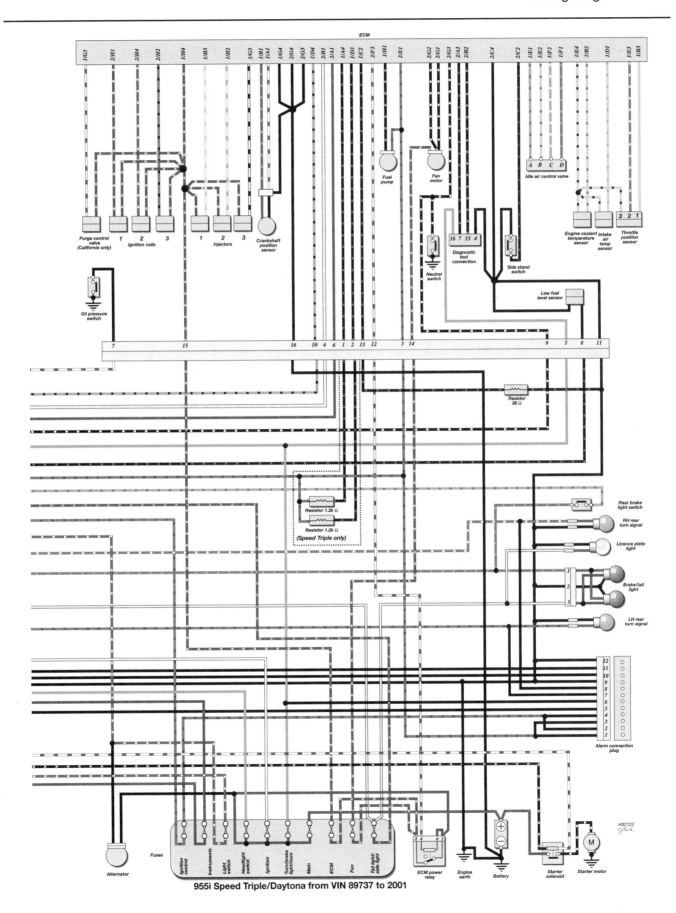

955i Speed Triple/Daytona from VIN 89737 to 2001

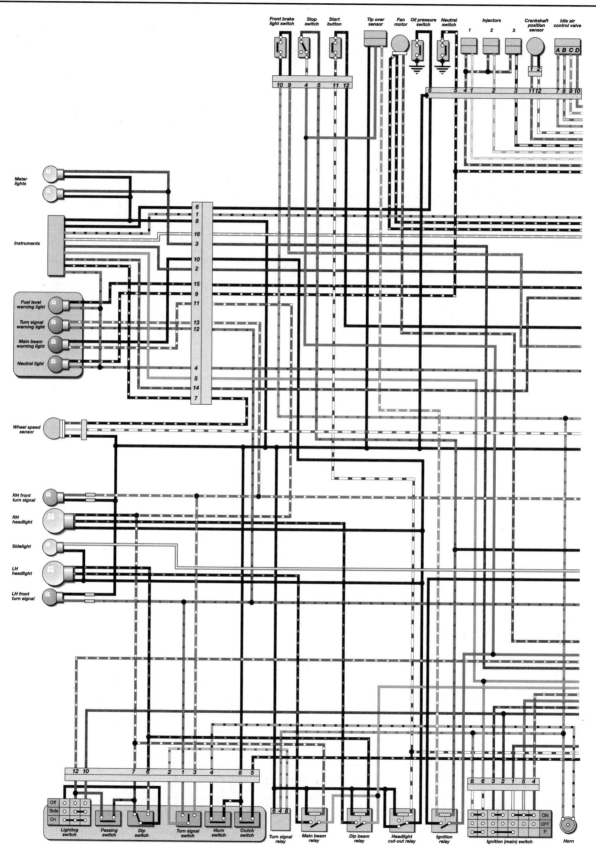

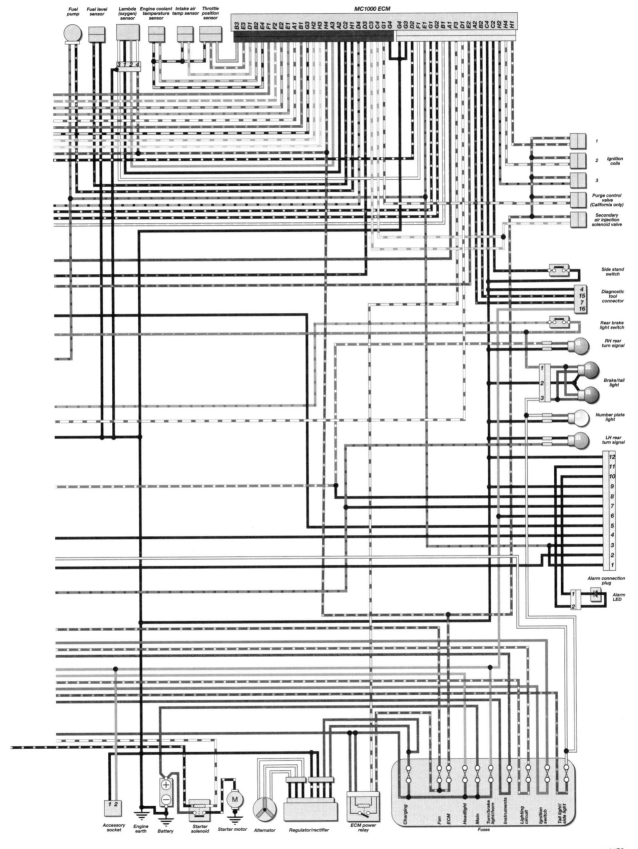

**Daytona 2002 - on**

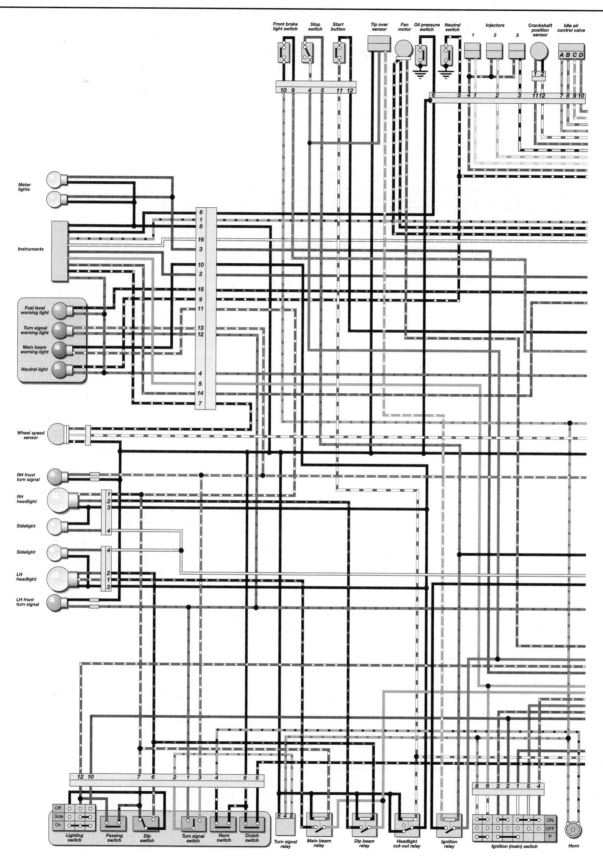

MTS
H33251

**Speed Triple 2002 - on**

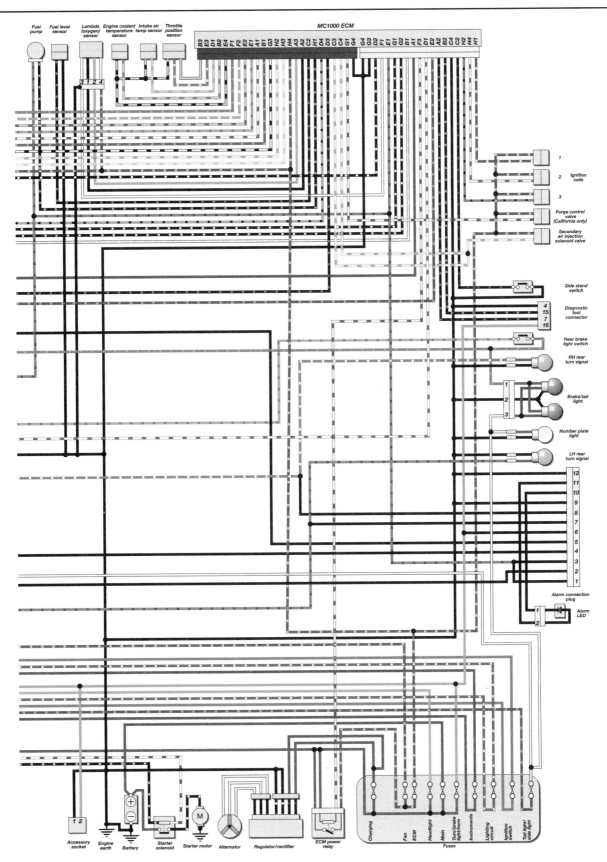

**Speed Triple 2002 - on**

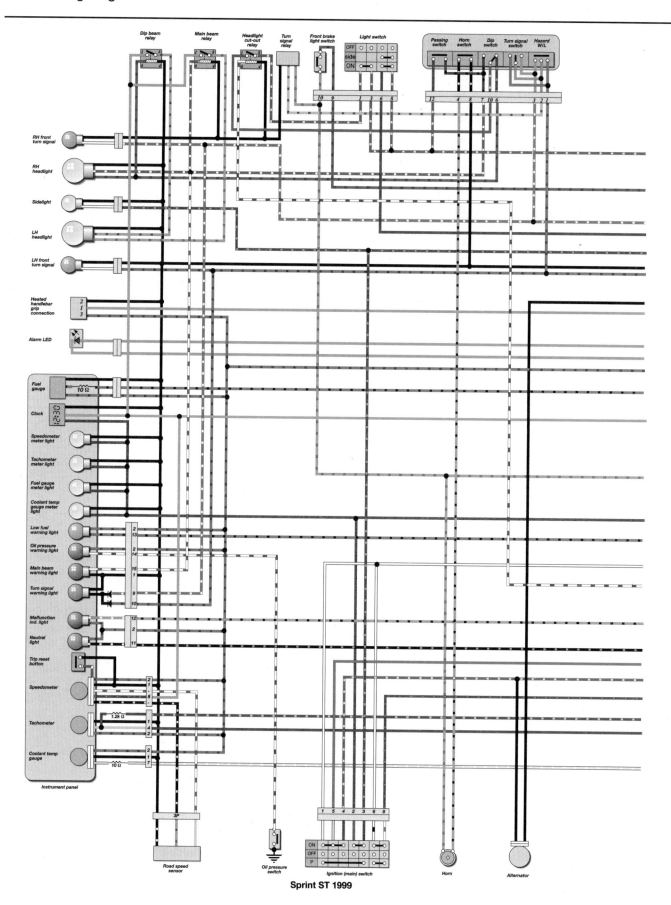

**Sprint ST 1999**

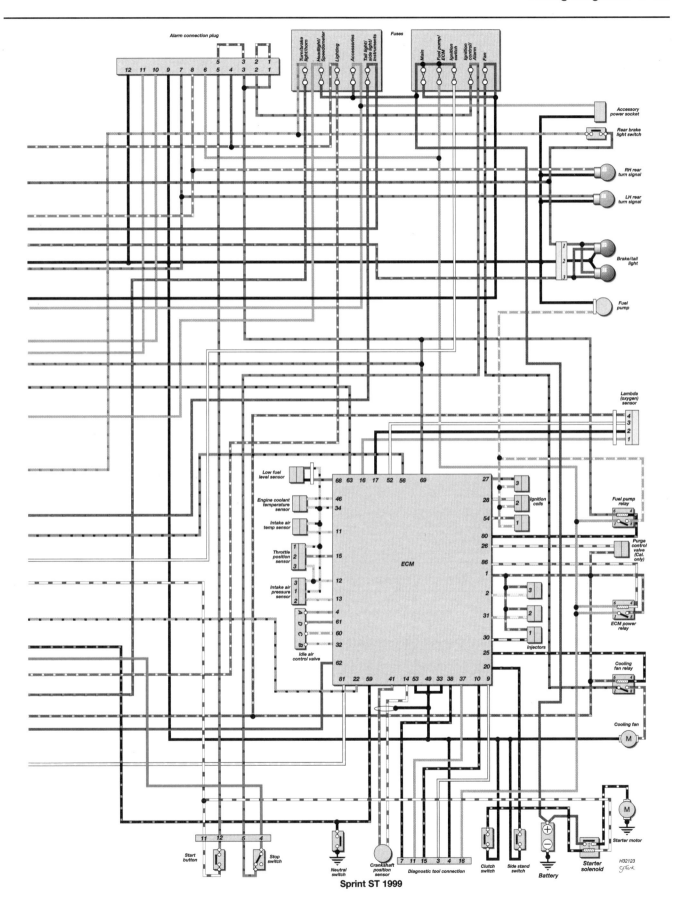

Sprint ST 1999

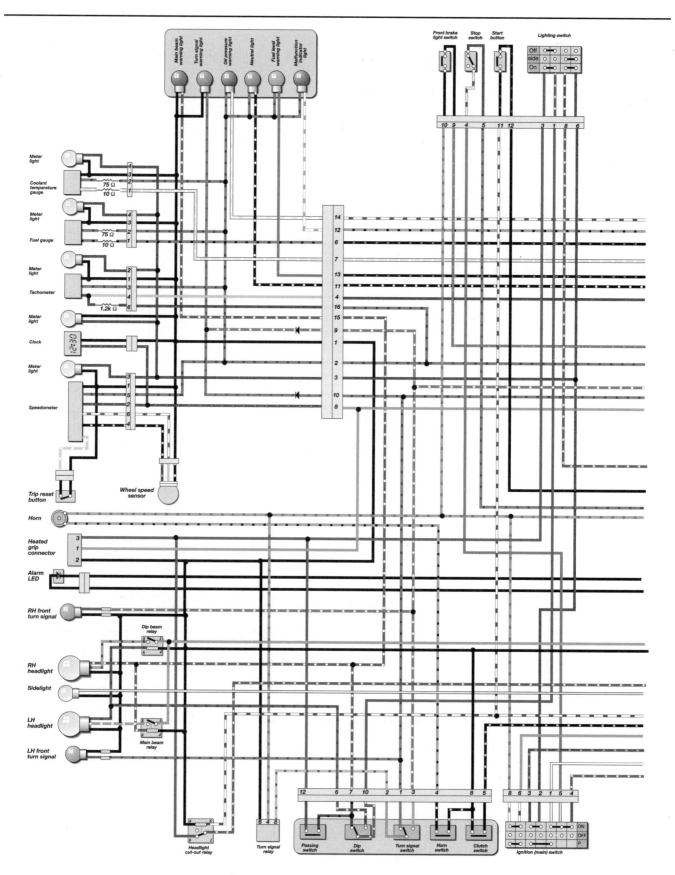

**Sprint ST 2000 to 2001**

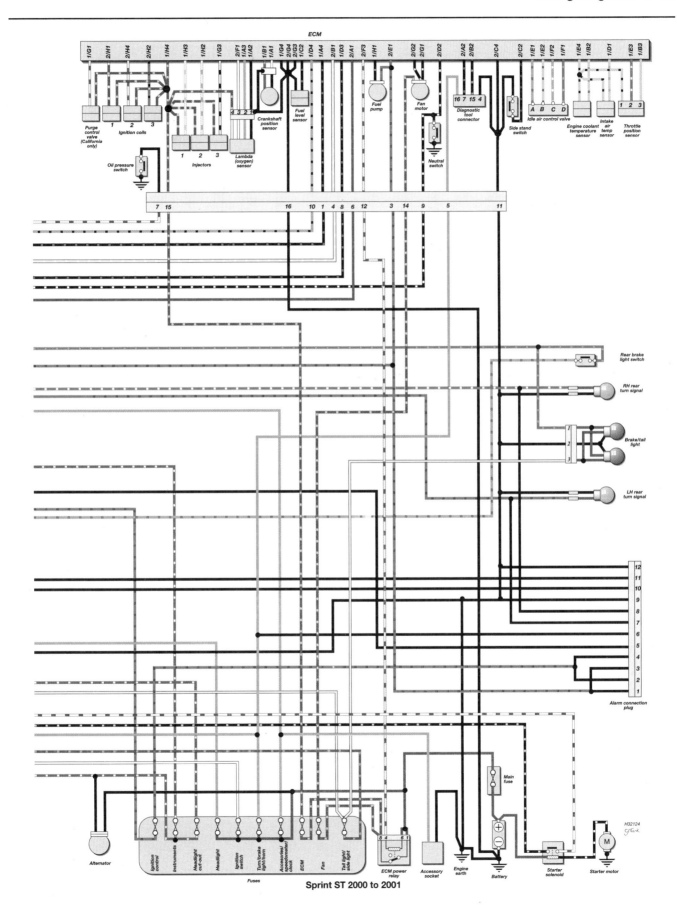

Sprint ST 2000 to 2001

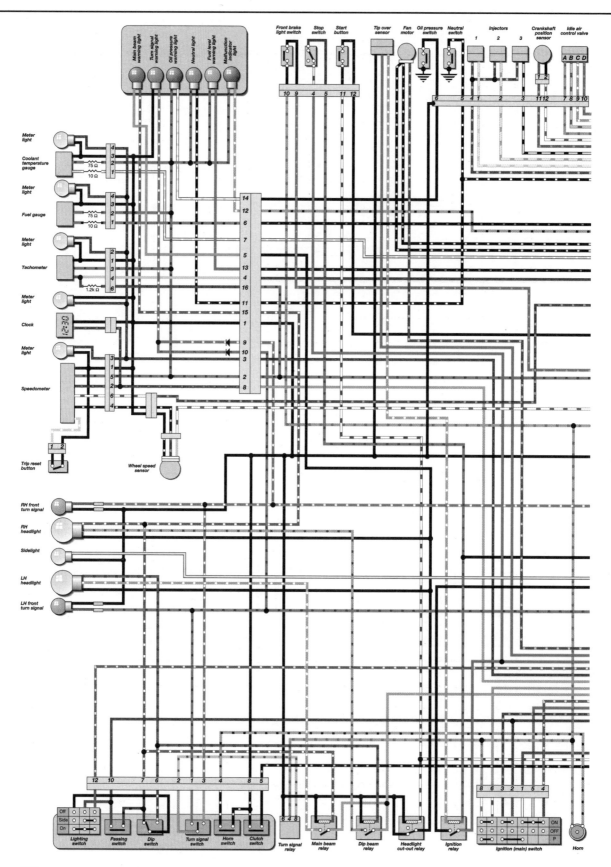

**Sprint ST 2002 to 2004**

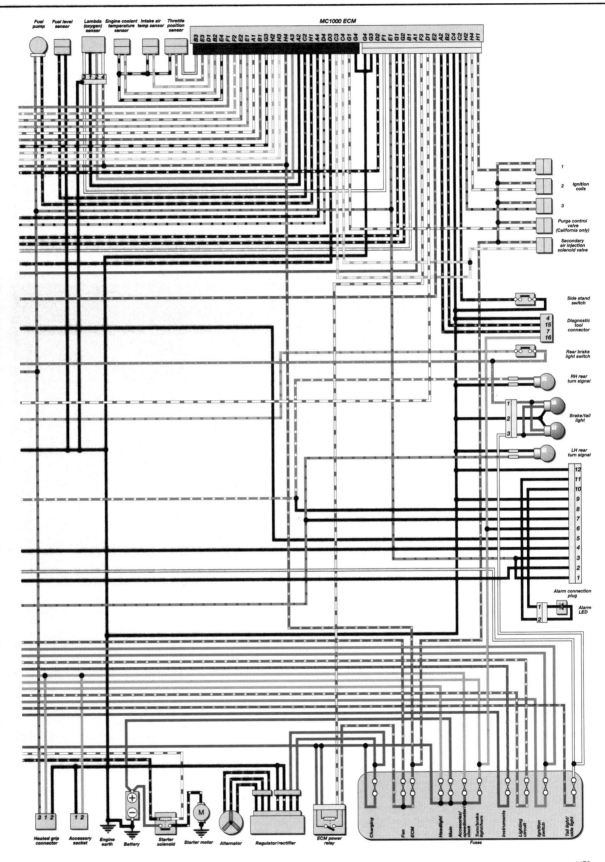

**Sprint ST 2002 to 2004**

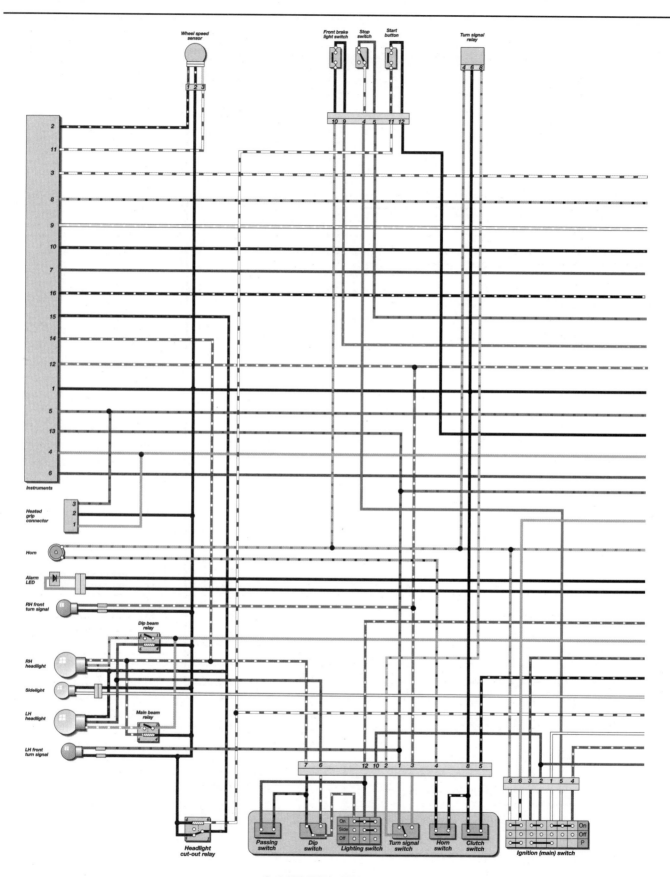

**Sprint RS 2000 to 2001**

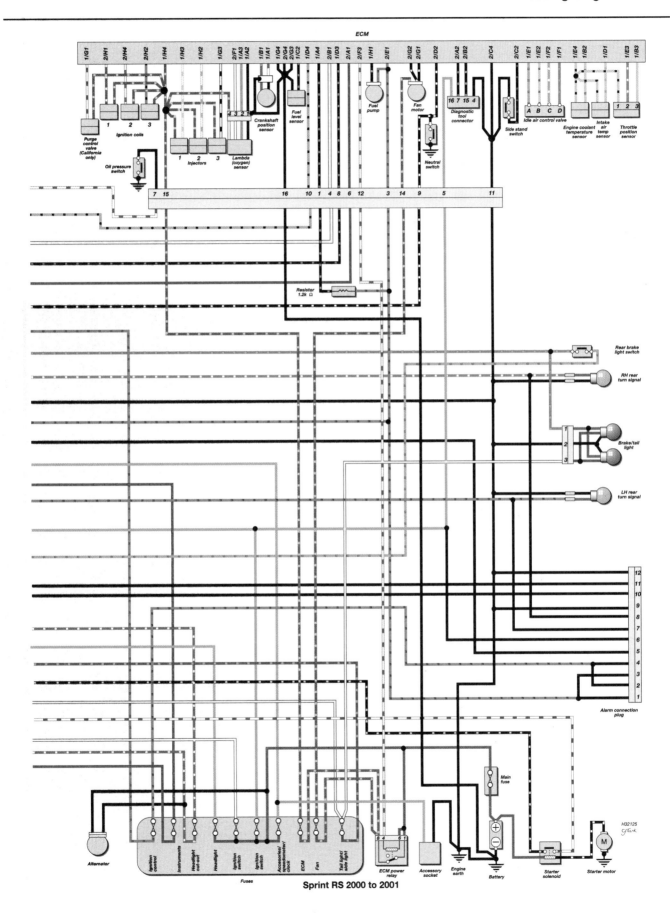

Sprint RS 2000 to 2001

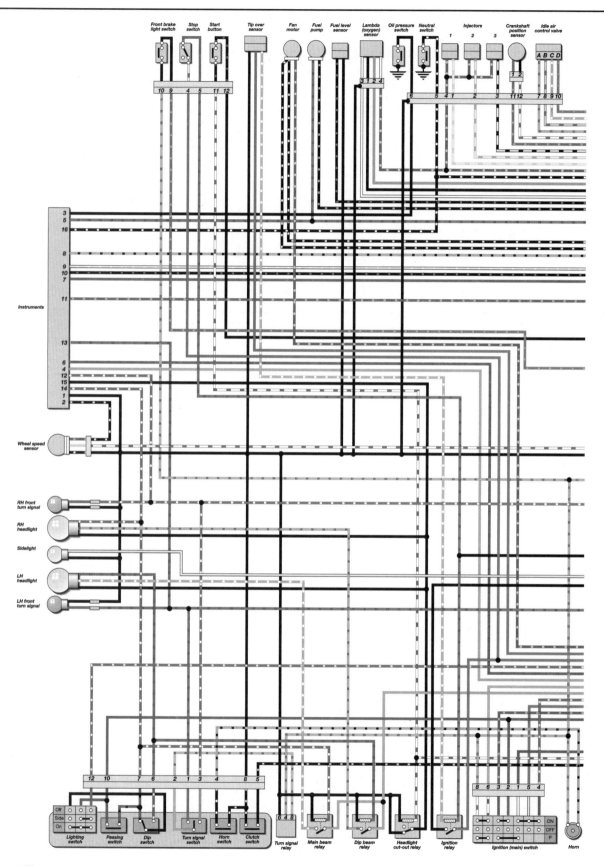

Sprint RS 2002 - on

MTS
H33247

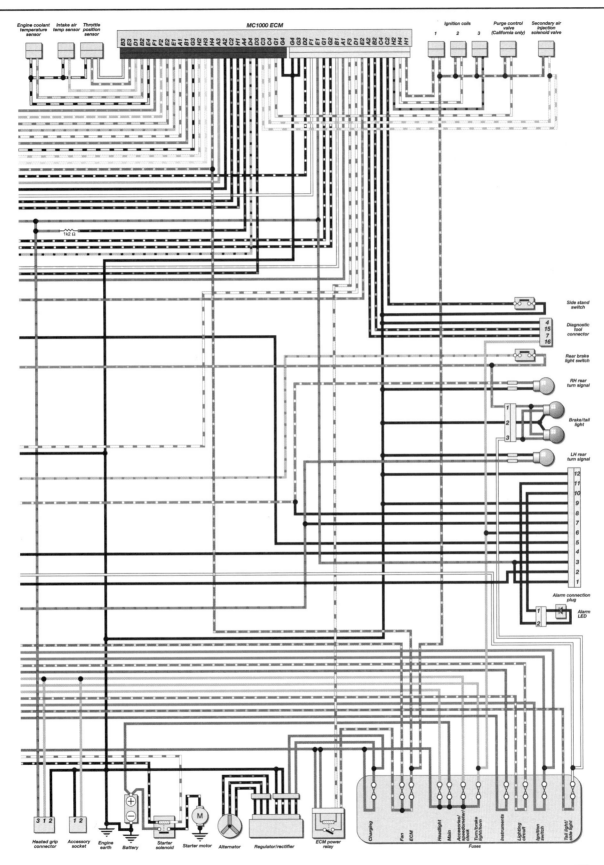

**Sprint RS 2002 - on**

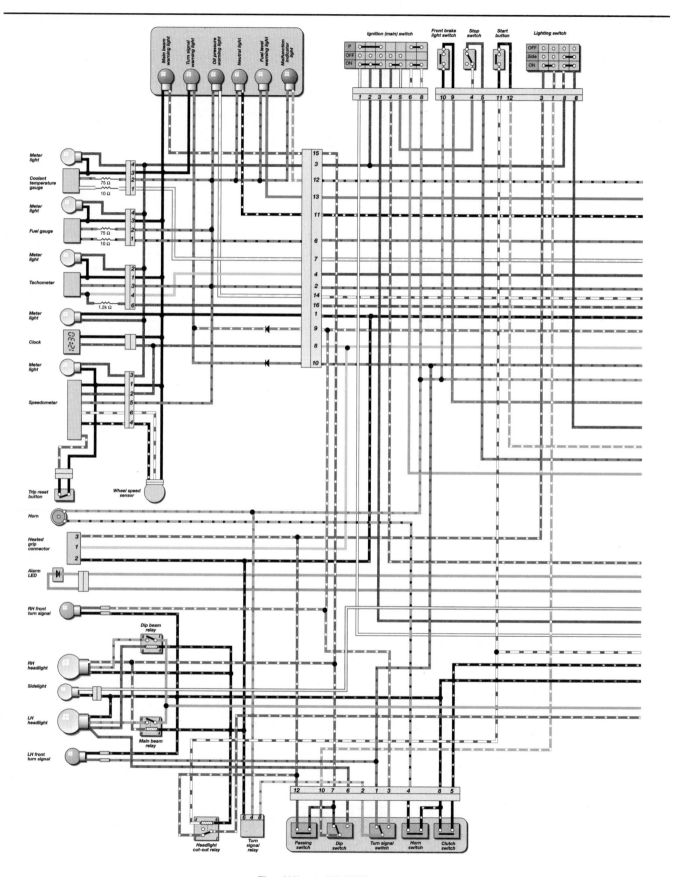

**Tiger 885i up to VIN 89736**

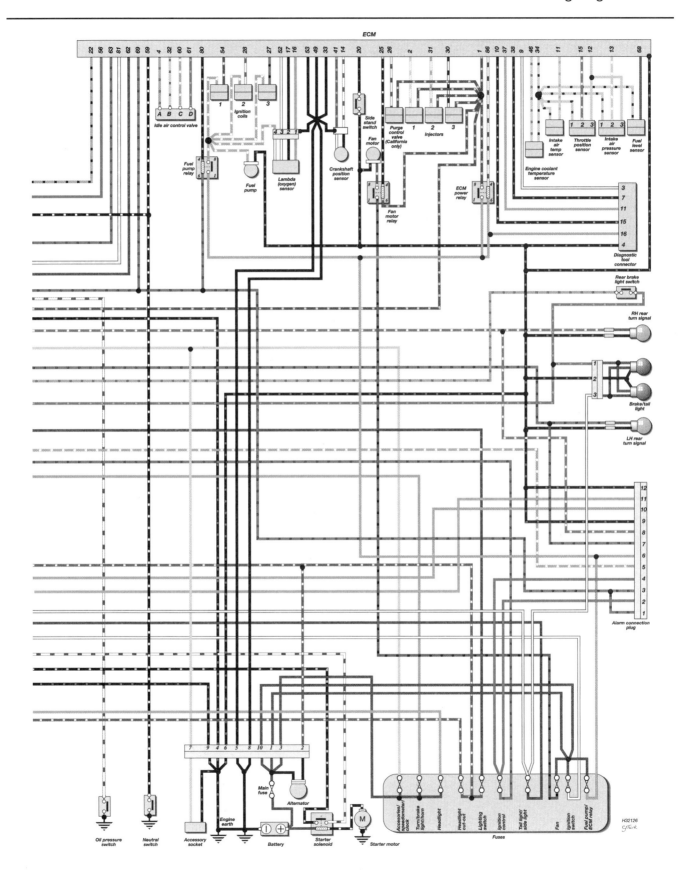

**Tiger 885i up to VIN 89736**

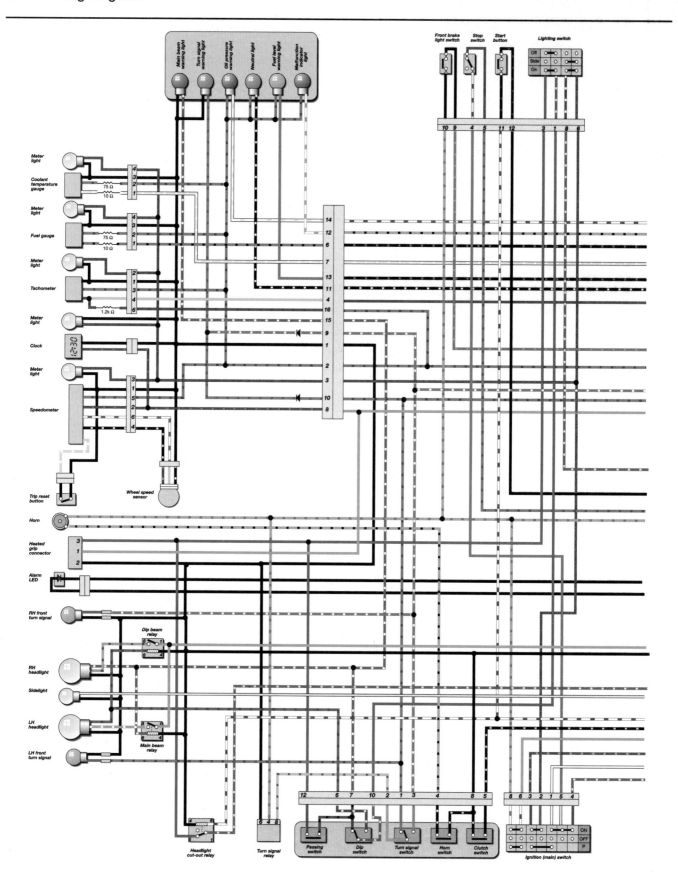

**Tiger 885i from VIN 89737**

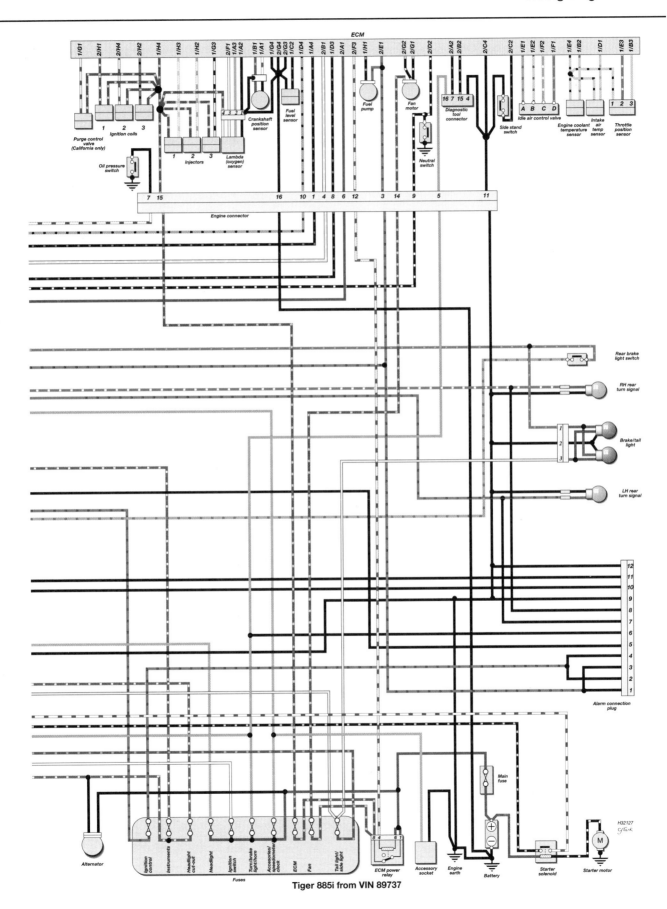

Tiger 885i from VIN 89737

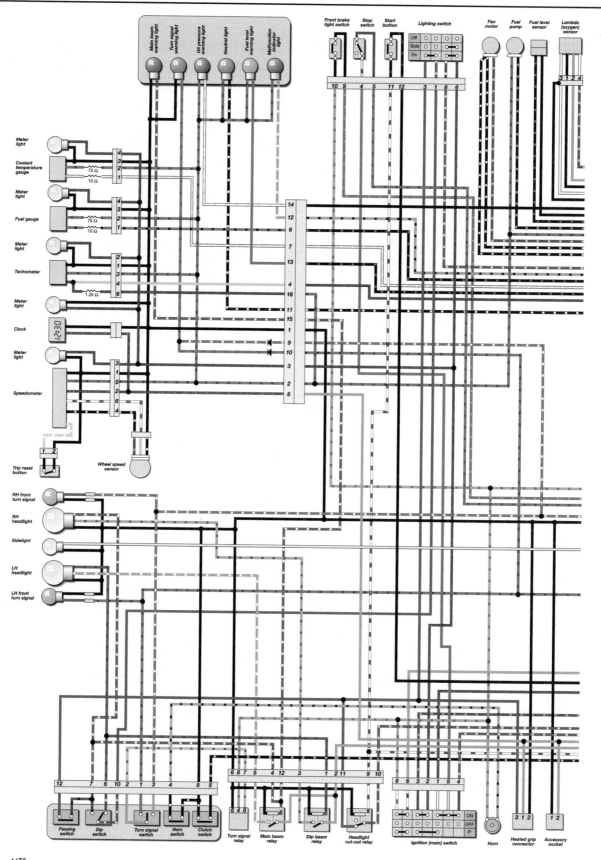

MTS
H33245

**Tiger 955i**

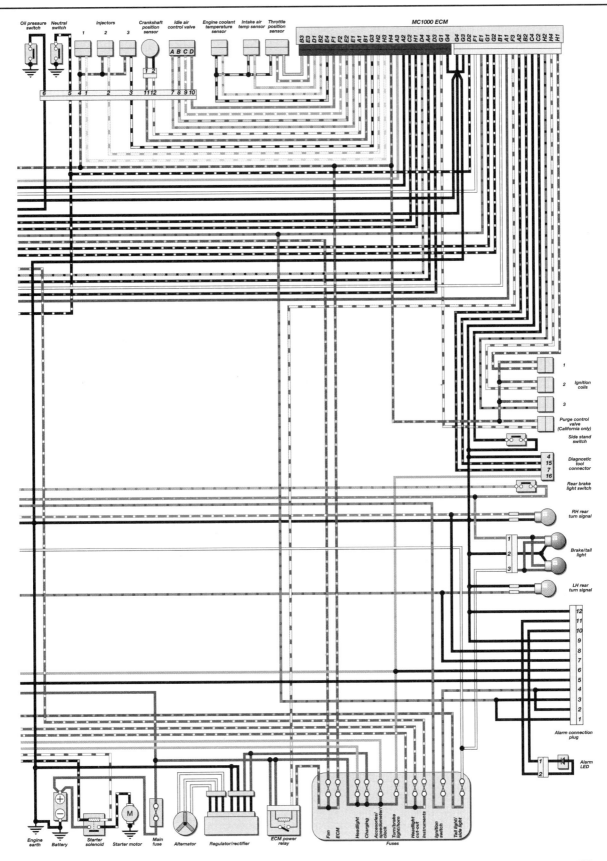

**Tiger 955i**

MTS
H33246

# Reference

## Buying tools

A toolkit is a fundamental requirement for servicing and repairing a motorcycle. Although there will be an initial expense in building up enough tools for servicing, this will soon be offset by the savings made by doing the job yourself. As experience and confidence grow, additional tools can be added to enable the repair and overhaul of the motorcycle. Many of the specialist tools are expensive and not often used so it may be preferable to hire them, or for a group of friends or motorcycle club to join in the purchase.

As a rule, it is better to buy more expensive, good quality tools. Cheaper tools are likely to wear out faster and need to be renewed more often, nullifying the original saving.

> ⚠️ **Warning: To avoid the risk of a poor quality tool breaking in use, causing injury or damage to the component being worked on, always aim to purchase tools which meet the relevant national safety standards.**

The following lists of tools do not represent the manufacturer's service tools, but serve as a guide to help the owner decide which tools are needed for this level of work. In addition, items such as an electric drill, hacksaw, files, soldering iron and a workbench equipped with a vice, may be needed. Although not classed as tools, a selection of bolts, screws, nuts, washers and pieces of tubing always come in useful.

For more information about tools, refer to the Haynes *Motorcycle Workshop Practice TechBook* (Bk. No. 3470).

## Manufacturer's service tools

Inevitably certain tasks require the use of a service tool. Where possible an alternative tool or method of approach is recommended, but sometimes there is no option if personal injury or damage to the component is to be avoided. Where required, service tools are referred to in the relevant procedure.

Service tools can usually only be purchased from a motorcycle dealer and are identified by a part number. Some of the commonly-used tools, such as rotor pullers, are available in aftermarket form from mail-order motorcycle tool and accessory suppliers.

# Maintenance and minor repair tools

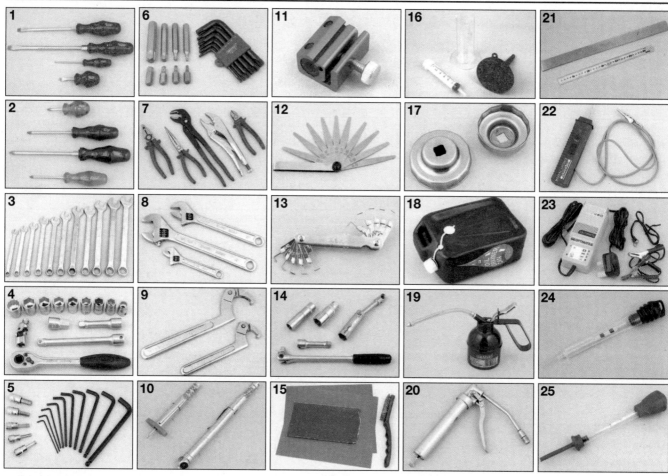

1. Set of flat-bladed screwdrivers
2. Set of Phillips head screwdrivers
3. Combination open-end and ring spanners
4. Socket set (3/8 inch or 1/2 inch drive)
5. Set of Allen keys or bits
6. Set of Torx keys or bits
7. Pliers, cutters and self-locking grips (Mole grips)
8. Adjustable spanners
9. C-spanners
10. Tread depth gauge and tyre pressure gauge
11. Cable oiler clamp
12. Feeler gauges
13. Spark plug gap measuring tool
14. Spark plug spanner or deep plug sockets
15. Wire brush and emery paper
16. Calibrated syringe, measuring vessel and funnel
17. Oil filter adapters
18. Oil drainer can or tray
19. Pump type oil can
20. Grease gun
21. Straight-edge and steel rule
22. Continuity tester
23. Battery charger
24. Hydrometer (for battery specific gravity check)
25. Anti-freeze tester (for liquid-cooled engines)

## Repair and overhaul tools

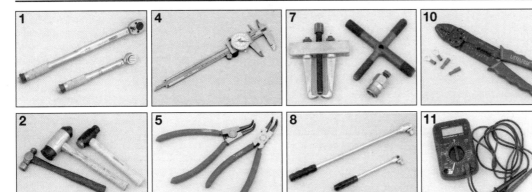

1 **Torque wrench**
   (small and mid-ranges)
2 **Conventional, plastic or**
   **soft-faced hammers**
3 **Impact driver set**

4 **Vernier gauge**
5 **Circlip pliers** (internal and
   external, or combination)
6 **Set of cold chisels**
   **and punches**

7 **Selection of pullers**
8 **Breaker bars**
9 **Chain breaking/**
   **riveting tool set**

10 **Wire stripper and**
   **crimper tool**
11 **Multimeter** (measures
   amps, volts and ohms)
12 **Stroboscope** (for
   dynamic timing checks)

13 **Hose clamp**
   (wingnut type shown)
14 **Clutch holding tool**
15 **One-man brake/clutch**
   **bleeder kit**

## Specialist tools

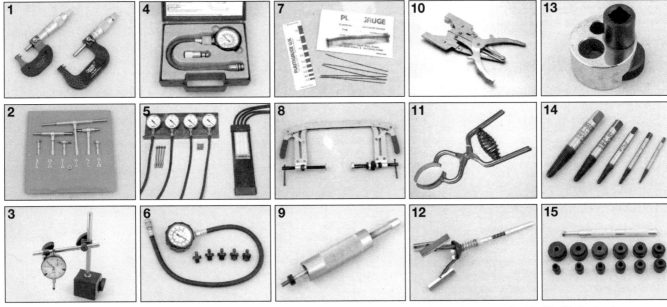

1 **Micrometers**
   (external type)
2 **Telescoping gauges**
3 **Dial gauge**

4 **Cylinder**
   **compression gauge**
5 **Vacuum gauges** (left) or
   manometer (right)
6 **Oil pressure gauge**

7 **Plastigauge kit**
8 **Valve spring compressor**
   (4-stroke engines)
9 **Piston pin drawbolt tool**

10 **Piston ring removal and**
   **installation tool**
11 **Piston ring clamp**
12 **Cylinder bore hone**
   (stone type shown)

13 **Stud extractor**
14 **Screw extractor set**
15 **Bearing driver set**

## 1 Workshop equipment and facilities

### The workbench

● Work is made much easier by raising the bike up on a ramp - components are much more accessible if raised to waist level. The hydraulic or pneumatic types seen in the dealer's workshop are a sound investment if you undertake a lot of repairs or overhauls **(see illustration 1.1)**.

**1.1 Hydraulic motorcycle ramp**

● If raised off ground level, the bike must be supported on the ramp to avoid it falling. Most ramps incorporate a front wheel locating clamp which can be adjusted to suit different diameter wheels. When tightening the clamp, take care not to mark the wheel rim or damage the tyre - use wood blocks on each side to prevent this.
● Secure the bike to the ramp using tie-downs **(see illustration 1.2)**. If the bike has only a sidestand, and hence leans at a dangerous angle when raised, support the bike on an auxiliary stand.

**1.2 Tie-downs are used around the passenger footrests to secure the bike**

● Auxiliary (paddock) stands are widely available from mail order companies or motorcycle dealers and attach either to the wheel axle or swingarm pivot **(see illustration 1.3)**. If the motorcycle has a centrestand, you can support it under the crankcase to prevent it toppling whilst either wheel is removed **(see illustration 1.4)**.

**1.3 This auxiliary stand attaches to the swingarm pivot**

**1.4 Always use a block of wood between the engine and jack head when supporting the engine in this way**

### Fumes and fire

● Refer to the Safety first! page at the beginning of the manual for full details. Make sure your workshop is equipped with a fire extinguisher suitable for fuel-related fires (Class B fire - flammable liquids) - it is not sufficient to have a water-filled extinguisher.
● Always ensure adequate ventilation is available. Unless an exhaust gas extraction system is available for use, ensure that the engine is run outside of the workshop.
● If working on the fuel system, make sure the workshop is ventilated to avoid a build-up of fumes. This applies equally to fume build-up when charging a battery. Do not smoke or allow anyone else to smoke in the workshop.

### Fluids

● If you need to drain fuel from the tank, store it in an approved container marked as suitable for the storage of petrol (gasoline) **(see illustration 1.5)**. Do not store fuel in glass jars or bottles.

**1.5 Use an approved can only for storing petrol (gasoline)**

● Use proprietary engine degreasers or solvents which have a high flash-point, such as paraffin (kerosene), for cleaning off oil, grease and dirt - never use petrol (gasoline) for cleaning. Wear rubber gloves when handling solvent and engine degreaser. The fumes from certain solvents can be dangerous - always work in a well-ventilated area.

### Dust, eye and hand protection

● Protect your lungs from inhalation of dust particles by wearing a filtering mask over the nose and mouth. Many frictional materials still contain asbestos which is dangerous to your health. Protect your eyes from spouts of liquid and sprung components by wearing a pair of protective goggles **(see illustration 1.6)**.

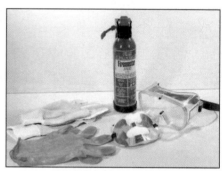

**1.6 A fire extinguisher, goggles, mask and protective gloves should be at hand in the workshop**

● Protect your hands from contact with solvents, fuel and oils by wearing rubber gloves. Alternatively apply a barrier cream to your hands before starting work. If handling hot components or fluids, wear suitable gloves to protect your hands from scalding and burns.

### What to do with old fluids

● Old cleaning solvent, fuel, coolant and oils should not be poured down domestic drains or onto the ground. Package the fluid up in old oil containers, label it accordingly, and take it to a garage or disposal facility. Contact your local authority for location of such sites or ring the oil care hotline.

**OIL CARE**
FOLLOW THE CODE
OIL BANK LINE
**0800 66 33 66**
www.oilbankline.org.uk

**Note: It is antisocial and illegal to dump oil down the drain. To find the location of your local oil recycling bank, call this number free.**

*In the USA, note that any oil supplier must accept used oil for recycling.*

## 2 Fasteners -
screws, bolts and nuts

### Fastener types and applications

#### Bolts and screws

● Fastener head types are either of hexagonal, Torx or splined design, with internal and external versions of each type **(see illustrations 2.1 and 2.2)**; splined head fasteners are not in common use on motorcycles. The conventional slotted or Phillips head design is used for certain screws. Bolt or screw length is always measured from the underside of the head to the end of the item **(see illustration 2.11)**.

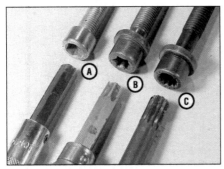

**2.1 Internal hexagon/Allen (A), Torx (B) and splined (C) fasteners, with corresponding bits**

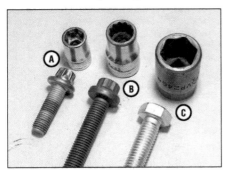

**2.2 External Torx (A), splined (B) and hexagon (C) fasteners, with corresponding sockets**

● Certain fasteners on the motorcycle have a tensile marking on their heads, the higher the marking the stronger the fastener. High tensile fasteners generally carry a 10 or higher marking. Never replace a high tensile fastener with one of a lower tensile strength.

#### Washers (see illustration 2.3)

● Plain washers are used between a fastener head and a component to prevent damage to the component or to spread the load when torque is applied. Plain washers can also be used as spacers or shims in certain assemblies. Copper or aluminium plain washers are often used as sealing washers on drain plugs.

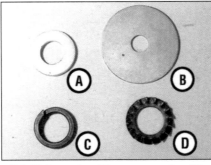

**2.3 Plain washer (A), penny washer (B), spring washer (C) and serrated washer (D)**

● The split-ring spring washer works by applying axial tension between the fastener head and component. If flattened, it is fatigued and must be renewed. If a plain (flat) washer is used on the fastener, position the spring washer between the fastener and the plain washer.

● Serrated star type washers dig into the fastener and component faces, preventing loosening. They are often used on electrical earth (ground) connections to the frame.

● Cone type washers (sometimes called Belleville) are conical and when tightened apply axial tension between the fastener head and component. They must be installed with the dished side against the component and often carry an OUTSIDE marking on their outer face. If flattened, they are fatigued and must be renewed.

● Tab washers are used to lock plain nuts or bolts on a shaft. A portion of the tab washer is bent up hard against one flat of the nut or bolt to prevent it loosening. Due to the tab washer being deformed in use, a new tab washer should be used every time it is disturbed.

● Wave washers are used to take up endfloat on a shaft. They provide light springing and prevent excessive side-to-side play of a component. Can be found on rocker arm shafts.

#### Nuts and split pins

● Conventional plain nuts are usually six-sided **(see illustration 2.4)**. They are sized by thread diameter and pitch. High tensile nuts carry a number on one end to denote their tensile strength.

**2.4 Plain nut (A), shouldered locknut (B), nylon insert nut (C) and castellated nut (D)**

● Self-locking nuts either have a nylon insert, or two spring metal tabs, or a shoulder which is staked into a groove in the shaft - their advantage over conventional plain nuts is a resistance to loosening due to vibration. The nylon insert type can be used a number of times, but must be renewed when the friction of the nylon insert is reduced, ie when the nut spins freely on the shaft. The spring tab type can be reused unless the tabs are damaged. The shouldered type must be renewed every time it is disturbed.

● Split pins (cotter pins) are used to lock a castellated nut to a shaft or to prevent slackening of a plain nut. Common applications are wheel axles and brake torque arms. Because the split pin arms are deformed to lock around the nut a new split pin must always be used on installation - always fit the correct size split pin which will fit snugly in the shaft hole. Make sure the split pin arms are correctly located around the nut **(see illustrations 2.5 and 2.6)**.

**2.5 Bend split pin (cotter pin) arms as shown (arrows) to secure a castellated nut**

**2.6 Bend split pin (cotter pin) arms as shown to secure a plain nut**

*Caution: If the castellated nut slots do not align with the shaft hole after tightening to the torque setting, tighten the nut until the next slot aligns with the hole - never slacken the nut to align its slot.*

● R-pins (shaped like the letter R), or slip pins as they are sometimes called, are sprung and can be reused if they are otherwise in good condition. Always install R-pins with their closed end facing forwards **(see illustration 2.7)**.

**2.7 Correct fitting of R-pin.
Arrow indicates forward direction**

### Circlips (see illustration 2.8)

● Circlips (sometimes called snap-rings) are used to retain components on a shaft or in a housing and have corresponding external or internal ears to permit removal. Parallel-sided (machined) circlips can be installed either way round in their groove, whereas stamped circlips (which have a chamfered edge on one face) must be installed with the chamfer facing away from the direction of thrust load **(see illustration 2.9)**.

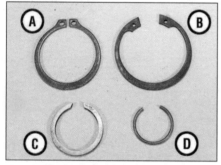

**2.8 External stamped circlip (A), internal stamped circlip (B), machined circlip (C) and wire circlip (D)**

● Always use circlip pliers to remove and install circlips; expand or compress them just enough to remove them. After installation, rotate the circlip in its groove to ensure it is securely seated. If installing a circlip on a splined shaft, always align its opening with a shaft channel to ensure the circlip ends are well supported and unlikely to catch **(see illustration 2.10)**.

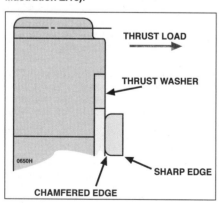

**2.9 Correct fitting of a stamped circlip**

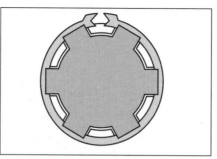

**2.10 Align circlip opening
with shaft channel**

● Circlips can wear due to the thrust of components and become loose in their grooves, with the subsequent danger of becoming dislodged in operation. For this reason, renewal is advised every time a circlip is disturbed.

● Wire circlips are commonly used as piston pin retaining clips. If a removal tang is provided, long-nosed pliers can be used to dislodge them, otherwise careful use of a small flat-bladed screwdriver is necessary. Wire circlips should be renewed every time they are disturbed.

### Thread diameter and pitch

● Diameter of a male thread (screw, bolt or stud) is the outside diameter of the threaded portion **(see illustration 2.11)**. Most motorcycle manufacturers use the ISO (International Standards Organisation) metric system expressed in millimetres, eg M6 refers to a 6 mm diameter thread. Sizing is the same for nuts, except that the thread diameter is measured across the valleys of the nut.

● Pitch is the distance between the peaks of the thread **(see illustration 2.11)**. It is expressed in millimetres, thus a common bolt size may be expressed as 6.0 x 1.0 mm (6 mm thread diameter and 1 mm pitch). Generally pitch increases in proportion to thread diameter, although there are always exceptions.

● Thread diameter and pitch are related for conventional fastener applications and the accompanying table can be used as a guide. Additionally, the AF (Across Flats), spanner or socket size dimension of the bolt or nut **(see illustration 2.11)** is linked to thread and pitch specification. Thread pitch can be measured with a thread gauge **(see illustration 2.12)**.

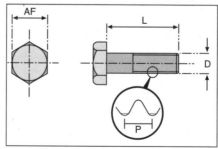

**2.11 Fastener length (L), thread diameter (D), thread pitch (P) and head size (AF)**

**2.12 Using a thread gauge
to measure pitch**

| AF size | Thread diameter x pitch (mm) |
|---------|------------------------------|
| 8 mm | M5 x 0.8 |
| 8 mm | M6 x 1.0 |
| 10 mm | M6 x 1.0 |
| 12 mm | M8 x 1.25 |
| 14 mm | M10 x 1.25 |
| 17 mm | M12 x 1.25 |

● The threads of most fasteners are of the right-hand type, ie they are turned clockwise to tighten and anti-clockwise to loosen. The reverse situation applies to left-hand thread fasteners, which are turned anti-clockwise to tighten and clockwise to loosen. Left-hand threads are used where rotation of a component might loosen a conventional right-hand thread fastener.

### Seized fasteners

● Corrosion of external fasteners due to water or reaction between two dissimilar metals can occur over a period of time. It will build up sooner in wet conditions or in countries where salt is used on the roads during the winter. If a fastener is severely corroded it is likely that normal methods of removal will fail and result in its head being ruined. When you attempt removal, the fastener thread should be heard to crack free and unscrew easily - if it doesn't, stop there before damaging something.

● A smart tap on the head of the fastener will often succeed in breaking free corrosion which has occurred in the threads **(see illustration 2.13)**.

● An aerosol penetrating fluid (such as WD-40) applied the night beforehand may work its way down into the thread and ease removal. Depending on the location, you may be able to make up a Plasticine well around the fastener head and fill it with penetrating fluid.

**2.13 A sharp tap on the head of a fastener
will often break free a corroded thread**

● If you are working on an engine internal component, corrosion will most likely not be a problem due to the well lubricated environment. However, components can be very tight and an impact driver is a useful tool in freeing them **(see illustration 2.14)**.

**2.14 Using an impact driver to free a fastener**

● Where corrosion has occurred between dissimilar metals (eg steel and aluminium alloy), the application of heat to the fastener head will create a disproportionate expansion rate between the two metals and break the seizure caused by the corrosion. Whether heat can be applied depends on the location of the fastener - any surrounding components likely to be damaged must first be removed **(see illustration 2.15)**. Heat can be applied using a paint stripper heat gun or clothes iron, or by immersing the component in boiling water - wear protective gloves to prevent scalding or burns to the hands.

**2.15 Using heat to free a seized fastener**

● As a last resort, it is possible to use a hammer and cold chisel to work the fastener head unscrewed **(see illustration 2.16)**. This will damage the fastener, but more importantly extreme care must be taken not to damage the surrounding component.

*Caution: Remember that the component being secured is generally of more value than the bolt, nut or screw - when the fastener is freed, do not unscrew it with force, instead work the fastener back and forth when resistance is felt to prevent thread damage.*

**2.16 Using a hammer and chisel to free a seized fastener**

## Broken fasteners and damaged heads

● If the shank of a broken bolt or screw is accessible you can grip it with self-locking grips. The knurled wheel type stud extractor tool or self-gripping stud puller tool is particularly useful for removing the long studs which screw into the cylinder mouth surface of the crankcase or bolts and screws from which the head has broken off **(see illustration 2.17)**. Studs can also be removed by locking two nuts together on the threaded end of the stud and using a spanner on the lower nut **(see illustration 2.18)**.

**2.17 Using a stud extractor tool to remove a broken crankcase stud**

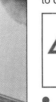

**2.18 Two nuts can be locked together to unscrew a stud from a component**

● A bolt or screw which has broken off below or level with the casing must be extracted using a screw extractor set. Centre punch the fastener to centralise the drill bit, then drill a hole in the fastener **(see illustration 2.19)**. Select a drill bit which is approximately half to three-quarters the

**2.19 When using a screw extractor, first drill a hole in the fastener . . .**

diameter of the fastener and drill to a depth which will accommodate the extractor. Use the largest size extractor possible, but avoid leaving too small a wall thickness otherwise the extractor will merely force the fastener walls outwards wedging it in the casing thread.

● If a spiral type extractor is used, thread it anti-clockwise into the fastener. As it is screwed in, it will grip the fastener and unscrew it from the casing **(see illustration 2.20)**.

**2.20 . . . then thread the extractor anti-clockwise into the fastener**

● If a taper type extractor is used, tap it into the fastener so that it is firmly wedged in place. Unscrew the extractor (anti-clockwise) to draw the fastener out.

> ⚠ *Warning: Stud extractors are very hard and may break off in the fastener if care is not taken - ask an engineer about spark erosion if this happens.*

● Alternatively, the broken bolt/screw can be drilled out and the hole retapped for an oversize bolt/screw or a diamond-section thread insert. It is essential that the drilling is carried out squarely and to the correct depth, otherwise the casing may be ruined - if in doubt, entrust the work to an engineer.

● Bolts and nuts with rounded corners cause the correct size spanner or socket to slip when force is applied. Of the types of spanner/socket available always use a six-point type rather than an eight or twelve-point type - better grip

**2.21 Comparison of surface drive ring spanner (left) with 12-point type (right)**

is obtained. Surface drive spanners grip the middle of the hex flats, rather than the corners, and are thus good in cases of damaged heads **(see illustration 2.21)**.

● Slotted-head or Phillips-head screws are often damaged by the use of the wrong size screwdriver. Allen-head and Torx-head screws are much less likely to sustain damage. If enough of the screw head is exposed you can use a hacksaw to cut a slot in its head and then use a conventional flat-bladed screwdriver to remove it. Alternatively use a hammer and cold chisel to tap the head of the fastener around to slacken it. Always replace damaged fasteners with new ones, preferably Torx or Allen-head type.

*A dab of valve grinding compound between the screw head and screwdriver tip will often give a good grip.*

### Thread repair

● Threads (particularly those in aluminium alloy components) can be damaged by overtightening, being assembled with dirt in the threads, or from a component working loose and vibrating. Eventually the thread will fail completely, and it will be impossible to tighten the fastener.

● If a thread is damaged or clogged with old locking compound it can be renovated with a thread repair tool (thread chaser) **(see illustrations 2.22 and 2.23)**; special thread

**2.22 A thread repair tool being used to correct an internal thread**

**2.23 A thread repair tool being used to correct an external thread**

chasers are available for spark plug hole threads. The tool will not cut a new thread, but clean and true the original thread. Make sure that you use the correct diameter and pitch tool. Similarly, external threads can be cleaned up with a die or a thread restorer file **(see illustration 2.24)**.

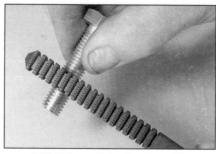

**2.24 Using a thread restorer file**

● It is possible to drill out the old thread and retap the component to the next thread size. This will work where there is enough surrounding material and a new bolt or screw can be obtained. Sometimes, however, this is not possible - such as where the bolt/screw passes through another component which must also be suitably modified, also in cases where a spark plug or oil drain plug cannot be obtained in a larger diameter thread size.

● The diamond-section thread insert (often known by its popular trade name of Heli-Coil) is a simple and effective method of renewing the thread and retaining the original size. A kit can be purchased which contains the tap, insert and installing tool **(see illustration 2.25)**. Drill out the damaged thread with the size drill specified **(see illustration 2.26)**. Carefully retap the thread **(see illustration 2.27)**. Install the

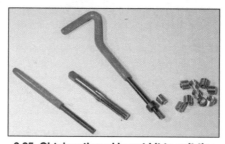

**2.25 Obtain a thread insert kit to suit the thread diameter and pitch required**

**2.26 To install a thread insert, first drill out the original thread . . .**

**2.27 . . . tap a new thread . . .**

**2.28 . . . fit insert on the installing tool . . .**

**2.29 . . . and thread into the component . . .**

**2.30 . . . break off the tang when complete**

insert on the installing tool and thread it slowly into place using a light downward pressure **(see illustrations 2.28 and 2.29)**. When positioned between a 1/4 and 1/2 turn below the surface withdraw the installing tool and use the break-off tool to press down on the tang, breaking it off **(see illustration 2.30)**.

● There are epoxy thread repair kits on the market which can rebuild stripped internal threads, although this repair should not be used on high load-bearing components.

## Thread locking and sealing compounds

● Locking compounds are used in locations where the fastener is prone to loosening due to vibration or on important safety-related items which might cause loss of control of the motorcycle if they fail. It is also used where important fasteners cannot be secured by other means such as lockwashers or split pins.

● Before applying locking compound, make sure that the threads (internal and external) are clean and dry with all old compound removed. Select a compound to suit the component being secured - a non-permanent general locking and sealing type is suitable for most applications, but a high strength type is needed for permanent fixing of studs in castings. Apply a drop or two of the compound to the first few threads of the fastener, then thread it into place and tighten to the specified torque. Do not apply excessive thread locking compound otherwise the thread may be damaged on subsequent removal.

● Certain fasteners are impregnated with a dry film type coating of locking compound on their threads. Always renew this type of fastener if disturbed.

● Anti-seize compounds, such as copper-based greases, can be applied to protect threads from seizure due to extreme heat and corrosion. A common instance is spark plug threads and exhaust system fasteners.

## 3 Measuring tools and gauges

## Feeler gauges

● Feeler gauges (or blades) are used for measuring small gaps and clearances (see illustration 3.1). They can also be used to measure endfloat (sideplay) of a component on a shaft where access is not possible with a dial gauge.

● Feeler gauge sets should be treated with care and not bent or damaged. They are etched with their size on one face. Keep them clean and very lightly oiled to prevent corrosion build-up.

**3.1 Feeler gauges are used for measuring small gaps and clearances - thickness is marked on one face of gauge**

● When measuring a clearance, select a gauge which is a light sliding fit between the two components. You may need to use two gauges together to measure the clearance accurately.

## Micrometers

● A micrometer is a precision tool capable of measuring to 0.01 or 0.001 of a millimetre. It should always be stored in its case and not in the general toolbox. It must be kept clean and never dropped, otherwise its frame or measuring anvils could be distorted resulting in inaccurate readings.

● External micrometers are used for measuring outside diameters of components and have many more applications than internal micrometers. Micrometers are available in different size ranges, eg 0 to 25 mm, 25 to 50 mm, and upwards in 25 mm steps; some large micrometers have interchangeable anvils to allow a range of measurements to be taken. Generally the largest precision measurement you are likely to take on a motorcycle is the piston diameter.

● Internal micrometers (or bore micrometers) are used for measuring inside diameters, such as valve guides and cylinder bores. Telescoping gauges and small hole gauges are used in conjunction with an external micrometer, whereas the more expensive internal micrometers have their own measuring device.

### External micrometer

**Note:** *The conventional analogue type instrument is described. Although much easier to read, digital micrometers are considerably more expensive.*

● Always check the calibration of the micrometer before use. With the anvils closed (0 to 25 mm type) or set over a test gauge (for

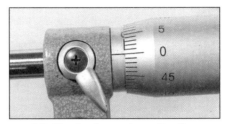

**3.2 Check micrometer calibration before use**

the larger types) the scale should read zero (see illustration 3.2); make sure that the anvils (and test piece) are clean first. Any discrepancy can be adjusted by referring to the instructions supplied with the tool. Remember that the micrometer is a precision measuring tool - don't force the anvils closed, use the ratchet (4) on the end of the micrometer to close it. In this way, a measured force is always applied.

● To use, first make sure that the item being measured is clean. Place the anvil of the micrometer (1) against the item and use the thimble (2) to bring the spindle (3) lightly into contact with the other side of the item (see illustration 3.3). Don't tighten the thimble down because this will damage the micrometer - instead use the ratchet (4) on the end of the micrometer. The ratchet mechanism applies a measured force preventing damage to the instrument.

● The micrometer is read by referring to the linear scale on the sleeve and the annular scale on the thimble. Read off the sleeve first to obtain the base measurement, then add the fine measurement from the thimble to obtain the overall reading. The linear scale on the sleeve represents the measuring range of the micrometer (eg 0 to 25 mm). The annular scale

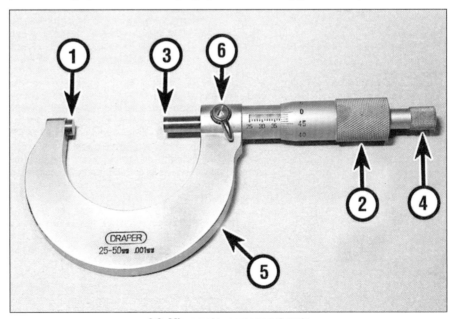

**3.3 Micrometer component parts**

| | | |
|---|---|---|
| 1 Anvil | 3 Spindle | 5 Frame |
| 2 Thimble | 4 Ratchet | 6 Locking lever |

on the thimble will be in graduations of 0.01 mm (or as marked on the frame) - one full revolution of the thimble will move 0.5 mm on the linear scale. Take the reading where the datum line on the sleeve intersects the thimble's scale. Always position the eye directly above the scale otherwise an inaccurate reading will result.

In the example shown the item measures 2.95 mm **(see illustration 3.4)**:

| | |
|---|---|
| Linear scale | 2.00 mm |
| Linear scale | 0.50 mm |
| Annular scale | 0.45 mm |
| Total figure | **2.95 mm** |

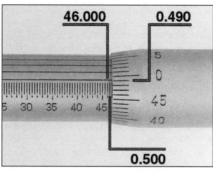

**3.5  Micrometer reading of 46.99 mm on linear and annular scales . . .**

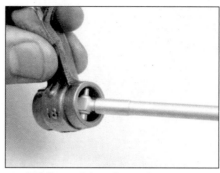

**3.7  Expand the telescoping gauge in the bore, lock its position . . .**

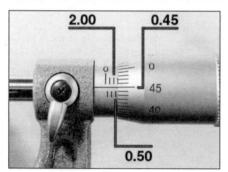

**3.4  Micrometer reading of 2.95 mm**

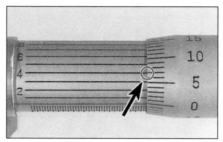

**3.6  . . . and 0.004 mm on vernier scale**

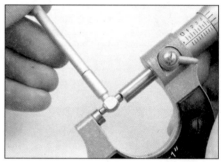

**3.8  . . . then measure the gauge with a micrometer**

Most micrometers have a locking lever (6) on the frame to hold the setting in place, allowing the item to be removed from the micrometer.

● Some micrometers have a vernier scale on their sleeve, providing an even finer measurement to be taken, in 0.001 increments of a millimetre. Take the sleeve and thimble measurement as described above, then check which graduation on the vernier scale aligns with that of the annular scale on the thimble **Note:** *The eye must be perpendicular to the scale when taking the vernier reading - if necessary rotate the body of the micrometer to ensure this.* Multiply the vernier scale figure by 0.001 and add it to the base and fine measurement figures.

In the example shown the item measures 46.994 mm **(see illustrations 3.5 and 3.6)**:

| | |
|---|---|
| Linear scale (base) | 46.000 mm |
| Linear scale (base) | 00.500 mm |
| Annular scale (fine) | 00.490 mm |
| Vernier scale | 00.004 mm |
| Total figure | **46.994 mm** |

### Internal micrometer

● Internal micrometers are available for measuring bore diameters, but are expensive and unlikely to be available for home use. It is suggested that a set of telescoping gauges and small hole gauges, both of which must be used with an external micrometer, will suffice for taking internal measurements on a motorcycle.

● Telescoping gauges can be used to

measure internal diameters of components. Select a gauge with the correct size range, make sure its ends are clean and insert it into the bore. Expand the gauge, then lock its position and withdraw it from the bore **(see illustration 3.7)**. Measure across the gauge ends with a micrometer **(see illustration 3.8)**.

● Very small diameter bores (such as valve guides) are measured with a small hole gauge. Once adjusted to a slip-fit inside the component, its position is locked and the gauge withdrawn for measurement with a micrometer **(see illustrations 3.9 and 3.10)**.

### Vernier caliper

**Note:** *The conventional linear and dial gauge type instruments are described. Digital types are easier to read, but are far more expensive.*

● The vernier caliper does not provide the precision of a micrometer, but is versatile in being able to measure internal and external diameters. Some types also incorporate a depth gauge. It is ideal for measuring clutch plate friction material and spring free lengths.

● To use the conventional linear scale vernier, slacken off the vernier clamp screws (1) and set its jaws over (2), or inside (3), the item to be measured **(see illustration 3.11)**. Slide the jaw into contact, using the thumbwheel (4) for fine movement of the sliding scale (5) then tighten the clamp screws (1). Read off the main scale (6) where the zero on the sliding scale (5) intersects it, taking the whole number to the left of the zero; this provides the base measurement. View along the sliding scale and select the division which

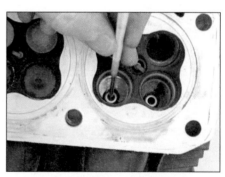

**3.9  Expand the small hole gauge in the bore, lock its position . . .**

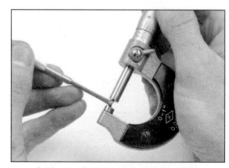

**3.10  . . . then measure the gauge with a micrometer**

lines up exactly with any of the divisions on the main scale, noting that the divisions usually represents 0.02 of a millimetre. Add this fine measurement to the base measurement to obtain the total reading.

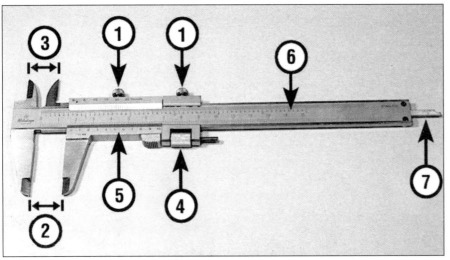

**3.11 Vernier component parts (linear gauge)**

| | | |
|---|---|---|
| 1 Clamp screws | 3 Internal jaws | 5 Sliding scale | 7 Depth gauge |
| 2 External jaws | 4 Thumbwheel | 6 Main scale | |

In the example shown the item measures 55.92 mm (**see illustration 3.12**):

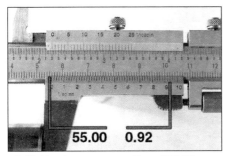

**3.12 Vernier gauge reading of 55.92 mm**

| | |
|---|---|
| Base measurement | 55.00 mm |
| Fine measurement | 00.92 mm |
| Total figure | **55.92 mm** |

● Some vernier calipers are equipped with a dial gauge for fine measurement. Before use, check that the jaws are clean, then close them fully and check that the dial gauge reads zero. If necessary adjust the gauge ring accordingly. Slacken the vernier clamp screw (1) and set its jaws over (2), or inside (3), the item to be measured (**see illustration 3.13**). Slide the jaws into contact, using the thumbwheel (4) for fine movement. Read off the main scale (5) where the edge of the sliding scale (6) intersects it, taking the whole number to the left of the zero; this provides the base measurement. Read off the needle position on the dial gauge (7) scale to provide the fine measurement; each division represents 0.05 of a millimetre. Add this fine measurement to the base measurement to obtain the total reading.

In the example shown the item measures 55.95 mm (**see illustration 3.14**):

| | |
|---|---|
| Base measurement | 55.00 mm |
| Fine measurement | 00.95 mm |
| Total figure | **55.95 mm** |

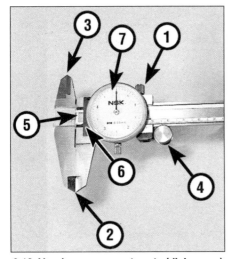

**3.13 Vernier component parts (dial gauge)**

| | |
|---|---|
| 1 Clamp screw | 5 Main scale |
| 2 External jaws | 6 Sliding scale |
| 3 Internal jaws | 7 Dial gauge |
| 4 Thumbwheel | |

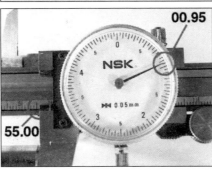

**3.14 Vernier gauge reading of 55.95 mm**

## Plastigauge

● Plastigauge is a plastic material which can be compressed between two surfaces to measure the oil clearance between them. The width of the compressed Plastigauge is measured against a calibrated scale to determine the clearance.

● Common uses of Plastigauge are for measuring the clearance between crankshaft journal and main bearing inserts, between crankshaft journal and big-end bearing inserts, and between camshaft and bearing surfaces. The following example describes big-end oil clearance measurement.

● Handle the Plastigauge material carefully to prevent distortion. Using a sharp knife, cut a length which corresponds with the width of the bearing being measured and place it carefully across the journal so that it is parallel with the shaft (**see illustration 3.15**). Carefully install both bearing shells and the connecting rod. Without rotating the rod on the journal tighten its bolts or nuts (as applicable) to the specified torque. The connecting rod and bearings are then disassembled and the crushed Plastigauge examined.

**3.15 Plastigauge placed across shaft journal**

● Using the scale provided in the Plastigauge kit, measure the width of the material to determine the oil clearance (**see illustration 3.16**). Always remove all traces of Plastigauge after use using your fingernails.

*Caution: Arriving at the correct clearance demands that the assembly is torqued correctly, according to the settings and sequence (where applicable) provided by the motorcycle manufacturer.*

**3.16 Measuring the width of the crushed Plastigauge**

### Dial gauge or DTI (Dial Test Indicator)

● A dial gauge can be used to accurately measure small amounts of movement. Typical uses are measuring shaft runout or shaft endfloat (sideplay) and setting piston position for ignition timing on two-strokes. A dial gauge set usually comes with a range of different probes and adapters and mounting equipment.

● The gauge needle must point to zero when at rest. Rotate the ring around its periphery to zero the gauge.

● Check that the gauge is capable of reading the extent of movement in the work. Most gauges have a small dial set in the face which records whole millimetres of movement as well as the fine scale around the face periphery which is calibrated in 0.01 mm divisions. Read off the small dial first to obtain the base measurement, then add the measurement from the fine scale to obtain the total reading.

In the example shown the gauge reads 1.48 mm (see illustration 3.17):

| | |
|---|---|
| Base measurement | 1.00 mm |
| Fine measurement | 0.48 mm |
| **Total figure** | **1.48 mm** |

**3.17  Dial gauge reading of 1.48 mm**

● If measuring shaft runout, the shaft must be supported in vee-blocks and the gauge mounted on a stand perpendicular to the shaft. Rest the tip of the gauge against the centre of the shaft and rotate the shaft slowly whilst watching the gauge reading **(see illustration 3.18)**. Take several measurements along the length of the shaft and record the

**3.18  Using a dial gauge to measure shaft runout**

maximum gauge reading as the amount of runout in the shaft. **Note:** *The reading obtained will be total runout at that point - some manufacturers specify that the runout figure is halved to compare with their specified runout limit.*

● Endfloat (sideplay) measurement requires that the gauge is mounted securely to the surrounding component with its probe touching the end of the shaft. Using hand pressure, push and pull on the shaft noting the maximum endfloat recorded on the gauge **(see illustration 3.19)**.

**3.19  Using a dial gauge to measure shaft endfloat**

● A dial gauge with suitable adapters can be used to determine piston position BTDC on two-stroke engines for the purposes of ignition timing. The gauge, adapter and suitable length probe are installed in the place of the spark plug and the gauge zeroed at TDC. If the piston position is specified as 1.14 mm BTDC, rotate the engine back to 2.00 mm BTDC, then slowly forwards to 1.14 mm BTDC.

### Cylinder compression gauges

● A compression gauge is used for measuring cylinder compression. Either the rubber-cone type or the threaded adapter type can be used. The latter is preferred to ensure a perfect seal against the cylinder head. A 0 to 300 psi (0 to 20 Bar) type gauge (for petrol/gasoline engines) will be suitable for motorcycles.

● The spark plug is removed and the gauge either held hard against the cylinder head (cone type) or the gauge adapter screwed into the cylinder head (threaded type) **(see illustration 3.20)**. Cylinder compression is measured with the engine turning over, but not running - carry out the compression test as described in

**3.20  Using a rubber-cone type cylinder compression gauge**

*Fault Finding Equipment*. The gauge will hold the reading until manually released.

### Oil pressure gauge

● An oil pressure gauge is used for measuring engine oil pressure. Most gauges come with a set of adapters to fit the thread of the take-off point **(see illustration 3.21)**. If the take-off point specified by the motorcycle manufacturer is an external oil pipe union, make sure that the specified replacement union is used to prevent oil starvation.

**3.21  Oil pressure gauge and take-off point adapter (arrow)**

● Oil pressure is measured with the engine running (at a specific rpm) and often the manufacturer will specify pressure limits for a cold and hot engine.

### Straight-edge and surface plate

● If checking the gasket face of a component for warpage, place a steel rule or precision straight-edge across the gasket face and measure any gap between the straight-edge and component with feeler gauges **(see illustration 3.22)**. Check diagonally across the component and between mounting holes **(see illustration 3.23)**.

**3.22  Use a straight-edge and feeler gauges to check for warpage**

**3.23  Check for warpage in these directions**

● Checking individual components for warpage, such as clutch plain (metal) plates, requires a perfectly flat plate or piece or plate glass and feeler gauges.

## 4 Torque and leverage

### What is torque?

● Torque describes the twisting force about a shaft. The amount of torque applied is determined by the distance from the centre of the shaft to the end of the lever and the amount of force being applied to the end of the lever; distance multiplied by force equals torque.

● The manufacturer applies a measured torque to a bolt or nut to ensure that it will not slacken in use and to hold two components securely together without movement in the joint. The actual torque setting depends on the thread size, bolt or nut material and the composition of the components being held.

● Too little torque may cause the fastener to loosen due to vibration, whereas too much torque will distort the joint faces of the component or cause the fastener to shear off. Always stick to the specified torque setting.

### Using a torque wrench

● Check the calibration of the torque wrench and make sure it has a suitable range for the job. Torque wrenches are available in Nm (Newton-metres), kgf m (kilograms-force metre), lbf ft (pounds-feet), lbf in (inch-pounds). Do not confuse lbf ft with lbf in.

● Adjust the tool to the desired torque on the scale (see illustration 4.1). If your torque wrench is not calibrated in the units specified, carefully convert the figure (see *Conversion Factors*). A manufacturer sometimes gives a torque setting as a range (8 to 10 Nm) rather than a single figure - in this case set the tool midway between the two settings. The same torque may be expressed as 9 Nm ± 1 Nm. Some torque wrenches have a method of locking the setting so that it isn't inadvertently altered during use.

**4.1 Set the torque wrench index mark to the setting required, in this case 12 Nm**

● Install the bolts/nuts in their correct location and secure them lightly. Their threads must be clean and free of any old locking compound. Unless specified the threads and flange should be dry - oiled threads are necessary in certain circumstances and the manufacturer will take this into account in the specified torque figure. Similarly, the manufacturer may also specify the application of thread-locking compound.

● Tighten the fasteners in the specified sequence until the torque wrench clicks, indicating that the torque setting has been reached. Apply the torque again to double-check the setting. Where different thread diameter fasteners secure the component, as a rule tighten the larger diameter ones first.

● When the torque wrench has been finished with, release the lock (where applicable) and fully back off its setting to zero - do not leave the torque wrench tensioned. Also, do not use a torque wrench for slackening a fastener.

### Angle-tightening

● Manufacturers often specify a figure in degrees for final tightening of a fastener. This usually follows tightening to a specific torque setting.

● A degree disc can be set and attached to the socket (see illustration 4.2) or a protractor can be used to mark the angle of movement on the bolt/nut head and the surrounding casting (see illustration 4.3).

**4.2 Angle tightening can be accomplished with a torque-angle gauge . . .**

**4.3 . . . or by marking the angle on the surrounding component**

### Loosening sequences

● Where more than one bolt/nut secures a component, loosen each fastener evenly a little at a time. In this way, not all the stress of the joint is held by one fastener and the components are not likely to distort.

● If a tightening sequence is provided, work in the REVERSE of this, but if not, work from the outside in, in a criss-cross sequence (see illustration 4.4).

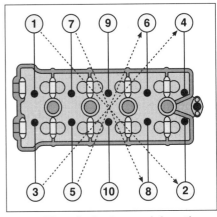

**4.4 When slackening, work from the outside inwards**

### Tightening sequences

● If a component is held by more than one fastener it is important that the retaining bolts/nuts are tightened evenly to prevent uneven stress build-up and distortion of sealing faces. This is especially important on high-compression joints such as the cylinder head.

● A sequence is usually provided by the manufacturer, either in a diagram or actually marked in the casting. If not, always start in the centre and work outwards in a criss-cross pattern (see illustration 4.5). Start off by securing all bolts/nuts finger-tight, then set the torque wrench and tighten each fastener by a small amount in sequence until the final torque is reached. By following this practice,

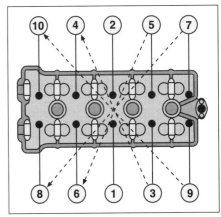

**4.5 When tightening, work from the inside outwards**

the joint will be held evenly and will not be distorted. Important joints, such as the cylinder head and big-end fasteners often have two- or three-stage torque settings.

## Applying leverage

● Use tools at the correct angle. Position a socket wrench or spanner on the bolt/nut so that you pull it towards you when loosening. If this can't be done, push the spanner without curling your fingers around it **(see illustration 4.6)** - the spanner may slip or the fastener loosen suddenly, resulting in your fingers being crushed against a component.

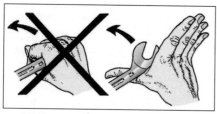

**4.6 If you can't pull on the spanner to loosen a fastener, push with your hand open**

● Additional leverage is gained by extending the length of the lever. The best way to do this is to use a breaker bar instead of the regular length tool, or to slip a length of tubing over the end of the spanner or socket wrench.
● If additional leverage will not work, the fastener head is either damaged or firmly corroded in place (see *Fasteners*).

## 5  Bearings

### Bearing removal and installation

#### Drivers and sockets

● Before removing a bearing, always inspect the casing to see which way it must be driven out - some casings will have retaining plates or a cast step. Also check for any identifying markings on the bearing and if installed to a certain depth, measure this at this stage. Some roller bearings are sealed on one side - take note of the original fitted position.
● Bearings can be driven out of a casing using a bearing driver tool (with the correct size head) or a socket of the correct diameter. Select the driver head or socket so that it contacts the outer race of the bearing, not the balls/rollers or inner race. Always support the casing around the bearing housing with wood blocks, otherwise there is a risk of fracture. The bearing is driven out with a few blows on the driver or socket from a heavy mallet. Unless access is severely restricted (as with wheel bearings), a pin-punch is not recommended unless it is moved around the bearing to keep it square in its housing.

● The same equipment can be used to install bearings. Make sure the bearing housing is supported on wood blocks and line up the bearing in its housing. Fit the bearing as noted on removal - generally they are installed with their marked side facing outwards. Tap the bearing squarely into its housing using a driver or socket which bears only on the bearing's outer race - contact with the bearing balls/rollers or inner race will destroy it **(see illustrations 5.1 and 5.2)**.
● Check that the bearing inner race and balls/rollers rotate freely.

**5.1  Using a bearing driver against the bearing's outer race**

**5.2  Using a large socket against the bearing's outer race**

#### Pullers and slide-hammers

● Where a bearing is pressed on a shaft a puller will be required to extract it **(see illustration 5.3)**. Make sure that the puller clamp or legs fit securely behind the bearing and are unlikely to slip out. If pulling a bearing

**5.3  This bearing puller clamps behind the bearing and pressure is applied to the shaft end to draw the bearing off**

off a gear shaft for example, you may have to locate the puller behind a gear pinion if there is no access to the race and draw the gear pinion off the shaft as well **(see illustration 5.4)**.

> **Caution: Ensure that the puller's centre bolt locates securely against the end of the shaft and will not slip when pressure is applied. Also ensure that puller does not damage the shaft end.**

**5.4  Where no access is available to the rear of the bearing, it is sometimes possible to draw off the adjacent component**

● Operate the puller so that its centre bolt exerts pressure on the shaft end and draws the bearing off the shaft.
● When installing the bearing on the shaft, tap only on the bearing's inner race - contact with the balls/rollers or outer race with destroy the bearing. Use a socket or length of tubing as a drift which fits over the shaft end **(see illustration 5.5)**.

**5.5  When installing a bearing on a shaft use a piece of tubing which bears only on the bearing's inner race**

● Where a bearing locates in a blind hole in a casing, it cannot be driven or pulled out as described above. A slide-hammer with knife-edged bearing puller attachment will be required. The puller attachment passes through the bearing and when tightened expands to fit firmly behind the bearing **(see illustration 5.6)**. By operating the slide-hammer part of the tool the bearing is jarred out of its housing **(see illustration 5.7)**.
● It is possible, if the bearing is of reasonable weight, for it to drop out of its housing if the casing is heated as described opposite. If this

**5.6 Expand the bearing puller so that it locks behind the bearing . . .**

**5.7 . . . attach the slide hammer to the bearing puller**

method is attempted, first prepare a work surface which will enable the casing to be tapped face down to help dislodge the bearing - a wood surface is ideal since it will not damage the casing's gasket surface. Wearing protective gloves, tap the heated casing several times against the work surface to dislodge the bearing under its own weight **(see illustration 5.8)**.

**5.8 Tapping a casing face down on wood blocks can often dislodge a bearing**

● Bearings can be installed in blind holes using the driver or socket method described above.

## Drawbolts

● Where a bearing or bush is set in the eye of a component, such as a suspension linkage arm or connecting rod small-end, removal by drift may damage the component. Furthermore, a rubber bushing in a shock absorber eye cannot successfully be driven out of position. If access is available to a engineering press, the task is straightforward. If not, a drawbolt can be fabricated to extract the bearing or bush.

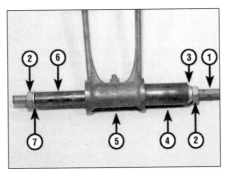

**5.9 Drawbolt component parts assembled on a suspension arm**

1  Bolt or length of threaded bar
2  Nuts
3  Washer (external diameter greater than tubing internal diameter)
4  Tubing (internal diameter sufficient to accommodate bearing)
5  Suspension arm with bearing
6  Tubing (external diameter slightly smaller than bearing)
7  Washer (external diameter slightly smaller than bearing)

**5.10 Drawing the bearing out of the suspension arm**

● To extract the bearing/bush you will need a long bolt with nut (or piece of threaded bar with two nuts), a piece of tubing which has an internal diameter larger than the bearing/bush, another piece of tubing which has an external diameter slightly smaller than the bearing/ bush, and a selection of washers **(see illustrations 5.9 and 5.10)**. Note that the pieces of tubing must be of the same length, or longer, than the bearing/bush.
● The same kit (without the pieces of tubing) can be used to draw the new bearing/bush back into place **(see illustration 5.11)**.

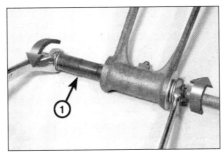

**5.11 Installing a new bearing (1) in the suspension arm**

## Temperature change

● If the bearing's outer race is a tight fit in the casing, the aluminium casing can be heated to release its grip on the bearing. Aluminium will expand at a greater rate than the steel bearing outer race. There are several ways to do this, but avoid any localised extreme heat (such as a blow torch) - aluminium alloy has a low melting point.
● Approved methods of heating a casing are using a domestic oven (heated to 100°C) or immersing the casing in boiling water **(see illustration 5.12)**. Low temperature range localised heat sources such as a paint stripper heat gun or clothes iron can also be used **(see illustration 5.13)**. Alternatively, soak a rag in boiling water, wring it out and wrap it around the bearing housing.

> ⚠ **Warning: All of these methods require care in use to prevent scalding and burns to the hands. Wear protective gloves when handling hot components.**

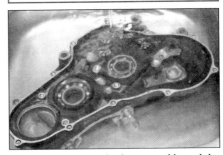

**5.12 A casing can be immersed in a sink of boiling water to aid bearing removal**

**5.13 Using a localised heat source to aid bearing removal**

● If heating the whole casing note that plastic components, such as the neutral switch, may suffer - remove them beforehand.
● After heating, remove the bearing as described above. You may find that the expansion is sufficient for the bearing to fall out of the casing under its own weight or with a light tap on the driver or socket.
● If necessary, the casing can be heated to aid bearing installation, and this is sometimes the recommended procedure if the motorcycle manufacturer has designed the housing and bearing fit with this intention.

● Installation of bearings can be eased by placing them in a freezer the night before installation. The steel bearing will contract slightly, allowing easy insertion in its housing. This is often useful when installing steering head outer races in the frame.

### Bearing types and markings

● Plain shell bearings, ball bearings, needle roller bearings and tapered roller bearings will all be found on motorcycles (see illustrations 5.14 and 5.15). The ball and roller types are usually caged between an inner and outer race, but uncaged variations may be found.

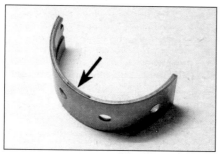

**5.14 Shell bearings are either plain or grooved. They are usually identified by colour code (arrow)**

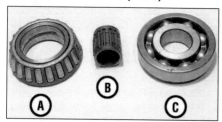

**5.15 Tapered roller bearing (A), needle roller bearing (B) and ball journal bearing (C)**

● Shell bearings (often called inserts) are usually found at the crankshaft main and connecting rod big-end where they are good at coping with high loads. They are made of a phosphor-bronze material and are impregnated with self-lubricating properties.
● Ball bearings and needle roller bearings consist of a steel inner and outer race with the balls or rollers between the races. They require constant lubrication by oil or grease and are good at coping with axial loads. Taper roller bearings consist of rollers set in a tapered cage set on the inner race; the outer race is separate. They are good at coping with axial loads and prevent movement along the shaft - a typical application is in the steering head.
● Bearing manufacturers produce bearings to ISO size standards and stamp one face of the bearing to indicate its internal and external diameter, load capacity and type (see illustration 5.16).
● Metal bushes are usually of phosphor-bronze material. Rubber bushes are used in suspension mounting eyes. Fibre bushes have also been used in suspension pivots.

**5.16 Typical bearing marking**

### Bearing fault finding

● If a bearing outer race has spun in its housing, the housing material will be damaged. You can use a bearing locking compound to bond the outer race in place if damage is not too severe.
● Shell bearings will fail due to damage of their working surface, as a result of lack of lubrication, corrosion or abrasive particles in the oil (see illustration 5.17). Small particles of dirt in the oil may embed in the bearing material whereas larger particles will score the bearing and shaft journal. If a number of short journeys are made, insufficient heat will be generated to drive off condensation which has built up on the bearings.

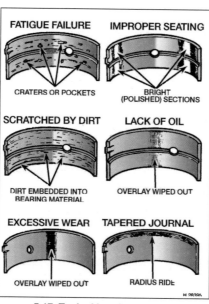

**5.17 Typical bearing failures**

● Ball and roller bearings will fail due to lack of lubrication or damage to the balls or rollers. Tapered-roller bearings can be damaged by overloading them. Unless the bearing is sealed on both sides, wash it in paraffin (kerosene) to remove all old grease then allow it to dry. Make a visual inspection looking to dented balls or rollers, damaged cages and worn or pitted races (see illustration 5.18).
● A ball bearing can be checked for wear by listening to it when spun. Apply a film of light oil to the bearing and hold it close to the ear - hold the outer race with one hand and spin the inner

**5.18 Example of ball journal bearing with damaged balls and cages**

**5.19 Hold outer race and listen to inner race when spun**

race with the other hand (see illustration 5.19). The bearing should be almost silent when spun; if it grates or rattles it is worn.

## 6 Oil seals

### Oil seal removal and installation

● Oil seals should be renewed every time a component is dismantled. This is because the seal lips will become set to the sealing surface and will not necessarily reseal.
● Oil seals can be prised out of position using a large flat-bladed screwdriver (see illustration 6.1). In the case of crankcase seals, check first that the seal is not lipped on the inside, preventing its removal with the crankcases joined.

**6.1 Prise out oil seals with a large flat-bladed screwdriver**

● New seals are usually installed with their marked face (containing the seal reference code) outwards and the spring side towards the fluid being retained. In certain cases, such as a two-stroke engine crankshaft seal, a double lipped seal may be used due to there being fluid or gas on each side of the joint.

● Use a bearing driver or socket which bears only on the outer hard edge of the seal to install it in the casing - tapping on the inner edge will damage the sealing lip.

### Oil seal types and markings

● Oil seals are usually of the single-lipped type. Double-lipped seals are found where a liquid or gas is on both sides of the joint.
● Oil seals can harden and lose their sealing ability if the motorcycle has been in storage for a long period - renewal is the only solution.
● Oil seal manufacturers also conform to the ISO markings for seal size - these are moulded into the outer face of the seal (see illustration 6.2).

**6.2 These oil seal markings indicate inside diameter, outside diameter and seal thickness**

## 7 Gaskets and sealants

### Types of gasket and sealant

● Gaskets are used to seal the mating surfaces between components and keep lubricants, fluids, vacuum or pressure contained within the assembly. Aluminium gaskets are sometimes found at the cylinder joints, but most gaskets are paper-based. If the mating surfaces of the components being joined are undamaged the gasket can be installed dry, although a dab of sealant or grease will be useful to hold it in place during assembly.
● RTV (Room Temperature Vulcanising) silicone rubber sealants cure when exposed to moisture in the atmosphere. These sealants are good at filling pits or irregular gasket faces, but will tend to be forced out of the joint under very high torque. They can be used to replace a paper gasket, but first make sure that the width of the paper gasket is not essential to the shimming of internal components. RTV sealants should not be used on components containing petrol (gasoline).
● Non-hardening, semi-hardening and hard setting liquid gasket compounds can be used with a gasket or between a metal-to-metal joint. Select the sealant to suit the application: universal non-hardening sealant can be used on virtually all joints; semi-hardening on joint faces which are rough or damaged; hard setting sealant on joints which require a permanent bond and are subjected to high temperature and pressure. **Note:** *Check first if the paper gasket has a bead of sealant*

*impregnated in its surface before applying additional sealant.*
● When choosing a sealant, make sure it is suitable for the application, particularly if being applied in a high-temperature area or in the vicinity of fuel. Certain manufacturers produce sealants in either clear, silver or black colours to match the finish of the engine. This has a particular application on motorcycles where much of the engine is exposed.
● Do not over-apply sealant. That which is squeezed out on the outside of the joint can be wiped off, whereas an excess of sealant on the inside can break off and clog oilways.

### Breaking a sealed joint

● Age, heat, pressure and the use of hard setting sealant can cause two components to stick together so tightly that they are difficult to separate using finger pressure alone. Do not resort to using levers unless there is a pry point provided for this purpose (see illustration 7.1) or else the gasket surfaces will be damaged.
● Use a soft-faced hammer (see illustration 7.2) or a wood block and conventional hammer to strike the component near the mating surface. Avoid hammering against cast extremities since they may break off. If this method fails, try using a wood wedge between the two components.

**Caution: If the joint will not separate, double-check that you have removed all the fasteners.**

**7.1 If a pry point is provided, apply gently pressure with a flat-bladed screwdriver**

**7.2 Tap around the joint with a soft-faced mallet if necessary - don't strike cooling fins**

### Removal of old gasket and sealant

● Paper gaskets will most likely come away complete, leaving only a few traces stuck on

*Most components have one or two hollow locating dowels between the two gasket faces. If a dowel cannot be removed, do not resort to gripping it with pliers - it will almost certainly be distorted. Install a close-fitting socket or Phillips screwdriver into the dowel and then grip the outer edge of the dowel to free it.*

the sealing faces of the components. It is imperative that all traces are removed to ensure correct sealing of the new gasket.
● Very carefully scrape all traces of gasket away making sure that the sealing surfaces are not gouged or scored by the scraper (see illustrations 7.3, 7.4 and 7.5). Stubborn deposits can be removed by spraying with an aerosol gasket remover. Final preparation of

**7.3 Paper gaskets can be scraped off with a gasket scraper tool . . .**

**7.4 . . . a knife blade . . .**

**7.5 . . . or a household scraper**

**7.6 Fine abrasive paper is wrapped around a flat file to clean up the gasket face**

**7.7 A kitchen scourer can be used on stubborn deposits**

the gasket surface can be made with very fine abrasive paper or a plastic kitchen scourer **(see illustrations 7.6 and 7.7)**.

● Old sealant can be scraped or peeled off components, depending on the type originally used. Note that gasket removal compounds are available to avoid scraping the components clean; make sure the gasket remover suits the type of sealant used.

## 8  Chains

### Breaking and joining final drive chains

● Drive chains for all but small bikes are continuous and do not have a clip-type connecting link. The chain must be broken using a chain breaker tool and the new chain securely riveted together using a new soft rivet-type link. Never use a clip-type connecting link instead of a rivet-type link, except in an emergency. Various chain breaking and riveting tools are available, either as separate tools or combined as illustrated in the accompanying photographs - read the instructions supplied with the tool carefully.

> ⚠ **Warning: The need to rivet the new link pins correctly cannot be overstressed - loss of control of the motorcycle is very likely to result if the chain breaks in use.**

● Rotate the chain and look for the soft link. The soft link pins look like they have been

**8.1 Tighten the chain breaker to push the pin out of the link . . .**

**8.2 . . . withdraw the pin, remove the tool . . .**

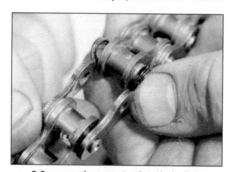

**8.3 . . . and separate the chain link**

deeply centre-punched instead of peened over like all the other pins **(see illustration 8.9)** and its sideplate may be a different colour. Position the soft link midway between the sprockets and assemble the chain breaker tool over one of the soft link pins **(see illustration 8.1)**. Operate the tool to push the pin out through the chain **(see illustration 8.2)**. On an O-ring chain, remove the O-rings **(see illustration 8.3)**. Carry out the same procedure on the other soft link pin.

> **Caution: Certain soft link pins (particularly on the larger chains) may require their ends to be filed or ground off before they can be pressed out using the tool.**

● Check that you have the correct size and strength (standard or heavy duty) new soft link - do not reuse the old link. Look for the size marking on the chain sideplates **(see illustration 8.10)**.

● Position the chain ends so that they are engaged over the rear sprocket. On an O-ring

**8.4 Insert the new soft link, with O-rings, through the chain ends . . .**

**8.5 . . . install the O-rings over the pin ends . . .**

**8.6 . . . followed by the sideplate**

chain, install a new O-ring over each pin of the link and insert the link through the two chain ends **(see illustration 8.4)**. Install a new O-ring over the end of each pin, followed by the sideplate (with the chain manufacturer's marking facing outwards) **(see illustrations 8.5 and 8.6)**. On an unsealed chain, insert the link through the two chain ends, then install the sideplate with the chain manufacturer's marking facing outwards.

● Note that it may not be possible to install the sideplate using finger pressure alone. If using a joining tool, assemble it so that the plates of the tool clamp the link and press the sideplate over the pins **(see illustration 8.7)**. Otherwise, use two small sockets placed over

**8.7 Push the sideplate into position using a clamp**

**8.8 Assemble the chain riveting tool over one pin at a time and tighten it fully**

**8.9 Pin end correctly riveted (A), pin end unriveted (B)**

the rivet ends and two pieces of the wood between a G-clamp. Operate the clamp to press the sideplate over the pins.

● Assemble the joining tool over one pin (following the maker's instructions) and tighten the tool down to spread the pin end securely **(see illustrations 8.8 and 8.9)**. Do the same on the other pin.

 *Warning: Check that the pin ends are secure and that there is no danger of the sideplate coming loose. If the pin ends are cracked the soft link must be renewed.*

### Final drive chain sizing

● Chains are sized using a three digit number, followed by a suffix to denote the chain type **(see illustration 8.10)**. Chain type is either standard or heavy duty (thicker sideplates), and also unsealed or O-ring/X-ring type.

● The first digit of the number relates to the pitch of the chain, ie the distance from the centre of one pin to the centre of the next pin **(see illustration 8.11)**. Pitch is expressed in eighths of an inch, as follows:

**8.10 Typical chain size and type marking**

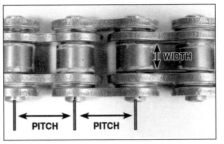

**8.11 Chain dimensions**

| |
|---|
| Sizes commencing with a 4 (eg 428) have a pitch of 1/2 inch (12.7 mm) |
| Sizes commencing with a 5 (eg 520) have a pitch of 5/8 inch (15.9 mm) |
| Sizes commencing with a 6 (eg 630) have a pitch of 3/4 inch (19.1 mm) |

● The second and third digits of the chain size relate to the width of the rollers, again in imperial units, eg the 525 shown has 5/16 inch (7.94 mm) rollers **(see illustration 8.11)**.

## 9 Hoses

### Clamping to prevent flow

● Small-bore flexible hoses can be clamped to prevent fluid flow whilst a component is worked on. Whichever method is used, ensure that the hose material is not permanently distorted or damaged by the clamp.

a) A brake hose clamp available from auto accessory shops **(see illustration 9.1)**.
b) A wingnut type hose clamp **(see illustration 9.2)**.

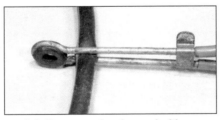

**9.1 Hoses can be clamped with an automotive brake hose clamp . . .**

**9.2 . . . a wingnut type hose clamp . . .**

c) Two sockets placed each side of the hose and held with straight-jawed self-locking grips **(see illustration 9.3)**.
d) Thick card each side of the hose held between straight-jawed self-locking grips **(see illustration 9.4)**.

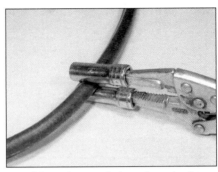

**9.3 . . . two sockets and a pair of self-locking grips . . .**

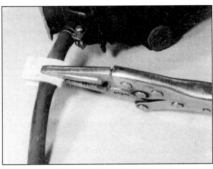

**9.4 . . . or thick card and self-locking grips**

### Freeing and fitting hoses

● Always make sure the hose clamp is moved well clear of the hose end. Grip the hose with your hand and rotate it whilst pulling it off the union. If the hose has hardened due to age and will not move, slit it with a sharp knife and peel its ends off the union **(see illustration 9.5)**.

● Resist the temptation to use grease or soap on the unions to aid installation; although it helps the hose slip over the union it will equally aid the escape of fluid from the joint. It is preferable to soften the hose ends in hot water and wet the inside surface of the hose with water or a fluid which will evaporate.

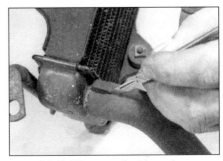

**9.5 Cutting a coolant hose free with a sharp knife**

## Introduction

In less time than it takes to read this introduction, a thief could steal your motorcycle. Returning only to find your bike has gone is one of the worst feelings in the world. Even if the motorcycle is insured against theft, once you've got over the initial shock, you will have the inconvenience of dealing with the police and your insurance company.

The motorcycle is an easy target for the professional thief and the joyrider alike and the official figures on motorcycle theft make for depressing reading; on average a motorcycle is stolen every 16 minutes in the UK!

Motorcycle thefts fall into two categories, those stolen 'to order' and those taken by opportunists. The thief stealing to order will be on the look out for a specific make and model and will go to extraordinary lengths to obtain that motorcycle. The opportunist thief on the other hand will look for easy targets which can be stolen with the minimum of effort and risk.

Whilst it is never going to be possible to make your machine 100% secure, it is estimated that around half of all stolen motorcycles are taken by opportunist thieves. Remember that the opportunist thief is always on the look out for the easy option: if there are two similar motorcycles parked side-by-side, they will target the one with the lowest level of security. By taking a few precautions, you can reduce the chances of your motorcycle being stolen.

# Security equipment

There are many specialised motorcycle security devices available and the following text summarises their applications and their good and bad points.

Once you have decided on the type of security equipment which best suits your needs, we recommended that you read one of the many equipment tests regularly carried out by the motorcycle press. These tests compare the products from all the major manufacturers and give impartial ratings on their effectiveness, value-for-money and ease of use.

No one item of security equipment can provide complete protection. It is highly recommended that two or more of the items described below are combined to increase the security of your motorcycle (a lock and chain plus an alarm system is just about ideal). The more security measures fitted to the bike, the less likely it is to be stolen.

### Lock and chain

**Pros:** *Very flexible to use; can be used to secure the motorcycle to almost any immovable object. On some locks and chains, the lock can be used on its own as a disc lock (see below).*

**Cons:** *Can be very heavy and awkward to carry on the motorcycle, although some types will be supplied with a carry bag which can be strapped to the pillion seat.*

● Heavy-duty chains and locks are an excellent security measure **(see illustration 1)**. Whenever the motorcycle is parked, use the lock and chain to secure the machine to a solid, immovable object such as a post or railings. This will prevent the machine from being ridden away or being lifted into the back of a van.

● When fitting the chain, always ensure the chain is routed around the motorcycle frame or swingarm **(see illustrations 2 and 3)**. Never merely pass the chain around one of the wheel rims; a thief may unbolt the wheel and lift the rest of the machine into a van, leaving you with just the wheel! Try to avoid having excess chain free, thus making it difficult to use cutting tools, and keep the chain and lock off the ground to prevent thieves attacking it with a cold chisel. Position the lock so that its lock barrel is facing downwards; this will make it harder for the thief to attack the lock mechanism.

Ensure the lock and chain you buy is of good quality and long enough to shackle your bike to a solid object

Pass the chain through the bike's frame, rather than just through a wheel . . .

. . . and loop it around a solid object

## U-locks

**Pros:** *Highly effective deterrent which can be used to secure the bike to a post or railings. Most U-locks come with a carrier which allows the lock to be easily carried on the bike.*

**Cons:** *Not as flexible to use as a lock and chain.*

● These are solid locks which are similar in use to a lock and chain. U-locks are lighter than a lock and chain but not so flexible to use. The length and shape of the lock shackle limit the objects to which the bike can be secured **(see illustration 4).**

**U-locks can be used to secure the bike to a solid object – ensure you purchase one which is long enough**

## Disc locks

**Pros:** *Small, light and very easy to carry; most can be stored underneath the seat.*

**Cons:** *Does not prevent the motorcycle being lifted into a van. Can be very embarrassing if you*

**A typical disc lock attached through one of the holes in the disc**

*forget to remove the lock before attempting to ride off!*

● Disc locks are designed to be attached to the front brake disc. The lock passes through one of the holes in the disc and prevents the wheel rotating by jamming against the fork/brake caliper **(see illustration 5).** Some are equipped with an alarm siren which sounds if the disc lock is moved; this not only acts as a theft deterrent but also as a handy reminder if you try to move the bike with the lock still fitted.

● Combining the disc lock with a length of cable which can be looped around a post or railings provides an additional measure of security **(see illustration 6).**

## Alarms and immobilisers

**Pros:** *Once installed it is completely hassle-free to use. If the system is 'Thatcham' or 'Sold Secure-approved', insurance companies may give you a discount.*

**Cons:** *Can be expensive to buy and complex to install. No system will prevent the motorcycle from being lifted into a van and taken away.*

● Electronic alarms and immobilisers are available to suit a variety of budgets. There are three different types of system available: pure alarms, pure immobilisers, and the more expensive systems which are combined alarm/immobilisers **(see illustration 7).**
● An alarm system is designed to emit an audible warning if the motorcycle is being tampered with.
● An immobiliser prevents the motorcycle being started and ridden away by disabling its electrical systems.
● When purchasing an alarm/immobiliser system, check the cost of installing the system unless you are able to do it yourself. If the motorcycle is not used regularly, another consideration is the current drain of the system. All alarm/immobiliser systems are powered by the motorcycle's battery; purchasing a system with a very low current drain could prevent the battery losing its charge whilst the motorcycle is not being used.

**A disc lock combined with a security cable provides additional protection**

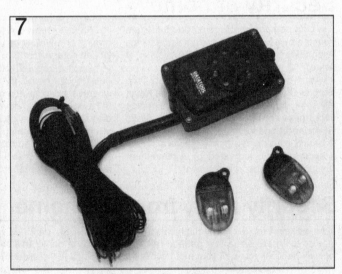
**A typical alarm/immobiliser system**

**Indelible markings can be applied to most areas of the bike – always apply the manufacturer's sticker to warn off thieves**

**Chemically-etched code numbers can be applied to main body panels . . .**

**. . . again, always ensure that the kit manufacturer's sticker is applied in a prominent position**

## Security marking kits

**Pros:** *Very cheap and effective deterrent. Many insurance companies will give you a discount on your insurance premium if a recognised security marking kit is used on your motorcycle.*

**Cons:** *Does not prevent the motorcycle being stolen by joyriders.*

● There are many different types of security marking kits available. The idea is to mark as many parts of the motorcycle as possible with a unique security number **(see illustrations 8, 9 and 10)**. A form will be included with the kit to register your personal details and those of the motorcycle with the kit manufacturer. This register is made available to the police to help them trace the rightful owner of any motorcycle or components which they recover should all other forms of identification have been removed. Always apply the warning stickers provided with the kit to deter thieves.

## Ground anchors, wheel clamps and security posts

**Pros:** *An excellent form of security which will deter all but the most determined of thieves.*

**Cons:** *Awkward to install and can be expensive.*

● Whilst the motorcycle is at home, it is a good idea to attach it securely to the floor or a solid wall, even if it is kept in a securely locked garage. Various types of ground anchors, security posts and wheel clamps are available for this purpose **(see illustration 11)**. These security devices are either bolted to a solid concrete or brick structure or can be cemented into the ground.

**Permanent ground anchors provide an excellent level of security when the bike is at home**

# Security at home

A high percentage of motorcycle thefts are from the owner's home. Here are some things to consider whenever your motorcycle is at home:
✔ Where possible, always keep the motorcycle in a securely locked garage. Never rely solely on the standard lock on the garage door, these are usual hopelessly inadequate. Fit an additional locking mechanism to the door and consider having the garage alarmed. A security light, activated by a movement sensor, is also a good investment.

✔ Always secure the motorcycle to the ground or a wall, even if it is inside a securely locked garage.
✔ Do not regularly leave the motorcycle outside your home, try to keep it out of sight wherever possible. If a garage is not available, fit a motorcycle cover over the bike to disguise its true identity.
✔ It is not uncommon for thieves to follow a motorcyclist home to find out where the bike is kept. They will then return at a later date. Be aware of this whenever you are returning

home on your motorcycle. If you suspect you are being followed, do not return home, instead ride to a garage or shop and stop as a precaution.
✔ When selling a motorcycle, do not provide your home address or the location where the bike is normally kept. Arrange to meet the buyer at a location away from your home. Thieves have been known to pose as potential buyers to find out where motorcycles are kept and then return later to steal them.

# Security away from the home

As well as fitting security equipment to your motorcycle here are a few general rules to follow whenever you park your motorcycle.
✔ Park in a busy, public place.
✔ Use car parks which incorporate security features, such as CCTV.

✔ At night, park in a well-lit area, preferably directly underneath a street light.
✔ Engage the steering lock.
✔ Secure the motorcycle to a solid, immovable object such as a post or railings with an additional lock. If this is not possible,

secure the bike to a friend's motorcycle. Some public parking places provide security loops for motorcycles.
✔ Never leave your helmet or luggage attached to the motorcycle. Take them with you at all times.

# Lubricants and fluids

A wide range of lubricants, fluids and cleaning agents is available for motor-cycles. This is a guide as to what is available, its applications and properties.

## Four-stroke engine oil

● Engine oil is without doubt the most important component of any four-stroke engine. Modern motorcycle engines place a lot of demands on their oil and choosing the right type is essential. Using an unsuitable oil will lead to an increased rate of engine wear and could result in serious engine damage. Before purchasing oil, always check the recommended oil specification given by the manufacturer. The manufacturer will state a recommended 'type or classification' and also a specific 'viscosity' range for engine oil.

● The oil 'type or classification' is identified by its API (American Petroleum Institute) rating. The API rating will be in the form of two letters, e.g. SG. The S identifies the oil as being suitable for use in a petrol (gasoline) engine (S stands for spark ignition) and the second letter, ranging from A to J, identifies the oil's performance rating. The later this letter, the higher the specification of the oil; for example API SG oil exceeds the requirements of API SF oil. **Note:** *On some oils there may also be a second rating consisting of another two letters, the first letter being C, e.g. API SF/CD. This rating indicates the oil is also suitable for use in a diesel engines (the C stands for compression ignition) and is thus of no relevance for motorcycle use.*

● The 'viscosity' of the oil is identified by its SAE (Society of Automotive Engineers) rating. All modern engines require multigrade oils and the SAE rating will consist of two numbers, the first followed by a W, e.g. 10W/40. The first number indicates the viscosity rating of the oil at low temperatures (W stands for winter – tested at –20°C) and the second number represents the viscosity of the oil at high temperatures (tested at 100°C). The lower the number, the thinner the oil. For example an oil with an SAE 10W/40 rating will give better cold starting and running than an SAE 15W/40 oil.

● As well as ensuring the 'type' and 'viscosity' of the oil match the recommendations, another consideration to make when buying engine oil is whether to purchase a standard mineral-based oil, a semi-synthetic oil (also known as a synthetic blend or synthetic-based oil) or a fully-synthetic oil. Although all oils will have a similar rating and viscosity, their cost will vary considerably; mineral-based oils are the cheapest, the fully-synthetic oils the most expensive with the semi-synthetic oils falling somewhere in-between. This decision is very much up to the owner, but it should be noted that modern synthetic oils have far better lubricating and cleaning qualities than traditional mineral-based oils and tend to retain these properties for far longer. Bearing in mind the operating conditions inside a modern, high-revving motorcycle engine it is highly recommended that a fully synthetic oil is used. The extra expense at each service could save you money in the long term by preventing premature engine wear.

● As a final note always ensure that the oil is specifically designed for use in motorcycle engines. Engine oils designed primarily for use in car engines sometimes contain additives or friction modifiers which could cause clutch slip on a motorcycle fitted with a wet-clutch.

## Two-stroke engine oil

● Modern two-stroke engines, with their high power outputs, place high demands on their oil. If engine seizure is to be avoided it is essential that a high-quality oil is used. Two-stroke oils differ hugely from four-stroke oils. The oil lubricates only the crankshaft and piston(s) (the transmission has its own lubricating oil) and is used on a total-loss basis where it is burnt completely during the combustion process.

● The Japanese have recently introduced a classification system for two-stroke oils, the JASO rating. This rating is in the form of two letters, either FA, FB or FC – FA is the lowest classification and FC the highest. Ensure the oil being used meets or exceeds the recommended rating specified by the manufacturer.

● As well as ensuring the oil rating matches the recommendation, another consideration to make when buying engine oil is whether to purchase a standard mineral-based oil, a semi-synthetic oil (also known as a synthetic blend or synthetic-based oil) or a fully-synthetic oil. The cost of each type of oil varies considerably; mineral-based oils are the cheapest, the fully-synthetic oils the most expensive with the semi-synthetic oils falling somewhere in-between. This decision is very much up to the owner, but it should be noted that modern synthetic oils have far better lubricating properties and burn cleaner than traditional mineral-based oils. It is therefore recommended that a fully synthetic oil is used. The extra expense could save you money in the long term by preventing premature engine wear, engine performance will be improved, carbon deposits and exhaust smoke will be reduced.

● Always ensure that the oil is specifically designed for use in an injector system. Many high quality two-stroke oils are designed for competition use and need to be pre-mixed with fuel. These oils are of a much higher viscosity and are not designed to flow through the injector pumps used on road-going two-stroke motorcycles.

## Transmission (gear) oil

● On a two-stroke engine, the transmission and clutch are lubricated by their own separate oil bath which must be changed in accordance with the Maintenance Schedule.
● Although the engine and transmission units of most four-strokes use a common lubrication supply, there are some exceptions where the engine and gearbox have separate oil reservoirs and a dry clutch is used.
● Motorcycle manufacturers will either recommend a monograde transmission oil or a four-stroke multigrade engine oil to lubricate the transmission.
● Transmission oils, or gear oils as they are often called, are designed specifically for use in transmission systems. The viscosity of these oils is represented by an SAE number, but the scale of measurement applied is different to that used to grade engine oils. As a rough guide a SAE90 gear oil will be of the same viscosity as an SAE50 engine oil.

## Shaft drive oil

● On models equipped with shaft final drive, the shaft drive gears are will have their own oil supply. The manufacturer will state a recommended 'type or classification' and also a specific 'viscosity' range in the same manner as for four-stroke engine oil.
● Gear oil classification is given by the number which follows the API GL (GL standing for gear lubricant) rating, the higher the number, the higher the specification of the oil, e.g. API GL5 oil is a higher specification than API GL4 oil. Ensure the oil meets or

exceeds the classification specified and is of the correct viscosity. The viscosity of gear oils is also represented by an SAE number but the scale of measurement used is different to that used to grade engine oils. As a rough guide an SAE90 gear oil will be of the same viscosity as an SAE50 engine oil.
● If the use of an EP (Extreme Pressure) gear oil is specified, ensure the oil purchased is suitable.

## Fork oil and suspension fluid

● Conventional telescopic front forks are hydraulic and require fork oil to work. To ensure the forks function correctly, the fork oil must be changed in accordance with the Maintenance Schedule.
● Fork oil is available in a variety of viscosities, identified by their SAE rating; fork oil ratings vary from light (SAE 5) to heavy (SAE 30). When purchasing fork oil, ensure the viscosity rating matches that specified by the manufacturer.
● Some lubricant manufacturers also produce a range of high-quality suspension fluids which are very similar to fork oil but are designed mainly for competition use. These fluids may have a different viscosity rating system which is not to be confused with the SAE rating of normal fork oil. Refer to the manufacturer's instructions if in any doubt.

## Brake and clutch fluid

● All disc brake systems and some clutch systems are hydraulically operated. To ensure correct operation, the hydraulic fluid must be changed in accordance with the Maintenance Schedule.
● Brake and clutch fluid is classified by its DOT rating with most motorcycle manufacturers specifying DOT 3 or 4 fluid. Both fluid types are glycol-based and can be mixed together without adverse effect; DOT 4 fluid exceeds the requirements of DOT 3

fluid. Although it is safe to use DOT 4 fluid in a system designed for use with DOT 3 fluid, never use DOT 3 fluid in a system which specifies the use of DOT 4 as this will adversely affect the system's performance. The type required for the system will be marked on the fluid reservoir cap.
● Some manufacturers also produce a DOT 5 hydraulic fluid. DOT 5 hydraulic fluid is silicone-based and is not compatible with the glycol-based DOT 3 and 4 fluids. Never mix DOT 5 fluid with DOT 3 or 4 fluid as this will seriously affect the performance of the hydraulic system.

## Coolant/antifreeze

● When purchasing coolant/antifreeze, always ensure it is suitable for use in an aluminium engine and contains corrosion inhibitors to prevent possible blockages of the internal coolant passages of the system. As a general rule, most coolants are designed to be used neat and should not be diluted whereas antifreeze can be mixed with distilled water to provide a coolant solution of the required strength. Refer to the manufacturer's instructions on the bottle.
● Ensure the coolant is changed in accordance with the Maintenance Schedule.

## Chain lube

● Chain lube is an aerosol-type spray lubricant specifically designed for use on motorcycle final drive chains. Chain lube has two functions, to minimise friction between the final drive chain and sprockets and to prevent corrosion of the chain. Regular use of a good-quality chain lube will extend the life of the drive chain and sprockets and thus maximise the power being transmitted from the transmission to the rear wheel.
● When using chain lube, always allow some time for the solvents in the lube to evaporate before riding the motorcycle. This will minimise the amount of lube which will

'fling' off from the chain when the motorcycle is used. If the motorcycle is equipped with an 'O-ring' chain, ensure the chain lube is labelled as being suitable for use on 'O-ring' chains.

## Degreasers and solvents

● There are many different types of solvents and degreasers available to remove the grime and grease which accumulate around the motorcycle during normal use. Degreasers and solvents are usually available as an aerosol-type spray or as a liquid which you apply with a brush. Always closely follow the manufacturer's instructions and wear eye protection during use. Be aware that many solvents are flammable and may give off noxious fumes; take adequate precautions when using them (see Safety First!).
● For general cleaning, use one of the many solvents or degreasers available from most motorcycle accessory shops. These solvents are usually applied then left for a certain time before being washed off with water.

**Brake cleaner** is a solvent specifically designed to remove all traces of oil, grease and dust from braking system components. Brake cleaner is designed to evaporate quickly and leaves behind no residue.

**Carburettor cleaner** is an aerosol-type solvent specifically designed to clear carburettor blockages and break down the hard deposits and gum often found inside carburettors during overhaul.

**Contact cleaner** is an aerosol-type solvent designed for cleaning electrical components. The cleaner will remove all traces of oil and dirt from components such as switch contacts or fouled spark plugs and then dry, leaving behind no residue.

**Gasket remover** is an aerosol-type solvent designed for removing stubborn gaskets from engine components during overhaul. Gasket remover will minimise the amount of scraping required to remove the gasket and therefore reduce the risk of damage to the mating surface.

## Spray lubricants

● Aerosol-based spray lubricants are widely available and are excellent for lubricating lever pivots and exposed cables and switches. Try to use a lubricant which is of the dry-film type as the fluid evaporates, leaving behind a dry-film of lubricant. Lubricants which leave behind an oily residue will attract dust and dirt which will increase the rate of wear of the cable/lever.

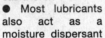

● Most lubricants also act as a moisture dispersant and a penetrating fluid. This means they can also be used to 'dry out' electrical components such as wiring connectors or switches as well as helping to free seized fasteners.

## Greases

● Grease is used to lubricate many of the pivot-points. A good-quality multi-purpose grease is suitable for most applications but some manufacturers will specify the use of specialist greases for use on components such as swingarm and suspension linkage bushes. These specialist greases can be purchased from most motorcycle (or car) accessory shops; commonly specified types include molybdenum disulphide grease, lithium-based grease, graphite-based grease, silicone-based grease and high-temperature copper-based grease.

## Gasket sealing compounds

● Gasket sealing compounds can be used in conjunction with gaskets, to improve their sealing capabilities, or on their own to seal metal-to-metal joints. Depending on their type, sealing compounds either set hard or stay relatively soft and pliable.

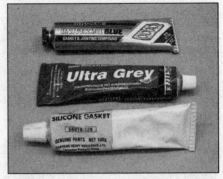

● When purchasing a gasket sealing compound, ensure that it is designed specifically for use on an internal combustion engine. General multi-purpose sealants available from DIY stores may appear visibly similar but they are not designed to withstand the extreme heat or contact with fuel and oil encountered when used on an engine (see 'Tools and Workshop Tips' for further information).

## Thread locking compound

● Thread locking compounds are used to secure certain threaded fasteners in position to prevent them from loosening due to vibration. Thread locking compounds can be purchased from most motorcycle (and car) accessory shops. Ensure the threads of the both components are completely clean and dry before sparingly applying the locking compound (see 'Tools and Workshop Tips' for further information).

## Fuel additives

● Fuel additives which protect and clean the fuel system components are widely available. These additives are designed to remove all traces of deposits that build up on the carburettors/injectors and prevent wear, helping the fuel system to operate more efficiently. If a fuel additive is being used, check that it is suitable for use with your motorcycle, especially if your motorcycle is equipped with a catalytic converter.

● Octane boosters are also available. These additives are designed to improve the performance of highly-tuned engines being run on normal pump-fuel and are of no real use on standard motorcycles.

# Conversion Factors

## Length (distance)

| | | | | |
|---|---|---|---|---|
| Inches (in) | x 25.4 | = Millimetres (mm) | x 0.0394 | = Inches (in) |
| Feet (ft) | x 0.305 | = Metres (m) | x 3.281 | = Feet (ft) |
| Miles | x 1.609 | = Kilometres (km) | x 0.621 | = Miles |

## Volume (capacity)

| | | | | |
|---|---|---|---|---|
| Cubic inches (cu in; in³) | x 16.387 | = Cubic centimetres (cc; cm³) | x 0.061 | = Cubic inches (cu in; in³) |
| Imperial pints (Imp pt) | x 0.568 | = Litres (l) | x 1.76 | = Imperial pints (Imp pt) |
| Imperial quarts (Imp qt) | x 1.137 | = Litres (l) | x 0.88 | = Imperial quarts (Imp qt) |
| Imperial quarts (Imp qt) | x 1.201 | = US quarts (US qt) | x 0.833 | = Imperial quarts (Imp qt) |
| US quarts (US qt) | x 0.946 | = Litres (l) | x 1.057 | = US quarts (US qt) |
| Imperial gallons (Imp gal) | x 4.546 | = Litres (l) | x 0.22 | = Imperial gallons (Imp gal) |
| Imperial gallons (Imp gal) | x 1.201 | = US gallons (US gal) | x 0.833 | = Imperial gallons (Imp gal) |
| US gallons (US gal) | x 3.785 | = Litres (l) | x 0.264 | = US gallons (US gal) |

## Mass (weight)

| | | | | |
|---|---|---|---|---|
| Ounces (oz) | x 28.35 | = Grams (g) | x 0.035 | = Ounces (oz) |
| Pounds (lb) | x 0.454 | = Kilograms (kg) | x 2.205 | = Pounds (lb) |

## Force

| | | | | |
|---|---|---|---|---|
| Ounces-force (ozf; oz) | x 0.278 | = Newtons (N) | x 3.6 | = Ounces-force (ozf; oz) |
| Pounds-force (lbf; lb) | x 4.448 | = Newtons (N) | x 0.225 | = Pounds-force (lbf; lb) |
| Newtons (N) | x 0.1 | = Kilograms-force (kgf; kg) | x 9.81 | = Newtons (N) |

## Pressure

| | | | | |
|---|---|---|---|---|
| Pounds-force per square inch (psi; lbf/in²; lb/in²) | x 0.070 | = Kilograms-force per square centimetre (kgf/cm²; kg/cm²) | x 14.223 | = Pounds-force per square inch (psi; lbf/in²; lb/in²) |
| Pounds-force per square inch (psi; lbf/in²; lb/in²) | x 0.068 | = Atmospheres (atm) | x 14.696 | = Pounds-force per square inch (psi; lbf/in²; lb/in²) |
| Pounds-force per square inch (psi; lbf/in²; lb/in²) | x 0.069 | = Bars | x 14.5 | = Pounds-force per square inch (psi; lbf/in²; lb/in²) |
| Pounds-force per square inch (psi; lbf/in²; lb/in²) | x 6.895 | = Kilopascals (kPa) | x 0.145 | = Pounds-force per square inch (psi; lbf/in²; lb/in²) |
| Kilopascals (kPa) | x 0.01 | = Kilograms-force per square centimetre (kgf/cm²; kg/cm²) | x 98.1 | = Kilopascals (kPa) |
| Millibar (mbar) | x 100 | = Pascals (Pa) | x 0.01 | = Millibar (mbar) |
| Millibar (mbar) | x 0.0145 | = Pounds-force per square inch (psi; lbf/in²; lb/in²) | x 68.947 | = Millibar (mbar) |
| Millibar (mbar) | x 0.75 | = Millimetres of mercury (mmHg) | x 1.333 | = Millibar (mbar) |
| Millibar (mbar) | x 0.401 | = Inches of water (inH₂O) | x 2.491 | = Millibar (mbar) |
| Millimetres of mercury (mmHg) | x 0.535 | = Inches of water (inH₂O) | x 1.868 | = Millimetres of mercury (mmHg) |
| Inches of water (inH₂O) | x 0.036 | = Pounds-force per square inch (psi; lbf/in²; lb/in²) | x 27.68 | = Inches of water (inH₂O) |

## Torque (moment of force)

| | | | | |
|---|---|---|---|---|
| Pounds-force inches (lbf in; lb in) | x 1.152 | = Kilograms-force centimetre (kgf cm; kg cm) | x 0.868 | = Pounds-force inches (lbf in; lb in) |
| Pounds-force inches (lbf in; lb in) | x 0.113 | = Newton metres (Nm) | x 8.85 | = Pounds-force inches (lbf in; lb in) |
| Pounds-force inches (lbf in; lb in) | x 0.083 | = Pounds-force feet (lbf ft; lb ft) | x 12 | = Pounds-force inches (lbf in; lb in) |
| Pounds-force feet (lbf ft; lb ft) | x 0.138 | = Kilograms-force metres (kgf m; kg m) | x 7.233 | = Pounds-force feet (lbf ft; lb ft) |
| Pounds-force feet (lbf ft; lb ft) | x 1.356 | = Newton metres (Nm) | x 0.738 | = Pounds-force feet (lbf ft; lb ft) |
| Newton metres (Nm) | x 0.102 | = Kilograms-force metres (kgf m; kg m) | x 9.804 | = Newton metres (Nm) |

## Power

| | | | | |
|---|---|---|---|---|
| Horsepower (hp) | x 745.7 | = Watts (W) | x 0.0013 | = Horsepower (hp) |

## Velocity (speed)

| | | | | |
|---|---|---|---|---|
| Miles per hour (miles/hr; mph) | x 1.609 | = Kilometres per hour (km/hr; kph) | x 0.621 | = Miles per hour (miles/hr; mph) |

## Fuel consumption*

| | | | | |
|---|---|---|---|---|
| Miles per gallon (mpg) | x 0.354 | = Kilometres per litre (km/l) | x 2.825 | = Miles per gallon (mpg) |

## Temperature

Degrees Fahrenheit = (°C x 1.8) + 32        Degrees Celsius (Degrees Centigrade; °C) = (°F - 32) x 0.56

*It is common practice to convert from miles per gallon (mpg) to litres/100 kilometres (l/100km), where mpg x l/100 km = 282*

## About the MOT Test

In the UK, all vehicles more than three years old are subject to an annual test to ensure that they meet minimum safety requirements. A current test certificate must be issued before a machine can be used on public roads, and is required before a road fund licence can be issued. Riding without a current test certificate will also invalidate your insurance.

For most owners, the MOT test is an annual cause for anxiety, and this is largely due to owners not being sure what needs to be checked prior to submitting the motorcycle for testing. The simple answer is that a fully roadworthy motorcycle will have no difficulty in passing the test.

This is a guide to getting your motorcycle through the MOT test. Obviously it will not be possible to examine the motorcycle to the same standard as the professional MOT tester, particularly in view of the equipment required for some of the checks. However, working through the following procedures will enable you to identify any problem areas before submitting the motorcycle for the test.

It has only been possible to summarise the test requirements here, based on the regulations in force at the time of printing. Test standards are becoming increasingly stringent, although there are some exemptions for older vehicles. More information about the MOT test can be obtained from the TSO publications, *How Safe is your Motorcycle* and *The MOT Inspection Manual for Motorcycle Testing*.

Many of the checks require that one of the wheels is raised off the ground. If the motorcycle doesn't have a centre stand, note that an auxiliary stand will be required. Additionally, the help of an assistant may prove useful.

Certain exceptions apply to machines under 50 cc, machines without a lighting system, and Classic bikes - if in doubt about any of the requirements listed below seek confirmation from an MOT tester prior to submitting the motorcycle for the test.

Check that the frame number is clearly visible.

> **HAYNES HiNT** *If a component is in borderline condition, the tester has discretion in deciding whether to pass or fail it. If the motorcycle presented is clean and evidently well cared for, the tester may be more inclined to pass a borderline component than if the motorcycle is scruffy and apparently neglected.*

# Electrical System

## Lights, turn signals, horn and reflector

✔ With the ignition on, check the operation of the following electrical components. **Note:** *The electrical components on certain small-capacity machines are powered by the generator, requiring that the engine is run for this check.*

a) *Headlight and tail light. Check that both illuminate in the low and high beam switch positions.*

b) *Position lights. Check that the front position (or sidelight) and tail light illuminate in this switch position.*

c) *Turn signals. Check that all flash at the correct rate, and that the warning light(s) function correctly. Check that the turn signal switch works correctly.*

d) *Hazard warning system (where fitted). Check that all four turn signals flash in this switch position.*

e) *Brake stop light. Check that the light comes on when the front and rear brakes are independently applied. Models first used on or after 1st April 1986 must have a brake light switch on each brake.*

f) *Horn. Check that the sound is continuous and of reasonable volume.*

✔ Check that there is a red reflector on the rear of the machine, either mounted separately or as part of the tail light lens.

✔ Check the condition of the headlight, tail light and turn signal lenses.

## Headlight beam height

✔ The MOT tester will perform a headlight beam height check using specialised beam setting equipment **(see illustration 1)**. This equipment will not be available to the home mechanic, but if you suspect that the headlight is incorrectly set or may have been maladjusted in the past, you can perform a rough test as follows.

✔ Position the bike in a straight line facing a brick wall. The bike must be off its stand, upright and with a rider seated. Measure the height from the ground to the centre of the headlight and mark a horizontal line on the wall at this height. Position the motorcycle 3.8 metres from the wall and draw a vertical

**Headlight beam height checking equipment**

line up the wall central to the centreline of the motorcycle. Switch to dipped beam and check that the beam pattern falls slightly lower than the horizontal line and to the left of the vertical line **(see illustration 2)**.

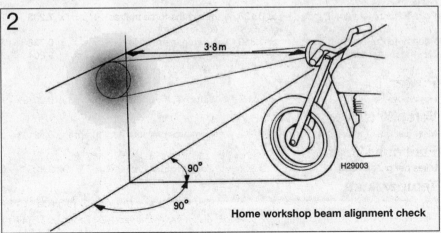

**Home workshop beam alignment check**

# Exhaust System and Final Drive

### Exhaust

✔ Check that the exhaust mountings are secure and that the system does not foul any of the rear suspension components.

✔ Start the motorcycle. When the revs are increased, check that the exhaust is neither holed nor leaking from any of its joints. On a linked system, check that the collector box is not leaking due to corrosion.

✔ Note that the exhaust decibel level ("loudness" of the exhaust) is assessed at the discretion of the tester. If the motorcycle was first used on or after 1st January 1985 the silencer must carry the BSAU 193 stamp, or a marking relating to its make and model, or be of OE (original equipment) manufacture. If the silencer is marked NOT FOR ROAD USE, RACING USE ONLY or similar, it will fail the MOT.

### Final drive

✔ On chain or belt drive machines, check that the chain/belt is in good condition and does not have excessive slack. Also check that the sprocket is securely mounted on the rear wheel hub. Check that the chain/belt guard is in place.

✔ On shaft drive bikes, check for oil leaking from the drive unit and fouling the rear tyre.

# Steering and Suspension

### Steering

✔ With the front wheel raised off the ground, rotate the steering from lock to lock. The handlebar or switches must not contact the fuel tank or be close enough to trap the rider's hand. Problems can be caused by damaged lock stops on the lower yoke and frame, or by the fitting of non-standard handlebars.

✔ When performing the lock to lock check, also ensure that the steering moves freely without drag or notchiness. Steering movement can be impaired by poorly routed cables, or by overtight head bearings or worn bearings. The tester will perform a check of the steering head bearing lower race by mounting the front wheel on a surface plate, then performing a lock to lock check with the weight of the machine on the lower bearing (see illustration 3).

✔ Grasp the fork sliders (lower legs) and attempt to push and pull on the forks (see

Front wheel mounted on a surface plate for steering head bearing lower race check

illustration 4). Any play in the steering head bearings will be felt. Note that in extreme cases, wear of the front fork bushes can be misinterpreted for head bearing play.

✔ Check that the handlebars are securely mounted.

✔ Check that the handlebar grip rubbers are secure. They should by bonded to the bar left end and to the throttle cable pulley on the right end.

### Front suspension

✔ With the motorcycle off the stand, hold the front brake on and pump the front forks up and down (see illustration 5). Check that they are adequately damped.

Checking the steering head bearings for freeplay

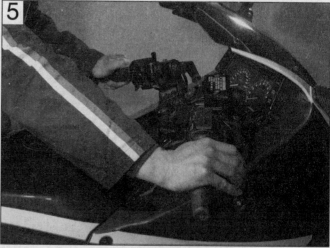

Hold the front brake on and pump the front forks up and down to check operation

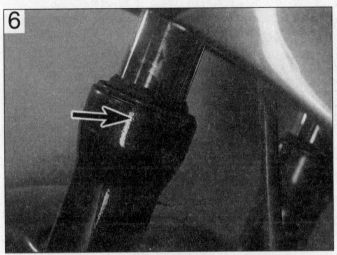

Inspect the area around the fork dust seal for oil leakage (arrow)

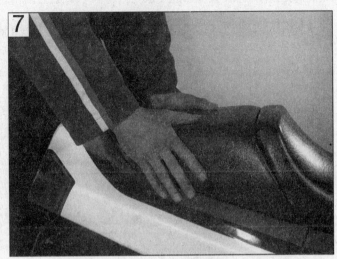

Bounce the rear of the motorcycle to check rear suspension operation

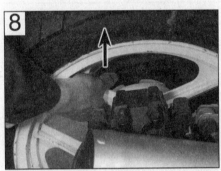

Checking for rear suspension linkage play

✔ Inspect the area above and around the front fork oil seals **(see illustration 6)**. There should be no sign of oil on the fork tube (stanchion) nor leaking down the slider (lower leg). On models so equipped, check that there is no oil leaking from the anti-dive units.

✔ On models with swingarm front suspension, check that there is no freeplay in the linkage when moved from side to side.

### Rear suspension

✔ With the motorcycle off the stand and an assistant supporting the motorcycle by its handlebars, bounce the rear suspension **(see illustration 7)**. Check that the suspension components do not foul on any of the cycle parts and check that the shock absorber(s) provide adequate damping.

✔ Visually inspect the shock absorber(s) and check that there is no sign of oil leakage from its damper. This is somewhat restricted on certain single shock models due to the location of the shock absorber.

✔ With the rear wheel raised off the ground, grasp the wheel at the highest point and attempt to pull it up **(see illustration 8)**. Any play in the swingarm pivot or suspension linkage bearings will be felt as movement. **Note:** *Do not confuse play with actual suspension movement.* Failure to lubricate suspension linkage bearings can lead to bearing failure **(see illustration 9)**.

✔ With the rear wheel raised off the ground, grasp the swingarm ends and attempt to move the swingarm from side to side and forwards and backwards - any play indicates wear of the swingarm pivot bearings **(see illustration 10)**.

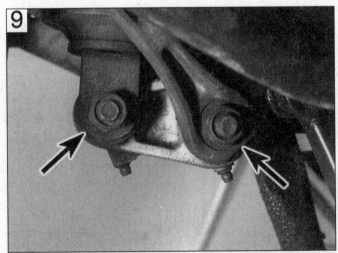

Worn suspension linkage pivots (arrows) are usually the cause of play in the rear suspension

Grasp the swingarm at the ends to check for play in its pivot bearings

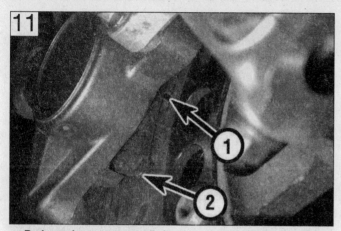

Brake pad wear can usually be viewed without removing the caliper. Most pads have wear indicator grooves (1) and some also have indicator tangs (2)

On drum brakes, check the angle of the operating lever with the brake fully applied. Most drum brakes have a wear indicator pointer and scale.

# Brakes, Wheels and Tyres

### Brakes

✔ With the wheel raised off the ground, apply the brake then free it off, and check that the wheel is about to revolve freely without brake drag.

✔ On disc brakes, examine the disc itself. Check that it is securely mounted and not cracked.

✔ On disc brakes, view the pad material through the caliper mouth and check that the pads are not worn down beyond the limit **(see illustration 11)**.

✔ On drum brakes, check that when the brake is applied the angle between the operating lever and cable or rod is not too great **(see illustration 12)**. Check also that the operating lever doesn't foul any other components.

✔ On disc brakes, examine the flexible hoses from top to bottom. Have an assistant hold the brake on so that the fluid in the hose is under pressure, and check that there is no sign of fluid leakage, bulges or cracking. If there are any metal brake pipes or unions, check that these are free from corrosion and damage. Where a brake-linked anti-dive system is fitted, check the hoses to the anti-dive in a similar manner.

✔ Check that the rear brake torque arm is secure and that its fasteners are secured by self-locking nuts or castellated nuts with split-pins or R-pins **(see illustration 13)**.

✔ On models with ABS, check that the self-check warning light in the instrument panel works.

✔ The MOT tester will perform a test of the motorcycle's braking efficiency based on a calculation of rider and motorcycle weight. Although this cannot be carried out at home, you can at least ensure that the braking systems are properly maintained. For hydraulic disc brakes, check the fluid level, lever/pedal feel (bleed of air if its spongy) and pad material. For drum brakes, check adjustment, cable or rod operation and shoe lining thickness.

### Wheels and tyres

✔ Check the wheel condition. Cast wheels should be free from cracks and if of the built-up design, all fasteners should be secure. Spoked wheels should be checked for broken, corroded, loose or bent spokes.

✔ With the wheel raised off the ground, spin the wheel and visually check that the tyre and wheel run true. Check that the tyre does not foul the suspension or mudguards.

✔ With the wheel raised off the ground, grasp the wheel and attempt to move it about the axle (spindle) **(see illustration 14)**. Any play felt here indicates wheel bearing failure.

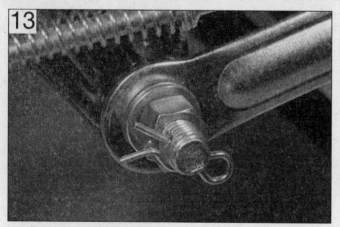

Brake torque arm must be properly secured at both ends

Check for wheel bearing play by trying to move the wheel about the axle (spindle)

**Checking the tyre tread depth**

**Tyre direction of rotation arrow can be found on tyre sidewall**

**Castellated type wheel axle (spindle) nut must be secured by a split pin or R-pin**

**Two straightedges are used to check wheel alignment**

✔ Check the tyre tread depth, tread condition and sidewall condition **(see illustration 15)**.
✔ Check the tyre type. Front and rear tyre types must be compatible and be suitable for road use. Tyres marked NOT FOR ROAD USE, COMPETITION USE ONLY or similar, will fail the MOT.

✔ If the tyre sidewall carries a direction of rotation arrow, this must be pointing in the direction of normal wheel rotation **(see illustration 16)**.
✔ Check that the wheel axle (spindle) nuts (where applicable) are properly secured. A self-locking nut or castellated nut with a split-pin or R-pin can be used **(see illustration 17)**.
✔ Wheel alignment is checked with the motorcycle off the stand and a rider seated. With the front wheel pointing straight ahead, two perfectly straight lengths of metal or wood and placed against the sidewalls of both tyres **(see illustration 18)**. The gap each side of the front tyre must be equidistant on both sides. Incorrect wheel alignment may be due to a cocked rear wheel (often as the result of poor chain adjustment) or in extreme cases, a bent frame.

# General checks and condition

✔ Check the security of all major fasteners, bodypanels, seat, fairings (where fitted) and mudguards.

✔ Check that the rider and pillion footrests, handlebar levers and brake pedal are securely mounted.

✔ Check for corrosion on the frame or any load-bearing components. If severe, this may affect the structure, particularly under stress.

# Sidecars

A motorcycle fitted with a sidecar requires additional checks relating to the stability of the machine and security of attachment and swivel joints, plus specific wheel alignment (toe-in) requirements. Additionally, tyre and lighting requirements differ from conventional motorcycle use. Owners are advised to check MOT test requirements with an official test centre.

# Preparing for storage

## Before you start

If repairs or an overhaul is needed, see that this is carried out now rather than left until you want to ride the bike again.

Give the bike a good wash and scrub all dirt from its underside. Make sure the bike dries completely before preparing for storage.

## Engine

● Remove the spark plug(s) and lubricate the cylinder bores with approximately a teaspoon of motor oil using a spout-type oil can **(see illustration 1)**. Reinstall the spark plug(s). Crank the engine over a couple of times to coat the piston rings and bores with oil. If the bike has a kickstart, use this to turn the engine over. If not, flick the kill switch to the OFF position and crank the engine over on the starter **(see illustration 2)**. If the nature on the ignition system prevents the starter operating with the kill switch in the OFF position,

remove the spark plugs and fit them back in their caps; ensure that the plugs are earthed (grounded) against the cylinder head when the starter is operated **(see illustration 3)**.

⚠️ *Warning: It is important that the plugs are earthed (grounded) away from the spark plug holes otherwise there is a risk of atomised fuel from the cylinders igniting.*

> **HAYNES HiNT** *On a single cylinder four-stroke engine, you can seal the combustion chamber completely by positioning the piston at TDC on the compression stroke.*

● Drain the carburettor(s) otherwise there is a risk of jets becoming blocked by gum deposits from the fuel **(see illustration 4)**.

● If the bike is going into long-term storage, consider adding a fuel stabiliser to the fuel in the tank. If the tank is drained completely, corrosion of its internal surfaces may occur if left unprotected for a long period. The tank can be treated with a rust preventative especially for this purpose. Alternatively, remove the tank and pour half a litre of motor oil into it, install the filler cap and shake the tank to coat its internals with oil before draining off the excess. The same effect can also be achieved by spraying WD40 or a similar water-dispersant around the inside of the tank via its flexible nozzle.

● Make sure the cooling system contains the correct mix of antifreeze. Antifreeze also contains important corrosion inhibitors.

● The air intakes and exhaust can be sealed off by covering or plugging the openings. Ensure that you do not seal in any condensation; run the engine until it is hot,

Squirt a drop of motor oil into each cylinder

Flick the kill switch to OFF . . .

. . . and ensure that the metal bodies of the plugs (arrows) are earthed against the cylinder head

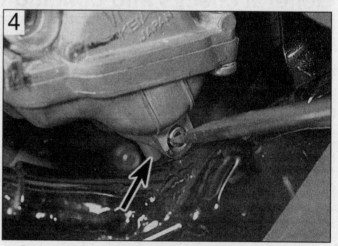

Connect a hose to the carburettor float chamber drain stub (arrow) and unscrew the drain screw

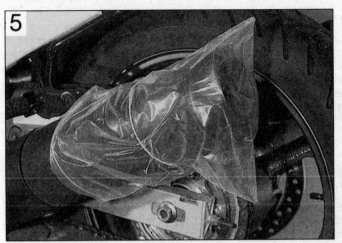

Exhausts can be sealed off with a plastic bag

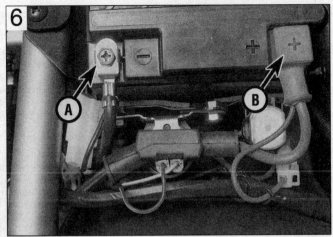

Disconnect the negative lead (A) first, followed by the positive lead (B)

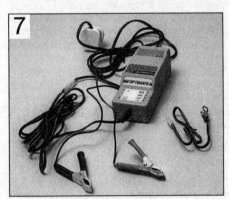

Use a suitable battery charger - this kit also assess battery condition

then switch off and allow to cool. Tape a piece of thick plastic over the silencer end(s) **(see illustration 5)**. Note that some advocate pouring a tablespoon of motor oil into the silencer(s) before sealing them off.

## Battery

● Remove it from the bike - in extreme cases of cold the battery may freeze and crack its case **(see illustration 6)**.

● Check the electrolyte level and top up if necessary (conventional refillable batteries). Clean the terminals.
● Store the battery off the motorcycle and away from any sources of fire. Position a wooden block under the battery if it is to sit on the ground.
● Give the battery a trickle charge for a few hours every month **(see illustration 7)**.

## Tyres

● Place the bike on its centrestand or an auxiliary stand which will support the motorcycle in an upright position. Position wood blocks under the tyres to keep them off the ground and to provide insulation from damp. If the bike is being put into long-term storage, ideally both tyres should be off the ground; not only will this protect the tyres, but will also ensure that no load is placed on the steering head or wheel bearings.
● Deflate each tyre by 5 to 10 psi, no more or the beads may unseat from the rim, making subsequent inflation difficult on tubeless tyres.

## Pivots and controls

● Lubricate all lever, pedal, stand and

footrest pivot points. If grease nipples are fitted to the rear suspension components, apply lubricant to the pivots.
● Lubricate all control cables.

## Cycle components

● Apply a wax protectant to all painted and plastic components. Wipe off any excess, but don't polish to a shine. Where fitted, clean the screen with soap and water.
● Coat metal parts with Vaseline (petroleum jelly). When applying this to the fork tubes, do not compress the forks otherwise the seals will rot from contact with the Vaseline.
● Apply a vinyl cleaner to the seat.

## Storage conditions

● Aim to store the bike in a shed or garage which does not leak and is free from damp.
● Drape an old blanket or bedspread over the bike to protect it from dust and direct contact with sunlight (which will fade paint). This also hides the bike from prying eyes. Beware of tight-fitting plastic covers which may allow condensation to form and settle on the bike.

# Getting back on the road

## Engine and transmission

● Change the oil and replace the oil filter. If this was done prior to storage, check that the oil hasn't emulsified - a thick whitish substance which occurs through condensation.
● Remove the spark plugs. Using a spout-type oil can, squirt a few drops of oil into the cylinder(s). This will provide initial lubrication as the piston rings and bores comes back into contact. Service the spark plugs, or fit new ones, and install them in the engine.

● Check that the clutch isn't stuck on. The plates can stick together if left standing for some time, preventing clutch operation. Engage a gear and try rocking the bike back and forth with the clutch lever held against the handlebar. If this doesn't work on cable-operated clutches, hold the clutch lever back against the handlebar with a strong elastic band or cable tie for a couple of hours **(see illustration 8)**.
● If the air intakes or silencer end(s) were blocked off, remove the bung or cover used.
● If the fuel tank was coated with a rust

Hold clutch lever back against the handlebar with elastic bands or a cable tie

preventative, oil or a stabiliser added to the fuel, drain and flush the tank and dispose of the fuel sensibly. If no action was taken with the fuel tank prior to storage, it is advised that the old fuel is disposed of since it will go off over a period of time. Refill the fuel tank with fresh fuel.

## Frame and running gear

● Oil all pivot points and cables.
● Check the tyre pressures. They will definitely need inflating if pressures were reduced for storage.
● Lubricate the final drive chain (where applicable).
● Remove any protective coating applied to the fork tubes (stanchions) since this may well destroy the fork seals. If the fork tubes weren't protected and have picked up rust spots, remove them with very fine abrasive paper and refinish with metal polish.
● Check that both brakes operate correctly. Apply each brake hard and check that it's not possible to move the motorcycle forwards, then check that the brake frees off again once released. Brake caliper pistons can stick due to corrosion around the piston head, or on the sliding caliper types, due to corrosion of the slider pins. If the brake doesn't free after repeated operation, take the caliper off for examination. Similarly drum brakes can stick

due to a seized operating cam, cable or rod linkage.
● If the motorcycle has been in long-term storage, renew the brake fluid and clutch fluid (where applicable).
● Depending on where the bike has been stored, the wiring, cables and hoses may have been nibbled by rodents. Make a visual check and investigate disturbed wiring loom tape.

## Battery

● If the battery has been previously removal and given top up charges it can simply be reconnected. Remember to connect the positive cable first and the negative cable last.
● On conventional refillable batteries, if the battery has not received any attention, remove it from the motorcycle and check its electrolyte level. Top up if necessary then charge the battery. If the battery fails to hold a charge and a visual checks show heavy white sulphation of the plates, the battery is probably defective and must be renewed. This is particularly likely if the battery is old. Confirm battery condition with a specific gravity check.
● On sealed (MF) batteries, if the battery has not received any attention, remove it from the motorcycle and charge it according to the information on the battery case - if the battery fails to hold a charge it must be renewed.

## Starting procedure

● If a kickstart is fitted, turn the engine over a couple of times with the ignition OFF to distribute oil around the engine. If no kickstart is fitted, flick the engine kill switch OFF and the ignition ON and crank the engine over a couple of times to work oil around the upper cylinder components. If the nature of the ignition system is such that the starter won't work with the kill switch OFF, remove the spark plugs, fit them back into their caps and earth (ground) their bodies on the cylinder head. Reinstall the spark plugs afterwards.
● Switch the kill switch to RUN, operate the choke and start the engine. If the engine won't start don't continue cranking the engine - not only will this flatten the battery, but the starter motor will overheat. Switch the ignition off and try again later. If the engine refuses to start, go through the fault finding procedures in this manual. **Note:** *If the bike has been in storage for a long time, old fuel or a carburettor blockage may be the problem. Gum deposits in carburettors can block jets - if a carburettor cleaner doesn't prove successful the carburettors must be dismantled for cleaning.*
● Once the engine has started, check that the lights, turn signals and horn work properly.
● Treat the bike gently for the first ride and check all fluid levels on completion. Settle the bike back into the maintenance schedule.

This Section provides an easy reference-guide to the more common faults that are likely to afflict your machine. Obviously, the opportunities are almost limitless for faults to occur as a result of obscure failures, and to try and cover all eventualities would require a book. Indeed, a number have been written on the subject.

Successful troubleshooting is not a mysterious 'black art' but the application of a bit of knowledge combined with a systematic and logical approach to the problem. Approach any troubleshooting by first accurately identifying the symptom and then checking through the list of possible causes, starting with the simplest or most obvious and progressing in stages to the most complex.

Take nothing for granted, but above all apply liberal quantities of common sense.

The main symptom of a fault is given in the text as a major heading below which are listed the various systems or areas which may contain the fault. Details of each possible cause for a fault and the remedial action to be taken are given, in brief, in the paragraphs below each heading. Further information should be sought in the relevant Chapter.

## 1 Engine doesn't start or is difficult to start

- [ ] Starter motor doesn't rotate
- [ ] Starter motor rotates but engine does not turn over
- [ ] Starter works but engine won't turn over (seized)
- [ ] No fuel flow
- [ ] Engine flooded
- [ ] No spark or weak spark
- [ ] Compression low
- [ ] Stalls after starting
- [ ] Rough idle

## 2 Poor running at low speed

- [ ] Spark weak
- [ ] Fuel/air mixture incorrect
- [ ] Compression low
- [ ] Poor acceleration

## 3 Poor running or no power at high speed

- [ ] Firing incorrect
- [ ] Fuel/air mixture incorrect
- [ ] Compression low
- [ ] Knocking or pinking
- [ ] Miscellaneous causes

## 4 Overheating

- [ ] Engine overheats
- [ ] Firing incorrect
- [ ] Fuel/air mixture incorrect
- [ ] Compression too high
- [ ] Engine load excessive
- [ ] Lubrication inadequate
- [ ] Miscellaneous causes

## 5 Clutch problems

- [ ] Clutch slipping
- [ ] Clutch not disengaging completely

## 6 Gear changing problems

- [ ] Doesn't go into gear, or lever doesn't return
- [ ] Jumps out of gear
- [ ] Overselects

## 7 Abnormal engine noise

- [ ] Knocking or pinking
- [ ] Piston slap or rattling
- [ ] Valve noise
- [ ] Other noise

## 8 Abnormal driveline noise

- [ ] Clutch noise
- [ ] Transmission noise
- [ ] Final drive noise

## 9 Abnormal frame and suspension noise

- [ ] Front end noise
- [ ] Shock absorber noise
- [ ] Brake noise

## 10 Oil pressure warning light comes on

- [ ] Engine lubrication system
- [ ] Electrical system

## 11 Excessive exhaust smoke

- [ ] White smoke
- [ ] Black smoke
- [ ] Brown smoke

## 12 Poor handling or stability

- [ ] Handlebar hard to turn
- [ ] Handlebar shakes or vibrates excessively
- [ ] Handlebar pulls to one side
- [ ] Poor shock absorbing qualities

## 13 Braking problems

- [ ] Brakes are spongy, don't hold
- [ ] Brake lever or pedal pulsates
- [ ] Brakes drag

## 14 Electrical problems

- [ ] Battery dead or weak
- [ ] Battery overcharged

# 1 Engine doesn't start or is difficult to start

## Starter motor doesn't rotate

☐ Engine kill switch OFF.
☐ Fuse blown. Check main, ignition and ECM fuses (Chapter 8).
☐ Battery voltage low. Check and recharge battery (Chapter 8).
☐ Starter motor defective. Make sure the wiring to the starter is secure. Make sure the starter solenoid clicks when the starter button is pushed. If the solenoid clicks, then the fault is in the wiring or motor.
☐ Starter solenoid faulty. Check it as described in Chapter 8.
☐ Starter button not contacting. The contacts could be wet, corroded or dirty. Disassemble and clean the switch (Chapter 8).
☐ Wiring open or shorted. Check all wiring connectors to make sure that they are dry, tight and not corroded. Also check for broken or frayed wires and wiring insulation that can cause a short to ground (earth) (see wiring diagrams, Chapter 8).
☐ Ignition (main) switch defective. Check the switch as described in Chapter 8. Replace the switch with a new one if it is defective.
☐ Engine kill switch defective. Check for wet, dirty, corroded or broken contacts. Clean or renew the switch as necessary (Chapter 8).
☐ Faulty neutral, sidestand or clutch switch. Check the wiring to each switch and the switch itself as described in Chapter 8.

## Starter motor rotates but engine does not turn over

☐ Starter clutch defective. Inspect and repair or renew (Chapter 2A or 2B).
☐ Damaged idler or starter gears. Inspect and renew the damaged parts (Chapter 2A or 2B).

## Starter works but engine won't turn over (seized)

☐ Seized engine caused by one or more internally damaged components. Failure due to wear, abuse or lack of lubrication. Damage can include seized valves, followers, camshafts, pistons, crankshaft, connecting rod bearings, or transmission gears or bearings. Refer to Chapter 2A or 2B for engine disassembly.

## No fuel flow

☐ No fuel in tank.
☐ Fuel tank breather hose obstructed.
☐ Fuel pump faulty, or strainer and/or filter is blocked (see Chapter 4).
☐ Fuel hose clogged, self sealing valve stuck closed, or unions not properly inserted in sockets. Remove the hoses and check them by blowing through from each end. If the valve is working, you should be able to blow in one direction only. To check the hose sockets on the fuel tank, first remove the tank and drain it (see Chapter 4), then blow through them – if the valve is good, you should be able to blow in one direction only.
☐ Fuel injector clogged or faulty. For all of the injectors to be clogged, either a very bad batch of fuel with an unusual additive has been used, or some other foreign material has entered the tank. Many times after a machine has been stored for many months without running, the fuel turns to a varnish-like liquid.

## Engine flooded

☐ Fuel injector stuck open. The Triumph diagnostic tool is required to check the injectors (see Chapter 4).
☐ Starting technique incorrect. Under normal circumstances (i.e., if the fuel injection system is sound) the machine should start with no throttle. When the engine is very cold, the throttle can be opened a little to aid starting, but should be closed again once the engine has fired.

## No spark or weak spark

☐ Ignition switch OFF.
☐ Engine kill switch turned to the OFF position.
☐ Battery voltage low. Check and recharge the battery as necessary (Chapter 8).
☐ Spark plugs dirty, defective or worn out. Locate reason for fouled plugs using spark plug condition chart on the inside rear cover and follow the plug maintenance procedures (Chapter 1).
☐ Spark plug cap/coil wiring faulty or connector loose. Check condition and connector fitting (Chapter 1).
☐ Electronic control module (ECM) defective. Check it, referring to Chapter 4 for details.
☐ Crankshaft position sensor (or camshaft sensor where fitted) defective. Check it, referring to Chapter 4 for details.
☐ Ignition HT coils defective. Check the coils, referring to Chapter 4.
☐ Ignition or kill switch shorted. This is usually caused by water, corrosion, damage or excessive wear. The switches can be disassembled and cleaned with electrical contact cleaner. If cleaning does not help, renew the switches (Chapter 8).
☐ Wiring shorted or broken in the ignition and starting circuit. Make sure that all connectors are clean, dry and tight. Look for chafed and broken wires (Chapters 4 and 8).

## Compression low

☐ Spark plugs loose. Remove the plugs and inspect their threads. Reinstall and tighten to the specified torque (Chapter 1).
☐ Cylinder head not sufficiently tightened down. If the cylinder head is loose, then there's a chance that the gasket or head is damaged. Tighten the cylinder head bolts to the correct torque in the proper sequence (Chapter 2A or 2B).
☐ Incorrect valve clearance. If the valve is not closing completely then engine pressure will leak past the valve. Check and adjust the valve clearances (Chapter 1).
☐ Cylinder and/or piston worn. Excessive wear will cause compression pressure to leak past the rings. This is usually accompanied by worn rings as well. A top-end overhaul is necessary (Chapter 2A or 2B).
☐ Piston rings worn, weak, broken, or sticking. Broken or sticking piston rings usually indicate a lubrication or fuelling problem that causes excess carbon deposits to form on the pistons and rings. Top-end overhaul is necessary (Chapter 2A or 2B).
☐ Piston ring-to-groove clearance excessive. This is caused by excessive wear of the piston ring lands. Piston renewal is necessary (Chapter 2A or 2B).
☐ Cylinder head gasket damaged. If the head is allowed to become loose, or if excessive carbon build-up on the piston crown and combustion chamber causes extremely high compression, the head gasket may leak. Retorquing the head is not always sufficient to restore the seal, so gasket renewal is necessary (Chapter 2A or 2B).
☐ Cylinder head warped. This is caused by overheating or improperly tightened head bolts. Machine shop resurfacing or head renewal is necessary (Chapter 2A or 2B).
☐ Valve spring broken or weak. Caused by component failure or wear; the springs must be renewed (Chapter 2A or 2B).
☐ Valve not seating properly. This is caused by a bent valve (from over-revving or improper valve adjustment), burned valve or seat (improper combustion) or an accumulation of carbon deposits on the seat (from combustion or lubrication problems). The valves must be cleaned and/or renewed and the seats serviced if possible (Chapter 2A or 2B).

# 1 Engine doesn't start or is difficult to start (continued)

### Stalls after starting

☐ Ignition malfunction. See Chapter 4.
☐ Fuel injection or engine management system malfunction. See Chapter 4.
☐ Fuel contaminated. The fuel can be contaminated with either dirt or water, or can change chemically if the machine is allowed to sit for several months or more. Drain the tank, fuel hoses and fuel rail (Chapter 4).
☐ Intake air leak. Check for loose throttle body-to-intake manifold connections or a leaking gasket (Chapter 4).
☐ Idle air control valve or one of its hoses faulty. First check that all hoses are securely connected at each end, and have no splits or cracks (Chapter 4). The idle air control valve can only be checked using the Triumph diagnostic tool (see Chapter 4).

### Rough idle

☐ Ignition malfunction. See Chapter 4.
☐ Idle air control valve or one of its hoses faulty. First check that all hoses are securely connected at each end, and have no splits or cracks (Chapter 4). The idle air control valve can only be checked using the Triumph diagnostic tool (see Chapter 4).
☐ Throttle bodies not synchronised. Adjust them with vacuum gauge or manometer set as described in Chapter 1.
☐ Fuel injection or engine management system malfunction. See Chapter 4.
☐ Fuel contaminated. The fuel can be contaminated with either dirt or water, or can change chemically if the machine is allowed to sit for several months or more. Drain the tank, fuel hoses and fuel rail (Chapter 4).
☐ Intake air leak. Check for loose throttle body-to-intake manifold connections or a leaking gasket (Chapter 4).
☐ Air filter clogged. Renew the air filter element (Chapter 1).

# 2 Poor running at low speeds

### Spark weak

☐ Battery voltage low. Check and recharge battery (Chapter 8).
☐ Spark plugs fouled, defective or worn out. Refer to Chapter 1 for spark plug maintenance.
☐ Spark plug cap/coil faulty or loose wiring. Check condition. Renew if cracks or deterioration are evident (Chapter 4).
☐ Electronic control module (ECM) defective. Check it, referring to Chapter 4 for details.

### Fuel/air mixture incorrect

☐ Fuel injector clogged or fuel injection system malfunction (see Chapter 4).
☐ Air filter clogged, poorly sealed or missing (Chapter 1).
☐ Air filter housing poorly sealed. Look for cracks, holes or loose clamps and renew or repair defective parts.
☐ Fuel tank breather hose obstructed.
☐ Intake air leak. Check for loose throttle body-to-intake manifold connections or a leaking gasket (Chapter 4).
☐ Idle air control valve or one of its hoses faulty. First check that all hoses are securely connected at each end, and have no splits or cracks (Chapter 4). The idle air control valve can only be checked using the Triumph diagnostic tool (see Chapter 4).
☐ Fuel injection or engine management system malfunction. See Chapter 4.

### Compression low

☐ Spark plugs loose. Remove the plugs and inspect their threads. Reinstall and tighten to the specified torque (Chapter 1).
☐ Cylinder head not sufficiently tightened down. If the cylinder head is loose, then there's a chance that the gasket or head is damaged. Tighten the cylinder head bolts to the correct torque in the proper sequence (Chapter 2A or 2B).
☐ Incorrect valve clearance. If the valve is not closing completely then engine pressure will leak past the valve. Check and adjust the valve clearances (Chapter 1).
☐ Cylinder and/or piston worn. Excessive wear will cause compression pressure to leak past the rings. This is usually accompanied by worn rings as well. A top-end overhaul is necessary (Chapter 2A or 2B).

☐ Piston rings worn, weak, broken, or sticking. Broken or sticking piston rings usually indicate a lubrication or fuelling problem that causes excess carbon deposits to form on the pistons and rings. Top-end overhaul is necessary (Chapter 2A or 2B).
☐ Piston ring-to-groove clearance excessive. This is caused by excessive wear of the piston ring lands. Piston renewal is necessary (Chapter 2A or 2B).
☐ Cylinder head gasket damaged. If the head is allowed to become loose, or if excessive carbon build-up on the piston crown and combustion chamber causes extremely high compression, the head gasket may leak. Retorquing the head is not always sufficient to restore the seal, so gasket renewal is necessary (Chapter 2A or 2B).
☐ Cylinder head warped. This is caused by overheating or improperly tightened head bolts. Machine shop resurfacing or head renewal is necessary (Chapter 2A or 2B).
☐ Valve spring broken or weak. Caused by component failure or wear; the springs must be renewed (Chapter 2A or 2B).
☐ Valve not seating properly. This is caused by a bent valve (from over-revving or improper valve adjustment), burned valve or seat (improper combustion) or an accumulation of carbon deposits on the seat (from combustion or lubrication problems). The valves must be cleaned and/or renewed and the seats serviced if possible (Chapter 2A or 2B).

### Poor acceleration

☐ Intake air leak. Check for loose throttle body-to-intake manifold connections or a leaking gasket (Chapter 4).
☐ Timing not advancing. The ECM or a sensor in the engine management system may be defective. If so, they must be renewed with new ones, as they can't be repaired. The systems can only be checked using the Triumph diagnostic tool – see Chapter 4 for details.
☐ Throttle bodies not synchronised. Adjust them with a vacuum gauge set or manometer (Chapter 1).
☐ Engine oil viscosity too high. Using a heavier oil than that recommended in Chapter 1 can damage the oil pump or lubrication system and cause drag on the engine.
☐ Brakes dragging. Usually caused by debris which has entered the brake piston seals, or from a warped disc or bent axle. Repair as necessary (Chapter 6).

# 3 Poor running or no power at high speed

### Firing incorrect

☐ Air filter restricted. Clean or renew the filter (Chapter 1).
☐ Spark plugs fouled, defective or worn out. See Chapter 1 for spark plug maintenance.
☐ Spark plug cap/coil or wiring defective. See Chapters 1 and 4 for details of the ignition system.
☐ Incorrect spark plugs. Wrong type, heat range or cap configuration. Check and install correct plugs listed in Chapter 1.
☐ Electronic control module (ECM) defective. Check it, referring to Chapter 4 for details.

### Fuel/air mixture incorrect

☐ Fuel injector clogged or fuel injection system malfunction (see Chapter 4).
☐ Air filter clogged, poorly sealed or missing (Chapter 1).
☐ Air filter housing poorly sealed. Look for cracks, holes or loose clamps and renew or repair defective parts.
☐ Fuel tank breather hose obstructed.
☐ Intake air leak. Check for loose throttle body-to-intake manifold connections or a leaking gasket (Chapter 4).
☐ Idle air control valve or one of its hoses faulty. First check that all hoses are securely connected at each end, and have no splits or cracks (Chapter 4). The idle air control valve can only be checked using the Triumph diagnostic tool (see Chapter 4).
☐ Fuel injection or engine management system malfunction. See Chapter 4.

### Compression low

☐ Spark plugs loose. Remove the plugs and inspect their threads. Reinstall and tighten to the specified torque (Chapter 1).
☐ Cylinder head not sufficiently tightened down. If the cylinder head is loose, then there's a chance that the gasket or head is damaged. Tighten the cylinder head bolts to the correct torque in the proper sequence (Chapter 2A or 2B).
☐ Incorrect valve clearance. If the valve is not closing completely then engine pressure will leak past the valve. Check and adjust the valve clearances (Chapter 1).
☐ Cylinder and/or piston worn. Excessive wear will cause compression pressure to leak past the rings. This is usually accompanied by worn rings as well. A top-end overhaul is necessary (Chapter 2A or 2B).
☐ Piston rings worn, weak, broken, or sticking. Broken or sticking piston rings usually indicate a lubrication or fuelling problem that causes excess carbon deposits to form on the pistons and rings. Top-end overhaul is necessary (Chapter 2A or 2B).
☐ Piston ring-to-groove clearance excessive. This is caused by excessive wear of the piston ring lands. Piston renewal is necessary (Chapter 2A or 2B).
☐ Cylinder head gasket damaged. If the head is allowed to become loose, or if excessive carbon build-up on the piston crown and combustion chamber causes extremely high compression, the head gasket may leak. Retorquing the head is not always sufficient to restore the seal, so gasket renewal is necessary (Chapter 2A or 2B).
☐ Cylinder head warped. This is caused by overheating or improperly tightened head bolts. Machine shop resurfacing or head renewal is necessary (Chapter 2A or 2B).
☐ Valve spring broken or weak. Caused by component failure or wear; the springs must be renewed (Chapter 2A or 2B).
☐ Valve not seating properly. This is caused by a bent valve (from over-revving or improper valve adjustment), burned valve or seat (improper combustion) or an accumulation of carbon deposits on the seat (from combustion or lubrication problems). The valves must be cleaned and/or renewed and the seats serviced if possible (Chapter 2A or 2B).

### Knocking or pinking

☐ Carbon build-up in combustion chamber. Use of a fuel additive that will dissolve the adhesive bonding the carbon particles to the crown and chamber is the easiest way to remove the build-up. Otherwise, the cylinder head will have to be removed and decarbonised (Chapter 2A or 2B).
☐ Incorrect or poor quality fuel. Old or improper grades of fuel can cause detonation. This causes the piston to rattle, thus the knocking or pinking sound. Drain old fuel and always use the recommended fuel grade.
☐ Spark plug heat range incorrect. Uncontrolled detonation indicates the plug heat range is too hot. The plug in effect becomes a glow plug, raising cylinder temperatures. Install the proper heat range plug (Chapter 1).
☐ Improper air/fuel mixture. This will cause the cylinders to run hot, which leads to detonation. Clogged injectors or an air leak can cause this imbalance, as could a fault in the engine management system which controls the fuel injection. See Chapter 4.

### Miscellaneous causes

☐ Throttles don't open fully. Check the cable and the twistgrip, and then the throttle bodies themselves (Chapters 1 and 4).
☐ Clutch slipping. May be caused by loose or worn clutch components. Refer to Chapter 2A or 2B for clutch overhaul procedures.
☐ Timing not advancing. The ECM or a sensor in the engine management system may be defective. If so, they must be renewed with new ones, as they can't be repaired. The system can only be checked using the Triumph diagnostic tool – see Chapter 4 for details.
☐ Engine oil viscosity too high. Using a heavier oil than the one recommended in Chapter 1 can damage the oil pump or lubrication system and cause drag on the engine.
☐ Brakes dragging. Usually caused by debris which has entered the brake piston seals, or from a warped disc or bent axle. Repair as necessary.

# 4 Overheating

## Engine overheats

- ☐ Coolant level low. Check and add coolant (Daily (pre-ride) checks).
- ☐ Leak in cooling system. Check cooling system hoses and radiator for leaks and other damage. Repair or renew parts as necessary (Chapter 3).
- ☐ Thermostat sticking open or closed. Check and renew as described in Chapter 3.
- ☐ Faulty radiator cap. Remove the cap and have it pressure tested.
- ☐ Coolant passages clogged. Drain and flush the system, then refill with fresh coolant (Chapter 1).
- ☐ Water pump defective. Remove the pump and check the components (Chapter 3).
- ☐ Clogged radiator fins. Clean them by blowing compressed air through the fins from the rear of the radiator.
- ☐ Cooling fan not cutting in. Cooling fan or fan relay fault (Chapter 3).
- ☐ Cooling fan not cutting in. Coolant temperature sensor faulty or ECM faulty (Chapter 4)

## Firing incorrect

- ☐ Air filter restricted. Clean or renew filter (Chapter 1).
- ☐ Spark plugs fouled, defective or worn out. See Chapter 1 for spark plug maintenance.
- ☐ Spark plug cap/coil or wiring defective. See Chapters 1 and 4 for details of the ignition system.
- ☐ Incorrect spark plugs. Wrong type, heat range or cap configuration. Check and install correct plugs listed in Chapter 1.
- ☐ Electronic control module (ECM) defective. Check it, referring to Chapter 4 for details.

## Fuel/air mixture incorrect

- ☐ Fuel injector clogged or fuel injection system malfunction (see Chapter 4).
- ☐ Air filter clogged, poorly sealed or missing (Chapter 1).
- ☐ Air filter housing poorly sealed. Look for cracks, holes or loose clamps and renew or repair defective parts.
- ☐ Fuel tank breather hose obstructed.
- ☐ Intake air leak. Check for loose throttle body-to-intake manifold connections or a leaking gasket (Chapter 4).
- ☐ Idle air control valve or one of its hoses faulty. First check that all hoses are securely connected at each end, and have no splits or cracks (Chapter 4). The idle air control valve can only be checked using the Triumph diagnostic tool (see Chapter 4).

- ☐ Fuel injection or engine management system malfunction. See Chapter 4.

## Compression too high

- ☐ Carbon build-up in combustion chamber. Use of a fuel additive that will dissolve the adhesive bonding the carbon particles to the piston crown and chamber is the easiest way to remove the build-up. Otherwise, the cylinder head will have to be removed and decarbonised (Chapter 2A or 2B).
- ☐ Improperly machined head surface or installation of incorrect gasket during engine assembly.

## Engine load excessive

- ☐ Clutch slipping. Can be caused by damaged, loose or worn clutch components. Refer to Chapter 2A or 2B for overhaul procedures.
- ☐ Engine oil level too high. The addition of too much oil will cause pressurisation of the crankcase and inefficient engine operation. Check Specifications and drain to proper level (Chapter 1).
- ☐ Engine oil viscosity too high. Using a heavier oil than the one recommended in Chapter 1 can damage the oil pump or lubrication system as well as cause drag on the engine.
- ☐ Brakes dragging. Usually caused by debris which has entered the brake piston seals, or from a warped disc or bent axle. Repair as necessary.

## Lubrication inadequate

- ☐ Engine oil level too low. Friction caused by intermittent lack of lubrication or from oil that is overworked can cause overheating. The oil provides a definite cooling function in the engine. Check the oil level (Daily (pre-ride) checks).
- ☐ Poor quality engine oil or incorrect viscosity or type. Oil is rated not only according to viscosity but also according to type. Some oils are not rated high enough for use in this engine. Check the Specifications section and change to the correct oil (Chapter 1).

## Miscellaneous causes

- ☐ Modification to exhaust system. Most aftermarket exhaust systems cause the engine to run leaner, which make them run hotter. Before installing an accessory exhaust system, always check with the exhaust manufacturer or Triumph themselves, as you may well need an adjustment to the engine management system, which can only be done using a diagnostic tool.

# 5 Clutch problems

## Clutch slipping

☐ Insufficient clutch cable freeplay. Check and adjust (Chapter 1).
☐ Friction plates worn or warped. Overhaul the clutch assembly (Chapter 2A or 2B).
☐ Plain plates warped (Chapter 2A or 2B).
☐ Clutch springs broken, sagged or weak. Replace the springs with new ones (Chapter 2A or 2B).
☐ Clutch release mechanism defective. Remove the clutch cover and check the mechanism (Chapter 2A or 2B).
☐ Clutch centre or housing unevenly worn. This causes improper engagement of the plates. Renew the damaged or worn parts (Chapter 2A or 2B).

## Clutch not disengaging completely

☐ Excessive clutch cable freeplay. Check and adjust (Chapter 1).
☐ Clutch plates warped or damaged. This will cause clutch drag, which in turn will cause the machine to creep. Overhaul the clutch assembly (Chapter 2A or 2B).

☐ Clutch spring tension uneven. Usually caused by a sagged or broken spring. Check and renew the springs as a set (Chapter 2A or 2B).
☐ Engine oil deteriorated. Old, thin, worn out oil will not provide proper lubrication for the plates, causing the clutch to drag. Change the oil and filter (Chapter 1).
☐ Engine oil viscosity too high. Using a heavier oil than recommended in Chapter 1 can cause the plates to stick together, putting a drag on the engine. Change to the correct weight oil (Chapter 1).
☐ Clutch housing sleeve seized on input shaft. Lack of lubrication, severe wear or damage can cause the sleeve to seize on the shaft. Overhaul of the clutch, and perhaps transmission, may be necessary to repair the damage (Chapter 2A or 2B).
☐ Clutch release mechanism defective. Remove the clutch cover and check the mechanism (Chapter 2A or 2B).
☐ Loose clutch centre nut. Causes housing and centre misalignment putting a drag on the engine. Engagement adjustment continually varies. Overhaul the clutch assembly (Chapter 2A or 2B).

# 6 Gear changing problems

## Doesn't go into gear or lever doesn't return

☐ Clutch not disengaging. See above.
☐ Selector fork(s) bent or seized. Often caused by dropping the machine or from lack of lubrication. Overhaul the transmission (Chapter 2A or 2B).
☐ Gear pinion(s) stuck on shaft. Most often caused by a lack of lubrication or excessive wear in transmission bearings and bushings. Overhaul the transmission (Chapter 2A or 2B).
☐ Selector drum binding. Caused by lubrication failure or excessive wear. Renew the drum and bearing (Chapter 2A or 2B).
☐ Gearchange lever return spring weak or broken (Chapter 2A or 2B).
☐ Gearchange lever broken. Splines stripped out of lever or shaft, caused by allowing the lever to get loose or from dropping the machine. Renew necessary parts (Chapter 2A or 2B).
☐ Gearchange mechanism stopper arm broken or worn. Full engagement and rotary movement of selector drum results. Renew the arm (Chapter 2A or 2B).
☐ Stopper arm spring broken. Allows arm to float, causing sporadic gearchange operation. Renew spring (Chapter 2A or 2B).

☐ Gearchange mechanism selector arm or pawl assembly broken or worn. Either the selector arm teeth aren't engaging correctly with the teeth on the pawl carrier, or the pawls themselves are not locating correctly in the selector drum end (due to weak or broken pawl springs, or worn cutouts in the drum end). Check the entire mechanism (Chapter 2A or 2B).

## Jumps out of gear

☐ Selector fork(s) worn. Overhaul the transmission (Chapter 2A or 2B).
☐ Gear groove(s) worn. Overhaul the transmission (Chapter 2A or 2B).
☐ Gear dogs or dog slots worn or damaged. The gears should be inspected and renewed. No attempt should be made to service the worn parts.

## Overselects

☐ Stopper arm spring weak or broken (Chapter 2A or 2B).
☐ Gearchange shaft return spring post broken or distorted (Chapter 2A or 2B).
☐ Gearchange mechanism stopper arm broken or worn. Full engagement and rotary movement of selector drum results. Renew the arm (Chapter 2A or 2B).

# 7 Abnormal engine noise

### Knocking or pinking

☐ Carbon build-up in combustion chamber. Use of a fuel additive that will dissolve the adhesive bonding the carbon particles to the piston crown and chamber is the easiest way to remove the build-up. Otherwise, the cylinder head will have to be removed and decarbonised (Chapter 2A or 2B).

☐ Incorrect or poor quality fuel. Old or improper fuel can cause detonation. This causes the pistons to rattle, thus the knocking or pinking sound. Drain the old fuel and always use the recommended grade fuel (Chapter 4).

☐ Spark plug heat range incorrect. Uncontrolled detonation indicates that the plug heat range is too hot. The plug in effect becomes a glow plug, raising cylinder temperatures. Install the proper heat range plug (Chapter 1).

☐ Improper air/fuel mixture. This will cause the cylinders to run hot and lead to detonation. Clogged injectors or an air leak can cause this imbalance. See Chapter 4.

### Piston slap or rattling

☐ Cylinder-to-piston clearance excessive. Caused by improper assembly. Inspect and overhaul top-end parts (Chapter 2A or 2B).

☐ Connecting rod bent. Caused by over-revving, trying to start a badly flooded engine or from ingesting a foreign object into the combustion chamber. Renew the damaged parts (Chapter 2A or 2B).

☐ Piston pin or piston pin bore worn or seized from wear or lack of lubrication. Renew damaged parts (Chapter 2A or 2B).

☐ Piston ring(s) worn, broken or sticking. Overhaul the top-end (Chapter 2A or 2B).

☐ Piston seizure damage. Usually from lack of lubrication or overheating. Renew the pistons and cylinder liners, as necessary (Chapter 2A or 2B).

☐ Connecting rod upper or lower end clearance excessive. Caused by excessive wear or lack of lubrication. Renew worn parts.

### Valve noise

☐ Incorrect valve clearances. Adjust the clearances by referring to Chapter 1.

☐ Valve spring broken or weak. Check and renew weak valve springs (Chapter 2A or 2B).

☐ Camshaft or cylinder head worn or damaged. Lack of lubrication at high rpm is usually the cause of damage. Insufficient oil or failure to change the oil at the recommended intervals are the chief causes. Since there are no replaceable bearings in the head, the head itself will have to be renewed if there is excessive wear or damage (Chapter 2A or 2B).

### Other noise

☐ Cylinder head gasket leaking.

☐ Exhaust pipe leaking at cylinder head connection. Caused by improper fit of pipe(s), loose nuts or broken gasket(s). All exhaust fasteners should be tightened evenly and carefully. Failure to do this will lead to a leak. If there is still a leak after tightening, remove the downpipe assembly and install new gaskets (Chapter 4).

☐ Crankshaft runout excessive. Caused by a bent crankshaft (from over-revving) or damage from a top-end component failure. Can also be attributed to dropping the machine on either of the crankshaft ends.

☐ Engine mounting bolts loose. Tighten all engine mount bolts (Chapter 2A or 2B).

☐ Crankshaft bearings worn (Chapter 2A or 2B).

☐ Camchain, guide blades or tensioner worn. Renew according to the procedure in Chapter 2A or 2B.

# 8 Abnormal driveline noise

### Clutch noise

☐ Clutch housing/friction plate clearance excessive (Chapter 2A or 2B).

☐ Loose or damaged clutch pressure plate and/or bolts (Chapter 2A or 2B).

### Transmission noise

☐ Bearings worn. Also includes the possibility that the shafts are worn. Overhaul the transmission (Chapter 2A or 2B).

☐ Gears worn or chipped (Chapter 2A or 2B).

☐ Metal chips jammed in gear teeth. Probably pieces from a broken clutch, gear or selector mechanism that were picked up by the gears. This will cause early bearing failure (Chapter 2A or 2B).

☐ Engine oil level too low. Causes a howl from transmission. Also affects engine power and clutch operation (Daily (pre-ride) checks).

### Final drive noise

☐ Chain not adjusted properly (Chapter 1).

☐ Front or rear sprocket loose. Tighten fasteners (Chapter 5).

☐ Sprockets worn. Renew sprockets and chain (Chapter 5).

☐ Sprocket coupling or hub assembly bearings worn, or loose axle nut, or damaged cush drive. Check and tighten or renew, according to model (Chapter 5).

# 9 Abnormal frame and suspension noise

### Front end noise

☐ Low fork oil level or improper viscosity. This can sound like spurting and is usually accompanied by irregular fork action (Chapter 5).

☐ Spring weak or broken. Makes a clicking or scraping sound. Fork oil, when drained, will have a lot of metal particles in it (Chapter 5).

☐ Steering head bearings loose or damaged. Clicks when braking. Check and adjust or renew as necessary (Chapters 1 and 5).

☐ Fork yokes loose. Make sure all clamp bolts are tightened to the specified torque (Chapter 5).

☐ Fork tube bent. Good possibility if machine has been dropped. Replace tube with a new one (Chapter 5).

☐ Front axle bolt or axle clamp bolts loose. Tighten them to the specified torque (Chapter 6).

☐ Loose or worn wheel bearings. Check and renew if necessary (Chapter 6).

### Shock absorber noise

☐ Fluid level incorrect. Indicates a leak caused by defective seal. Shock will be covered with oil. Renew shock or seek advice on repair from a Triumph dealer or suspension specialist (Chapter 5).

☐ Defective shock absorber with internal damage. This is in the body of the shock and can't be remedied. The shock must be replaced with a new one (Chapter 5).

☐ Bent or damaged shock body. Replace the shock with a new one (Chapter 5).

☐ Loose or worn suspension linkage components. Check and renew if necessary (Chapter 5).

### Brake noise

☐ Squeal caused by pad shim not installed or positioned correctly (where fitted) (Chapter 6).

☐ Squeal caused by dust on brake pads. Usually found in combination with glazed pads. Clean using brake cleaning solvent (Chapter 6).

☐ Contamination of brake pads. Oil, brake fluid or dirt causing brake to chatter or squeal. Clean or renew pads (Chapter 6).

☐ Pads glazed. Caused by excessive heat from prolonged use or from contamination. Do not use sandpaper, emery cloth, carborundum cloth or any other abrasive to roughen the pad surfaces as abrasives will stay in the pad material and damage the disc. A very fine flat file can be used, but pad renewal is suggested as a cure (Chapter 6).

☐ Disc warped. Can cause a chattering, clicking or intermittent squeal. Usually accompanied by a pulsating lever and uneven braking. Renew the disc (Chapter 6).

☐ Loose or worn wheel bearings. Check and renew if necessary (Chapter 6).

# 10 Oil pressure warning light comes on

### Engine lubrication system

☐ Engine oil pump defective, blocked oil strainer gauze or failed relief valve. Carry out oil pressure check (Chapter 2A or 2B).

☐ Engine oil level low. Inspect for leak or other problem causing low oil level and add recommended oil (Daily (pre-ride) checks).

☐ Engine oil viscosity too low. Very old, thin oil or an improper weight of oil used in the engine. Change to correct oil (Chapter 1).

☐ Camshaft or journals worn. Excessive wear causing drop in oil pressure. Renew cam and/or/cylinder head. Abnormal wear could be caused by oil starvation at high rpm from low oil level or improper weight or type of oil (Chapter 1).

☐ Crankshaft and/or bearings worn. Same problems as above. Check and renew crankshaft and/or bearings (Chapter 2A or 2B).

### Electrical system

☐ Oil pressure switch defective. Check the switch according to the procedure in Chapter 8. Renew it if it is defective.

☐ Oil pressure warning light circuit defective. Check for pinched, shorted, disconnected or damaged wiring (Chapter 8).

# 11 Excessive exhaust smoke

### White smoke

- ☐ Piston oil ring worn. The ring may be broken or damaged, causing oil from the crankcase to be pulled past the piston into the combustion chamber. Replace the rings with new ones (Chapter 2A or 2B).
- ☐ Cylinders worn, cracked, or scored. Caused by overheating or oil starvation. Install new liners (Chapter 2A or 2B).
- ☐ Valve stem seal damaged or worn. Remove valves and replace seals with new ones (Chapter 2A or 2B).
- ☐ Valve guide worn. Perform a complete valve job (Chapter 2A or 2B).
- ☐ Engine oil level too high, which causes the oil to be forced past the rings. Drain oil to the proper level (Daily (pre-ride) checks).
- ☐ Head gasket broken between oil return and cylinder. Causes oil to be pulled into the combustion chamber. Renew the head gasket and check the head for warpage (Chapter 2A or 2B).
- ☐ Abnormal crankcase pressurisation, which forces oil past the rings. Clogged breather is usually the cause.

### Black smoke

- ☐ Air filter clogged. Clean or renew the element (Chapter 1).
- ☐ Fuel injection system or idle air control valve malfunction (Chapter 4). These systems can only be checked using the Triumph diagnostic tool. Refer to Chapter 4 for further information.
- ☐ Fuel pressure too high. Check the fuel pressure regulator (Chapter 4).

### Brown smoke

- ☐ Fuel pump faulty or pressure regulator stuck open (Chapter 4).
- ☐ Throttle body-to-intake manifold bolts loose or gasket broken (Chapter 4).
- ☐ Air filter poorly sealed or not installed (Chapter 1).
- ☐ Fuel injection system malfunction (Chapter 4).

# 12 Poor handling or stability

### Handlebar hard to turn

- ☐ Steering head bearing adjuster nut too tight. Check adjustment as described in Chapter 1.
- ☐ Bearings damaged. Roughness can be felt as the bars are turned from side-to-side. Renew bearings and races (Chapter 5).
- ☐ Races dented or worn. Denting results from wear in only one position (e.g. straight-ahead), from a collision or hitting a pothole or from dropping the machine. Renew races and bearings (Chapter 5).
- ☐ Steering stem lubrication inadequate. Causes are grease getting hard from age or being washed out by high pressure car washes. Disassemble steering head and repack bearings (Chapter 5).
- ☐ Steering stem bent. Caused by a collision, hitting a pothole or by dropping the machine. Renew damaged part. Don't try to straighten the steering stem (Chapter 5).
- ☐ Front tyre air pressure too low (Daily (pre-ride) checks).

### Handlebar shakes or vibrates excessively

- ☐ Tyres worn or out of balance (Chapter 6).
- ☐ Swingarm bearings worn. Renew worn bearings (Chapter 5).
- ☐ Wheel rim(s) warped or damaged. Inspect wheels for runout (Chapter 6).
- ☐ Wheel bearings worn. Worn front or rear wheel bearings can cause poor tracking. Worn front bearings will cause wobble (Chapter 6).
- ☐ Handlebar clamp bolts loose (Chapter 5).
- ☐ Fork clamp bolts loose in yoke(s). Tighten them to the specified torque (Chapter 5).
- ☐ Engine mounting bolts loose. Will cause excessive vibration with increased engine rpm (Chapter 2A or 2B).

### Handlebar pulls to one side

- ☐ Frame bent. Definitely suspect this if the machine has been dropped. May or may not be accompanied by cracking near the bend. Renew the frame (Chapter 5).
- ☐ Wheels out of alignment. Caused by improper location of axle spacers or from bent steering stem or frame (Chapter 5).
- ☐ Swingarm bent or twisted. Caused by age (metal fatigue) or impact damage. Renew the arm (Chapter 5).
- ☐ Steering stem bent. Caused by impact damage or by dropping the motorcycle. Renew the steering stem (Chapter 5).
- ☐ Fork tube bent. Disassemble the forks and renew the damaged parts (Chapter 5).
- ☐ Fork oil level uneven. Check and add or drain as necessary (Chapters 1 and 5).

### Poor shock absorbing qualities

Too hard:
- a) Fork oil level too high (Chapter 5).
- b) Fork oil viscosity too high. Use a lighter oil (see the Specifications in Chapter 5).
- c) Fork tube bent. Causes a harsh, sticking feeling (Chapter 5).
- d) Rear shock shaft or body bent or damaged (Chapter 5).
- e) Fork internal damage (Chapter 5).
- f) Rear shock internal damage.
- g) Tyre pressure too high (Daily (pre-ride) checks).

Too soft:
- a) Fork or shock oil insufficient and/or leaking (Chapter 5).
- b) Fork oil level too low (Chapter 5).
- c) Fork oil viscosity too light (Chapter 5).
- d) Fork springs weak or broken (Chapter 5).
- e) Rear shock internal damage or leakage (Chapter 5).

# 13 Braking problems

### Brakes are spongy, don't hold

- ☐ Air in brake line. Caused by inattention to master cylinder fluid level or by leakage. Locate problem and bleed brakes (Chapter 6).
- ☐ Pad or disc worn (Chapters 1 and 6).
- ☐ Brake fluid leak. Locate leak and renew faulty seals or hose as necessary (Chapter 6).
- ☐ Contaminated pads. Caused by contamination with oil, grease, brake fluid, etc. Renew the pads. Clean disc thoroughly with brake cleaner (Chapter 6).
- ☐ Brake fluid deteriorated. Fluid is old or contaminated. Drain system, replenish with new fluid and bleed the system (Chapter 6).
- ☐ Master cylinder internal parts worn or damaged causing fluid to bypass (Chapter 6).
- ☐ Master cylinder bore scratched by foreign material or broken spring. Repair or renew master cylinder (Chapter 6).
- ☐ Disc warped. Renew disc(s) (Chapter 6).

### Brake lever or pedal pulsates

- ☐ Disc warped. Renew disc(s) (Chapter 6).
- ☐ Axle bent. Renew axle (Chapter 6).

- ☐ Brake caliper bolts loose (Chapter 6).
- ☐ Brake caliper slider pins damaged or sticking (sliding type caliper only), causing caliper to bind. Lubricate the sliders or renew them if they are corroded or bent (Chapter 6).
- ☐ Wheel warped or otherwise damaged (Chapter 6).
- ☐ Wheel bearings damaged or worn (Chapter 6).

### Brakes drag

- ☐ Master cylinder piston seized. Caused by wear or damage to piston or cylinder bore (Chapter 6).
- ☐ Lever balky or stuck. Check pivot and lubricate (Chapter 6).
- ☐ Brake caliper binds (sliding type caliper only). Caused by corrosion or inadequate lubrication or damage on caliper slider pins (Chapter 6).
- ☐ Brake caliper piston seized in bore. Caused by wear or ingestion of dirt past deteriorated seal (Chapter 6).
- ☐ Brake pad damaged. Pad material separated from backing plate. Usually caused by faulty manufacturing process or from contact with chemicals. Renew pads (Chapter 6).
- ☐ Pads improperly installed (Chapter 6).

# 14 Electrical problems

### Battery dead or weak

- ☐ Battery faulty. Caused by sulphated plates which are shorted through sedimentation. Also, broken battery terminal making only occasional contact (Chapter 8).
- ☐ Battery cables making poor contact (Chapter 8).
- ☐ Load excessive. Caused by addition of high wattage lights or other electrical accessories.
- ☐ Ignition (main) switch defective. Switch either earths (grounds) internally or fails to shut off system. Renew the switch (Chapter 8).
- ☐ Regulator/rectifier defective (Chapter 8).
- ☐ Alternator defective (Chapter 8).
- ☐ Wiring faulty. Wiring earthed (grounded) or connections loose in ignition, charging or lighting circuits (Chapter 8).

### Battery overcharged

- ☐ Regulator/rectifier defective. Overcharging is noticed when battery gets excessively warm (Chapter 8).
- ☐ Battery defective. Replace battery with a new one (Chapter 8).
- ☐ Battery amperage too low, wrong type or size. Install manufacturer's specified amp-hour battery to handle charging load (Chapter 8).

## Checking engine compression

● Low compression will result in exhaust smoke, heavy oil consumption, poor starting and poor performance. A compression test will provide useful information about an engine's condition and if performed regularly, can give warning of trouble before any other symptoms become apparent.
● A compression gauge will be required, along with an adapter to suit the spark plug hole thread size. Note that the screw-in type gauge/adapter set up is preferable to the rubber cone type.
● Before carrying out the test, first check the valve clearances as described in Chapter 1.
1 Run the engine until it reaches normal operating temperature, then stop it and remove the spark plug(s), taking care not to scald your hands on the hot components.
2 Install the gauge adapter and compression gauge in No. 1 cylinder spark plug hole **(see illustration 1)**.

Screw the compression gauge adapter into the spark plug hole, then screw the gauge into the adapter

3 On kickstart-equipped motorcycles, make sure the ignition switch is OFF, then open the throttle fully and kick the engine over a couple of times until the gauge reading stabilises.
4 On motorcycles with electric start only, the procedure will differ depending on the nature of the ignition system. Flick the engine kill switch (engine stop switch) to OFF and turn the ignition switch ON; open the throttle fully and crank the engine over on the starter motor for a couple of revolutions until the gauge reading stabilises. If the starter will not operate with the kill switch OFF, turn the ignition switch OFF and refer to the next paragraph.
5 Install the plugs back in their coil/caps and arrange the plug electrodes so that their metal bodies are earthed (grounded) against the cylinder head; this is essential to prevent damage to the ignition system **(see illustration 2)**. Position the plugs well away from the plug holes otherwise there is a risk of

All spark plugs must be earthed (grounded) against the cylinder head

atomised fuel escaping from the plug holes and igniting. As a safety precaution, cover the cylinder head cover with rag and disconnect the fuel pump wiring connector (see Chapter 4). Turn the ignition switch and kill switch ON, open the throttle fully and crank the engine over on the starter motor for a couple of revolutions until the gauge reading stabilises.
6 After one or two revolutions the pressure should build up to a maximum figure and then stabilise. Take a note of this reading and on multi-cylinder engines repeat the test on the remaining cylinders.
7 Typical pressures are given in Chapter 1. If the results fall within the specified range and on multi-cylinder engines all are relatively equal, the engine is in good condition. If there is a marked difference between the readings, or if the readings are lower than specified,

inspection of the top-end components will be required.
8 Low compression pressure may be due to worn cylinder bores, pistons or rings, failure of the cylinder head gasket, worn valve seals, or poor valve seating.
9 To distinguish between cylinder/piston wear and valve leakage, pour a small quantity of oil into the bore to temporarily seal the piston rings, then repeat the compression tests **(see illustration 3)**. If the readings show

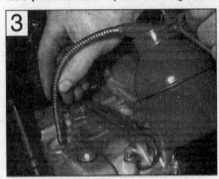

Bores can be temporarily sealed with a squirt of motor oil

a noticeable increase in pressure this confirms that the cylinder bore, piston, or rings are worn. If, however, no change is indicated, the cylinder head gasket or valves should be examined.
10 High compression pressure indicates excessive carbon build-up in the combustion chamber and on the piston crown. If this is the case the cylinder head should be removed and the deposits removed. Note that excessive carbon build-up is less likely with the used on modern fuels.

## Checking battery open-circuit voltage

 *Warning: The gases produced by the battery are explosive - never smoke or create any sparks in the vicinity of the battery. Never allow the electrolyte to contact your skin or clothing - if it does, wash it off and seek immediate medical attention.*

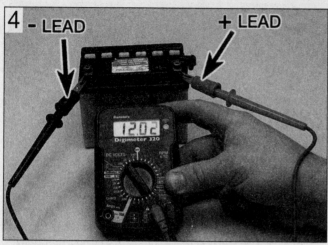

Measuring open-circuit battery voltage

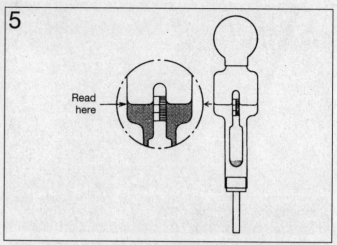

Float-type hydrometer for measuring battery specific gravity

● Before any electrical fault is investigated the battery should be checked.

● You'll need a dc voltmeter or multimeter to check battery voltage. Check that the leads are inserted in the correct terminals on the meter, red lead to positive (+ve), black lead to negative (-ve). Incorrect connections can damage the meter.

● A sound fully-charged 12 volt battery should produce between 12.3 and 12.6 volts across its terminals (12.8 volts for a maintenance-free battery). On machines with a 6 volt battery, voltage should be between 6.1 and 6.3 volts.

**1** Set a multimeter to the 0 to 20 volts dc range and connect its probes across the battery terminals. Connect the meter's positive (+ve) probe, usually red, to the battery positive (+ve) terminal, followed by the meter's negative (-ve) probe, usually black, to the battery negative terminal (-ve) **(see illustration 4)**.

**2** If battery voltage is low (below 10 volts on a 12 volt battery or below 4 volts on a six volt battery), charge the battery and test the voltage again. If the battery repeatedly goes flat, investigate the motorcycle's charging system.

## Checking battery specific gravity (SG)

⚠️ *Warning: The gases produced by the battery are explosive - never smoke or create any sparks in the vicinity of the battery. Never allow the electrolyte to contact your skin or clothing - if it does, wash it off and seek immediate medical attention.*

● The specific gravity check gives an indication of a battery's state of charge.

● A hydrometer is used for measuring specific gravity. Make sure you purchase one

which has a small enough hose to insert in the aperture of a motorcycle battery.

● Specific gravity is simply a measure of the electrolyte's density compared with that of water. Water has an SG of 1.000 and fully-charged battery electrolyte is about 26% heavier, at 1.260.

● Specific gravity checks are not possible on maintenance-free batteries. Testing the open-circuit voltage is the only means of determining their state of charge.

**1** To measure SG, remove the battery from the motorcycle and remove the first cell cap. Draw

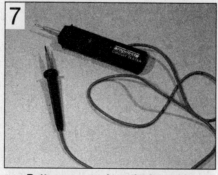

Digital multimeter can be used for all electrical tests

some electrolyte into the hydrometer and note the reading **(see illustration 5)**. Return the electrolyte to the cell and install the cap.

**2** The reading should be in the region of 1.260 to 1.280. If SG is below 1.200 the battery needs charging. Note that SG will vary with temperature; it should be measured at 20°C (68°F). Add 0.007 to the reading for every 10°C above 20°C, and subtract 0.007 from the reading for every 10°C below 20°C. Add 0.004 to the reading for every 10°F above 68°F, and subtract 0.004 from the reading for every 10°F below 68°F.

**3** When the check is complete, rinse the hydrometer thoroughly with clean water.

## Checking for continuity

● The term continuity describes the uninterrupted flow of electricity through an electrical circuit. A continuity check will determine whether an **open-circuit** situation exists.

● Continuity can be checked with an ohmmeter, multimeter, continuity tester or battery and bulb test circuit **(see illustrations 6, 7 and 8)**.

Battery-powered continuity tester

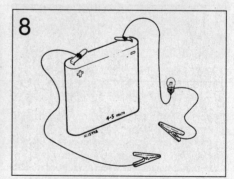

Battery and bulb test circuit

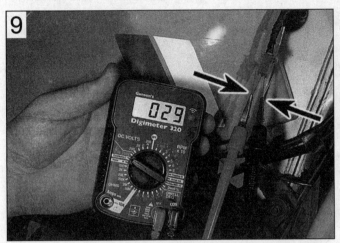

**Continuity check of front brake light switch using a meter - note split pins used to access connector terminals**

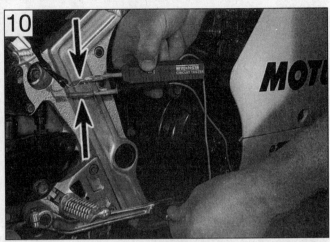

**Continuity check of rear brake light switch using a continuity tester**

● All of these instruments are self-powered by a battery, therefore the checks are made with the ignition OFF.

● As a safety precaution, always disconnect the battery negative (-ve) lead before making checks, particularly if ignition switch checks are being made.

● If using a meter, select the appropriate ohms scale and check that the meter reads infinity (∞). Touch the meter probes together and check that meter reads zero; where necessary adjust the meter so that it reads zero.

● After using a meter, always switch it OFF to conserve its battery.

### Switch checks

**1** If a switch is at fault, trace its wiring up to the wiring connectors. Separate the wire connectors and inspect them for security and condition. A build-up of dirt or corrosion here will most likely be the cause of the problem - clean up and apply a water dispersant such as WD40.

**2** If using a test meter, set the meter to the ohms x 10 scale and connect its probes across the wires from the switch **(see illustration 9)**. Simple ON/OFF type switches, such as brake light switches, only have two wires whereas combination switches, like the ignition switch, have many internal links. Study the wiring diagram to ensure that you are connecting across the correct pair of wires. Continuity (low or no measurable resistance - 0 ohms) should be indicated with the switch ON and no continuity (high resistance) with it OFF.

**3** Note that the polarity of the test probes doesn't matter for continuity checks, although care should be taken to follow specific test procedures if a diode or solid-state component is being checked.

**4** A continuity tester or battery and bulb circuit can be used in the same way. Connect its probes as described above **(see illustration 10)**. The light should come on to indicate continuity in the ON switch position, but should extinguish in the OFF position.

### Wiring checks

● Many electrical faults are caused by damaged wiring, often due to incorrect routing or chaffing on frame components.

● Loose, wet or corroded wire connectors can also be the cause of electrical problems, especially in exposed locations.

**1** A continuity check can be made on a single length of wire by disconnecting it at each end and connecting a meter or continuity tester across both ends of the wire **(see illustration 11)**.

**2** Continuity (low or no resistance - 0 ohms) should be indicated if the wire is good. If no continuity (high resistance) is shown, suspect a broken wire.

### Checking for voltage

● A voltage check can determine whether current is reaching a component.

● Voltage can be checked with a dc voltmeter, multimeter set on the dc volts scale, test light or buzzer **(see illustrations 12 and 13)**. A meter has the advantage of being able to measure actual voltage.

● When using a meter, check that its leads are inserted in the correct terminals on the meter, red to positive (+ve), black to negative (-ve). Incorrect connections can damage the meter.

● A voltmeter (or multimeter set to the dc volts scale) should always be connected in parallel (across the load). Connecting it in series will not harm the meter, but the reading will not be meaningful.

● Voltage checks are made with the ignition ON.

**Continuity check of front brake light switch sub-harness**

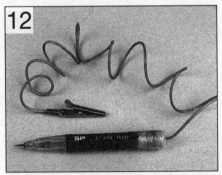

**A simple test light can be used for voltage checks**

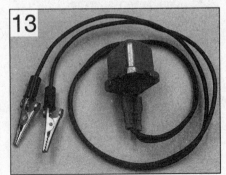

**A buzzer is useful for voltage checks**

**Checking for voltage at the rear brake light power supply wire using a meter . . .**

**1** First identify the relevant wiring circuit by referring to the wiring diagram at the end of this manual. If other electrical components share the same power supply (ie are fed from the same fuse), take note whether they are working correctly - this is useful information in deciding where to start checking the circuit.

**2** If using a meter, check first that the meter leads are plugged into the correct terminals on the meter (see above). Set the meter to the dc volts function, at a range suitable for the battery voltage. Connect the meter red probe (+ve) to the power supply wire and the black probe to a good metal earth (ground) on the motorcycle's frame or directly to the battery negative (-ve) terminal **(see illustration 14)**. Battery voltage should be shown on the meter

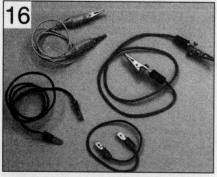

**A selection of jumper wires for making earth (ground) checks**

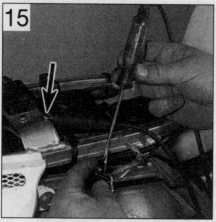

**. . . or a test light - note the earth connection to the frame (arrow)**

with the ignition switched ON.

**3** If using a test light or buzzer, connect its positive (+ve) probe to the power supply terminal and its negative (-ve) probe to a good earth (ground) on the motorcycle's frame or directly to the battery negative (-ve) terminal **(see illustration 15)**. With the ignition ON, the test light should illuminate or the buzzer sound.

**4** If no voltage is indicated, work back towards the fuse continuing to check for voltage. When you reach a point where there is voltage, you know the problem lies between that point and your last check point.

## Checking the earth (ground)

● Earth connections are made either directly to the engine or frame (such as sensors, neutral switch etc. which only have a positive feed) or by a separate wire into the earth circuit of the wiring harness. Alternatively a short earth wire is sometimes run directly from the component to the motorcycle's frame.

● Corrosion is often the cause of a poor earth connection.

● If total failure is experienced, check the security of the main earth lead from the negative (-ve) terminal of the battery and also the main earth (ground) point on the wiring harness. If corroded, dismantle the connection and clean all surfaces back to bare metal.

**1** To check the earth on a component, use an insulated jumper wire to temporarily bypass its earth connection **(see illustration 16)**. Connect one end of the jumper wire between the earth terminal or metal body of the component and the other end to the motorcycle's frame.

**2** If the circuit works with the jumper wire installed, the original earth circuit is faulty. Check the wiring for open-circuits or poor connections. Clean up direct earth connections, removing all traces of corrosion and remake the joint. Apply petroleum jelly to the joint to prevent future corrosion.

## Tracing a short-circuit

● A short-circuit occurs where current shorts to earth (ground) bypassing the circuit components. This usually results in a blown fuse.

● A short-circuit is most likely to occur where the insulation has worn through due to wiring chafing on a component, allowing a direct path to earth (ground) on the frame.

**1** Remove any bodypanels necessary to access the circuit wiring.

**2** Check that all electrical switches in the circuit are OFF, then remove the circuit fuse and connect a test light, buzzer or voltmeter (set to the dc scale) across the fuse terminals. No voltage should be shown.

**3** Move the wiring from side to side whilst observing the test light or meter. When the test light comes on, buzzer sounds or meter shows voltage, you have found the cause of the short. It will usually shown up as damaged or burned insulation.

**4** Note that the same test can be performed on each component in the circuit, even the switch.

# Haynes Motorcycle Manuals – The Complete List

| Title | | Book No |
|---|---|---|
| **APRILIA** RS50 (99 – 06) & RS125 (93 – 06) | | 4298 |
| Aprilia RSV1000 Mille (98 – 03) | ♦ | 4255 |
| Aprilia SR50 | | 4755 |
| **BMW** 2-valve Twins (70 -96) | ♦ | 0249 |
| BMW F650 | ♦ | 4761 |
| BMW K100 & 75 2-valve models (83 - 96) | ♦ | 1373 |
| BMW F800 (F650) Twins (06 – 10) | ♦ | 4872 |
| BMW R850, 1100 & 1150 4-valve Twins (93 – 06) | ♦ | 3466 |
| BMW R1200 (04 – 09) | ♦ | 4598 |
| BMW R1200 dohc Twins (10 – 12) | ♦ | 4925 |
| **BSA** Bantam (48 – 71) | | 0117 |
| BSA Unit Singles (58 – 72) | | 0127 |
| BSA Pre-unit Singles (54 – 61) | | 0326 |
| BSA A7 & A10 Twins (47 – 62) | | 0121 |
| BSA A50 & A65 Twins (62 – 73) | | 0155 |
| **CHINESE**, Taiwanese & Korean Scooters | | 4768 |
| Chinese, Taiwanese & Korean 125cc motorcyles | | 4781 |
| Pulse/Pioneer Adrenaline, Sinnis Apache, Superbyke RMR (07 – 14) | ◊♦ | 5750 |
| **DUCATI** 600, 620, 750 & 900 2-valve V-twins (91 – 05) | ♦ | 3290 |
| Ducati Mk III & Desmo singles (69 – 76) | ◊ | 0445 |
| Ducati 748, 916 & 996 4-valve V-twins (94 – 01) | ♦ | 3756 |
| **GILERA** Runner, DNA, Ice & SKP/Stalker (97 – 11) | | 4163 |
| **HARLEY-DAVIDSON** Sportsters (70 – 10) | ♦ | 2534 |
| Harley-Davidson Shovelhead & Evolution Big Twins (70 -99) | ♦ | 2536 |
| Harley-Davidson Twin Cam 88, 96 & 103 models (99 – 10) | ♦ | 2478 |
| **HONDA** NB, ND, NP & NS50 Melody (81 -85) | ◊ | 0622 |
| Honda NE/NB50 Vision & SA50 Vision Met-in (85-95) | ◊ | 1278 |
| Honda MB, MBX, MT & MTX50 (80 – 93) | | 0731 |
| Honda C50, C70 & C90 (67 – 03) | | 0324 |
| Honda XR50/70/80/100R & CRF50/70/80/100F (85 – 07) | | 2218 |
| Honda XL/XR 80, 100, 125, 185 & 200 2-valve models (78 – 87) | | 0566 |
| Honda H100 & H100S Singles (80 – 92) | ◊ | 0734 |
| Honda 125 Scooters (00 – 09) | | 4873 |
| Honda ANF125 Innova Scooters (03 -12) | ♦ | 4926 |
| Honda CB/CD125T & CM125C Twins (77 – 88) | ◊ | 0571 |
| Honda CBF125 (09 – 14) | ♦ | 5540 |
| Honda CG125 (76 – 07) | ◊ | 0433 |
| Honda NS125 (86 – 93) | ◊ | 3056 |
| Honda CBR125R (04 – 10) | | 4620 |
| Honda CBR125R, CBR250R & CRF250L/M (11 – 14) | ♦ | 5919 |
| Honda MBX/MTX125 & MTX200 (83 – 93) | ◊ | 1132 |
| Honda XL125V & VT125C (99 – 11) | | 4899 |
| Honda CD/CM185 200T & CM250C 2-valve Twins (77 – 85) | | 0572 |
| Honda CMX250 Rebel & CB250 Nighthawk Twins (85 – 09) | ◊ | 2756 |
| Honda XL/XR 250 & 500 (78 – 84) | | 0567 |
| Honda XR250L, XR250R & XR400R (86 – 04) | | 2219 |
| Honda CB250 & CB400N Super Dreams (78 – 84) | ◊ | 0540 |
| Honda CR Motocross Bikes (86 – 07) | | 2222 |
| Honda CRF250 & CRF450 (02 – 06) | | 2630 |
| Honda CBR400RR Fours (88 – 99) | ◊♦ | 3552 |
| Honda VFR400 (NC30) & RVF400 (NC35) V-Fours (89 – 98) | ◊♦ | 3496 |
| Honda CB500 (93 – 02) & CBF500 (03 – 08) | ◊ | 3753 |
| Honda CB400 & CB550 Fours (73 – 77) | | 0262 |
| Honda CX/GL500 & 650 V-Twins (78 – 86) | | 0442 |
| Honda CBX550 Four (82 – 86) | ◊ | 0940 |
| Honda XL600R & XR600R (83 – 08) | ♦ | 2183 |
| Honda XL600/650V Transalp & XRV750 Africa Twin (87 – 07) | ♦ | 3919 |
| Honda CB600 Hornet, CBF600 & CBR600F (07 – 12) | ♦ | 5572 |
| Honda CBR600F1 & 1000F Fours (87 – 96) | ♦ | 1730 |
| Honda CBR600F2 & F3 Fours (91 – 98) | ♦ | 2070 |
| Honda CBR600F4 (99 – 06) | ♦ | 3911 |
| Honda CB600F Hornet & CBF600 (98 – 06) | ◊♦ | 3915 |
| Honda CBR600RR (03 – 06) | ♦ | 4590 |
| Honda CBR600RR (07 -12) | ♦ | 4795 |
| Honda CB650 sohc Fours (78 – 84) | | 0665 |
| Honda NTV600 Revere, NTV650 & NT650V Deauville (88 – 05) | ◊♦ | 3243 |
| Honda Shadow VT600 & 750 (USA) (88 – 09) | | 2312 |
| Honda NT700V Deauville & XL700V Transalp (06 -13) | ♦ | 5541 |
| Honda CB750 sohc Four (69 – 79) | | 0131 |
| Honda V45/65 Sabre & Magna (82 – 88) | | 0820 |
| Honda VFR750 & 700 V-Fours (86 – 97) | ♦ | 2101 |
| Honda VFR800 V-Fours (97 – 01) | ♦ | 3703 |
| Honda VFR800 V-Tec V-Fours (02 – 09) | ♦ | 4196 |
| Honda CB750 & CB900 dohc Fours (78 – 84) | | 0535 |
| Honda CBF1000 (06 -10) & CB1000R (08 – 11) | ♦ | 4927 |
| Honda VTR1000 Firestorm, Super Hawk & XL1000V Varadero (97 – 08) | ♦ | 3744 |
| Honda CBR900RR Fireblade (92 – 99) | ♦ | 2161 |
| Honda CBR900RR Fireblade (00 – 03) | ♦ | 4060 |
| Honda CBR1000RR Fireblade (04 – 07) | ♦ | 4604 |
| Honda CBR1000RR Fireblade (08 – 13) | ♦ | 5688 |
| Honda CBR1100XX Super Blackbird (97 – 07) | ♦ | 3901 |
| Honda ST1100 Pan European V-Fours (90 – 02) | ♦ | 3384 |
| Honda ST1300 Pan European (02 -11) | ♦ | 4908 |
| Honda Shadow VT1100 (USA) (85 – 07) | | 2313 |

| Title | | Book No |
|---|---|---|
| Honda GL1000 Gold Wing (75 – 79) | | 0309 |
| Honda GL1100 Gold Wing (79 – 81) | | 0669 |
| Honda Gold Wing 1200 (USA) (84 - 87) | | 2199 |
| Honda Gold Wing 1500 (USA) (88 – 00) | | 2225 |
| Honda Goldwing GL1800 | ♦ | 2787 |
| **KAWASAKI** AE/AR 50 & 80 (81 – 95) | | 1007 |
| Kawasaki KC, KE & KH100 (75 – 99) | | 1371 |
| Kawasaki KMX125 & 200 (86 – 02) | ◊ | 3046 |
| Kawasaki 250, 350 & 400 Triples (72 – 79) | | 0134 |
| Kawasaki 400 & 440 Twins (74 – 81) | | 0281 |
| Kawasaki 400, 500 & 550 Fours (79 – 91) | | 0910 |
| Kawasaki EN450 & 500 Twins (Ltd/Vulcan) (85 – 07) | | 2053 |
| Kawasaki ER-6F & ER-6N (06 -10) | ♦ | 4874 |
| Kawasaki EX500 (GPZ500S) & ER500 (ER-5) (87 – 08) | ♦ | 2052 |
| Kawasaki ZX600 (ZZ-R600 & Ninja ZX-6) (90 – 06) | ♦ | 2146 |
| Kawasaki ZX-6R Ninja Fours (95 – 02) | ♦ | 3451 |
| Kawasaki ZX-6R (03 – 06) | ♦ | 4742 |
| Kawasaki ZX600 (GPZ600R, GPX600R, Ninja 600R & RX) & ZX750 (GPX750R, Ninja 750R) (85 – 97) | ♦ | 1780 |
| Kawasaki 650 Four (76 – 78) | | 0373 |
| Kawasaki Vulcan 700/750 & 800 (85 – 04) | ♦ | 2457 |
| Kawasaki Vulcan 1500 & 1600 (87 – 08) | ♦ | 4913 |
| Kawasaki 750 Air-cooled Fours | | 0574 |
| Kawasaki ZR550 & 750 Zephyr Fours (90 – 97) | ♦ | 3382 |
| Kawasaki Z750 & Z1000 (03 – 08) | ♦ | 4762 |
| Kawasaki ZX750 (Ninja ZX-7 & ZXR750) Fours (89 – 96) | ♦ | 2054 |
| Kawasaki Ninja ZX-7R & ZX-9R (94 – 04) | ♦ | 3721 |
| Kawasaki 900 & 1000 Fours (73 – 77) | | 0222 |
| Kawasaki ZX900, 1000 & 1100 Liquid-cooled Fours (83 – 97) | ♦ | 1681 |
| Kawasaki ZX-10R (04 – 10) | ♦ | 5542 |
| **KTM** EXC Enduro & SX Motocross (00 – 07) | ♦ | 4629 |
| **LAMBRETTA** Scooters (58 – 00) | ♦ | 5573 |
| **MOTO GUZZI** 750, 850 & 1000 V-Twins (74 – 78) | | 0339 |
| **MZ** ETZ models (81 – 95) | ◊ | 1680 |
| **NORTON** 500, 600, 650 & 750 Twins (57 – 70) | | 0187 |
| Norton Commando (68 – 77) | | 0125 |
| **PEUGEOT** Speedfight, Trekker & Vivacity Scooters (96 – 08) | ◊ | 3920 |
| Peugeot V-Clic, Speedfight 3, Vivacity 3, Kisbee & Tweet (08 – 14) | ◊♦ | 5751 |
| **PIAGGIO** (Vespa) Scooters (91 – 09) | ◊ | 3492 |
| **SUZUKI** GT, ZR & TS50 (77 – 90) | ◊ | 0799 |
| Suzuki TS50X (84 – 00) | ◊ | 1599 |
| Suzuki 100, 125, 185 & 250 Air-cooled Trail bikes (79 – 89) | | 0797 |
| Suzuki GP100 & 125 Singles (78 – 93) | ◊ | 0576 |
| Suzuki GS, GN, GZ & DR125 Singles (82 – 05) | ◊ | 0888 |
| Suzuki Burgman 250 & 400 (98 – 11) | ♦ | 4909 |
| Suzuki GSX-R600/750 (06 – 09) | ♦ | 4790 |
| Suzuki 250 & 350 Twins (68 – 78) | | 0120 |
| Suzuki GT250X7, GT200X5 & SB200 Twins (78 – 83) | ◊ | 0469 |
| Suzuki DR-Z400 (00 – 10) | ♦ | 2933 |
| Suzuki GS/GSX250, 400 & 450 Twins (79 – 85) | | 0736 |
| Suzuki GS500 Twin (89 – 08) | ♦ | 3238 |
| Suzuki GS550 (77 – 82) & GS750 Fours (76 – 79) | | 0363 |
| Suzuki GS/GSX550 4-valve Fours (83 – 88) | | 1133 |
| Suzuki SV650 & SV650S (99 – 08) | ♦ | 3912 |
| Suzuki DL650 V-Strom & SFV650 Gladius (04 – 13) | ♦ | 5643 |
| Suzuki GSX-R600 & 750 (96 – 00) | ♦ | 3553 |
| Suzuki GSX-R600 (01 – 03), GSX-R750 (00 – 03) & GSX-R1000 (01 – 02) | ♦ | 3986 |
| Suzuki GSX-R600/750 (04 – 05) & GSX-R1000 (03 – 06) | ♦ | 4382 |
| Suzuki GSF600, 650 & 1200 Bandit Fours (95 – 06) | ♦ | 3367 |
| Suzuki Intruder, Marauder, Volusia & Boulevard (85 – 09) | ♦ | 2618 |
| Suzuki GS850 Fours (78 – 88) | | 0536 |
| Suzuki GS1000 Four (77 – 79) | | 0484 |
| Suzuki GSX-R750, GSX-R1100 (85 – 92) GSX600F, GSX750F, GSX1100F (Katana) Fours (88 – 96) | ♦ | 2055 |
| Suzuki GSX600/750F & GSX750 (98 – 02) | ♦ | 3987 |
| Suzuki GS/GSX1000, 1100 & 1150 4-valve Fours (79 – 88) | | 0737 |
| Suzuki TL1000S/R & DL V-Strom (97 – 04) | ♦ | 4083 |
| Suzuki GSF650/1250 Bandit & GSX650/1250F (07 – 14) | ♦ | 4798 |
| Suzuki GSX1300R Hayabusa (99 – 14) | ♦ | 4184 |
| Suzuki GSX1400 (02 – 08) | ♦ | 4758 |
| **TRIUMPH** Tiger Cub & Terrier (52 – 68) | | 0414 |
| Triumph 350 & 500 Unit Twins ( 58 – 73) | | 0137 |
| Triumph Pre-Unit Twins (47 – 62) | | 0251 |
| Triumph 650 & 750 2-valve Unit Twins (63 – 83) | | 0122 |
| Triumph 675 (06 – 10) | ♦ | 4876 |
| Triumph Tiger 800 (10 – 14) | ♦ | 5752 |
| Triumph 1050 Sprint, Speed Triple & Tiger (05 -13) | ♦ | 4796 |
| Triumph Trident & BSA Rocket 3 (69 – 75) | | 0136 |
| Triumph Bonneville (01 – 12) | ♦ | 4364 |
| Triumph Daytona, Speed Triple, Sprint & Tiger (97 – 05) | ♦ | 3755 |
| Triumph Triples & Fours (carburetor engines) (91 – 04) | ♦ | 2162 |
| **VESPA** P/PX125, 150 & 200 Scooters (78 – 12) | | 0707 |
| Vespa GTS125, 250 & 300 (05 – 10) | | 4898 |
| Vespa Scooters (59 – 78) | | 0126 |

| Title | | Book No |
|---|---|---|
| **YAMAHA** DT50 & 80 Trail Bikes (78 – 95) | ◊ | 0800 |
| Yamaha T50 & 80 Townmate (83 – 95) | ◊ | 1247 |
| Yamaha YB100 Singles (73 – 91) | ◊ | 0474 |
| Yamaha RS/RXS 100 & 125 Singles (74 – 95) | | 0331 |
| Yamaha RD & DT125LC (82 – 87) | ◊ | 0887 |
| Yamaha TZR125 (87 – 93) & DT125R (88 – 07) | ◊ | 1655 |
| Yamaha TY50, 80, 125 & 175 (74 – 84) | ◊ | 0464 |
| Yamaha XT & SR125 (82 – 03) | ◊ | 1021 |
| Yamaha YBR125 & XT125R/X (05 – 13) | | 4797 |
| Yamaha YZF-R125 (08 – 11) | ♦ | 5543 |
| Yamaha Trail Bikes (81 – 03) | | 2350 |
| Yamaha 2-stroke Motocross Bikes (86 – 06) | | 2662 |
| Yamaha YZ & WR 4-stroke Motorcross Bikes (98 – 08) | | 2689 |
| Yamaha 250 & 350 Twins (70 – 79) | | 0040 |
| Yamaha XS250, 360 & 400 sohc Twins (75 – 84) | | 0378 |
| Yamaha RD250 & 350LC Twins (80 – 82) | | 0803 |
| Yamaha RD350 YPVS Twins (83 – 95) | | 1158 |
| Yamaha RD400 Twin (75 – 79) | | 0333 |
| Yamaha XT, TT & SR500 Singles (75 – 83) | | 0342 |
| Yamaha XZ550 Vision V-Twins (82 – 85) | | 0821 |
| Yamaha FJ, FX, XY & YX600 Radian (84 – 92) | | 2100 |
| Yamaha XT660 & MT-03 (04 – 11) | ♦ | 4910 |
| Yamaha XJ600S (Diversion, Seca II) & XJ600N Fours (92 – 03) | ♦ | 2145 |
| Yamaha XJ6 & FZ6R (09 – 15) | ♦ | 5889 |
| Yamaha YZF600R Thundercat & FZS600 Fazer (96 – 03) | ♦ | 3702 |
| Yamaha FZ-6 Fazer (04 – 08) | ♦ | 4751 |
| Yamaha YZF-R6 (99 – 02) | ♦ | 3900 |
| Yamaha YZF-R6 (03 – 05) | ♦ | 4601 |
| Yamaha YZF-R6 (06 – 13) | ♦ | 5544 |
| Yamaha 650 Twins (70 – 83) | | 0341 |
| Yamaha XJ650 & 750 Fours (80 – 84) | | 0738 |
| Yamaha XS750 & 850 Triples (76 – 85) | | 0340 |
| Yamaha TDM850, TRX850 & XTZ750 (89 – 99) | ◊♦ | 3450 |
| Yamaha YZF750R & YZF1000R Thunderace (93 – 00) | ♦ | 3720 |
| Yamaha FZR600, 750 & 1000 Fours (87 – 96) | ♦ | 2056 |
| Yamaha XV (Virago) V-Twins (81 – 03) | ♦ | 0802 |
| Yamaha XVS650 & 1100 Drag Star/V-Star (97 – 05) | ♦ | 4195 |
| Yamaha XJ900F Fours (83 – 94) | ♦ | 3239 |
| Yamaha XJ900S Diversion (94 – 01) | ♦ | 3739 |
| Yamaha YZF-R1 (98 – 03) | ♦ | 3754 |
| Yamaha YZF-R1 (04 – 06) | ♦ | 4605 |
| Yamaha FZS1000 Fazer (01 – 05) | ♦ | 4287 |
| Yamaha FJ1100 & 1200 Fours (84 – 96) | ♦ | 2057 |
| Yamaha FJR1300 (01 – 13) | ♦ | 5607 |
| Yamaha XJR1200 & 1300 (95 – 06) | ♦ | 3981 |
| Yamaha V-Max (85 – 03) | ♦ | 4072 |
| **ATVs** | | |
| Honda ATC 70, 90, 110, 185 & 200 (71 – on) | | 0565 |
| Honda Rancher, Recon & TRX250EX ATVs | | 2553 |
| Honda TRX300 Shaft Drive ATVs (88 – 00) | | 2125 |
| Honda Foreman (95 – 11) | | 2465 |
| Honda TRX300EX, TRX400EX & TRX450R/ER ATVs (93 – 06) | | 2318 |
| Kawasaki Bayou 220/250/300 & Prairie 300 ATVs (86 – 03) | | 2351 |
| Polaris ATVs (85 – 97) | | 2302 |
| Polaris ATVs (98 – 07) | | 2508 |
| Suzuki/Kawasaki/Artic Cat ATVs (03 – 09) | | 2910 |
| Yamaha YFS200 Blaster ATV (88 – 06) | | 2317 |
| Yamaha YFM350 & YFM400 (ER & Big Bear) ATVs (87 – 09) | | 2126 |
| Yamaha YFZ450 & YFZ450R (04 – 10) | | 2899 |
| Yamaha Banshee and Warrior ATVs (87 – 10) | | 2314 |
| Yamaha Kodiak and Grizzly ATVs (93 – 05) | | 2567 |
| ATV Basics | | 10450 |
| **SCOOTERS** | | |
| Twist and Go (automatic transmission) Scooters Service and Repair Manual | ◊ | 4082 |
| **TECHBOOK SERIES** | | |
| Motorcycle Basics Techbook (2nd edition) | | 3515 |
| Motorcycle Electrical Techbook (3rd edition) | | 3471 |
| Motorcycle Fuel Systems Techbook | | 3514 |
| Motorcycle Maintenance Techbook | | 4071 |
| Motorcycle Modifying | | 4272 |
| Motorcycle Workshop Practice Techbook (2nd edition) | | 3470 |

◊ = not available in the USA ♦ = Superbike

The manuals on this page are available through good motorcycle dealers and accessory shops.
In case of difficulty, contact: **Haynes Publishing**
(UK) **+44 1963 442030** (USA) **+1 805 498 6703**
(SV) **+46 18 124016**
(Australia/New Zealand) **+61 2 8713 1400**

# Preserving Our Motoring Heritage

< The Model J Duesenberg Derham Tourster. Only eight of these magnificent cars were ever built – this is the only example to be found outside the United States of America

Almost every car you've ever loved, loathed or desired is gathered under one roof at the Haynes Motor Museum. Over 300 immaculately presented cars and motorbikes represent every aspect of our motoring heritage, from elegant reminders of bygone days, such as the superb Model J Duesenberg to curiosities like the bug-eyed BMW Isetta. There are also many old friends and flames. Perhaps you remember the 1959 Ford Popular that you did your courting in? The magnificent 'Red Collection' is a spectacle of classic sports cars including AC, Alfa Romeo, Austin Healey, Ferrari, Lamborghini, Maserati, MG, Riley, Porsche and Triumph.

## A Perfect Day Out

Each and every vehicle at the Haynes Motor Museum has played its part in the history and culture of Motoring. Today, they make a wonderful spectacle and a great day out for all the family. Bring the kids, bring Mum and Dad, but above all bring your camera to capture those golden memories for ever. You will also find an impressive array of motoring memorabilia, a comfortable 70 seat video cinema and one of the most extensive transport book shops in Britain. The Pit Stop Cafe serves everything from a cup of tea to wholesome, home-made meals or, if you prefer, you can enjoy the large picnic area nestled in the beautiful rural surroundings of Somerset.

> John Haynes O.B.E., Founder and Chairman of the museum at the wheel of a Haynes Light 12.

< The 1936 490cc sohc-engined International Norton – well known for its racing success

The Museum is situated on the A359 Yeovil to Frome road at Sparkford, just off the A303 in Somerset. It is about 40 miles south of Bristol, and 25 minutes drive from the M5 intersection at Taunton.
Open 9.30am - 5.30pm (10.00am - 4.00pm Winter) 7 days a week, *except Christmas Day, Boxing Day and New Years Day*
Special rates available for schools, coach parties and outings  Charitable Trust No. 292048